Elements of Marketing

**ANTHONY R MORDEN MBA, Dip. Inst. Marketing,
M. Chartered Inst. Marketing, M. Marketing Society**

Principal Lecturer
Teesside Polytechnic UK

DP Publications

Aldine Place, 142/144 Uxbridge Road
Shepherds Bush Green, London W12 8AW
1991

ACKNOWLEDGEMENTS TO THE FIRST EDITION

I wish to express my thanks:

* to Sue Hill, who wordprocessed the book; and to Mabel Chrimes and Bernie Emery who assisted in the preparation of the draft.

* to the Editors of *Marketing Intelligence and Planning*, *Quarterly Review of Marketing*, *British Baker* and *Baking Today* for permission to reproduce material originally published in their journals. Particular thanks must go to the Editor of *Marketing* for permission to reproduce material from that journal.

* to the following for their advice or assistance:-
  # Terry Darlington (Research Associates Ltd)
  # Ken Morgan (Morgan Insurance Brokers Ltd)
  # John Mustoe (Lucy Foods Ltd)
  # Derek Turpin (Yorton Honey Farms Ltd)
  # John Whitehead (CACI Market Analysis PLC)

* to the following professional institutes for permission to reproduce past examination questions:-
  Chartered Institute of Marketing (CIM)
  Marketing Institute of Ireland (IIM)
  Marketing Institute of Singapore (IOMS)
  Institute of Purchasing and Supply (IPS)
  Institute of Export (IOE)
  Chartered Institute of Management Accountants (CIMA)
  Chartered Association of Certified Accountants (ACCA)
  Chartered Building Societies Institute (CBSI)
  Institute of Bankers in Scotland (SCOB)
  Society of Sales Management Administrators (SSM)
  Association of Business Executives (ABE)

The source of the past examination questions to be found at section-ends is acknowledged by the use of the acronyms listed above and to the right of the full title of the institute. The full postal addresses of these institutes will be found in the "Useful addresses" section at the end of this book.

First Edition 1987, reprinted 1989
Second Edition 1991, reprinted 1991

ACKNOWLEDGEMENTS TO THE SECOND EDITION

I wish to express my thanks:

* to the Editors of *InterCity Magazine*, the *Darlington and Stockton Times* and the *Middlesbrough Evening Gazette* for permission to reproduce material originally published in their journals. Particular thanks must again go to the Editor of *Marketing* for permission to reproduce material from that journal.

* to the following for their advice or assistance:-

Robin Bellis-Jones (Develin and Partners)   Northallerton Health Authority
Margaret Dibben   Taylors Tea and Coffee Ltd,
Margaret Hutchinson (Darlington Health Authority)   Harrogate, UK

A CIP Catalogue Record is available from the British Library.

ISBN 1 870 941 70 5

Copyright A.R. Morden © 1991

Printed in Great Britain by
The Guernsey Press Co. Ltd, Guernsey, Channel Islands

Contents

Preface

AIMS

1. This book provides a broad and comprehensive introduction to the principal ideas, concepts and applications of the theory and practice of marketing.

2. This book gives guidance to students in the construction of answers to a sample of typical examination questions set by a variety of professional institutes.

3. This book gives value for money to the customer.

TARGET MARKETS

1. Students taking *Certificate* level examinations of the major professional institutes in marketing, namely:

* Chartered Institute of Marketing
  — Certificate Part 1 "Fundamentals of Marketing"
  — Certificate Part 2 "Practice of Marketing Management"
* Marketing Institute of Ireland
  — Certificate Part 1 "Marketing I"
  — Certificate Part 2 "Marketing Research"

2. Students taking *Diploma* level examinations of the Chartered Institute of Marketing and the Marketing Institute of Singapore; and *Graduateship* examinations of the Marketing Institute of Ireland.

3. Students taking equivalent examinations of other major professional institutions that include the study of marketing within their syllabus, for example:

* Institute of Purchasing and Supply
* Institute of Export
* Chartered Institute of Cost and Management Accountants
* Chartered Association of Certified Accountants
* Chartered Building Societies' Institute
* Institute of Bankers/Institute of Bankers in Scotland
* Society of Sales Management Administrators
* Association of Business Executives

4. Students on full-time and part-time courses in business and management studies at post-experience, undergraduate and higher diploma/certificate level in universities, polytechnics, colleges of higher and further education.

5. Students on full or part-time courses in design, engineering, operations management or applied science which contain a significant element of business and management studies.

6. Practising managers and specialists in industry, commerce and the private sector, and especially those undergoing training and development.

APPROACH TAKEN

The treatment of the material in this book is broad, comprehensive and reader-orientated. It is written with the needs of the professional, post-experience, undergraduate and higher diploma/certificate student in mind. The subject-matter of the book, and the approach taken are based on the needs of the student who has to study, do coursework assignments, revise and take internal or professional examinations.

The material in this book is structured around sections and chapters which deal with the various specific concepts and topics. Each chapter has its own summary, and each section has questions for self-review and sample examination questions. The reader is offered frequent opportunities to pause and reflect on the material upon which he or she is working. The process of summary, thought and self-review is essential to the development of the reader's understanding. It is particularly important in developing his or her ability to deal with questions written under the pressure of the examination situation.

A variety of case study material is included within the text. This material serves to illustrate the application of the particular concept or practice to which it is appropriate.

As with any other subject, the study of marketing has its own range of technical terms and jargon. The book attempts to avoid the excessive use of jargon, but the reader cannot escape learning technical terms, abbreviations (etc) and applying them where their use would be customary or expected. The appropriate use of necessary technical terms (etc) indicates that the examination candidate, in particular, understands the concepts that underlie these terms. It also indicates that he or she is able to apply them to situations, problems, or requirements to comment and discuss, in which they are needed and where the examiner will expect to see them.

The book can be used as a class text-book; as a text for students studying on an independent basis; and as a manual for practising managers and specialists undergoing in-company training and development. In each case, the questions for self-review, examination questions and sample assignments will be useful for monitoring and encouraging learning, assisting revision, and developing examination and problem-solving technique.

FORMAT

1. Related groups of chapters are assembled into sections. Each section has its questions for self-review and sample examination questions listed at the section-end.

2. Suggested outline answers are given in Appendix I to some of the sample examination questions. Readers will gain most benefit if they consult these suggested answers *after* having made their own attempt at answering the question.

3. The sample examination questions reproduced in this book are numbered in a *consecutive order*. The suggested outline answers carry the same number as the examination question to which they refer.

4. Appendix I does *not* contain answers to *all* of the examination questions reproduced in this book. Suggested outline answers to some of the examination questions will instead be found in a special supplement available only to lecturers on direct application to the publisher. This means that the reader will in a number of cases have to rely entirely on his or her own resources in order to write an answer. The development of self-reliance and self-confidence that comes from thorough study and personal application is an essential pre-requisite to examination success.

SUGGESTIONS AND CRITICISMS

The author welcomes constructive comments and suggestions from readers and institutions about the content and format of this book.

Notes to the Second Edition

The second edition of *Elements of Marketing* has been reviewed and updated. It now contains:

* a completely revised chapter on marketing strategy and planning.

* a major new section on the marketing of services, appropriate to both the commercial and non-profit/public sector.

* a new chapter on Green Marketing, reflecting the growing importance of this topical subject.

* additional sample assignments and group projects. These will be suitable for student-centred learning, whether at post-experience, undergraduate or BTEC Higher level.

Elements of Marketing is recommended by CIMA, ACCA and the Society of Sales Management Administrators.

The Fundamentals of Marketing

The first three chapters of this text introduce some of the major areas of study within the theory and practice of marketing. The section begins by outlining what the marketing function actually does. It defines marketing and introduces "the marketing concept", contrasting this with other less market-orientated approaches to the business activity. Some examples of the marketing concept in practice are given. The role and function of marketing management are examined, within the context of both profit and non-profit making organisations. The final chapter in this section defines consumer and industrial markets, and differentiates the two in terms of marketing policy and practice.

1 The Marketing Concept

"Turn a deaf ear and a blind eye to your market, and wait for your customers to be struck dumb."

INTRODUCTION

This chapter describes in outline what the marketing function actually does, using a simple example. The marketing function is responsible for:

* identifying market opportunities and needs;
* keeping abreast of relevant technological developments;
* managing products;
* choosing and motivating the channels of distribution, such as retail outlets;
* advertising and promoting its products;
* obtaining sales of its products;
* setting prices and terms of supply;
* planning the marketing activity.

The chapter introduces and defines the "marketing concept" as a common sense managerial orientation that understands the needs and wants of customers in the market, and adapts the operations of the organisation to deliver the right goods and services more effectively than the company's competitors. This is put into two practical perspectives, namely:

* company management remaining sensitive to market needs;
* company management operating the enterprise in a market-orientated manner.

The marketing orientation towards business activity is then contrasted with three alternatives. These are production, product and sales orientations.

CHAPTER CONTENTS

1) What is marketing ?
2) Two definitions of marketing
3) What does marketing actually do ?

1) WHAT IS MARKETING ?

Marketing links two basic functions in the community, namely those of *production* and *consumption*. As society has become more complex, and the processes of manufacture and supply more varied, so the *means* by which the community is supplied with the goods and services it demands has itself become more complicated and important. Within the business enterprise it is the marketing activity which should provide this means, by ensuring that the enterprise supplies its market with goods or services that customers wish to buy.

From the viewpoint of the business enterprise, therefore, marketing is an activity which is directed at satisfying the needs and wants of customers through *exchange* processes which occur in the market. An exchange process actually means the transaction between buyer and seller, in which the buyer purchases a product and pays the supplier an agreed price for his wares. The market itself is made up of all the actual or potential buyers of these products or services.

2) TWO DEFINITIONS OF MARKETING

The definition given above is that:

Marketing is an activity directed at satisfying customer needs and wants through exchange transactions in the market.

The U.K. Institute of Marketing's definition is that:

Marketing is the management process responsible for identifying, anticipating and satisfying customer requirements profitably.

3) WHAT DOES MARKETING ACTUALLY DO ?

The management and staff of a company's marketing department would be responsible for a number of inter-related activities. Let us assume for a moment that the company manufactures and sells a range of *consumer durable* products, such as televisions, radios and Hi-Fi's. The marketing department might be responsible for

a) *identifying market opportunities:* it should research the needs and wants of the different types of customer to be found in the market. This is called "Market Research". At the same time it needs to be aware of *technological developments* taking place outside the company, and of "Research and Development" activities being undertaken by the enterprise itself. Indeed, as we shall see in later chapters, the marketing function has an important role to play in shaping the content of the Research and Development activity.

From its market research and its scanning of technological developments, the marketing function should be in a position to identify (or forecast):-

* trends in the demand pattern for existing products;

* market opportunities for new products, for example such as personal Hi-Fi's like the Sony Walkman;

* detailed needs for new product development that the company should undertake.

b) *managing products:* the marketing function should be responsible for forecasting and managing the rate of supply and distribution of the company's *existing products.* Equally important will be its prime role in determining what *new products* should be developed by the company and launched into its various markets. These new products should be designed in such a way as to meet the differing requirements of differing sections or "segments" of the total market. For instance, the marketing function in this case might have to decide which Hi-Fi ranges must be adapted to contain compact disc players, or whether to introduce an entirely new range of car stereo equipment incorporating the latest design and circuit features.

c) *choosing and motivating the channels of distribution:* a manufacturer of televisions and Hi-Fi could not possibly supply all of its retail customers direct. So it must use retailers to stock and sell its products on its behalf. It must select those retailers who will best look after its interests, and put most effort into selling its products to those retail customers who wish to buy such merchandise from amongst the wide choice of competing suppliers.

These retailers are an important "channel of distribution". Because they are separate companies, only rarely owned by the manufacturer, their efforts must be encouraged and supported by that manufacturer. After all, the final sale of the company's products to the retail customer is not (in this particular case) in the hands or control of the manufacturer, but in someone else's hands, those of the retailer.

d) *advertising and promoting its products:* the marketing function will be responsible for communicating to its *target market customers* the existence of its products and the benefits to be obtained from purchasing them. The advertising and promotional process is aimed at the target customer group so that it:-

* communicates to the customer;
* persuades the customer;
* encourages the customer to examine the product and understand its benefits;
* supports the retailer in selling the product to the customer;
* reassures the customer that he or she has made the correct purchase decision;
* encourages the customer to make further purchases of the company's products.

Advertising and promotional effort aims to stimulate the potential buyer into becoming *interested in purchasing,* which it will in this case be the retail salesperson's job to change into a *decision to purchase,* so that the sale is made.

e) *setting prices and terms of supply:* the marketing activity will be closely involved in agreeing and setting market prices, terms of supply and payment conditions. Other functional activities, such as finance and credit control, will also be involved in this important business area. For it is essential to the achievement of successful and profitable trading that:-

* prices are quoted both to the retailer, and to the final customer, that encourage them to buy the company's products, yet allow the company to make an adequate return on the funds that it has invested in the business. At the same time, the transaction must be financially rewarding to the retailer, whilst the customer must perceive that the prices being charged are reasonably competitive in comparison with the prices of other manufacturers of televisions or Hi-Fi's.

5

* conditions of supply and terms of payment are established with the retailer so that (i) the retailer is given adequate credit to encourage him to stock and sell quantities of the merchandise; yet (ii) he pays for the goods within a reasonable period after their receipt. Otherwise the manufacturer will suffer from the problem of having too much of its working capital tied up by *debtors* (businesses or customers who have taken delivery of products but have not yet paid for them).

f) *planning the marketing activity:* planning is an important and essential part of the operation of any business. Marketing planning must cover, in detail, items such as:-

* the time scale of new product development and launch onto the market;

* annual sales forecasting, which is the vital first step in company budgetary planning and control;

* the annual amount and rate of cashflow expenditure on advertising and promotion;

* the rate at which customers can be encouraged to pay for the goods they have received. The quicker that payment is received, the better;

* the actual cost and cashflow expenditure of the marketing activity as a whole.

Some of these activities are summarised in Figure 1.1.

4) THE MARKETING CONCEPT

The "Marketing Concept" may be defined thus:

The most important managerial task within the organisation is that of understanding the needs and wants of customers in the market, and of adapting the operations of the organisation to deliver the right goods and services more effectively and efficiently than its competitors.

This means that management in the business enterprise has two main areas of responsibility:

i) *remaining sensitive to market needs:* the management of the business must be aware of the nature of market demand, and of changes that occur in it. The nature of market demand, and the need to supply it effectively yet profitably, *should be the driving force behind the decisions*

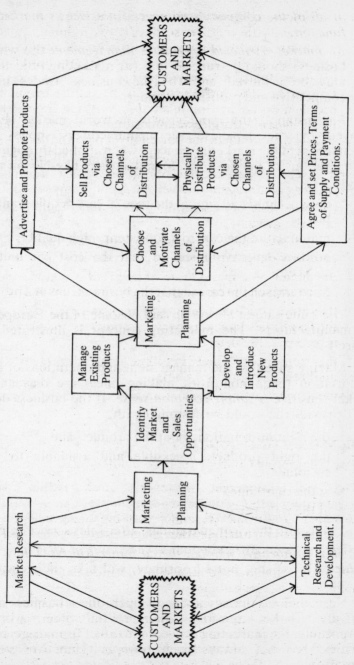

Figure 1.1. What Does Marketing Actually Do?

of all of the company's managers, not just its marketing function.

ii) *market-orientated operations management:* the whole business should be run so that (a) marketing objectives may be achieved and (b) the business trades in a competitive and profitable manner.

For instance, the rapid growth in world market share enjoyed by the Japanese car manufacturers shows the effectiveness of the marketing concept when applied throughout the operations of the business. Manufacturers like Nissan and Toyota

* design, build and supply the type of cars people want to buy;
* manufacture the cars to a consistent, high quality;
* produce large volumes, so that the cost per unit is reduced;
* price and sell the cars so that the business runs at a profit.

The same cannot always be said of some of the European car manufacturers! The marketing concept is illustrated in Figure 1.2.

Making sure that the management and operations of any organisation (even non-profit making ones) are reasonably market sensitive *is simple common sense.* If the business does NOT provide the would-be customer with:

* the right information about the product, and
* the right product, accessible and available to the customer
* at the right time
* at the right price
* and with the right guarantees, after-sales service (etc)

then, in a competitive market, the customer will NOT buy the product. He or she, not surprisingly, will take their custom elsewhere.

Nevertheless, the advantage of operating a business in a relatively market sensitive manner (in other words, incorporating the marketing concept into all of its management activities) has not always been obvious. Here are some alternatives.

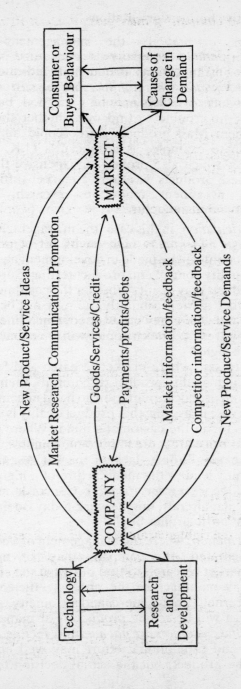

Figure 1.2. The Marketing Concept.

4.1 Some alternative business orientations

a) *production orientation:* the management in a production-orientated company is concerned with its manufacturing arrangements, productivity indicators, cost and volume. *It makes what it thinks that the customer will buy.* The products it makes may be very good, but it will take little or no trouble to find out whether there is a market for them. Mass-produced stereoscopic cameras are one unfortunate example; as is Sinclair's U.K. electric cycle, the C5, which also proved an expensive flop. For neither of these products was there a market sufficient to justify the investment made in research, design, development and manufacture.

b) *product orientation:* in this case, the management places *product design and quality* high on its list of priorities. Heavy investment will be made in development and design capability, quality control and product testing. Superb and efficient products may result. Whether the customer needs them is another matter. Similarly, he may not be able to buy them if and when they are wanted, since (inevitably) delivery delays result. The customer will have to wait until the product is right!

Needless to say, where market research and feedback show that a high quality product *is* required , then market orientation and product orientation go hand in hand. But it is not always wise to assume that product quality is the most important factor in the customer's mind. Where product availability or price are more important, compromises will have to be made. Worse, lack of market research and forecasting may lead to the manufacture of a high quality product *with the wrong specification.* Concorde may be a more spectacular aircraft, but the work-a-day Boeing 747 is the plane that most airlines buy!

c) *selling orientation:* where the management of a company is sales orientated, the company may, or may not undertake market research to find out what the customer wants. It may manufacture the product efficiently and remain concerned about merchandise quality. But its prime concern will be *selling products.* For management *will assume that customers are not naturally inclined to buy.* Advertising and promotional effort may well create an interest in the product, but the actual decision to buy is seen as a *negative* one (or at the very best, non-negative). Would-be customers, therefore, have to be pushed into making the purchase decision (which they would, it is assumed, prefer to avoid). This requires a strong and energetic *sales push*. Hence, the task of the business is to make, package, price and promote the product, *and then to sell it hard*. The sales department becomes a central function in the business, and expenditure on promotional and sales effort forms the main part of the company's investment.

This approach to business is seen in the UK in the market for Life Assurance, and in the area of Home Improvements, such as replacement windows, house insulation, showers and fitted kitchens.

Evidently, each of these three alternative business orientations contain common sense. Products must be made to the right quality and within budgeted cost, and there must be appropriate arrangements for manufacture and supply. Often the potential customer will not make up his or her mind without some sales pressure, and indeed may rely on the salesperson to reinforce an existing favourable (or unfavourable) attitude towards the product. But any one of these orientations is inadequate. It would be highly risky to invest in manufacturing plant and design capability *before* finding out about market requirements. Many customers will accept a compromise between quality and price. Other customers will arrive at a purchase decision without the presence of a salesperson, and indeed may resent or dislike "the hard sell".

A company management that is market-orientated, and marketing-orientated, will therefore take *all* of these factors into account, and will manage its affairs in the more systematic way already described. *In this way, it will put the marketing concept into practice.*

SUMMARY

The contents of this chapter are summarised in Table 1.3

TABLE 1.3
Summary : Chapter One

SECTION	MAIN POINTS
1. What is marketing?	Marketing links the production and purchase/consumption of goods and services through exchange processes.
2. Definition of marketing	Marketing is an activity directed at satisfying customer needs and wants through exchange transactions in the market.
3. What does marketing do?	The marketing function is responsible for (i) identifying market opportunities and needs; (ii) keeping abreast of relevant technological developments; (iii) managing products; (iv) choosing and motivating the channels of distribution (such as retail outlets); (v) advertising and promoting the company's products; (vi) selling its products; (vii) setting prices and terms of supply; (viii) planning the marketing activity.
4. The marketing concept	The marketing concept may be defined thus : "the most important managerial task within the organisation is that of understanding the needs and wants of customers in the market, and of adapting the operations of the organisation to deliver the right goods and services more effectively and efficiently than its competitors." This involves the business in (i) remaining sensitive to market needs; (ii) managing operations on a market-orientated basis. The marketing concept can be contrasted with production, product and selling orientations.

2 Marketing Management

INTRODUCTION

This chapter looks at the responsibility of company and marketing management for implementing the marketing concept. This responsibility is explained and described on the basis of the four standard management functions of planning, organising, motivating and controlling.

The chapter goes on to take a brief look at marketing orientations within non-profit making organisations, and concludes with three short examples of the marketing concept and marketing orientation put into practice.

CHAPTER CONTENTS

1) Marketing Management
   1.1) The functions of marketing management
2) Profit and non-profit making organisations
3) Some case examples of the marketing concept in operation
   3.1) Amstrad wordprocessors
   3.2) Air inclusive package tours
   3.3) Family recreation experiences

Summary

1) MARKETING MANAGEMENT

To recap what was said in the previous chapter, marketing management is responsible for putting the marketing concept into practice by:

* making sure that *all* of the activities of the business (including production and financial management, as well as marketing), identify, anticipate and satisfy customer requirements in an effective and profitable manner;

* making sure that *all* of the activities of the business operate in a market-orientated manner, relative to the company's financial objectives and obligations.

It will actually do this by incorporating the marketing concept into all of the management functions for which it is responsible.

1.1 The functions of marketing management

It is usual to identify four main *management functions*. Any manager, in any corporate or functional area, is responsible for

> PLANNING
> ORGANISING
> MOTIVATING, GUIDING OR DIRECTING
> CONTROLLING

a) *Planning:* Marketing Management has three main responsibilities here. The first is its contribution to the process of corporate (or company-wide) business planning. The marketing function should have a major influence on such issues as what businesses the company should be in, what markets it should serve, what products or services it should offer, and what investments it should make. The second is the provision of detailed market and sales forecasts for the company's annual operating and budget plans. The third is the detailed planning of marketing and sales activities over which it has direct control. The *planning horizons* or time scale of these three responsibilities will vary from a few weeks or months ahead, up to several years in the case of the development of new products or new businesses.

b) *Organising:* Marketing Management has two main responsibilities under this heading. The first responsibility is that of managing its functional and corporate relationship to the other main business functions (manufacturing or operations management, physical distribution, credit control and financial management, personnel etc), *so that these other functions themselves* (i) remain sensitive to market needs and (ii) operate in a market sensitive manner. The second responsibility is that of the cost effective organisation of those marketing and sales activities over which there is direct (or line) control.

The organisational role of the marketing function is analysed in the section entitled *"Marketing within the organisation"* later in this book. It is an area that many other marketing texts fail properly to deal with, yet it is crucial to effective marketing management, *and to the implementation of the marketing concept right throughout the enterprise.*

c) *Motivating, Guiding or Directing:* Managers are responsible for motivating and guiding the people who carry out the work of the organisation, so that its objectives are achieved. Sometimes employees (and managers) need firm direction, whilst at other times consultation and participation will achieve the desired level of motivation and activity.

Marketing management will again have two main responsibilities. The first will be to guide and motivate the management of the other main business functions into maintaining an effective level of market orientation. Marketing management may achieve this by influence and persuasion, by exhortation, or by otherwise reminding other functional managers of the risks of becoming insensitive to the company's markets. Marketing management will also have to develop political and bargaining skills to make sure that its views are well represented in decision-making at the highest levels of the business. It must in any case be in a position to exercise a major influence at Board of Directors level over the formulation of corporate policies and decisions, and over their implementation in practical terms.

Secondly, marketing management must guide and motivate the efforts of those staff directly involved in implementing marketing policies and decisions, so that the functional or departmental objectives of the marketing activity are achieved.

d) *Controlling:* Managers are responsible for monitoring and adjusting the operations of the business so that its objectives are achieved. This is the *control process.* Marketing management will be responsible for the achievement of its own direct departmental objectives. These will take the form of unit volume and sales revenue achieved, new products launched onto the market, the creation of effective advertising campaigns, etc. Secondly, marketing management will have a direct responsibility for the fulfillment of enterprise-wide goals for cash flow, profitability and return on assets employed. This is because the marketing activity, and its relationship to the other business functions, will play a key role in the achievement of the enterprise's financial objectives, and therefore on its capacity to meet its obligations to shareholders, suppliers and employees, and hence to the community in which it operates.

2) PROFIT AND NON-PROFIT MAKING ORGANISATIONS

It is usual to think of marketing, market-orientation and the marketing concept within the context of profit making, and business environments. However, these concepts can apply just as much to non-profit making organisations where:

* there are clients or "customers" for the product or service;
* there is some kind of benefit available to the client/ customer;
* there is need for communication of these available benefits;
* there are costs involved in the provision of these benefits, even if they are indirect and are financed by taxation.

If the marketing concept is applied to such situations, the client or customer is seen as the "target market" and the organisation should be adapted such that it meets the needs of the target within its financial constraints. So, for instance, there would be:

i) accurate targeting of communications on specific groups (for instance, health communications to male smokers aged forty and above who run a disproportionately high risk of heart disease);

ii) an attempt to provide the range and level of service required by clients (for instance by a drastic reduction of U.K. National Health Service treatment waiting lists to a level comparable with private health care);

iii) an appropriate extension of the services provided (for instance by the provision of low-cost annual health check-ups carried out at people's place of work);

iv) an attempt to improve cost effectiveness. This might also involve changes in the funding basis, for instance by requiring additional financial contributions from the client, or privatising the suppliers of the service. Most institutions of higher education in the U.K. and the Commonwealth are themselves required to seek and obtain at least some of the funds they need. These additional funds may come from industry and commerce, from benefactors and charitable trusts, or even from past students. Such changes in the funding basis of these non-profit making organisations are based on the recognition that:

– there are advantages to both client and institution of an improved service, and:
– available funds are inadequate and need supplementing, and:
– therefore, improved cost-effectiveness is vital to achieving improved service and minimising the need for supplementary funds.

3) SOME CASE EXAMPLES OF THE MARKETING CONCEPT IN OPERATION

Here are three brief examples of the marketing concept put into practice. Each shows a clear case of market sensitivity and market orientation.

3.1) Amstrad Wordprocessors.

The introduction by Amstrad of its low priced wordprocessor onto the U.K. market undoubtedly caught the public imagination. The availability and effectiveness of a complete wordprocessor system for under £500 at the time of launch clearly met a market need, whether in office, small business or domestic environments. The complete system was competitive in price with electric typewriters, and yet provided all the added-value features of wordprocessing and storage that have made the wordprocessor concept such a universally popular one.

3.2 Air inclusive package tours

The air inclusive package tour concept was originally pioneered in the U.K. during the late 1940's and the 1950's. Instead of being required to make separate bookings for accommodation and transport, holidaymakers were offered the convenience of making one single integrated booking for all of the elements making up their holiday. Secondly, the large volumes of business generated meant that tour operators could obtain large discounts on bulk accommodation and flight bookings. These savings were passed on to the customer, who found that air inclusive package tours, whether it be to Spain, Greece, Hong Kong, Singapore, Malaysia or wherever, became highly price competitive. Increased volume and competition in turn generated further bulk discounts and resulted in long term price stability, with *real prices* (from which the effects of inflation are excluded) which have shown resistance even to increases caused by rising aircraft fuel costs, or currency value fluctuations.

3.3) Family recreation experiences

The past decade has seen the development of "theme parks", "fantasy lands" and the like, offering family recreation experience or "adventure" with a high level of novelty and excitement. Well known examples include Disneyland and the EPCOT Centre (USA), Legoland (Europe), Santa Claus land (Scandinavia) and Alton Towers (U.K.). The concept can be widened to include working museums, safari parks and preserved railways. U.K. examples include the Jorvik Viking centre, the Ironbridge Trust, Gladstone Pottery Museum, Longleat and the National Garden Festivals. The popularity of these recreation centres is shown by their massive visitor and sales turnover figures. They have identified and filled a major gap in the provision of exciting, escapist or nostalgic family recreation.

SUMMARY

The contents of this chapter are summarised in Table 2.1

TABLE 2.1
Summary : Chapter Two

SECTION	MAIN POINTS
1. Marketing management	Marketing management is responsible for putting the marketing concept into practice by ensuring that all activities of the business (i) identify, anticipate and satisfy customer requirements in an effective and profitable manner; (ii) remain sensitive to market needs; (iii) operate in a market-sensitive manner, relative to the company's financial objectives and obligations.

Its functions include (a) *planning* marketing activity, and being involved in corporate and budgeting planning; (b) *organising* the marketing function, and that function's relationship with other business functions (production, finance etc), such that the whole business operates in a market-sensitive manner; (c) guiding and *motivating* the staff in the marketing function, and those other business functions affected by the need to remain market-orientated; (d) *controlling* the marketing function and its relationship with other functions such that the company's marketing and financial objectives are achieved.

2. Non-profit making organisations

The marketing concept can be applied to non-profit making organisations if a "target market" can be identified and its required satisfactions established. Customer satisfaction gained from the right products or services positioned on target groups is just as desirable an objective as in commercial organisations, especially where the organisation is funded by the taxpayer. Attempts to improve customer service in such organisations may have financial implications and call for additional fundraising

3 Consumer and Industrial Marketing

INTRODUCTION

In this chapter, consumer and industrial markets for goods and services are defined, and the differences between the two are illustrated by a variety of examples. The kinds of items purchased in each type of market are outlined, and the differences between the two are then analysed in detail, using a range of selected criteria.

A key factor in differentiating the two types of market is the derived nature of demand in industrial markets. The meaning of derived demand is explained, and the vulnerability of industrial markets to *cyclical variations* in line with the general business cycle is identified.

Another important matter for consideration is the *organisational nature of buying decisions* in industrial markets. Those people that wish to sell into such markets must understand the policies and processes determining what, when and how their customers will buy.

The chapter goes on to consider the prices, terms and conditions of trade in the two market types. Whilst these may be straightforward in consumer goods markets, they may be much more complex and influential in industrial markets, where they are usually determined by negotiation between the suppliers and the purchaser.

The chapter concludes with a brief comparison between the approaches to marketing policy and practice adopted by companies in the two different types of market. That section anticipates material dealt with in greater detail later in the book.

CHAPTER CONTENTS

1) Consumer and Industrial Markets

2) What do people buy in consumer markets?

3) What do people buy in industrial markets?

4) Some differences between consumer and industrial markets

    4.1) Criteria for differentiation

    4.2) Significant differences between consumer and industrial markets

1) CONSUMER AND INDUSTRIAL MARKETS

Consumer markets consist of all the individuals and households who purchase goods and services for their own, *personal consumption. Industrial markets,* on the other hand, are made up of individuals and organisations who buy products and services that will be used *in manufacture or business,* or eventually *resold* to other customers. Ford and General Motors sell cars in both markets. The cars they make are sold to individual private owners, and also to fleet owners who are in business to hire out cars to their own customers. Nescafé is sold mainly in consumer markets, (although sales to vending machine operators would count as an industrial or business market). JCB, however, sell the vast majority of their earthmoving equipment to construction companies, local government authorities, farmers and the like.

2) WHAT DO PEOPLE BUY IN CONSUMER MARKETS?

There are three distinct categories within consumer markets. These are:

a) *non durable products,* purchased on a relatively frequent basis and consumed or used within a reasonably short period after purchase. Examples: foodstuffs, fuels, toiletries, paint. Sometimes called "fast moving consumer goods" (f.m.c.g.).

b) *durable goods,* purchased less frequently and used over a longer period of time (perhaps for several or many years). Examples: clothing, electrical goods, cars, furniture, housing.

c) *services,* which are activities whose purchase will secure specific benefits or satisfactions sought by the consumer. These services are often personal, and since the demand for them may occur at any time their supplier must be able to offer them on a continuous basis. Examples:

hairdressing, car repairs, painters and decorators, entertainments and recreation.

3) WHAT DO PEOPLE BUY IN INDUSTRIAL MARKETS?

i) *consumable products,* purchased on a relatively frequent basis and generally used shortly after purchase (especially where a company is attempting to minimise its holdings of stock of such products in order to minimise its expenditure of working capital). Examples: fuels and lubricants, welding rods, edible oils and ingredients for foodstuffs manufacture.

ii) *capital goods,* purchased infrequently and used over a longer period of time. Examples: ships, plant, machinery, vehicles, land and buildings.

iii) services, which comprise work activities needed to carry out specific tasks that the organisation must undertake in order to achieve its commercial or operational objectives. Again, suppliers must be able to offer these services on a continuous basis. Examples: support services for oil rigs, road hauliers, machinery repairers, advertising agencies, business consultants.

4) SOME DIFFERENCES BETWEEN CONSUMER AND INDUSTRIAL MARKETS

There are a number of significant differences between consumer and industrial markets, and these are examined in sections (4.1) to (4.3). Their implications for a company's marketing policy are then briefly analysed in section (5). Further analysis is given in the following chapters, as appropriate.

4.1) Criteria for differentiation

A number of criteria can be used to differentiate between consumer and industrial markets. They include:

* type of demand;
* type of product;
* use of product;
* type of buyer (individual, group or organisational);
* number of buyers;
* place of purchase;
* terms and conditions of purchase.

4.2) Significant differences between consumer and industrial markets

a) *demand in industrial markets is "derived":* goods and services are purchased as *inputs* to a manufacturing or operational process whose objective is the supply of a product to another customer. This customer might be an individual in a consumer goods market, or it might be another industrial customer. For instance, the manufacturers of edible oils sell their products to biscuit manufacturers, who sell biscuits into consumer markets. But a manufacturer of specialist electronic circuits might sell his control systems to machinery manufacturers, who sell foodprocessing equipment to the biscuit maker. Thus, *market prospects depend on the demand for the product sold to the next customer in the chain of supply.*

It is inevitable, therefore, that industrial markets will suffer from a *variable demand pattern.* There are often pronounced swings in the demand for products like merchant ships, engineering machinery, steel plants or oil drilling rigs. These variations and swings follow the pattern of the *business cycle,* which reflects the state of the total economy at the time. Where there is a reduction in consumer demand during a recession, then there is likely to be a more than proportionate decrease in the derived demand within the industrial markets dependent on that consumer demand. Similarly, in boom conditions, industrial markets may be swamped with orders that the manufacturers simply cannot meet quickly. These variations are illustrated in Figure 3.1.

The most severe effect is felt by suppliers of *basic products* like fuel, steel and manufacturing machinery. Recession works backwards against these suppliers, as each link in the supply chain to the final consumer pushes his problems backwards towards them. Similarly, they may receive far too many orders at the peak of a boom, since everyone wants additional supplies to meet their own increased demand. (Economists describe this principle as "the accelerator", which describes the dynamics of demand patterns).

The worst problems of derived demand are faced by the manufacturers of machine tools, who are at "the end" of the business cycle and who cannot respond quickly either in conditions of boom or slump.

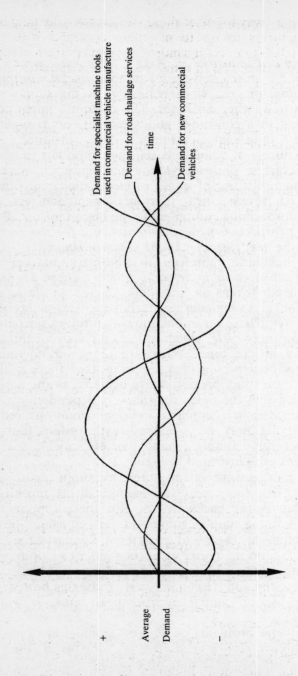

Figure 3.1. An Example of Cyclical Demand Variations. Demand for Road Haulage Services.

The only way to offset these variations in demand is for manufacturers to try to negotiate contracts with their industrial customers for a more consistent pattern of supply over a stated period of time. Such *smoothed* patterns will help suppliers during recession, and benefit customers during booms, since their orders will take priority.

b) *size and frequency of purchase:* purchases in consumer goods markets are usually frequently made, and the value of each transaction will be relatively small. The purchase of grocery products is one good example. Compare this with the purchase of a mighty Foden, Volvo or Peterbilt truck. Large commercial vehicles will be purchased by any one customer on an infrequent basis. But the order value of the transaction may run into many thousands of pounds or dollars.

c) *number of potential customers:* foodstuffs manufacturers face consumer markets containing millions of buyers. This means that they must undertake a massive or "dense" distribution operation so that the product is available in relatively small quantities in many wholesale and retail outlets. The manufacturer cannot deal face to face with the customer, and needs to *promote* the product by advertising, or offering price incentives to encourage shoppers to buy. Manufacturers or suppliers in consumer goods markets also rely on "intermediaries" (wholesalers and retailers) to stock and sell the product, and to receive payments from customers.

Computer manufacturers like IBM and ICL on the other hand, do have many thousands of customers for mainframe computer systems, *but a relatively small proportion of these customers will buy a large proportion of the total output.* Amongst their customers will be departments in central and local government, utilities such as electricity supply, and industrial giants like Shell or General Foods. In this kind of industrial market, direct contact between supplier and customer is essential, and the product will be supplied direct. Indeed, an extreme case is the market for railway equipment and locomotives, in which manufacturers usually face only one major buyer in those countries that have a unified, state-run railway network.

d) *technical buying decisions:* purchase decisions in industrial goods markets have a technical as well as an economic dimension. Technical factors will influence the product supplied, its price and the conditions of its supply and demand. They will also complicate the costing of the product, and make accurate *cost estimation* and *sales forecasting* an essential ingredient to the achievement of commercial success.

e) *organisational purchasing motives:* as we have seen already, business, governmental or administrative organisations do not buy for personal consumption, but to obtain goods or services necessary to the achievement of their operational objectives. More people get involved in any one organisational buying decision than do in consumer markets, and amongst these different decision makers there may be a variety of organisational responsibilities and perceptions that influence attitudes towards the product and the potential supplier. The organisational buyer is in any case likely to be subject to laid-down purchase evaluation criteria, which are based on the particular policies and constraints under which the organisation operates.

Thus, the seller must anticipate and understand the *organisational factors* that determine what products are purchased, when investments will be made, and who makes the final choice. Above all, the seller must understand how the purchase decision is made. For example, local or central government authorities may put major orders out "to tender" to selected companies. These companies will be the only ones permitted to tender. The order may then be placed with the company which has quoted the lowest price! Or, a component company wishing to supply a car or commercial vehicle manufacturer may have *first* to equip its delivery fleet with some of the vehicles manufactured by that company. Only then may it be allowed to quote for business.

f) *buying procedures:* organisational buyers will require suppliers to conform to a variety of formalised and standardised buying procedures. These may include formal requests for quotations, verbal and written presentations of sales proposals, and detailed negotiation of contractual arrangements. Buying procedures and documentation may become much more complex in overseas markets, especially in centralised planned economies such as Russia and China. Specialist expertise is usually required when dealing with sales to such countries.

4.3) Prices, terms and conditions of trade

i) *consumer goods markets:* the terms and conditions of supply to consumers are usually fixed in Western markets. The consumer will normally be required to pay the full price, or a proportionate deposit, in cash, upon order or delivery. Any outstanding balance of payments for, say, a suite of furniture might then be made on a Hire Purchase basis (that is, using borrowed money upon which interest is to be paid). There will usually be little scope for negotiation between supplier and customer over terms and conditions, and only marginally more over the price itself. Prices in consumer markets are often "fixed", in contrast to the moveable prices in the kasbah in Tangier, the bazaar in Istanbul, or the crowded markets of the Far East! Bargaining over price does occur in the UK in the area of house purchase, the purchase of major items of home improvement (such as fitted kitchens or double glazing), and in car purchase.

Generally speaking, however, the fixed price is the norm in the West. This situation is made the more likely given the effect of price competition between retail outlets and their need to cover their own operating and capital costs.

ii) *industrial goods markets:* dealings in industrial goods markets are usually standardised and formalised. They follow set procedures and normally involve the signing of formal contracts and agreements. Industrial markets are often characterised by the use of *loans and credit facilities* which finance the transactions involved. In this way the supplier and customer are tied together, since financial provisions are often included in the contractual arrangements regulating the transaction. Indeed, it is common to find that agreement to a deal between a supplier and a buyer is largely dependent upon the supplier offering appropriate and adequate credit terms to the buyer, and the negotiation of the credit terms will be an important part of the final deal. Other relevant factors include:

* the process by which the actual *price* is negotiated: this will depend upon the relative bargaining strengths of the parties involved, the relative importance of the transaction to each, and the

    costing/pricing policy of the supplier (this is dealt with in later chapters, on Pricing)
* contractual inducements (incentives) for early delivery, and financial penalties for late delivery. Such "encouragements" are often found in international trading agreements.
* provisions for cost or price variations caused by currency value fluctuations beyond the supplier's control.

In those overseas trading markets which are generally judged to be "unreliable", suppliers may require government guarantees or other security against payments not being made by customers. Alternatively, buyers may demand the right to delay any payment until after the agreed work has been completed.

Certainly, a major consideration in any industrial market will be the financial consequences of the deal on both supplier and customer. Of special importance will be the effect on:

– cashflow movements involved in manufacture, supply or purchase.
– the total available working capital: for example can the manufacturer actually supply the product without "overtrading" (operating beyond his financial resources)?

5) APPROACHES TO MARKETING POLICY AND PRACTICE

Table 3.2 gives some examples of the differences in marketing policy and practice to be found between consumer and industrial markets. These examples anticipate the more complete analysis to be found under the relevant headings in later chapters, where more specific and detailed comparisons will be made.

Table 3.2
A comparison of some examples of approaches to marketing policy and practice

MARKETING POLICY/ PRACTICE	CONSUMER MARKETS	INDUSTRIAL MARKETS
Number of final customers for product	Often very many (eg grocery and foodstuffs market)	Often relatively few (eg market for ceramics kilns)
Closeness of relationship to final customer	Usually remote	Often very close
Product specificity in market	Relatively low; broad specifications generally acceptable	Relatively high; often customer specified
Technical content of marketing function	Low	High
Importance of sales-force	Important	Very important
Use of salesforce	Sell to intermediaries (wholesalers, retailers)	Sell to intermediaries and direct to customers
Importance of advertising	Very important	Less important
Expenditure on media advertising and promotion	High	Less high
Main types of advertising and promotion used	Commercial television and radio; mass circulation newspapers and magazines, posters; coupons and money-off incentives; on-pack offers (etc)	Specialist trade press; technical data sheets and sales literature; trade exhibitions; specialist/technical conferences (etc)
Terms and conditions of supply	Fixed	Negotiated contracts
Payment conditions	Cash based; payment on collection or delivery	Negotiated, credit and delivery terms agreed in contract

SUMMARY

The contents of this chapter are summarised in Table 3.3

TABLE 3.3
Summary : Chapter Three

SECTION	MAIN POINTS
2. Consumer markets	Consumer markets consist of all the individuals and households who purchase goods/services for their own, personal use/consumption. These people buy (i) non durable goods (eg foodstuffs, paint) purchased and used relatively frequently; (ii) durable goods (eg clothing, electrical products) purchased less frequently but used over longer periods of time; (iii) services (eg hairdressing, car repairs) whose purchase secures specific benefits or satisfactions, sought mainly to meet personal demands that may occur at any time.
3. Industrial goods markets	Industrial goods markets consist of individuals and organisations who buy products/services used in manufacture or business, or eventually resold to other customers. These people buy (i) consumable products, purchased frequently and used up after purchase (eg welding rods, fuel oil); (ii) capital goods purchased infrequently and used over a period of time (eg land/buildings, plant/machinery); (iii) services needed to enable the organisation to carry out specific tasks relevant to the achievement of its objectives (eg machinery repairers, advertising agencies)

4. Differences between consumer and industrial markets	Demand in industrial goods markets is "derived": goods/services are purchased as inputs to a manufacturing or operational process whose objective is the supply of a product/service to another customer. As a result, market prospects depend on the demand for the product sold to the next customer in the chain of supply. In consequence, industrial markets tend to suffer from variable demand patterns manifest as "business cycles". There are often pronounced swings in demand for products like merchant ships or engineering machinery, because where there is a reduction in consumer demand (or increased competition amongst suppliers) during a recession, there is likely to be a more than proportionate decrease in the derived demand within industrial markets dependent on that consumer demand. Other differences include (i) relative size and frequency of purchase; (ii) number of potential customers; (iii) technical content of buying decisions; (iv) organisational purchasing motives; (v) buying procedures; (vi) prices, terms and conditions of trade.

QUESTIONS FOR SELF REVIEW

1) Compare and contrast production, product, sales and marketing orientations towards the market served by a business enterprise.

2) Define and comment on the "Marketing Concept".

3) What is the function of marketing management?

4) Outline and comment on the role of marketing management within the wider context of the operation of a business enterprise as a whole unit.

5)   *In what ways is the marketing concept relevant to non profit-making organisations?*

6)   *Compare and contrast consumer and industrial markets for goods and services.*

7)   *What is "derived demand?" Why is it an important factor in industrial marketing decisions? (Also see Chapters 14 and 15).*

8)   *Why should the management of an industrial or organisational buying department take the "derived" nature of industrial demand into account when deciding on the timing and pattern by which it will purchase goods and services? (Also see Chapters 14 and 15).*

9)   *"Credit is as important as price in marketing to industrial customers." Comment on this statement. (Also see Chapter 40).*

EXAMINATION QUESTIONS

Q1   *What is marketing?*

                                                                    (SSM)

Q2   *What is the 'marketing concept'? Comment on its relationship to other business orientations.*

                                                                    (ACCA)

Q3   *"The marketing concept is applicable to all business organisations irrespective of size or nature of the goods and services marketed". Discuss this statement.*

                                                                    (IIM)

Q4   *Outline and discuss those factors which you believe have given rise to the need for companies to be marketing orientated.*

                                                                    (CIM)

Q5   *Evaluate, using examples, the main differences between consumer marketing and industrial marketing.*

                                                                    (IPS)

Market Research

Market research can be described as a process which provides a business organisation with its basic information and market intelligence. This information concerns the customer or client, and seeks to find out who he or she is, what they will buy, or what services they are seeking. This section looks at the kind of information sought by market researchers. It describes the two main sources of market intelligence, which are desk research and field research. Field research methods are analysed, and the construction of questionnaires is given detailed consideration. The role of sampling is discussed, and sampling methods are analysed. Finally, an overview of the whole market research process is given.

4 Market Research

"The business graveyard is full of marketing people who didn't listen to their customers!"

INTRODUCTION

Market research can be defined as the process which provides a business (or indeed any organisation which deals with the public) with its basic information. This information concerns the customer and who he or she is, and what they will buy. Market research information is needed to make a whole variety of marketing and operational decisions.

This chapter outlines the kind of information sought by market researchers, and looks at who may actually be responsible for obtaining it. It examines the two main sources of information, which are desk (or secondary) research and field (or primary) research.

Desk or secondary research involves the investigation and analysis of (i) internal company data, and (ii) external published information, such as trade and government statistics.

There are four main types of field or primary research used to obtain market information. They are (i) the personal interview, (ii) the telephone interview, (iii) the postal survey, and (iv) consumer panels. These sources of information are described, and their relative advantages and disadvantages are listed. The factors relevant to the market researcher's choice amongst these field methods are also described.

Other issues in market research are dealt with in Chapters Five and Six.

CHAPTER CONTENTS

1) Market research defined
2) What are the results of market research?
3) Who carries out market research?
4) Sources of information: desk or secondary research
   4.1) Internal company data
   4.2) External published data

5) Sources of information: field or primary research
   5.1) Choice of field research method
   5.2) The personal interview
   5.3) The telephone interview
   5.4) The postal survey
   5.5) The panel

Summary

1) MARKET RESEARCH DEFINED

Market research means finding out who the customer is, and what he or she will buy. *Market research provides a business with its basic information. This basic market information is needed to make a whole variety of marketing and operational decisions.* It is so important that it has been placed in this first part of the book, for without adequate market research the issues dealt with in its later stages cannot, in practical terms, be resolved. For instance, how can you set prices if you have no idea about the income levels of prospective customers, nor any idea of *their* perceptions about what price reflects good "value for money"? How can you design new products if you have no idea about how people will treat these products, or use them? Indeed, how will you know in the first place whether they will even consider buying them?

The absolute importance to a business of carrying out adequate, and *continuous* market research can be illustrated by a medical parallel. A firm that ignores the need to carry out market research is like a doctor who prescribes treatment without undertaking any diagnosis of the patient, and then refuses to consider the effects!

2) WHAT ARE THE RESULTS OF MARKET RESEARCH?

Market research activities aim to find answers to some of the following questions:

* who and where are the customers, and what are they like?
* who are the non-customers and why do they not buy?
* how is the market made up?
* how is the market divided into separate sections or "segments"?

* what are the patterns of market behaviour and why does this behaviour occur?
* what are the patterns of market demand?
* what products or services are demanded, and in what qualities and quantities?
* what is the size and economic viability of these markets?
* what changes are taking place in these markets?
* (etc)

3) WHO CARRIES OUT MARKET RESEARCH?

Market research activities may be carried out by the marketing function, or it may instead make use of an external market research *agency*. These agencies are specialists, and may be able to call upon a level of technical expertise and data processing facilities in which an individual company could not justify the investment *on its own*. Commonly, a company's marketing department and its chosen market research agency will work closely together on a teamwork basis.

4) SOURCES OF INFORMATION: DESK OR SECONDARY RESEARCH

There are two main sources of market information that can be obtained from Desk or Secondary Research. They are:

– Internal company data.
– External published data.

Each will be described in turn.

4.1) Internal company data

Market information can be gained from *objective sales records,* and *subjective assessments* made by anyone who is in contact with customers and the marketplace generally. This, of course, assumes that objective sales records are compiled and maintained, and subjective assessments (say, made by sales representatives) are actually written down, kept, and read! Internal company data may include:

* customer sales records;
* customer payment records, lists of debtors by amount and time outstanding;
* unsuccessful bids and quotations;

* sales representatives' reports;
* assessments of competitor effectiveness;
* customer guarantee documents;
* correspondence with individual customers;
* internal assessments of market and technological changes;
* (etc)

Business enterprises usually generate large quantities of information that can be of use to the market researcher. This potential for usefulness will depend on whether such information:

– is recognised as being relevant and useful for market research purposes;
– is categorised, sorted, summarised and stored;
– is accessible to the researcher;
– is deemed valuable *as an information resource in its own right*.

The impact of Information Technology (for instance through the use of *databases)* on the achievement of the *potential* offered to the market researcher by internal sources of information may be considerable. But this anticipates the subject matter of a later chapter.

4.2) External published data

There is available a whole variety of published (or purchasable) information which may be relevant to the market researcher. This "secondary" information will itself vary widely in the degree to which it is general or specific. These sources include:

a) *trade information:* which comprises the trade press, trade association reports and surveys, and independently published reports and surveys. There are also specialist publishers (such as Mintel and the Economist Intelligence Unit) who compile and sell periodic reports and surveys on different markets, which from time to time they update.

b) *company reports and accounts:* annual company reports and accounts may give a clue to what competitors plan to do, and hint at their interpretation of market trends. There are also specialist publishers who collect and publish company ratios and performance trends. This comparative information may again give a clue towards emerging market behaviour and trends.

c) government publications, national and international statistics: these include census data, family expenditure surveys, national income statistics, trade and manufacturing trends. Whilst such information suffers from a high level of generalisation, and time delays in compilation, it has obvious use as basic information input and structure in market research concerned with:

* demographic (population) distribution and categorisation;

* export into new overseas markets;

* broad market trends, say related to income level, employment and available leisure time;

* (etc).

d) *retail audit data:* in this case a market research agency will undertake a continuous sample audit of retail stocks of particular product types and categories. By analysing delivery notes and stocks, an estimate of retail sales of these products can be made. Depending upon the size of the sample of retail shops included in the audit, relatively accurate estimates can be made of (i) the total market size and market shares of the different manufacturers within it, (ii) the proportion of retail outlets stocking various brands, and (iii) the overall trends in retail stock levels and sales of the product category in question.

5) SOURCES OF INFORMATION – FIELD OR PRIMARY RESEARCH

Field or primary research is actually undertaken within the market itself. It is "original" and is designed to obtain *specific information* in response to specific questions or lines of enquiry. It therefore concentrates on a *selection of people* who can correctly be categorised as actual or potential buyers in the market, and whose responses to the line of enquiry are therefore *relevant* to the market research and the decisions to be based upon it.

For instance, a manufacturer of garden tools and equipment would research the attitude of trade and retail customers towards existing types and makes of (say) lawnmowers before designing a new prototype of its own, and before setting a target price at which the product would be sold. Actual market research showed that many users of electric hover mowers considered them "messy", as the grass cuttings were blown all over the place. Some manufacturers then redesigned the mower so the grass cuttings were blown into a collecting box, which could be emptied just like those on traditional cylinder mowers.

There are four main methods by which field (or primary) research may be carried out. They are:

5.2) the personal interview.
5.3) the telephone interview.
5.4) the postal survey.
5.5) the panel.

These are described in detail below. The choice of method will depend on a number of factors, thus:-

5.1) Choice of field research method

This will depend on:

a) the budget available for the field research; which is related to:

b) the time available for the field work, since methods vary in the amount of time they require for completion; which is also related to:

c) the accuracy of the results required, since some methods are more accurate than others. However, the more accurate the method, the more expensive it is likely to be.

d) the kind of people to be surveyed, for different methods will suit different types of people or different circumstances. For instance, people vary in their literacy, and some people are also fearful of completing written questionnaires because they equate this with "official snooping" on their privacy.

e) the geographical spread of the sample of people to be surveyed. If the sample is geographically scattered, some methods are more economic than others to operate.

5.2) The personal interview

The personal interview is a widely used method of contact and communication in market research. It is a direct form of investigation, in which an interviewer obtains information from selected respondents on a face-to-face basis. The interview is normally structured around a formal questionnaire (see Chapter 5), upon which responses are recorded and later correlated with all the other interview results.

a) *advantages of the personal interview method:*

* the personal interview yields a high percentage of acceptable responses;
* there is a low refusal rate;
* the sample can be statistically accurate (see Chapter 6);
* the information can be accurate, as the interviewer can immediately clarify contradictory statements or misunderstandings;
* the interviewer can assess cases when incorrect information is given deliberately;
* through observation, additional information on respondent characteristics can be noted, e.g age, social class;
* the respondent is likely to give spontaneous answers;
* personal questions can be asked;
* the questionnaire can be longer than with any other method.
* visual material can be used;
* a list of individual adults (the electoral register, or its equivalent outside the UK) is available.

b) *disadvantages of the personal interview method:*

* the high cost per interview, including interviewers' fees, maintenance, travelling expenses, etc;
* through personal contact the interviewer may influence the answers given, (this is called interviewer bias);
* inaccuracy in recording the replies may occur, especially if the respondent is in a hurry, or shows a negative attitude towards the interviewer whilst answering the questions;

* the decentralised nature of personal interviews, such that control and supervision are costly, and both organiser and interviewer have frequently to rely on written instructions;
* the expensive organisation and administration needed for selecting, training and supervising interviewers;
* the number of interviews per day is restricted:
  – by the time taken to contact appropriate respondents; and
  – by the length of the interviews themselves;
* it may be necessary to conduct interviews in the evenings and at weekends, which increases the cost for overtime payments, overnight accommodation, etc.

5.3) The telephone interview

The telephone interview method is restricted to a sample population which also happen to be telephone subscribers. There are still wide regional, national and international variations in the proportion of the total populations who have telephones installed in their homes, or indeed have access to telecommunications systems in their place of work. The method is most widely used in North America, whilst its use in the U.K. is largely restricted by mistrust on the part of householders, who will often refuse to answer telephone requests for market research information.

Where the telephone interview method is used, contact is established by telephone and respondents are asked a set list of questions based on the research questionnaire. The results are recorded and correlated.

a) *advantages of the telephone interview:*
* a relatively large number of interviews can be conducted within a short time;
* the interviewers can be located in one place;
* the interviewers can be supervised directly;
* centralisation means that interviewer briefing/training is consistent, and the interviewing process is continuously supervised;
* the selection of respondents is effectively outside the control of the interviewer;

41

* the cost per interview is low;
* the sample can be spread over the country, since no travelling expenses are incurred;
* the method is particularly satisfactory where the sample population consists of the higher social classes only, the majority of whom are likely to be telephone subscribers;
* people who might otherwise be inaccessible can be interviewed, since the interview can be brief and arranged for a time which is convenient to the respondent.
* centralisation facilitates the use of computer-aided interviewing technology, which may improve the quality of the response.

b) *disadvantages of the telephone interview:*

* not everyone has a phone, so population coverage by this method is incomplete;
* telephone subscribers may not be representative of the general population;
* only a short questionnaire is likely to be feasible;
* observation is not possible, so that for example the age and class of the respondent cannot be obtained unless personal questions are asked. Respondents may refuse to answer such questions over the phone;
* visual stimuli cannot be easily used;
* non-verbal communication cannot be evaluated;
* the interviewer cannot pace the interview to suit the respondent;
* it is not easy to sample individuals — telephone directories only list one household name;
* the times during the day or evening when respondents can be called are limited, if they are not to be antagonised. It is difficult to predict such times;
* interviewers will have quickly to communicate and explain their identity, establish credibility with the respondent, and establish sufficient trust so that the respondent will answer questions;
* some subscribers are not listed in public directories ie they are "ex-directory".

* response rates tend to be lower than with personal interview method.

5.4) The postal survey

The approach to respondents is usually made by post. Letters are sent to the sample population, and include a questionnaire to be completed and returned. After a certain period of time has elapsed, a follow-up letter may be sent, along with the questionnaire, to those who have not replied. Sometimes a small gift or product offer (say, an additional discount on purchasing one of the company's products) is enclosed as an incentive. Postal questionnaires may also be enclosed in periodicals, or attached to the guarantee documentation for a product purchased by a consumer. The questionnaire itself should be simple, concise, attractively presented and easy to follow. The instructions to the respondent on how to complete the questionnaire *must be crystal clear!* Otherwise it is likely to end up in the waste-paper bin!

a) *advantages of the postal survey:*

* a widely spread sample may be reached without proportionately increased costs, as postal rates do not usually vary with distance within any one country;

* the postal survey may be much cheaper than the personal interview survey as field expenses are not incurred;

* no investigator training is involved;

* investigator bias is avoided;

* certain groups which cannot be reached easily or without undue expense by other methods, can be reached by post;

* the respondent can consider his/her answers at leisure.

b) *disadvantages of the postal survey:*

* respondents are a self-selecting group and may not be fully representative of the population, (although personal interviews with non-respondents, if they can be arranged, can give a basis for estimating the difference);

* the refusal rate is invariably much higher than with any other method of inquiry. Returns may range from five or ten to fifty per cent, although they may sometimes be higher than this; well presented letters and questionnaires which encourage the respondents can improve the rate of return;

* the respondents may misinterpret the questions and give contradictory or misleading answers since there is not an interviewer present to clarify the actual questions for them;

* the amount of information which can be obtained is limited by the need to keep the questionnaire short and simple, and by the fact that little additional writing can be expected from the respondents;

* up-to-date address lists are expensive to obtain and maintain;

* the last returns tend to come in slowly, so that a substantial margin of time must be allowed before the next step of the survey is undertaken;

* as personal questions may serve to antagonise the respondents, they should be kept to a minimum or omitted altogether;

* the answers given on returns may not be those of the respondent, but instead come from one or several other people. For the intended respondent is free to consult anyone before returning the questionnaire.

5.5) The panel

The panel method differs from the three previous types in that the *same informants* are used *over a period of time*. There are several types of panel, for example:

i) consumer purchasing panels — which regularly report on their buying patterns, purchase intentions and attitude towards products. The data is collected either by interview, by the panel member maintaining a "diary" or record of purchases, by completing periodic postal questionnaires, or by the electronic recording and transmission of packaging bar code information.

ii) consumer product testing panels — which are asked to test new products and report on their reaction to them.

iii) radio and television audience panels — where listening and viewing patterns are monitored by specialist audience research agencies. The findings are used by both the media involved, and by advertisers planning to use commercial television or radio.

The important point about panels is that they allow the researcher *to study the same people over a period of time*, or even on a continuous basis. They can be used to provide a variety of information. They may report on a particular group of products (such as groceries), or provide information on a wide range of markets, according to the particular demands placed on the research agency at the time. They may be restricted to monitoring the media. They may be established for a limited period, for instance during a "test market" (see later chapters); or last for many years. Their geographical spread may range from regional to national, and even to international.

a) *advantages of the panel method:*

* the method is especially useful for research into trends, as the respondents are the same individuals over a period of time;
* the data gathered over a period of time can be accumulated and the factors underlying changes in trend can be analysed;
* case histories of panel members can be established to give relevant background material to responses.

b) *disadvantages of the panel method:*

* losses of members of the panel will occur
  - for natural reasons such as death, or moving to another area;
  - due to loss of interest of the members;
  In both instances, the composition of the panel as it was established is disturbed;
* The composition of the panel sample will affect the validity of the exercise. Refusals to join a panel may limit its representativeness, as it has been shown that it is more often the less literate sector of the population which will not join panels and that the buying and listening habits of this sector differ from those of the whole population. Such refusals for example stem from the fear of showing low levels of literacy when faced with completing the diary supplied;
* membership of a panel over a long period of time may render its member self-conscious. Their reactions may then no longer be typical behaviour;

* the original recruiting drive is usually expensive and the resources invested take a long time to yield useful results;

* to ensure replacements for lost panel members, personal interviews have to be conducted almost continuously, which is costly;

* panel members must be visited from time to time to monitor their activity and reliability, which is expensive;

* usually a small reward is given to panel members, which adds to the overall cost. This acts as an inducement. It could take the form of gifts, shopping vouchers or subscriptions to magazines. There may also be incentives for the prompt completion and return of diaries and questionnaires.

SUMMARY

The contents of this chapter are summarised in Table 4.1

SECTION	MAIN POINTS
1 Market research defined	Market research provides an enterprise with basic information about who the customer is, and what he or she will buy. This information is needed to make a whole variety of marketing and operational decisions.
2 What are the results of market research?	Market research should provide answers to such questions as who and where are the target customers, and what are they like; how the market is divided up or segmented; what products/services are demanded and in what qualities and quantities.
3 Who carries out |market research?	Market research may be carried out by the marketing function, or by a market research agency, or by both in co-operation.

4 Desk (or secondary) research	Desk or secondary research yields information from two sources, namely internal company data and external published data. Internal data includes sales and customer records, customer accounts, sales representatives' reports (etc). External sources include trade information, company reports and accounts, government publications, national and international statistics, retail audit data. Each information type will have varying value in terms of objectivity, specificity, generality, accuracy, time relevance (etc), depending upon the objectives of the information search.
5 Field (or primary) research	Field or primary research is original and is undertaken within the market. It is specific to the market research objective. It concentrates on a relevant selection of people in that market. There are four methods, namely the personal interview, telephone interview, postal survey, and consumer panel. The choice of method depends on the available finance, time available, accuracy of results required, the kind of people to be surveyed, and their geographical spread.

5 Market Research Questionnaires

INTRODUCTION

This second chapter on market research concentrates on some of the detailed techniques and processes used to carry out market investigations. It takes a detailed look at the questionnaires that form the basis of field research. The actual construction of the questionnaire is described. The choice between closed, open, direct and indirect questions is described and illustrated. The applications, advantages and drawbacks associated with each type of question are analysed. Consideration is then given to the recording of respondent attitudes and opinions. This gives rise to the need for specialist techniques which allow respondents to articulate and express attitudes and opinions in a meaningful way for market research purposes. Examples of question structures are given.

CHAPTER CONTENTS

1) Questionnaire design
   1.1) Questionnaire construction
   1.2) Structured questionnaires
   1.3) Unstructured questionnaires
   1.4) Recording attitudes and opinions

Summary

Appendix to Chapter Five

1) QUESTIONNAIRE DESIGN

In Chapter Four, four main types of field research were identified. These methods are used to obtain basic (or "primary") market data. The four methods were:

- the personal interview;
- the telephone interview;
- the postal survey;
- the panel.

In all four cases, questionnaires will be used to record (and later to collate) responses from the chosen population sample. The questionnaire may be completed by an interviewer (who might interview you in the High Street or in the home), or instead be completed directly by the respondent. The questionnaire, therefore, is itself an important item. A well constructed questionnaire will elicit more information than a badly constructed one, because clarity, simplicity and logic will make answering it easy. Market research activities must always avoid frustrating or antagonising respondents, since compliance is voluntary and non-co-operation means no information.

1.1) Questionnaire construction

Questionnaires are constructed on the basis of four main question types, namely:

– closed questions
– open questions
– direct questions
– indirect questions

a) *closed questions:*
Where closed questions are used, the respondent must choose the particular response he or she thinks appropriate from a *given list* on the questionnaire. If there are only *two* possible answers (for instance, "Yes" or "No") the question is termed "dichotomous".

For example:

"Have you purchased life assurance on your own life?"   YES/NO

"Have you purchased life assurance on your wife's life?"   YES/NO

Where more than two possible answers are required, the questions are termed "multi-choice". For example:

"Have you purchased life assurance on your own life?"   YES/NO

"Did you buy it from a sales representative who came to visit you in your own home?"   YES/NO

"Did you buy it by post, in response to an advertisement in the press?"   YES/NO

"Did you buy it from a local agent?"   YES/NO

It is also usual to add an extra category, the DON'T KNOW, for those respondents who do not understand the question, have no preference, or simply just don't know! Thus:

"Have you purchased life assurance on your own life or that of your wife? YES/NO/DON'T KNOW

"Has your wife purchased life assurance on your life or on her own life?" YES/NO/DON'T KNOW

b) *open questions:*

In this case, the respondent is required to answer the question as he or she thinks fit, without any given structure. The interviewer simply writes down (or records) the answer. For example:

"What do you think are the advantages to you and your family of purchasing life assurance?"

c) *direct questions:*

Direct questions require an exact and specific response. All of the questions in paragraphs (a) and (b) above are direct questions. They either elicit a YES or a NO answer, or structure the answer to a question in a clear and specific way. A final example should make the point, thus:

"Thank you for purchasing this Anglepoise lamp. Please tell us in the space below your reasons for purchasing it."

d) *indirect questions:*

Indirect questions may be used to elicit apparently generalised individual responses about (for example) attitudes or behaviour patterns. From these generalised responses the interviewer may be able to deduce the specific attitudes or behaviour patterns of the respondent, about which it might not be easy (or wise) to ask direct questions. Let us return to our life assurance example, and assume a market researcher is talking to a husband and wife (who have several children) and has ascertained that:

* the family has no life assurance;

* the husband sees no need for it (many men consider they are immortal and do not like thinking about their own death or its consequences for their family!);

* the wife is worried about the lack of life assurance and her husband's apparent attitude towards it.

The market researcher might ask indirect questions like:

"What do you think life assurance is for?"

"Why do you think people buy life assurance?"

"Do you know anything about the attitudes of housewives to life assurance?"

"How do you think your sons and daughters will get on at school/college/polytechnic/university?"

"What jobs do you think your children will get?"

The objective might be to build up a detailed picture of the husband's attitude towards the purchase of life assurance, and to explain the reasons underlying it.

Open and indirect questions are usually only likely to be used where the market researcher has the objective of, and the opportunity for, carrying out *in depth* investigations of the subject of the research. This will be an expensive and time consuming activity, but it may reveal basic and fundamental attitudes towards products and services which will be of crucial importance to product or service planning. For instance, market research has shown that:

* car owners see vehicle servicing as a major irritant. Reliable cars with long intervals between services have, as a consequence, become the norm.

* intercity rail passengers in the UK prefer frequent fast services to infrequent but luxurious ones (as found for example, in Europe and the Far East).

These, then, are the four question types by which market research questionnaires may be constructed. Most frequently, information is collected by the use of direct closed and open questions contained in a *structured questionnaire*.

1.2) Structured questionnaires

These contain a series of direct closed and/or open questions in an order that the interviewer is to follow. The interviewer must keep to this order and may not alter the questions. Where closed questions are used, all the interviewer has to do is to tick a box, or circle a computer code number representing the answer.

1.3) Unstructured questionnaires

In-depth interviews may, as described above, be carried out on the basis of an *unstructured questionnaire*. This contains a selection of direct or indirect open questions from which the interviewer may select as appropriate. The interviewer may choose to ask questions in whatever order seems sensible. The questionnaire acts as a guide, or series of cues, by which to assist and encourage the respondents to talk about the issues involved.

1.4) Recording attitudes and opinions

Market research may have to record and correlate people's *attitudes and opinions* about products and services, since these will be important determinants of purchase behaviour. For instance, Japanese products are rated highly in the UK for their quality, irrespective of the fact that many British and European products are just as good. British consumers have a *positive attitude* towards Japanese products.

People's attitudes reflect their background, their experience and their disposition. Attitudes develop from learning and experience at home and in education, at work and in buying goods and services. These attitudes influence opinions and reactions towards products, advertising messages and purchasing behaviour. They will determine the fate of a new product launched on to the market, and when existing products may start to lose popularity. For instance, health fears might make skin tanning less popular. Such a change of attitude could have a knock-on effect on the sales of skin tanning preparations and lotions, and even on holiday destinations.

There are two well-known techniques for measuring and recording respondent attitudes in market research. These are:

– Likert scales
– Semantic Differential scales

a) *Likert scales:* respondents are asked to indicate the extent to which they agree or disagree with a series of statements. It is usual to give the respondent a choice of five or six options on a scale ranging from "strongly agree" to "strongly disagree". The total of the responses are then correlated. Such a table might look like this:

SUBJECT:

Double glazed replacement window systems:	Improve your Home	Increase the value of your Home	Are a good value for money purchase
Strongly agree	---	---	---
Tend to agree	---	---	---
Neither agree or disagree	---	---	---
Tend to disagree	---	---	---
Strongly disagree	---	---	---

Figure 5.1. A Likert rating scale

b) *Semantic Differential scales:* respondents are asked to rate the variables under consideration on a relative basis, using a seven point scale. For example, many holidaymakers will have seen something like this:

Please rate the hotel in which you stayed under the following headings, on a scale from 1 to 7

comfortable bedroom	7 6 5 4 3 2 1	uncomfortable bedroom
excellent cleanliness	7 6 5 4 3 2 1	unhygienic and dirty
good food, well presented	7 6 5 4 3 2 1	bad food, poor service
courteous hotel staff	7 6 5 4 3 2 1	ill mannered staff
good facilities	7 6 5 4 3 2 1	poor facilities
excellent for families	7 6 5 4 3 2 1	not suitable for families

Figure 5.2. A Semantic Differential scale

The market researcher would aggregate the totals for each of the headings, and when compared with the results for other hotels, these might indicate:

* which hotels had a higher rating per capita in total;
* which hotels had higher ratings per capita under individual headings (eg perceived as better for families);
* what were the perceived strengths and weaknesses of the hotels used by the tour operator.

Semantic Differential scales are particularly popular because it is relatively easy for respondents using them to compare and rate *specific attributes,* such as quality of restaurant service or suitability for children. For, any product or service is designed to offer specific (and presumably desirable) attributes or characteristics to the

53

buyer. *The market researcher may want to find out whether or not, and how strongly, these desirable characteristics are actually associated with the product in the mind of the respondent.* A tour operator offering family holidays will want to know whether customers actually experienced what was *to them* an appropriate holiday in suitable surroundings. Does what he has on offer in his brochure actually live up to the reputation of the company as it was when the customer booked his package tour? In other words, does the actual product live up to customer expectations?

1.5) A questionnaire example

An example questionnaire is shown in the Appendix to this chapter. The example is taken from an actual industrial attitude research study, undertaken in the UK.

SUMMARY

The contents of this chapter are summarised in Table 5.3

TABLE 5.3
Summary : Chapter Five

SECTION	MAIN POINTS
1. Questionnaire design	Questionnaires are used to record and collate responses from the chosen population sample.
1.1 Questionnaire to 1.3 construction	Four main question types are used, namely closed, open, direct, indirect. The choice depends upon the market research objective; the size of the population sample; and the available budget. Market research objectives of wide coverage may conflict with demands for in-depth investigation. A trade-off will be needed at any given level of available funding. Most frequently, information is sought by means of structured questionnaires using direct closed and open questions.

1.4 Recording attitudes and opinions	Attitudes and opinions are measured on Likert scales or Semantic Differential scales. On Likert scales the respondent is asked to indicate the extent to which he/she agrees or disagrees with a series of statements. On Semantic Differential scales the respondent is asked to rate the variable under consideration on a relative basis, using (for example) a seven point scale. Semantic Differential scales are popular because they constitute an easy method by which respondents can compare and rate specific attributes to the buyer. The market researcher will want to find out whether or not, and how strongly, these desirable characteristics are actually associated with the product in the mind of the respondent.

APPENDIX TO CHAPTER FIVE

This appendix to chapter five contains an example of a questionnaire which was used in an attitude survey carried out in the UK. The study was concerned with an assessment of the effect of central and local government requirements on the operations of small businesses, on the attitude of owners and managers to these requirements, and on what the respondents thought should be done to relieve unnecessary burdens placed upon their business activities. Permission to reproduce the questionnaire has kindly been granted by Research Associates Ltd of Stone, Staffordshire.

DISCUSSION SCHEDULE FOR EXECUTIVE INTERVIEWS

Please fill in carefully and legibly under all appropriate headings. Use back of sheets if space is insufficient.

Interviewer .... Date ....

Respondent's name including all initials   Sales £ ....

.... Year org set up

Job Title ....

Company name in full   Sole trader ....
                                             Partnership ....
.... Private Ltd ....
                                             Public Ltd ....
Full address and postcode   plc ....

....

....

Telephone number ....

Other respondents and job titles

....

....

Quota frame – please circle appropriate entry

	Retail	W/S	Other Services	Const	Manuf
1	1	1	1	1	1
2-10	1	1	1	1	1
11-50	1	1	1	1	1
51-200	1	1	1	1	1

Explain that Research Associates is an industrial research consultancy, carrying out in-depth policy studies for major British companies and government departments. This survey is concerned with the effect of central and local government requirements on small businesses. Individual confidence will be respected at all times.

Any notes for the tabulating team? ....

....

Requirements hindering and helping business – unprompted

This section examines the current state of business among small firms and identifies government requirements which hinder or help them.

_____

How is business?

What is making business good for you? (Unprompted)

What is making business bad for you? (Unprompted)

Which central or local government requirements have hindered your business? Please list. (Unprompted)

Which government requirements or schemes have helped your business? Please list. (Unprompted)

Requirements hindering small businesses – unprompted

This section examines in depth those requirements which have already been mentioned as hindering small businesses.

Requirement Area A ....

How has it affected your business, and when/how often?

Attitude/image. Give 3 words to describe your personal attitude to it.

....

How much time is/has been spent dealing with it by yourself or your staff?

Management time .... Other time ....

Expenses £ ....

What could be done to reduce the burden/problem?

How serious is the effect of this requirement? (0 not serious, 10 extremely serious) Please circle.

0   1   2   3   4   5   6   7   8   9   10

Requirement Area B ....

How has it affected your business, and when/how often?

Attitude/image. Give 3 words to describe your personal attitude to it.

....

How much time is/has been spent dealing with it by yourself or your staff?

Management time .... Other time ....

Expenses £ ....

What could be done to reduce the burden/problem?

How serious is the effect of this requirement? (0 not serious, 10 extremely serious) Please circle.

0   1   2   3   4   5   6   7   8   9   10

ENTRIES ON THE SHUFFLE CARDS USED WHEN PROMPTING

This is a note of the words on the shuffle cards which will be used to prompt responses on requirements not already mentioned.

VAT

PAYE AND NATIONAL INSURANCE CONTRIBUTIONS (SEPARATE IF APPROPRIATE)

STATUTORY SICK PAY

FILLING IN GOVERNMENT STATISTICAL FORMS EG PRODUCTION CENSUS, EMPLOYMENT STATISTICS

HEALTH & SAFETY AT WORK REQUIREMENTS

LOCAL AUTHORITY PLANNING REQUIREMENTS

LOCAL AUTHORITY BUILDING REGULATIONS

ENVIRONMENTAL REGULATIONS

FIRE REGULATIONS

DATA PROTECTION REQUIREMENTS

EMPLOYMENT PROTECTION LEGISLATION EG UNFAIR DISMISSAL, REDUNDANCY PAY, MATERNITY PAY/ RIGHTS ETC

MINIMUM WAGE LAWS (WAGES COUNCILS)

CONSUMER LAW – ENFORCED BY LOCAL TRADING STANDARD OFFICERS

COMPANY LAW (INCLUDING AUDITING AND DEPOSIT OF ACCOUNTS)

RESTRICTIVE TRADE PRACTICES LEGISLATION

EMPLOYED/SELF EMPLOYED TAX TREATMENT

ANY OTHER REQUIREMENTS

Other requirements affecting small businesses – prompted

This section examines respondents' attitude to other government requirements that have not previously been mentioned.

_____

Show respondent shuffle pack and ask, have any of these requirements hindered your business? In what way? How seriously? What could be done about it?

Requirement Area 1 How affected? ....

....

How much time is/has been spent dealing with it by yourself or your staff?

Management time .... Other time ....

Expenses £ ....

How seriously?

0   1   2   3   4   5   6   7   8   9   10

What could be done to reduce the burden/problem? ....

....

_____

Requirement Area 2 How affected? ....

....

How much time is/has been spent dealing with it by yourself or your staff?

Management time .... Other time ....

Expenses £ ....

How seriously?

0   1   2   3   4   5   6   7   8   9   10

What could be done to reduce the burden/problem? ....

....

Have government requirements influenced you at any time in deciding whether to take on more staff or drop staff off? If so how and to what extent?

How? ....

....

How many jobs? ....

....

Looking at all the requirements together, how serious a burden are they in relation to your other business problems?

0   1   2   3   4   5   6   7   8   9   10

6 Sampling and the Market Research Process

INTRODUCTION

This third chapter on market research commences with an analysis of sampling. Surveys carried out for market research purposes cannot normally cover the whole of the relevant population, so a representative sample of it has to be taken. Such samples are either based on a random, quota or judgement basis, and each type is illustrated, explained and compared. The statistical viability of random sampling is then compared with the non or semi-statistical viability of the other two techniques, which, in turn, may be more cost effective relative to market research objectives.

The overall process of market research is summarised, and emphasis is placed upon the relationship between the approach and method to be used, and the marketing objective and budgeted cost of the investigation.

Finally, some examples of Information Technology in market research are given, anticipating a later chapter on Marketing and Information Technology.

CHAPTER CONTENTS

1) THE CHOICE OF SAMPLE

Surveys carried out for market research purposes cannot (usually) realistically cover the *whole* of the relevant population, so a "sample" of it has to be taken. The objective is to achieve a selection of individuals from the total relevant population *that is representative of it*. The "relevant population" might be consumers, industrial buyers, retail outlets, government buying agencies etc. The "population" can be very large (eg: all purchasers of consumer durable goods in Hong Kong), or it can be very small (eg: all institutional buyers of kidney dialysis machines in Belgium).

The sample chosen should exhibit the characteristics and variations in attitude, behaviour, purchasing capability (etc) that are relevant to the line of enquiry being undertaken by the market research (and to its marketing objective). And the sample should exhibit these characteristics and variations *in much the same proportions as in the total population from which the sample has been drawn*. There are two main ways in which such a representative sample can be constructed. These are:

- random samples.
- quota samples.

Each is described in turn, below.

1.1) Random samples

These are samples of the relevant population chosen completely at random. Random samples are *objectively determined* and their "sampling error" can be calculated to indicate the degree to which they are representative of the relevant population. They will be used where a high degree of statistical accuracy is needed, such as in substantiating claims for market share, or in the development of new products that are to be positioned (targeted) accurately on relatively small market segments. Such products may have to contain specific properties (attributes) that match exactly the demand pattern of a specific group of customers. It will be necessary to determine in detail what are the constituents of this demand pattern. Carefully constructed random samples may yield such an accurate response.

Random sampling, as a method, however faces a major problem. This is the problem of making such samples *manageable* where the relevant population is large or widely dispersed. A full scale sample, to be representative, may mean carrying out many interviews over a geographically dispersed area. This may not be cost effective. The solution is to restrict the sample in one or both of two ways, as follows:

a) *stratified samples:* in this case, a random sample is taken of a particular "strata" (or part) of the total relevant population. This is viable because the statistical proportions of such strata are well known, the information coming from basic sources like the Census of Population and, in the UK, the Classification of Residential Neighbourhoods (**ACORN** – see later chapter). For instance, a car manufacturer who wished to find out about UK attitudes towards diesel engines might research only those strata from which it already knows that it derives (say) 80% of its sales. In the case of Mercedes Benz, BMW and Volvo, this might mean restricting the investigation to the population strata categorised on *socioeconomic* grounds as:

A   Higher managerial, administrative or professional.

B   Intermediate managerial, administrative or professional.

(This classification will be explained more fully in a later chapter.)

These two categories make up about 15% of the total UK population. But the sample might be restricted to males only (say 7½%) if these companies knew that most of their sales were made to male customers.

The example might be further refined if these manufacturers knew that most of their cars were sold to men between the ages of (say) 35 and 55. The chosen strata might then comprise:

Males aged 35 to 55 in socioeconomic classes A and B.

A random sample of this strata might then be carried out.

b) *cluster samples*

Cluster samples are a means by which random sampling may be made even more manageable in terms of administrative effort and cost-effectiveness. The relevant population is divided up into manageable groupings (or "clusters") and then randomly sampled, perhaps on a strata-only basis as in (a) above. Clusters may be based on geographical variables such as:

– county, city, district or parish boundaries.

- commercial television franchise regions.
- electoral constituencies.
- classifications of residential neighbourhoods.

The statistical significance of the area chosen must, of course, be known. The total population and its distribution into socioeconomic classes, income or occupational categories must be known. This information will, again, come from government census statistics, classifications of residential neighbourhoods etc. In the case of UK commercial television franchise regions, accurate economic and demographic (population) data is available and there are specialist agencies who monitor and publish details of television viewing behaviour within these regions.

So, the cluster is based upon a proportion of a population, or a strata of it, whose "vital statistics" (in demographic terms) are already known. Here are some examples:

* a cluster based on a random sample of the entire population in the counties of Shropshire, Staffordshire and Cheshire.

* a cluster based on a national market segment. For instance, this might be all organisational buyers of cars for own fleet use only, or all organisational buyers of cars for fleet and individual hire only.

* a cluster based on a variety of factors. For instance, to return to our Mercedes Benz, BMW and Volvo example (paragraph 1.1(a) above), the market researcher might know that (say) at least 50% of UK sales are made in London and the South East of England (since this is the wealthiest part of the country). The final choice, based on a regional cluster, might be:

Males aged 35 to 55 in socioeconomic classes A and B resident only in (i) areas of recent growth (modern middle status housing); (ii) high status inner city areas of multi-occupancy; (iii) traditional high status suburban areas; (iv) seaside and retirement resorts; (v) rural areas; all within the boroughs of London and the counties of Berkshire, Buckinghamshire, Hertfordshire, Essex, Kent, Surrey, Sussex and Wiltshire.

A random sample of the clustered strata might then be carried out.

c) *Information Technology*

There are now available in the UK computer programs (for instance based on **ACORN**) that ensure that, when sampling locations are chosen, the sample generated has the requisite variety in economic and social circumstances. That is, it is statistically representative to the required degree.

1.2) Quota Samples

Quota sampling is widely used in market research as it is cost-effective. The method of sampling, however, is *not* based on random chance, and no quantification of statistical sampling error is possible. In other words, a quota sample is not statistically representative of the relevant population.

However, the method is viable *because the sample may be matched to objective criteria or proportions in a manner that is appropriate to the particular research exercise.* As we have already seen above, in countries like the UK, West Germany, Singapore (etc) a good deal is known about the population structure, and records are regularly updated by government agencies and professional, industrial and trade associations. So, an attempt can be made to introduce "representativeness" by stratifying the quota sample in terms of objective and known population characteristics such as:

- age, sex and family status;
- socioeconomic group;
- occupation;
- income level;
- ethnic background;
- householder/houseowner status;
- (etc)

Indeed, quota samples may now be accurately constructed on the basis of classifications like **ACORN** using computer programs, simply because such classifications are based on objective distributions of statistical variation in demographic, housing and occupational factors. Here is a very simple example:

i) As part of a wider market research exercise, a UK bread manufacturer wishes to find out more about peoples' preferences between white, brown and wholemeal bread. He knows, from objective statistics, the relative demographic proportions of each socioeconomic strata. He also knows, from trade statistics, the approximate proportions of each loaf type purchased by housewives in each socioeconomic category. He also knows of the existence of at least half a dozen hypermarkets which have a shoppers' profile that includes every socioeconomic category, and which sell all three types of bread. His calculations might be as shown in Figure 6.1.

The calculations assume that a total of respondents from five hypermarkets is deemed to be adequate, that is 380. The distribution of the five hypermarkets is itself a variable. A national orientation would be obtained if each of the five outlets were located in (say) the South, the Midlands, the North, Scotland and Wales. Alternatively, regional preferences would dominate the findings if the survey was restricted to only one of these regions.

Such a sample of 380 housewives should yield a useful cross section of attitudes towards the purchase and consumption of the different types of bread. Although it is not statistically valid, it is based on objective data. And it may well fit the budget of the bread manufacturer, who could have other lines of market research enquiry which it would also like to pursue, for which funding must also be made available.

1.3 Judgement samples

A variation on the quota method is called the "judgement" sample. This is used in trade and industrial market research. The method is not statistically valid, but is viable in the same way as quota sampling, in that it may be based on objective proportions. For instance, the basic variable in an industrial market research enquiry might be the output or turnover of the firms in that trade. It would not be the number of establishments, since many of these will account for only a relatively small proportion of the total output. ICI and Du Pont are only two of the firms in the chemical industry, but their output is rather more significant than their number would suggest!

A judgement sample, therefore, would be based on a selection of companies representing the different scales of

Socioeconomic categories	UK Population distribution across socioeconomic categories (%)		Percentage of total bread purchases comprising white bread		Respondents required in each location		Hypermarket locations required (say) five:		Total respondents needed
AB	16	×	.65	=	10	×	5	=	50
C1	22	×	.75	=	17	×	5	=	85
C2	32	×	.77	=	25	×	5	=	125
DE	30	×	.79	=	24	×	5	=	120
TOTAL	100%								380

Figure 6.1. A simple quota sample calculation

operation (or strata) within the industry as a whole. For instance:

20 buyers in a trade comprising 100 firms purchase 80% of the output of industry "X" sold into that trade. A judgement sample might therefore include 5 of these 20 major companies, plus 20 buyers from the remaining 80 firms. These 20 buyers would be chosen from a representative cross section of firms, according to the numbers in each level of output category. This total sample of 25 buyers should give a reasonably representative view of events in this particular market for product "X", since between them they purchase 25% of the total, but in order sizes varying from large to small, in proportion to the structure of the trade.

2) THE MARKET RESEARCH PROCESS

Market research investigations will tend to follow a series of stages. These stages are described below, and are summarised in Figure 6.2.

a) *objective and approach:*
The objective of the research will follow from the particular requirement for information identified by the marketing function. The objective will show in detail how the information is to be obtained within the cost constraints imposed by the marketing budget. Thus, terms of reference for the study will be established, and the scope and extent of the investigation defined. The process of establishing objective and approach may be assisted by the carrying out of a preliminary investigation, particularly where the investigation will be complex and resource constraints make it important to follow only the most promising lines of enquiry.

It is essential that both the person authorising the research, and the individual or agency carrying it out, are in agreement about the objectives of the exercise and the approach to be taken to carry it out within the requisite cost constraints.

b) *collection and classification of information:*
One part of this process is the obtaining of information by *Desk Research*, which was described in Chapter 4. The other part involves *Field Research*, described in detail in Chapters 4 and 5.

It may be important to carry out a preliminary field research exercise to identify:

* who are the "relevant population" and what they are like in general terms;
* what type of research method will prove most cost-effective;
* what should be the structure and content of the questionnaire, and how researchers should use it;
* how the information collected is to be collated and classified.

Once this preliminary or "pilot" research has been carried out, the main field investigation can be constructed and then carried out, using the various techniques already described in Chapter 3 and in this chapter.

c) *collation and analysis of information*
Once information starts to flow in, it will be combined, compiled and summarised, so that *market intelligence* or knowledge can emerge under the various category headings used to classify the data. It is at this stage that a useful picture of the market should emerge, that picture being appropriate to the particular requirements of the marketing objective established in (a) above. Typically, much of this classification, compilation and summary will be carried out on computer packages specially written for market and statistical research purposes.

d) *presentation of market research findings:*
The final step will be the presentation of the findings of the investigation. A written (and usually also a formal verbal) report will state:

* Objectives and terms of reference;
* Summary of main findings and conclusions;
* Detailed analysis of main findings;
* Detailed reasoning behind main conclusions;
* Appendices, tables, detailed supporting data and results (etc).

A final point of note here is that the purpose of market research in consumer and industrial markets is the same. However, given the differences between the two types of market, there will be variations in the techniques, detail and points of emphasis. For example, researchers may

71

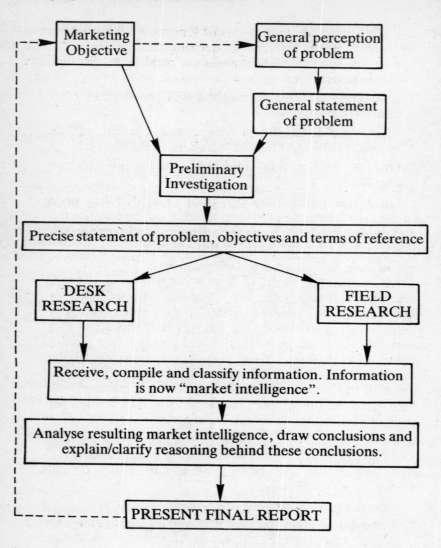

Figure 6.2. Stages in the Market Research Process.

attempt to obtain a series of lengthy in-depth interviews with senior buyers or decision-makers in industrial organisations, whilst consumer market research might concentrate on getting a limited amount of specific information from as large a sample as possible from the relevant population.

3) MARKET RESEARCH AND INFORMATION TECHNO-LOGY

The impact of Information Technology on marketing will also be dealt with in a later chapter. As far as market research is concerned, a brief mention of three items can be made, thus:

a) *electronic data processing (EDP) of market research results:* EDP is frequently used for compiling, categorising and summarising the results of survey investigations. This has two advantages. One is that relatively lengthy questionnaires can be used to increase the quantity or detail of information obtained. The other is the potential for numerically large surveys, assuming that the interviewer resources are available. EDP does put a premium on questionnaires which are constructed of direct closed questions which can be coded for data entry.

b) *electronic interviewing:* where direct interactive systems based upon telecommunication networks (or cable television) are available, market research based on direct, closed questions is possible. The value of such systems would perhaps lie in their *immediacy,* for instance in assessing reaction to a television advertising campaign whilst it was actually being carried out. Needless to say, electronic interviewing remains at an early stage in its development. It is expensive to operate because of the hardware involved. Additionally, respondents must be both television subscribers and telephone subscribers.

c) *databases for desk research:* databases are briefly dealt with in the chapter on marketing and Information Technology. Databases have an obvious use as an information source for desk research. The weekly UK journal *"Marketing"* noted that "computer power ... takes larger, geographically organised databases, of which published Census statistics are the most important, and links them to other sets of marketing information, intelligence and research data. The result is computer systems that can provide new insights into marketing patterns and marketing opportunities. (For instance) over the years retailers have accessed Census statistics with increasing sophistication to evaluate site and market potential and to target new and expensively developed retail propositions. Demographics permit local market sizes to be quantified with a precision that was previously impossible. Databases detailing the size and distribution of retail competitors can then build an even more complete picture of the marketplace. Large grocery multiples and the oil companies have led the way in retail modelling, and some now reckon to be able to predict new store or site performance to within a few percentage points."

SUMMARY

The contents of this chapter are summarised in Table 6.3.

TABLE 6.3
Summary : Chapter Six

SECTION	MAIN POINTS
1. The choice of sample	Market research surveys cannot realistically cover the whole of the relevant population, so a "sample" of it has to be taken. This sample must be "representative" ie exhibit characteristics and variations in attitude, behaviour, purchasing capability (etc) (i) relevant to the line of market research enquiry; (ii) in much the same proportions as the total population from which the sample is drawn. Sampling may be "random". Such samples are objectively determined and the sampling error can be calculated (ie their degree of statistical representativeness of the population can be indicated). Such samples may be "stratified", based on population groupings or "clusters" to make them

more manageable. Sampling may instead be based on "quotas". Quota samples are not based on random choice and so they are not statistically objective. Quota samples are, however, used because the sample can be *matched* to the objective proportions that are appropriate to the objective of the investigation. As such, they are cost-effective, since their construction can be tailor made to fit the relevant population and its geographical distribution, the budget available (etc). A variation on quota sampling is the "judgement" sample, which is based on objective proportions within industrial markets.

2. The market research process

The market research process follows these stages; (i) set objective and agree approach; (ii) carry out pilot survey; (iii) collect and classify information; (iv) collate and analyse information; (v) present findings.

RECOMMENDED READING

Crimp M. The Marketing Research Process. Prentice Hall International.

QUESTIONS FOR SELF REVIEW

1.   What is market research, and why does it play an important role in the marketing function?

2.   List, describe and compare the main sources of information from which desk research may be carried out. What are some of the advantages and disadvantages of these different sources?

3.   What is the role of field research within the market research process?

4.   Describe and compare the four main methods by which field research may be carried out. What factors will influence the researcher's choice amongst the methods actually available to him or her?

5. What major factors are relevant to the design and construction of a market research questionnaire?

6. What are the relative advantages and disadvantages in questionnaire construction of closed and open questions?

7. What are the relative advantages and disadvantages in questionnaire construction of direct and indirect questions?

8. What are "attitudes" and "opinions"? What are the particular problems in market research of recording respondent attitudes and opinions? How may the market researcher overcome these difficulties?

9. Why do market researchers make use of "samples" of the "relevant population"? How might the relevant population be defined?

10. Describe and comment on the technique of random sampling. What are its advantages and disadvantages?

11. Describe and comment on the techniques of quota and judgement sampling. What are their advantages and disadvantages?

12. Compare and contrast random and quota sampling methods in market research.

13. Compare and contrast random and quota sampling methods in consumer goods market research.

14. Compare and contrast random and quota sampling methods in industrial goods market research.

EXAMINATION QUESTIONS

Q6   What is Market Research and how is it carried out? Why is it an important input to setting objectives and judging enterprise performance?

(ACCA)

Q7   'A firm cannot be considered to be genuinely marketing-orientated unless it has a thorough understanding of its markets, its customers and their problems.' Comment with reference to the role of market research within the business firm. Describe the four basic research methods in common use.

(SCOB)

Q8   Identify the major steps involved in carrying out a marketing research exercise, briefly identifying the problems associated with each stage.

(ABE)

Q9   What factors should be taken into account when designing questionnaires so that they may be efficiently and accurately analysed?

(CIM)

Q10   Why is quota sampling used in survey research extensively, in preference to the theoretically superior random sampling?

(CIM)

Q11   In what ways do techniques of market research differ between capital goods and consumer goods markets? How are these differences accounted for?

(CIM)

Sales and Market Forecasting

"When you can measure what you are speaking of, and express it in numbers, you know that on which you are discoursing. But when you cannot measure it and express it in numbers, your knowledge is of a very meagre and unsatisfying kind."

Lord Kelvin

This section begins by looking at the role of sales and market forecasting in the operation of the business. It continues by putting sales and market forecasting into the wider context of the role and purpose of company planning and forecasting. Forecasting techniques can be divided into two main types, namely quantitative and qualitative. Each category is explained and analysed within the context of marketing and business planning, and their application is illustrated by a variety of examples.

7 Sales and Market Forecasting

INTRODUCTION

This chapter commences by putting sales and market forecasting into the wider context of the role and purpose of forecasting within the business enterprise. Planning assumptions and future expectations are compared, and the relationship between the two is analysed. The advantages to a business of making use of planning and forecasting techniques are then described.

The role of the sales or market forecast in the operation of the business is also explained, particularly within the context of the budgetary planning and control process.

Other issues in sales and market forecasting are dealt with in Chapters Eight and Nine.

CHAPTER CONTENTS

1) The role and purpose of forecasting
   1.1) Planning assumptions and future expectations
   1.2) The advantages of planning and forecasting

2) Sales and market forecasting

Summary

1) THE ROLE AND PURPOSE OF FORECASTING

Forecasting is a basic ingredient of business and marketing planning. *A business cannot plan without making forecasts, and it cannot make forecasts without having some kind of plan to act as a framework for forecasters to use.*

Forecasting is an attempt to visualise or anticipate the kind of future environment in which company plans and actions are likely to be implemented. It makes assumptions about known and unknown future conditions that are likely to determine the success of these plans. And it will attempt to predict the specific outcome from the implementation of company plans. For instance, will the introduction of fuel-efficient petrol engines by some car manufacturers mean that car buyers will come to insist on fuel efficiency *as the norm* in future years? What will be the effect on other manufacturers who will have to commit substantial funds to developing new engines, or to buy-in new engines from other makers (so losing control over a major item of added value in their profit creation process)

1.1 Planning assumptions and future expectations.

Planners will distinguish between forecasts that are *planning assumptions,* and those that are *future expectations. Planning assumptions* are predictions about the probable environments in which plans are expected to operate. Indeed, such predictions might be described in terms of *the probability* with which their occurrence may be estimated. For instance, planners might attempt to estimate the probability of the following:

* further significant increases/decreases in the price of crude oil;
* increases in the number of terrorist attacks on civilian airliners in those Mediterranean countries which have large tourist trades;
* the likelihood of political change in South Africa, and the chances of continuing economic stability in that country.

These planning assumptions, therefore, are an attempt to predict future business conditions and the sales volumes that might be obtained from them.

However, decisions based upon these assumptions may then lead to forecasts of *future expectations,* for example in terms of probable ranges of costs, revenues, profits and cashflows. For instance, investment decisions taken in response to planning assumptions will yield future expectations about financial viability and success. In this case, planning assumptions are a prerequisite of planning, and forecasts of future expectations are a result of planning.

1.2 The advantages of planning and forecasting.

It is not enough for a business to be responsive only to its present environment. A business must plan for the future. *Effective management will attempt to anticipate the environment in which its plans will operate.* This means forecasting what elements in that environment will affect such plans. It also means being prepared to alter plan, or course, as circumstances develop. Clearly, those businesses that foresee the critical changes that will affect plans, and are flexible enough to do something about them, will have a far better chance of being successful than those who cannot or will not.

The advantages to be gained from effective planning and forecasting, and a company willingness to adapt to changing circumstances, stems from three main factors; as follows:

a) the making of forecasts, and their eventual review, forces managers to think ahead, to look to the future, and to use their experience to provide for it. Decision-making is often about future plans and events, yet nobody knows with certainty what will happen in the future. An effective and systematic attempt at forecasting may reduce some of this uncertainty, and render the future more manageable. After all, experienced marketers and managers know what has happened in the past. They should, as a result, be able to predict the probability of occurrence of at least some future events, and their consequences. The company should know what are the future consequences of its *existing* investments and commitments, and ought to be able to describe, at least in broad terms, some of the most probable *scenarios* it is likely to face during the next few years. There is no reason why it should not limit the uncertainty contained in the future to those most unpredictable or surprising events, which will almost always be impossible to forecast.

b) the making of explicit forecasts will involve systematic thought and analysis. Such an intellectual process is likely to be of great value in business organisations which have a tendency to be long on action, but short on thought! Sales and market forecasting will focus attention upon the basic influences on the marketplace, and on the relationships within it. For instance, how valid are the company's assumptions about:

* customer sensitivity to price changes (price elasticity of demand);

* the effectiveness of its advertising in stimulating customer demand, and in maintaining its share of the total market;

* the relationship of per capita real income to demand for its products (for instance, people with increasing incomes tend to eat a wider variety of foodstuffs than

hitherto, yet their per capita expenditure on food tends to decline as a proportion of their total personal expenditure).

The forecasting process opens up basic assumptions, and past marketing strategies, for review, appraisal and criticism.

c) systematic forecasting will help to unify and co-ordinate the wider process of market research and planning. There will have to be agreement about the significance and relationship between the variables involved in the planning process, before these variables can be accepted as those for which research must be carried out, and forecasts made. For instance, the relatively high costs of a quality-orientated operation can only be justified if forecasts of market demand show that customers will remain insensitive to price increases, but sensitive to variations in product quality. This, for example, is a problem for tyre manufacturers. Will commercial vehicle operators buy long-lasting, reliable but expensive quality tyres, or cheap, short-life imports and re-moulds? What are the different types of market demand (or *segments* – see later chapter) to be forecasted, and is there agreement about the basic reasons for that demand?

2) SALES AND MARKET FORECASTING

The sales forecast is a key part of the company's plans. It is important both in long term or "corporate" (company wide) planning, and in the budgetary planning and control process which is carried out on an annual basis. *Budgetary planning and control* is used as the framework for detailed operational planning and control.

* a budget may be defined as a *quantitative and financial plan of the activity to be pursued during the financial year to achieve that year's objectives.*

* *the budgetary planning and control process may be defined as the establishment of budgets which relate the responsibilities of departments and employees to the requirements of plans and policies; and the continuous comparison of actual results with the budgeted targets, so that the latter may be achieved, or amendments made to the objectives upon which they were based.*

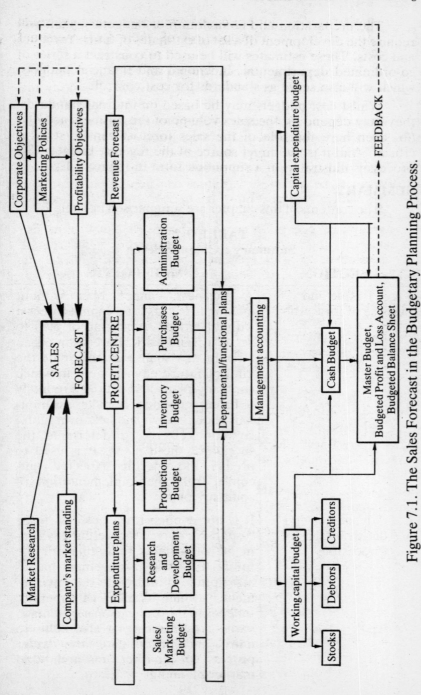

Figure 7.1. The Sales Forecast in the Budgetary Planning Process.

The preparation and compilation of budgetary plans will require the development of a set of estimates of future revenues and costs. These estimates will be used to construct a series of co-ordinated departmental, functional and financial budgets, which will also serve as standards for cost control.

Whilst cost budgets may be based on internal standards, they may depend on the sales volume of the business activity. So, even here the role of the sales forecast can be seen as crucial. And it is the direct source of the revenue budget. The process is illustrated in a simplified form in Figure 7.1.

SUMMARY

The contents of this chapter are summarised in Table 7.2.

TABLE 7.2
Summary : Chapter Seven

SECTION	MAIN POINTS
1 & 1.1 Role and purpose of forecasting	A business cannot plan without making forecasts, and cannot forecast without having some kind of plan to act as a framework. Forecasting is an attempt to visualise or anticipate the kind of future environment in which company plans and actions are likely to be implemented. It makes assumptions about known and unknown future conditions likely to determine the success of these plans. It is used to predict the specific expected outcomes from the implementation of company plans.
1.2 Advantages and disadvantages of forecasting	It is not enough for a business to be responsive only to its present environment. A business must plan for the future. Effective management means attempting to anticipate the environment in which its plans will operate. It needs to think ahead on a systematic basis. And forecasting also helps to unify and co-ordinate the wider process of market research and market planning.

2 Sales and market forecasting

Sales and market forecasting plays an essential part in budgetary planning and control, which is "driven" by annual sales forecasts and periodic amendments thereto. It is also an important ingredient of company-wide or "corporate" planning.

8 Quantitative Forecasting Techniques

INTRODUCTION

This second chapter on sales and market forecasting deals with quantitative forecasting techniques. These techniques are based on subjective, statistical and explanatory methods. Whatever the method chosen, these quantitative techniques are used for the construction of specific sales and market forecasts, whether it be at the level of the sales territory, market segment, national or even international market. The time scale for which such forecasts may be calculated may vary from one month to several years ahead.

CHAPTER CONTENTS

1) Forecasting techniques

2) Quantitative forecasting techniques

3) Subjective forecasting techniques
   3.1) Sales force composite method
   3.2) Juries of executive opinion
   3.3) Surveys of buyer intentions

4) Statistical forecasting techniques
   4.1) Moving averages
   4.2) Exponential smoothing
   4.3) Decomposition or time-series analysis
   4.4) Trend extrapolation and curve fitting

5) Explanatory forecasting techniques
   5.1) Operational research models
   5.2) Management System Dynamics
   5.3) Macroeconomic and econometric forecasting

Summary

1) FORECASTING TECHNIQUES

There is a wide variety of forecasting techniques, which can usefully be divided into two categories, namely *quantitative* and *qualitative*. Each will be analysed separately. The point should also be made that many of these techniques are statistically and technically complex, often requiring computerised operation. A detailed analysis of such techniques is beyond the scope of this book, and so the coverage given to them will be generally limited to their marketing applications. The techniques to be considered are listed in Table 8.1. Qualitative techniques are analysed in Chapter Nine.

Table 8.1
Forecasting Techniques

QUANTITATIVE	QUALITATIVE
Subjective methods	Technological forecasting
– sales force method	Social Forecasting
– juries of executive opinion	
– surveys of buyer intentions	Political forecasting
Statistical methods	
– moving averages	Methods include
– exponential smoothing	– scenario development
– decomposition analysis	– Delphi techniques
– trend extrapolation and	– cross-impact analysis
curve fitting	– value profiles
Explanatory techniques	
– operational research	
– management system	
dynamics	
– macroeconomic and	
econometric forecasting	

2) QUANTITATIVE FORECASTING TECHNIQUES

Quantitative forecasting techniques comprise three main groups, each of which will be considered in turn. These groups are:

* Subjective
* Statistical
* Causal

Whatever the method chosen, these techniques are used for the construction of specific sales and market forecasts, whether it be at the level of the sales territory, market segment (see later chapter), national or even international market. The time scale for which such forecasts may be calculated may vary from one month to several years ahead.

3) SUBJECTIVE FORECASTING TECHNIQUES
3.1) Sales force composite method.

One of the more commonly used methods of sales forecasting is to obtain from salesforce personnel and sales managers their combined view of sales to be expected during the forecast period. Before making their individual territory estimates, the salesforce may be briefed on past trends, and on significant factors that the company thinks are likely to affect total sales during the forthcoming period. The estimates made by each salesperson for his or her territory are then aggregated and reviewed by regional and head office sales managers, marketing managers associated with particular products or brands, and advertising staff.

After all, salesforce personnel are in close contact with the people who actually make up the market, and ought to have the most detailed knowledge about how it is likely to behave in the near future. Indeed, many sales personnel would be offended if sales forecasts were made *without* any attention being paid to their knowledge and opinion! However, the salesforce composite method also has a number of disadvantages, which include:

* limited perspectives – salesforce estimates may tend to over-emphasise prevailing conditions, reacting (or over-reacting) to localised or short run trends. They may also be shaped by personal reaction to the passage of events. This may take the form of individual optimism or pessimism about likely future events within the territory. Such feelings, however, may not accurately represent the movement of trends. Indeed, they may (unwittingly) hide the reality so that no account is taken of it in the forecast. Similarly, individual members of the salesforce may be too close to their territory to perceive wider patterns within marketplace trends, and there will be a need for an overview to balance this intimate and territory biased view.

* lack of knowledge of regional, national or international trends – individual salespeople are not likely to be in a position to possess a broad knowledge of the market. The value of their estimates lies in specificity and detail. But this must be balanced by an overview about trends in customer behaviour, economic conditions (etc) that are likely to affect longer term market conditions. The

provision of such an overview is the responsibility of the company's marketing and corporate planning functions.

* forecasts and targets – individual territory forecasts may be viewed with scepticism when an individual salesperson suspects that his forecast will become his sales target. In this case, the figure may be adjusted downwards so that it may more easily be achieved, especially when commission payments are based on the full achievement of sales target or quota.

Despite these disadvantages, forecasts submitted by the salesforce are an essential *grass-roots* starting point to the forecasting process. Sales territory forecasting is also dealt with in later chapters.

3.2) Juries of executive opinion.

These are groups of senior managers and/or outside trade representatives brought together to offer a combined judgement about market trends and the viability of internal and external sales and market forecasts. Such juries bring together on an integrated basis a variety of relevant experience and opinion. They may question and qualify the company's internal sales forecast, however it is formulated. They may advise or warn the forecasters about trends or events that are likely to influence sales performance. They may be asked to react to the implications of the forecast and the means to be employed by the enterprise to achieve it. And they may be asked to play the role of "devil's advocate", preventing forecasters and marketers alike from becoming complacent and insular, losing sight of the continuous impact of the external environment on the business.

3.3) Surveys of buyer intentions.

Suppliers operating in industrial markets dominated by a small number of large companies may find it possible to base their annual and long term forecasts on the expected purchases of these customers. After all, the number of such buyers is small and past purchase patterns may be known in great detail (from internal sales information, and from trade association statistics covering the whole market). And where there is a stable and well established relationship between buyer and supplier, it may be in the interest of both to allow the supplier to build up an accurate sales forecast. This way the buyer need not fear a situation in which the supplier will run out of essential stock, and the supplier can plan on the long term to optimise his conditions of supply. Stable contracts will permit cost reductions and capital investment to improve the quality and reliability of supply. Contract marketing is dealt with in a later chapter. More generalised surveys of industrial buyer intentions can also be useful. For instance, in the UK the Confederation of British Industry publishes on a four monthly basis a national survey of the opinions of a large sample of companies whether they expect their sales, exports, production, employment and investment to remain stable or change. Similar opinion surveys are carried out throughout the European Economic Community and are published by the European Commission.

Regular surveys of industrial and consumer confidence are also published by the *Financial Times* in the UK, and by other specialist media such as the trade press and market research organisations. In some other countries, these kinds of surveys are carried out and published by Chambers of Commerce, government ministries (etc).

4) STATISTICAL FORECASTING TECHNIQUES

This is a particularly complex issue, largely beyond the scope of this book. Readers might wish to consult *Quantitative Techniques* by T. Lucey (DP Publications); whilst a useful summary of the marketing applications of statistical forecasting techniques will be found in the article by Makridakis and Wheelwright, entitled "Forecasting: Issues and challenges for Marketing Management" *Journal of Marketing* Vol 41 No. 4 October 1977. A number of techniques are briefly summarised below.

4.1) Moving averages.

Where it is unreasonable to assume that sales in period $t+1$ will be the same as at time t (the present), or that the increase/decrease in sales over the period t to $t+1$ will be the same as during the period $t-1$ to t, a moving average may be calculated. This bases the forecast for time $t+1$ on the average of several past values of the actual sales figure achieved. For instance, a forecast for sales in month $t+1$ might be based on the actual figures for months $t-4$ to $t-1$ inclusive. Each of these values would be given a weight of ¼ and the sum of these values would be the forecast. If sales for the last four months were 42, 36, 41, 45 units respectively, the forecast for next month would be $((42+36+41+45) \div 4)=41$ units.

As each new actual value becomes available, it is then incorporated into the averaging formula, so that the value calculated "moves" through time. Moving averages would normally be used for short term forecasting, perhaps up to a maximum of a few (say 3 to 6) months ahead.

4.2) Exponential smoothing.

This differs from the moving average in that it does not use equal weightings for the past values chosen. Rather, an exponentially decreasing set of weights is used so that the more recent values receive more weight than older ones. Common sense (or observation) may show that the pattern of behaviour requires the forecaster to give progressively less weight to values the further back in time they occur.

Exponential smoothing would again normally be used for short term forecasting, for periods up to six months ahead.

4.3) Decomposition or time series analysis.

This assumes that patterns and trends which can be identified in past (historical) sets of data may be projected forward, especially under stable economic, market and organisational conditions, for the purpose of forecasting perhaps up to one year ahead. The forecaster would search past *time-series* of data for consistent evidence of:-

* seasonal variations (which are for instance marked in the case of holiday or toy sales) over a period of a year.

* cyclical variations, which are longer term and may lack the consistency and predictability of seasonal variations. Nevertheless, many sales forecasters will need to predict the general movement of the relevant cycle during the forthcoming year.

* variations which can be attributed to the occurrence of identifiable and non-random events, such as bad weather, strikes or adverse publicity. The forecaster must decide whether to exclude such events from the analysis of trends where these are being used to forecast for the future.

* longer term (or "secular") trends indicated by past time-series of data. These might include market growth or decline. A forecaster would be interested in their source (for instance growth in personal disposable income combined with long-term taste changes favouring a new product type), and their likely degree of permanence or duration, before fully accepting them.

4.4) Trend extrapolation and curve fitting.

These are techniques that may be used for longer term forecasting, perhaps for periods of two or more years ahead. They are in part based upon the statistical techniques described above, but use whatever mathematical form of extrapolation (forward projection) that the forecaster considers will be most valid in achieving a prediction. The projection may be linear or exponential, or may incorporate more complex calculations which make allowance for variation in the basic parameters assumed to remain constant in the simpler equations. Or they may incorporate values for the degree of error of past forecasts when compared with actual results achieved.

Methods of correlation and regression analysis may be incorporated, along with variations in outcome probability. A variety of techniques are also available to produce curves that "fit" data and extrapolate it forwards for forecasting purposes.

5) EXPLANATORY FORECASTING TECHNIQUES

There are two main categories of explanatory (or "causal") forecasting techniques. These are based on:

* operational research models, including management system dynamics;
* macroeconomic/econometric models.

These techniques are normally used to assist, augment and inform the quantitative forecasting process. Their role is to give depth, colour and understanding to the issues at hand, and to provide a broad context (or "environment") by which to guide the more specific calculation of quantitative forecasts described above.

5.1) Operational research models.

These are an *abstraction* of real systems or processes which are used to represent the basic variable and constant features.

The purpose is to allow exploration and explanation of the behaviour of the system or process, for instance:-

* as the values of its variables are changed, for instance on a "what if?" basis;
* as the system or process operates through time;
* as it is affected by the incorporation of probabilistic measures of outcome risk and uncertainty.

Operational Research (OR) models are used to *simulate* the workings of a real life system, so that the model builder, planner or manager can "experiment" with alternative processes, policies and plans. Two main approaches can be used. The first is called *algorithmic,* which comprises a procedure or series of instructions used to solve a specific type of problem. The second is called *heuristic,* which is an exploratory approach to problem solving and simulation that uses repeated (iterative) trial and error, each solution being assessed and used to modify successive attempts, until a final solution is achieved. This solution must satisfy specific criteria of outcome viability.

Both approaches will incorporate *controllable* and *uncontrollable* variables, the proportion and relative importance of each type varying with the type of system or process being modelled. This may be described in the general formula

$$U = f(X,Y)$$

where U is the decision function, which has to be operated in conjunction with controllable variables X and uncontrollable variables Y.

Where OR models are used in sales and market forecasting, it is likely that there will be more relevant uncontrollable variables Y than in, say, a production line scheduling problem comprising controllable variables X.

R. L. Ackoff and others have classified OR techniques in terms of the *general applications for which they may be used.* These applications include:

queueing problems	allocation problems
inventory problems	search problems
replacement and maintenance problems	competition problems
scheduling and routing problems	

Several of these applications will be relevant to specific sales and market forecasting requirements. For instance, annual sales forecasting for a manufacturing activity undertaking a wide variety of large complex engineering work on a unit and small batch basis may be carried out using a combination of queueing, scheduling and inventory based methods.

More specifically, four main categories of OR models can be identified on the basis of their general objective. Each is listed below, together with a sales forecasting example.

5.1 a) *Models used to describe and analyse the structure, inter-relationships, functioning and behaviour of systems.* For instance, a model may be constructed to represent the main factors determining a company's proportionate share of a specific market. If operation of the model can, to some degree, accurately represent the workings of the market then an individual company may be able to gain a deeper understanding of the relative position that it has in that market. It may then be able to forecast more clearly the outcome of variations in its product and marketing policies, advertising expenditures (etc) in terms of possible sales.

5.1 b) *Models used to make predictions under given sets of probabilities and assumptions about the basic relationships between variables, and their relative influence on each other.* An obvious example is that of pricing policy. A company may attempt to measure the degree to which the market is sensitive to price changes, that is to understand its price *elasticity.* Where it knows that it will suffer increases in its costs, it may wish to use a model to predict what will be the effect of a series of increasingly large price rises upon its sales. To do this it will have to make assumptions about the price elasticity of demand for competitors' products, again under a series of increasing price rises. This, of course, will involve the modeller in finding out about how price competitive the market is, so that reasonable assumptions can be made about the influence of price competition on the sales of any one supplier, and on sales in the market as a whole.

5.1 c) *Models used to calculate the optimum outcomes from a specific set of variables.* These are called "optimising models" and are best known from their application to queueing, scheduling and routing problems. Such a model could be used for sales forecasting purposes in the following way. A company might wish to study the specific effect of its promotional activities (dealt with in detail in a later chapter) on its sales. At any given level of expenditure £n it may wish to optimise its "mix" of expenditure on the various promotional methods available to it, so as to maximise the level of sales to be obtained at the level of promotional expenditure £n. The model might be represented thus:-

$$S = f((Tvad + Psad + Slsfce + Slsfcecomm + Dsincve) + C)$$

where S = sales level to be optimised
  Tvad = television advertising
  Psad = press advertising
  Slsfce = Salesforce size and deployment
  Slsfcecomm = sales commission paid to salesforce
  Dsincve = distributor discounts and incentives
  C = factors assumed to remain constant for the purpose of the exercise.

Constant factors "C" might include the activities of competitors, and company price competitiveness and product acceptability. The model might be illustrated as in Figure 8.2.

5.1 d) *Models used to indicate time – dependent behaviour.* For instance a dynamic model may be used to show the effect of changes in advertising expenditure on sales. One example of such a model is that of Vidale and Wolfe who related the rate of change of sales to advertising by the equation:

$$\frac{ds}{dt} = \frac{rA(M-S) - \lambda S}{M}$$

where S = sales at time t
  ds/dt = rate of change of sales at time t
  A = advertising expenditure at time t
  r = sales response factor (sales generated per unit of advertising expenditure)
  λ = sales decay factor (rate of sales loss per unit of time)
  M = saturation level of sales (sales maximum)

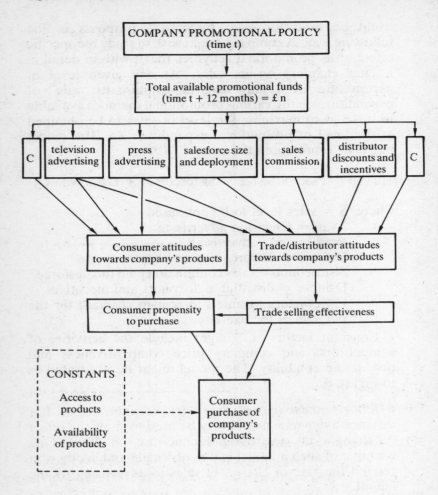

Figure 8.2. A Promotional Mix Model.

This simple model shows an exponential increase in sales during the period of the advertising campaign, and an exponential decay after it has ended. It is, of course, assumed that all other marketing factors remain constant in their impact on sales. It is illustrated in Figure 8.3.

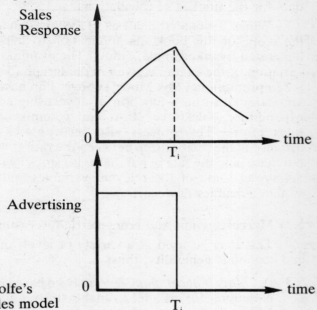

Figure 8.3.
Vidale and Wolfe's
advertising-sales model

5.2) Management System Dynamics.

This is an underused but powerful and versatile OR tool. Management system dynamics is mainly concerned with the time-varying behaviour of processes or systems, but it may be used to carry out modelling and investigation under any of the four OR categories described in section (5.1) above. Its particular advantage to the marketer is that it may be used without extensive training in mathematics or computer programming, since programming is done by the package itself when in operation. The user, therefore, can concentrate on the structure and behaviour of the system under consideration, rather than on the technical aspects of the modelling process.

The technique is based on the University of Bradford *DYSMAP* package. Dysmap compiles and carries out continuous simulation models and is particularly suited to modelling situations whose *dynamic* nature is based on *feedback* processes. Dysmap works by solving a large number of simultaneous equations at specified time intervals, using the information already calculated for the previous time interval as the basis for the current series of calculations. This means that initial conditions need to be specified so as to provide the data for the first set of calculations.

Whilst a detailed analysis of system dynamics is beyond the scope of this book, its application to sales forecasting is illustrated by an example, below. The example to be used is a variation of the example given in paragraph (5.1 c) and Figure 8.2 (a promotional Mix Model) above. Purchases by customers are assumed to be a function of advertising and promotional expenditure, salesforce effort and commission, and retailer sales effort. The process also incorporates feedback, for instance in the relationship between the rate at which customers purchase, and the rate of purchases for stock by retailers. Figure 8.4 shows some of the relevant variables and feedback in a system dynamics flowchart.

5.3) Macroeconomic and econometric forecasting.

This may be used at a variety of levels of sophistication and economic generality, thus:

5.3 i) *Models at company level* may be based on econometric equations, for instance to analyse the relationship between price and demand, perhaps using the model

$$Q = aP^{-b} \text{ (or log Q = log a-b log P) where}$$

Q = demand
P = price
b = price elasticity

Another example is quoted by Milne (T.E. Milne *Business Forecasting : a managerial approach.* Longman) of the owner of a chain of ten shops who suspected that his level of sales was a function of the number of shoppers per hour passing by in the street, and the floor area of a given store. The owner wished to find out whether such a relationship could be formulated and used to predict sales in other shops which he was considering adding to his chain. Data was collected on the three variables for the existing shops and the following model emerged:

£ Sales per week = 193 + 0.23 x shoppers + 0.118 x floor area

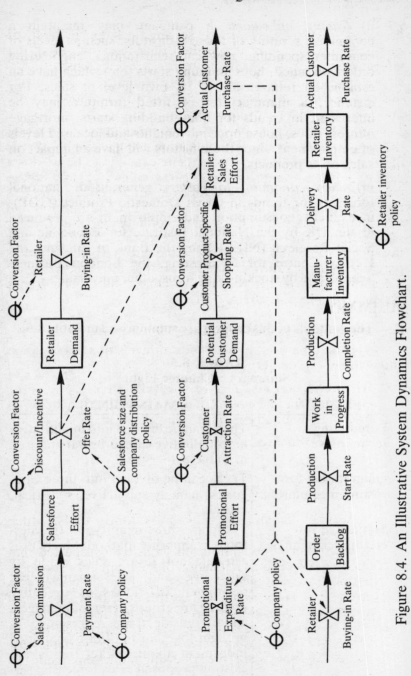

Figure 8.4. An Illustrative System Dynamics Flowchart.

5.3 ii) *leading indicators:* a company may maintain a continuous scrutiny of those indicators, such as levels of consumer spending, new car registrations, engineering orders obtained, housebuilding starts (etc) which have an established relationship to its own level of sales. For instance, a manufacturer of fitted furniture may be interested in trends for housebuilding starts, mortgage interest rates, house price movements and localised levels of employment, since these factors will have an impact on sales of its products.

5.3 iii) *macroeconomic forecasts:* generalised national forecasts for trends in Gross Domestic Product (GDP), investment, consumption and employment are produced in the UK by the National Institute for Economic and Social Research (NIESR), by the Bank of England, the Henley Centre for Forecasting, the London Business School, and by stockbroking firms, other universities etc.

SUMMARY

The contents of this chapter are summarised in Table 8.5.

TABLE 8.5
Summary : Chapter Eight

SECTION	MAIN POINTS
1. Forecasting techniques	These can be divided into quantitative and qualitative categories summarised in Table 8.1
2. Quantitative fore-casting techniques	These can be divided into three categories, namely subjective, statistical, causal.
3. Subjective fore-casting techniques	There are three main types: (i) sales-force composite method which uses estimates of future sales made by salesforce and sales management personnel; (ii) juries of executive opinion are groups of senior managers and/or outside trade representatives brought together to offer a combined judgement about market trends and existing/proposed sales forecasts; (iii)

	surveys of buyer intentions are taken from industrial markets dominated by small numbers of large buyers, whose expected or forecast purchases provide the basis for the survey.
4. Statistical forecasting techniques	Comprise (i) moving averages; (ii) exponential smoothing; (iii) decomposition or time-series analysis; (iv) trend extrapolation and curve fitting. Mainly used for short-term forecasting.
5. Explanatory forecasting techniques	These techniques are used to assist, augment and inform the quantitative forecasting process, giving depth, colour and understanding to the issues at hand. They provide a broad context by which to guide the more specific calculations and assumptions made by other quantitative techniques. Two main types: (i) Operations Research models, which are an abstraction of real systems or processes which are used to represent the basic variable and constant features of the reality, so that its behaviour or process can be explored, explained and simulated; (ii) Macroeconomic and econometric models which may be used at a company level, or at a more general industry or economy level.

9 Qualitative Forecasting Techniques

INTRODUCTION

This third chapter on sales and market forecasting deals with qualitative forecasting techniques. Qualitative forecasting techniques are used to assist and augment the quantitative forecasting process described in the previous chapter. Their role is to give depth and colour to the issues at hand, and to provide a broad context or environment by which to guide the more specific calculation of quantitative forecasts.

Consideration is then given to the marketer's choice of forecasting method, and the chapter concludes by examining an alternative forecasting basis, that of market share. This will require the forecasting of both the size of the total market into which the enterprise trades, and its likely share of that market. Target customer forecasting is dealt with in a later chapter.

CHAPTER CONTENTS

1) Qualitative forecasting techniques
   1.1) Scenario development
   1.2) Delphi techniques
   1.3) Cross-impact analysis
   1.4) Value profiles
2) Choice of forecasting method
3) Forecast of market share

Summary

Questions for self-review

Examination questions

1) QUALITATIVE FORECASTING TECHNIQUES

The application of qualitative techniques is a recognition that sales or market forecasting is not carried out in isolation from the external environment in which the enterprise operates. Indeed, qualitative forecasting is often termed *environmental forecasting*. It involves an analysis of environmental trends likely to affect sales levels, and a detailed examination of those environmental conditions (such as changes in people's life-style, standard of eduction (etc)) for which specific forecasts have to be constructed. Environmental forecasting may be used to "inform" the market forecasting process, or to provide the basis for more detailed quantification. It is more likely to be relevant to medium and long term planning and forecasting, especially (as far as this book is concerned) as regards market development, growth and decline. The areas for which environmental forecasting may be carried out are described in Figure 9.1.

Forecasts of the *economic environment* have already been analysed in the previous chapter. *Technological forecasting* deals with the projected impact of scientific developments on the future state of technology, and attempts specifically to examine how these developments will affect the company's products, processes or markets. For instance, the high rate of scientific and technological development in the field of semiconductors during the past two or three decades has meant that technological forecasting has become a crucial part of sales and market forecasting for companies manufacturing electronic and telecommunication products, computers etc. There is a direct link between technological development, new product design and performance, price, and a company's standing in such markets.

Social and *political forecasting* involves a company in attempting to predict how changes in social, ethical and political attitudes will have direct market effects on the enterprise. Such market effects may be caused by changing consumer attitudes, for instance in the UK to the wearing of fur or seal-skin clothing; or by direct legislative interference. As one example of the latter, social disapproval of cigarette smoking has led to advertising restrictions and mandatory warnings on cigarette packets in the UK; whilst many third world governments control the manufacture or supply of tobacco products and (for financial reasons) almost encourage people to smoke!

A variety of techniques are used in qualitative or environmental forecasting. These include:

* scenario development
* Delphi techniques
* cross-impact analysis
* value profiles

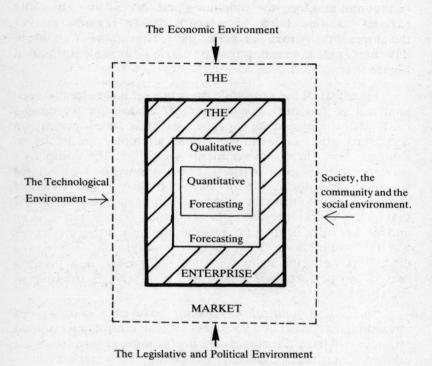

Figure 9.1. Environmental Forecasting.

1.1) Scenario development.

This involves the construction or simulation of a number of alternative possible "futures". These future scenarios should permit deductions to be made about the particular environmental variable in view, whether this be technological, economic or whatever. Because common sense (and cost) suggest that there will be a limit to the number of scenarios that are worth developing, the number may be restricted to three. The first will be based on a projection of known and stable trends, using statistical extrapolation (as described in the previous chapter), and will represent a "surprise-free" scenario. The other two scenarios will be developed around this first one, one being *optimistic* and the other *pessimistic*. Each will incorporate various measures of probability of the forecasted events occuring.

1.2) Delphi techniques.

These are based on the views of a panel of experts, perhaps drawn both from inside and outside of the ranks of the organisation. This panel provides views about the issue to be forecast, each member working independently from his or her colleagues. The initial opinions are collated and compiled, and then fed back to the panel. With the information to hand, each member makes a further assessment until, after the process has been repeated perhaps three times, some convergence of opinion may appear. The forecast may then be based on this synthesis of informed and developed opinion, perhaps reformulated on a quantitative basis.

1.3) Cross-impact analysis.

This is an attempt to explore and analyse the potential interaction between events. Social changes or technological developments necessarily create market opportunities in all sorts of different directions, some established and some completely new. Here are a couple of examples:

* the development of computer technology called for parallel developments in printer technology. At the personal computer level, Epson has specialised in the economy printer market and has become one of the market leaders.

* changes in the UK population structure may have radical effects on the markets for housing, accomodation and personal pension finance, as the age structure of the population becomes dominated by more and more people aged 40 plus.

1.4) Value profiles.

Of considerable current interest to forecasters are the values that inspire the attitudes and consumption patterns of the people who make up society. As we shall see in the next few chapters, changes in values and attitudes will cause changes in the kinds of products that people buy. Forecasters may attempt to identify shifts as between, say:

* preferences towards work and leisure orientations;
* preferences for individually determined as opposed to governmentally determined expenditure (eg pressure for tax reductions, restricting local government expenditure etc);
* traditional authority/religious personal ethics as opposed to personal freedom and individualistic behaviour.

There is no doubt that enormous changes have occured in the social and cultural values of the western world, for instance emphasising individual freedom and material well-being. Whilst the consequences of these changes may be hotly debated, their marketing impact on business enterprises has been immense. Hence the need for general forecasts about them to be included in the marketing process.

2) CHOICE OF FORECASTING METHOD

The choice of sales and market forecasting method will depend on a number of factors, including:

a) *forecasting objectives:* within the context of this book, the objective of the forecasting process will mainly be to assist marketing planning and, as outlined in Chapter Seven, to co-ordinate operational and budgetary planning with anticipated levels of sales. Sales and market planning will also, of course, form a crucial part of the corporate planning and strategic management process.

b) *time scale:* different forecasting methods will have different value according to the time scale for which they are being applied. Commonly, sales forecasting for a period of up to one year ahead is differentiated from sales and market forecasting for longer periods. Forecasting for periods of three to five years ahead is as much a part of the corporate planning activity.

c) *the importance of the forecast:* the more important the forecast, the more informed must be the choice of method, and the more likely will be the need to use *several* forecasting methods. In particular, annual sales forecasts may be based on a series of different methods, whether these be subjective, statistical or qualitative. The relative importance of a forecast can be gauged in terms of the consequences of its degree of error. This is why the annual sales forecast that "drives" operational and budgetary planning may be subject to monthly revisions, thereby minimising the impact of forecasting error. This is related to:-

d) *the degree of accuracy required:* the sophistication (and cost) of a single or composite forecasting process will determine the resulting accuracy. Accuracy must be defined within the forecasting objective in terms of methods to be used, time scale and the relative importance of the forecast.

e) type of data required: will be determined by the forecasting methods to be employed and the budget available for finding and assembling such information.

f) *availability of data:* there will be limits to the kind of information that is readily accessible, and to the finance available to obtain it. As in all business calculations, the cost of obtaining such information needs to be balanced against its benefits, (and against the consequences of limiting the search to a point where the forecaster does not know whether the information foregone is more or less than marginally useful).

g) *access to forecasting skills and methods:* the quality and accuracy of the forecasting process will in part be a function of skills and methods available. Larger scale enterprises are likely to be in a better position than smaller ones in this respect, although the forecasting situation they face will, correspondingly, be more complex.

h) *company experience with forecasting:* the more that a company, large or small, can build up forecasting information and experience, the more successful it is likely to be in achieving effective forecasts. Experience may offset a lack of access to sophisticated and costly specialist skills. However, since experience is *person-centred* the enterprise will have to reward and retain the loyalty of those company specialists or managers who have built up this expertise. Small companies do not have the option of "buying-in" specialist skills to which their larger brethren can resort.

3) FORECAST OF MARKET SHARE

So far, the assumption has been made that the forecasting process is *concerned directly with sales*. The sales forecast is then used to "drive" the annual marketing, operational and budgetary planning process. These direct sales forecasts may be constructed using the methods described in this chapter, and Chapter Eight.

An alternative approach (which will, of course, have the same organisational role) *is to prepare a forecast of the company's likely market share for the forecast period in view*. From this forecast market share a sales figure may be derived for operational and budgetary planning purposes. The alternative approach has two stages, thus:-

i) forecast the likely total available market for the period;

ii) forecast the likely share of this total market to be obtained by the company.

A forecast of the likely total available market for the period can be achieved in one of two ways, thus:-

a) *the total market:* may be estimated from statistics made available by trade associations, government statistical publications and specialist market research agencies. These estimates may be adjusted upwards, using judgement and experience, where they are not thought exactly to represent the total potential available market. For instance, increased advertising and improved product availability through distributors or retailers may have led to an increase in the total potential market since the initial statistics were published.

Alternatively, where published statistics are not available, the forecaster may attempt to construct estimates of the total available market. Such estimates may be based on calculations which use the determining variables. For instance, the value of the total toy market is a function of the number of children of the relevant ages, the access of these children (as permitted by their parents) to retail outlets, and industry or market research figures for per capita expenditure per child on toys, suitably adjusted for inflation, increases in personal disposable income (etc).

b) *individual market segments:* market segmentation is a major issue in the study of marketing and marketing management, and is the subject of a later chapter. Market segments are distinct groupings of different customer types, each with different demand patterns and behaviour. Estimates of the total market value of each segment may be compiled on the basis of those determining variables used to define and quantify the segment. For instance, forecasts for the total sales of bread, cakes and other bakery products in the UK can be calculated for any particular segment on the basis of trade and census data on the number of people in different socioeconomic classes (see later chapters), their per capita consumption of bakery products, and trends in the consumption pattern as between standard lines, such as wrapped white bread, and value added lines such as wholemeal bread, cream cakes, crispbread etc.

Once a forecast for the likely total available market has been prepared, company sales for the forecast period may then be calculated from either:-

* the expected market share, which should result from the various selling and marketing activities to be implemented during the period; or

* the target market share, which will be used to determine the level of activity of the sales and marketing function, and take into account the impact of competitors in the marketplace. Customer targeting is dealt with in a later chapter.

In both of these cases, the forecaster must have a clear understanding about the workings and relationship of those variables which will determine a company's relative market share. The forecaster and the marketing manager must be clear about, for instance, the impact on market share of advertising, pricing policy, levels of distribution, and customer access to products, salesforce efforts, and the need for segment-specific products. Each of these issues will be dealt with in detail in later chapters.

SUMMARY

The contents of this chapter are summarised in Table 9.2.

Table 9.2
Summary : Chapter Nine

SECTION	MAIN POINTS
1. Qualitative forecasting	This involves the analysis of environmental trends likely to affect market sales levels, and a detailed examination of those environmental conditions for which specific forecasts have to be constructed. This kind of "environmental" forecasting may be used to inform the marketing forecasting process, or provide the basis for more detailed quantification. It is more likely to be relevant to medium and long term forecasting and planning than quantitative techniques. Qualitative forecasting includes economic forecasts (dealt with in Chapter Eight), and technological, social and political forecasting. The actual techniques for the latter three include (i) scenario development; (ii) Delphi techniques; (iii) cross-impact analysis; (iv) value profiles.
2. Choice of forecasting method	The choice of method will depend on (i) forecasting objectives; (ii) time scales required; (iii) the relative importance of the forecast; (iv) the degree of accuracy required; (v) the type of data required; (vi) the availability of data; (vii) access to forecasting skills and methods; (viii) company experience with forecasting.

| 3. Forecast of market share | This involves two stages. The first is to forecast the likely total available market for the period (on a total or segment basis). The second is to forecast the likely share of this total market to be obtained by the company. |

QUESTIONS FOR SELF REVIEW

1) Why must a business plan ahead, making use of sales and market forecasts?

2) Describe and comment on the role of the sales forecast in the operation of a business.

3) Compare and contrast quantitative and qualitative approaches to sales and market forecasting.

4) Analyse and compare the main techniques of quantitative forecasting.

5) Analyse and compare the main techniques of qualitative forecasting.

6) What is the purpose of qualitative forecasting when taken in a sales and marketing context?

7) Describe and explain some of the factors which will determine the choice or combination of forecasting methods used by a company for constructing sales and market forecasts.

8) How might a company construct a forecast of its likely share of the market in which it trades?

9) "Planning ahead is as much a waste of time for my business as it is for me. I live and work for today!" Comment on this statement.

EXAMINATION QUESTIONS

Q12 Comment on the role of forecasting in the marketing planning process.

(IIM)

Q13 "Realistic annual forecasts of sales are essential for the successful compilation of budgets throughout the enterprise".

Describe the methods which could be used to arrive at an annual forecast of sales.

(IPS)

Q14   *Why would it be dangerous to base a Marketing Plan upon statistical sales forecasts alone? What other information should be used to supplement such forecasts?*

(CIM)

Q15   *What are the advantages and shortcomings of statistical approaches to sales forecasting? What should management do in order to compensate for the shortcomings?*

(CIM)

Q16   *Exponential smoothing and time series analysis generally have one set of applications in forecasting, whilst econometric modelling and scenario writing have another. Describe the two sets of situations to which each set of techniques is appropriate, showing why this should be so.*

(CIM)

Q17   *Identify the major environmental factors which are responsible for producing change in markets. Explain the potential significance of each factor, illustrating your answer by reference to products and/or markets of your own choice.*

(ABE)

Consumer Behaviour

The study of consumer behaviour is a crucial issue in marketing. It is essential for the marketer to understand the behavioural determinants of people's attitudes and purchase behaviour. These determinants include motivation, culture, social class, the family and so on. This section contains a detailed analysis of the behavioural determinants. This analysis is extended by the examination of theoretical models of buying behaviour, and is illustrated by a major case study. This is concerned with the consumer behaviour associated with the purchase and use of cotton wool.

10 Consumer Behaviour

INTRODUCTION

Chapter Ten begins with a brief outline of the *economic* determinants of consumer demand. An extensive treatment of this issue is not the concern of this book, and it is assumed that the reader has *already* made a study of it elsewhere, usually in some introductory study of economics.

The chapter then turns to a detailed analysis of the *behavioural* determinants of consumer demand. Firstly, the role of individual personal motivation is examined by means of the "Hierarchy of Needs" and "Self-Image Theory". Secondly, the impact of individual personality traits are considered. Thirdly, the significance of culture is analysed. Culture is generally regarded as a key determinant of consumer demand and purchase pattern. Finally, life-style is given brief consideration. The significance and measurability of life-style as a determinant of demand is a controversial issue, and so its discussion is kept to an introductory level.

The analysis of behavioural determinants of consumer demand is continued in Chapters eleven, twelve and thirteen.

CHAPTER CONTENTS

1) Determinants of demand
    1.1) Economic determinants of consumer demand
    1.2) Behavioural determinants of consumer demand
2) Behavioural determinants of demand
    2.1) Individual motivation
    2.2) Individual personality
    2.3) Culture
    2.4) Life-style

Summary

1) DETERMINANTS OF DEMAND

Markets are not inanimate objects or systems, although at one time it was fashionable to regard them as being so. *Markets, in reality, comprise the interactions and behaviour of people.* The publisher of this book estimates that there will be a market for this book, having carried out market research.

He has done his market forecasts and commissioned the author to write the book. It has been stocked by booksellers, and it has been purchased by a variety of people. Different readers have purchased this book for different reasons, whether it be to pass a professional examination, to commence undergraduate studies in marketing, or to train for a new job in the company's sales or marketing department.

It is essential, therefore, for the marketer to understand some of the reasons which cause people in the market to behave as they do. Why do people buy some kinds of products, and not others? *What are the reasons for buyer behaviour?* These four chapters concentrate on buyer behaviour in consumer markets, and chapters fourteen and fifteen deal with purchase behaviour in industrial markets.

1.1) Economic determinants of consumer demand.

People's purchase behaviour will, in part, be determined by basic economic factors such as:-

* the real disposable income available to them for expenditure on consumer goods and services;
* the price of the available products;
* basic personal perceptions of what constitutes good "value for money";
* the relative prices of "substitute" products, whose purchase might become preferred;
* the relative prices of "complementary" products (whose purchase is in some way related to the original purchase). For instance, colour films and processing are relatively expensive in comparison with the original expenditure on a basic camera.

1.2) Behavioural determinants of consumer demand.

People's purchase behaviour will also be determined by a whole series of *behavioural factors,* which are used to explain why buyers *need* or *want* certain products. The marketer must understand why people want or need products, so that he or she can:-

* group (or "segment") different people according to those reasons for purchase (see chapter sixteen);

* design and distribute products which will deliver the required "satisfactions" for these needs or wants;
* target promotional activities on these different people so that they become aware of the satisfactions on offer from the supplier, and are encouraged to make the actual purchase.

Behavioural determinants of consumer demand include:

* individual motivation;
* individual personality;
* culture;
* life-style;
* social class;
* groups and reference groups;
* family life cycle.

Each of these are considered in some detail in section two, below. The analysis is continued in chapter eleven.

2) BEHAVIOURAL DETERMINANTS OF DEMAND

2.1) Individual motivation.

To study individual motivation means *studying those forces that move a person to behave in a particular way*. Motivation links needs and personal objectives, thus:

need or want – motivation – attitude – behaviour pattern – objective (to satisfy the need or want)

For instance, a married couple may want a bigger and better house, so they are motivated into purchasing one. This may involve the following behavioural changes:-

* the wife may return to full-time work to increase the family's total income;
* expenditure on other items, such as cars or holidays, may for the time be reduced;
* the couple may place an increased value on the enhanced personal prestige attached to the ownership of the larger property, and will be prepared to accept the financial consequences of enjoying this enhanced prestige. This may involve a *change of attitude* towards the kind of housing that interests them.

The marketer, therefore, needs to understand the needs or wants that inspire individual motivation, and give rise to particular forms of purchase behaviour. There are a number of ways in which this can be done, and they include:

a) A. H. Maslow's HIERARCHY OF NEEDS : which is illustrated in Figure 10.1.

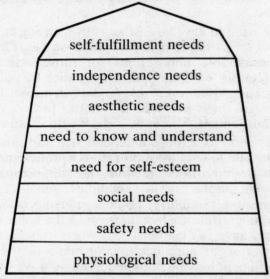

Figure 10.1. A.H. Maslow's Hierarchy of Needs.

In this theory, wants and needs are "pre-potent", that is potential higher level needs emerge and influence purchase behaviour only after there has been an opportunity for the satisfaction of lower level needs.

Purchase behaviour is motivated by a series of different levels of need or want. The most basic motivations stem from needs to eat, rest, have a home, feel secure and wanted, and to have the company of one's fellow men. For these reasons, people buy food and drink, pay rent or buy a house, purchase insurance, and meet up with their friends in clubs, pubs, churches, professional institutions and so on.

Once these kinds of needs are satisfied, the theory suggests that individual motivations will be shaped by behaviour that is associated with:-

* the need to gain self-esteem in the eyes of other people, for instance through the possession of prestigious

objects, taking expensive holidays, making donations to charity, etc.

* the need to know and understand what is going on around them. This perhaps accounts for the expenditure on news media such as newspapers, teletext etc, and the continuous radio and television news programmes operated commercially in the USA, and planned for the UK.

* the need to have an aesthetically pleasing environment, and to get rid of ugliness, pollution etc. This need has considerable implications for those activities which affect our environment, for instance by polluting it or creating visual eyesores. And it has meant that product design has become a major factor in product management. This issue is dealt with in later chapters.

* the need to achieve independence and self-fulfilment. The purchase of the motor car is a prime example, for its ownership offers freedom and an escape from the regimentation (and sometimes squalor) of public transport. Similarly, home ownership offers freedom from interference by others, since the home owner does not have a landlord to worry about, nor local government bureaucrats controlling his destiny. Self-fulfilment may be obtained in many ways. It may come from a beautiful home, leisure activities or sport, hobbies or continuing education, (etc).

b) SELF IMAGE THEORY:

Maslow's hierarchy isolates needs for *self-esteem* as a separate motivating category. Self-esteem is important in western culture for two reasons. Firstly, western culture places a high value on material acquisition and its display, because this reflects hard work and thrift. Hard work, thrift, and the enjoyment of income earned are the hallmark of the "protestant work ethic" that is still characteristic of many western societies.

Secondly, the achievement of self-esteem involves earning the respect of others. It is characteristic of our society that a high value is placed upon achieving self-respect and prestige. Whilst there are many ways in which prestige and respect can be obtained, the possession or use of certain types of goods and services are likely to increase individual status. Such goods or services might include homes and cars, private education or higher degrees, holidays in the Caribbean, objets d'art, eating out or membership of the golf-club.

This emphasis on self-respect and self-esteem leads to the concept of *self-image*. Consumers' self-image is an important clue to purchase behaviour, for around it cluster wants and needs that serve to defend and enhance *the idealised perceptions that most individuals have about themselves*. Self-image theory accepts that purchase behaviour will in part be determined by the need to satisfy physiological, safety and social needs. But it also recognises a series of emotional and psychological needs concerned with bolstering self-image and obtaining self-respect relative to others.

The "self" is an individual person's image of himself or herself. Within this self are various drives and motivations, the most important of which serve to maintain and enhance this image. Goods and services may be purchased because they "fit" these particular motivations. For instance many products are promoted as being the "in thing", whose consumption will make you "one of the crowd". Others are purchased because the buyer feels that ownership will confer separateness and status.

The individual will also interpret his or her environment in terms that suit or enhance the self-image. The choice of clothing, music or even places to shop will be made so that the individual's interaction with the external environment is structured in a particular way. This personal interaction with the environment can easily be illustrated by the success of clothing retail chains like "Next", "Chelsea Girl" and "Top Shop" in the UK, and international companies like Laura Ashley, C. and A. Modes, and Marks and Spencer. Each company sells clothes which have a clear identity allowing the wearer to convey a particular image to the outside world.

Thus, purchase behaviour and shopping patterns are seen under this motivation theory to support and enhance personal self-identity. The manufacturer, marketer and retailer will need to design, promote and retail products in such a way that images are produced which are consistent with those sought by prospective customers.

The components of the self-image are illustrated in Figure 10.2.

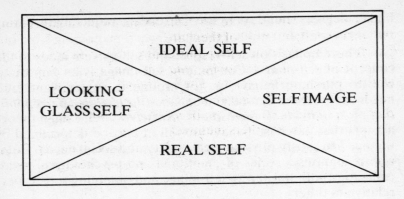

Real Self – you as you actually are.
Looking Glass Self – you as you think others see you.
Ideal Self – you the way you would like to be.
Self-Image – you the way you see yourself.

Figure 10.2. The Self Image.

2.2) Individual Personality.

An individual's personality is the sum total of those *traits* which define his or her individuality, and which cause one person to be different from another. Personality traits are particular characteristics or aspects of this total personality. They give rise to behavioural responses to external stimuli that are enduring and consistent within a person's psychological constitution. These traits are, in fact, *ingrained and stable dispositions to respond to certain situations in particular ways characteristic of the personality.* For instance, personality variations account for the wide range of reactions towards a salesperson. Some people will act in a submissive and respectful manner, automatically accepting that the salesperson is honest and trustworthy. Others will be hostile and critical; whilst those readers who have bargained in the bazaars of North Africa or the East will have recognised that the customer and the shopkeeper are expected to play a negotiating game, jousting with each other until there is agreement and mutual respect. Some people's natural politeness makes such bargaining difficult or "embarrassing".

The traits which make up the individual's personality have two main sources. Some of them are inherent, coming from our parents. (This was the viewpoint of Freud and Jung). Others come from *social conditioning and personal experience.* (This was the viewpoint of Adler). The emergence of the personality is a lengthy process, which continues throughout maturity into old age, with some traits becoming more developed or pronounced, whilst others mellow.

A description of personality traits is beyond the scope of this book, but they may be *categorised* in a simple manner under three headings, thus:-

* role traits: which are those parts of the personality which determine how an individual will react or behave in particular situations, and will react to the expectations of others in that situation.

* sociometric traits: which are those parts of the personality which will shape individual reactions to the behaviour of other people, and their relationship to them.

* expressive disposition: which will determine an individual's self-expression, both in response to particular situations, and towards other people.

The marketer may take account of personality variables in the following way. Many people will have similar types of personality, or similar sets of traits. The market can be divided (or "segmented") on the basis of these "typical" personalities or *stereotypes,* and products and promotional activities targeted upon them. The marketer may well expect that there will be a sufficient number of people who conform to these stereotypes to make this course of action viable. For instance:-

i) products may be consistent with widely accepted behaviour patterns which maintain or enhance the traits associated with self image. This is most certainly the case with the purchase of clothing and drinks, and the following of a particular style of life (see below).

ii) products or services may be consistent with traits associated with compliance. The air inclusive package tour holiday requires a certain amount of compliant behaviour in order to work. Customers must adhere to the laid down schedule for travel, and accept the accomodation offered. The package tour is particularly appropriate to the personality traits of compliance and sociability which make up the typically British temperament.

iii) suppliers may market products or services which are widely consistent with personality traits associated with *extraversion* (outward going and highly visible behaviour) and aggression. Sports cars, pop music and sporting products and services are all attractive to these personality traits.

iv) suppliers may market products or services which are widely consistent with personality traits associated with *introversion* (inward looking and self-sufficient behaviour) and personal detachment. Music, self-catering and "get away from it all" holidays, book publishing, and creative pastimes such as painting, model building (etc) are all attractive to these personality traits.

2.3) Culture.

Culture will play an important part in shaping purchase behaviour, because culture determines many of our patterns and standards ("norms") of behaviour. For instance, the purchase and consumption of alcohol is an important feature of western life. Indeed, the symbolic consumption of wine lies at the heart of Christianity, in the form of Communion and Mass. Alcohol, on the other hand, is forbidden to Muslims, and islamic societies are often characterised by an absence of the alcoholic beverages which are so familiar elsewhere.

a) *Culture and its impact:* culture can be defined as distinctive patterns of behaviour which result from basic beliefs and traditions. The impact of culture on individual behaviour is summarised in Figure 10.3.

Culture stems from a society or community's experience, traditions, basic beliefs, aspirations and ambitions. Any one individual is *socialised* into the prevailing culture, whose values and standards are integrated into that person's motivation, personality and life-style (see below). Socialisation is thus a process that integrates the individual into the ways and standards of the community of which he or she is a part. And that person's consumption habits and purchase behaviour will be as much affected by this socialisation process as any other form of individual and social behaviour. For instance, the acceptance of new types or brands of product may, in part,

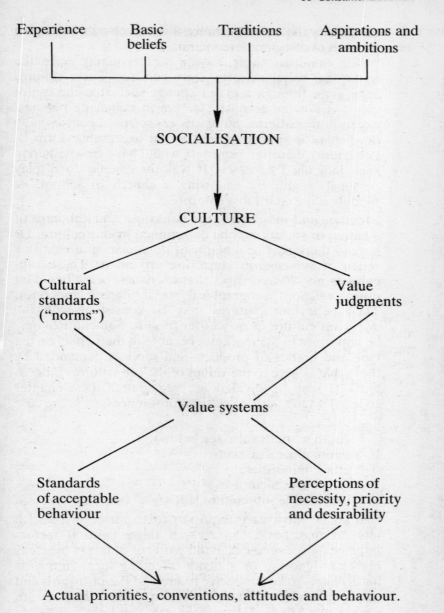

Figure 10.3. The Impact of Culture on Individual Behaviour.

depend on the cultural implications involved in changing patterns of consumption.

For example, thrift, saving and economy were the traditional hallmarks of western cultures. These cultures have gone through a major change such that the use of credit is now an accepted feature in managing personal expenditure patterns. Similarly, *conspicuous consumption* or display is now regarded as an acceptable form of behaviour. Victorian propriety would have frowned upon such individual excesses. It was then better to display personal wealth by endowing a church or school, or funding some charitable enterprise.

b) *culture and sub-culture:* the behaviour and standards of a nation or society may be determined by one culture. Or instead there may be a major or *dominant* culture, with a series of *sub-cultures* clustering around it. These sub-cultures may have distinct characteristics, being based on ethnic, religious, geographical, social or age factors (etc). Their behaviour patterns may be consistent with the dominant culture or may differ from it. Sub-cultures may be important to the marketer because of their effect on the type and brands of products and services demanded by those that adhere to the values of the sub-culture. Indeed, markets may be divided or "segmented" (see chapter sixteen) on the basis of cultural differences, as in the case of:-

* youth markets (also see below);
* senior citizen markets;
* ethnic minorities;
* religious sub-cultures;
* identifiable sub-culture "life style" (see below);

It will be particularly important for exporters involved in international trade to research those cultural factors influencing consumer demand patterns in target overseas markets. Ignoring or actually offending local culture is hardly likely to be conducive to success! Beautiful girls and champagne may be powerful western symbols, but they are useless in a Middle Eastern context. Similarly, wholesale buyers may only deal with those who can speak the local language, refusing in principle to use an international language like English, French or Chinese.

c) *culture and language:* culture finds its expression in the language used by adherents to that culture or sub-culture. Indeed, *language is the tool of culture.* The marketer will have to understand and use the "right" language if he is to achieve an effective communication to the market. This choice of language is for example particularly important in communicating to youth and senior citizen markets. Both cultures are easily discouraged or bored by language and concepts that they perceive as unfashionable, trendy, patronising, disturbing or just plain out of date!

d) *traditional, achieving and affluent cultures:* one way in which cultures can be categorised for marketing purposes is to differentiate between traditional, achieving and affluent cultures, thus:-

* *traditional cultures* are rooted in the past. They will often be characterised by a strong deference to religious and moral customs; traditional hierarchies of authority and family relationships; social stratification and class structures; and low levels of per capita gross national product. Purchase and consumption habits will be firmly anchored in customary patterns, which it will be difficult to break. Attacking such cultures can have unpredictable results, for instance as in Iran where the break-down of traditional patterns and the establishment of western customs has been suppressed, and a form of religious dictatorship established.

* *achieving cultures* are cultures that have begun to break away from the traditions of the past, in order to develop and grow. Achieving cultures, based on principles of self-help and free enterprise, were characteristic of the USA and north Europe during the period 1800 to 1960. Purchasing patterns may alter significantly from the traditional roots, emphasising personal material possession and display, the possession of prestigious homes and objects, "one-upmanship" etc. Where achieving cultures are growing out of traditional ones there will inevitably be tension between the two, and the occasional conflicts will affect marketing development and growth.

* *affluent cultures* include the post second world war industrial societies of the USA, Japan and Western Europe. Whilst personal achievement and material

possession remain important, such societies can afford sophisticated social welfare systems, providing a minimum welfare "safety net" for all of the population, rich or poor. This means that in addition to personal expenditure on goods and services, there are major opportunities for marketing products and services associated with health and welfare provision.

e) *cultural trends:* culture is generally a dynamic phenonemon. This accounts for the attempts of fiercely traditional societies, for instance those based upon fundamental islamic principles, to turn the clock back to the past. In general, cultures undergo a slow evolution and development. This will have an effect on consumption and expenditure patterns. For instance, in western societies women have become economically more important than hitherto. Many women are equal (in economic terms) with men as earners and consumers. Similarly, cultural and population dynamics have meant that there is now a major youth culture, with its associated markets. Later on during this century a massive senior citizen culture is likely to emerge in the west, and this again will present its marketing opportunities.

2.4) Life-style.

Life-style refers to *distinctive ways of living adopted by particular communities or sub-sections of society*. Life-style is a *manifestation* of a number of behavioural factors, such as motivation, personality and culture, and depends on the economic status of the people in question. *If a life-style can be accurately described, and the numbers of people following it quantified, then marketers can assign and target products and promotion upon this particular target life-style group*. Life-style is a controversial issue, and a full analysis of the arguments is beyond the scope of this book. The implications of life-style for marketing, and the problems of definition involved, can perhaps best be illustrated by some examples.

One simple example generalises life-style in terms of four categories, thus:-

i) *upwardly mobile, ambitious:* seeking a better and more affluent life-style, principally through better paid and more interesting work, and a higher material standard of living. Such a life-style will be prepared to try new products.

ii) *traditional and sociable:* compliance and conformity to group norms bring social approval and reassurance to the individual. Purchasing patterns will therefore be "conformist".

iii) *security and status seeking:* stressing "safety" needs and "ego-defensive" needs. This life-style links status, income and security. It encourages the purchase of strong and well known products and brands, and emphasises those products and services which confer status and make life as secure and predictable as possible. These would include insurance, membership of the AA or RAC etc. Products that are well established and familiar inspire more confidence than new products, which will be resisted.

iv) *hedonistic preference:* placing emphasis on "enjoying life now" and the immediate satisfaction of wants and needs. Little thought is taken for the future.

Two more complex life-style analyses are shown in Box 10.4. These sets of analysis are based on empirical attitude research, and the agencies that have constructed them use them to advise their clients on how best to design and position existing and new products on target segments made up of people who have similar life-style patterns.

Box 10.4
Life-style categories

McCann-Erickson Men	Women
Avant Guardians. Concerned with change and well-being of others, rather than possessions. Well educated, prone to self-righteousness.	Avant Guardians. 'Liberal left' opinions, trendy attitudes. But outgoing, active, sociable.
Pontificators. Strongly held, traditional opinions. Very British, and concerned about keeping others on the right path.	Lady Righteous. Traditional, 'right-minded' opinions. Happy, complacent, with strong family orientation.
Chameleons. Want to be contemporary to win approval. Act like barometers of social change, but copiers not leaders.	Hopeful seekers. Need to be liked, want to do 'right'. Like new things, want to be trendy.
Self-admirers. At the young end of the spectrum. Intolerant of others and strongly motivated by success and concerned about self-image.	Lively ladies. Younger than above, sensual, materialistic, ambitious and competitive.
Self-exploiters. The 'doers' and 'self-starters', competitive but always under pressure and often pessimistic. Possessions are important.	New unromantics. Generally young and single, adopting a hard-headed and unsentimental approach to life. Independent, self-centred.
Token triers. Always willing to try new things to 'improve their luck', but apparently on a permanent try-and-fail cycle. Includes an above average proportion of unemployed.	Lack-a-daisy. Unassertive and easy-going. Try to cope but often fail. Not very interested in the new.
Sleepwalkers. Contented under-achievers. Don't care about most things, and actively opt out. Traditional macho views.	Blinkered. Negative, do not want to be disturbed. Uninterested in conventional success – in fact, few interests except TV and radio.
Passive endurers. Biased towards the elderly, they are often economically and socially disenfranchised. Expect little of life, and give little.	Down-trodden. This group is shy, introverted, but put-upon. Would like to do better. Often unhappy and pressurised in personal relationships.

Taylor Nelson
Self-explorers. Motivated by self-expression and self-realisation. Less materialistic than other groups, and showing high tolerance levels.
Social resistors. The caring group, concerned with fairness and social values, but often appearing intolerant and moralistic.
Experimentalists. Highly individualistic, motivated by fast-moving enjoyment. They are materialistic, pro-technology but anti-traditional authority.
Conspicuous consumers. They are materialistic and pushy, motivated by acquisition, competition, and getting ahead. Pro-authority, law and order.
Belongers. What they seek is a quiet, undisturbed family life. They are conservative, conventional rule followers.
Survivors. Strongly class-conscious, and community spirited, their motivation is to 'get by'.
Aimless. Comprises two groups, (a) the young unemployed, who are often anti-authority, and (b) the old, whose motivation is day-to-day existence.

Source : Marketing

SUMMARY

The contents of this chapter are summarised in Table 10.5.

Table 10.5
Summary : Chapter Ten

SECTION	MAIN POINTS
1.1 Economic determinants of consumer demand	Include real disposable income, product price, price of substitute and complementary goods, basic personal perceptions of what constitutes "value for money".
2.1 Individual motivation	To study individual motivation means studying the forces that move a person to behave in a particular way. Motivation links needs and personal objectives, thus:- need/want – motivation – attitude – behaviour pattern – objective. Motivation is then analysed by using Maslow's "Hierarchy of Needs", and "Self-image" theory. Purchase behaviour is a key behavioural pattern and can, in part, be explained by these theories.
2.2 Individual personality	This is the sum total of those "traits" which define individual character. Personality traits are particular aspects of the total character. These traits are ingrained and stable dispositions to respond to certain situations in particular ways characteristic of the personality. The marketer can take account of personality variables by grouping personality types as "stereotypes", and targeting products and promotion on them.

2.3 Culture

Culture determines patterns and standards ("norms") of behaviour. It derives from basic beliefs and traditions. Individuals are socialised into the prevailing culture, and its values and norms are integrated into the person's motivation, personality and life-style. This will affect consumption habits and purchase behaviour. Subcultures often cluster around the main culture. Language is the tool of culture. Cultures may be traditional, achieving or affluent, since culture is a dynamic phenomenon.

2.4 Life-style

Life-style refers to distinctive ways of living, purchase and consumption habits (etc) adopted by particular groups in society. Life-styles can be upwardly mobile; traditional and sociable; security and status-seeking; hedonistic.

11 Behavioural Determinants of Demand

INTRODUCTION

This chapter continues the analysis of consumer behaviour commenced during the previous chapter. It continues the examination of the behavioural determinants of demand, by looking first at the role and significance of social class. Social class and social stratification are major influences on consumer purchase behaviour. Groups and their influence on the individual are considered next. Thirdly, the family constitutes a major determinant of consumer behaviour, whether in terms of its influence on the individual, direct family purchasing, or through the movement of individuals across the family life cycle.

Reference groups and opinion leaders are discussed, and their influence on purchase behaviour illustrated by youth culture and other age-related examples.

The chapter then moves on to consider multi-individual buying behaviour. Here, purchase decisions are influenced by a variety of different roles, each of whose relative importance needs to be understood by the marketer selling goods and services subject to such multiple influences.

CHAPTER CONTENTS

1) Behavioural determinants of demand (continued)

   1.1) Social class

   1.2) Groups

   1.3) The Family

   1.4) Reference groups

   1.5) Opinion leaders

   1.6) The family life cycle

2) Multi-individual buying behaviour

Summary

This chapter continues the analysis of consumer behaviour, commenced in Chapter Ten. Chapter Ten commenced with a brief examination of the economic determinants of consumer demand, and then turned to a detailed analysis of the following behavioural determinants of consumer demand, namely:

* individual motivation;
* individual personality;
* culture;
* life-style.

1) BEHAVIOURAL DETERMINANTS OF DEMAND

1.1) Social class

Social class is a major behavioural determinant of consumer buying behaviour, and its importance is widely acknowledged by marketers. Marketers will have to take into account the fact that expenditure and consumption patterns are often differentiated by the membership of social classes.

It is normal for societies to be divided up into different social groups or **classes.** This division is called **social stratification.** One cause of such stratification can be illustrated by a simple example. As societies developed, so did the need for particular occupations and trades, such as the warrior, the priest, the merchant trader, the doctor, the farmer and the lawyer. These occupations called for specialised skill, training and personal persistence. They had a major impact on the community, and attracted authority, wealth and prestige. They became the traditional "upper" or "professional" classes.

A social class may be defined as a **psychological-social grouping,** within which social, economic, educational and political interests tend to coincide. These interests may be different from other social classes, in which case the society may become stratified, that is, made up of a series of social classes differentiated by status and prestige. The "membership" of any one social class may be determined by such factors as:

– traditions
– family
– beliefs, values, and attitudes
– occupation
– education
– wealth or income
– personal aspirations

The social stratification that results may be ill-defined (as in North American societies) or may be fully institutionalised, as in India where a rigid "caste" system operates. In some

133

countries it may in part be based on social/ethnic background. In South America the upper classes tend to be European in origin, whilst the lower classes tend to be the negro descendants of slaves. In between is the mulatto, the product of centuries of inter-marriage between the white and coloured races.

Social classes often have their own particular behaviour, purchase and consumption patterns, and tend to limit their closest relationships, social intercourse and friendship to their own kind. This serves to reinforce group standards and norms, confers a feeling of identity, solidarity and belonging, and permits the achievement of psychological and physical protection. It also means that they will favour particular types of product, service or shopping, and will constitute a viable market for these particular products or retail outlets.

   a) *a UK classification of social class:* one of the best known classifications divides the UK population as follows:-

Classi-fication	Social Class	Occupation
A	Upper/upper middle class	Higher managerial; professional; administrative.
B	Middle class	Intermediate managerial; professional; administrative.
C1	Lower middle class	Supervisory; junior managerial or administrative; clerical.
C2	Skilled working class	Skilled manual.
D	Working class	Semi-skilled and unskilled.
E	Those at the lowest level of subsistence	State pensioners; casual workers; unemployed

This classification has been simplified for use by the UK General Household Survey, which uses the following categories:-

1 Professional
2 Employers and managers
3 Intermediate and junior non-manual
4 Skilled manual
5 Semi-skilled manual and personal service
6 Unskilled manual; unemployed; those who have not worked.

Whilst a detailed discussion of the advantages and disadvantages of such classifications is beyond the scope of this book, their widespread use shows that:

* they give a generally reliable picture of the relationship between occupation and income;

* they do indicate differences in purchase and consumption patterns, although the total disposable income as between any two categories may be similar (especially where husband and wife are both working)

* those categories are stable and enduring.

Some examples of social class-related expenditure priorities in the UK might include:-

– private health care and private education   A, B
– caravans and caravanning   C1, C2
– air inclusive package tours to the Costa Brava and the Costa del Sol in Spain   C1, C2, D
– membership of working mens' clubs   C2, D, E

b) *Social mobility:* in western societies it is common to find that individuals aspire to "move up" to the next social class above. This *social mobility* is a characteristic feature, and has two implications. The first is that if a country's economy can support a widespread increase in per capita income, then people will move out of the "lower" classes and these may become less significant in population and marketing terms. Some European and Middle Eastern countries have for many years responded to the resultant labour shortages by "importing" immigrant labour to perform relatively menial and unskilled tasks. These immigrant groups then tend to become part of the lower classes, unless there are so many that they form a separate sub-culture (as is the case with Turks in West Germany). Eventually, immigrant workers (like the Irish, Poles and Germans in the UK) tend to become assimilated, lose their separate identity, and move upwards in the social scale.

Secondly, those people who have the means to achieve upward mobility will exhibit purchase and consumption patterns similar to the social class to which they aspire. This may increase the size and value of the market higher up the scale. For instance, there may be an increase in demand for:-

- owned homes, as opposed to rented ones (which will affect both the market for housing and mortgage finance);
- prestigious foreign saloon cars (in the UK the demand for prestige German cars has had a significant effect on the sales of luxury UK produced saloon cars, such as Triumph (now extinct) and Rover);
- private education, for which UK demand is now very high;
- air inclusive package tours to resorts that were hitherto exclusive (such as Marbella in Spain, the French Caribbean, the Greek Islands etc).

1.2) Groups

Within any particular society, with its cultures, social classes and life-styles, there will be many different social groupings. A social group comprises any number of people who interact with each other in some way, and whose behaviour is a composite of both individual and group influences. Group members will tend to conform to group standards or norms, especially where such conformity is the result of a general acceptance of the basic beliefs, attitudes and values of the group. This level of conformity is likely to be a function of two factors:-

* the level of *dependence* on the group;
* the *benefits* (or acceptance) of conformity, and the risk of *sanction* (or loss of benefits) arising from non-conformity.

It should be self-evident, therefore, that where individual behaviour can be so extensively influenced by conformity to the standards of the social groups that make up our community and its social strata, then there will be major implications for the marketer. Purchase and consumption behaviour will be as much influenced by social groups as by any other form of behavioural determinant. But given the considerable importance of purchase behaviour, this relative influence may be particularly great.

If you are not sure about this influence, *think about the clothes you wear at work and at leisure.* Ask yourself why you wear such clothes. Was it purely your choice? How might your boss react if you turned up to work in your best disco gear? Why did you buy a dress with this year's fashion colour!

The influence of the group on purchase behaviour can be studied in two ways. The first deals with the role of the family (section 1.3 below). The second looks at the influence of "reference groups" (section 1.4 below).

1.3 The Family

The family is a basic social grouping, and it has an all pervading influence over its members. The families of a nation have an enormous collective purchasing power over a very wide range of products and services. Indeed, some goods are usually only purchased within a family context. Such goods include suites of furniture, children's clothing and children's foodstuffs. So how is a "family" defined? Let us look at Phil and Maggie Jones, who have just got married. Maggie's maiden name was Smith.

a) *family of origin:* Phil is a member of the Jones family, and Maggie is a member of the Smith family. Both families will retain some influence over Phil and Maggie.

b) *family of marriage:* the Jones (Phil and Maggie) are now a family of marriage. The creation of a family of marriage usually means that, in Western societies at least, a "household" will be established. This has major marketing implications, for the Jones will now become active members in the markets for housing, mortgage finance, furniture and home applicances, do—it-yourself and gardening products, insurance (etc).

c) *nuclear family:* once the Jones have children, the family becomes a "nuclear" one. Phil and Maggie are the nucleus of a new Jones family. This also has major marketing implications as the Jones will become active members of the markets for larger housing, washing machines, children's foodstuffs, clothes, toys and books, family holidays (etc).

d) *extended family:* Phil and Maggie Jones, plus offspring, are part of the wider Jones clan, comprising Phil's parents (and grandparents if they are still alive), brothers and sisters (and their families) and other relatives. A large extended family may have a few dozen members.

The family situation will have specific marketing implications, as in the purchase of housing, washing machines or children's clothes. But family purchase behaviour will also be subject to *family influence* (or even interference) over the choice and direction of the expenditure of any one individual. For instance:-

i) the influence of children on family purchases may be product or service specific. They may choose what breakfast cereals or brand of baked beans they will eat, and have some discretionary expenditure within their pocket money. Nevertheless, parents will often impose their judgement, for instance condemning some pop music as "decadent" or just plain crude, and insisting that some children's food brands are a rip-off!

ii) the influence of teenagers, especially within "Youth" culture, is harder to discern. The family will have to decide on how much its teenage members will be allowed to spend, and how much discretion they have in making their own choice of clothes, records, holidays or motor cycles. Many readers will readily recognise that such purchase decisions are often fraught with difficulty and argument. The seventeen year old does not always want to listen to the views of his father and mother, particularly if he has his heart set upon a motorbike!

iii) the young housewife will be subject to a whole variety of influence and advice. Notwithstanding her relationship to her husband, the young housewife is likely to pay particular heed to the views of her own mother, especially in expenditures on housewares and domestic consumer durables like cookers, freezers (etc). This maternal influence on the housewife is likely to decline with age, experience and maturity, but, as far as marketers are concerned, *its influence is strongest at a point in the couple's life when heavy expenditure may be incurred* to establish the "household".

iv) the mother in a nuclear family may come to play a *pivotal role* in all major expenditure decisions, especially if the husband relies upon her to manage the household budget. Purchase decisions will be referred to her, and discussion of them will take place around her. In many cases she will have the last word. This pivotal role is much more obvious in matriarchical societies in which it is accepted that the mother or grandmother must make the final decision about such expenditures.

v) the experience of older family members may be deferred to before purchase decisions are made. Grandfather or grandmother's opinion may be communicated in a subtle manner, but even in today's western society the opinion of the elders still carries great weight. The older generation can ask the most awkward questions whilst giving less offence than younger members, who may feel it incumbent upon themselves to appear more reticent in giving advice. Indeed, the younger generation may look to its elders to play "the devil's advocate" before important decisions are made.

1.4 Reference Groups

Reference groups *are groups with which an individual closely identifies*. Depending on the strength of identification with the reference group, an individual may conform to its standards and norms. Purchase behaviour will, again, be altered so as to come into line with the customary behaviour of the reference group. Specifically, a reference group may influence an individual person's behaviour:-

* by establishing "conventional" patterns of behaviour and purchase satisfaction;

* by influencing individual expectations and aspirations, which will shape people's attitude towards consumption and satisfaction;

* by defining and shaping individual personal taste;

* by supplying the consumer with information about particular products or services, in situations where the individual has minimal prior knowledge. Reference group and "word of mouth" recommendation is highly influential. Advertisers know this, and attempt to use promotional messages to shape the general attitude and opinion of the target reference group.

An illustration should make this influence clear. Once they have an adequate income, many British men and women aged, say, between thirty five and fifty, tend to adopt reference-group orientated life-styles. They buy the "right" type of car (currently the BMW or Jaguar!), go to particular resorts in Spain or Greece, play golf, eat out at certain types of restaurant, and read the 'Sunday Times' on Sunday. They are identifying with the type of people who lead a life-style which is attractive to them.

Earlier influences on their expenditure pattern (family etc) become less important.

But, above all, the impact of the reference group is seen most clearly in the life-style adopted by youth. Here, the conformity can be zealous or even excessive. Marketers have proved adept at catching the mood of the age range sixteen to twenty four, supplying products like jeans, cola drinks, music, cars and motorcycles which become the mode, the "in thing", the product to have. Here, the reference group can be all powerful in influencing purchase behaviour.

1.5 Opinion leaders

Reference groups may contain individuals who as "opinion leaders" appear to exercise a disproportionate influence in forming and shaping the opinions of those other people who orientate their behaviour'towards that of the reference group. Such individuals may be expert in a limited field, or expert across a variety of fields of interest relevant to those who will as a result, tend to follow the opinion leader. Opinion leaders are influential for two reasons:-

* they are psychologically "open" or receptive to new ideas, wherever these come from. They are less resistant to innovation than the average person, who tends (at least initially) to put up barriers to the adoption and assimilation of new ideas.
* they are perceived as authoritative. This personal authority can come from the holding of a traditionally authoritative role, or it can come from age, experience, personality and qualification.

The views of opinion leaders are often taken very seriously by reference group members, and "word of mouth" recommendation is regarded as just about the most powerful tool of promotion (or condemnation) that there is. Marketers interested in the development and introduction of new products will be particularly interested in the attitude of opinion leaders to these products, for their general market acceptance can be slowed down or speeded up by the views of such people. This issue is dealt with in a later chapter.

It may also be true that social and market changes may "filter down" from the higher social classes (such as the AB's in the UK) who are often first to perceive the need or desirability for a particular change. These higher social classes may themselves act as opinion leaders for other social classes, who, over a period of time, may adopt the change. This filtering down of influence seems in the UK to be visible in the trend towards more "healthy" eating patterns. This development is not a fad, but has been an established trend indicated by objective demographic and food survey statistics. As time has gone by, the desirability of an improved diet, less smoking (etc) has filtered down throughout the social class structure, after originating with people whose opinions and experience (for instance in the medical and other professions, the media and senior business management) is, in any case. likely to be authoritative.

Table 11.1
The family life cycle

I	II	III	IV	V
Bachelor Stage: young single people not living at home	Newly married couples: young, no children	Full nest I: youngest child under six	Full nest II: youngest child six or over	Full nest III: older married couples with dependent children
Few financial burdens. Fashion/opinion leader led. Recreation orientated. Buy: Basic kitchen equipment, basic furniture, cars, equipment for the mating game, holidays. Experiment with patterns of personal financial management and control.	Better off financially than they will be in the near future. High levels of purchase of homes and consumer durable goods. Buy: Cars, refrigerators, cookers, life assurance, durable furniture, holidays. Establish patterns of personal financial management and control.	Home purchasing at peak. Liquid assets/savings low. Dissatisfied with financial position and amount of money saved. Reliance on credit finance, credit cards, overdrafts, etc. Child dominated household. Buy necessities: washers, dryers, baby food and clothes, vitamins, dolls and toys, books, etc.	Financial position better. Some wives return to work. Child dominated household. Buy necessities: foods, cleaning materials, clothes, bicycles, sports gear, music lessons, pianos, holidays, etc.	Financial position still better. More wives work. School and examination dominated household. Some children get first jobs; others in further/higher education. Expenditure to support children's further/higher education. Buy: New, more tasteful furniture, non-necessary appliances, boats etc; holidays.

VI	VII	VIII	IX
Empty nest I: older married couples, no children living with them, head of family still in labour force.	Empty nest II: older married couples, no children living at home, head of family retired.	Solitary survivor in labour force.	Solitary survivor(s) retired
Home ownership at peak. More satisfied with financial position and money saved. Interested in travel, recreation, self-education. Make financial gifts and contributions. Children gain qualifications; move to Stage I. Buy luxuries, home improvements, e.g. fitted kitchens, etc.	Significant cut in income. Keep home. Buy: medical appliances or medical care, products which aid health, sleep and digestion. Assist children. Concern with level of savings and pension. Some expenditure on hobbies and pastimes.	Income still adequate but likely to sell family home and purchase smaller accommodation. Concern with level of savings and pension. Some expenditure on hobbies and pastimes. Worries about security and dependence.	Significant cut in income. Additional medical requirements. Special need for attention, affection, and security. May seek sheltered accommodation. Possible dependence on others for personal financial management and control.

1.6 The family life cycle

Quite apart from the influence of reference groups, opinion leaders and family members, purchase behaviour will be shaped by the stage reached by individuals and families within the *family life cycle*. Table 11.1 shows the nine suggested stages of this life cycle, and analyses some of the changing income and expenditure patterns across these stages. Put simply, purchase behaviour will be a function of the different variables already analysed in this and the previous chapter, but will vary in emphasis and priority according to the stage reached by individual and family.

2) MULTI-INDIVIDUAL BUYING BEHAVIOUR

This and the previous chapter have concentrated on an analysis of some of the major behavioural influences and determinants of individual demand. The study of individual purchase motivations and behaviour may, however, be complicated *where a number of individuals become involved in the purchase decision*. In this case, a wider variety of the kinds of influences dealt with in these two chapters will come into play. The marketer will, therefore, have to adapt his promotional and distribution arrangements (etc) to meet this additional complication. Three examples are given in Table 11.2. The various multi-individual influences on the purchase decision take the form of a number of *roles* which are:-

* the initiator – who originates the purchase process, having given expression to the need or want that motivates it.

* the influencer – individuals whose influence over the purchase decision is in some way significant or authoritative. The influencer may, for instance, change the purchase objective, or act as a catalyst to render the original purchase motivation more practical or feasible.

* the decider – who actually determines what the outcome of the purchase motivation will be.

* the purchaser – who physically carries out the purchase transaction.

* the user – who receives and uses the product or service.

Any number of people may be involved in these roles, whilst it would be quite normal for one person to fulfil more than one of these roles.

SUMMARY

The contents of this chapter are summarised in Table 11.3

ROLE EXAMPLE	INITIATOR	INFLUENCER	DECIDER	PURCHASER	USER
(i) child's toy	child.	parents, other relatives, parents' friends, salesperson.	parents.	mother.	child.
(ii) family car	father, salesperson.	mother, family, father's friends, salesperson.	father, mother.	father.	father, mother.
(iii) retirement home	retired couple, children.	children, friends, acquaintances, doctor, salesperson.	husband, wife.	husband, son.	retired couple.

Table 11.2. Multi-Individual Purchase Roles.

TABLE 11.3
Summary : Chapter Eleven

SECTION	MAIN POINTS
1.1 Social class	Social class is defined as a psychological – social grouping within which social, economic, educational and political interests tend to coincide. Societies are usually divided up or "stratified" into different social groups or classes. These classes are differentiated by status and prestige differences, which may give rise to the desire for upward movements within the class structure. This is called "social mobility". Expenditure and consumption patterns are often differentiated by membership of these different social classes.
1.2 Groups	Behaviour within social groups will tend (to some degree) to conform to group attitudes, standards and pressures. This will affect the purchase and consumption patterns of group members, according to the level of identification/dependence on the benefits of conformity, and the risk of loss of benefits from non-conformity.
1.3 The family	The family is a basic social grouping, and has a pervasive influence over its members' behaviour. The families of a nation have an enormous collective purchasing power, and many goods are normally only sold within a family context.
1.4 Reference groups	These are groups with which an individual closely identifies. Depending on the strength of identification with the reference group, an individual's purchase behaviour may follow the customary pattern found within that reference group.

1.5 Opinion leaders	Reference groups may contain individuals who as opinion leaders appear to exercise a disproportionate influence in forming and shaping the opinions of others who orientate their behaviour towards that of the reference group. Opinion leaders tend to be receptive to new ideas, and are perceived by others as authoritative. Opinion leaders are important "where word of mouth" recommendation (or condemnation) is likely to affect attitudes and purchase behaviour.
1.6 Family life cycle	Purchase patterns and behaviour will be shaped by the stage reached by individuals and families within the family life cycle. See Table 11.1
2 Multi-individual buying behaviour	Purchase behaviour may be complicated where a number of individuals are involved in a purchase decision. Multi-individual buying behaviour may be analysed on the basis of a number of roles, namely the initiator; influencer; decider; purchaser; user.

12 Models of Buying Behaviour

INTRODUCTION

This third chapter on consumer behaviour concentrates on conceptual and theoretical models of buying behaviour. Such models comprise theoretical constructs of variables which are inter-related, and significant in influencing the outcome of a purchase motivation. They are used to clarify the relationships that exist between the variables that influence the buying situation, and to predict the outcome of change to these variables.

CHAPTER CONTENTS

1) Models of buying behaviour

    1.1) Decision process models

    1.2) A theoretical model : the Howard and Sheth model

Summary

Recommended Reading

Questions for self-review

Examination Questions

1) MODELS OF BUYING BEHAVIOUR

It should by now be clear to the reader that the purchase decision may turn out to be a highly complex one, subject to a wide variety of inter-related economic and behavioural influences. One way of recognising and analysing this complexity is that of constructing *models of buying behaviour*. Such models comprise theoretical constructs of variables which are inter-related and significant in influencing the outcome of a purchase motivation. These models may be of use to marketers in dealing with particular problems, such as the relative importance of advertising or price in influencing consumer purchase behaviour. A model attempts to clarify the relationship between variables influencing the buying situation, and may assist the marketer to predict the outcome from some planned change, such as the introduction of a new brand, or a change in advertising policy. Two approaches to the construction of buying behaviour models will be considered.

1.1) Decision process models

Decision process models analyse the buying process *as a series of sequential steps*. Since there will be distinct patterns of behaviour at each step, the marketer can identify specific opportunities or activities that will assist the decision-making process, and orientate the would-be buyer towards his particular product or brand. A simple decision process model might contain the following steps:

NEEDS/WANTS → RECOGNITION OF NEEDS OR WANT → PURCHASE MOTIVATION → INFORMATION

SEARCH → EVALUATION OF ALTERNATIVES → CHOICE → PURCHASE PROCESS → POST-PURCHASE

EVALUATION → FEEDBACK → NEEDS/WANTS.

The model assumes that the buyer will pass through this series of steps, whether it be consciously or unconsciously, until the purchase is (or is not) made. It also assumes (reasonably enough) that since the average consumer is not stupid, he or she will *learn* on an accumulative basis from the purchase experience. This learning process will focus in particular on a comparison of:-

* the evaluation of the alternatives made prior to the purchase;
* the claims made by the supplier for the product that was eventually purchased;
* the performance or acceptability of the product actually purchased, relative to the purchase motivation and the needs/wants that gave rise to it.

In other words, consumers will learn from their buying successes and failures, and this experience will inform future buying decisions. It will be important for marketers to assess the experience of customers with their particular product, in case it possesses some unsatisfactory performance or operating characteristic to which customers will eventually build up resistance. Market research should assess consumer satisfaction, whilst consumer likes and preferences that stem from use or consumption of the product should be fed back into the advertising, promotion and product differentiation that are important inputs at the *information search* and *evaluation of alternatives* stages in the model.

Advertising and promotional activity will be important at the *information search* stage, since this will ensure that the potential customer is kept aware of the existence of the product or brand. Advertising and promotion will also be used to influence the *evaluation of alternatives,* and will be used to build up particular preferences in the mind of the potential purchaser. *Product differentiation* will also be important at this stage in the model. *Product differentiation is the process by which specific features, characteristics and attributes are built in to the product or service so that the consumer perceives it to be in some way different from (and preferably superior to) competing products.* For instance, the first Japanese cars imported for sale in the UK market were differentiated from much of the competition by including "optional extras" in the basic specification and price. At that time, customers for British-made cars had to pay extra for "optional" items like heated rear windows, reversing and fog lamps, and even windscreen wipers, heaters and demisters. It is little wonder that this policy, coupled with their reliability, soon established the popularity of Japanese cars, and such product specification rapidly became the norm throughout the market.

Product differentiation will be used to increase the likelihood of specific product recognition (from amongst competing brands) and preference at the *evaluation stage*. The sooner the potential customer selects a particular product or brand as meeting his or her purchase needs, the more successful has been its marketing.

a) *decision process speed:* the speed at which the individual (or group of individuals in the case of multi-individual buying situations) moves through the decision process will depend on a number of factors, including :-

* whether the decision involves *a simple or routine purchase,* in which case routine response or impulse behaviour will occur. Such situations might include the routine repeat purchase of washing up liquid, sweets or cigarettes.

* whether the decision involves *a modification to previous purchasing patterns,* for instance when the usual product purchased has been re-formulated, an apparently attractive new brand introduced, or the purchaser's *usage context* for the product has changed. In this case, the decision process will be slowed down by the need for

some limited consideration or problem-solving behaviour.

* whether the decision involves a *major purchase,* in which case there may be prolonged reflection, consultation and problem-solving behaviour. The reader can choose his or her own examples to illustrate the point. The purchase process for a new house, car, cooker or video recorder may have been a quite lengthy process.

Certainly, as far as the marketer is concerned, the build-up of consistent and long-term customer loyalty towards a particular brand (*brand loyalty*) may have the (desirable) effect of speeding the individual through the decision process sequence, and minimising the degree to which alternative brands or products are given serious consideration. Brand loyalty is also said by marketers to make the process of evaluation and choice less difficult, particularly where this process gives rise to anxiety or uncertainty on the part of the consumer. The marketer will try to encourage brand loyalty as a means of rendering the purchase process more comfortable and more satisfying. After all, fear of the purchase process *itself* is hardly likely to be conducive to the build-up of positive feelings about the eventual product or service to be bought.

1.2 A theoretical model : the Howard and Sheth model

Theoretical models of consumer behaviour attempt to show the inter-relationship between the various behavioural and economic factors that are involved. Within these models, typically, information is processed by the individual; economic, socio-cultural and psychological influences are evaluated and related; and a purchase/no purchase decision is the result. One of the best known models was constructed by *J. A. Howard and J. Sheth,* and has since undergone substantial testing and development. The model is described and explained in a simplified form, thus:

i) *inputs:* information inputs about the alternative products or services available to the interested individual/ potential customer will include *the facts* about those products (brands available, product specification, quality, price etc). They will also include the images or feelings created by those products, and by the promotional activity surrounding them.

150

ii) *purchase attitudes and intentions* will be shaped by *basic behavioural determinants* already discussed in this and the previous chapter. These include :-

* personality
* culture
* social class

These attitudes and intentions will also be influenced by the importance of the purchase decision to the individual.

iii) *perceptual variables* will determine the individual's reaction to the information inputs referred to in paragraph (i) above. For a start, an individual is likely to be more positive towards information he or she has actively sought, whereas there may be *perceptual bias* against unsought information. Secondly, the degree of individual interest in (or "sensitivity" to) information may be determined by the source, content and authority of that information. Thirdly, irrespective of the source or priority of the information, any particular individual will psychologically "filter" out what he or she does not think important, or what he or she *does not want to know*. The result of these three components will be the individual's perceptual reaction towards information inputs. This bias will shape the individual's reaction to that information.

iv) *processing determinants* will include:

* motivation – which includes the specific motives for the purchase, and the additional but non-specific advantages that will result. For instance, a sales representative needs a car, but if he is able to buy a BMW, Mercedes, Jaguar or Rover then he may gain a bonus in the form of status or prestige enhancements.

* available satisfactions and past experience – the psychological processes involved in a purchase decision will take into account the available satisfactions relevant to the purchase motivation, and accumulated experience of past consumer satisfaction from the product or service in view.

* judgemental criteria – by which the individual evaluates the alternatives available in the market to which he or she has access.

151

v) *inhibitors* which are external constraints on actual or potential purchase behaviour. These include:-
– price of product or brand;
– availability of product or brand;
– financial status of the individual;
– time constraints which limit the time available to deal with the purchase.

vi) *outputs* which may lead to a purchase decision. These outputs take the form of personal attitude and intention to purchase which, if favourable, will lead to the purchase decision being made.

The Howard and Sheth model is reproduced in a simplified form in figure 12.1.

This kind of model has a number of advantages, of which the most important is its indication of the complex nature of many purchase situations. It emphasizes the need for marketers to analyse the satisfactions being sought by individuals through their purchase and consumption patterns, and to gain a clear understanding of individual purchase motivations. It suggests that marketers need to offer products or services that offer satisfactions, or solve the consumer's purchase problems, *at a variety of levels at the same time*. These levels include the economic and physical, cultural, emotional and environmental. For all these kinds of factors are involved in the determination of consumer attitude, motivation and purchase behaviour. And, finally, it points to the importance of external constraints *(inhibitors)* in permitting the individual to satisfy his or her purchase motivations. These are often so important that they require the marketer to find direct means of dealing with them, so as to minimise their effect on the satisfaction of consumer demand. So, for example, the credit card and the financial "package-deal", one-stop shopping and the direct mail catalogue all contribute to lessening the impact of these constraints, and facilitate the marketer's direct concern with supplying and selling his product to the customer.

SUMMARY

The contents of this chapter are summarised in Table 12.2.

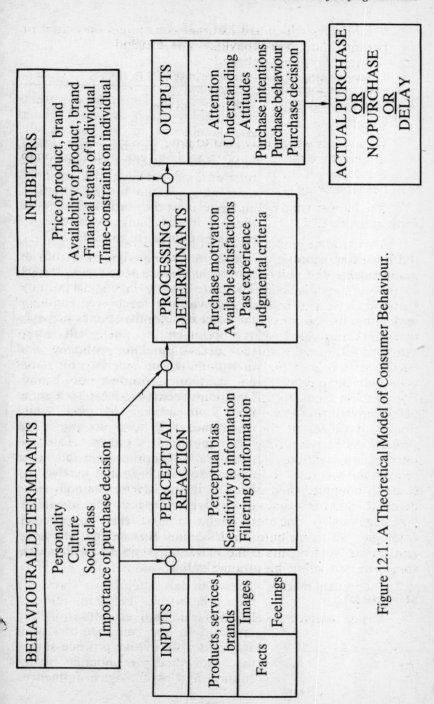

Figure 12.1. A Theoretical Model of Consumer Behaviour.

TABLE 12.2
Summary : Chapter Twelve

SECTION	MAIN POINTS
1. Models of buying behaviour	These comprise theoretical constructs of variables which are inter-related and significant in influencing the outcome of a purchase motivation. Such models attempt to clarify the relationships between the variables that influence the buying situation, and may assist the marketer to predict the outcome of change in any one or a number of purchase variables.
1.1 Decision-process models	These models analyse the buying process as a series of sequential steps. There are likely to be distinct patterns of behaviour at each step, and the marketer can identify specific activities or opportunities that will assist the decision-making process, and orientate the would-be buyer towards his particular product or brand. Decision-process models also assume that consumer learning and experience will build up and affect future purchase situations. Decision process models are also affected by the degree to which brand loyalty has been built up and maintained, since brand loyalty speeds the individual through the decision process sequence, and lessens the degree to which alternative products or brands are evaluated.
1.2 Theoretical models	These models attempt to show the inter-relationship between relevant behavioural and economic factors involved in the purchase decision. Typically, information is processed by the individual; economic, socio-cultural and psychological influences

> are evaluated and related; and a purchase/no purchase decision is the result. Such models are illustrated by the Howard and Sheth model.

RECOMMENDED READING

Chisnall P. M. Marketing: a behavioural analysis. McGraw-Hill.

QUESTIONS FOR SELF-REVIEW

1)   Describe and comment on some of the major economic determinants of consumer demand.

2)   Describe and comment on the role of individual personal motivation as a behavioural determinant of consumer demand.

3)   How may Maslow's Hierarchy of Needs assist the Marketer to understand some of the behavioural reasons for consumer demand?

4)   How may a study of Self-Image Theory assist the Marketer to understand some of the behavioural reasons for consumer demand?

5)   What is "personality"? How may an individual's personality shape his or her demand for goods and services?

6)   What is "culture"? Why is it an important determinant of purchase behaviour?

7)   What is "life-style"? What is its significance as a determinant of consumer purchase behaviour?

8)   "There is no such thing as life-style". Comment.

9)   What is "social class"? Why is it a significant determinant of consumer buying behaviour?

10)   Outline and comment on some of the marketing consequences of social mobility.

11)   What is the significance of the group as a determinant of consumer purchase behaviour?

12)   Describe and comment on family purchase behaviour and pattern. Use your own family background to illustrate your answer.

13)   How important is the family in determining individual purchase patterns?

14) What is a "reference group"? What is its significance in determining the nature of consumer purchase behaviour?

15) Why are "opinion leaders" important in determining people's purchase behaviour?

16) Describe and comment on multi-individual buying behaviour. Describe some of the roles involved in such purchase patterns. Use your own family and social background to illustrate your answer.

17) Compare and contrast "decision-process" and "theoretical" models of consumer behaviour.

EXAMINATION QUESTIONS

Q18 What behavioural factors should be taken into account by the marketing manager who wishes to change consumer attitudes towards a product or service?   (IIM)

Q19 "Successful marketing of goods and services of all kinds should be based on a fundamental appreciation of motivation." Explain.   (IIM)

Q20 Why is it important to understand family roles and decision making processes for products and services that are consumed by the household as a unit?   (IIM)

Q21 In what ways are consumers influenced by their group memberships and by their reference groups?   (IIM)

Q22 What are opinion leaders and how do they affect market processes? Using a specific example, show how opinion leaders might be identified and influenced through a marketing strategy?   (IIM)

Q23 What advantages does life-style analysis have over more traditional types of consumer analysis?   (IIM)

13 Consumer Behaviour – A Case Study

CONSUMER NEEDS AND ATTITUDES IN THE USE OF COTTON WOOL.

(1) INTRODUCTION

The objective of this chapter is to illustrate in practical terms some of the material contained in the three previous chapters. The case study is based on an actual consumer behaviour investigation carried out a few years ago by a leading market research agency.

2) THE PRODUCT

The product under investigation was COTTON WOOL.

3) THE RESEARCH OBJECTIVE

The research objective included an investigation (i) of consumer attitudes towards the purchase and use of cotton wool, and (ii) of the reasons that underpinned these attitudes and usage patterns. In other words, why did consumers purchase the product, and what needs were satisfied by its use?

4) THE RELEVANT CUSTOMERS

The investigation concentrated on the main consumer group that purchases cotton wool, namely women aged between sixteen and forty-five.

5) THE METHOD OF INVESTIGATION

The investigation was based on *in-depth group discussions*. These discussions were structured around a predetermined format whose objective was to elicit the respondents' motives and attitudes towards the product.

The discussions took place in the homes of some of the respondents, and appeared to be carried out in a relaxed and informal manner. Respondents were encouraged to relax and to contribute to the discussion at will. The aim of the approach was to avoid the tension of the individual interview, and to obtain group influence on the response of individuals. Consumer attitudes and behaviour towards a product like cotton wool are to a considerable extent shaped by the views and actions of other people.

6)THE RESPONDENTS

Eight discussion groups were held in various parts of the U.K. Each group contained between seven and eleven respondents. The criteria for inclusion were:

* age;
* marital status;
* socio-economic class.

The distribution of these eight discussion groups was as follows:-

	Single girls	Mothers with children at home
A B	2	2
C1 C2 D	2	2

6) THE FINDINGS

In the minds of many respondents, cotton wool was perceived as one of those indispensable household requisites which is necessary for some tasks and handy for a great many more.

As a rule, the mothers in both upper and lower socio-economic groups regarded cotton wool as:

* an essential product for care of babies;
* a useful product for care of children;

Its uses in babycare include:-

– cleaning eyes, ears and nose;
– sponging face;
– general body cleaning;
– cleansing the bottom, especially if sore, when nappy is changed;
– to apply cream to bottoms;
– to apply talc when baby is small;

Uses in childcare; its mainly medicinal role includes:-

– bathing cuts and grazes;
– dabbing calamine lotion on heat spots;
– stopping up the ears when the child has earache;

but also

– stuffing the toes of new shoes which are bought, deliberately, slightly too large (lower socio-economic groups).

Cosmetic uses included:-

– removing make-up.

The mothers used cotton wool for cosmetic purposes because they had already purchased it for child and babycare, and it is to hand. Sometimes, it depended on the location of the product; if the cotton wool is not kept in the place where make-up is removed then tissues tend to be used instead.

Mothers and the lower socio-economic single girls used soap and water for facial cleansing most of the time, and less frequently used cotton wool with cleansing cream or cleansing milk. Upper socio-economic single girls were much more likely to say that they did not use soap and water because it would ruin their skin. They used cleansing products often with cotton wool because it is "the only natural thing to use".

Other cosmetic uses included:-

– removing nail varnish;
– as a powder puff (mostly lower socio-economic mothers);
– in hair care: cotton wool was used in conjunction with lotions and in permanent waving. Cotton wool was placed between rollers and the scalp at night to prevent rollers sticking into the head, thus disturbing sleep or making marks (mostly lower socio-economic girls);
– bathing the ears if pierced (mostly lower socio-economic single girls).

Other uses:-

Cotton wool has a diverse number of other household uses which include:

– packing delicate things in (such as jewellery);
– decorations at Christmas;
– filter material.

7) THE USAGE CONTEXT

This section looks at the context of product use; what customers are doing, thinking and feeling when they use cotton wool.

In babycare, several of the significant routine *care activities* involve the use of cotton wool. *The emotional investment in these activities is high, involving as they do the powerful maternal drive.* Mothers set themselves exacting standards, either because of their own inner motives or because of social forces acting upon them. Because babies are delicate and vulnerable and because the mother – for all kinds of reasons – is compelled to succeed in caring for the child, the situation has a potential for much distress on the mother's part if anything goes wrong. Mothers of young babies want the products they use in babycare to be absolutely "right"; either (i) the product should be well known, widely recognised and easy to understand or (ii) it must have the endorsement of authoritative sources. Cotton wool falls into the first category.

In childcare, the situation is a rather more relaxed one. Mothers enjoy protective and caring episodes in dealing with their children as much as they enjoy seeing them grow more independent. Such episodes are a simple and direct affirmation of the maternal role. Cotton wool is a material which can be used at such times; respondents thought of this context when talking about cotton wool.

Cotton wool plays a secondary part, on the whole, in cosmetics. Most respondents found it a useful medium for aiding some cosmetic task or other. Nevertheless, skin care assumes considerable importance in the woman's mind, so that even a secondary association can be a significant one.

Overall, the patterns and contexts of use indicated a restriction in the respondents' minds about the nature and purpose of cotton wool. It could very easily be that the accidents of product development and distribution have led to an almost exclusive focus on *skin care* as the function of cotton wool.

Customer needs in different kinds of use:-

7.1) In Babycare

The paramount need is for a quality of softness, something which is entirely compatible with its use on babies' skins. The product should be:

– soft enough not to irritate or harm.

Two other characteristics which mostly attracted indirect mention but which, nevertheless, were important included:

– purity, in the sense of not containing other substances;
– dependability, in the sense that the product can always be relied upon to meet the mothers' standard (viz softness, non-irritant, pure).

Mothers were generally confident enough about the product not to show much spontaneous concern, but these characteristics were of significance to them.

A property which did, however, find frequent mention was:
- absorbency

The fact that cotton wool can "mop up" larger amounts of liquid or semi-liquid matter than anything else of a remotely similar nature is the most important functional property it has.

There is also a marked convenience element in the use of the product. Respondents typically stated that cotton wool is:

- "economical" or
- "works out cheaper".

but did not say that it is more convenient than washing and re-using facial flannels or cloths. It is likely that the implication of mothers saving effort or time over the care of babies produces some anxiety (guilt) in them, unless the rationale is very acceptable. For the housewife, however, being economical and especially finding a particular way of reducing expenditure gives satisfaction.

7.2) In Childcare.

There are few needs specific to the use of cotton wool; most of the interest centred on the mother's more general needs as she uses the product.

Certainly, the significant properties as they relate to these needs are:
- cotton wool is more specific to the purpose (than cloths); it has a "medicinal" property.
- it is soft enough to clean broken or damaged skin;
- it is intrinsically very clean and thus appropriate to use.

Thus, if the child appears with a bleeding wound the cotton wool not only performs well in staunching the flow, but it gives satisfaction because the mother has no fears about its cleanliness, and because the use of the material represents a special act of care.

7.3) Cosmetic use

From a practical point of view the need is for:
- absorbency

both in order to take up cosmetics and cleansing agents, and at the same time to hold sufficient of the cleansing agents whilst they are being applied.

In addition, much of what has been previously said about softness (and purity and dependability) in relation to skin care of babies applies here too.

Single girls particularly spoke about skin care as a specific problem for which special products are required. There is a particular form of satisfaction for many in seeing the dirt on the cotton wool after the skin has been cleaned, as a demonstration that their care has been effective.

The mothers appeared to be less particular, but were still susceptible to the argument that skin care is a special and personal problem. They were more likely to use paper tissues , mainly because of the convenience but often more simply because of the location of tissues in the house. A final point of note here was that in cosmetic use there was no substantial resistance to the idea of convenience in use.

8) WHAT DOES THE CASE STUDY TELL US ABOUT CONSUMER BEHAVIOUR?

The case study shows that respondent attitudes towards the purchase, usage context and use of cotton wool are subject to a number of the behavioural influences discussed in chapters ten, eleven, and twelve. These are listed below.

a) individual personal motivation: the use of cotton wool assisted the individual to satisfy *caring needs* in looking after babies and children. Maternal needs and instincts are amongst the most potent human motivations, and the product is strongly associated with the context in which these needs are expressed and satisfied.

b) individual personality: the cosmetic use of the product is associated with personality traits concerned with *physical appearance* and *personal presentation*. Some respondents could only visualise facial cleanliness (a key component of personal appearance) in terms of cleansing with lotions applied with cotton wool. Other products (flannels, tissues) were perceived as inadequate in this role.

c) life-style: respondents in the single girl upper socio-economic categories indicated that they achieved facial cleanliness with lotions and cotton wool because it is the only natural thing to use. The life-style of such girls increasingly emphasises the use of *safe and natural products* for cosmetic and presentational purposes, particularly where the usage context is an intimate one.

d) culture: mothers are under massive social and cultural pressure *to succeed in their maternal role*. There is therefore the potential for personal distress if anything goes wrong. Products will be sought that minimise the risk of failure, however small, and carry general acceptance in a particular role. Cotton wool fulfils these criteria; paper tissues (which disintegrate more easily and leave "bits") do not. Cotton wool is a familiar and *re-assuring* product.

e) social class: the study revealed variations in attitude and usage pattern as between the various social classes. For instance, there were variations in attitude towards the use of cotton wool in cosmetic and facial cleansing activities, and in hair care.

f) family: the basic perception of cotton wool is as a product used in a family context, associated with *care episodes*. This is hardly surprising since it is mainly purchased by women between certain ages, and is associated with baby and child care.

g) reference groups and opinion leaders: the life-style adopted by some of the single girls clearly indicates an orientation towards a particular type of reference group and opinion leader associated with encouraging "the use of natural products", personal grooming and beauty (etc). Similarly, mothers of babies and children tend to look towards the experience and activities of those women whom they perceive as "successful", "caring" and "attractive" in the maternal role. Again, given the cultural pressure on women with children, it is hardly surprising to find that successful mothers provide a point of reference and fulfil an opinion leader role.

Industrial Buying

This section analyses individual and company buying behaviour in industrial goods markets. It examines some of the factors which influence industrial buying and purchase behaviour. It differentiates the various purchase types to be found within the industrial situation, and examines the importance to marketers in supplier companies of selling under contract. It analyses the problem of marketing to multi-individual buying structures, and concludes by looking at the applications of industrial purchase behaviour models.

14 Buying Behaviour in Industrial Goods Markets

INTRODUCTION

This chapter analyses company and individual buying behaviour in industrial goods markets. It begins by defining the augmented nature of the product or service being purchased, and looks at the derived characteristics of demand for goods and services in these industrial markets.

It examines the scope and limitations of such markets, and remarks briefly upon the impact of business cycles on demand and purchase patterns. This discussion is then broadened into an analysis of contingency or situational factors which will have both a general and a specific impact on individual company purchasing.

The chapter goes on to outline the main purchase types, and looks at the importance of contract markets in many industrial buying situations.

The analysis of buying behaviour in industrial goods markets is continued in Chapter Fifteen.

CHAPTER CONTENTS

1) Derived demand and augmented products
2) Business cycles
3) The scope of industrial goods markets
4) Contingency factors
5) Purchase types
6) Contract markets
Summary

Chapters Ten to Thirteen dealt with consumer purchasing behaviour. This chapter turns to an analysis of buying behaviour in industrial goods markets. It does not include any consideration of the buying activities of retail companies, which is an issue dealt with in later chapters.

1) DERIVED DEMAND AND AUGMENTED PRODUCTS

This chapter, then, concentrates on buying behaviour in organisations such as manufacturing concerns, large agricultural co-operatives, the construction industry, mining, government services and so on. *The processes by which these organisations purchase the goods and services they need are radically different from those in consumer markets. The value of their buying, furthermore, is enormous.* Just think of the capital investment required to manufacture cars, steel or cornflakes. All that plant and equipment was purchased by the organisations requiring them. Products are sold in industrial goods markets to organisations that need them as INPUTS. These products and services are purchased *in order that some specific organisational objective may be achieved,* whether it be to make a new product, hold greater stocks, improve service and quality, or increase profitability. The same logic is true for non-profit making organisations like government agencies or local government authorities. These too make purchase decisions that are related to specific objectives.

Demand in industrial goods markets is therefore described as DERIVED. The concept of derived demand was introduced in an earlier chapter. Industrial goods and services are usually purchased *to allow the organisation to satisfy demand from its own customers.* The demand for these goods and services derives from that final market. So, a car manufacturer sells its products to the customer. To do this, it will have a derived demand for manufacturing equipment, components, steel, lubricants and the like, so that it can satisfy its own customers.

The industrial buyer is therefore acutely aware that he or she is building-in, or using, *someone else's product* so that the final customer's demands can be met. It is therefore no use if the steel is of poor quality, the paint is full of grit, or the machinery keeps breaking down. Organisational buyers, therefore, may seek an AUGMENTED PRODUCT. An augmented product is more than just a tangible product or service. It is a *collection of related benefits.* These benefits to the buyer may include:-

* exact specification and reliability;
* stringent and effective supplier quality control;
* after-sales service; rapid remedy for defects in delivered products;
* supplier reputation for consistent and predictable meeting of customer needs;
* length of supplier experience in the trade.

2) BUSINESS CYCLES

Industrial goods markets, and therefore the buying patterns within them, are usually subject to fluctuations caused by cyclical market behaviour. Such fluctuations have an effect on both:

* sales levels; which determine production levels plus
* stock or inventory levels, which provide a buffer between sales and production levels.

During downward fluctuations in demand (which give rise to *recessionary* economic conditions), the organisation supplying the next or final customer will reduce his production and inventory levels, as demand for his product declines. The result will be a cut-back in his derived demand for inputs. Recession, therefore, has the unfortunate and *cumulative* effect of working backwards. Each link in the chain pushes its problems backwards in the chain of supply, so that demand patterns become progressively more erratic until the final source is reached. Thus, the demand patterns for products like coal, steel and heavy goods vehicles decline rapidly in a recession, (and may be subject to a level of demand during boom conditions that they simply cannot meet).

The machine tool industry meets the worst of the problem, as it is at the end of the manufacturing cycle and cannot respond quickly either in recession or in a boom, because of the long lead-times involved in production and delivery. Indeed, the machine tool industry is often regarded as a good barometer of the state of the economy as a whole.

These kinds of cyclical dynamics are illustrated in Figure 14.1, using the example of the building industry.

Whilst the demand for buildings shows a considerable variation around the movement of the economy, the most violent swings may be felt by the manufacturers of specific products like bricks, concrete, roof-tiles and the like.

One of the only ways around this problem is for suppliers in industrial goods markets to encourage their customers to buy on a consistent and long term basis, *under contract*. Such a contract may, to some extent, even out (or "smooth") the worst of the cyclical fluctuations experienced by the trade.

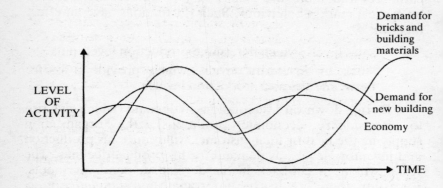

Figure 14.1. Cyclical Demand Patterns in the Building Industry.

3) THE SCOPE OF INDUSTRIAL GOODS MARKETS

Companies that supply industrial goods markets enjoy one significant advantage over those that trade into consumer markets. This advantage stems from the fact that *the companies and organisations that make up the market tend to be clustered together,* for instance on a geographical basis, or by product type. This allows suppliers to specialise and to develop an intimate knowledge of customer needs and wants. At the same time it permits cost-effectiveness, for instance in terms of marketing and distribution costs. An example should make the point:

* a large proportion of the UK output of ceramic products comes from one geographic area (the North Midlands). Equipment suppliers can concentrate their efforts within a relatively small area.

*   specialist suppliers of manufacturing equipment will find such a concentrated market economic to supply, since within one region there will be a relatively large and varied demand for highly specialised machinery. At the same time, equipment suppliers can keep abreast of market and technological developments within the industry upon which it depends. This will be much more difficult where an industry is geographically diffused, or where the supplier (say, the steel industry) faces a very wide range of market demands.

On the other hand, *demand in industrial goods markets is limited in terms of the total number of buying organisations*. There are relatively few customers for industrial kilns, but many consumers buying tins of baked beans! Therefore, each individual customer is relatively important to the supplier, *and sensitivity to his needs* (which is fundamental to the Marketing Concept) is an essential pre-requisite to survival. Investment decisions made by just a few organisations can make or break a supplier.

This restriction on the scope of industrial goods markets has become more significant given the degree of industrial and commercial concentration that has taken place since, say, 1945. There are fewer organisations in the market than hitherto (although the demands of each have increased proportionately). This concentration is made more of a problem for suppliers where large scale organisations *centralise their buying function*. One office may be responsible for many millions of pounds worth of purchase orders. The significance of centralised buying will be most clearly seen in later chapters which deal with buying by retail companies.

Such concentration means that the industrial marketer *may be faced with a relative increase in buyer power*. The trading consequences of such a development possibly means that the supplier risks becoming a "captive", subject to a potentially catastrophic threat of the withdrawal of the buyer's patronage. This threat of withdrawal of large volume business may restrict the supplier's freedom of manoeuvre, both with any one customer, and in the marketplace generally. For instance, such suppliers may find that customers dictate the terms and conditions of trade, the prices to be paid, and the arrangements for supply.

Alternatively, buying organisations may themselves be faced with concentration amongst suppliers, and find that there are fewer alternative sources of domestic supply. In such cases:

* buyers may deliberately use two suppliers (this is called using a *dual source*);

* buyers may take over their suppliers completely. For instance, some foodstuffs manufacturers are dependent on their supplies of edible oils. They might see it as better to take-over their main supplier, even if it means that company losing some existing orders from competing manufacturers of food products;

* buyers may deliberately seek international suppliers, so as to maintain their choice and retain some degree of control over the prices and terms of supply.

Buying behaviour in industrial goods markets also tends to be conservative. Those people responsible for buying will often place a limit on the range and number of alternatives they are prepared to consider, particularly where they are happy with their existing suppliers. Much buying takes place *under contract* and this also tends to limit the search and investigation of alternative suppliers. Buyers often develop strong loyalties to suppliers, preferring not to make changes unless they are unavoidable. This is hardly surprising where the supplier consistently meets the customer's needs, and where the customer buys a wide variety of products from many different suppliers, thereby incurring a major management and monitoring task.

In any case, where the supplier offers competitive or preferential credit terms and loan finance to the customer, the two parties become tied together by *the financial packaging* of contractual terms between the two parties. The offering of the appropriate financial assistance and credit to the customer *will then become a key part of the supplier's marketing policy*. For instance, the major suppliers of earthmoving plant, backhoe loaders, excavators (etc) have their own finance houses, who can offer attractive loan finance or leasing packages to the manufacturer's existing and potential customers.

4) CONTINGENCY FACTORS

Marketers in companies supplying industrial goods markets have therefore to accept that the situations faced by their companies in these markets are subject to a variety of different *contingencies* (or specific circumstances). Each marketing response will have to take the relevant contingencies into account, so that (to use the jargon) it is situationally relevant. Generalised responses will not be adequate, and marketing policy will need to be accurately informed about particular circumstances prevailing at particular times within the target markets in view. So far, the following contingencies have been identified:

* industrial structure; number of potential customers; market structure;
* centralised buying; contract business;
* risk of supplier dependency on customer; unbalanced customer profile; loss of market initiative;
* risk of takeover by customer;
* threat of competition from international suppliers.

Other examples of possible contingencies could include:

* the deliberate exercise of *buyer power,* influencing the prices, terms and conditions of supply;
* large customers seeking smaller companies as suppliers, so that again buyer power can be exercised. The ability to influence supplier costs, price and conditions of delivery may be seen as worth the extra managerial, administrative and quality assurance cost incurred in buying from a large number of small suppliers;
* large customers who pursue a deliberate policy of delaying payment for goods or services received. Some local authorities in the UK are notorious for doing this! Such delaying tactics can have a serious impact on the supplier's working capital cycle and cashflow management;
* the working capital and cashflow implications of large orders obtained. This may lead to the investigation by a potential customer of the supplier's working capital, financial and management expertise before large orders are placed. Those who place orders will not normally accept any great degree of risk that the supplier will go out of business before the order is delivered, nor will they place large orders with firms whose working capital and liquidity appears unsound or badly managed;

* the placing of conditions on potential orders such that suppliers:-

– must conform to specified quality control procedures such as those specified by the UK quality standard BS 5750. This is now a quite normal condition to impose on suppliers, whose output quality may be rigorously tested by customers prior to the acceptance of batches of products;

– undertake (*and pay for*) specified research, development and design activities needed to meet the specifications laid down by the customer. This, again, is quite usual, say in the automotive industry;

* meeting stringent specifications laid down by the customer. The best UK example is the Ministry of Defence (M.O.D.) specification for products purchased for military service and use. All such products must conform with the appropriate M.O.D. and N.A.T.O. specifications, as a condition of acceptance by the military authorities.

5) PURCHASE TYPES

Purchase decisions in industrial markets can be categorised thus:-

(i)*straight re-buy decisions:* these are standard, routine and repetitive. They would include orders for routine raw materials such as steel stock; screws, nuts and bolts; lubricants and fuel oil. Such purchases are often made under long term contracts, and may be enacted by computerised stock control programs when current stock levels reach a minimum "safety level". The computer program is triggered by a decision-rule and a purchase order is automatically raised.

ii) *modified re-buy decisions:* relate to purchase situations in which some kind of review is called for. Whatever the reason for the review, the purchasing function will be required to examine alternative sources of supply, or alternative products capable of meeting an existing or predictable need. The need for a review of the existing supply arrangements might be occasioned by mounting dissatisfaction with current suppliers, or concern at increasing price levels. Alternatively, organisational processes such as "value analysis" may have shown that the specific requirement can be met in a different way, this alternative being either cheaper or offering better value for money. Witness for instance the use in car manufacture of self-tapping screws rather than nuts and bolts, the use of circlips instead of nuts to secure bolts, or plastic body sections and panels to reduce both body weight and manufacturing costs.

iii) *new task purchasing:* which relates to new types of goods or services never purchased before. In such cases there is the greatest need for effective search, analysis, evaluation and selection by those people involved in the making of purchase decisions, particularly where the item to be purchased is complex. New task purchasing, with its inherent lack of previous experience of the product to be purchased, contains the greatest risk for the organisation. It may therefore provide the incentive for the most thorough pre-purchase behaviour, and marketers hoping to supply such products may have to be prepared for extensive enquiry and investigation before they will manage to sell any of them.

6) CONTRACT MARKETS

Some industrial markets are dominated by trade *which takes place under contract.* Such markets present suppliers and marketers with substantial problems. Typically, the products involved are standardised and cannot be differentiated. Indeed, they may have to be manufactured to exact customer specifications.

Such products include fuel oil, paint, building materials and fitments, and electronic components. The markets in which they are sold often include a small number of very large customers, such as, for example in the UK:-

* fuel oil — Ministry of Defence, British Railways; P and O, Sealink and other large shipping companies (etc);

* paint – Central and local government authorities, British Railways, car manufacturers (etc).

Before individual suppliers may submit tenders for orders from these kinds of customers, they must be accepted as *capable* and reliable. This will involve the submission and testing of their product by the potential customer, who will ensure that it meets his technical and operating requirements. Only then may the supplier's product be classified as satisfactory, and, perhaps after a number of years of further product tests have elapsed, the supplier may be added to the list of *recognised contractors*. Only then can the supplier tender for orders.

Competition between recognised contractors is then solely based on PRICE. Product quality and specification, and delivery capacity, are assumed by the supplier to be the same in the case of all recognised contractors. What results is high volume business which carries low profit margins. Indeed, competition may be so fierce that pricing is based on a Contribution basis, that is, covering variable costs and only a proportion of the business' fixed costs. The supplier will seek his profits in other markets, hoping that the volume at which he can operate in the contract market will make his product highly competitive in price and cost terms elsewhere. Contract markets, therefore, may be sought for the volume and unit cost savings they bring, rather than profitability itself.

Contract markets therefore force the supplier to operate in a cost effective manner. Once the product and marketing managers have gained the company a foothold in such markets, it will be up to production and operations management to produce and deliver the right quality goods at the budgeted cost.

SUMMARY

The contents of this chapter are summarised in Table 14.2.

TABLE 14.2
Summary : Chapter Fourteen

SECTION	MAIN POINTS
1. Derived demand and augmented products	Goods and services are usually purchased in industrial goods markets to facilitate the process by which the organisation satisfies the demand from its own customers. The demand for these goods and services derives from that final market. An augmented product is more than just a tangible product or service. It is a collection of related benefits.

2. Business cycles	Buying patterns within industrial goods markets are usually subject to upward or downward fluctuations caused by cyclical market behaviour. Such fluctuations affect the level of sales, production and stockholding. These fluctuations can have a cumulative effect, particularly on the demand for such products as steel, bricks, heavy goods vehicles and machine tools.
3. The scope of industrial goods markets	The companies and organisations that make up industrial markets tend to be clustered together, whether by geographical region, or product (or both). However, demand in industrial goods markets is limited in terms of the total number of buying organisations. Industrial concentration may lead to a relative increase in buyer power. Industrial buying behaviour tends to be conservative, based on contracts, preferential credit terms and loan finance.
4. Contingency factors	Industrial market conditions are usually subject to a variety of contingencies, such as the development of buyer power, large buyers seeking small customers, the placing of conditions on specification and terms of supply, etc. Each marketing response will have to take into account the relevant contingencies, so that it is situationally relevant.
5. Purchase types	Purchase decisions can be categorised into straight re-buy decisions; modified re-buy decisions; new task purchasing.
6. Contract markets	Products are supplied to exact customer specifications on the basis of open competition amongst recognised contractors. Suppliers not on the list of

recognised contractors cannot submit tenders for the order. Competition is based on price. Commonly, the products involved are standardised and cannot be differentiated.

15 Marketing to Multi-Individual Industrial Buying Structures

INTRODUCTION

This chapter commences with an analysis of multi-individual buying behaviour. This is important because much organisational purchasing is influenced and determined by a number of individuals and roles, rather than by any one person. Buying process roles are considered, and attention is then turned to the issue of how suppliers may effectively sell products to companies using multi-individual buying procedures.

The chapter concludes with a brief examination of decision process and behavioural models of industrial purchasing. Two simplified versions of such theoretical models are described and illustrated.

CHAPTER CONTENTS

1) MULTI INDIVIDUAL BUYING BEHAVIOUR AND THE DECISION MAKING UNIT

Purchase decisions, particularly on a straight re-buy basis, may be made by a company's buying department. But in industrial goods markets the role of the buying function may vary from significant to relatively insignificant. In general terms:-

* the more complex the decision, the more people will be involved as a *Decision Making Unit* (DMU), and the less important will be the role of the buying department;
* the more expensive the decision, the more will senior management be involved and the less important will be the role of the buying department.

Given the likely involvement of a variety of people as a Decision Making Unit in purchase decisions, and the likelihood of particular contingencies affecting its outcome, it will be important for the marketing function in supplier companies to:-

* understand how buying decisions are made;
* understand how the Decision Making Unit is constituted;
* find out who are the most influential figures in the decision-making process.

For instance, decisions on investment in plant and machinery will at least be informed (if not influenced) by the advice and views of engineers and operations managers, even though such people may not *formally* be included in the actual Decision Making Unit. The problem for the marketing function of a potential supplier will eventually resolve itself into the specific issue of *how to promote and sell the product* to the Decision Making Unit. Promotional and sales effort will need to find the right target (which may not necessarily be the buying department), otherwise it may be wasted. These targets may be analysed on the basis of *buying process roles,* as follows.

1.1 Buying process roles

Five roles may be identified in the buying process. These are:

(a) *The Gatekeeper:* who builds up, maintains and filters information used by the other four roles. Purchase decisions may need substantial information flows, whilst a well-organised enterprise will also keep up-to-date on the main trends, developments and events involving the companies from which it buys its inputs. It may know as much about its suppliers (and their competitors) as it does about its own markets. This is one of the benefits of a professional approach to industrial buying and *supply management.* The gatekeeper role may be fulfilled by the buying department but, as like as not, that role will be shared by influential members of technical and operating departments whose expertise and experience renders their technical knowledge indispensable to the making of purchase decisions.

b) *The User:* the concern of the user or recipient of the product will centre on whether or not the alternatives available meet the required operating or performance specifications. Increasingly, they are also likely to be interested in the budgeted cost of the purchase, and the return they obtain from it (perhaps measured in terms of *payback or discounted cash flow*). The user will be the role most concerned with the purchase of *the augmented product,* since, for instance:

* the user has perhaps to budget for the cost of the item, and will wish to maximise the value for money he or she can obtain from the expenditure;
* the user has to cope with the consequences of late delivery, faulty products, breakdowns and servicing requirements (etc);
* the user will be concerned with product reliability and supplier reputation.

c) *The Influencer:* purchase decisions may be subject to a variety of influences. It may be very difficult for the supplier's marketing department to identify all of the individual sources of influence, or to evaluate their relative significance. Nevertheless, two categories of influence role can be identified:
* external influences, which can include:-
  – your company's salespeople;
  – salespeople from competing suppliers;
  – journalists and professionals writing in trade and specialist journals;
  – individual representatives at trade shows and exhibitions;
  – influential individuals in companies competing with the potential purchaser's company;

– influential associates and people with significant reputations whose opinions are listened to and adopted, perhaps in professional bodies such as engineering, computing, marketing, accountancy, etc.

* internal influences, which may of course include gatekeepers and users, described above. Inevitably, once the company gets near to making a purchase decision, the influence exercised by senior management will increase, whether within functional departments, or at a divisional or general management level. This is hardly surprising, since ultimately the responsibility for the decision eventually made, and its consequences, will fall to them. This is why industrial buying tends to have a "conservative" philosophy. Senior managers *do not want things to go wrong,* and will not take what they consider to be unnecessary risks in recommending one supplier as opposed to another.

d) *The Decision Maker:* where decisions take the form of modified re-buys or new task purchasing, it is most likely that senior functional, divisional or general management will take the actual decision to purchase, and choose the supplier, specification and product. Obviously, the wishes of the user will be taken into account, as will the various sources of influence described above. Where major investment decisions are concerned (say, in the purchase of a completely new computer-based data processing and management information system), the Board of Directors is likely to take the responsibility. Again, this is hardly surprising, since in organisational terms the authority and responsibility distribution will determine how the final decision is to be taken, and who is to be involved. Marketers in supplier companies will have to find out the nature of these organisational arrangements before they can have any hope of making a sale.

(e) *The Buyer:* who is responsible for the actual details involved in placing the order and monitoring the delivery process. Typically this task will be carried out by the company's buying department. Whether senior buyers are able at the same time to exercise an influencing and decision making role *will depend on organisational factors.* These will determine:-

* the status and authority of senior buyers;

* the degree to which they are consulted by influencers and decision-makers;

* the degree to which they are actually involved in decision making.

Certainly, one of the organisational reasons for centralising the buying function in a company is that it gives senior buyers *more clout*. At this level it may become essential to involve the senior buyer in high level buying decisions, in view of the large sums of money going through the department. Ideally, the top professional buyer will seek Board status as the company's senior buyer, since this ensures his or her involvement in all major purchase decisions.

2) MARKETING TO MULTI INDIVIDUAL BUYING STRUCTURES AND DECISION MAKING UNITS

Supplier companies wishing to sell their products to industrial markets must try to establish a pattern or "mix" of inter-related activities. The initial target in any potential industrial customer may be the *gatekeeper* role. The supplier needs to build up awareness, understanding and interest in his products in the mind of the gatekeeper, whether this be a buying department, technical specialist, or both. Otherwise the gatekeeper role may filter out awareness of the supplier, and so his promotional effort will fail at the first hurdle! And in any case, the buying department of the potential customer must be informed about the basic mechanics of how to deal with the supplier. It must know about product ranges and specifications, production and servicing arrangements, the names of salespeople, addresses, phone numbers (etc).

Supplier companies must then determine how they are going to inform, promote or persuade *influencers* and *decision makers* within the Decision Making Unit. This is much more difficult. For a start, the supplier's marketing department must try to identify and reach technical specialists, engineers, technical buyers (etc). This will depend on how accessible these people are, and on how effective are the gatekeepers whose role includes filtering out what they, or the influencer, deem to be undesirable or unnecessary information. *A strong gatekeeper role will limit sales access to influencers and decision takers* in the way laid down by company policy, and it may not be until that policy is changed that an individual supplier may be permitted sales access to present his wares. We have already seen this effect in the section on contract markets in the previous chapter. Evidently, it presents the marketer with a circular or "chicken and egg" argument; if you have no access it will be difficult to persuade policy makers to change their attitude towards giving you access!

The problem is most difficult when it comes to the supplier's sales and marketing people gaining access to decision-makers. The access will in part be determined by gatekeepers and influencers. It will be made more difficult where a number of senior individuals are actually involved in making a purchase decision. And it will be further complicated by status differences. Senior management may not be prepared to deal with ordinary salespeople, or even sales managers.

So how can the supplier mitigate the effects of this limitation on access? There are a number of possibilities, as follows.

2.1) Catalogues

A well constructed and well presented catalogue, sent to selected gatekeepers, technical managers (etc) acts as a detailed source of information about the supplier and his products. Indeed many catalogues become prestigious reference works, updated by the supplier, which are used by the customer to frame purchase proposals. For example, so detailed was the Texas Instruments integrated circuit catalogue that at one time it was the standard specification reference work for electronic component buyers. Its product categories were used by other manufacturers. A good catalogue, therefore, makes life easy for its user, and so builds up the supplier's reputation.

2.2) Trade and technical press

People who work in a particular business tend to read the relevant trade and technical press, whether in the UK it be The Grocer, Marketing, Electronics Weekly, the British Baker, or whatever. Whilst they may not take too much notice of advertisements which promote goods and services used in that trade, readers will tend to notice when advertisements by their suppliers *are absent*. Buyers and influencers expect to see their suppliers (and *their* competitors) represented.

Editorial comment will be widely read and taken seriously, whilst favourable or unfavourable references to supplier companies tend to be spotted and remembered in the trade. This is hardly surprising. Senior people like talking about their work, and read the trade and technical press both for reasons of professional *and* personal interest. *A good professional knows what is going on, both within his own company, and outside it in its trade environment.*

2.3) Public Relations

Public relations and the building of *corporate image* are dealt with in a later chapter. Suffice it to say that a company may use public relations activities, and what is called "corporate advertising" to try to build up an image in the minds of target individuals and groups who are likely to be influential in purchase decision-making. This image might be one of reliability and technical competence, of innovation or sensitivity to customer needs (etc). It is essential that this image be transmitted through media (communication methods) *that will reach those people who hold influencer or decision making roles*. So, prestige newspapers and television might be used, as well as the trade and technical press, to secure editorial comment and carry out direct advertising. Similarly, trade shows, exhibitions and sponsored events may be used to build up such a favourable image.

2.4) Peer group promotion

At the same time as using catalogues, trade and technical press, and public relations, supplying companies may use a two-pronged sales effort. Sales staff and sales managers will attempt to get access to such influencer and decision-making roles as they can, presenting the supplier's products and making the sales effort. Where senior management refuses access to the sales force, the supplying company *can involve its own senior management to make its presentation on a peer group basis*. The supplying company will attempt to respond on a *status to status* basis, such that its products are presented and promoted to equals by equals.

In other words, senior sales, technical and general management in the supplying company will need to get out to present, promote and sell the company's products. This may mean a change in management attitudes and practice within the supplying company. Promotion and sales may not have been seen as a high status activity deserving of such high level management attention. *Yet what is more deserving of anyone's attention than getting the sales orders upon which the survival of the enterprise depends?* It is a question of priorities: some industrial customers may not be prepared to deal with salespeople, and may insist on granting access only to people of their own status and organisational level. This way, they may reason, they can get to the heart of the supplier's promotional and sales pitch, and re-assure themselves that they are getting the right deal.

3) MODELS OF INDUSTRIAL PURCHASE BEHAVIOUR

Models of buying behaviour were introduced in an earlier chapter as a means of analysing and explaining purchase decisions. In industrial markets these decisions are subject to a wide variety of inter-related economic, marketing, technical and behavioural influences. Models were described as comprising theoretical constructs of variables which are inter-related and significant in influencing the outcome of a purchase requirement. Two approaches to the construction of buying behaviour models will again be considered.

3.1) Decision process models

Decision process models analyse the buying process *as a series of sequential steps*. These would typically include:-

a) recognition or anticipation of the need to make the purchase;

b) classification of the nature of the purchase requirement into straight re-buy, modified re-buy or new task category;

c) determination of the characteristics and quantity of the required item(s);

d) specification and description of the characteristics of the required item, and the quantity to be actually purchased;

e) search for possible sources, and investigation of alternative products/augmented products available;

f) acquisition and evaluation of supplier sales proposals and terms;

g) selection of supplier;

h) agreement on terms and conditions of supply, order placed;

i) receipt of product;

j) post purchase evaluation and FEEDBACK into future decisions.

The nature of the progress through this series of sequential steps will be influenced (or determined) by the buying process roles described in section (1.1) above. This influence can be summarised in diagrammatic form, as shown in figure 15.1.

3.2) Behavioural models

The objective of behavioural models is the same in both industrial and consumer goods markets. Theoretical models of buyer behaviour attempt to show the inter-relationship between the various behavioural and economic factors that are involved. Within the context of industrial goods markets, organisational factors must be added to the list of relevant variables.

One of the best known models was constructed by *J. Sheth,* and this model is described and explained in a simplified form, thus:

i) *information sources:* a variety of information sources will be available, (some of which have already been discussed in detail in this and the previous chapter). They include sales representatives, advertising and promotion, trade exhibitions and trade news, professional and technical conferences and journals, word of mouth opinion (etc). Each information source will be subject to some degree of *filtering* and *perceptual distortion* by members of the buying organisation.

ii) *contingency factors:* include the relevant economic and market circumstances that are likely to influence product investigations and purchase decisions.

iii) *product-specific factors:* are those factors which will determine the nature, timing, risk and technical content of the buying process.

iv) *company-specific factors:* include such variables as :-

– organisation size and degree of centralisation;

– official purchase decision-making procedures and processes;

– role of buying department and other buying process roles;

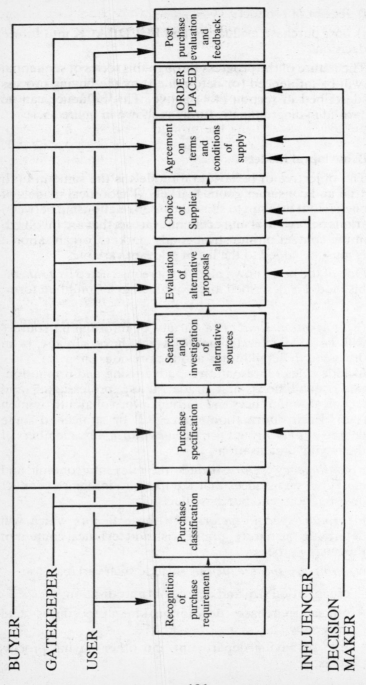

Figure 15.1. A Decision Process Model of Industrial Purchase Behaviour.

- means of resolving conflicts or differences that appear within the Decision Making Unit during the buying decision-making process.

v) *expectations and past experience:* there may be a variety of expectations about products and purchase decisions to be found at different places within the buying organisation. Similarly, there may be variations in people's experience of purchasing and using the product or service in question. How are these expectations and experiences articulated? How are they communicated? What influence do they have? And by what means does the organisation interpret, choose between, and make use of these expectations and this experience?

vi) *individual objectives and behavioural factors:* the Sheth model focuses on such factors as:-

- individual role and expectations;
- individual background, training and motivation;
- individual objectives in the purchasing process.

The Sheth model is reproduced in a simplified form in Figure 15.2.

SUMMARY

The contents of this chapter are summarised in Table 15.3.

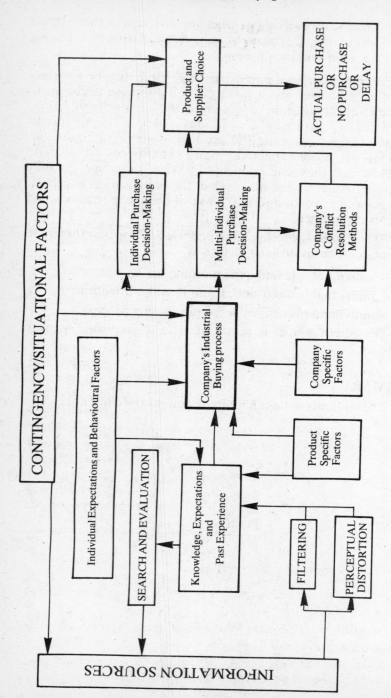

Figure 15.2. A Theoretical Model of Industrial Purchase Behaviour.

TABLE 15.3
Summary : Chapter Fifteen

SECTION	MAIN POINTS
1. Multi-individual buying behaviour and the DMU	A variety of people or roles may be involved as a Decision Making Unit in industrial or organisational purchase decisions. These may be analysed in terms of five influential roles, namely the gatekeeper, the user, the influencer, the decision-maker and the buyer.
2. Marketing to multi-individual buying structures and DMU's	Supplier companies will have to determine how most effectively to market their products to the various roles identified in the previous section. This may involve them in attempting to secure access to influencers and decision-makers. This may be difficult if both gatekeepers and policy in the buying company aim to restrict such access. Limitations on access may be mitigated by the use of: effective and useful technical catalogues; trade and technical press; public relations activities; peer group promotion.
3. Models of industrial purchase behaviour	Two approaches to the construction of industrial buying behaviour models were described, namely (i) decision process models (comprising a series of sequential steps); and (ii) behavioural models (such as that constructed by J. Sheth).

QUESTIONS FOR SELF-REVIEW

1)   What is "derived demand"? Comment on its significance in the study of marketing.

2)   Describe and comment on the significance of the concept of the "augmented product".

3)   What are business cycles? How do they affect demand patterns in industrial goods markets?

4) How may the scope and structure of industrial goods markets affect the selling and buying activities and policies of supplier and purchasing companies?
Illustrate your answer by an example with which you are familiar.

5) What are "contract markets", and why may they be significant in industrial goods marketing?

6) Comment on the importance to the marketer of the buying department in any firm to which he or she would like to sell goods or services.

7) Why may it be difficult for a supplier to sell his products to a company that makes use of a multi-individual Decision Making Unit to make purchase decisions? How may it attempt to overcome these difficulties?

EXAMINATION QUESTIONS

Q24   Dependent on how a product is purchased, it may be described as a consumer product or as an industrial product. For example, a ball point pen may be purchased for personal use or by a company for use in its business. What differences would you expect to find in the buying behaviour of an individual buying the same product for his/her own use and also on behalf of an organisation?
(ABE)

Q25   Discuss the importance of identifying the Decision Making Unit (DMU) in the marketing of industrial products. Use examples to illustrate your answer.
(ABE)

Q26   How might the composition of the Decision Making Unit (DMU) vary between:
a) A new capital purchase decision and
b) A repeat supplies purchase?
Use examples of products/markets to illustrate your answer.
(IPS)

Q27   Research has shown that industrial buyers are reluctant to change from an existing regular supplier even if the new supplier can offer a price reduction.
How might the marketing department of the new supplier meet this particular challenge?
(IPS)

Market Analysis

This section commences with a detailed examination of market segmentation. Market segmentation is the analysis of a particular total market demand into its constituent parts, so that sets of buyers or "segments" can be differentiated. These segments are used as targets against which appropriate products or services can be positioned, and upon which an appropriate promotional mix may be focussed. The analysis is illustrated by a variety of case examples and case studies.

The second chapter in the section turns to the specific application of consumer targeting as a detailed example of market segmentation in practice. Within the context of this section, consumer targeting is described in terms of the application of the **ACORN** system.

16 Market Segmentation

INTRODUCTION

Market segmentation is a vital issue in the study of marketing. Market segmentation means the analysis of a particular total market demand into its constituent parts, so that sets of buyers can be differentiated. Segmentation has significance *both* as a marketing tool, and as a basic input to marketing and business planning. This chapter examines the role of market segmentation as a marketing tool. Its use in marketing planning is the subject of a later chapter.

The chapter begins by explaining the importance of market segmentation within the study of marketing. Market segmentation is then defined and two main segmentation criteria are explained. These criteria are based firstly on *consumers/users,* and secondly on *products/benefits.* There is an analysis of how these criteria may be used to identify segment boundaries. Market segments are then used as targets against which appropriate products or services can be positioned, if the forecast revenues are likely to exceed the costs to be incurred. Similarly, segments are used as targets upon which an appropriate promotional mix may be focussed.

A number of practical examples are given to illustrate the principles explained in this chapter, and the chapter ends with a case study of how market segmentation might be implemented.

CHAPTER CONTENTS

1) THE IMPORTANCE OF MARKET SEGMENTATION

Market segmentation means *the analysis of a particular market demand on the basis of its constituent parts, so that sets of buyers can be differentiated.* It is an important input to marketing planning because it can be used to formulate company "product-market" objectives, by which the enterprise may:

* define its markets;
* position ranges of brands and product varieties;
* identify gaps which offer significant opportunities for expansion or new product positioning;
* rationalise policies for existing brands, products and mixes.

Market segmentation plays a dual role, namely (i) as a marketing tool, and (ii) as a basic input to business planning. Its role in business planning is dealt with in a later chapter.

There are three main reasons for the importance of market segmentation. These are:

(a) *market fragmentation,* caused by demographic and lifestyle changes, new product and process developments and intense market competition. Some markets, which once had a homogeneous character, have tended to splinter into a variety of consumer groups, each with different tastes and preferences; for instance, see Box 16.1.

BOX 16.1
FRAGMENTATION IN THE UK FOOD MARKETS

Food markets in the UK tended, in the past, to have a homogeneous character. There were mass markets for a relatively limited variety of fresh and processed foodstuffs. Many people lived on a similar diet, and changes took place

---

slowly. After the end of the second world war, however, a series of technological developments in farming, preserving, packaging, distributing and presenting foodstuffs made possible radical changes in foodstuff consumption habits.

These technological and distribution changes ran parallel to an increase in real income available to the consumer. Families had greater incomes to spend, and whilst the relative proportion of income spent on foodstuffs has not increased greatly, the absolute sums spent have risen as a a result. In other words, people were able to purchase a wider variety of foodstuffs. Other changes have included:

* an increasingly imaginative use of the technologies available;

* a substantial increase in the rate at which manufacturers have introduced new products;

* changes in the *relationship between volumes and values* purchased (for instance, less yellow fat is now eaten in the UK, but the value of fats consumed has not declined because more high value or value-added products, such as polyunsaturated fats, are being consumed);

* acceptance of the refrigerator as an essential kitchen item; introduction of freezer cabinets, microwave ovens (etc);

* increased priority of food preparation convenience, encouraging suppliers to market value-added foodstuffs (such as pizzas, frozen ready cooked meals and so on);

* use of additives to preserve products, lengthen shelf-life etc. This process may be further developed by the introduction of techniques of food irradiation;

* increased public concern with nutrition, food value and food health. Hence the changes in attitude towards the fibre, fat and additive content of foodstuffs, the increased interest in healthy foods, consumer reaction to intensive farming and environmental concerns over the use of pesticides, (etc).

These changes, coupled with increased marketing activity from producer and retailer alike, have caused the once mass food markets to *fragment into a wide range of market segments,* upon each of which are positioned a whole variety of different foodstuffs. There are convenience segments, children's segments, fresh food segments, health food and vegetarian segments, traditional segments, catering segments and so on. Food is consumed at home, in restaurants or burger bars (etc), or eaten "on the hoof" from takeaways.

These segments vary in volume and value from very large to very small. There are manufacturers, distributors and retailers geared up to supply them all, from multinational companies like Nestlé to small healthfood firms manufacturing grain, nut and honey crunch bars. Each has a place in such a varied marketplace.

(b) *the development of retailer power,* in which the relative advantage obtained from bulk buying, the use of retailers' "own brands", and policy limitations on the range of items stocked have all combined to put the manufacturer or supplier at a disadvantage. At the same time concentration has occurred amongst retail companies, leaving a small number of very large companies as well as a large number of smaller retailers.

(c) *the volume trap,* in which markets for commodity type products (like plant-baked bread) may become dominated by suppliers capable of volume production and distribution to retail multiple chains bulk-buying on a centralised basis.

In each case, market segmentation offers an answer to the marketer. For instance, non-standard or value-added lines are now frequently targeted on customer segments which seek to avoid the purchase of standardised products, whether these are foodstuffs, clothes, computers or industrial machinery. Alternatively, production arrangements may be designed to be flexible enough to supply target markets in a large number of relatively small and specialised niches, such as in the market for industrial or aviation control systems.

Technological developments in product design, manufacturing, distribution and retailing have also been essential to meeting these market developments. Technological developments have permitted product differentiation, and made possible more flexible production and supply arrangements. Such changes are needed if the demands of an increasing number of market segments are to be met, especially if they are relatively small in volume and value.

Let us look at two examples of these market changes in more detail.

1.1) Distributor and retailer power in consumer goods markets.

The exploitation of the relative advantage obtained from *bulk buying,* the use of retailer "own brands", and limitations on the number and range of items and brands stocked have all combined to put the manufacturer at a disadvantage.

Grocery chains in particular require stock lines to meet sales turnover objectives, which if not met will result in the discontinuing of the line. At the same time the manufacturer is expected to support his product with adequate promotional expenditure. One of the defences possessed by the manufacturer *against the retailer determining the nature of supply* is the accurate positioning of products and brands, derived from effective market research, against target market segments known to be an important constituent of the retailer's customer profile. Effective promotional activity may then leave the retailer with little choice but to stock the brand on a continuous basis. This may be true whether the product is a "blockbuster" (such as Nescafé), or aimed at specific smaller segments, as is currently the case in the UK with some health food ranges.

1.2) Volume commodity markets.

The second explanation involves the *volume trap*. Where a product is effectively a "commodity" (as is the case with many foodstuffs), or the consumer perceives a number of alternative brands to be easily substituted (as with paint, do-it-yourself products, electronic calculators, video recorders or home computers), then volume production and marketing may determine who will dominate the market.

This is the case with the UK bread market in which two bakery companies (Allied Bakeries and Rank Hovis McDougall) supply 60% of all bread sold in the UK. Volume, price and market share are inter-related. Those with the highest volume in this market can control price, negotiate from a position of strength with retailers, and so build market share, which in turn increases the volume sold. For those smaller plant plant bakery companies who cannot compete in these volume stakes the choice is quite clear. They need in addition to aim non-standard or value-added product lines (such as quality wholemeal bread, malted, muesli or "breakfast" loaves, croissants, cakes, sandwiches, catering lines or hot bread) at those specific local or regional markets in which their location and lower distribution costs give them an advantage, and at those market segments which seek non-standard or differentiated products. Only by so doing can their business activity generate an adequate return.

2) SEGMENTATION DEFINITIONS

Market segmentation means THE ANALYSIS OF A PARTICULAR TOTAL DEMAND IN TERMS OF ITS CONSTITUENT PARTS, SO THAT SETS OF BUYERS CAN BE DETERMINED. These sets of buyers should possess distinguishing characteristics, so that:

* they may be used as marketing targets against which products are positioned to meet segment customer need;

* a marketing mix appropriate to a particular segment may be selected.

Segmentation starts with the notion that a "global" analysis of total market demand needs to be broken down into its component parts. These are likely to be more effective for marketing and operational planning purposes. The mass producer (who may be production, quality or sales orientated) may attempt to supply all, or a substantial part of this total demand, and in so doing may consider that he can obtain a price, volume or distribution advantage relative to smaller scale producers. However, this mass producer is then forced to market a product range that is limited to a demand pattern of hypothetical "average consumers". At the same time he will miss out on segments of the market which in mass production or distribution terms are not thought economic to supply. This strategy has two basic flaws :

* it assumes that the profile of the "average consumer" is adequately representative of the majority of buyers within the market. This may mean that a production orientated company is (paradoxically) dependent on the effectiveness of its marketing skills in selling and promotion to sell adequate volumes in the marketplace. Yet in industrial goods markets there may be no such thing as an average consumer; each buyer's demand pattern and requirement may be different.

* a significant proportion of the market may comprise consumers who require non-standard products simply because they are not able or willing to conform to standardised purchasing patterns.

Two simple illustrations may be given. The first is the wide variation in specification and finish that are standard practice in the motor industry. The second is the dilemma faced by national UK brewers in deciding the content and distribution of their product range. Should they market keg beers under national brand names or should they return to localised brewing and brand names? Ultimately, what should be their response to the fragmenting of demand in the different directions of "real ale", pilsener lager, the decline of mild ale, and the increased consumption of wine and cocktail drinks?

Market segmentation, therefore, represents a recognition that people as buyers and consumers differ in their needs, tastes, family and cultural background, motivation, lifestyle and attitudes towards products and purchases. So how is market segmentation carried out?

3) SEGMENTATION CRITERIA

There are two main categories of segmentation criteria. The first *is based on the characteristics of the consumer or user*. The second, called "product segmentation", *focuses on how consumers or buyers perceive, group together and differentiate between available brands, products or services*. Products or services may then have to be positioned according to these perceptions. Both types are summarised in Table 16.2.

4) CONSUMER/USER CHARACTERISTICS

In this case, consumers or users are allocated into different groupings according to the way they may be categorised, thus:

4.1) Consumer Goods Markets

* Geographic Distribution – for instance, a substantial proportion of total UK demand is concentrated in London and the South East. Geographic segments are also important in rendering manageable a worldwide export marketing activity. Export marketing might be concentrated for example on South East Asian countries that have relatively high per capita income and large concentrations of population in cities such as Singapore, Hong Kong, Manila, Canton or Djakarta.

* Demography – in which the population is categorised according to age, sex, socio-economic group, income, housing, family characteristics and stage in family cycle.

	CONSUMER GOODS MARKETS	INDUSTRIAL GOODS MARKETS
CONSUMER/USER CHARACTERISTICS	Geographic distribution. Demography (age, sex, socio-economic group, occupation, income, family characteristics etc). Life-style. Personality (significant in the diffusion of new products). Consumption rate.	Geographic distribution. Customer size (the marketing process may have to vary with customer size, especially for very large industrial concerns). Usage rate. Industry classification (e.g. for steel marketing).
PRODUCT SEGMENTATION	Principal benefit sought within perceived usage context.	Principal benefit sought within perceived usage context. Vendor segmentation (usage requirements of customers of firms supplied). £ Contribution per unit of limiting factor (such as square metres of supermarket floor space).

Table 16.2. Segmentation Criteria.

* Life-Style (or "psychographics") – which was described in an earlier chapter as a reflection of deeper sociological and behavioural influences on people's attitudes and activities. The relevant population may be categorised on the basis of distinct patterns of work, leisure, or attitude to consumption of particular goods or services.

For example, an analysis of geographic distribution, demographic and life-style characteristics might be used to segment the market for value-added furnishing or food products, and determine appropriate distribution channels to be sought.

* Personality – which is believed to be significant in the "trickle down" process (or diffusion) of new products. In particular, *opinion leaders* may be important in increasing the level of recognition and acceptance of a new product, or in situations where innovatory behaviour is required of the consumer (for example in purchasing a completely new car model as soon as it is launched).

* Consumption Rate —consumers may be segmented on the basis of the volume and frequency of purchase. They might, for example, fall into any of the following six categories:-

USERS   NON USERS

Light   Convinced non-users
Medium   Non-potential accidental users
Heavy   Potential users.

The objective of marketing strategy towards these six segments would be (i) to maintain and increase the incidence of medium and heavy consumption of the company's products or brands; and (ii) to upgrade the other categories in the company's favour. For instance, a manufacturer of household detergents might aim to increase the housewife's use of any one of its proprietary brands, and also persuade her to purchase other company products for other household cleaning, such as washing up or spray polishing.

4.2) Industrial Goods Markets

* Geographic Distribution – this is particularly important where personal selling by sales representatives is the

main element of the company's promotional mix. Personal selling is a very expensive activity to maintain, and it may be best suited to relatively concentrated markets, such as in the UK for ceramics or steel manufacture, or those in which buying is carried out on a centralised basis.

* Customer Size – the various industrial customers may be grouped according to their size, and potential purchase quantity. The nature of the marketing process may have to vary with customer size; paint manufacturers will for instance have to get themselves onto a list of approved contractors before they can even bid for orders to major customers such as the railways or car manufacturers.

* Usage Rate – the supplier may attempt to increase the purchase rate of the customer, so that the customer becomes a heavier user, or may instead try to increase his proportion of the customer's total order for the product.

* Industry Classification – steel marketing is often segmented on this basis, since the UK Standard Industrial Classifications are readily understood and market data is frequently based upon them. Such classifications render the process of categorising diverse market opportunities more manageable. After all, steel is purchased by every industrial sector in the economy.

5) PRODUCT SEGMENTATION

This second approach focuses on how consumers or buyers perceive, group together, and differentiate between the available products, brands or services. Products or services may then have to be fitted or positioned according to these perceived market patterns. This segmentation basis can be explained thus:

* people may seek the *benefits* that products provide, rather than the products themselves. Market Research should be able to establish the nature of these benefits.

* consumers may consider the available alternatives from the vantage point of the *usage contexts* with which they have experience, or the specific applications they are considering. *It is the usage requirement which dictates the benefit being sought.*

Segmentation based on usage contexts is held to be particularly efficient because it permits product and marketing planning to be based on *customer perceptions of what is required of, or desirable in that product*. It is not based on the preconceived characteristics of (some possibly arbitrary) category of customer delineated on demographic or income criteria, or media data.

Three examples of Product Segmentation are given below.

5.1) Segmentation by Benefit.

Products are grouped according to the *principal benefit* which customers perceive that their purchase will bring. Thus, for example, the UK travel market could be segmented on the basis of desirable combinations or permutations of factors such as speed, frequency of service, comfort, cost and freedom from undesirable features such as seasickness or football supporters! The relatively low cost of long distance inter-city bus services, combined with their comfort and strict passenger control has, for instance, made them a highly competitive force when looked at from the viewpoint of older or economy conscious passengers.

A first variation on this theme will be product segmentation based on customer perceptions of "value for money". Product segmentation of this sort is visible in clothes retailing, and the distribution of fitted kitchens and bedroom furniture.

A second variation applicable to industrial goods markets will be customer perceptions of operating characteristics, which may carry greater weight than the technical specifications that may form the basis of the supplier's sales pitch. Buyers of commercial vehicles or heavy trucks, for instance, may prefer to buy products that they know will "feel right" to drivers, and which at the same time are straightforward for their maintenance crews to service.

5.2) Vendor Segmentation

It may be necessary for suppliers in industrial goods markets to sharpen the focus of their own market segmentation policy *by studying the specific demands and usage perceptions of the customers of the firms they supply*. Thus, not only are their own customers in focus, but the demands of the next group of customers "down the line" are part of the segment. This is called Vendor Segmentation.

After all, the supplier's products are only of benefit to his customer because the "end user" perceives them to be acceptable. This is obviously the case in markets such as civil or electrical engineering, but the principle is widely applicable; for instance see Box 16.3 below.

Box 16.3

PERKINS ENGINES

Perkins Engines are a major (UK) supplier of diesel engines. The company "sells to people who have factories" and "under-stand(s) what their problems are". That understanding lies at the heart of the company's market segmentation policy.

Selling engines to original equipment manufacturers (OEMs), such as vehicle builders, agricultural and mechanical handling equipment manufacturers, and producers of generating sets and compressors means selling to customers who are building somebody else's product into the heart of their own machines. Knowing what the customer wants is essential to this kind of business. Anticipating his future power unit needs and helping him to achieve them is the key to tomorrow's survival in OEM industries hard pressed by recession and overseas competition.

Perkins also claims that it is making a segment virtue out of necessity. It is using its applications engineering resources by offering "a total engine package" to those of its customers whom recession has forced to run down their own development activities.

Ultimately, segmentation policy may lead Perkins to a market situation where it may no longer see itself as "an engineering company selling an engineering product" but instead is "moving towards a service company approach" in which "the ability to work with customers must be a high priority."

(Source : Marketing.)

5.3) Contribution Targets

Retail outlets will view the products that they buy from manufacturers or wholesalers as items that *should provide the maximum Contribution per unit of limiting factor,* which is floor space. The usage context or benefit is simply one in which the total stock type, taken together, should bring in as much Contribution as possible per square metre. Lines that fail to meet minimum Contribution targets are eliminated from the stock range, unless their presence (for instance as loss leaders or long-established lines maintained for customer goodwill purposes) supports the achievement of the overall Contribution objective.

6) SEGMENTATION TECHNIQUES AND PRODUCT POSITIONING

A market segment may be identified and analyzed using the reasons for demand, whether these reasons are consumer or product orientated. Two examples are given below, thus:

* *Consumer criteria:* UK demand segment for low cost European travel:-

  age range : concentrated between 18 to 30;
  sex : both male and female;
  socio-economic class : A B1 B2 C1;
  occupation : predominantly full-time student;
  source of finance : parental; casual holiday or part-time earnings;
  special factors : access to discount arrangements; hold student travel cards;
  personality indicators : innovative behaviour, tendency to extraversion, high tolerance of low standards of travel and accommodation modes.

* *Product criteria* : UK demand segment for high season air inclusive tour package family holidays :-

  principal benefit sought : sunshine, warmth, comfortable accommodation, relaxed atmosphere;
  retail price : (say) between £200 to £500 for one or two weeks, per person;
  duration : 7, 10 or 14 days, with emphasis on departure/ return on Fridays, Saturdays or Sundays;
  location and climatic requirements : Mediterranean coast, guaranteed sunshine, warmth;
  mode of transport : air charter flights;
  mode of accommodation : two, three and four star equivalent hotels or self catering apartments. High standards of plumbing, sanitation and hygiene;

special factors : school summer holiday peak demand; operator reliability and continuity; English spoken by guides and hotel staff; airport security and aircraft safety; access to long term airport car parking.

This process of identification and analysis may be carried out in a number of ways, for instance :

* by using intuition based upon an interpretation of existing knowledge of the market;

* by using any of the wide array of market research techniques, based on internal sources of information about the market, and field research. The information so obtained may then have to be re-arranged to show segment differences, and again this process of interpretation may be subjective or objective, depending on how statistically valid the end product must be;

* by using an analysis of attribute sets. Attribute sets are analysed in section 6.1 below.

6.1) Attribute Sets

Attribute sets are combinations of individual reasons for demand. Complex statistical multivariate procedures can be used to correlate and group market research data so as to give a statistically accurate identification of :-

* the size of segment groups and their similarities;
* the differences between the various groupings of attribute sets;
* the relationship of these groups to important consumer, market or product/benefit requirements.

These statistical procedures have two components. The first is *Factor Analysis* which examines the correlations between variables across the respondents or products surveyed. The second is *Cluster Analysis* which seeks correlations between respondents or products across the segmentation variables being used.

Various distributions of attribute sets are possible. But where Cluster Analysis can show the existence of sufficiently large groupings of respondents, or product/benefit requirements which have similar attribute sets, then these may be used as MARKETING TARGETS, if the benefits of selling into them are likely to exceed the cost. Three simple examples are given in Figures 16.4, 16.5 and 16.6.

6.2) Product Positioning and differentiation

The company should then use the segments that it has defined *as targets against which products may be positioned*. The product range or "mix" (defined in a later chapter) should emphasise those product attributes or differences which are appropriate to the characteristics and requirements of clusters or segments that are seen as most viable in commercial terms. Similarly, an appropriate promotional "mix" may be formulated to provide the most effective communication to, and persuasion of those specific people who make up the segment, or are likely to seek the product or its benefits within the purchase contexts that the analysis has identified.

First class UK inter-city rail services provide an example to illustrate the point. These services have been positioned against a particular segment within the diffused travel market, and are promoted accordingly. This segment is that represented by long-distance business travellers and executives. The best track, rolling stock and journey times are to be found on the main intercity routes, where timetables and the provision of first class carriages and full catering services are aimed at the needs of the business community. Promotional activity stresses safety, speed and comfort (by direct comparison with the use of cars to cover the same type of journey), and the central location of termini (compared with the relative isolation of airports).

The logic for this *product differentiation* has already been explained, but it is worth repeating because it is *a direct means of implementing the marketing concept*. People seek the benefits that products provide, rather than the products or brands themselves. Specific products or brands should therefore be differentiated by those combinations of benefits and costs sought by a particular set of potential customers. It may be impracticable and unrealistic in segmentation terms for a company to try to incorporate into one product all the benefits and costs sought by *all* potential customers. Similarly, it may be highly risky if the product or brand contains only those benefits and costs selected on a subjective basis by the supplier, without reference to the marketplace itself.

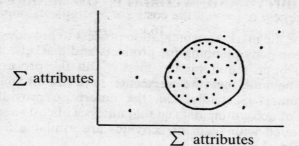

* one cluster; forming a "homogeneous" market;
  e.g. analgesics (headache and proprietary pain relief products), car oil, paint.

Figure 16.4. A "Homogeneous" Market.

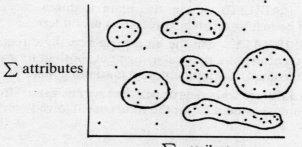

* several clusters, forming a "diffused" market; e.g. TV, radio, and hi-fi; other household electrical goods.

Figure 16.5. A "Diffused" Market.

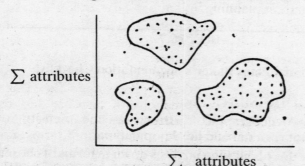

* few, concentrated clusters, forming a "concentrated" market; e.g. floor/carpet cleaners, cars.

Figure 16.6. A "Concentrated" Market.

7) THE VALIDITY AND VIABILITY OF MARKET SEGMENTATION

In order for the market segmentation process to provide a valid input to company planning for products and markets, it must fulfil two basic requirements. Firstly, can the process identify, describe and measure segments in a useful and meaningful manner? Secondly, can the enterprise provide adequate flows of accounting data so that analysis of costs and revenues associated with segment activities are available for planning and control purposes?

Hence, the four standard tests of segment VALIDITY:

IDENTIFICATION – does the segmentation process discriminate meaningfully between sets of buyers, and does it pick out differences in market demand patterns?

MEASURABILITY – can the main features of each segment be measured and expressed in useful terms?

ACCESSIBILITY – can the enterprise actually direct its marketing effort at a particular segment, both in terms of product/product development, and marketing mix?

VIABILITY – to what degree will the revenue gained from selling into a segment offset the total cost involved?

8) A PRACTICAL EXAMPLE

Box 16.7 contains a checklist which describes the steps a medium-sized business (in this case a UK regional plant baker) might take in order to provide a market segmentation input to its product and market planning:

BOX 16.7

A Regional Plant Baker's Segmentation Checklist

STEP REQUIREMENT

(1) Analyse geographic distribution and density of relevant regional and local population.

(2) Break this population analysis down in terms of chosen demographic variables and significant consumer life-style variations. For example:
(a) age, housing and home ownership patterns;
(b) socio-economic class distribution;

    (c) significant patterns and trends of income distribution;

    (d) family/non family orientations (e.g. : family dominated, middle class owned suburban residential areas; working class family rented residential areas; inner city rented singles/students' bed sit/flat accommodation; and so on);

    (e) significant shopping pattern variations relative to retail provision (and trends therein);

    (f) significant variations in purchase behaviour influences (e.g.: children's tastes in bread/cakes influencing mother's purchase patterns; acceptance of high fibre diet and concern with weight, smoking and heart disease among middle aged, middle class men; major competitor promotional campaigns).

(3)   Research and/or describe type and purchase patterns of consumers showing heavy, medium and light/casual purchase rates of bread and cakes, relative to item (1) and (2) above.

(4)   In the case of new/modified products (e.g.: high fibre muesli loaves), locate and identify types of innovative buyers and opinion leaders, and their shopping patterns.

(5)   Obtain relevant sample consumer perceptions about:
    (a) food purchase priorities and influences;
    (b) your own products;
    (c) competitor's products;
    (d) relevant retail provision relative to user type (item (3) above).

(6)   Locate, list and describe relevant local, regional, and national retail outlets and:
    (a) describe their trading, buying and pricing policy as if affects bakery products;
    (b) describe their attitude to manufacturer's brands/own brands, and ranges.

(7)   List and describe main and secondary competitors, and:
    (a) describe their segmentation policy (if this can be identified);
    (b) describe their trading policy (product positioning and marketing mix variables).

(Source : Baking Today October 1984).

SUMMARY

The contents of this chapter are summarised in Table 16.8.

TABLE 16.8
Summary : Chapter Sixteen

SECTION	MAIN POINTS
1. The importance of market segmentation	The increasing importance of market segmentation as a marketing tool can in part be explained by: market fragmentation; the development of retailer power (which is based on concentration, and on the relative advantage obtained from centralised bulk buying); the development of volume based markets for commodity-type products (such as plant baked bread).
2. Segmentation definitions	Market segmentation means the analysis of a particular total demand in terms of its constituent parts, so that sets of buyers can be determined. These sets of buyers should possess distinguishing characteristics so that (i) they may be used as marketing targets against which products are positioned to meet segment customer need; (ii) a marketing mix appropriate to a particular segment may be selected.
3. Segmentation criteria	There are two main categories of segmentation criteria. The first is based on the characteristics of the consumer or user. The second, called "product segmentation", focuses on how consumers or buyers perceive, group together and differentiate between available brands, products or services.
4. Consumer/user characteristics	Summarised in Table 16.2.

5. Product segmentation	This focuses on how consumers or buyers perceive, group together and differentiate between available brands, products or services. It is used where (i) people seek the benefits that products provide, rather than the products themselves; and (ii) where customers consider the available alternatives from the viewpoint of the usage contexts with which they have experience, or the specific applications they are considering. The usage requirement dictates the benefit being sought. Three examples are given, namely: segmentation by benefit; vendor segmentation; contribution targets.
6. Segmentation techniques and product positioning	This may be carried out on the basis of (i) intuition and interpretation; or (ii) use of market research data (suitably re-arranged and interpreted); or (iii) using an analysis of attribute sets. Attribute sets are combinations of individual reasons for demand. They are correlated by Factor Analysis and Cluster Analysis. Cluster analysis may reveal segments with sufficiently large groupings of respondents, or product/benefit requirements with similar attributes. These clusters are then used as targets against which products should be positioned. The product range and promotional mix should emphasise products or usage attributes required/sought by the people making up the segment.
7. Validity of market segmentation	The four standard tests of segment validation are Identification, Measurability, Accessibility, Viability.

17 Consumer Targeting and the Acorn System

INTRODUCTION

There are a number of methods by which knowledge about a market segment can be built up. Some of these methods have been described in previous chapters, which dealt with market research, sales forecasting, analysis of consumer and buyer behaviour and so on.

Additional market segmentation intelligence can be gained from the technique of **consumer targeting.** Consumer targeting has been made possible by developments in demographics and statistics, and Information Technology applications in these areas. Consumer targeting has been pioneered in the UK by **CACI Market Analysis** using:

* official UK Census of Population statistics;
* official Post Office postcodes;
* profiles of retail outlets and shopping centres.

Consumer targeting may be based on **ACORN** ("A Classification of Residential Neighbourhoods"). **ACORN** is a classification system which divides blocks of 150 addresses throughout Great Britain into 38 different types of residential neighbourhood, according to their demographic, housing and socio-economic characteristics.

This chapter describes the **ACORN** system in some detail, and examines some of its specific applications to market segmentation and consumer targeting. These applications include customer profiling, the analysis of retail catchment areas, sales forecasting and retail branch siting.

This chapter has been prepared and written with the help of CACI Market Analysis. The author wishes to acknowledge the assistance given by that company.

CHAPTER CONTENTS

1) Marketing intelligence and consumer targeting
2) Demographic data and consumer targeting
3) ACORN described

4)   Market research
5)   Customer profiles
6)   Area analysis
7)   Retail catchment areas
8)   Market forecast modelling
9)   Retail branch customer profiling
10) Retail branch siting
11) Shopping centre planning
12) Leafleting
Summary
Questions for self-review
Examination Questions
Chapter Appendix One: Shopping Centre Planner

1) MARKETING INTELLIGENCE AND CONSUMER TARGETING

Previous chapters have dealt at length with market research, sales and market forecasting, consumer behaviour and market segmentation. These chapters made extensive reference to how *marketing intelligence* (or knowledge) could be built up. Each of these chapters contained at least some description of how the concepts and techniques they described could be put to practical use to build up market knowledge. Companies need to analyse, segment, research and forecast the likely patterns and behaviour of the markets into which they wish to trade. They need to do this for a number of reasons, which include:

*   identifying the characteristics and attributes of customers and market segments;
*   developing and positioning products and services which are appropriate to customer needs and purchasing patterns;
*   maximising sales penetration potential through distribution and retail channels;
*   focusing the most cost-effective promotional activity (advertising, exhibitions, sponsorship etc) as accurately as possible on target market segments.

The process by which detailed analysis is carried out, and accurate knowledge or intelligence of the market is built-up is a crucial one in marketing. Without such market intelligence a company cannot remain sensitive to its market. *Market intelligence is fundamental to market-orientated company operations and planning.*

Each of the previous chapters on market research, sales and market forecasting, consumer behaviour and market segmentation have included practical illustrations of how the principles outlined in these chapters can contribute to the build-up of market intelligence.

This chapter concentrates on *consumer targeting*. Techniques of consumer targeting are an important additional input to market analysis, segmentation and planning. Such techniques may be used to assist and augment the processes of market segmentation, research and forecasting. They have been made possible in consumer markets by developments (i) in the study of demographics and statistics; and (ii) in Information Technology applications.

These techniques of consumer targeting are now so widely applied that a separate chapter must be devoted to them. Nevertheless, it is worth repeating that their essential role is to assist and augment the processes of market analysis, research, segmentation and forecasting.

2) DEMOGRAPHIC DATA AND CONSUMER TARGETING

Whilst a variety of *geodemographic* systems of market analysis are now available, geographic and demographic data for consumer targeting was pioneered in the UK by **CACI Market Analysis PLC**, a leading marketing analyst. The raw material for consumer targeting includes:

a) official UK Census of Population statistics, which may be sorted, permutated and aggregated according to the analysis requirements.

b) official Post Office "postcodes": all UK addresses have a postcode which was originally designated to permit automated sorting of mail. Postcodes are a basic geodemographic unit, groups of which are contained within *postal sectors* and *census enumeration districts. CACI have built-up a geographically based postcode database which permits the analyst to match postal addresses to census demography.* This identifies the demographic features of geographic areas *as identified by customer addresses.* Using customer addresses to define target markets is basic to the approach and method used in customer targeting.

c) profiles of retail outlets, which categorise shopping centres in terms of the number, type and size of shops, and identify the branch outlets of every retail multiple company.

Consumer targeting is largely based on **ACORN,** which is a system that classifies every address in Great Britain into one of thirty-eight types, according to the demographics of its immediate neighbourhood. This classification makes it possible, for instance, for the analyst to use individual customer lists and market research survey data to identify the types of neighbourhood with the heaviest consumption of a particular product or service. Such detailed market analysis then makes possible a very accurate targeting of retail and product distribution, product promotion and advertising on specific geographical demographic customer segments.

3) ACORN DESCRIBED

ACORN stands for "A Classification of Residential Neighbourhoods". **ACORN** is a classification system which divides units of 150 addresses throughout Great Britain into 38 different types of residential neighbourhood, according to their demographic, housing and socio-economic characteristics. The system is based on the Census of Population in Great Britain, and Post Office address postcodes. Its categories are shown in Table 17.1.

1984 ACORN Profile – Great Britain

Acorn groups		1984 population	%
A	Agricultural areas	1,830,000	3.4
B	Modern family housing, higher incomes	9,004,000	16.8
C	Older housing of intermediate status	9,422,000	17.6
D	Poor quality older terraced housing	2,240,000	4.2
E	Better-off council estates	7,009,000	13.1
F	Less well-off council estates	4,934,000	9.2
G	Poorest council estates	3,975,000	7.4
H	Multi-racial areas	2,060,000	3.8
I	High status non-family areas	2,227,000	4.2
J	Affluent suburban housing	8,531,000	15.9
K	Better-off retirement areas	2,042,000	3.8
U	Unclassified	389,000	0.7

Acorn types		
A	1	Agricultural villages
A	2	Areas of farms and smallholdings

215

B	3	Cheap modern private housing
B	4	Recent private housing, young families
B	5	Modern private housing, older children
B	6	New detached houses, young families
B	7	Military bases
C	8	Mixed owner-occupied and council estates
C	9	Small town centres and flats above shops
C	10	Villages with non-farm employment
C	11	Older private housing, skilled workers
D	12	Unimproved terraces with old people
D	13	Pre-1914 terraces, low income families
D	14	Tenement flats lacking amenities
E	15	Council estates, well-off older workers
E	16	Recent Council estates
E	17	Council estates, well-off young workers
E	18	Small council houses, often Scottish
F	19	Low rise estates in industrial towns
F	20	Inter-war council estates, older people
F	21	Council housing for the elderly
G	22	New council estates in inner cities
6	23	Overspill estates, high unemployment
G	24	Council estates with overcrowding
G	25	Council estates with worst poverty
H	26	Multi-occupied, terraces
H	27	Owner-occupied terraces, with Asians
H	28	Multi-let housing with Afro-Caribbeans
H	29	Better-off multi-ethnic areas
I	30	High status areas, few children
I	31	Multi-let big old houses and flats
I	32	Furnished flats, mostly single people
J	33	Inter-war semis, white collar workers
J	34	Spacious inter-war semis, big gardens
J	35	Villages with wealthy older commuters
J	36	Detached houses, exclusive suburbs
K	37	Private houses, well-off elderly
K	38	Private flats with single pensioners
U	39	Unclassified

TABLE 17.1
ACORN CLASSIFICATIONS

Organisations which have used customer addresses to define
ACORN types cover a number of sectors. Large users include
direct mail order suppliers; financial organisations and building
societies, which hold addresses for every account holder; gas
and electricity companies and TV rental companies which
maintain customer accounting information; multiple retailers
who operate their own credit cards; travel companies; motor
appliance and furniture manufacturers who retain addresses for
warranty or guarantee purposes; manufacturers who obtain

addresses from special on-pack promotion or coupon drops; even charities and political parties.

For insurance companies, building societies, credit operators and direct mail houses, **ACORN** is used to identify the types of customer it is most profitable to serve. They are able to identify from their own records those types who are the loyal customers – where average order value is highest, where bad debt is lowest, and where responsiveness to mailshots is highest.

Sometimes, an **ACORN** type may score well on one of the criteria, but badly on others. For instance, high status retirement areas (type 37) are usually of poor or average order value, but good on loyalty; modern council estates (type 16) are good on mailing responsiveness, but bad on debt.

Since age distribution and family life-cycle stage both play a very important part in determining the **ACORN** codes, it is possible to distinguish pre-family areas (of relatively high disposable income and low commitments), young family areas (with a high level of mortgage, hire purchase and overdraft debt), post-family areas (with high levels of saving, low use of credit and high incomes), and retirement areas (with low income, but significant investment income).

Once an advertiser knows the **ACORN** types he wants to aim at, he has a number of options. This is because research information, which gives the media types preferred by different **ACORN** types, is widely available. For instance, although *Daily Telegraph* and *Guardian* readers are not dissimilar in social class, the *Telegraph* scores very much higher in the established high-status suburbs and high-status retirement areas; while the *Guardian* leads in high-status, non-family areas in inner cities and especially in inner London.

National market research organisations such as the British Market Research Bureau and JICNARS (Joint Industry Committee for National Readership Surveys), which are dealt with in a later chapter, code their surveys by **ACORN** to enable the advertiser to identify titles whose profiles best match his own, and to see what share of this target market that title reaches.

The marketing companies for local radio and local press also supply information showing the **ACORN** composition of the areas served by these media.

Another medium that can be used selectively is direct

marketing, a fact which has been vigorously promoted by the Post Office. (Direct marketing is dealt with in more detail in a later chapter.) For instance, a number of building societies have used **ACORN** to promote premium savings services only to those account holders who live in particularly affluent neighbourhoods; an electricity board promotes electric central heating only to those of its consumers living in agricultural **ACORN** types (beyond the reach of gas). Some manufacturers have taken advantage of the willingness of leaflet contractors to deliver coupons to selected **ACORN** types only.

Another important capability enables the advertiser to mail each address in any town, or indeed Great Britain, falling into the appropriate **ACORN** categories. This has proved a particularly useful option for retailers who wish to use direct marketing within relatively restricted catchment areas. Other retail multiples use targeted mailshots to support new branches that they are opening.

While **ACORN's** most obvious application is in market analysis, advertising and direct marketing, CACI argues that it is equally relevant to the sales manager for setting equitable targets for different sales territories. All too easily, he or she forms subjective opinions about the relative sales potential of different territories, but lacks an objective framework for setting sales quotas. Now, by analysing a sample of customer addresses by **ACORN** he or she can set sales targets for each **ACORN** type; and by allowing for the population in each type in each sales territory, he or she can set quotas which relate directly to the potential for business in each area.

Another important application area is site location, using an **ACORN** profile of each shopping centre to minimise the risk of opening an unprofitable shop. Many retailers also use **ACORN** to evaluate the product ranges that should be stocked at different stores. Conversely, information about local consumer preferences can be used by manufacturers' sales forces in selling to a retail outlet those lines which its local customer profile is most likely to purchase. (Channels of distribution are dealt with in detail in a later chapter.)

4) MARKET RESEARCH

ACORN can be used for market research purposes in survey analysis and sampling. *Market surveys* which contain respondents' addresses and postcodes can be related to the appropriate **ACORN** categories. Then each respondent's **ACORN** category becomes a variable against which his or her responses can be cross-tabulated, for instance for market segmentation purposes. It can also be used to establish the propensity of different **ACORN** categories to buy different products or services, or to use them at particular rates; and to analyse their exposure and reaction to different forms of promotional and advertising media. For instance:

* **ACORN** analyses are available for some of the major U.K. consumer panels. The use of consumer panels is described in other chapters:

* The National Readership Survey, administered by JICNARS (defined above), provides extensive information on the exposure of different **ACORN** categories to published and broadcast media. The issue of advertising effectiveness is dealt with in a later chapter.

ACORN classifies areas on the basis of a number of attributes which can be used to construct *stratified quota samples*. These attributes include *direct strata indicators* such as social class, housing type and neighbourhood, and *indirect* indicators such as region, parliamentary constituency and media area. The design and use of samples was discussed in an earlier chapter. Samples may be specified on the basis of postcode sectors, census enumeration districts or electoral wards and constituencies. The results may then be cross-referenced back to the **ACORN** codes that are supplied with the sample, for aggregation and analysis.

5) CUSTOMER PROFILES

Many U.K. companies maintain large customer databases. The addresses held therein may already have postcodes, and there are specialist agencies that will add postcodes to addresses by computer where customer records are incomplete. From the postcode of any address, CACI can categorise the customer record by its **ACORN** type.

By taking a sample profile of its customers, the company can then discover which of its **ACORN** categories are its most valuable in terms of sales. It can use its customer records to indicate what people in the different categories buy, how much they spend per capita, how they pay and whether they are repeat customers. Using this kind of information, promotional messages and direct mailshots can be more selectively targeted on those categories which are the company's best and most consistent customers.

A recent addition to this customer profiling capability is CACI's use of *age* as a discriminating variable. CACI's MONICA system uses *first name* as an indicator of age, relying upon the fact that at different times different first names are in fashion. The reader can test this assumption for himself or herself. If you are called Sharon or Tracey or Kevin or Wayne you are probably under 30 years of age. First names come and go in the popularity stakes, and your elderly grandmother or aunt is more likely to be called Violet, Ada or Ethel.

CACI suggest that the importance of indicating age as a segmentation variable can be illustrated in the context of one of the more affluent **ACORN** categories by expenditure on holidays. Whilst the majority of households are likely to take at least one holiday per year, the type of holiday taken may depend on age group. The under-25's are most likely to take a skiing holiday, the 25−44 age group to take their car to Europe on the ferry, and the over 45's to take a package holiday abroad.

6) AREA ANALYSIS

Area analysis can be used to provide a company with information about the different types of people living in a particular area. The area defined might be:

* a catchment area around a particular retail store;
* sales territories;
* official media coverage areas.

Area analysis would then provide details of:

* population according to Census statistics and population updates;
* population by **ACORN** category;
* statistics for the number of people who work in that area (which may be significantly larger than the resident population).

Once the company has defined its target market segment by **ACORN** type(s), area analysis will help find those locations in which these types are most concentrated, or most easily accessible. The company may then target its efforts on these preferred locations.

CACI give the example of Haywards Heath, in West Sussex. Over 40% of the population in this area are classified as category J, which is a high status, high income group. This compares with the average of 16% in the U.K. as a whole. Companies wishing to sell up-market financial services, cars, consumer goods (etc) would concentrate their efforts on such areas.

RETAIL CATCHMENT AREAS

CACI have divided Great Britain into a series of retail catchment areas, based on a shopping centre with a Crown post office. For each of these zones it can provide:

* population statistics;
* population by **ACORN** category;
* consumer expenditure potential;
* details of retail competition;
* a postcode index for matching to a postcoded customer file.

By using this information, retail companies may (i) site branch stores, and (ii) allocate their product mix according to the kinds of customer type to be found in these catchment areas. In so doing, retailers can find answers to such questions as:

- do enough people shop in Hanley to support a "Next" shop?
- how many bicycles should my Chester store be capable of selling in a year?
- in which towns in the Tyne Tees TV region does my company have the most/fewest customers per 1000 population?

8) MARKET FORECAST MODELLING

Effective consumer target marketing depends in part on finding or forecasting the areas of highest sales potential for any particular product. Such a forecast of sales potential may be a crucial input into sales, production and budgetary planning. If a company can ascertain the **ACORN** categories which make up its target market segments, this can be matched up with the distribution of **ACORN** types living in any area. The relationship between these two factors can be an indication of sales potential. This indication can then be compared with a national base of 100 to indicate whether a particular area is better or worse than average for finding buyers or owners of any product which is already specifically measured in existing national market research surveys.

For instance, a national fuel distributor or utility might wish to identify the location of homes with electric or oil-fired central heating on a town-by-town basis outside the domestic gas supply network. Once combined with the relevant **ACORN** types, the distributor may be in a position:

* * to set sales targets for regional and local sales management;
* * to identify towns in which to establish local retail branches or service depots;
* * to identify appropriate regional and local media for targeting promotional messages;
* * to select the postal sectors in which to aim a leaflet drop using the U.K. Post Office Household Delivery Service.

9) RETAIL BRANCH CUSTOMER PROFILING

Retail companies may want to know the answers to the following kinds of questions:

* ● how far do its customers travel to a specific store or branch?
* ● what is the direction from which they travel?
* ● in what type of area do they live?
* ● what are their lifestyles and purchasing habits?
* ● how much of a town or area remains untapped by a shop located in it?

CACI's **BRANCHPLAN** can assist in answering these questions by analysing addresses held by the branch. The basis of the analysis is the customer's postcode, which may be held on existing computerised customer records. Branchplan then indicates which **ACORN** types contain people most likely to use the store; which contain people who will travel long distances to do their shopping; and how quickly customer traffic falls off as distance from the outlet increases.

For instance, Figure 17.2 shows that most shoppers at one particular supermarket live within 1.5 kilometres of the store. This information is relevant to plans for local advertising, leaflet distribution, and for determining the potential for opening another branch to be sited a few kilometres away.

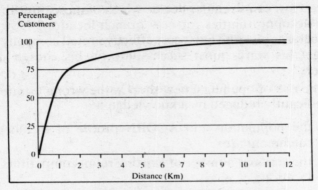

Figure 17.2. Customer Residence Proximity.

Similarly, Branchplan can be used to generate a plot of customer distribution around a particular store location. Figure 17.3 shows clearly the failure of the store (marked X) to draw from the north-west of the city in which it is situated. From this analysis the company should be able to evaluate the untapped potential to the north-west, and forecast the viability of opening another outlet on that side of the city centre.

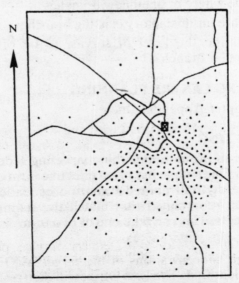

Figure 17.3. Customer Distribution Plot.

223

10) RETAIL BRANCH SITING

There are over one thousand shopping centres in Great Britain. How can a retailer decide which of these offer the most profitable opportunities for new branch location? How can a manufacturer pick the most cost effective retail company to use to target his wares most successfully on his chosen market segments?

The risk of opening a new shop in the wrong location may be significantly reduced by a knowledge of:

* the population and **ACORN** profile of the location's catchment area;
* the size and number of existing retail competitors in the location;
* the "normal" level of retail competition in shopping centres of a similar type.

This information is available from the **ACORN** programs, and from specific retail census statistics, and market surveys. These can be combined in a modelling program which compares and forecasts branch performance in groups of shopping centres, each with similar characteristics. The objective is to assist retailers to:

– decide where to open new branches;
– relocate unsatisfactory existing branches;
– determine the level of service to be offered at any particular branch.

11) SHOPPING CENTRE PLANNING

See Chapter Appendix One.

12) LEAFLETING

The role of promotion within marketing is dealt with in a later chapter. One simple but often effective form of promotion is that of the door to door distribution of leaflets. Delivery schedules can be obtained that match the required **ACORN** customer targets. This can take one of two forms in the U.K.

a) *Post Office Household Delivery Service:* postal sectors with high concentrations of the target **ACORN** category can be identified. The Post Office will then restrict delivery of leaflets to these specific target locations.

b) *Leafleting contractors:* CACI can map any town or part of Great Britain and identify the location of target **ACORN** neighbourhoods. The client's leafleting contractors can use these maps to isolate those sections of the town or country for selective distribution. Alternatively, for distribution which requires very precise targeting, CACI lists the streets that fall within the specific **ACORN** neighbourhoods.

SUMMARY

The contents of this chapter are summarised in Table 17.4

TABLE 17.4
Summary : Chapter Seventeen

SECTION	MAIN POINTS
1. Marketing intelligence and consumer targeting	There are a number of ways in which knowledge about market, or "market intelligence", can be built up. These include market research, market segmentation, sales forecasting, analysis of consumer or buyer behaviour. Chapter seventeen concentrates on consumer targeting as a source of market intelligence. Consumer targeting has been made increasingly effective by developments in demographics and statistics, and Information Technology applications. Whatever its source , however, market intelligence is fundamental to market-orientated company operations and planning.
2. Demographic data and consumer targeting	Consumer targeting makes use of (i) official UK Census of Population statistics; (ii) official Post Office postcodes; (iii) profiles of retail outlets, which categorise shopping centres in terms of number, type and size of shop, branch outlets etc.

225

3. **ACORN** described	**ACORN** stands for "A Classification of Residential Neighbourhoods". **ACORN** is a classification system which divides units of 150 addresses throughout Great Britain into 38 different types of residential neighbourhood, according to their demographic, housing and socio-economic characteristics.
4. **ACORN** applications	Consumer targeting intelligence may be built up using the **ACORN** system to carry out (4) market research; (5) the construction of customer profiles; (6) area analysis; (7) analysis of retail catchment areas; (8) market forecast modelling; (9) retail branch customer profiles; (10) retail branch siting; (11) shopping centre planning; (12) leafleting.

QUESTIONS FOR SELF-REVIEW

1)   What is Market Segmentation, and why is it an important marketing tool?

2)   Compare and contrast Consumer and Product based segmentation criteria.

3)   "Highly specialised companies are highly risky companies". Comment on this statement.

4)   "Mass producers do not need Market Segmentation policies, only a large salesforce". Comment on this statement.

5)   Comment on the role of customer targeting within the process by which a company builds up its marketing intelligence.

*6)   What is **ACORN**? Explain and comment on the principles upon which it is based.*

*7)   Why is **ACORN** of great value to retail companies?*

*8)   Why is **ACORN** of great value to companies making use of direct marketing? (also see later chapter).*

*9)   Why is **ACORN** of great value to media buyers and suppliers? (also see later chapter).*

EXAMINATION QUESTIONS

Q28 (a) *What is the purpose of dividing a market into segments?*

(b) *Describe the likely ways in which:*

(i) *a manufacturer of diesel engines and*

(ii) *a manufacturer of breakfast cereals might segment their markets.*   *(CIMA)*

Q29 *Examine the main dimensions or bases which a marketing manager might use to segment his market.(IIM)*

Q30 *How useful is social class as a variable for segmenting consumer markets?*   *(IIM)*

Q31 *What do you understand by "Product Positioning"? Select a product as an example and show how positioning can be used in the marketing of that product.*   *(IIM)*

Q32 *What is the relationship between market segmentation, market targeting and product positioning?*   *(CIM)*

Q33 *'Market segmentation and product differentiation are really two sides of the same coin and businesses seek to match products to market segments.'*
How true do you think this is of bank marketing? Illustrate by means of examples from your own bank.
                    (SCOB)

CHAPTER APPENDIX ONE
Shopping Centre Planner

CACI's Shopping Centre Planner identifies 230 areas of retail activity in Great Britain, varying from major city centres down to small local shopping parades. CACI have derived catchment areas for these centres using gravity modelling techniques and drive-time analysis.

CACI are able to provide simple summary reports on standard catchment areas around each centre, giving local statistics on population, housing and other key demographic indicators.

CACI are also able to build more advanced studies looking at the specific market sectors that a client may be interested in. Typically this will involve detailed catchment area research, and competition analysis.

Shopping Centre Definition

CACI have identified 2380 areas of concentrated retail activity and have thus created a comprehensive picture of retailing in Great Britain. Each of these centres can be analysed according to its size, both in retail composition and in area covered on the ground.

CACI used computer techniques to build up shopping centre analyses from raw data which covered a representative sample of all retail activity. The sample included information on the locations of supermarkets, banks and selected outlets which take Access credit cards (about 140,000 outlets in all).

The centres are segmented into two categories based on the scores developed for each area. There are 1446 main shopping areas covering all well known centres down to the level of small local centres. CACI also identified a further 934 centres of low but significant retail concentration.

The planner is concerned with shopping centres rather than out-of-town retailing so that stand-alone stores or retail parks with few stores are not represented. These retail areas can be built into the Planner in advanced projects.

Catchment Area definition

CACI have used a gravity model in order to build up catchment areas around each defined shopping centre. This model looks at each postal sector in Great Britain and answers the question 'where do people go shopping?'. Clearly people use a number of centres of different sizes. Some centres may be visited every week, some only once a year. Some visits may only be for convenience shopping and some for comparison. To address this problem CACI's gravity model looks at all the centres around each sector. Each centre will have a particular attractiveness and will be within a particular drive-time (eg 15 minutes) from the sector. On the basis of this information proportions of population are allocated to each centre giving a realistic model of how people shop.

For simple use of a Shopping Centre Planner CACI have developed a standard calibration of the model described above. This standard Planner is designed to give a general purpose catchment for each centre and is not designed for a specific retail sector. The calibration is based on CACI's long experience in the field of catchment area study across all retail sectors, and is therefore best viewed as relating to the catchment area of the centre as a whole.

Advanced Shopping Centre Planner Applications

CACI have also developed the Shopping Centre Planner with a view to undertaking advanced analysis projects. These advanced studies build into the planning model information which is specifically relevant to a chosen retail market sector. There are two primary areas where the planner can be modified to fit more exactly with a particular market. Firstly, CACI can build on to the shopping centres additional information relating to those outlets in a particular retail sector - this might be in terms of floorspace allocations, number of outlets or other attractiveness measures. Secondly, CACI can specifically assess the catchment areas faced by any particular centre or retailer by analysing survey data, credit card data or other sources of customer information.

It is also possible to add in new centres in order to look at the impact of potential new developments, including 'What-if' analysis based around the attractiveness of the new centre.

(Reproduced with permission)

18 The Marketing Mix

INTRODUCTION

This chapter defines and describes the Marketing Mix. It then places this concept within the wider context of the marketing management process, and describes the role of the Marketing Mix in achieving the company's marketing objectives. The chapter acts as the introduction to the next (and largest) section of this manual, in which the four constituent elements of the Marketing Mix (the *"Four P's"*) are described in detail.

CHAPTER CONTENTS

1) The Marketing Mix defined
2) The Marketing Mix in context
3) The Marketing Mix
4) The Four P's
5) Interdependence within each category
6) Interdependence between each category
7) Managing the Marketing Mix

Summary

Questions for self-review

Examination Questions

1) THE MARKETING MIX DEFINED

The Marketing Mix can be defined as *the combination of detailed strategies; tactics; operational policies, programmes, techniques and activities, to which resources may be allocated such that the company's marketing objectives are achieved.*

2) THE MARKETING MIX IN CONTEXT

Up to this point, this book has:

* introduced the marketing concept and defined the role of marketing management;

* looked at how a company can research and identify its target markets and market segments;

* analysed consumer and buyer behaviour within these target markets;

* examined the methods by which a company can construct some kind of demand forecast.

These concepts, activities and techniques will yield market intelligence and marketing information. This information will be used as a vital input to the corporate strategic planning and strategic marketing planning processes, from which will come the company's basic marketing objectives.

The Marketing Mix is concerned with the realities and practicalities of how these marketing objectives may be turned into specific marketing plans and activities. *The role of the marketing mix is to move objectives and plans into the reality of implementation and achievement.* As a result, the marketing mix must have:

- *strategic elements* (for instance, the company must decide what kinds of products or services it wishes to produce, given the choices it has made about the target markets it wants to satisfy. Such decisions will, inevitably, preclude other markets and products, given the limitation on resources available to it.)
- *planning elements* (for instance, what time-scales should be applied to new product development activities?)
- *tactical elements* (for instance, to what extent should the company allow discounts to volume buyers, and how widely should its pricing policy be publicised within the trade?)
- *operational and implementation elements* (for instance, should marketing management expect to be involved in the formulation of detailed advertising copy being undertaken by the company's advertising agency?)
- *resource commitment* (for instance, upon what basis should advertising and sales promotion budgets be constructed: or over what time scale should new products be expected to pay-back the Research and Development costs incurred in their development?)

The importance and complexity of the Marketing Mix, therefore, explain why it is such a major subject in the theory and practice of marketing. A detailed study of the Marketing Mix comprises a substantial proportion of the total content of this manual.

3) THE MARKETING MIX

The Marketing Mix was defined in Section 1 above as the combination of detailed strategies; tactics; operational policies, programmes, techniques and activities, to which resources may be allocated such that the company's marketing objectives are achieved.

This complex of elements and activities should be managed such that it ensures that the *right product* is available at the *right price* in the *right place* at the *appropriate time* to satisfy the needs of target customers in the chosen market segments. This management process will also require the creation of customer awareness about the product, its price and availability. It may also involve some degree of persuasion that the customer should consider purchasing the product, or should actually make the purchase. The need for *appropriate promotion* of the product or service is, therefore, also an important part of the Marketing Mix.

(4) THE FOUR P's

The Marketing Mix may effectively be described and analysed on the basis of the *Four P's*. These are:

PRODUCT
PRICE
PLACE
PROMOTION

This is the order in which they are analysed in this manual. Each comprises a major section with chapters listed as follows:

a) *PRODUCT*
Ch. 19   The Product Life Cycle
Ch. 20   Product planning and development
Ch. 21   Brand and product management

b) *PRICING*
Ch. 22   Pricing determinants
Ch. 23   Prices and costs
Ch. 24   Pricing policy

c) *PLACE*
Ch. 25   Channels of distribution
Ch. 26   Physical distribution management and customer service
Ch. 27   Direct marketing

5) INTERDEPENDENCE WITHIN EACH CATEGORY

The various elements or component activities which make up each of the four Marketing Mix categories are interdependent. For instance, the larger the sales force, the less the need for heavy advertising expenditure. Similarly, a product which is marketed under a prestigious brand name may enjoy a much longer market life than basically similar products which lack a strong brand image. In consequence, product planning, and research and development activities may concentrate resources on the product and the brand, so further strengthening its position relative to the competition.

6) INTERDEPENDENCE BETWEEN EACH CATEGORY

The four Marketing Mix categories are themselves significantly interdependent. A number of examples can be used to illustrate this interdependence, for instance:

* the size of the salesforce (*Promotion*) depends on the distribution channel (*Place*) to be used. The more intensive is to be the distribution, the larger will be the salesforce. Alternatively, the more the company wishes to rely on wholesalers, agents or trade distributors, the smaller will be the salesforce but the more important becomes advertising to the final customer group;

* brand image (*Product*) must be reinforced by the pricing policy (*Price*) applied to the brand. Customers will expect to pay more for a reputable brand, but they will also expect the price charged to be consistent with their perceptions of the product;

* the amount and style of advertising and sales promotion (*Promotion*) will influence the consumer's perception of the product, which in turn must influence on-going company product and brand development activities (*Product*).

7) MANAGING THE MARKETING MIX

The effective management of the Marketing Mix must take this interdependence into account. Alterations to one element of the Marketing Mix can have repercussions within each category, or elsewhere within the Marketing Mix. Marketing Management must therefore take care to ensure that the alteration, which in itself appears to be sensible, does not adversely affect other significant components of the mix. For instance, an ill-judged price reduction may have an opposite effect to that desired. The price reduction, for instance carried out "on-pack", may have the effect of damaging the brand's market image and positioning. Or it may give rise to a level of customer price-sensitivity which was hitherto absent in the target market segment.

Conversely, a problem in one sector of the Marketing Mix may be solved by an adjustment in another. For instance, a product may carry a price which cannot easily be reduced or discounted, for instance because of the need to cover heavy Research and Development costs. This price might initially appear uncompetitive, but may be justified in the market place by additions to the features associated with the product such that consumers perceive the product to be effectively differentiated from the alternatives available. As long as the price and the product differentiation are perceived in a consistent or positive light, then the extra price will be viable.

The skill of the marketing manager therefore lies in understanding how the four categories of the Marketing Mix interact, and in being able to combine them in the most cost-effective manner such that the company's marketing objectives are satisfactorily achieved.

SUMMARY

The contents of this chapter are summarised in Table 18.1.

TABLE 18.1
Summary : Chapter Eighteen

SECTION	MAIN POINTS
1. The Marketing Mix defined	The Marketing Mix can be defined as the combination of detailed strategies; tactics; operational policies, programmes, techniques and activities, to which resources may be allocated such that the company's marketing objectives are achieved.
2. The Marketing Mix in context	The Marketing Mix is concerned with the realities and practicalities of how the company's marketing objectives may be turned into specific marketing plans and activities. The role of the Marketing Mix is to move objectives and plans into the reality of implementation and achievement.
3. The Marketing Mix	The Marketing Mix should be managed such that it ensures that the right product is appropriately promoted at the right price in the right place at the appropriate time so as to satisfy the needs of target customers in the chosen market segments.
4. The Four P's	The Marketing Mix can be described and analysed on the basis of the "Four P's", namely Product, Price, Place, Promotion.
5. Interdependence within each category	The various elements or component activities which make up each category are interdependent.
6. Interdependence between each category	The four Marketing Mix categories are themselves significantly interdependent.
7. Managing the Marketing Mix	The effective management of the Marketing Mix must take these interdependencies into account. Alterations to one element of the Marketing Mix can have repercussions

within each category, or elsewhere in the mix. Conversely, a problem in one area may be solved by an adjustment elsewhere in the mix. The skill of the marketing manager lies in understanding how the four categories of the Marketing Mix interact, and in being able to combine them in the most cost-effective manner such that the company's marketing objectives are satisfactorily achieved.

QUESTIONS FOR SELF REVIEW

1.   What is the Marketing Mix?

2.   Why is interdependence an important feature of the Marketing Mix? How should this interdependence be managed?

EXAMINATION QUESTIONS

Q34   Define what is meant by the term 'Marketing Mix' and explain its significance to marketing management.

(ABE)

Q35   Marketing mix decisions are among the most complex decisions facing marketing management. Discuss. (CIM)

Q36   'The marketing mix is not static, but must be responsive to changes in both the target market and the external business environment.' Discuss this statement.   (IIM)

Products
and
Product Management

"No product, no sale. Wrong product, no sale. Lousy support, no sale."

The next three chapters look at the management and development of the company's products or services. This activity is central to the management of the marketing mix. Whilst successful product management needs the effective support of the other activities involved in marketing management, no amount of high quality advertising, sales effort or dealer incentives will make up for poor quality products, badly designed or ineptly packaged. The customer may try the product once, but he or she will not come back for more!

19 The Product Life Cycle

INTRODUCTION

This chapter commences with a basic definition of product and service, and introduces the terminology used to describe the range of the company's products and brands.

The remainder of the chapter is devoted to an analysis of the Product Life Cycle, which is a fundamental concept within the theory and practice of marketing. The product life cycle shows the trends in sales and profitability of a particular product over its life cycle or evolution. The product life cycle concept represents a recognition of the fact that most products will have a finite market life, be it short or long.

This life span has clearly separate stages, just like the life span of an individual human being. These stages are described and analysed in detail, and summarised at the end of the chapter.

The analysis of the company's products and services, and the manner in which they are managed within the total marketing mix, is continued in chapters twenty and twenty-one.

CHAPTER CONTENTS

1) Definitions

2) The Product Mix

3) The Product Life Cycle

   3.1) Stages in the product life cycle

   3.2) The Introduction stage

   3.3) The Growth stage

   3.4) The Maturity stage

   3.5) The Decline stage

   3.6) The product life cycle stages summarised

Summary

1) DEFINITIONS

A product is defined *as something that is capable of satisfying a customer need or want*. That need or want may already exist, or it may be latent, that is, awaiting the development of the right product to meet this need. The Sony

"Walkman" personal hi-fi is a classic example of a product that met a latent need.

The term "service" has the same definition, and throughout this book the terms product and service are used interchangeably.

2) THE PRODUCT MIX

The product mix is *the range of the company's products and brands*. The nature and characteristics of these products and brands should be adapted to, and positioned on the demand patterns of the various target market segments into which the firm wishes to sell its goods. Market segmentation, customer targeting and product positioning were described in detail in earlier chapters. The product mix comprises the following elements:

* PRODUCT MIX – which is the complete range of the company's products, services and brands aimed at *all* of the relevant target markets and market segments;

* PRODUCT LINE– which are products, or ranges of products aimed at any one target market or customer type;

* MIX WIDTH – which is the number of Product Lines contained in the Product Mix;

* MIX DEPTH – which is the number of products within any *one* Product Line;

* MIX CONSISTENCY – which describes the relationship between Product Lines within the Product Mix. Are these lines complementary, as in the case of a confectionery manufacturer whose product lines are all based on chocolate? Or are they different, requiring widely differing investment and skills of manufacture, marketing and distribution? The UK company Thorn-EMI PLC, for example, manufactures a wide variety of industrial and consumer products, using a variety of technologies, processes and raw materials.

3) THE PRODUCT LIFE CYCLE

The Product Life Cycle is an important tool for analysis and planning of the marketing activity. *It shows the trends in SALES and PROFITABILITY of a particular product over its life cycle.* The product life cycle represents a recognition of the fact that most products will only have a finite market life, be it short as in the case of fashion goods, or long as in the case of certain types of industrial equipment. This life span, further, has clearly separate stages, *just like the life span of an individual human being.* These stages are shown in figure 19.1.

The shape of the curves in Figure 19.1 are based on a "normal" distribution. The *actual* shape of the curve, and the length of duration of the four constituent stages will, of course, vary for each product or brand. They will depend on the interaction of many variables, including:-

a) the emergence, growth or disappearance of markets and segments.

b) trends in available buyer spending capacity, real disposable income (etc).

c) technological developments which may lengthen or shorten the life cycle stages, for instance by permitting the rejuvenation of products, or rendering them obsolete.

d) changes in the tastes and preferences of consumers or buyers.

e) the effect of manufacturing or distribution cost changes on the price to the consumer, and relative movements in the price of competing or substitute products.

3.1) Stages in the product life cycle

There are four main stages in the product life cycle, namely:

INTRODUCTION

GROWTH

MATURITY

DECLINE

These four stages are described in detail below.

3.2) The Introduction stage

This stage will be dominated *by the need to establish the product in the market by building buyer and distributor*

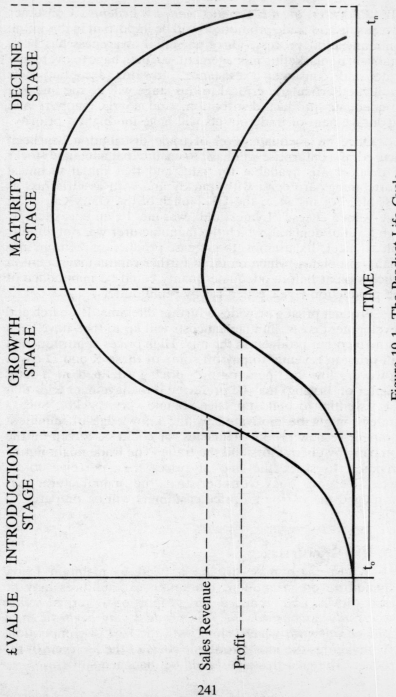

Figure 19.1. The Product Life Cycle.

AWARENESS of the product and its benefits. Consumer advertising and trade promotions will be important in this initial communication process. Once an initial awareness has been established, marketing management will then have to overcome trade and consumer "resistance" towards accepting new products. Particularly critical to this stage will be the building of adequate product distribution, and so the support and encouragement of trade outlets will have the highest priority.

Once an adequate level of trade distribution has been secured, the enterprise will have to ensure that adequate stocks of product are available for sale, and that initial technical shortcomings are dealt with quickly and with as little fuss as possible. For instance, the UK launch of the Dairy Crest soft blue-veined cheese "Lymeswold" was met by an unexpectedly high level of demand, which the manufacturer was not initially able to meet. Its attempts to increase production then ran into quality problems, which required further capital investment in process plant before adequate quality could be maintained at the production levels called for by retail outlets.

Product pricing provides a further dilemma. Research and development costs, and launch costs will up to then have been borne by other products in the mix. High prices at introduction will bring in revenue to pay off some of these R and D costs. However, low or "penetration" pricing (defined in a later chapter on Pricing) may be preferred if management feels that it is essential to build up sales volume very quickly. Such a strategy might be motivated by the knowledge of imminent competitive new product launches, or could be forced on the company by distributors and the trade. The trade might not be prepared to stock the line at prices they perceive to be "excessive", or may consider that the manufacturer has misjudged the maximum price customers will be prepared to pay.

3.3) The Growth stage

Whilst there may still be a need to maintain heavy expenditure on promotion, marketing expenditures may be eased down and reduced in proportional terms. *Once successfully established, the new product may begin to enjoy rapid sales growth* which, along with the lack of competition, may make this the most profitable stage of the life cycle of the product. The growth stage should be managed so that:

* a full demand base is built in the market.
* there is selective building of customer demand at the expense of existing or substitute product types marketed by competitors.
* there is the beginning of a search for other target market segments into which the product, once modified or differentiated, can be sold.

The growth stage is likely to see the emergence of competitive pressures, and the beginnings of downward pressure on high introductory prices if these have been used.

3.4) The Maturity stage

It is essential to company profitability and cash flow *that this stage be prolonged for as long as possible.* For well-established products and brands this should be a time for consolidation. Competition in the market place is mainly concerned with market share, so critical marketing activities need to be managed:

i) to maintain product distribution and customer access to the product.

ii) to maintain customer loyalty to the brand or product, and hence the rate of repurchase.

Whilst competitors in mature markets prefer if possible to avoid price competition (which in the end generally benefits none of them), competition over market share is likely to mean increased promotional costs, higher discounts to distributors or retailers (etc). Downward pressures on profit margins will be the result.

Attempts may be made to "stretch" the duration of the product's maturity. *Product stretching means finding new uses or applications for the product, so that its usefulness is prolonged and further market segments opened up.* For instance, whilst the market for monochrome television receivers is now generally limited in the UK, the product has found widespread application (and an entire new market) as the Visual Display Unit (VDU) and monitor for use with personal computers. Similarly, Lea and Perrins Worcester Sauce has found new favour as a flavouring for potato crisps and other snacks.

Alternatively, the product may undergo extensive modification with the aim of "recreating" both its market and its entire life cycle. Product modification and market extension are examined in more detail in Chapter Twenty.

3.5) The Decline stage

Whether for reasons of technical obsolescence, changes in customer or trade attitudes towards the product, over-familiarity with it, or the emergence of a better product elsewhere in the market, a stage may be reached when sales and profitability start a consistent and perhaps irreversible decline. Once management has recognised and accepted the inevitable, it has a number of choices, which include:

a) withdrawing all expenditure on the product above its variable cost of production, and perhaps raising its price. Demand for the product is then left to wither away, whilst the company diverts the remaining revenues from it towards other products or activities.

b) eliminating the product or service once demand for the product has dropped below a pre-determined threshold, particularly that where it is no longer bringing in any Contribution, (which is the difference between net sales revenue and total variable cost).

c) maintaining production and sale of the product on a restricted basis, for instance in those market segments in which there is still some residual brand loyalty. Marketing management may maintain the product's price and quality, protect the product or brand, and await developments. There are two reasons for doing this. The first is that marketers will protect and encourage brand loyal purchasing behaviour, since its discouragement can have undesirable knock-on effects elsewhere. The second is the hope that demand for the product may eventually increase again, especially where the market is affected by fashion cycles and trends. For instance, whilst the demand for long established food products like Marmite and Horlicks declined in the 1960's and 1970's, radical changes in food purchasing patterns have led to the re-emergence of favour for such traditional and healthy foodstuffs in the 1980's.

3.6) The Product Life Cycle Stages summarised

The four stages described above are summarised and compared in Table 19.2.

	INTRODUCTION	GROWTH	MATURITY	DECLINE
Sales	Low	Fast growth	Slow growth	Decline
Profits	Negligible	Peak levels	Declining	Low or zero
Cash Flow	Negative	Moderate	High	Laggardly
Research and Development Costs	Borne by other products	Borne by product	Borne by product, until paid off. Costs of modification or "stretching" may be incurred.	Paid off.
Customers	Innovative	Mass market	Mass market	Latecomers, laggards
Competitors	Few	Growing	Many rivals	Declining number
Management objective	Expand market	Market penetration	Defend share, extend duration of stage.	Operational productivity, minimise costs.
Marketing expenditure	High	High	Adequate to maintain market share and brand loyalty	Low
Marketing emphasis	Product awareness	Brand preference	Brand loyalty	Selected segments
Distribution	Patchy	Intensive	Intensive	Selected outlets
Price	High; or penetration(?)	Lower	Lowest	Low; or rising(?)
Product	Basic	Improved	Differentiated	Rationalized

Table 19.2. Product Life Cycle Stages.

SUMMARY

The contents of this chapter are summarised in Table 19.3.

TABLE 19.3
SUMMARY : CHAPTER NINETEEN

SECTION	MAIN POINTS
1. Definitions	A product or service is defined as something that is capable of satisfying a customer need or want.
2. The product mix	The product mix is the range of the company's products and brands. The product mix comprises the product line, mix width, mix depth and mix consistency.
3. The product life cycle	The product life cycle shows the trends in sales and profitability of a particular product over its life cycle. The life cycle represents a recognition of the fact that most products will only have a finite market life, whether this be short or long. The product life cycle has four main stages, namely Introduction, Growth, Maturity, Decline. These stages are shown in Figure 19.1 and summarised in Table 19.2.
3.2 Introduction Stage	This stage will be dominated by the need to establish the new product in the market by building buyer and distributor awareness of the product and its benefits.
3.3 Growth stage	Once successfully established, the new product may enjoy rapid sales growth which, together with the lack of competition, may make this stage relatively profitable.
3.4 Maturity stage	This stage is characterised by competition over market share, consolidation, and the encouragement of customer loyalty towards the product.

	It is essential to company profitability and cash-flow that this stage be prolonged for as long as possible.
3.5 Decline stage	Sales and profitability begin to decline, due to product obsolescence, changes in customer attitude or taste, over-familiarity with the product (etc), or the emergence of a better product elsewhere in the market.

20 Product Planning and Development

INTRODUCTION

This chapter on products and product management concentrates on two major issues. The first is concerned with the planning and development of new and existing products. As existing products near the end of their life cycle, they will either have to be revitalised, or replaced by new products. One of the major roles of the product management process within the marketing mix is to ensure the development of a smooth flow of new or updated products and services to replace those that will soon become obsolete.

Product development strategies may be either proactive (leading) or reactive (following). The success of new product introductions will depend on having an effective source of new ideas and innovations, which can be incorporated as unique selling propositions. These unique selling propositions must be relevant to the characteristics of the market segments on which the product is to be targeted, and must effectively differentiate the product so as to give it purchase appeal.

The chapter then goes on to examine the process by which new or rejuvenated products are actually developed, test marketed and launched. The critical relationship between new product development and cashflow management is highlighted. As new product development becomes more and more expensive, the need for existing products to contribute adequate cashflows becomes an increasingly important management priority.

CHAPTER CONTENTS

1) Product planning and development

    1.1) Implications of the product life cycle for marketing management

    1.2) Proactive product development strategies

    1.3) Reactive product development strategies

    1.4) Unique selling propositions

    1.5) New product sources

2) The product development process
    2.1) Test marketing and product launch
    2.2) Product modification and market extension
    2.3) Cashflow and product planning

Summary

Chapter Appendix 20(1): Protecting a new product

1) PRODUCT PLANNING AND DEVELOPMENT

1.1) Implications of the Product Life Cycle for Marketing management

A business enterprise needs to phase the introduction of new products so that its product mix is well distributed across the various stages of the product life cycle, without an undue concentration at any one point. Too many products at the same stage may age together, and present the risk of simultaneous obsolescence to a substantial proportion of the total product range.

Ideally, a business should have a product mix which has a varied "age structure", so that it has a range of products from "young" through "mature", and manages those products which are "elderly" so that their obsolescence does not unduly damage the future commercial prospects of the enterprise.

The business must therefore plan for a flow of profitable and cash generating products to maintain and support this age distribution, and to offset the development costs of new products.

1.2) Proactive product development strategy

The decision may be taken to undertake product development strategies that are *proactive*. This means deliberately taking the lead in new developments, and being the first to break new ground. Such a policy carries with it both the maximum risk of failure, and the greatest opportunity for the generation of profit and cash. Examples of proactive development strategies in the UK have included:

* the Barclaycard – the first UK credit card;
* the hovercraft;
* the Sinclair home computers (ZX 80 and its successors);
* Dairy Crest "Lymeswold" and "Melbury" cheeses.

249

The launch by Dairy Crest of its soft "Lymeswold" and "Melbury" cheeses met a clear market need. This was the increasing UK consumption of soft cheeses relative to the traditional hard cheeses such as Cheddar. The problem faced by Dairy Crest was that most of the soft cheeses consumed in the UK were imported, whilst most of the UK's production was of hard cheeses. Dairy Crest therefore created an entirely new type of product, which broke with the traditions of UK cheesemaking. Its two soft cheese brands are positioned in such a way as to meet the consumption patterns of UK soft cheese buyers, and have not only successfully taken market share from European competitors, but may well have increased the size of the UK soft cheese market as well.

1.3) Reactive product development strategy

Product development strategies may be designed to react to, or follow developments elsewhere. Such a strategy lessens the risk of product development, since the enterprise will try to learn from the mistakes and failures of its more adventurous competitors. At the same time, proactive strategies carry the risk of delayed market acceptance. Companies using reactive strategies will wait until someone else has prepared the ground, and launch under more favourable circumstances.

Examples of reactive development strategies in the UK have included:

* The Access card, which was launched onto a market made more favourable by the pathfinding efforts of the Barclaycard.
* the ICL and IBM personal computers, which followed in the wake of the Apple, Commodore "Pet" and Tandy TRS 80 microcomputers.
* the Vauxhall "Astra", whose aerodynamic shape exploits the lengthy and costly period of market familiarisation created by the Ford "Sierra".

Reactive development strategies can also take the form of *fast seconding*. This means the development and marketing of competitive products shortly after their introduction by other companies. Fast seconding is sometimes described as "me too" marketing. It exploits the promotional activity undertaken by rivals, especially where the fast seconder is able to gain intensive distribution on a very short time scale. Fast seconding is common in toy marketing, where one range of electronic or space toys, action figures (etc) is rapidly followed by other ranges of very similar toys.

1.4) Unique Selling Propositions

New or modified products often fail to obtain market acceptance. *One of the key factors in determining the likely acceptance and success of new products lies in the degree to which they possess significant advantages over competing products.* Such advantages are sometimes described as Unique Selling Propositions (USP's) or "Product Plusses" and some examples are listed below:

a) *accurate product or brand positioning* on the wants and requirements of specific target market segments. For instance, simple and reliable electrically powered hover mowers perform a similar function to vacuum cleaners in the home. They meet the needs of people who have small garden lawns and wish to keep their grass tidy at the minimum expense of money, time and effort. These people are not particularly concerned with lawn appearance (cylinder mowers leave attractive "stripes" after lawn mowing but hover mowers do not), and gardening is more likely to be perceived by them as a "chore" than an enjoyable hobby or pastime.

b) *functional advantages*. These attributes include product or service form, design, quality and reliability. These should relate to the usage context in which the purchaser will make use of the product.

c) *performance*. How well does the product or service perform within the usage context for which it was purchased, relative to customer requirements or expectations of its performance (and manufacturer claims)? The success of Land Rover or Foden Trucks stems from the capacity of their product to stand up to the demands of the most rigorous operating conditions, for instance in military applications.

d) *purchaser psychology*. How well does the product or service accord with the role and motivational needs of the customer in buying and using it? This issue was dealt with in an earlier chapter. Does ownership of the product make life easier by reducing the amount of personal effort in accomplishing   particular   tasks?   Fully   automated

251

household appliances (central heating, washing machines and driers, cookers, freezers, etc) are marketed on the basis of freeing the housewife from domestic drudgery, and allowing her opportunities (unheard of to past generations of exhausted mothers) to better care for her family. Alternatively, does use of the product enhance the customer's ego, self esteem or ambition? Or does it confer the respect of others or enhance self-image?

e) *product philosophy*. What are the customer's perceptions about the product and "what it does best"? How does this perception, or the philosophy presented by promotional media, fit the perceptions of the target market segments? For instance, is Glenfiddich whisky perceived as "superior" and does its purchase confer status on the host who offers it to his guests? Is first class rail travel simply "better than second class" or is it supposed to be "de luxe"? Should first class rail travel really mean de luxe? Is the extra fare incurred in travelling first class really worthwhile compared with the service and fares on internal passenger flights?

f) *product presentation*. A product or service may derive significant selling advantage if its presentation combines and enhances all of the product's advantages, and builds up its philosophy in the mind of the potential customer. Similarly it may reinforce brand loyal behaviour by maintaining a favourable image in the minds of existing customers.

g) *market advantage*. This will be based upon favourable cost, volume and price factors relative to competing and substitute products already on the market.

h) *consistency of positioning, packaging and presentation*. Consumers like consistency and stability. People hate change for change's sake. Maintaining a consistent and stable policy of product positioning, packaging and presentation may produce a perception by the consumer *that he or she can rely on the brand*. It always looks the same, it performs the same, it always delivers the same image or philosophy, and gives the same satisfaction. Consumers like to be able to rely on brands and to treat them as old and trusted friends. One UK example of such consistency is Black Magic chocolate (introduced in 1934), which has remained the consistent brand leader in the luxury plain chocolate market. Another example is Persil washing powder, with its caring, family image.

1.5) New product sources

Product development and modification must, of course, be related to (i) market research findings, (ii) company knowledge of consumer and buyer behaviour, and (iii) product positioning requirements of market segmentation and customer targeting. Actual sources of new products and new product ideas are many, but they can be divided into two main sources, internal and external, as in Table 20.1.

Whatever source is used, marketing management needs to ensure that new concepts and ideas can be developed by the company *amid an organisational climate or culture that positively encourages innovation, achievement and success*. Indeed, many experts have suggested that obtaining effective innovatory behaviour in new product development and marketing has proved to be one of the most difficult organisational problems faced by manufacturing companies in the UK, and especially in those that operate in industrial markets.

2) THE PRODUCT DEVELOPMENT PROCESS

Once the enterprise has identified the opportunity or need for a particular new product or new service development (NPD), its response (let us call it a new product "idea") must pass three basic hurdles. These are described in turn, thus:

a) *organisational capacity* – can the enterprise actually turn the idea into reality? Can it make and market the product, and does it have the resources (operational and financial) and the expertise to make a success of the exercise? If the company cannot achieve success on its own, can it find a partner to assist it, or can it licence the development and manufacture to someone else, retaining the marketing rights?

b) *concept testing* – new product ideas are often subjected to basic "concept testing". This is an attempt to gauge consumer or buyer reaction to the concepts making up the new product idea, and occurs at a very early stage in the development process. Nowadays, concept testing is usually carried out by specialist agencies who have developed skills at assessing the likely acceptability of the product.

| | EXTERNAL SOURCES | |
INTERNAL SOURCES	Planned Use	Non Planned Use
(1) Market research findings, market feedback, trade comments (etc);	(1) Product development agencies, design agencies;	(1) Unsponsored inventors;
(2) Company knowledge of consumer and buyer behaviour;	(2) Sponsored inventors;	(2) Patent agents;
(3) Product positioning requirements from market segmentation studies;	(3) Sponsored research and development;	(3) Published sources (trade and technical press, etc);
(4) Market gap analysis (seeking unexploited gaps, segments or niches within the market);	(4) Bringing in ideas from overseas markets and establishing them in the U.K.;	(4) Exhibitions and trade fairs;
(5) Market, sales and technological trends and forecasts (e.g. demographic trends; changing patterns of home ownership, food consumption or purchase of consumer durables, (etc));	(5) Licensing from other companies;	(5) New material developments or new process developments;
(6) Developing new images or brands for existing own products;	(6) Franchising from other companies;	(6) Companies relinquishing products or brand names; companies undertaking divestments.
(7) Development or modification of existing products (own or competitive);	(7) Following up expired patents;	
(8) Copies of competitive products; fast seconding;	(8) Joint development programmes e.g. with government departments, military authorities, other companies (etc);	
(9) Joint developments with major customers;	(9) Mergers with other companies who have desirable product ranges, brands or processes;	
(10) Company Research and Development function.	(10) Takeovers of other companies with desirable product ranges, brands or processes (e.g. the purchase by Beecham of Horlicks, Bovril, Lucozade, Macleans and Aquafresh).	

Table 20.1. New Product Sources.

Two examples can be given. The concept of marmalades containing whisky flavour or other flavours taken from alcoholic beverages was rejected at an early stage, as being unlikely to achieve mass popularity! On the other hand, the concept of flavoured potato crisps was accepted with enthusiasm, and flavoured crisps are now the mainstay of the crisp market.

c) *product testing* – this is the detailed testing and evaluation of prototypes and pre-production models. Again, the services of specialist agencies are often used. The people selected for the testing process will be asked to respond to, and evaluate the various characteristics and attributes of the product samples they are given. An attempt is also made to evaluate their likely "intention to buy", when the product is compared with its competitors at a variety of suggested prices. Detailed product testing is widely used in the development of new motor car models, and considerable reliance is placed on the findings.

These three hurdles are part of a detailed process by which the enterprise learns, develops and modifies the product or service. *At the same time, the marketing support for the new product should be developed, so that it is complementary to, and supportive of the product.*

As the development of the product and its marketing support gather momentum, it will become essential to seek and obtain:

i) *detailed consumer reaction to pre-production and production samples.* This would be needed to make sure that no obvious faults have been overlooked, and to gauge precisely the kind of approach that should be taken in promotional activity undertaken at "test marketing", (see section 2.1 below)

ii) *trade support.* Dealer/wholesaler/retailer support of a new product is essential. The trade must be happy with the product, with the after-sales service policy, and with the marketing and promotional support to be given to the new product by the manufacturer. Otherwise it will be negative towards the product and refuse to give it shelf-space. And even if the trade takes the product, the appearance of being reluctant to endorse the product, or a lack of enthusiasm can nullify the effects of even the most brilliant (and costly) promotional campaigns.

Whilst negative reactions at any point in the development process may result in the abandonment of the product, it will be of particular importance to make a GO AHEAD/ TERMINATE decision prior to the decision to submit the product to test marketing. Test marketing is dealt with in Section 2.1 below.

The sequence of events in new product development (NPD) is summarised in Figure 20.2.

2.1) Test marketing and product launch.

Test marketing means putting the new product or service on sale in a test region. It will be supported by the kind of promotion, dealer incentives (etc) that have been proposed for the eventual nationwide launch of the product. It is used to check on:

* consumer and trade reaction to the product;
* the effectiveness of the marketing support;
* the likely commercial viability of the product.

The choice of test location provides a problem. Commonly, television (IBA) or radio (ILR) areas will be used, since audience figures in them are available. This is important if television or radio are the main promotional media to be used for advertising. Alternatively, specific company retail audit areas may be used, which give comparative sales statistics for stores in different locations.

The ideal test area will contain a reasonable cross-section of the new product's likely purchasers, so demographic factors such as age distribution, socioeconomic and income patterns and regional lifestyle will have to be taken into account. Similarly, the area should contain a reasonably representative selection of trade, wholesale or retail outlets, so that trade reaction to the product can be gauged. It will also be important to learn how the trade treats the product and handles customer reaction to it.

The decision to launch the product on a wider regional, or nationwide basis will depend on two sets of results from the test market. The first will comprise qualitative data about consumer and trade reaction to the product and its support. For instance, the retail trade might not like the packaging, or consumer reaction might indicate that the price at launch could be increased. The second comprises *the relationship between (i) trial first purchase rate and (ii) the trial repurchase rate.* This relationship is described in Table 20.3.

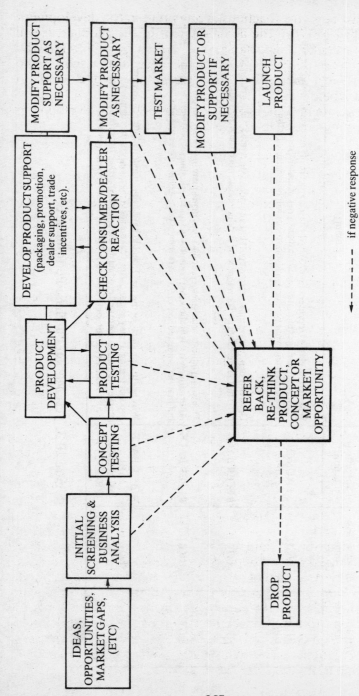

Figure 20.2. The New Product Development Process.

if negative response

Trial first purchase rate	Trial repurchase rate	Suggested action	Comment
HIGH	HIGH	LAUNCH	Was the test market representative? Was the test market really necessary? Is there a risk of over-estimating eventual demand? Is there a risk of under-estimating total demand after launch and what production level, stocks will be available by then?
HIGH	LOW	REFER BACK	Does this signify good marketing support but an inadequate product? Does the product need further research and development? Product should not be launched yet.
LOW	HIGH	REFER BACK	This would indicate a satisfactory product, but inadequate marketing support. Alternatively it might show that both product and marketing support were adequate, but that the estimated size of the market must be re-examined or reduced.
LOW	LOW	REFER BACK OR ABANDON PRODUCT	Why has this product got this far? It should have been abandoned after concept or product testing. It may also show up weaknesses in the quality of the company's marketing management and product development expertise. It is probably time to call in a consultant or recruit some better qualified and more experienced staff.

Figure 20.3. Test Market Purchase Performance.

Once the lessons of the test market have been learned, adequate distribution secured and the marketing support scaled-up to cope with a wider regional, or national launch, the final decisions can be taken. The product may be launched and a new life cycle commenced.

2.2) Product modification and market extension

The product life cycle, and common sense, indicate that marketing management cannot expect endless performance from its products or brands. At some point, the rate of growth of sales will slacken, stagnate or decline. Whilst management should by then have ensured that its new product development programme will provide new and vigorous products to augment or replace older or perhaps near-exhausted ones, it may prove difficult to relinquish long-established products or brands. Large sums may have been spent on the development of market acceptance and brand loyalty, and on the building of good relationships with the various channels of distribution.

The problem of product decline or withdrawal may further be complicated where the company markets a wide range of goods and services. A number of products may be manufactured on the same plant, or joint-products or by-products may be produced. In such cases, it may not be feasible to withdraw these products, since they result from processes required for the manufacture of other products. Therefore, an alternative to product withdrawal may have to be sought. This alternative is that of *product modification and market extension,* and includes the following possibilities:

a) continue manufacturing and pass on the marketing rights to another business which has greater market access, complementary products (etc).

b) continue marketing the product, but cease manufacture. The product might be imported from a low cost producer (say, in the Far East) and demand stimulated by price reductions.

c) undertake more detailed market segmentation studies, allowing a suitably modified product to be positioned on a series of new segments or niches.

d) export the product into the lesser developed economies, perhaps establishing a manufacturing base there and importing adequate supplies for the existing home market.

e) re-vitalise the product, and extend its demand (that is, moving it back as far as possible to the left of the life cycle pattern shown in Figure 19.1) by any of, or a combination of:–

* style changes;
* functional changes;
* quality changes;
* brand name changes.

2.3) Cashflow and product planning

New product development is often a very costly business. The Ford Sierra cost £600 million, Philips' Compact Disc £100 million. Such expenditure needs to be supported by cashflows brought in by sales of products in their growth and maturity stages. *One of the most critical tasks of marketing management is that of ensuring a long term flow of products across the life cycle, each of which is managed in such a way as to maximise the cashflows it generates. And satisfactory cashflows will only result from the right products profitably positioned on the right markets, correctly priced, distributed and supported by promotional activities. Ineffective product planning and management may result in cashflows inadequate to support the kind of product development that the market calls for.*

As the new product development stakes in the market increase, and the need to ensure adequate future cashflows becomes more urgent, the role of cashflow management within the product planning strategy becomes more and more essential. It is an issue which is dealt with in a later chapter.

SUMMARY

The contents of this chapter are summarised in Table 20.4.

TABLE 20.4
Summary : Chapter Twenty

SECTION	MAIN POINTS
1.1 Implications of the Product Life Cycle for marketing management	A business enterprise needs to phase the introduction of new products so that its product mix is well distributed across the various stages of the product life cycle, without an undue

concentration at any one point. Ideally, a business should have a product mix with a varied age structure, and must therefore plan for a flow of profitable and cash generating products to maintain this age distribution, and offset the development costs of new products.

1.2 Proactive product development strategy	This means deliberately taking the lead in new product development, and being the first to break new ground.
1.3 Reactive product development strategy	This reacts to, or follows developments made elsewhere. Such a strategy is likely to be less risky. Reactive strategies may take the form of "fast-seconding", which means the development and marketing of products similar to those recently launched by competitors.
1.4 Unique selling propositions (USP's)	One of the key determinants of new product acceptance and success lies in the degree to which new products possess significant advantages over competing products. These advantages are called "unique selling propositions". They include (a) accurate product or brand positioning: (b) functional advantages; (c) performance; (d) purchaser psychology; (e) product philosophy; (g) market advantage; (h) consistency of positioning, packaging and presentation.
1.5 New product sources	New product sources may be internal or external. They are summarised in Table 20.1. New concepts and ideas need to be developed in an organisational climate or culture that encourages innovation and success.
2 Product development process	Summarised in Fig. 20.2. A new product idea must pass three basic hurdles, namely (a) analysis of organisational capacity; (b) concept testing;

(c) product testing. At the same time, the marketing support for the new product should be developed, so that it is complementary to the product. The new product development process must also obtain (i) detailed consumer reaction to pre-production and production samples; (ii) trade support.

2.1 Test marketing and product launch

Test marketing means putting the new product or service on sale in a "test region". It will be supported by the kind of promotion, dealer incentives (etc) that have been proposed for the eventual nationwide launch. It is used to check on consumer and trade reaction to the product, the effectiveness of the marketing support, and the likely commercial viability of the product. The final decision on full launch will depend on qualitative data about trade and consumer reaction, and quantitative data on the relationship between (i) trial first purchase rate and (ii) trial repurchase rate (Table 20.3).

2.2 Product modification and market extension

Where it may prove difficult to relinquish long-established products near the end of their life cycle, product modification and market extension may be considered as an alternative to product withdrawal.

2.3 Cashflow and product planning

New product development is often very expensive. Such expenditure needs to be supported by cashflows brought in by the sales of products in their growth and maturity stages. Cashflow management is therefore of critical importance both to company and marketing management.

CHAPTER APPENDIX 20(1)
PROTECTING A NEW PRODUCT

If the specification and/or design of a new product is not properly protected, it leaves the way open for anyone to make a copy and *legally* to claim it as their own.

There are three main methods in the UK of protecting any innovation from such abuse by others. These are:

    i)   patenting

    ii) trade mark registration

    iii) industrial design registration

Each is briefly described below.

i) Patenting

A patent is 'a document issued by the Patent Office giving the proprietor monopoly rights relating to an invention, and effective within the United Kingdom. In return the inventor must provide a full disclosure of his invention.'

Once granted, a patent gives the patentee the right to prevent exploitation of the innovation by others. It allows High Court action to be taken against anyone who exploits the invention without consent, and enables claims to be made for any damages to which the patentee may be legally entitled. The existence of a patent may also deter a potential infringer.

Once a patent is granted it gives the patentee the right to prevent exploitation in the UK for up to 20 years. However, a patent must also be taken out for *any other country* in which the patentee wishes the innovation to be protected.

Is the invention patentable?

Not all inventions qualify for the grant of a patent. The UK Patent Act 1977 lays down that, to be patentable, an invention must

    (a)   be new

    (b)   involve an inventive step

    (c)   be capable of industrial application; and

    (d)   not be 'excluded'

a) Is the invention new?

To be patentable, an invention must never have been disclosed publicly in any way, anywhere, before the date on which the originator files an application for a patent.

It is surprising how often 'new' ideas have been thought of already, so it is always advisable to check whether the invention really is new, especially if you do not have a thorough and wide knowledge of the technical field in which it resides.

To check whether an idea has been published anywhere in the world may be an expensive undertaking. But for practical purposes, and for most types of invention, a sensible first step would be to check through trade and technical magazines, text books and reference books. If you want to go further than this and attempt a more comprehensive search you are advised to consult a *patent agent* or a professional patent searcher. (Or instead, obtain the booklet 'Patents: a source of technical information', available from the Patent Office. This booklet gives advice on searches. It also lists those libraries in the UK which hold collections of patent specifications, abridgements or abstracts).

b) Inventive step

An invention involves an inventive step if, when compared with what is already known, it would not be obvious to someone with a good knowledge and experience of the subject.

c) Industrial application

In order to be patentable an invention *must be capable of being made or used in some kind of industry*. This means that the invention must take the practical form of an apparatus or device, a product — such as some new material or substance, or an industrial process or method of operation. 'Industry' should be understood in its broadest sense of including any useful, practical activity as distinct from purely intellectual or aesthetic activity and does not necessarily imply the use of a machine or the manufacture of an article. It includes agriculture.

d) 'Excluded' inventions

No matter how ingenious, unusual or beneficial an idea may be, an invention is not patentable if it is *merely* a discovery;

scientific theory or mathematical method; mental process; literary, artistic or aesthetic creation; a scheme or method for doing a mental act; playing a game; doing business or presenting information. Of course, if it necessarily involves more than the mere mental aspect, so that it has physical features, for example special apparatus needed to play a new game, and so is capable of industrial application, then it may be patentable.

However, even if the invention meets all of these requirements you still cannot get a patent for it if it is a new animal or plant variety, or a method of diagnosis practised on the human or animal body or of treatment thereof by therapy or surgery, nor if the publication or exploitation of it would generally be expected to encourage offensive, immoral or anti-social behaviour. (Certain plant varieties may, however, be protected in the United Kingdom under the Plant Varieties and Seeds Act 1964, but the Patent Office does not deal with this. It is administered by the Plant Variety Rights Office).

ii) Trade Mark Registration

A trade mark is 'a mark used on or in relation to goods to identify a connection in the course of trade between the goods and a manufacturer or merchant, thus distinguishing those goods from others, i.e. a trade mark is used to identify goods as the product of a particular manufacturer or as merchandise of a particular trader.

A trade mark is a valuable asset in marketing, and as such should be protected. *A firm uses the chosen symbol and words to establish an identity and reputation for its goods.* By always relating, say, high quality or good value for money to a product and its trademark, the firm can encourage the consumer to buy the product on recognition of the mark, *in preference to a similar one.*

Such brand loyalty is of crucial importance to the company. If someone else were to use (abuse) the trademark this would lead to 'confusion and deception of the public', who might associate the wrong goods with the trademark and reputation attaching to their rightful owner. It could also 'deprive the rightful user of some of his business.'

Obviously, then, it is worthwhile to protect a trademark by *registering* it. This allows the registrant 'the exclusive right to use the mark in relation to the goods for which it is registered.' Any

infringement of this right allows the owner of the trademark to take
action through the courts.

iii) Industrial Design Registration

If a design relies on its visual appeal, it can be protected against
imitation by registering an industrial design. 'A *design* as protected
by registration . . . is the outward appearance of an article. Only
the appearance given by its actual shape, configuration, pattern or
ornamentation can be protected, not any general underlying idea.'

This form of protection differs from patenting in that it does
not have to involve an inventive step. Design registration has two
other advantages:

* it is relatively inexpensive in the UK;
* it gives the proprietor 'the sole right in the United Kingdom
  . . . for an initial period of five years, to make or import
  for sale, hire or use in business such articles bearing the
  design as registered or a design not substantially different'.

Infringement of these terms allows the proprietor to take High Court
action against any offender. Thus, for significantly less than the cost
of patenting, the standard of protection afforded is still substantial.

As with patenting, it is necessary to take similar protective measures
in any other country, identified as a potential market, in which design
registration is possible.

REFERENCES

Introducing patents — a guide for inventors
Patent Office

Basic facts about patents for inventions in the UK
Patent Office

Basic facts series — Patent Office, on:
    Patents
    Registered Trade and Service Marks
    Registered Designs
    Copyright

Search and Advisory Service — Patent Office

What is Intellectual Property? — Patent Office

Protecting innovation DTI for Patent Office

Trade marks, registered trade marks and patent agents
Chartered Institute of Patent Agents, London

Protection of industrial designs HMSO

Introducing design registration DTI for Patent Office

USEFUL ADDRESSES

The Patent Office
State House
66-71 High Holborn
London WC1R 4TP

Institute of Patent Agents
Staple Inn Building
London WC1V 7PZ

Institute of Trade Mark Agents
69 Cannon Street
London EC4N 5AB

21 Brand and Product Management

INTRODUCTION

The final chapter on products and product management deals with a variety of issues. It begins with an analysis of brand strategy and management. A brand is a name given by a manufacturer or supplier to one (or a number) of its products or services. These products may also carry a specific name, in addition to the brand name. Brand and product names are used to identify and differentiate products from their competitors. They facilitate recognition, and where customers have built-up a favourable attitude towards the product, may speed the individual buyer through the purchase decision process. Individual purchasers will filter out unfavoured or unknown brands, and the continued purchase of the branded product will reinforce the brand-loyal behaviour.

The chapter then turns to a brief look at the functional and marketing value of packaging. It continues with an analysis of some of the general problems involved in new product planning and development, and the analysis is illustrated with a case study based upon the UK foodstuffs industry.

CHAPTER CONTENTS

1) Brand strategy
   1.1) Multiproduct brands
   1.2) Multibrand products
   1.3) Manufacturer's brand and retailer's own brand

2) Product names
   2.1) Trademarks

3) Packaging

4) Problems of new product planning and development

5) An illustrative case study

Summary

Recommended Reading

Questions for self-review

Examination questions

1) BRAND STRATEGY

A "Brand" is a name given by a manufacturer to one (or a number) of its products or services. It might be the manufacturer's own name, such as Heinz or Philips. It might be a name unconnected with the name of the manufacturer (or provider of the service), such as Golden Wonder, Horlicks, or Next. Or it might be a name used by a retailer, such as Marks and Spencer, Sainsbury's or British Home Stores, who do not manufacture products themselves.

Brands are used to differentiate products from their competitors, and to facilitate recognition. The potential influence a brand name can have is enormous. For instance, the products of Kelloggs, Nestlé and Heinz, well supported as they are by advertising and promotion, are market leaders in the grocery field, and are to be found stocked on the shelves of almost every supermarket and food retailer in the land. Everyone has heard of names such as Hoover, Rolls Royce or Toshiba. Everyone knows that Cadbury makes and markets chocolate confectionery, and most children will have drunk Coca Cola!

Indeed, the use and promotional support of brand names is a major factor in sustaining manufacturer capacity to identify and market its own consumer goods in the face of pressure from retailers, and their preference for retail "own brands". *Consumer recognition and perceptions of different products are affected by their response to brand names.* Different brand names will cause them to see broadly similar products or services in different ways. People regard Kellogg's cornflakes or Nescafé as "better" than their competitors and will pay more for them. Some people perceive Volvo cars as superior because they are Swedish. Others will only buy branded Japanese hi-fi equipment because Japanese origin is seen as synonymous with quality.

Brand names are important to consumer behaviour because they "speed" the potential customer through the kind of decision process described in an earlier chapter. Customers seeing a favoured brand (to which they may exhibit *brand-loyal* behaviour), may cut short the analysis of alternatives prior to the purchase decision, and proceed more rapidly towards the purchase. Brand loyal behaviour may lessen the perceived "difficulty" or "confusion" of the purchase process to the would-be buyer. *Therefore suppliers will be at pains to build-up, encourage and reinforce brand-loyal behaviour.*

1.1) Multiproduct brands

Where multiproduct or "family" brands are used, one or a limited number of brand names is applied to a variety of products. Examples include Heinz foodstuffs, ICL computers or Mattel toys. Multiproduct or family brands have a promotional advantage in that awareness and reputation can be built up over a whole range of products or services that carry the same brand name. As a result, new products may more speedily find trade and consumer acceptance, as long as the market perceives the product as being appropriate to the brand range. On the other hand, a poor product can have a disproportionate effect in damaging the reputation of the brand. *Effective and consistent brand management,* as in the UK case of Black Magic chocolate or Persil washing powder, then becomes a key task of the company's marketing management.

1.2) Multibrand products

Where multibrand products are used, one company will use a range of different brand names, and may even have several brand names within one particular product line. United Biscuits and General Foods employ a wide variety of brand names, such as McVitie's, Huntley and Palmer, and Maxwell House. Similarly, soap manufacturers use many different brand names, such as Palmolive, Imperial Leather, Lux and Sunlight.

Separate brands may be regarded as appropriate where products have been developed for, and positioned on clearly defined target market segments, and marketing policy is aimed at developing a clear and identifiable *brand-segment relationship.* For instance, in the UK, Sunlight washing up liquid is formulated and aimed at purchasers with families, who have regular and heavy amounts of washing up to do. Fairy Liquid is aimed at younger housewives who are concerned with their appearance, and who may also be caring for young children.

1.3) Manufacturer's brand and retailer's "own" brand

Some manufacturers make products which are sold under a *retailer's own brand or label* (eg Sainsbury's or Marks and Spencer), as well as (or instead of) products sold under their own brand name. Contracts to manufacture for retail sale under "own" brand may permit the building of production volume, encourage cost reduction and bring in Contribution. Such contracts *may* permit stable production planning and long production runs, which are then sold without incurring much marketing or promotional expenditure. Indeed, it may be the only way in the UK to supply retail chains such as Sainsbury, Marks and Spencer or Waitrose, because such firms mainly sell products under their own label.

However, supplying for own brand sale puts the retailer in a powerful position, since the retailer controls the distribution, pricing and marketing of the product. The supplier may have little control over the price he receives from the retailer for his products, and indeed may find that his customer demands the right to determine and control his costs. At the same time he will have to conform exactly to the specifications, stock levels and delivery pattern laid down at the time he signed the contract. In the end, not only can the supplier lose control over the marketing of his products, but he can lose control over the running of the whole business itself if he becomes too dependent on any one retailer customer. This is a fundamental issue in marketing management, and it is also examined in later chapters.

2) PRODUCT NAMES

In addition to brands, products often carry a specific name, such as the Austin-Rover Group's "Montego", or Parker "Arrow" pens. *The use of a name reinforces the product differentiation value of the brand, and assists in the exact recognition and recall of the product by the purchaser.*

Again, the product name assists the capacity of the brand name to speed the would-be buyer through the purchase decision process. The customer can develop loyalty towards a named product, which can easily be recognised and selected from amongst a potentially confusing variety of competing or substitute products. The likelihood of such favoured or selective treatment will be encouraged where the product name establishes a *specific image* by which the customer perceives the product and can relate to it. This attitude formation and identification was analysed in the earlier chapters on consumer and buyer behaviour.

A product name must be appropriate to the product and the image it is trying to communicate to a potential purchaser. One car manufacturer markets a car called a "Violet", but in the UK would it call another model a "Pansy"? One UK chain of clothing retailers is called "Richard Shops", but might it

271

have been called "Herbert Shops" instead? The wrong name could ruin an otherwise perfect launch: Fiat introduced into the UK market a car called the "Argenta". The car was launched here during the Falklands conflict between the UK and Argentina. Another, more English, name might have been better received!

The product name is used to assist product positioning and to convey some kind of feeling, quality or promise. For instance, the retail chain store name "Next" aims to imply mobility, a clothes store to move on to, *and up to,* being targeted at men and women between (say) 18 and 30 with a relatively high level of real disposable income to spend on suitably fashionable clothes. *In other words, the name should contain some hint of the benefit to be gained from purchase.* For example, the name might accord with the purchaser's personality. The Sony Walkman is not intended for those of a sedentary disposition! A name might instead be aspirational, as in the case of Pomagne and Babycham, which are inexpensive substitutes for the real thing (!), champagne.

If, on the other hand, the name is meaningless (like Omo or BL Cars) then the benefits of the product have to be more fully communicated and promoted, incurring extra expense and effort. Such names offer no marketing benefit.

2.1) Trademarks

To be protected from unauthorised use, brands and product names have to be registered as *trademarks.* Perhaps the most famous of all is Rolls Royce, unauthorised commercial use of which name is fiercely prosecuted whenever it occurs. There are about 250,000 "live" trademarks and registered names in the UK, the oldest of which belong to the brewers Bass. There are another million names on the official register. These names cannot be used unless an effective legal challenge is made to their owner, or the owner is prepared to sell.

The registration of trademarks and names sometimes presents problems. Names that would deliberately confuse or mislead customers would not be accepted by the authorities. Female names cannot be registered for cosmetics in the UK, and the use of a colour, on its own, would now raise eyebrows (!) Older readers may remember Pink Paraffin and Esso Blue? The brand name would be protected if registered, but generally the use of a colour word would not.

The registered name or trademark of a successful product or service can become a valuable and appreciating asset. It has identity, visibility, personality and recognition value. It can be franchised, licensed or merchandised. For instance, many luxury products carry the name "Dunhill" or "Orient Express". Its potency can be enhanced by advertising and promotion, yet it can itself exert a powerful effect on that promotional activity. Successful names include Beecham's "Night Nurse", Lever Brothers' "Persil", Rowntree's "Black Magic", Nestlé's "Nescafé" and Ford's "Cortina", "Escort" and "Sierra".

As in other areas of marketing management, there are now many specialist agencies to assist in finding product names. These agencies also deal with the complexities of legal registration and protection of trademarks. Their work is a recognition of the increasingly demanding and professional role that marketing management must nowadays play in the affairs of the business in which they work.

3) PACKAGING

The packaging of both consumer and industrial products has become an important part of the product management activity. In the consumer goods area, changes in retail patterns towards self-service and supermarket/hypermarket organisation, the increase in the number and variety of products available, and the growth of retailer power have meant *that packaging must give any one product an impact in situ*. In the industrial goods field, packaging must be attractive yet strong enough to withstand all but the most abusive handling in shipment, and be light enough to minimise transport costs. Packaging needs to fulfil a number of requirements, including:

i) *protection of the product* – the product will need protection from its environment, to prevent oxidation, damage or deterioration, loss of colour or flavour (etc), and from the handling it receives in shipment or at the point of sale. Its packaging will need to fit the physical requirements of storage and transport, for instance where cases are stacked on pallets and moved in standard container loads. It may also have to withstand wide variations in climatic conditions in export markets.

ii) *trade appeal* – the physical properties of the packaging, and the image it conveys must appeal to the trade. Otherwise they may not feel it is a suitable item to stock, since

273

they are interested in a high rate of stock turnover. Well presented, well protected and undamaged goods will be a basic trade requirement.

iii) *consumer convenience* – the packaging must be safe and convenient for the consumer to use. Can the packaging be opened relatively easily? Can it be reclosed or resealed while the contents are being consumed, and keep the products fresh? Does it actually add to the qualities of the product, for instance in assisting its processing or consumption? For instance, polystyrene sleeves around glass soft drinks bottles fulfil three objectives:-

* they identify and promote the product;
* they protect the glass container;
* they assist insulation, for instance keeping the contents cool after the bottle has been taken out of the refrigerator.

iv) *sales promotion* – packaging is used to communicate information about the product to the customer, and build perceptions about it. It may enhance the appearance of the product and differentiate it from its competitors. Everyone in the UK has seen the bright gold and shiny black packets used by two well known competing brands of king size cigarettes! Certainly, the packaging should be co-ordinated with, and assist, the wider promotional efforts of advertising and in-store promotion. Similarly, the higher the product price, the more likely is the customer to expect luxurious packaging, as in the perfume or luxury gifts markets.

v) *design co-ordination* – the relationship between marketing and design is dealt with in a later chapter. There should be a relationship between the form and design of the product, and its packaging. Whilst this need is obvious in consumer goods markets, it is also true of industrial goods markets where, for instance, pre-formed wood and polystyrene packaging, covered with polythene film, is increasingly used in trade outlets to show off the shape, design and attractiveness of the product.

vi) *image co-ordination* – the relationship between marketing and corporate image is dealt with in a later chapter. Both product and packaging design should be co-ordinated with, and complementary to the corporate image portrayed by the organisation as a whole. This is particularly important where the enterprise wishes to establish in the mind of the purchaser a link between the product (or service) and its manufacturer. Such a link may serve to:-

* offset the development of retailer power and its influence over consumer goods marketing;

* make the customer aware of other products or services marketed by the supplier. Satisfaction with one product may lead to trying others, and build up a favourable image of the supplier in the mind of the buyer. This is particularly important in industrial goods markets where buying is often controlled by centralised purchasing departments. Such departments monitor the quality and reliability of their suppliers, and also depend on requisitioning departments for an assessment of products and suppliers when there is a new, or changed buying requirement.

4) PROBLEMS OF NEW PRODUCT PLANNING AND DEVELOPMENT

Up to three out of every four new products that are launched onto the market do not achieve commercial success. Where are "Strand" cigarettes, the "Brabazon" airplane or the Ford "Edsel" now?! Product planning and development are risky and uncertain activities. For a start, there will always be a problem of forecasting the future. To what extent can marketing management foresee:

* technical obsolescence of a product;

* changes in product demand elasticities, relative to price and consumer income;

* the effect of changes in price and consumer income on preferences for substitute goods;

* what will be the effect of changes in consumer taste and fashion (for instance in the purchase of foodstuffs, clothes, alcoholic and non-alcoholic beverages, cigarettes, eating-out, travel etc)?

Similarly, to what extent can the enterprise draw up accurate forecasts of the risks and returns involved in product development, so that it can carry out appraisal of the necessary investment, perhaps using Payback or Discounted Cash Flow?

Effective product planning and development response may be made harder to achieve where there is *internal organisational resistance to change*. This might take the form of a lack of enthusiasm to take on new product development risks. Such an attitude could result from product orientation, managerial inertia, complacency or remoteness from market feedback. It could instead simply result from a corporate inability to plan ahead. Other problems include:

a) *the capacity of existing or new competitors* to undertake product development. They may have greater capacity and available resources. At the same time a larger scale may permit them to gain lower unit costs as a result of greater investment in operational facilities, more highly productive manufacturing equipment (etc) to make and distribute the new product. This is the case with the larger Japanese car manufacturers, whose volume of sale and cashflow permits them to increase their market advantage by frequent model changes and modifications, manufactured on the most modern and productive plant at costs below any of their competitors. This kind of capacity may put the new product development activities of smaller competitors at increased risk, and in so doing enhances the total operating risk with which the business, committed to funding these developments, is faced.

b) *trade and consumer reaction* to the abandonment of a well known product or brand and its replacement by something new. There is risk of resentment, with the customer taking his business elsewhere, for instance to existing competitors of the original product.

c) *trade, consumer and media reaction* to a new product may help or hinder its acceptance. For instance, see Box 21.1, below.

Box 21.1

NEW SYSTEM PERSIL AUTOMATIC WASHING POWDER

Within a few months of its UK launch, New System Persil Automatic washing powder became associated with skin problems on the part of some of its users. This necessitated the re-launch of the earlier, non-biological product, Persil Automatic, to cover a sizeable segment of the market which

---

will not use enzyme based washing powders. Unknown to Persil's product planners, many of these customers were using Persil Automatic before it was withdrawn, and some of them suffered reaction to its biological replacement product. There was considerable media comment on the issue, and, in addition to relaunching Persil Automatic, the New System product had to be supported through an extended acceptance period. This involved substantial extra promotional expenditure and additional discounts to retailers.

There were very good reasons for the introduction of the new product. There is a trend to washing synthetic fibres at low temperatures, and low temperature washing also saves energy. This makes essential an enzyme base to the washing powder. The new product eventually settled into a market leadership place, and studies found that there was no more risk of dermatological problems with New System Persil Automatic than with any other enzyme based washing powder. Neverthless, the new product introduction initially proved less predictable than was anticipated, and more expensive than budgeted.

d) *attention to detail.* New products must be as right or appropriate as possible before they are launched on to the market. The last thing the company wants is customers pointing out (or suffering) errors or shortcomings that it should have spotted or rectified first. Faulty new products can cause immense damage to brand reputation. Before the successor to British Rail's "tilting train", the APT, reappears on the newly electrified East Coast line in the 1990's, the traveller can be sure that all of its faults will have been sorted out. Flying soup bowls or seasickness will no longer be a high speed hazard in the railway dining car!

e) *cash flow.* The business must be able to meet, control and manage the cash consumption rate of new product development, launch and support. For example, the pharmaceutical development activities of the Beecham Group are supported by cash flows from its portfolio of well known packaged consumer brands. Such brands function as "cash cows", a concept which is explained in a later chapter.

f) *market scale.* Company and marketing management must decide whether new product planning and development, and the business opportunities and costs associated with it, *are aimed at UK markets, European and/or US markets, or world markets.* The scale of market research, financial resources and planning skill must all be adapted accordingly. The larger the scale, the more skill must be shown by marketing (and financial) management in initiating and controlling the activity.

5) AN ILLUSTRATIVE CASE STUDY : BOX 21.2

BOX 21.2

NEW PRODUCT DEVELOPMENT IN THE FOODSTUFFS INDUSTRY

It is estimated that there is a 90% failure rate amongst the two thousand new food and drink products launched annually in the UK. Part of the reason is that product research and development is *not* market orientated, and hence is not in tune with customer buying patterns and decisions, nor with usage patterns within target market segments.

Factors likely to contribute to trade and market acceptance of new foodstuff products include:

a) exploiting existing brands/brand awareness (eg Heinz; Gold Blend).

b) superior product characteristics and perceptions.

c) technological advance (eg the introduction by RHM Ingredient Supplies Ltd. of new crumb coating products and technology, which had the effect of widening the crumb coating market).

d) expanding accepted usage patterns beyond traditional perceptions of the product. This is a key to the expansion of the relatively static bread market in the UK, and depends on brown and wholemeal bread becoming identified as a "staple healthy food".

e) a consistent record of success with earlier products which are now widely accepted by the trade and the customer.

f) correct product positioning against market segments. For example, in the UK bread market, Allied Bakeries has always been relatively successful in the white bread market. But RHM's British Bakeries counter-attacked strongly in the

---

more rapidly growing brown bread sector of the market. It launched its "Windmill" range during Autumn 1980. This range comprises a series of brown and wholemeal breads, and rapidly established a significant market share, thus:

Brown/wholemeal bread market (March)	1980	1981	1982
Market Volume Index	100	117	119
Windmill % market share	–	13	16

This market has two broad segments (if the market is segmented on the basis of product usage). One is economy, family breads (brown versions of existing white loaves). The other is wheatmeal and wholemeal breads, eaten by dedicated brown bread eaters and those consumers interested in the fibre content of the product. The Windmill range was launched in the middle of these two areas, with enough variety to appeal to most of the customer segments within these two broad market sectors.

Food product rating criteria include:

* formulation;   * consumer expectations of product;
* appearance;   * unique advantage/relative advantage;
* taste;   * price and perceptions of value for money;
* smell/aroma;   * choice of channel of distribution;
* packaging;   * shelf-life;
* instructions for handling/cooking/storage/freezing;
* attention to detail.

SUMMARY

The contents of this chapter are summarised in Table 21.3.

TABLE 21.3
Summary : Chapter Twenty One

SECTION	MAIN POINTS
1 Brand strategy	Brand names are used to differentiate products, facilitate recognition and assist in the build-up of customer loyalty to the product. Customers seeing a favoured brand may cut short the analysis of alternatives prior to the purchase decision, and go more rapidly to its purchase. One brand name may be used to cover a range

	of products (eg Heinz), or instead a number of brand names may be used within that range (eg as in biscuits, groceries etc). Choice between these two strategies depends in part on the nature of the brand-segment relationship, and on the degree to which retailer own-brands are in use.
2 Product names	Product names reinforce the product positioning, differentiation and image building value of the brand, and assist in recognition and recall by consumers. Again, this speeds consumers through the purchase decision process. The name may hint at the benefit to be gained from the purchase. Product names need to be protected, and "trademarks" are used for this purpose.
3 Packaging	Packaging must serve a functional purpose, and at the same time be consistent with other elements in the marketing mix. Packaging has a major recognition and promotional value, especially where the product is displayed alongside competing products.
4 Problems of new product planning and development	Product planning and development is made more difficult by the need to forecast market risk and return; to overcome organisational and trade resistance/inertia towards new products; to forecast competitor response; and to manage the cash flow consequences of product planning and development.

RECOMMENDED READING

Oliver G.   Marketing Today.   Prentice Hall International

QUESTIONS FOR SELF-REVIEW

(1) What is the Product Life Cycle? Why is it an important tool in the product management process?

2) *Compare and contrast proactive and reactive product development strategies.*

3) *What steps can marketing management take to achieve successful market acceptance of a new product or service?*

4) *What is a "brand"? What is the role of the brand in the product management process?*

5) *"Company cashflow is the key to successful new product development". Comment on this statement.*

6) *"An acid test of the quality of marketing management is its skill in managing and stretching long established products, and those in the decline phase". Comment on this statement.*

7) *Outline and comment on the relationship within the product management process between market segmentation, product positioning, product life cycle and new product development. What constraints does each place upon the other, and how do these constraints affect the total marketing planning activity?*

EXAMINATION QUESTIONS

Q37 *Product life cycle theory suggests that marketing activities should change as the product progresses through the life cycle. Describe the main features of the Product Life Cycle and for a product of your own choice, explain how and why the marketing activities would be expected to change.*

(ABE)

Q38 *'There is nothing the manager can do once a product reaches the decline stage of the product life cycle.' Comment on this statement, explaining why you either agree or disagree with it.*

(ABE)

Q39 *Describe the stages of the new product development process.*

(IIM)

Q40 *(a) What is meant by brand image?*
(b) What are the required characteristics of a good brand name?

(IIM)

Q41   (a) *What do you understand by 'own label' brands?*

(b) *Why have such brands been developed?*

(c) *What effect has their development had on the structure of the market for consumer goods?*

(CIMA)

Q42   *Suggest reasons for the increased importance of packaging as an element of the marketing mix.*

(IIM)

Pricing

"Ask thy purse what thou shouldst buy"

The next three chapters take an in-depth look at Pricing, as it affects the marketer and the management of the marketing mix. Pricing is a vital subject, not only for the marketer, but for the enterprise as a whole. The financial performance of the business will be determined by the company's effectiveness at pricing its goods and services so that:

* customers will perceive that these prices are reasonable, or offer value for money;
* the company's objectives for profitability can be met.

Ineffective pricing policies can have very serious commercial consequences, and could lead to bankruptcy or liquidation.

22 Pricing Determinants

INTRODUCTION

This chapter commences by defining the meaning of "price", and indicates where prices are charged. It looks at the relationship between pricing and the financial objectives of the business. Pricing situations vary widely as between consumer and industrial goods markets, and also vary widely within each of the two market types.

The chapter then continues with an analysis of the main determinants of price. These include the level of market demand, the nature of market competition, the characteristics of market segments and so on.

The analysis of pricing is continued in the next two chapters.

CHAPTER CONTENTS

1) What is a price?

2) Where are prices charged?

3) Pricing and the financial objectives of the business.

4) The variety of pricing situations.

5) Pricing determinants.

   5.1) Level of market demand.

   5.2) Nature of market competition.

   5.3) Customer types and market segments.

   5.4) Consumer behaviour and perceptions.

   5.5) Impact of channels of distribution.

   5.6) Research and development costs.

   5.7) Cost definitions and formulations.

   5.8) Macroeconomic trends.

Summary

1) WHAT IS A PRICE?

A price is a value, or sum of money, at which a supplier of a product or service, and a buyer agree to carry out an exchange transaction. The prices at which such exchange transactions take place may either be:

i) *fixed* to the buyer – the customer either agrees to the price, or does not undertake the purchase;

ii) *negotiable* – in which case the supplier and customer bargain together until they arrive at a mutually agreed price at which the transaction can take place.

2) WHERE ARE PRICES CHARGED?

Prices are charged between sellers and buyers at various points in the *chain of distribution*. Channels of distribution are analysed in a later chapter within the section on the marketing mix. Prices are charged between:

* the original supplier   – and the final customer; OR
                            – a wholesaler or agent; OR
                            – a retailer.
* a wholesaler or agent – and a retailer.
* a retailer   – and the final customer.

The price paid to a retailer by the final customer, say for a fridge-freezer, will therefore be based on two constituent prices paid:-
   – between the manufacturer and the electrical goods wholesaler;
   – between the wholesaler and the retailer.

For instance, both the wholesaler and the retailer may add a *percentage mark-up* to the price at which they purchased the refrigerator, and these mark-ups will determine the price to the final customer. For instance, if the ex-works price of the freezer was £200, the wholesaler's mark-up was 25% and the retailer's mark-up was 35%, the price to the final customer would be:

£200 x 1.25 = 250 x 1.35 = £337.50 + VAT

3) PRICING AND THE FINANCIAL OBJECTIVES OF THE BUSINESS

Whilst there are many ways of defining the financial objective of a business enterprise, it is common enough to find that financial performance is measured in terms of:

* the percentage margin on sales revenue (or "turnover") earned; OR

  * the percentage rate of return on the net operating capital
     employed (which is defined as the value of fixed assets
     plus current assets minus current liabilities).

In either case, the sales revenue calculation is one of the
critical variables. And the generation of sales revenue is, in
part, dependent on the prices set by the supplier or distributor
for his goods. So, the pricing policies used by an enterprise are
*an essential determinant of the degree to which its financial
objectives can be met.*

A business can have good products and manufacturing
facilities, excellent distribution and effective advertising. Yet
it may fail to achieve its revenue and financial targets because
it sets prices that are too high or too low, or uses prices that
confuse the distributor or final customer. It may even fail to
integrate its product costing with its price setting procedure,
so that its prices fail to cover costs. Setting the right prices,
and following a coherent and thought-out pricing policy, is
essential to the achievement of financial objectives, and indeed
to the very survival of the enterprise itself.

4) THE VARIETY OF PRICING SITUATIONS

The factors that determine prices, and pricing policies,
vary widely according to the particular commercial environment
in which the enterprise is operating. Pricing decisions have to
be made by foodstuffs manufacturers who wish to sell their
products to national retail multiples, such as (in the UK)
Sainsbury, Tesco or Safeway. Retailers have to fix the prices
at which they will sell these products to consumers who shop
in their stores. Other companies must agree prices with their
industrial customers to supply complex technological
equipment or capital plant. Not only will cost forecasts have
to be made in such cases, but the agreement of the customer
to the profit margin to be charged must also be obtained. There
is a whole range of commercial considerations to be taken into
account within the many different pricing situations, each of
which will be characterised by its own particular customs,
practices and expectations.

5) PRICING DETERMINANTS

There are a number of basic determinants which shape
and constrain the pricing process. These are listed below.

5.1) Level of market demand

All pricing decisions are, in the end, dependent on the level of market demand, and on "what the market will bear". The market demand for Rolls Royce cars is very small, and so is the supply. Supply and demand meet at a very high price, because the Rolls Royce is a luxury product for which a few customers are willing to pay a lot extra because of its prestige value (etc). On the other hand, most customers for toothpaste are only prepared to pay a relatively small amount for each tube, rationalising that there is a limit to the value added potential of the product, which in any case they purchase relatively frequently.

5.2) Nature of market competition

The more competitive a market is, the more competitive will be the pricing policies pursued by the suppliers in that market. Ultimately, a market can develop into a state of what economists call "perfect competition", in which market competition leads to prices being established at the point at which supply equals demand. Economists also identify markets which are "imperfectly competitive", "oligopolistic" and "monopolistic" and, again, price is deemed to result from the competitive (or non-competitive) situations described by these conditions.

Certainly, the room for price variation on the part of any one supplier will depend on *pricing expectations* in the market. Suppliers will have to estimate the reaction of their competitors to any change in price that they wish to make. And they will have to forecast the reaction of consumers to such price changes. Economists describe this degree of consumer sensitivity towards price as *price elasticity of demand*. A price increase which is not fully matched by the competition will immediately put any one supplier at a disadvantage; whilst a cut in price may result in "cut-throat" competition all round. There is no guarantee that such competition will result in a significant increase in consumer demand, especially when the consumer equates price and quality. Low price may be perceived as a reflection of low quality.

5.3) Customer types and market segments

Where customers can be clearly differentiated by segment, then the products positioned on these target segments should be appropriate to the particular demand requirements and usage contexts associated with the segments. Price may be only one of a number of relevant factors which determine the nature of segment demand, and influence the acceptability (or otherwise) of products targeted on that demand. For instance, a market which emphasises product availability, reliability and after-sales service may rate price as a relatively less important factor when comparing the available alternatives.

This point was made in an earlier section. Marketing management must identify those characteristics of segment demand that are most important to target customers, and build-in appropriate product attributes. Product price should reflect the importance of price within the total constituent of segment demand.

5.4) Consumer behaviour and perceptions

Research into consumer and buyer attitudes, perceptions and behaviour (examined in earlier chapters) will show three things:

a) the relative importance of product price in shaping consumer or buyer attitudes towards particular products or purchase situations;

b) the relative importance of product price in determining the outcome of actual purchase behaviour;

c) the relative role of product price in shaping basic consumer perceptions of *value for money*.

Blanket judgements or generalisations about consumer sensitivity to price are usually inappropriate, not only because they ignore market segmentation, but because they ignore the variety of consumer and buyer attitudes towards price. Some consumers equate low price with value for money. Others relate the quality, reliability or availability of products to their price, and arrive at an entirely different perception of value for money. An expensive product which outperforms its cheaper rivals, lasts longer and needs less maintenance (because it breaks down less often) may be perceived as representing better value for money from a buyer who is concerned with the output and reliability of that product. Commercial vehicle operators, for example, buy Volvo, Foden or Mercedes trucks because they can be sure of the reliability and durability of the product.

5.5) Impact of channels of distribution

The impact of channels of distribution has already been noted in Section (2) above. Where a product passes through a channel of distribution, it will have its price both at different stages in the channel, and to the final customer. Often these prices will be subject to percentage mark-ups; for instance:-

P = (pxw + m (1...n)) where

P is the price to the final customer;

pxw is the ex-works price charged by the manufacturer (or original supplier);

m(1...n) is the number of mark-ups added in the channel of distribution.

Such a price might look like this:-

* *manufacturer–(pxw)–wholesaler–(pxw+m1)–retailer–(pxw+m1+m2)–customer.*

Within consumer goods markets, however, there is likely to be a further complication. This will be the degree to which the price obtained by the manufacturer or wholesaler is subject to *trade discount*. This will *decrease* the price they obtain for the product. The decrease may show up as:

* additional wholesaler or retailer profit where the reduction is not passed on to the consumer; OR
* a lower than expected price to the consumer where the reduction is passed on to the final consumer.

The effect of trade discounts may be described thus. The manufacturer or supplier is at the beginning of the channel of distribution, shown diagramatically in Figure 22.1.

The price received by the supplier (pxw) is:

pxw = (supplier's costs + (profit margin less trade discount))

where: trade discount = f(volume purchased by whole-saler or retailer)

where: volume purchased = f(wholesaler or retailer's turnover) where: turnover = f(wholesaler or retailer size, number of outlets, number of customers, market share, promotional effectiveness and other marketing mix factors)

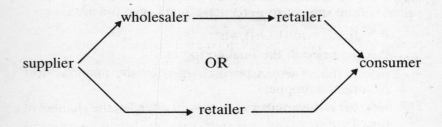

Figure 22.1. A Channel of Distribution.

The larger and more powerful the wholesaler or retailer is relative to the supplier, or the larger the order being placed on him, the greater is the pressure on the supplier to yield discounts which are volume-related. This *bulk buying* pressure is an issue dealt with in later chapters.

5.6) Research and development costs

Reference was made in an earlier chapter on the Product Life Cycle to the need for newly introduced products to make a financial contribution towards the research and development costs incurred by their introduction. This may mean that the price at launch may be a high one. This high price may be maintained until competitive pressures eventually force it down. Certainly, it must be true in general terms that the prices charged within the product mix must cover the total research and development costs incurred by the enterprise over a particular period, given the forecasted and actual sales volumes achieved.

5.7) Cost definitions and formulations

The price received by a supplier was defined in section (5.5) above as:

pxw = (supplier's costs + net profit margin)

The cost structure applied to the product is therefore of critical importance to the establishment of price. The cost proportion of the final price will depend upon the cost formulation method chosen. Various formulations are available and these are analysed in more detail in the next chapter.

5.8) Macroeconomic trends

It will be generally true that price levels will be affected by such macroeconomic and fiscal trends and events as:

* changes in the price of basic raw materials (such as oil, steel, petrochemical products etc);
* changes in labour productivity and labour costs;
* changes in the rate of inflation;
* changes in government policy towards Value Added Tax;
* use of price control as a tool of government policy;
* (etc).

SUMMARY

The contents of this chapter are summarised in Table 22.2.

TABLE 22.2
Summary : Chapter Twenty Two

SECTION	MAIN POINTS
1 What is a price?	A price is a value, or sum of money, at which a supplier of a product or service, and a buyer agree to carry out an exchange transaction. The prices at which such exchange transactions take place may either be fixed or negotiated.
2 Where are prices charged?	Prices are charged between sellers and buyers at various points in the chain of distribution.

3 Pricing and the financial objectives of the business	The generation of sales revenue is critical to the achievement of financial objectives. This is, in part, dependent on the level of prices charged for these goods. So, the pricing policies used by an enterprise are an essential determinant of the degree to which its financial objectives can be met.
4 The variety of pricing situations	The factors that determine prices and pricing policies vary widely according to the particular commercial environment in which the enterprise is operating.
5 Pricing determinants	Listed as 5.1 to 5.8 below.
5.1 Level of market demand	All pricing decisions are, in the end, dependent on the level of market demand, and on what the market will bear.
5.2 Nature of market competition	Price and the level of competition are related. Economists identify perfect, imperfect, oligopolistic and monopolistic markets. Pricing will also be affected by customer and competitor expectations and reactions.
5.3 Customer types and market segments	Pricing policy should reflect the importance of price as a product attribute within the total constituent of segment demand.
5.4 Consumer behaviour and perceptions	Price is relevant to consumer/buyer attitude formation to purchase behaviour, and to perceptions of value for money.
5.5 Channels of distribution	Use of percentage mark-ups at stages in the channel of distribution. Importance of trade discounts and bulk buying in price formulation.
5.6 Research and development costs	May lead to the setting of high prices at the introduction stage for new/rejuvenated products at the beginning of the product life cycle.

| 5.8 Macroeconomic trends | Trends in raw material costs, labour productivity, inflation, government fiscal/taxation policy (etc) will affect general price levels and enterprise pricing policy. |

23 Prices and Costs

INTRODUCTION

This chapter concentrates on the various ways in which commercial enterprises may define their costs and profit margins, so that they can set prices which will allow them to achieve their marketing and financial objectives.

The simplest pricing structure involves the addition of a mark-up to the total cost of producing or obtaining the product. This technique is widely used by wholesale and retail suppliers.

A company may instead attempt to achieve its financial objectives by using a profit margin calculated on the basis of the desired target rate of return. The degree to which this approach will be successful will depend on market demand and competition.

Whatever the mark-up or margin being used, the calculation of price will also depend on the means by which costs are defined and formulated. A major part of the chapter, then, is concerned with an explanation and comparison of the two main costing methods, which are "absorption" and "contribution" costing respectively. Contribution costing is illustrated by a number of examples contained in the chapter appendices.

CHAPTER CONTENTS

1) COST DEFINITIONS AND PRICING

The manner in which costs are formulated and defined is a complex subject. So far, price structure has been simply explained in the following terms:

price = total cost + percentage markup; OR

price = total cost + profit margin; OR

price = total cost + (gross profit margin less discount = net profit margin).

The previous chapter did not define the concept of *total cost,* nor did it attempt to explain the *basis for calculating* mark-up or profit margin. These issues will now be considered.

2) PROFIT MARGINS

2.1) Percentage mark-up

The percentage mark-up added to the supplier's costs may be based upon:

* what the supplier can reasonably charge, which in turn depends upon what the market will bear; OR

* "traditional" or "normal" mark-ups found within the trade. Such patterns of mark-up expectations would be characteristic of long-established and stable trading relationships; OR

* supplier target rate of return criteria: see section (2.2) below.

2.2) Target rate of return

Some companies calculate their prices on the basis of a *specified rate of return to be achieved over a period of time.* This target rate of return is related to the investment in operational and marketing capacity, and to the degree of risk attaching to the manufacture, supply and sale of the product. The target rate of return will therefore be used to calculate the percentage mark-up or acceptable net profit margin to be added to unit cost.

Rate of return pricing is used to achieve a pre-determined rate of return on investment over a given period of time. The process will involve:

* an attempt to forecast sales volume at various stages through the product life cycle;

* the application of *variable* mark-ups or net profit margins over the life-cycle, such that the sales volume yields the profitable revenue flows that constitute the required rate of return. For instance, the profit margin will decline over the life cycle, so it will be important that the company maximises its profit on that product for at least some part of the product's life, so as to offset the inevitable effect of downward pressure on its net margins.

Rate of return pricing demands relatively accurate forecasting and costing in terms of level of output and marketing expenditure. It is probably only suitable for relatively stable markets if its long term use is planned, and it will inevitably be subject to unpredictable variations caused by changes in market demand.

However, target rate of return pricing may be used in *unstable and risky markets* where the supplier aims to cover his investment within a very short period of time. Here, the relationship between risk and price becomes the over-riding factor in price calculations.

3) COST CALCULATIONS

3.1) Absorption costing

The manner in which responsibility for pricing decisions is allocated within particular organisations varies widely, but in general terms it is often true that in UK production-orientated manufacturing industries, *accountants are a dominating influence.* The "heavier" manufacturing industries (such as steel making, heavy engineering, petrochemicals and so on) are usually suppliers to other businesses, and because of the nature of their activities they tend to be strongly *cost-orientated.* This cost-orientation is a traditional one, encouraged by the high status and prestige of the accountant in the UK's commercial culture. Contracts are negotiated or renewed in these industrial markets on the basis of costs that have been ascertained by long-established procedures of *cost-accounting.* The use of such procedures has been encouraged by the need to recover both manufacturing costs, and the considerable capital cost of investments in plant and machinery required to operate the business.

The approach to pricing that is used tends to be conditioned by the accountant's training in these techniques of costing. Such techniques are based on the assumption that a detailed *unit cost* of manufactured products (and hence their prices) can be calculated by the use of widely-accepted rules of cost accounting practice. These rules assume that in addition to the *direct materials element* of cost in a unit of output, there can also be calculated the unit costs of the *labour element,* and *overhead element* involved in the manufacturing process.

Thus, if the labour costs which are incurred during a period of production are divided by the resulting output quantity produced, then the resulting unit cost of labour can be regarded as a *cost standard* (or "standard cost" in cost accounting terminology). Similarly, factory overhead costs (rent, rates, power, maintenance, head office and salary costs, etc) which relate to the period of production are allocated to the production departments and production lines. By dividing the allocated overhead costs by the quantities produced there is derived a standard unit overhead cost.

Such an approach to pricing is termed *absorption costing.* At any predetermined (standard) level of output, price might be calculated per unit of output as follows:-

unit price = standard direct materials cost + standard labour cost + overhead allocation + profit margin.

The profit margin may well be calculated, at that level of output, to yield a total profit which gives a target percentage rate of return *that is equal to, or greater than the percentage cost of the capital required to produce that output*. Let us assume that the capital costs of the production system were £1 million, and that it "costs" £100,000 per year in dividends to reward the shareholders who have provided that capital. It also "costs" £100,000 per year to replace or "depreciate" this capital in the accounts of the company. So, the percentage return must be at least 20% to cover these capital costs and depreciation. Any return above 20% will yield additional profits which can be re-invested in the business, or used to increase shareholder dividends.

However, the main distinguishing feature of absorption costing is that *it allocates overhead costs to the productive process on a basis that is proportionate to the volume of work carried out.* Prices which result will therefore include an allocation of fixed costs, calculated according to the rules of cost accounting. Absorption costing attempts to account for all production and overhead costs *by absorbing them directly into the units of output produced*. As a pricing tool this is its major weakness, for it can tie the marketer's hands in a situation in which the enterprise must be flexible in the face of market pressures. It is not a method of cost calculation which is particularly suited to commercial environments which require a degree of market orientation, and in which pricing decisions must be made on the basis of competitive response. In such circumstances, pricing decisions are, in any case, more likely to be made by the marketing function. There are two other main criticisms of absorption costing, as follows.

i)   as a consequence of the widespread use of traditional cost-accounting conventions, the concept of "cost" used in the context of absorption costing has taken on a connotation of accuracy which cannot be justified. In reality, the cost of an individual unit of volume-produced manufacture is an elusive concept, not capable of being completely accurately measured.

ii) the concept of absorption costing makes use of a number of assumptions and conventions which involve the allocation of expenditures which are often *fixed*. Such expenditures include rent, rates and salaries. These costs are *fixed period costs* and bear no relationship to variations in the volume of output. Indeed, in the short and medium term such costs would be incurred even if output fell by a drastic proportion.

3.2) Contribution costing

The main alternative to absorption costing is known as *contribution costing* (or "marginal costing"). This approach takes a more pragmatic view that the only positively identifiable elements of cost in a unit of volume-produced output comprise:

*   direct materials used;
*   direct labour actually required to make the product;
*   other directly attributable costs such as power, packaging, lubricants (etc).

All other costs are assumed to be *fixed* in the short and medium term, and are not expected to show significant variations, irrespective of the level of output being produced.

This approach accords with the realities of business life, because even in times of recession expenditures on rent, rates, salaries, maintenance, sales and marketing costs, administration (etc) show little direct relationship to variations in output volume.

The use of contribution costing in product pricing represents a recognition of these realities. In most business situations market demand will always be a prime factor in determining price levels. Although monopolies do exist, for instance in the state owned sector of the economy, and cartel (price-fixing) arrangements remain in sectors like international civil aviation, outside of these situations price is a function of the demand expressed in the market place.

The competitive pressures that are evident in markets such as those for branded consumer products, and household goods, ensure that suppliers have to price to the market demand. As a result, these suppliers have to attempt to restrict their costs within a revenue ceiling, so as to produce as large a profit margin as their efficiency and productivity will permit. It is for this reason that the marketing influence on pricing policy is strongest in this kind of business enterprise.

Contribution costing, therefore, recognises two main categories of cost. These are:

a) *Variable costs:* which are associated directly with the manufacture or provision of the product or service. These costs will vary in direct proportion to the volume produced, most simply on a one to one basis, or with proportionate decreases due to economies of scale becoming operational once volume has reached a particular level. Within a manufacturing context, such costs might include:-

* direct material;
* direct labour;
* units of electric power/energy;
* directly attributable costs such as packaging, lubricants (etc).

Variable costs *may* also include *directly attributable* costs incurred in:-

* research and development connected only with that specific product or service;
* sales and marketing activities directly attributable to that product, especially at the time of its introduction and launch on to the market;

299

* market segment-specific activities (promotion etc) directly related to the distribution and sale of the product in its target market.

b) *fixed costs:* which are associated with the operation of the business as a whole, rather than with specific products. Within a manufacturing context, fixed costs might include:-

* property costs (rent, rates);
* marketing costs;
* indirect operating costs (indirect labour associated with the manufacturing process, power and light, postal and telephone costs, etc);
* maintenance costs, insurance;
* salary costs of administrative and managerial staff;
* information system and data processing;
* head office costs.

Contribution is itself defined as the difference between net sales revenue and total variable cost, thus:

Contribution = Net Sales Revenue − Variable Cost.

The significance of this concept lies in the relationship between the contribution yield from sales revenue and the total of fixed costs which must be recovered from this sum. The profit margin (if any) is included in this contribution yield, *but the focus of the business is placed on the generation of contribution rather than specified profit margins* since, in any case, competitive conditions may make impractical the achievement of the kind of target rate of return described in section (2.2) above.

Contribution, therefore, is used to pay for the fixed costs of the operation and provides the profit margin. Fixed costs are treated differently from the method used in absorption costing, as they are simply attributed to the TOTAL ACTIVITY over the time period in view. The point may be illustrated by the standard break-even chart thus:

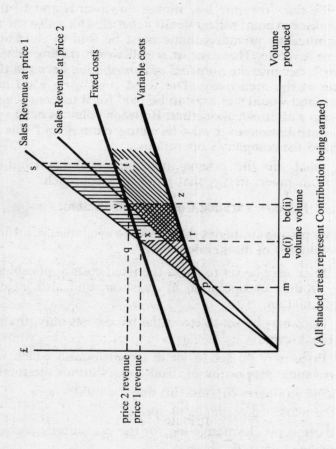

Figure 23.1. Contribution Break-Even Chart.

(All shaded areas represent Contribution being earned)

At price 1 the volume *be(i)* is sold and the contribution earned is *q-r*, which equals the fixed costs at that level of output. The total contribution earned between output m and output *be(i)* is *p-q-r*. Beyond volume *be(i)* the business covers its fixed costs and earns a profit, for instance *q-s-t*.

If, however, market pressures force the price down to price 2, the sales revenue line moves downwards and to the right. Break-even point will now shift to *be(ii)*, which also shows that a significantly greater volume must be sold to yield any increase in revenue. However, it is still worth trading at this new price 2, because *the only loss of contribution* between the two prices is the area *q-x-y*. The fixed costs *q-r-z-y* do not disappear, and would still have to be paid for if this particular product was withdrawn altogether. Between volumes *be(i)* and *be(ii)* a contribution of *x-r-z-y* is being earned and this is beneficial to the company's operations.

So, what are the pricing implications of contribution costing? Remember, firstly, that under this approach:

Price = Variable Cost + Contribution

Three pricing strategies then become available, according to the conditions of market demand:

i) Price may be set to cover the fixed costs applicable to the product or operation in question, and also yield a profit margin.

ii) Price may be set to cover the fixed costs only, that is, to break-even.

iii) Price may be set to yield a contribution which will cover some proportion of fixed costs, but not the total.

Pricing strategies (ii) and (iii) may be used where:

*   the market determines the price;

*   there is no alternative use for the operational capacity being employed;

*   fixed costs cannot be reduced, for instance because other fixed cost components relevant to different activities are inter-dependent with these particular fixed costs (that is, they are not "avoidable").

*   other products yield contribution in excess of their fixed cost burden, such that *the total contribution earned by the operation as a whole during the accounting period*

is equal to or greater than the fixed costs of the operation as a whole during that time.

The general pricing objective, therefore, is to maximise the contribution yield from the products or services sold into the market. Prices will be set such that they are competitive, yet, taken together, maximise the contribution available to cover fixed costs and general profit. This has implications for sales management. Sales staff need to be encouraged, for instance though their commission (payment by results achieved) structure *such that they put most effort into selling products or services with the highest ratio of contribution to sales price.*

Some illustrative examples of the application of contribution costing to the pricing situation are given in the Appendices to this chapter. The first chapter appendix looks at the way the price for a new product might be set. The second chapter appendix illustrates the pricing of a new product which will compete with an existing line. The third and final chapter appendix illustrates how the contribution approach can simplify pricing and production decisions which have been confused by the application of techniques of absorption costing.

SUMMARY

These profit margin formulations, and the two main approaches to calculating cost are summarised in Table 23.2 below.

TABLE 23.2
Summary : Chapter Twenty Three

SECTION	MAIN POINTS
2.1 Percentage mark-up	A straight percentage mark-up is added to the supplier's costs. Mark-up is dependent on what the market will bear, or on "normal", "traditional" or "expected" mark-ups used in the trade. Such mark-ups are particularly characteristic of wholesale and retail distributors, especially where there is a stable pattern of trade, and supplier-distributor relationships are long-established.

2.2 Target rate of return	Prices are based on margins over cost calculated on the basis of a specified rate of return to be achieved by the business over a period of time. Target is related to investment in operational and marketing capacity, and degree of risk attaching thereto, over the life of the product. Liable to be subject to market and competitive fluctuations.
3.1 Absorption costing	Assumes that a detailed unit cost of a manufactured product can be calculated on the basis of direct materials and labour required, plus an allocation of overhead costs. This allocation is proportionate to the volume of work carried out. Absorption costing attempts to account for all production and overhead costs incurred, by absorbing them directly into the units of output produced. Prices therefore include this allocation of overhead cost.
3.2 Contribution costing	Differentiates those costs which vary with output (Variable Cost) and those which are fixed over a period of time (Fixed Cost). Prices are calculated on the basis of Variable Cost plus Contribution. Contribution is Sales Revenue minus Variable Cost. Contribution is used to cover Fixed Cost and the profit margin needed. Represents a more flexible approach to cost and price decisions, and is more viable in competitive and variable market conditions.

CHAPTER APPENDIX 23(1)

PRICING A NEW RANGE

Elliots make and sell a range of tools bought by retailers and a variety of manufacturers. Bedrock, the marketing manager, wants to introduce a new range of tools based on the "Long Arm", a product with which a mechanic can reach the parts of a machine that other tools cannot reach. His sample survey of customers, assessment of demand (based on analysis for similar products) and forecast of competition have enabled him to estimate the volume of sales which Elliots should make, at different price levels. The results are shown in columns (a) and (c) in the table below.

Having engineered the Long Arm to a high degree of perfection, the cost estimate is:

Variable costs, including sales commission and promotional expenditure £12

What price should Bedrock show in the price list which must be finalised next week?

The table below shows the contribution that is expected at each price level.

(a) Net price	(b) Unit contribution = (a) − £12	(c) Unit sales forecast	(d) Contribution forecast
£	£		£000
36	24	15,000	360
34	22	20,000	440
32	20	25,000	500
30	18	28,000	504
28	16	30,000	480
26	14	32,000	448

This indicates that a net price of £30 is the one to aim for. At £30 the contribution will reach a maximum of £504,000. If average trade discounts applicable to Long Arm sales are expected to be 20%, the list price should be £36 (£30 x 1.2) and that is the price Bedrock decides to show.

CHAPTER APPENDIX 23(2)
PRICING A NEW PRODUCT

For the last four years Elliots have successfully sold its "Standardplane". Foreign competition is threatening to penetrate the upper end of the market for planes and Elliots have now perfected a programmable 'three-in-one' "Wonderplane". Bedrock has carried out a market survey and has made his estimates of the extent to which Wonderplanes will supplant Standardplanes, a situation bound to occur the nearer the Wonderplane price comes to that of the Standardplane, which is £18 net of discounts and which he does not plan to increase. His figures show that for next year, sales levels are expected to be:

WONDERPLANE		STANDARDPLANE	Both planes
Unit price	will sell	sales reduction	net sales
£			
42	14,000	–	14,000
40	18,000	1,000	17,000
38	23,000	2,000	21,000
36	28,000	4,000	24,000
34	33,000	8,000	25,000
32	40,000	14,000	26,000

The variable costs, which include sales commission and promotional expenditure, per unit are forecast to be £15 for the Wonderplane and are £8 for the Standardplane. What is the net price that should apply to the Wonderplane next year?

The table below shows the contribution from sales of Wonderplanes at different price levels, less the lost contribution arising from the reduction in sales of Standardplanes, on each of which the contribution is £10, ie £18 less £8.

(a)	(b)	(c)	(d)	(e)	(f)	(g)
	WONDERPLANES				STANDARDPLANES	
Unit Price	Contrib'n per unit = (a)–15	Unit sales forecast	Forecast contrib'n = (b)x(c)	Forecast loss of sales in units	Forecast loss of contrib'n = (e)x£10	Net contrib'n = (d)–(f)
£	£		£000		£000	£000
42	27	14,000	378	–	–	378
40	25	18,000	450	1,000	10	440
38	23	23,000	529	2,000	20	509
36	21	28,000	588	4,000	40	548
34	19	33,000	627	8,000	80	547
32	17	40,000	680	14,000	140	540

The unit price to aim for is shown to be between £36 and £34. At £35 the net contribution will reach a maximum of £550,000. If average trade discounts applicable to Wonderplane sales are expected to be 15%, the list price should be £40.25 (£35 x 1.15). But Bedrock wants the price to reflect the quality of the product and considers that, at £41 (a mere 2% higher), Elliots will sell just as many Wonderplanes, so he sets the list price at this level.

CHAPTER APPENDIX 23(3)

THE POTBANK COMPANY

The Potbank Company currently sells three products whose quantity, selling price and variable cost are given below:

Product	Quantity	Selling Price	Variable Cost
110	5,000	£15	£14
111	10,000	£16	£10
112	15,000	£25	£18

The company's fixed costs total £120,000 p.a. and the accountant has *allocated* these on the basis of the total units produced. He has therefore calculated the fixed cost per unit by dividing the total fixed cost by the units produced, thus:

$$£120,000 \div 30,000 \text{ units} = £4 \text{ per unit}$$

Potbank are currently operating at full capacity and each unit produced requires the same production time. The sales manager has seen the following cost report for product 110:

	£	£
selling price		15
variable cost	14	
fixed cost	4	18
loss		(3)

This report causes the sales manager (who does not understand accountancy) to argue that product 110 should be dropped from the product line.

Requirement One: if no alternative exists for the use of production capacity, should product 110 be dropped?

Requirement Two: if more of product 111 can be sold at its existing price, should product 110 be dropped?

Requirement Three: how much would the selling price of product 110 have to be raised to make it as desirable as product 111?

Assume the same conditions as stated above, except that if product 110 is dropped, no additional units of 111 or 112 can be sold. The sales manager then finds another product 113, which can be sold at a price of £10 each and has a variable cost of £9.75 but only takes one third of the time to produce, as compared with product 110.

The sales manager argues that 113 should be added and 110 dropped. He reasons that "it's true that the margin per unit is 75p less on 113 than on 110 (25p compared with £1), but since more units of 113 can be produced the fixed cost per unit will also go down. As a matter of fact, the fixed cost per unit on all units will drop by £1, that is from £4 (£120,000 ÷ 30,000units) to £3 (£120,000 ÷ 40,000 units), if we switch to product 113."

Requirement Four: Is the sales manager right? How much would the price of 113 have to be increased before it would be as profitable as 110? Explain to the sales manager the error in his reasoning.

ANSWERS:

Requirement One

No, since Fixed Costs remain the same. Product 110 yields £5,000 contribution which would otherwise be lost if the line was dropped, thus:

Product	Contribution £		Volume	With Product110 £	Without Product 110 £
110	1	x	5,000	5,000	NIL
111	6	x	10,000	60,000	60,000
112	7	x	15,000	105,000	105,000
TOTAL CONTRIBUTION				170,000	165,000
Less Fixed Costs				120,000	120,000
NET PROFIT				50,000	45,000

Requirement Two

Yes, since the unit contribution of product 111 is £6 compared with £1 for product 110.

Requirement Three

Increase price of product 110 by (£6-1 = £5) to £20 per unit.

Requirement Four

The sales manager's argument is incorrect, as the changes mentioned do not affect the total fixed costs. If the volume of sales of Product 113 is three times that of product 110, 15,000 units of Product 113 will be sold, with the following result:

Product 113   15,000 x (£10-9.75=25p) = £3,750

which is less than the contribution from Product 110 at £5,000. Product 113 should not be added unless the price is at least raised to:

£9.75 + (100p÷3) = £9.75 + 33p = £10.08p

24 Pricing Policy

INTRODUCTION

This final chapter on pricing concentrates on the policy and practice of companies when making decisions on price level and structure. Firstly, the relationship between product and price is considered, for instance in terms of brand management. Pricing of new products provides a particular problem, as do the dynamics of price movements over the life-cycle of the product. The relationship between price and market segment, seasonality, quality and customer attitude is analysed, and the importance of taking buyer psychology into account is noted.

Another major factor facing suppliers and distributors is the impact of channels of distribution on price. This issue has also been dealt with in the previous two chapters. The chapter concludes by taking a brief look at the strategic implications of pricing within the context of market competition.

CHAPTER CONTENTS

1) Price and product
   - 1.1) Price and quality
   - 1.2) Price and brand
   - 1.3) Product line pricing
   - 1.4) After-sales service

2) Price and the product life cycle
   - 2.1) Research and the product life cycle
   - 2.2) Unique selling propositions

3) Price and market segments

4) Variable pricing

5) Price and the customer
   - 5.1) Price stability and consistency
   - 5.2) The psychology of pricing
   - 5.3) Price clarity and price confusion

6) Price and the channels of distribution

7) Price and competition
   - 7.1) Competitive position

8) Price-quality strategies

Summary

Recommended reading

Chapter Appendix 24(1) : Price lists

Questions for self review

Examination questions

1) PRICE AND PRODUCT

1.1) Price and quality

Consumers and buyers will normally expect that there will be a consistent relationship between the *quality* of a product and its price. The higher the quality, the higher will be the price that the purchaser will expect to have to pay. If a supplier underprices his product, the purchaser may come to the conclusion that its quality is suspect. Similarly, an excessive price will cause the potential customer to think hard about what value he is getting for his money. However he rationalises his thoughts and perceptions he will conclude that the price and the quality on offer are inconsistent. Price-quality strategies are dealt with in section (8) below.

1.2) Price and brand

Brands and brand management were described in an earlier chapter. Companies, particularly in consumer goods markets, will invest heavily in building and maintaining *customer awareness of, and loyalty* to particular brands. They will have therefore to maintain a relationship between brand image, quality and price that is consistent from the viewpoint of the consumer, relative to:

* other brands marketed by that company; AND
* competing brands.

So, for instance, consumers would expect to pay more for a long established brand which has the leading share of the market. This is because they perceive the product not only to be the best in its class, *but the best brand*. Price and the product differentiation established by the brand must be consistent. The brand leader will try to build a perception in the mind of the customer that cheaper competitive brands are poorer products, and that the brand leader's product sets the standard for others to follow.

1.3) Product line pricing

Companies that sell a range of products within the product line may look at their pricing policy from the viewpoint of that range, rather than individual products. For instance:

* some products are priced (relative to expected demand and consumer sensitivity to price) to yield a relatively high unit contribution. These products are used to support those others which yield a lower unit contribution. The objective, of course, is to cover the fixed costs and profit requirements *of the product line as a whole*.

* some products may yield little or no contribution, but stimulate the buying of more profitable lines. Such products (called loss leaders where they yield *little or no* contribution) are a feature of retailing operations. For example, cheap white sliced bread attracts people into a grocery supermarket, where they are likely to purchase other, more profitable items.

* some low-priced products yield a relatively small unit contribution, *but serve to introduce customers into the range*. For instance, car buyers tend to replace their models with new ones of the same make, particularly if they get advantageous used car trade-in prices. Eventually, many customers will "trade up" to more expensive models within the same manufacturer's model range.

* when setting prices for a range of products, a supplier may select a *bench-mark price,* around which the prices of other products in the range will be adjusted. The bench-mark price will be that of the most popular model. The purchaser will then perceive that the logic of the price structure relates to this model, with which he or she is in any case most likely to be familiar.

1.4) After-sales service

For many products, and particularly the categories of consumer durable appliances and industrial equipment, a major selling point will be the availability of an effective after-sales service. The objective of this service will be to deal with guarantee and warranty claims, and to provide routine maintenance and servicing facilities.

The provision of such facilities will usually entail significant and continuing expenditure. This cost needs to be taken into account when the company is setting its prices.

2) PRICE AND THE PRODUCT LIFE CYCLE

The chapter on the Product Life Cycle noted that there is likely to be a price-stage relationship. For instance, at the stage of:

* introduction – "penetration" pricing may be used to achieve large sales volume and establish market share; or "premium" pricing may instead be used to generate profit and pay for Research and Development costs.

* maturity – companies may seek price stability and compete on a "non-price" basis, for instance making heavy use of advertising and techniques of sales promotion.

* decline – price reductions may occur, and price competition may be undertaken.

"Penetration" prices are low prices which are used to obtain as large a market share as possible in the the shortest possible time. Penetration prices can only be used where:

i) the market is price sensitive;

ii) production costs will fall significantly in line with increases in output (for instance where a fixed cost burden can be spread over more and more units);

iii) competitors are likely, at least for some time, to be discouraged from following the same policy, and causing a "price war" which could damage either or both of the protagonists;

iv) buyers perceive a logical relationship between the price set, the brand, and its quality and availability.

2.1) Research and development costs

An alternative to penetration pricing is the use of high or "premium" prices which may be set during the early period of the product's life so as to permit the recovery of some, or all of the marketing and research and development costs incurred by the product's introduction. After all, when a development period has entailed heavy expenditure there is bound to be a strong argument for aiming to recover these costs in as short a period as the market price will bear. Sooner or later, competitors are going to bring out their own version of a new product that has successfully demonstrated its market appeal, and in general terms it would seem to be a sounder policy for the pioneer to make the most of his opportunity. This means pricing up to the potential level of demand while that opportunity lasts. No doubt this will encourage competitors to enter the market, but if the pioneer has by then already earned a substantial contribution he will be in a good position to contemplate the necessary price reductions.

2.2) Unique selling propositions

The argument stated in paragraph (2.1) above is reinforced where it becomes clear that a product possesses a significant advantage because of its special features or unique selling proposition. The marketing function will have to decide whether to maximise the pricing opportunity open to them before competitors are able to bring out their own versions, or whether instead to use penetration pricing to achieve a rapid increase in market share.

3) PRICE AND MARKET SEGMENTS

Where a company's products are targeted on specific market segments, and supported by segment-specific promotion, there may well be scope for *segment-sensitive* pricing policies. Price is one of the attributes of a product or service, and the marketing concept suggests that products should be developed so that their specific characteristics are appropriate to the particular requirements of the target segment upon which they are positioned.

Market research should identify the relative importance of price as a product attribute within any particular market segment. That market research should also identify the degree to which demand is price-elastic (sensitive to changes in price), and make some assessment of the consumers' attitude towards price and price changes.

The result may indicate that some segments are less sensitive to price than others. In some such segments a *skimming price* may be set. These are high prices paid by customer segments who are relatively insensitive to price. Books are often introduced as high-price hardbacks. These are purchased by customer segments who might comprise:

* long-standing devotees of the author's work;
* academics and critics who have a particular interest in that work;
* public libraries meeting the demands of their borrowers.

Eventually, lower-priced paperback editions are introduced to meet the more general demand of the book-buying public.

Similarly, cosmetics, perfumes, clothes and many luxury items are developed for, and promoted to specific target market segments. The price policy pursued will, again, depend on likely customer attitude towards price relative to the other features of the product, such as exclusivity, fragrance, feel, image and so on. This was a point made by an earlier chapter. Effective product differentiation based upon accurate market segment-ation may enable the supplier to get away from the problem of price competition in mass markets.

4) VARIABLE PRICING

Variable or differential pricing is applied to products or services whose demand pattern is characterised by well-known seasonal variations or time-dependent behaviour. For instance, reduced tariffs apply in the UK to electricity supply and telephone calls taken during *off-peak* periods. Electricity and telecommunications utilities are keen to encourage off-peak consumption because this:

* reduces the pressure on supply facilities during peak periods;
* increases the usage of supply facilities outside peak periods, which reduces the degree to which such facilities would otherwise remain idle.

315

Hoteliers and holiday tour operators also make use of variable pricing. They charge reduced prices for bargain breaks and cheap rate tours during the "low season", when their more lucrative "high season" trade is not available. The objective of off-peak or low season charges will be to cover variable cost, and to make some contribution to the continuing fixed costs of the business. Tour operators also know that off-season breaks "introduce" customers to hotels and resorts, to which they may eventually return at the more profitable peak season.

5) PRICE AND THE CUSTOMER

5.1) Price stability and consistency

It is a reasonable enough assumption for the marketer to make that *the customer hates change for change's sake!* This is particularly true of prices. The enterprise should aim to avoid unnecessary price changes, and should try to maintain as stable a price structure as possible. This is impossible during times of rising inflation, and the company raising its prices is the first recipient of the general public's understandable antipathy towards inflationary conditions!

Similarly, the buying public should be able to perceive a consistent relationship within the price structure of the goods or services on offer. Understandable antagonism is likely to occur where prices for similar products within the product line differ widely, or the prices for different sizes are significantly inconsistent. Customers will for instance expect that the larger the size, pack or quantity, the lower the unit price will be.

5.2) The psychology of pricing

There is a certain amount of psychology attached to pricing in consumer goods markets. For instance, there is an advantage in setting prices just below a round sum, eg £19.95 rather than £20. This makes the price "look" lower than it is. A car priced at £5995 really costs about £6000, but the first figure the customer sees is a 5, not a 6. This makes it seem rather less expensive! This is related to:-

5.3) Price clarity and price confusion

Some companies operating in competitive markets may wish to hide from their competitors the prices *that their customers are actually paying* for the product. This means that the marketer will deliberately avoid using clear prices, and will introduce an element of confusion. He or she will, of course, have to explain the pricing realities to the customer, and use promotional techniques to offset the inevitable initial confusion that the customer will have about the price he must pay. These requirements will be fulfilled by the company's advertising, and the salesperson selling the product.

Price confusion can be operated by the use of *discounts, and variable trade-in values* (where the sale is dependent on the trade-in of an existing product). These items can be varied, so that in deducting their worth from the stated *gross price*, a variable and competitive *net price* can be reached. The exchange transaction will take place at this net price, and it is important to inform the customer of that fact. The value of the discount or the trade-in will, of course, depend upon:

* competitive pressures in the marketplace;
* supplier incentives to sell one product rather than another;
* the relative bargaining skills of the customer and salesperson during the completion of the transaction.

6) PRICE AND THE CHANNELS OF DISTRIBUTION

The role of channels of distribution within the marketing mix is dealt with in the next section of this book. Where manufacturers or suppliers depend upon wholesalers or retailers for the distribution of their products, it is not uncommon for them to invoice their deliveries at a *marked-up gross price*. The invoice also shows the *trade discount* which they allow the distributor. This is deducted from the gross price to give the *net price*. The wholesaler or retailer will then add his mark-up, as explained in the two preceding chapters, until the final price paid by the customer is reached.

The trade discount allowed to the distributor will depend on:

i) the status of the distributor;

ii) the size of the order value ie. the larger the quantity purchased, the larger the discount.

The marketer in the supplying company is often faced with a *distributor expectation of discount*. Where the giving of discounts has become a long-established practice, distributors may automatically expect that it will continue. The supplier will always have to calculate the net price he will receive, from a notional gross price less trade discount, irrespective of how pointless or irrelevant this exercise has become. As we shall see in a later chapter, it is very hard for suppliers to overcome the inertia of traditional practices that are often found in the channels of distribution with which they have to deal.

This expectation of discount may become a problem when the supplier's costs increase, and there is a need for a price increase. Retail or wholesale costs are less susceptible to change than those of the manufacturer, who must face increases in material costs and variations in the volume of output. Existing discounts may still be demanded by distributors, leading to the manufacturer suffering either or both:

* consumer resistance to the increase in price;
* decreased margins and reductions in profitability.

7) PRICE AND COMPETITION

Companies will set their prices after considering the price structures and price policies used by their competitors. They must then decide whether to set prices which are above, below, or in line with the competition. However, the more closely a company's price policy is geared to match, or undercut competitive prices, the more important it becomes to match the productivity and cost structures of competing companies, and to be prepared to accept lower profit margins and a lower rate of return.

This price-cost relationship becomes most critical in competitive markets for products which can only ineffectively be differentiated, and worst of all in *commodity markets* in which undifferentiated or standardised products are sold.

The price-cost relationship becomes progressively less serious as the degree to which:

* the product can be differentiated increases, and brand loyal purchasing behaviour encouraged;
* effective market segmentation can be undertaken.

Ideally, the business should aim to market a range of products and brands, each in some way differentiated from competing products, which are positioned on a wide variety of

318

different market segments and market niches. This way, a consumer goods manufacturer may at the same time be able:

* to supply supermarket chains under own-brand label at a competitive price, thereby obtaining long production runs and avoiding heavy promotional expenditure;
* to supply a range of branded products at higher prices to other market segments, using a broader range of wholesale and retail outlets, suitably supported by promotional expenditure.

7.1) Competitive position

Dominant and powerful producers or distributors may be in a market position to set the "going rate" for price. Thus, they act as *price leaders*. Other powerful enterprises may be in a position to meet these prices, and seek *price parity* as a matter of pricing policy. Weaker suppliers must accept the going rate, that is they will be *price takers*. Their survival in such competitive markets will depend upon their ability to maintain a competitive cost structure and accept whatever profit margin and percentage rate of return is available to them.

These pricing policies reflect the choice of corporate strategy towards price. Companies may choose between *offensive* (attacking) or *defensive* pricing strategies. The degree to which such strategies will succeed depends on many factors, such as dominance and size in the market, product advantages, cost competitiveness and so on.

8) PRICE-QUALITY STRATEGIES

Section (1.1) noted that consumers and buyers will normally expect that there will be a consistent relationship between the quality of a product or service, and its price. The extent to which suppliers can satisfy this *expectation* will, however, be a function of the *price-quality strategy* that they follow. Some examples of price-quality strategies are shown in Table 24.1.

	PRICE		
	HIGH	**MEDIUM**	**LOW**
HIGH	PREMIUM STRATEGY	PENETRATION STRATEGY	SUPER VALUE FOR MONEY STRATEGY
MEDIUM	OVER-PRICING STRATEGY	AVERAGE PRICE – QUALITY STRATEGY	VALUE FOR MONEY STRATEGY
LOW	HIT AND RUN STRATEGY	SHODDY GOODS STRATEGY	CHEAP GOODS STRATEGY

QUALITY

Table 24.1. Price – Quality Strategies.

The choice of price-quality strategy will depend upon such factors as:

* the market segment upon which the product or service is targeted;

* stage in Product Life Cycle. Price-quality strategy will be crucial in establishing demand in the Growth stage, and in maintaining it during the Maturity stage. Companies wishing to maintain brand loyalty are likely to pursue consistent "value for money" strategies, so that customers do not come to perceive that the goods are over-priced, or have been subject to lowered quality as time has passed;

* the likelihood of repeat purchase behaviour. The entire bottom line of the matrix shown in Table 24.1 will be unsuitable to the build-up and maintenance of brand-loyal repeat purchase patterns. "Hit and run" strategies (offering poor quality products at high prices) will in particular generate strong customer resentment, and even attract the interest or intervention of government departments and consumer agencies (etc);

* competitive circumstances. For instance, the extensive introduction of own brands in consumer goods markets, priced on a penetration or value for money basis, has led many manufacturers to add "up-market" or "value-added" products to their product mix, which are *priced at a premium*. Own brands (except perhaps for brands like St. Michael) do not compete well with such products which are sold on brand name and are heavily promoted by their manufacturers. These products carry higher margins and help the manufacturer to sell his products in a market environment dominated by the activities of large retail multiples. At the same time, however, product specification, quality and price must be carefully positioned against well-researched and accurately defined market segments, if a premium price-quality strategy is to succeed.

SUMMARY

The contents of this chapter are summarised in Table 24.2

TABLE 24.2
Summary : Chapter Twenty Four

SECTION	MAIN POINTS
1 Price and product	Price set must be appropriate to quality and brand management objectives. Price of any one product must be consistent with other prices within the product line. Price calculation must include allowance for after-sales service, warranty claims (etc).
2 Price and product life cycle	There must be an appropriate price-stage relationship. Prices at introduction may have to bring in sufficient revenue to pay for research and development costs. Unique selling propositions may mean higher prices can be charged.
3 Price and market segments	Price is a product attribute; attributes should be appropriate to the target market segment upon which the product/service is positioned.
4 Variable pricing	Price may be varied where demand is seasonal or time dependent.
5 Price and the customer	Customers prefer clear and stable prices, which "appear" as low as possible. Sometimes, however, competitive pressures force suppliers to "hide" their net prices behind variable discounts and trade-in values.
6 Price and channels of distribution	Distributors add mark-ups. They also expect discounts from suppliers. These discounts are usually volume related, but can also indicate channel tradition or inertia.
7 Price and competition	Suppliers may adopt offensive or defensive price strategies. As a result they may be price leaders, seek price parity or remain price takers.

8 Price-quality strategies	Consumers and buyers will normally expect that there will be a consistent relationship between the quality of a product or service, and its price. The extent to which suppliers can satisfy this expectation will, however, be a function of the price-quality strategy they follow. Price-quality strategies are illustrated in Table 24.1.

RECOMMENDED READING

Gabor A.   Pricing – Principles and Practices.   Heinemann

Sizer J.   An Insight into Management Accounting.   Penguin

Winkler J.   Pricing for Results.   Heinemann

CHAPTER APPENDIX 24(1)

PRICE LISTS

1) THE OBJECTIVE OF A PRICE LIST

For a business that sells products from stock, or provides standard services, one of its most important external documents will be the *price list* it issues to its customers and the trade. How this price list is formulated and structured, and the prices it contains, will have a significant effect on the earning of company revenue and profits. When drawing up a price list, it is important that its main purpose is identified and made clear to salesperson, trade distributor and customer alike. The company will have to decide whether the price list is to be:

a) a list of fixed prices which all customers, other than perhaps a few large ones, must pay?

b) a list of basic or recommended (retail) prices from which all customers can obtain specified or negotiable discounts dependent upon:-
– size of order?
– placing orders early in the season?
– accepting delivery out of season or during unsociable working hours? (some petrol suppliers distribute their products on a 24 hour, 7 days a week basis).

c) a list of basic prices from which customers can negotiate suitable discounts with the salesperson? Often in such cases the list is not shown to the customer but acts as the salesperson's guide before the negotiating process commences.

2) PRICE LIST DESIGN FACTORS

There are a number of design factors relevant to the structure and presentation of a price list. These include:-

i)   the advantage of letting smaller customers know what their bigger competitors have to pay, be it the same price, or one determined by volume related discounts.

ii) the advantage of keeping the price list separate from the products catalogue, which avoids unnecessary printing and postage costs each time a price change is necessary.

iii) the need to present the price list in the same order as the products listed in the catalogue. This order might be determined by the product range, the products themselves, their age or measurements, and order quantities.

iv) the use of different price lists for different:
* types of customer;
* geographical and delivery areas of the country;
* categories of goods or services;
* units of measurement (eg imperial or metric);
* levels of order volume;
* types and size of packaging;
* methods of delivery, or prices "ex-works";
* Value Added Tax (VAT) inclusive prices.

v)   the need to design the list(s) *to assist the user,* be this the customer or the salesperson, to ascertain the net price per unit/measure with as little effort as possible.

vi) percentage mark-ups, additions to price for extras or packaging and carriage, being shown at the end of the section of the list to which they apply, with prominent reference to them being made on each page of the relevant list.

vii) likewise, discounts and the criteria by which they are given should be shown separately and clearly cross-referenced.

viii)sample price calculations. If the customer is required to undertake calculations to arrive at the net price he must pay, it is helpful to provide examples of how these calculations should be carried out.

ix) avoiding too many variations and exceptions, which make calculations difficult for the customer and prevent the salesperson from offering speedy price quotations.

3) PRICE LIST CLARITY

Clarity of price list presentation may be obtained if:

a) the date from which it applies is prominently shown;

b) columns and rows are clearly titled and explained;

c) descriptions are concise, accurate and do not mislead;

d) unit measurements are clearly shown (eg per "unit", "per thousand", "per kg" etc). Similarly, awkward units like "per gross" (12x12=144) or "per 25 yds" should be avoided;

e) the amount of information on any one page is limited; and

f) different typefaces, print colours and other techniques of presentation and display are used.

4) A BAD PRICE LIST

Slapiton sells paint of different types, colours and tin sizes. Its undated price list has just been circulated to its 5,000 trade customers. The extract for "midnight blue" appears as follows:

Order	2	5	10
10+	2.27	5.30	10.30
30+	2.15	5.20	9.85
60+	2.05	4.95	9.50

What is wrong with this price list?

* it assumes that all customers realise that the figures 2,5 and 10 refer to litre sized cans, rather than gallon or pint measurements;

* it assumes that the "£" sign and the word "each" are superfluous;

* it is not clear whether ten is the minimum order quantity;

* it does not state whether the price of 35 x 2 litre cans is
  - 29 at £2.27 + 6 at £2.15 = £78.73   OR
  - 35 at £2.15 = £75.25;

* assuming that the latter applies (ie 35 x £2.15), the company has left it to customers to work out for them-

selves that the absence of "marginal relief" makes an order of 58 x 5 litres (58 x £5.20 = £301.60) more expensive than a larger order of 60 x 5 litres (60 x £4.95 = £297). Is that what is intended?

* the list structure is inconsistent. For example, 12 x 10 litres (12 x £10.30 = £123.60) costs more than 60 x 2 litres (60 x £2.05 = £123). But the cost of the 60 small tins must be greater than that of the 12 large ones, although the volume of paint is the same in both cases.

QUESTIONS FOR SELF-REVIEW

1)   Describe and comment on the determinants of the prices a company can set for its products or services.

2)   To what extent must the price setting process take into account prevailing market and competitive conditions?

3)   What are the advantages and disadvantages of using (i) percentage mark-ups; (ii) target rate of return in establishing selling prices?

4)   Compare and contrast the absorption and contribution approaches to defining and calculating cost.

5)   Why is the contribution approach to costing more suitable for use in pricing decisions than the absorption method?

6)   What costing and pricing decisions have to be taken before a new product is launched onto the market?

7)   In what ways must price, product and brand be related?

8)   Why must a company's pricing policy be sensitive to its customers and their attitude towards product price?

9)   What is the effect of channels of distribution on product prices and the price-setting process?

EXAMINATION QUESTIONS

Q43   List and evaluate the factors which a marketing manager must take into account when setting price for his product.

(IIM)

Q44   Review the different basic pricing policies open to the marketing executive.

(IIM)

Q45   Distinguish between Market-Skimming pricing and Market Penetration pricing, and discuss the factors which will tend to favour each of these approaches to pricing.

(CIM)

Q46   'Effective pricing decisions rely more upon a knowledge of costs than estimates of likely demand.'
Discuss this view of pricing decisions, explaining the extent to which it is, or should be, a true reflection of reality.

(ABE)

Q47   Many companies decide on a selling price for their products by adding a percentage to their costs. Comment briefly on this approach to pricing, indicating the other factors which should be taken into account when deciding on the price of a new product.

(IPS)

Q48   Compare and contrast cost-based and demand-based pricing.

(CIM)

Place

"Give me a firm place to stand, and I will move the earth."

The next five chapters are concerned with the role of Place in marketing. A study of Place deals with how the product is made accessible and available to the customer. Product availability, and the level of customer service offered are important determinants of how well a manufacturer or supplier can compete in the marketplace. They will require the marketer to manage the relationship between his or her company, and those enterprises or "intermediaries" who actually make up the channels of distribution to be used.

25 Channels of Distribution

INTRODUCTION

This chapter defines the meaning of "channels of distribution" and analyses the objectives that the marketer needs the channels of distribution to fulfil. It describes the main channel types, and examines some of their advantages and disadvantages. It then turns to the specific issue of retailing and consumer goods marketing, using the UK grocery market as an illustrative example.

CHAPTER CONTENTS

1) Definition
2) The marketer's channel objectives
3) Channel types
   3.1) Direct supply
   3.2) Merchant supply
   3.3) Short channel
   3.4) Long channel
4) Retailing and consumer goods marketing
   4.1) The UK grocery market

Summary

1) DEFINITION

Channels of distribution provide the link between production or supply, and consumption. They are used to make products or services accessible and available to consumers or buyers. In consumer goods markets, in particular, they also provide the means by which the customer can obtain servicing, repairs (etc) for the products he or she has purchased. As a product or service passes through its channel of distribution *it gains added value* (or value enhancement) because it becomes available to the consumer when and where it is wanted.

2) THE MARKETER'S CHANNEL OBJECTIVES

The supplier of a product or service will have clear marketing objectives that he or she will want the chosen channel of distribution to fulfil. These are listed below, and summarised in Table 25.2. Whether these objectives will *actually* be achieved on a consistent and continuous basis may be another matter, as we shall see in the later section in the chapter on retail management.

a) *appropriate and adequate distribution:* the supplier will use his channels of distribution to achieve the level of product distribution that meets his objective for market penetration, market share and competitive position. This will determine:-

b) *access to the market, and to target customer segments:* the distribution channels used must be capable of giving access to the target market segments. Do these channels serve the appropriate geographic-demographic areas? Is the coverage of the market to be *intensive,* with the product or service being widely available; or is it to be *selective,* restricted to target locations containing specific customer types? This level of access will be determined by:-

c) *relative cost-effectiveness in access and transaction value:* the supplier will attempt to use a channel of distribution which yields some net benefit or advantage relative to the costs or disadvantages incurred in employing it. The objective will be to maximise the benefits to be obtained, given any particular level of cost or disadvantage incurred. Remember, the more "expensive" the channel, the greater the difference between the revenue per unit received by the supplier, and the price per unit paid by the final customer. The chapters on Pricing showed how, with cost-plus pricing, the giving of trade discounts (etc), this "cost" will come about. Ideally, of course, the supplier wants to minimise the difference in transaction value as between his basic supply price and the final price the customer has to pay. The more complex, or powerful, the channel of distribution used, the greater will be this difference in transaction value between the two.

d) *competitive representation and reseller effort:* the choice or availability of channel type will be a key determinant of how the supplier can actually implement his competitive strategies. Can he or she gain a level of representation in the marketplace such that the product can compete on equal terms with similar goods or services? Does the channel of distribution used actually give competitive advantage, and what is the "cost" of that advantage? Is the product displayed and promoted *in situ* such that it will be perceived in an advantageous light by the potential customer? After all, products can be displayed and promoted by retailers, for instance, in a variety of ways. Some retailers will be more effective in this process than others, and will sell more. And what sales effort is made by retailers or distributors?

The business enterprises that operate within the channels of distribution are *resellers. Resellers are also known as "channel intermediaries" or "middlemen"*. They purchase goods or services from their original suppliers, or act as agents on their behalf in selling them to the final customer. The original supplier must try to ensure that the reseller's stock holding, promotion and selling activities are complementary to, and supportive of his or her own marketing objectives. *For there is a limit to the degree to which the original supplier can manage, direct or control the activities of an independent reseller or intermediary.* This fact has serious implications for the marketer, especially in consumer goods markets.

e) *reseller motivation:* part of the supplier's channel objectives will be its strategy and capacity for motivating resellers. Generally, resellers are independent enterprises which may stock a wide range of merchandise, some of which will be directly competing. The marketer will have to decide:

* how the distributor is to be motivated into achieving consistent and effective sales of the company's products;
* how the distributor is to be motivated into putting more effort into selling your products when he stocks a variety of directly competing merchandise. In other words, how is the supplier to maintain *his* products in a *priority position* in the reseller's strategy?

f) *revenue returns from resellers:* the supplier will want to maximise or optimise his revenue returns from the intermediaries used. His capacity to achieve this will be interdependent with the achievement of some of the other objectives listed in this section. For instance, the more effective is the channel at selling the product, the more expensive it will be, the less the risk to the supplier, and the lower will be his returns. See Figure 25.1.

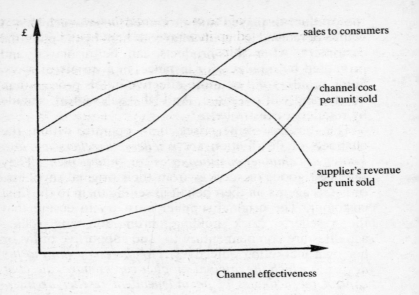

Figure 25.1. A Supplier's Revenue Returns.

The revenue returns will also depend on the pricing policies pursued by the supplier and the distributor (which is why it is worth repeating the contention of an earlier chapter that pricing is such an important issue to any business enterprise.) *Revenue returns will also be influenced by the financial and marketing objectives of the reseller, over whom the supplier may have little or no control.*

g) *cost-effectiveness in physical distribution:* physical distribution is concerned with the actual movement of goods to their point of sale, and to locations of storage before sale. It is dealt with in the next chapter. The choice of any particular pattern of distribution will entail the use of an appropriate transportation and storage system. This in turn will affect production and supply activities. The enterprise will try to seek the most cost-effective physical distribution strategy, consistent with the other channel objectives it has set itself. Again, some kind of trade-off or compromise will be needed. For instance, the faster and more reliable is to be the supply of cars and spare parts to garages and motor repairers, the more expensive must be the physical distribution network, and the greater will be the amount of the manufacturer's and main dealers' working capital tied up in unsold cars, and stocks in warehouses and dealerships.

h) *customer access to repair and servicing facilities:* buyers in consumer goods markets usually rely on retailers, dealers (etc) for repairs and servicing activities. Part of the product's competitive advantage relative to its competitors may be the *availability of repairs and servicing* (as well as its quality, cost etc). The higher the *customer service objective* (defined in the next chapter), the more distributors there will have to be who are trained and equipped to cope with servicing and repair activities. Again, this will incur cost, so, finally:-

j) *cost-effectiveness of customer service:* the supplier will have to balance the cost of providing the necessary level of service to the customer within its channels of distribution, against the marketing and competitive benefit to be gained by offering an accessible and efficient standard of customer service.

3) CHANNEL TYPES

There are four main types of channel of distribution. They are:

> Direct Supply
> Merchant Supply
> Short Channel
> Long Channel

3.1) Direct Supply

The supplier or manufacturer supplies the customer direct, thus:-

MANUFACTURER/SUPPLIER → CUSTOMER

This channel type is common in industrial goods markets. For instance, UK manufacturers of heavy electric power generating equipment supply the CEGB (electricity generating utility) direct. Industrial companies usually purchase machine tools, computers and bulk consumables like fuel oil or paint directly from their manufacturers. This is why the *technical sales representative* is so important in promoting and selling such products under conditions of direct supply. The role of the salesperson is examined in a later chapter.

	OBJECTIVE	SUMMARY
(a)	Appropriate and adequate distribution.	To achieve objectives for market penetration and competitive position.
(b)	Access to the market.	To gain access to target markets, however these are distributed.
(c)	Cost-effectiveness in access to the market.	To maximise the benefits obtained from the chosen channel, relative to the costs incurred by using that channel.
(d)	Competitive representation and reseller effort.	Will the channel chosen, and the reseller effort that it contains, allow the supplier to implement his or her competitive strategy, relative to competing suppliers? Will the channel actually add competitive advantage to the product or service?
(e)	Reseller motivation.	To motivate the distributor into making the maximum effort on behalf of the supplier's products, and to place them in a priority position within his own reselling strategy.
(f)	Revenue return from resellers.	To maximise the revenue returns, given (i) the channel structure chosen, and (ii) the inter-dependent effect of other channel objectives on revenue returns obtainable.
(g)	Cost-effective physical distribution.	To achieve the most cost-effective physical distribution of goods, given the distribution channel chosen.
(h) and (j)	Customer service.	To offer a cost-effective level of customer service, whilst at the same time maximising the competitive advantage to be gained from offering consistent and reliable customer service.

Table 25.2. Channel of Distribution Objectives.

In consumer goods markets, direct supply can usually take one of two forms. One is "direct marketing", described in Chapter Twenty Seven. The other is the use of agencies or retail outlets owned or controlled by the supplier. This is a fairly unusual situation in the UK, but retail examples include Boots the Chemist, and Wimbush, Chatwins and other retailers owned by the major bakery companies. Older readers (!) may remember Brentford Nylons, Singer sewing machines and the Rootes Group, all of whom owned their retail outlets.

a) *advantages of direct supply:* there are two main advantages. The first is the direct contact and communication with the customer. This assists product and sales promotion, and leads to effective customer feedback. Companies using direct supply should be able to maintain an effective level of customer sensitivity. The second advantage lies in the absence of the reseller or "middleman". The revenue received by the supplier will equal the purchase price paid by the customer, less the costs incurred in direct supply or retailing.

b) *disadvantages of direct supply:* there are two main disadvantages. The first is the difficulty of product display. Companies that supply direct to consumer markets, without their own retail outlets or agencies, cannot easily display their wares. Direct marketers must rely on catalogues, pictures and descriptions. But customers cannot touch, feel or "experience" the product in the way that is possible in retail outlets, and without this reassurance may be reluctant to buy. Direct supply is in any case impossible in mass or "fast-moving" consumer goods markets, such as those for groceries and household products. There are too many customers, and the low relative value of each transaction (say in the purchase of a few tins of baked beans) makes direct supply uneconomic.

3.2) Merchant Supply

The supplier or manufacturer supplies the customer through a merchant, who acts as the reseller, thus:

MANUFACTURER/SUPPLIER → MERCHANT →
CUSTOMER

This channel type is also common in industrial goods markets, typically to supply trade customers. It is widely used because it is cost-effective for the manufacturer or supplier. Merchants will buy bulk quantities of such products as building products, manufacturing consumables like welding rods, or steel stock. They then break these down into smaller unit sizes for resale to the customer. Typically they will sell such products in conjunction with other complementary products also purchased in bulk. For instance, builders' merchants will sell bricks, sand, cement, roof tiles and rainwater goods (gutters etc) to building companies large and small.

This channel type is also widely used in export markets. Exporters often use *Import Agents* who fulfil the kind of role just described. Export marketing is described in Chapter Twenty Eight.

a) *advantages of merchant supply:* these are three-fold. Firstly, supply to the merchant (or agent) takes place on a bulk basis, which is economic. The manufacturer does not have to deal with, or distribute, small orders. Secondly, regular payments will be received from merchants. Thirdly, there is very little risk of payment default or Bad Debts, since the trading record of the merchant (which may be a long-established company) will be reliable and known.

b) *disadvantage of merchant supply:* the manufacturer or supplier is dependent upon the marketing and selling effort of the merchant or agent. Merchants may need periodic motivation! This is especially difficult and expensive in scattered export markets in which the manufacturer is dependent upon the efforts of his import agent.

3.3) Short Channel

The supplier or manufacturer supplies the customer in a consumer goods market through a retailer, who acts as the reseller or intermediary, thus:-

MANUFACTURER/SUPPLIER → RETAILER → CUSTOMER

Whilst the supplier is not in direct contact with the customer, this channel type minimises the loss of contact; whilst at the same time it maximises the supplier's influence and control over the retail intermediary or agent. For instance, in some consumer markets the supplier and the retailer will agree to co-operate in funding, designing or specifying:

* promotional activity, whether it be external advertising or in-store sales promotion;
* store layout and product display;
* training of shop sales staff.

a) *disadvantages of the short channel:* there are a number of disadvantages. Firstly, the supplier may be maximising the number of separate accounts with which he or she has to deal. This in turn maximises the administrative cost of supplying these accounts, and controlling the flow of revenue from them. It may also maximise the physical distribution cost of supplying direct to a large number of retailers. Large vehicle delivery fleets, regional warehouses and complex, computerised inventory control and picking systems may be the result. Secondly, the supplier will be maximising the risk of payment default and Bad Debts, since it will be statistically inevitable that a significant proportion of retail intermediaries will suffer from ineffective financial management and control, or go out of business altogether. Thirdly, *it exposes the supplier to the bulk-buying power of large-scale retailers.* Such retailers will demand large trade discounts, and can interrupt the smooth flow of production by arbitrary changes in the rate at which they order. Indeed, as we shall see later in this chapter, small manufacturers may actually be in peril when they deal with the retail giants like Tesco, Sainsbury or Marks and Spencer.

3.4) Long Channel

The supplier or manufacturer supplies the customer in a consumer goods market through a set of two intermediaries, thus:-

MANUFACTURER/SUPPLIER → WHOLESALER → RETAILER → CUSTOMER

The supplier sells his merchandise on a bulk basis to the wholesaler, who in turn breaks these bulk orders down and supplies smaller quantities to retail outlets. At the same time, the wholesaler is able to supply a range of complementary products to the retailer, who stocks his shop entirely from one or a small number of wholesale outlets.

a) *advantages of the long channel:* the long channel is a cost-effective means whereby the supplier or manufacturer can get his product into a large number of small retail outlets, since each does not have to be supplied direct as in (3.3) above. The supplier will receive bulk orders, which will be paid for reliably on a regular basis by their wholesale purchasers. Such bulk orders will minimise operational uncertainty, assist in smooth production planning, and minimise the requirement for the manufacturer or supplier to hold large stocks. They will also simplify the physical distribution problem, cutting down the need for delivery

fleets and warehouse facilities that may be a feature of
the Short Channel. Bulk supply to wholesalers will also
minimise the number of accounts, and reduce the risk of
payment default and Bad Debts to a very low level.

b) *disadvantage of the long channel:* as in section (3.3)
above, the supplier is exposed to the bulk-buying power
of the purchaser (in this case the wholesaler). Given the
structure of trade discounts and the effect of cost-plus
pricing, this channel type may maximise the difference
between the unit price received by the supplier, and that
paid by the final customer in the retail outlet. Whilst the
manufacturer may not be exposed to the worst problems
of bulk-buying by national retail companies that can arise
within the Short Channel, it may nevertheless be an
expensive channel in which to operate.

4) RETAILING AND CONSUMER GOODS MARKETING

Retailers, as resellers, are *independent intermediaries.*
There is a limit to the extent to which their activities can be
controlled by the manufacturer or supplier. Retail companies
pursue strategies that are developed in their own interest, not
in the interests of their suppliers. The retail trade in the UK,
the USA and parts of Western Europe, has been characterised
by the following developments:

i) concentration, so that in some consumer goods
markets there is a relatively small number of large retail
intermediaries;

ii) the emergence of RETAIL MANAGEMENT as a
highly effective, customer-responsive and technically
sophisticated development. There is a school of thought
which suggests that some retail companies learned and
benefitted greatly from the major economic recession of
the early 1980's, emerging stronger, leaner and fitter from
the experience than the manufacturing companies who
supply them.

Large retail companies (and to a lesser extent large wholesalers) capitalise on the market strength that they can obtain
from BULK BUYING. It is sometimes the case that 20% of
the retail outlets in a channel of distribution purchase 80%
of the products sold through that channel. The larger the retailer
is relative to its competitors, the more it can exert pressure on

its suppliers to offer it extra trade discounts, special prices and delivery terms. Indeed, some retail companies prefer to seek supplies from small manufacturers, over whom they may then proceed to exercise some or all of the following controls:

a) they specify the products to be supplied, and their delivery schedule (which influences production planning);

b) they specify the cost structure, and the profit margin (or contribution) they will allow the supplier;

c) they specify the quality of output to be achieved, and make regular inspections of both product quality and supplier premises;

d) they will not guarantee future orders, leaving the supplier in a potentially catastrophic position. The supplier may have devoted (say) 80% of his productive capacity to fulfil a large order for a retailer, for which he may have had to install new plant and machinery. Once this order is completed, *should he lack his own well-known brand name to differentiate his products,* he may have little or no further work. He may even have to lay off his employees until he can secure further orders. And the price of securing such orders may be low or non-existent profit margins. In the worst case, all the supplier may hope to earn is some Contribution towards his fixed costs, perhaps to break-even.

The relative power of retailers as compared with suppliers *varies widely,* especially if the retail trade has not become concentrated, or remains fragmented with many small independent retailers still dominating the channel of distribution. For instance, whilst in the UK there is a small number of very large electrical goods retailers, their relative market power is offset by the existence of:

* a large number of independent high-street electrical goods retailers;

* supermarket and hypermarket chains selling electrical goods;

* very strong manufacturer and brand names, (such as those of Hotpoint, Thorn, Philips, Sony and Technics) supported by these manufacturers with effective product differentiation and promotion.

4.1) The UK grocery market

The emergence of retailer power in its most extreme form can be illustrated by the example of the UK grocery trade, where a very large proportion of manufactured foodstuffs and household products like detergents, soap, polish and disinfectants (etc) are sold through a small number of very large retail and wholesale intermediaries.

Buyer power can be exerted on the manufacturer by any of the following:

* foodstuffs/grocery retail multiples such as Sainsbury, Tesco or Asda;

* major wholesalers (trade delivery) such as Linfoods, Wheatsheaf or Booker;

* major wholesale trade "cash and carry" companies, such as Booker;

* the Co-operative Wholesale Society, which supplies Co-operative retail outlets.

The development of buyer power in this market, which offers the opportunity for price discounting to the retail customer as a means of securing competitive advantage, has even led to a reaction from many smaller independent retailers.

Many of these retailers have voluntarily joined together in "symbol groups" and collectively employ bulk buying. This is done through sponsoring wholesalers, such as the Booker Group, under names such as "V.G." or "Spar". The result is that such retailers can:

i) offer competitive discounts to the customer;

ii) offer products carrying the symbol group name, which may be supported by regional or national promotion; and which help differentiate their products, thereby enhancing their collective identity.

The exercise of buyer power is illustrated in Figure 25.3.

The relationship between the supplier, the marketer and the retail intermediary is also dealt with in later chapters.

SUMMARY

The contents of this chapter are summarised in Table 25.4.

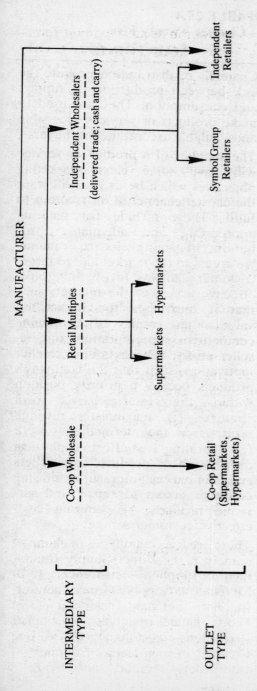

Points at which intermediary bulk-buying power can be exercised over the manufacturer are underlined with broken lines.

Figure 25.3. Foodstuffs/Grocery Intermediary Buyer Power.

TABLE 25.4
Summary : Chapter Twenty Five

SECTION	MAIN POINTS
1. Definition	Channels of distribution provide the link between production or supply, and consumption. They are used to make products or services accessible and available to consumers or buyers.
2. The marketer's channel objectives	The supplier of a product or service will have some clear marketing objectives which he or she will want the chosen channel of distribution to fulfil. These include (a) securing appropriate and adequate distribution; (b) gaining selective or intensive access to the market and to target customer segments; (c) obtaining cost-effective access to the market, such that it maximises the transaction values that result; (d) obtaining competitive representation and re-seller effort; (e) maximising reseller motivation, such that the company's products occupy a priority position within the intermediary's own strategy; (f) maximising revenue returns from the intermediaries used; (g) operating cost-effective physical distribution of products to resellers and the final customer; (h) optimising customer access to repair and servicing facilities; (j) offering cost-effective customer service.
3. Channel types	There are four main types of channel, namely (3.1) Direct Supply (manufacturer/supplier – customer); (3.2) Merchant Supply (manufacturer/supplier – merchant – customer); (3.3) Short Channel (manufacturer/supplier – retailer – customer); (3.4) Long Channel (manufacturer/supplier – wholesaler – retailer – customer).

| 4. Retailing and consumer goods marketing | Retailers, as resellers, are independent intermediaries and pursue strategies in their own interest. Where concentration has occurred amongst retailers, they may be able to influence supplier/manufacturer activities and revenues by: obtaining extra discount through bulk buying; determining specifications, costs and margins; controlling delivery (and therefore production arrangements). An extreme case is the UK foodstuffs/grocery market where distribution is dominated by a small number of large retail and wholesale intermediaries. |

26 Physical Distribution Management and Customer Service

"Q. When is a refrigerator not a refrigerator?
A. When it's in Birmingham but wanted in London."

INTRODUCTION

This chapter looks at physical distribution management and its relationship to customer service. It defines the role and purpose of physical distribution in terms of the achievement of the company's customer service objectives. Customer service is defined by the specification and performance of the places at which the product will be made available, and the frequency with which it will be available to the customer. The higher is the requirement for customer service, the more widely must the product or service be made available to the customer, the more dense must be the distribution network, the more frequently or continuously must it be available, and the more reliable must be the distribution system and the channel intermediaries. The cost of distribution and stock-holding will therefore rise proportionately with the customer service requirement.

In looking at the relationship between physical distribution and the achievement of customer service objectives, the chapter concentrates particularly on inventory management and transportation.

CHAPTER CONTENTS

1) PHYSICAL DISTRIBUTION

Within the context of this manual, the term "Physical Distribution" may be taken to include operational and managerial activities associated with some or all of the following:

a) the physical storage and transportation of goods; or the physical process of making a service type activity available (such as the test flying of new civil or military aircraft).

b) the holding of base or "buffer" stocks, via distribution warehouses and goods in transit, to "smooth" the relationship between the rate of production and the demand from channel intermediaries.

c) stocks held by intermediaries within the channel of distribution.

d) customer ordering procedures.

e) warehouse picking and order collection systems.

f) distribution control systems.

The choice and specification of physical distribution facilities is dependent on the objectives set by the enterprise for its desired level of customer service, thus:

Physical distribution system specification = f(customer service objectives)

This is analysed in Section Two, below. The specification of a physical distribution system is a "mix" which has to be designed (i) to assist the achievement of customer service objectives; and (ii) to operate that level of customer service on a cost-effective basis. Inevitably, this will involve compromise and trade-offs between the resources available and what they can be expected to achieve. For instance:

* the more frequent the delivery schedule, the lower the supplier or intermediary stockholdings;
* the fewer the distribution centres or warehouses, the greater the transportation cost;
* the larger the distribution centres or warehouses, the more effectively can they incorporate cost-effective

operational, picking and control systems, and the greater their operational productivity;

* the more sensitive and responsive the ordering system and the operational system are to each other, the lower will be the need for stocks;

* (etc).

2) CUSTOMER SERVICE

Customer service objectives are basically defined by the specification of two marketing variables. The first is *the place of product or service availability*. The second is *the frequency with which the product is available to the customer*. Two contrasting examples may be given:

i) a prospective purchaser of a new Rolls Royce will expect to travel some distance to a main dealer, and is likely to have to wait for his or her new car to be delivered, having ordered it. Rolls Royce, for obvious reasons, does not keep large stocks of its cars around! This is an example of *selective* distribution.

ii) the same buyer, popping into his local supermarket for a pack of instant coffee, will expect to find his favourite brand on the shelves. If it is not there he is likely to purchase another brand. Buyers of coffee do not expect to have to travel far to buy the product, nor to wait for it. Coffee is distributed on an *intensive* basis.

The specification of place and frequency of availability is likely to have an effect both on market demand and the competitive response that the supplier can make in that market. This relationship is shown in an illustrative form in Figure 26.1.

The determinants of the specifications for place and frequency include the following:

a) *stated corporate or marketing objectives:* for instance one UK manufacturer of earthmoving equipment states that where one of the machines it has supplied has broken down in a working situation, its dealers or servicing agents should submit orders for the required replacement parts at any time, day or night, or at weekends. They should expect that 99% of these orders will be despatched from the factory within 24 hours of receipt of the order (except

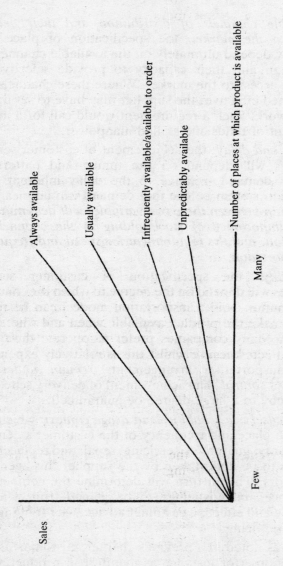

Figure 26.1. Sales Effect of Place and Frequency of Availability.

Labels within figure:
Always available
Usually available
Infrequently available/available to order
Unpredictably available
Number of places at which product is available
Many
Few
Sales

for Sundays). This has implications both for stockholding policy and production planning. An urgent replacement part order will take priority over all other manufacturing activities.

b) *available channels of distribution and their density relative to the market:* the specification of place and frequency depend ultimately on the available channels of distribution and their capacity to provide selective or intensive access to the market. Where these channels are not deemed effective, the supplier may have to set up his own network. Such a requirement would call for a major investment of funds and skilled manpower.

c) *timing and delay:* the achievement of customer service objectives will depend on the timing and pattern of customer demand, relative to the delay inherent in a distribution system before that demand can be met. *The relationship between these two variables will determine the relative importance of stockholding in the channels of distribution, and the requirement for speed and frequency of transportation.*

d) *reliability:* the specification of customer service objectives will depend on the degree to which the channels of distribution, and transportation modes, can be relied upon to make the product available when and where it is required. Many companies prefer to operate their own delivery fleets because whilst this is relatively expensive, their transportation arrangements *remain under the company's control.* The achievement of delivery schedules can thereby to a large degree be guaranteed.

e) *product/service reliability and usage context:* which will affect the place and frequency of the customer's demand for warranty, guarantee, servicing, repair and replacement activities to be undertaken by the supplier, his agents or distributors. This in turn will determine the competitive importance and advantage to be gained from offering accessible and effective customer advice, user training and product servicing.

f) *price:* as noted in a previous chapter, customer service specifications (for instance as manifest in product avail--ability; customer or operator training; product warranties, servicing and repair facilities etc.) need to be reflected in the price paid by the customer. A highly price-sensitive market may limit the scope for offering high quality customer service, which may under such circumstances have to be restricted to its bare necessities. Alternately, a market may be characterised by competition in the quality of customer service offered; this is the case for first class air travel, de luxe hotels, television repairs being carried out on the same day that the fault was notified, etc.

g) *cost:* the specification of place and frequency (and hence quality of service) will need to be cost-effective in the manner in which the determinants listed above are actually used. For instance, whilst it might be desirable to establish one's own distribution networks in export markets, the cost might be prohibitive, especially where an existing and effective agent is already available.

2.1) Customer service performance

Levels of customer service performance achieved can be indicated in a number of ways, including:

* percentage of customers satisfied in a specific period, relative to total demand;
* average waiting period or delivery delay before the customer's order is supplied;
* percentage of customer orders satisfied after a quoted delivery/availability period;
* percentage of total demand that can be satisfied within a given time limit.

The performance achievement, as indicated by these measurements, can be compared with buyer reactions (feedback) to the level of customer service offered by the enterprise. This will indicate necessary modifications or improvements to the number of supply points accessible to the market, the level of stocks to be held by supplier or intermediary, and the frequency of delivery (which, together with stockholding, determines the frequency of availability).

The higher the performance level to be achieved (whether this be to fulfil stated objectives or to meet customer reaction to existing levels of service provision), the higher will be the cost to the supplier. For instance, see Figure 26.2.

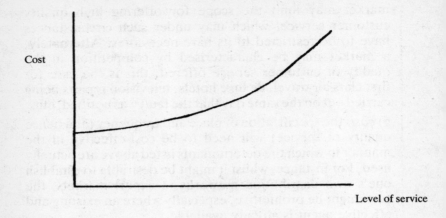

Figure 26.2. Customer Service – Cost Relationship.

The sources of this increased cost will include:

i) the requirement for an intensive or dense distribution network, with numerous distribution outlets.

ii) appropriate levels of stockholding throughout the chain of distribution, accompanied by an effective system of inventory management and control. This will reduce the likelihood of stock shortages or stockouts, or the build-up of excess stockholdings.

iii) appropriate delivery systems to maintain buffer stocks and intermediary stock levels. Such delivery systems will need to operate with such frequency and flexibility that the likelihood of either delivery delays or stockouts is minimised or eliminated.

iv) periodic requirements for delivery systems to deliver smaller than usual unit loads, which is uneconomic when compared, for instance, with large unit load trunking over "optimum" distances.

Conceptually, therefore, two basic choices of customer service level are available to the decision-maker. They are shown as points X and Y on Figure 26.3.

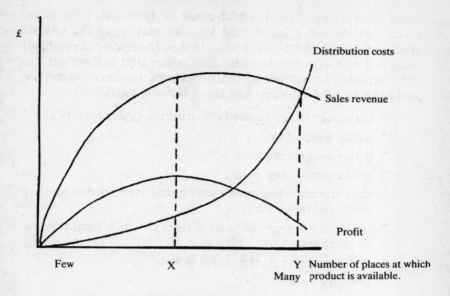

Figure 26.3. Customer Service Decision Alternatives.

Assuming that the marketer was sufficiently free from competitive pressures to actually be in a position to make the choice, he or she could choose between a profit maximising position at X, or a sales maximising position at Y. At point Y the marginal distribution cost of one sales unit equals the marginal sales revenue obtained from it. Beyond point Y the cost of distribution exceeds the sales revenue, whilst unit profit declines after point X. Nevertheless, the area X to Y does yield additional profit or contribution, dependent on the nature of the product cost-volume-profit relationships involved.

3) INVENTORY MANAGEMENT

Stock or inventory is held for three main reasons. The first is the achievement of marketing objectives for customer service. The second aim is the protection of production processes from variations in demand, so that production levels may be stabilised in spite of demand fluctuations around the planning norm or forecast. The third aim is to permit the manufacture or supply of items in economic quantities.

High buffer stocks, and well-stocked channel intermediaries are good for customer service purposes but incur major investment of working capital, which must be financed. Low stock levels, on the other hand, cost less but may incur the risk of stockouts (stock shortages) and lost sales. In seeking to establish what is a cost-effective stockholding policy that will permit the achievement of customer service objectives, the decision-maker will have to take into account the following variables:

* customer order quantity/distributor order quantity;
* order frequency;
* order processing cost;
* order processing delay;
* unit stockholding cost (warehouse cost, order picking cost, insurance etc);
* the minimum size of "safety stocks" which limit the risk of stockouts;
* delivery delay to the order point;
* delivery cost.

Where the manufacturer or supplier meets customer or distributor demand from his base or "buffer" stock, it will be in his interest to persuade customers (perhaps using some kind of incentive discount or favourable delivery terms) to call off an *Economic Order Quantity* (EOQ). The EOQ minimises the supplier's stockholding and order processing costs, as is shown in Figure 26.4.

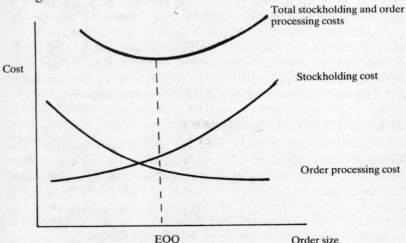

Figure 26.4. Economic Order Quantity.

Stockouts can be avoided by having minimum or safety stock levels at appropriate points in the channel of distribution. Safety stock levels can be calculated on the basis of past customer demand rate patterns, weighted with the appropriate probabilities so that stock shortages or stockouts will be statistically unlikely to a specified *nth* degree. It will be the role of the customer service objective to determine what this specified *nth* degree should be. Conceptually, desired safety stock levels can be shown as in Figure 26.5.

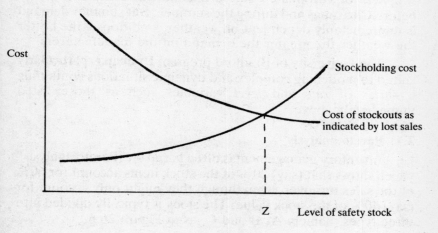

Figure 26.5. Desired Safety Stock Level.

The safety stock level Z is the optimum, since it equates stockholding cost with the cost of stockouts as indicated by lost sales or sales foregone.

The calculation of Economic Order Quantities and desired safety stock levels is complicated by the need to establish stockholding levels *throughout the chain of distribution.* The decision maker will therefore have to inter-relate (or model) the following variables:

* manufacturer production rate, and production rate flexibility;
* manufacturer/supplier's base or buffer stocks;
* channel intermediary stockholding policy;
* stocks held by channel intermediaries;
* customer demand rate;

* rate of stock movement through distribution system;
* speed of stock delivery/replenishment by manufacturer or supplier.

If the supplier cannot inter-relate these variables, it may be difficult to establish an EOQ and even more difficult to prevent stock imbalances or stockouts within the channel of distribution. This risk is highest in those markets characterised by marked seasonal fluctuations in demand. For instance, suppliers of carbonated soft drinks will face demand peaks before Christmas and during the summer. But summer demand is unpredictably dependent on weather conditions – the hotter the weather the greater the demand on the manufacturers.

The University of Bradford program **Dysmap** is particularly suited to modelling complex and dynamic situations containing a series of *rate* and *level* variables such as those listed immediately above.

3.1) Pareto analysis

Inventory management is often based on "Pareto analysis" which shows that (say) 20% of the stock items account for 60% of the sales turnover, even though they might only account for (say) 40% of the stock value. The stock is typically divided into three types, namely A, B and C, as in Figure 26.6.

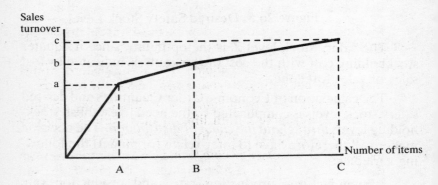

Figure 26.6. Pareto Stock Analysis.

Inventory management concentrates most on stock type A, less on B and least on C. This is a sensible approach because it ensures that the investment and control of stocks is concentrated on the most essential items, whilst at the same time making sure that customer service objectives are met and that stockouts, especially in stock type A, do not occur. Effectively, this process embodies the principle of "management by exception", since management attention is concentrated on the most important part of the total stock mix.

3.2) Adjusting demand to supply

Inventory decisions usually attempt to adjust production or supply to the rate of market demand. But under certain circumstances *demand may have to be adjusted to supply*. These circumstances include:-

a) a supply which is fixed over a period of time, (for instance where investments in new manufacturing capacity take a long time to come into operation).

b) the operation of time constraints, as in the case of perishable goods.

c) the operation of *limiting factors,* such as productive capacity maxima, or "special orders". Special order production is carried out for specific operational or marketing reasons. These include taking advantage of supplies of raw materials, foodstuffs (etc) which are usually difficult to obtain. Or it might be designed to use up old or excess stocks of raw materials (etc), the resulting production being sold at prices which will ensure that all the stock is cleared, even if excess demand results.

Methods by which demand may be adjusted to supply include:-

i) *restricting place availability,* so that the customer must make some conscious effort to gain access to the product.

ii) *restricting time availability,* only making the product or service available within limited time periods, thereby restricting the opportunity for customer access.

iii) *using differential pricing,* which was described in an earlier chapter. Price can be used to restrict the place and time of customer demand, for instance by charging "high season" prices for summer holidays taken in popular Mediterranean resorts, or restricting access to low price services for pensioners to off-peak hours.

iv) *restricting access only to "qualifying" customers,* who receive preferential access to the limited supply. The "qualification" might be based upon the customer's previous purchase record, or membership of some club, society or association.

4) TRANSPORTATION

Reference has already been made to the role of transportation within the physical distribution system, and within the management of stock levels and inventory. The choice of transportation modes is a function of some or all of the following variables:-

a) *customer service objectives for place and frequency of availability:* the chosen transportation mode must meet frequency and/or speed requirements, so that products are available to the customer where and when they are demanded. Frequency and speed of delivery are also major determinants of stockholding policy, both for supplier base or buffer stock, and for intermediary stock levels.

b) *volume and distance:* different transportation modes have different economics dependent on the volume and value of goods to be carried, and the distance of carriage.

c) *product life:* in the case of perishable goods to be sold fresh, rapid transportation from source to outlet will be needed. Specialist containment will be needed, for instance to carry refrigerated or chilled goods, hence:

d) *containment type:* certain types of products may need to be carried in specialist containment, or stored in a specific manner. Transportation capacity, frequency and speed may then depend on the appropriate investment in containment and storage facilities. The need for refrigerated or chilled transport and storage for perishable foodstuffs has already been mentioned. Other examples include:

* liquid gas transported and stored under pressure;
* corrosive or dangerous materials;
* delicate and sensitive products, mainframe computers, etc;
* fuel.

There are various transportation modes available, and each has specific advantages within the context of the contribution of the physical distribution system to meeting objectives for customer service. They include:

i) *air:* cost effective over long distances for low volume, high unit value items requiring rapid delivery. Frequency may depend on flight schedules and availability, whilst reliability may depend on speed of clearance from the airport of flight destination.

ii) *rail:* cost effective over intermediate to long distances for high volume loads (of high or low unit value); and also for "parcels" type deliveries requiring rapid and frequent delivery. The denser the railway network, the more efficient is its parcels service, since this minimises the length of onward road journeys to make final delivery.

iii) *road:* cost effective over short to intermediate distances for a wide variety of unit load types. Road transportation has the critical advantage of *flexibility and reliability,* since it is not dependent on fixed routes as in the case of rail or air. Road transportation can also be cost-effective over long distances if a return load can be carried, or "groupage" business obtained. Groupage is the consolidation of a number of different loads carried to a particular destination, and, ideally, from that destination back to the point of origin.

iv) *ship or canal:* cost-effective for low unit value, high volume loads not requiring rapid delivery. Such loads include coal, fuel oil, iron ore, steel, wheat etc.

SUMMARY

The contents of this chapter are summarised in Table 26.7

TABLE 26.7
Summary : Chapter Twenty Six

SECTION	MAIN POINTS
1. Physical distribution	Comprises operational and managerial activities associated with: customer ordering; the physical transportation, storage and delivery of goods; making services available; stockholding policy, the level of supplier base or buffer stock, the level of channel intermediary stockholding; management and control systems for ware-

housing and distribution. Physical distribution is a function of customer service objectives. The specification of a physical distribution system is a mix, requiring compromise and trade-off in the selection of components, and in judging what is cost-effective.

2. Customer service

Customer service is defined by the specification, quality and performance of (i) the place of product availability; and (ii) the frequency with which the product is available to the customer. The higher the requirement for customer service, the more widely must the product/service be available to the customer, the more dense the distribution network, the more frequently/continuously must it be available, and the more reliable must be the distribution system and the channel intermediaries. The cost of distribution will rise proportionately with the customer service requirement.

3. Inventory management

The management of stocks or inventory has three objectives, namely: (i) the achievement of marketing objectives for customer service; (ii) the protection of production processes from variations in demand; (iii) to permit the manufacture or supply of items in economic quantities. The higher the stock levels, the better the customer service and the greater the cost (and vice versa). Inventory may be divided into three types (fast moving; less fast; and slow moving) and managed on a Pareto basis, which concentrates attention on stock flows that account for the majority of sales turnover. In some cases, inventory management is based on a need to adjust demand to supply.

4. Transportation	Transportation modes include air, rail, road, canal and ship. The choice of transportation mode depends on customer service objectives for place and frequency of availability; volume and distance; product life; product type and containment.

RECOMMENDED READING

Wild R.   Operations management – a policy framework.
                                    Pergamon Press

Wild R.   Production and operations management.
                          Holt, Rinehart and Winston

Taff C A.   Management of physical distribution and
                 transportation.   Irwin

27 Direct Marketing

INTRODUCTION

This chapter deals specifically with Direct Marketing. Direct Marketing is a form of direct supply, which involves a direct promotional, sales and supply relationship between the enterprise and the customer. The chapter describes the main types of direct marketing, and explains some of the reasons for their development.

The chapter then moves on to a consideration of the importance of customer databases and presentation techniques to effective direct marketing. It examines some of the current UK trends in direct marketing, paying particular attention to the interest of retail companies in mail order, and to the importance of accurate target market segmentation. It concludes with a case study based on the effective use of direct mail in the UK insurance market.

CHAPTER CONTENTS

1) Direct marketing defined
2) Types of direct marketing
   2.1) Mail order
   2.2) Direct response advertising
   2.3) Direct mail
   2.4) Junk mail
3) Reasons for the development of direct marketing
4) Databases and direct marketing
5) Direct marketing lists
6) Presentation
7) Mail order trends and UK retailing
8) An illustrative case example – direct mail in the insurance market

Summary

Recommended Reading

Chapter Appendix 27(1) – Direct mail and the **ACORN** system

Questions for self-review

Examination Questions

1) DIRECT MARKETING DEFINED

Direct marketing is a form of *direct supply*. Direct supply was described in some detail in Chapter Twenty Five. Direct marketing involves a direct promotional, sales and supply relationship between the enterprise and the customer, which does not normally involve the use of any intermediaries within the chain of distribution. Amongst the basic business objectives of direct marketing is the elimination of:-

* control losses;
* revenue losses;

that are inherent in any channel of distribution in which other commercial interests are involved.

Proponents of direct marketing also claim that its techniques can be used *to increase the level of communication and interaction between customer and supplier*. Traditionally, a supplier of products or services has, of necessity, to communicate *indirectly* with its customers through retailers and dealer networks for supply, and through promotional media such as television or the press. The basic shortcoming of this process is that it does not always allow for direct dialogue with the customer. With the so-called 'information revolution' the consumer has started to seek much more information about products and services than either the retailer, distributor or promotional message has hitherto been able to provide. With the fragmentation of demand into an increasing variety of market segments (a process described in Chapters 16 and 44), and the increasing demand for individually 'tailored' products or services, have come customer requirements that reject standardised mass-market offerings. There is now widespread preference for differentiated products and services which can variously be described (and positioned) as *segment-specific, niche, premium quality* or *personalised*. The provision of detailed information about these products and services is a role which, *if the technique is used sensitively and appropriately to achieve two-way communication,* direct marketing may effectively promote and fulfill.

Direct marketing is best known in the UK, Europe and the USA for its application to consumer goods markets. But it is also found in marketing to industrial and business organisations. It has been estimated that £7 billion worth of goods and services were sold in 1988 as a result of the application of direct marketing techniques to UK consumer goods markets.

2) TYPES OF DIRECT MARKETING

There are three main types of direct marketing. They are:-

* mail order;
* direct response advertising;
* direct mail.

Each is analysed in turn.

2.1) Mail Order

Mail order is generally based upon the issue of *catalogues* through the postal system to target recipients. The catalogues are used to describe and display the products on sale, and contain information about ordering and delivery procedure, dealing with returned goods, obtaining refunds (etc).

The catalogue may be the only selling device involved. Or, instead, the supplier may make use of part-time agents to carry out the order-taking process. This is a well-known system in the UK in the case of clothing, housewares and cosmetics. Catalogue-agent marketing is used in the UK by major mail order houses such as Grattan, Freemans and Littlewoods, and the cosmetic manufacturer Avon. Catalogue-only marketing is used by such retail companies as Next, Damart, Kaleidoscope and Marks and Spencer.

Alternatively (and more controversially), catalogue marketing may be based upon "party selling". In this case an agent invites potential customers to his or her own home (or someone else's), where the catalogue products are displayed. The invited guests are encouraged to examine the merchandise and to place orders. Party selling is used in the marketing of plastic kitchen and housewares, ceramic tableware and china, lingerie, shoes, toys and wine. In the latter case, guests are invited to sample the various vintages on offer, and to order by the case.

Mail order has a long history in Europe and the USA. Its fortunes have varied in the UK, but it now seems to be enjoying something of a renaissance. This rejuvenation is examined in a later section of this chapter.

2.2) Direct Response Advertising

The objective of direct response advertising is to sell products or services direct to the public, using advertisements which describe the item, its price and method of supply. These advertisements may appear in such media as the newspapers, magazines or television. This technique may be effective where the product or service is well-known and understood. For instance, popular records are sometimes sold by television advertising. Customers are asked to specify the title, whether they want record, tape or compact disc, and to send their address and the correct remittance. Ideally, customers will place credit card orders by telephone. So the advertisement must contain clear address and telephone number information.

Readers will be able to think of your own examples. Look for them in the colour supplements to Sunday newspapers, in magazines and professional journals, in the Radio Times or TV Times (etc). The value of the items they are selling may vary from a few pounds, to complete fitted kitchens costing several thousand pounds.

2.3) Direct Mail

The term direct mail covers a number of direct marketing approaches, but all are based on *the usage of the postal system*. Direct mailings or "mailshots" use letters, brochures and other printed material, but not catalogues. Often these letters are *personalised*. Whilst much of this unsolicited mail will be ignored by its recipients, carefully targeted and well presented mailings can be an effective method of promoting and selling products or services, or at least causing the recipient to enquire further about the offer. Some examples of direct mail are given in later sections of this chapter.

Direct mail is used in consumer goods/services markets by such UK organisations as the Automobile Association and Royal Automobile Club, Readers Digest, National Geographic magazine, insurance companies, unit trusts and banks. It can also be used to good effect in marketing products or services to industrial and business prospects (a "prospect" is a potential customer). Take for instance a winner in the business-to-business category in the British Direct Marketing Association/ Royal Mail awards. The supplier was British Telecom Mobile Phones, whose agency created a briefcase size mock-up of a car's dashboard, in which it was suggested that the only important thing missing was a car phone. Further information could be obtained by pressing the button of a cassette recorder concealed inside, and the taped message told the car dealer who had been sent the package why he should stock British Telecom car phones. An additional benefit was that the package could also be used at *point of sale* (a promotional technique described in a later chapter). The other side of the tape relayed a different message to interested people who had come into the showroom to look at the cars on offer. One mailing of this package was sent to 1,200 Ford dealers and generated 300 enquiries, 34% of which led to sales of the product (which cost up to £2000 each!)

2.4) Junk Mail

The direct mailing of letters, brochures and other printed materials appears however to have one basic disadvantage. Such mailings are often perceived by the recipient as *unsolicited mail*. The quantity of such direct mailings has increased dramatically during recent years in the UK. This appears to have generated a negative reaction from the general public, who have come to describe many of the offerings of direct mail as 'junk mail'. *This negative reaction threatens to devalue direct mail as a tool of direct marketing*. Indeed, the Chairman of the UK Post Office went as far in 1989 as 'laying down a challenge to all users of our medium: stop junk mail. By junk mail, I mean direct mail advertising which is poorly targeted and of a poor creative standard. The term has been used to refer to all direct mail advertising. This is clearly wrong, but there can be no denying some direct mail is junk. This is the mail that does not respect individuals, but deluges them with unwanted and untargeted paper to their irritation and the detriment of the medium as a whole.

The medium is in danger of becoming devalued by messages which do not use it with sufficient discrimination. Direct marketing should not be used as a broadcast medium, aiming for blanket coverage with insensitive and unselective mailshots. It is a unique medium, going into every household in the UK and allowing the advertiser to treat every customer as an individual. Marketing needs to be more selective, more targeted, and more attentive to the individual needs of its customers and thus more respectful of the individual'.

3) REASONS FOR THE DEVELOPMENT OF DIRECT MARKETING

Mail order is a long established method of marketing. Despite variations in its fortunes, and the development of an efficient and aggressive retail sector, it has survived and even prospers. The use of direct response advertising and direct mail has expanded greatly during the last decade. There are two main reasons for these developments:

i) direct marketing cuts out the use of channel intermediaries or reduces dependence on them, and (to some degree) protects the supplier from increases in the relative power that they enjoy. At the same time, the use of direct marketing may have the effect of widening the available market.

ii) technological and applications developments in computing hardware and software, information systems and databases, residential-lifestyle classifications such as **ACORN,** and letter printing systems (for instance, see the appendix to this chapter).

4) DATABASES AND DIRECT MARKETING

Computing and database developments mean that large volumes of information about customers and the market can be categorised and stored. Such customer databases can include demographic information about individual customers, and their purchase history of the company's products. For example:

* car manufacturers can now record the life of a vehicle, and its owner(s) with some precision. They can support their agents and dealers by sending personalised mailings to customers encouraging servicing or replacement, and by promoting new models or accessories when these are introduced. They can sell their customer lists to other companies who are directly promoting and marketing complementary products, such as insurance, designer clothes, travel and credit facilities. Rover Group, for instance, have a large database which can be used to contact each customer personally and accurately at low cost, compared with direct sales contact by dealers.

A customer database may be built up from information received from any of the following:

i) order forms.

ii) guarantee cards and warranty documents.

iii) account customer documentation.

iv) enquiry coupons.

v) on-pack offers giving name and address.

vi) subscriptions to magazines, motoring organisations, professional bodies, clubs and societies (etc).

Alternatively, *lists* may be purchased. Customer lists are analysed in the next section. Basic customer information will comprise:

CUSTOMER	VARIABLE	INFORMATION
Mr	Title	Gender; marital status
Barry	First name	Ethnic origin, age
Ward	Surname	Ethnic origin
38	House number	) Area
Morningside Rise	Street name	) demographics
Lymington	Town	) based on Census data,
Hampshire	County	) for instance expressed
SO4 7NR	Postcode	) as **ACORN** categories.

Other customer information included in the database record could include any of the following:

* *Frequency:* how often does the customer purchase the product?

* *Time:* when did the customer last purchase the product?

* *Value:* how much is the customer's business worth?

* *Payment:* when does the customer pay, and how does he/she pay?

* *Loyalty:* how long has the individual been a customer?

A customer database can be used for direct marketing purposes in one of two ways. The first is *non-selective*. The mailing or catalogue is sent to all of the individuals in the particular database or list. This assumes that the mailing is appropriate to all of these individuals, or that the listing makes accessible a desired set of target recipients. Where the enterprise cannot be sure that the database or list meets these two criteria, it must accept the risk that many of the recipients will ignore the mailing. Much of it will end up in the wastepaper bin, adjudged to be the junk mail described in section (2.4) above.

The second application is *selective*. The recipients of the mailing must be *targeted* by the application of selection criteria to screen out those individuals to whom the catalogue or message is inappropriate. An earlier chapter has already described the use of the **ACORN** system to achieve such a selection. The **ACORN** system will require the database or list

366

to contain the postcodes of the potential recipients. Alternatively, the selection criteria may be based upon additional customer information, such as value or frequency of purchase. The more accurate and precise is to be the selection and targeting of individuals for direct mail purposes, the more detailed and up-to-date must be the customer data, and the more expensive will be the compilation and maintenance of the database.

5) DIRECT MARKETING LISTS

Lists are compiled from customer databases, and generally take the form of tapes or discs which can be accessed by computerised systems that print personalised letters, envelopes or address labels. The direct marketer may be in a position to access his or her own company database, using a *database management system,* to produce customer lists. Or instead, he or she may purchase lists from specialist agencies who compile databases from customer information purchased from other companies. Needless to say, the purchaser of a customer list will have to make sure that:

* the list is relevant to the objective and the target recipients of the mailing;
* the list is accurate;
* the list is up-to-date.

6) PRESENTATION

Whichever form of direct marketing is used, whether it be mail order catalogues, media advertisements or direct mail communications, *the quality of presentation is of critical importance.* The catalogue, advertisement, letter or package needs to be attractive and appealing. It should make it easy for the potential customer to understand the message, and to act upon it if he or she so chooses. It should not confuse the recipient, or give rise to questions, since these will frustrate or annoy. Ideally, it should not contain too much dense or complicated text, since this will cause the recipient to "switch-off" and ignore the item. Once a recipient has switched-off, a direct mailing is likely to end up in the bin or at the waste-paper recycler!

As a result, direct mail catalogues are often printed in full colour on high quality paper. They may feature creative photography, and contain easy-to-follow ordering instructions. They will often encourage customers to make use of telephone ordering using credit or charge cards. Direct mail communications, on the other hand, may be accompanied by personalised letters, produced by high speed wordprocessors and laser printers which give a typeface and finish as acceptable as many printing systems.

7) MAIL ORDER TRENDS AND UK RETAILING

The UK mail order business accounts for over 4% of total UK retail trade. Mail order, therefore, is a highly significant component of the retail scene in this country. Its development has been boosted by the debut of major retail chains as direct mail order suppliers. Retail companies such as Marks and Spencer (with a home furnishings catalogue), Next (up-market clothes) and High and Mighty (clothes for large or tall men) have moved into the mail order business.

This development has three main sources. The *first* is mergers between retail companies and mail order houses (such as Next and Grattan), or direct takeovers of mail order business by retail companies. The second is the modernisation of mail order operating systems. Modern computerised systems have streamlined and speeded up trading operations. And customer databases provide a wealth of information about who is buying what from their catalogues. The result is an increasing capacity to position catalogues on selected customer segments. *For these customer databases are ideal tools by which to carry out detailed market segmentation activities*. Market segmentation was analysed in an earlier chapter, but the frequent references to it throughout this book should reinforce its importance in the study and practice of marketing and marketing management.

The *third* reason is the level of retailer demand for prime high street sites. Such is the pressure of demand for good sites that rents and rates (property taxes) are becoming prohibitive. For instance, the annual rent and rates for a reasonably sized shop premise in Princes Street, Edinburgh, can be in excess of £1 million! The cost and availability of such sites constitute a major *limiting factor* on the expansion of retail chains.

In addition to the traditional "all-purpose" catalogues, mail order companies are introducing specialised catalogues or "specialogues" targeted on specific customer segments. There are catalogues, for example, for short women, tall men, babies and children, women aged 35 plus, and so on. These catalogues are used to market clothes, shoes and accessories; household goods and soft furnishings; motoring accessories; books; toys; holidays; and luxury goods. The target segments vary right across the socio-economic scale, from the traditional target groups C and D (once the main mail order catalogue market) right up to the A and B groups. For instance, one mail order house has found direct marketing success in selling up-market clothes and accessories to young, fashion-conscious working women. On the other hand, Marks and Spencer, commenting on the problem and cost of prime retail site availability, is of the opinion that the catalogue offers a convenient alternative method of reaching customers. The use of mail order is of especial relevance to firms like Marks and Spencer who operate their own credit or charge cards, since these companies already hold customer details on their databases and can make use of their customer accounts as a ready made and credit-worthy payment system. Such companies can offer restricted lines to specific target segments, or they can offer extensive ranges of merchandise, as displayed in their retail outlets, to a wider market.

The mail order industry has traditionally been the poor relation of the UK retail trade. Mail order enjoyed profitable trading during the 1960's and 1970's, but was hit badly by the recession of the early 1980's. Between 1980 and 1985 mail order companies had, along with hardware stores, the lowest increase in turnover in the non-food retail sector.

The mail order companies' traditional market in the UK has been the lower socio-economic groups C and D, which meant that when the recession tightened its grip, mail order companies were hit harder than most. With a strong customer base in the North of the country, where unemployment was, and continues to be, running at high levels, the effects of the recession were further exacerbated. Added to which, in the words of one senior executive, mail order companies "were providing slow service, had a bad image, and were competing against the very competitive high street retailers. We wouldn't have survived if we had continued in the way we were going."

Various strategies have been pursued as a result. There have been mergers between retailers and mail order houses. Attempts have been made to move the mail order business up-market, and improve its service and efficiency. The range of goods on offer increased dramatically, and the mail order business has attracted a wide range of new customer types and segments. And the image of mail order has improved. These changes and innovations have had something of the desired effect, and a once stagnant sector of the retail trade seems to have taken on a new lease of life.

8) AN ILLUSTRATIVE CASE EXAMPLE

BOX 27.1

Direct mail in the insurance market

According to the insurance industry, there is a high degree of *under-insurance* in the UK. For instance, something like 35% of the adult population has no life cover whatsoever, which means that should they die leaving mortgages or debts unpaid, these will be transferred to their inheritors. Established methods of promoting and selling insurance in the UK cannot therefore be seen as completely effective. These methods include expensive media advertising, and direct selling by insurance agents and brokers.

However, the use of *carefully targeted direct mailings* has proved effective. Users of such mailings include the AA (Automobile Association), Avon Insurance and the RAC (Royal Automobile Club). Such mailings must:-

* identify a genuine market need;
* be consistent with customer motives for seeking insurance;
* offer an effective and consistent answer to this identified need;
* explain the insurance service clearly and precisely;
* be well presented and free from errors.

The potential for direct marketing success will lie with the *specificity of the offer, and the preciseness of targeting.* The individual recipient is free from direct sales pressure (well-known where life assurance is concerned!), and is able to study the proposal at leisure in his or her own home. Specific insurance packages can be put together that directly satisfy target customer motives for seeking insurance. Such motives could include:

* fear of loss of income for the self-employed;
* the need to anticipate wedding or funeral expenses;
* a desire to cover one's family for private medical treatment.

One insurance company targeted an income protection policy on General Practitioners (doctors in public practice). In the UK, GPs must provide a locum (a replacement doctor) to cover their work if they are ill, and they must pay the locum's fee themselves. The insurance policy was targeted on subscribers to a magazine called "Pulse", which is distributed to GPs, and met a very favourable response. Many policies were sold, indicating that the insurance company had discovered a specific but important insurance need.

SUMMARY

The contents of this chapter are summarised in Table 27.2

TABLE 27.2
Summary : Chapter Twenty Seven

SECTION	MAIN POINTS
1. Direct marketing defined	Direct marketing is a form of direct supply. It involves a promotional, sales and supply relationship between the enterprise and the customer, which does not normally include the use of any channel intermediary.
2. Types of direct marketing	These include (i) mail order (based on catalogues), which may make use of part-time agents to collect orders (etc); (ii) direct response advertising; (iii) direct mail.
3. Reasons for development of direct marketing	Are two-fold: (i) to cut out the use of channel intermediaries and thereby reduce revenue and control losses; (ii) make use of developments in computing hardware and printing systems, information systems and databases, and residential-lifestyle classifications such as **ACORN.**
4. Databases and direct marketing	Customer databases can include demographic information, and the customer's purchase history of the company's products. Databases can

371

	be used non-selectively; or selectively, in which case customer targets or segments are selected on the basis of specific criteria of appropriateness.
5. Direct marketing lists	Lists are compiled from customer databases, and take the form of tapes or discs which can be accessed by computerised systems that print personalised letters, envelopes or address labels.
6. Presentation	Presentation quality is of critical importance to the achievement of effective direct marketing.
7. Mail order trends and UK retailing	Mail order accounts for a significant proportion of UK retail trade. After a period of stagnation it is showing signs of expansion as retail companies move into mail order, and specialist catalogues are positioned on accurately defined market segments. These developments have three sources, namely (i) mergers involving mail order and retail companies; (ii) computerised operating systems and customer databases making possible accurate market segmentation and customer targeting; (iii) retailer demand for prime retail sites, and the cost and availability of such sites constituting a major limiting factor on the expansion of retail chains.

RECOMMENDED READING

Graham J.W. and Jones S.K.   Selling by Mail.   Macmillan

CHAPTER APPENDIX 27(1)

DIRECT MAIL AND THE ACORN SYSTEM

"Direct Mail is one of ACORN'S most powerful application areas. Many million ACORN selections from the electoral roll have been mailed successfully by all types of client organisation.

Users include financial, retail and mail order companies, normally for customer acquisition but also for building local store traffic and at a more sophisticated level, for pre-screening offers of credit.

The new ACORN List is compiled from the largest source of up-to-date names and addresses in Great Britain — the electoral register — 43 million adults.

Each name and address is matched, via the postcode, to an ACORN neighbourhood type, plus numerous geographic boundaries. This database is held on CACI's computer installation for list rental selections. So, if you know the ACORN type of your target market, CACI can supply a tailor made list of names and addresses of prime consumer prospects within any combination of retail and media areas.

You can select names and addresses as follows:

Volume:
Between 10,000 and 18 million names and addresses.

Lifestyle:
By an individual or a combination of ACORN neighbourhood types.

Area:
By town/Local Expenditure Zone/County/IBA or ILR region/ or simply a circle around your retail outlet.

Output:
On labels, magnetic tape or personalized letters.

The list can be further refined by selecting:

Mobility:
House movers since the last Voters Roll.

Age:
18 year olds newly entitled to vote.

Credit:
Those on the Voters Roll without County Court Judgements.

ACORN is used by all major direct mail companies. It has proved particularly effective for retailers wishing to support individual branches by local mailing, for motor manufacturers in support of specific distributors and for direct selling organisations wishing to expand their customer base."
(Reproduced with permission.)

QUESTIONS FOR SELF REVIEW

1)   What is the role of the channels of distribution in the supply of goods or services to the customer?

2)   What marketing objectives are fulfilled by the channels of distribution?

3)   Describe and compare the four main types of channel of distribution. What are the advantages and disadvantages of each type, when seen from the viewpoint of a manufacturing or supplying company?

4)   In what ways may channel intermediaries make it difficult for a manufacturing or supplying company to achieve its commercial and marketing objectives?

5)   In what ways can the development of large scale retail chains pose a threat to manufacturers or suppliers in a consumer goods market?

6)   What are the marketing objectives of the physical distribution process? Describe some of the main elements of the physical distribution process.

7)   What is customer service? How can it be specified and measured?

8)   Describe and comment on the relationship between the quality and the cost of customer service objectives.

9)   What are the marketing objectives of holding stocks?

10) How may inventory be best managed by a manufacturer or supplier? What compromises will have to be made in this inventory management process?

11) What are the main transportation modes used in physical distribution? What are their advantages and disadvantages?

12) What is direct marketing? Why is it an important means of promoting and selling goods and services?

13) Describe and compare the three main types of direct marketing.

14) What is a customer database and how might it be constructed? Why is the customer database a vital element in direct marketing?

EXAMINATION QUESTIONS

Q49 *What major factors influence the distribution channels adopted by a company? For each factor identified, explain how different product types may affect the decision choice of management.*

(ABE)

Q50 *What are some of the advantages and disadvantages of using intermediaries in channels of distribution?*

(CIM)

Q51 *Outline the circumstances in which a manufacturer might use the following, giving examples to illustrate your answers:*

a) Selective distribution

b) Intensive distribution?   *(IPS)*

Q52 *How do you account for the increasing emphasis given to the management of physical distribution? Using examples, illustrate some of the key decisions to be made in this area.*

(CIM)

Q53 *How do you account for the fact that non-shop selling has, in recent years, been one of the fastest growing areas of distribution.*

(CIM)

28 International Marketing

"Where am I? What place is this?" British export salesman overheard by the author in the foyer of the Hotel Cinar, Istanbul, Turkey.

INTRODUCTION

This chapter begins by looking at some of the reasons why companies undertake international marketing activity. This is followed by an analysis of some of the factors that the exporter must take into consideration when analysing markets. These factors are listed as "the 12 C's". The analysis of international marketing is continued in Chapter Twenty Nine.

CHAPTER CONTENTS

1) Why international marketing?
2) Analysing international markets – the 12 C's.
   2.1) Country
   2.2) Culture and consumer behaviour.
   2.3) Concentration.
   2.4) Communication.
   2.5) Channels of distribution.
   2.6) Capacity to pay.
   2.7) Currency.
   2.8) Control and co-ordination.
   2.9) Commitment.
   2.10) Choices.
   2.11) Contractual obligations.
   2.12) Caveats.
3) The 12 C's summarised.

1) WHY INTERNATIONAL MARKETING?

Any business enterprise, whether great or small, must choose between two alternative trading policies. These are:

* to trade in the domestic or national economy within which the enterprise is located;

* to trade in its domestic economy and/or to trade on an international basis.

If a company decides to trade on an international basis, it will become involved in export marketing and international operations. But why should a company choose to trade on such a basis? There are a number of explanations, including:

a) *to achieve growth:* where the domestic market is static, or showing only a slow rate of growth, or is characterised by high levels of competition, international marketing may be used to achieve business growth and expansion. By looking at international markets the company can widen its horizons, and increase its scope. It will be aiming at a larger target, and this target will increase the size of the potential market available to it.

b) *to achieve economies of scale:* there is a direct relationship between volume of output and the cost per unit. It is a reasonable generalisation to state that *lower than competitor unit costs* give the supplier a significant competitive advantage. But given the limitations of any one domestic market, the supplier may have to trade on an international basis to gain a level of sales that will support the necessary investment in plant and technology required to yield these unit cost reductions. An obvious example is the motor vehicle trade. Most manufacturers operate on an international basis as a matter of necessity.

c) *international competition:* where national markets have become dominated by suppliers who operate on an international basis, then other suppliers will have little choice but to follow suit. Failure to compete on equal terms may bring about the elimination of the supplier, or at best his relegation to some kind of "second division" status. This perhaps might involve carrying out assembly or sub-contract operations for major manufacturers in markets where these indigenous enterprises have political guarantees of protection, subsidy and survival.

d) *national necessity:* international trade is a national necessity. Many economies are not self-sufficient, and must import raw materials, fuel, foodstuffs, machinery, technology and so on. They must therefore export other goods in order to earn the currency to pay for the imports they need. Some countries need to import oil or foodstuffs, and export manufactured goods to pay for these vital imports. National and international economies are inter-related, and the health of one influences the health of the other. Restrictions on one will have some kind of effect in the other. These "knock-on" effects may be hard to predict. Indeed, international trade and international stability are themselves closely linked. Times of trade are times of peace!

2) ANALYSING INTERNATIONAL MARKETS – THE 12 C's

Any analysis of international markets in a text such as this must, of necessity, be limited in its scope and depth. Indeed, a considerable number of textbooks are available which deal only with this subject. For convenience, therefore, twelve sub-headings have been chosen. These sub-headings deal with a number of important areas but, inevitably, others have had to be left out. For ease of reading and revision purposes each of these sub-headings begins with the capital letter 'C', so that this section of the chapter is based on *the 12 C's* of international marketing.

2.1) Country

The marketer must obtain a thorough understanding of the country with which he or she proposes to trade. Three vital components of this knowledge include:

a) *policy towards imports:* are there stated government policies about the range and type of imports that will be accepted into the country; the degree to which home ("indigenous") suppliers or manufacturers will be protected against foreign competition; and the proportion of total product value that must derive from home produced or manufactured content of products marketed by foreign companies? Does the government impose tariff duties or quotas upon imports? Is its policy towards foreign companies consistent, visible and predictable? Is there any way in which the exporter can protect himself against unpredictable uncertainties arising from overseas government policy, and what help do home agencies (such as the Department of Trade and Industry, Export Councils, Chambers of Commerce (etc)) have to offer to reduce the risk and uncertainty associated with international marketing?

b) *import regulations:* the marketer (or his export agent if he uses one) must have an intimate knowledge of the regulations imposed by the target country on all products imported from abroad. The exporter will have to fulfil all of the legal and financial regulations laid down; complete all of the necessary shipping, insurance and import documentation that is required; and generally cope with whatever other bureaucratic necessities come his way. This may be a complex and expensive process, and many companies make use of specialist agencies who are skilled at coping with the different paperwork requirements of different export markets.

c) *the marketing and commercial infrastructure:* the marketer or his agent must understand the structure and functioning of the country's trade and commercial infrastructure. This may be similar to that used in his or her own domestic market, or it may be radically different. For instance, buying and distribution in centrally planned socialist economies requires an entirely different export marketing strategy compared with that used, say, by British companies selling draught beer in Holland, or German companies selling cars in the USA. Again, specialist agencies, government departments and embassies, chambers of commerce (etc) may provide help and assistance to the exporter in working out how best to understand and come to terms with the particular commercial infrastructure in question. Similarly, the exporter must understand *the marketing and distribution structures* used by the particular trade in the target country. What marketing agencies are available and what market intelligence can be gained? What channels of distribution are available and how may the product best be promoted? All of the issues dealt with throughout this book will be relevant to building up such an understanding of the way in which the product can be marketed and sold.

2.2) Culture and consumer behaviour

Chapters 10 to 13 contained a detailed analysis of consumer and buyer behaviour. Of particular relevance to the export marketer will be the relative influence of the different behavioural determinants of demand. For instance:-

    * how important is individual motivation as compared with group norms and the influence of the family in purchase decisions? Individual motivations are important in western cultures; family influences are much stronger in eastern ones;

    * what kinds of life-style are prevalent in the target country, and what forms of reference group are influential in determining the acceptance (or otherwise) of new products?

    * what pattern does the family life-cycle take, and how does this affect purchasing decisions? For instance, what is the effect of having to pay school and college fees on family disposable income in some overseas markets? How large are the dowries payable on the marriage of a daughter, and what will her wedding cost? What kind of housing is available, and how is it financed?

Of particular importance to the international marketer is the *culture* of the target country. Reference was made in Chapter 10 to the difference between *traditional, achieving* and *affluent cultures*. Culture, in turn, was related to life-style. The international marketer must attempt to understand the culture prevailing in the country in which he is interested, so that he can gauge the relevance of his product and the likely reaction to it. Will the product be acceptable in its present form, or will it need modification? And how best may it be promoted and sold, given the particular cultural values and traditions of the society in question? Two examples can be given.

i) whilst the use of *consumer credit* is encouraged in western economies, other societies may frown on the borrowing of money for expenditure on consumer goods. People may expect to have to build up savings from their personal income, and to purchase the product for cash. The rate of consumer spending may therefore appear relatively slow in comparison with western economies.

ii) developing economies may, in any case, encourage *saving* rather than expenditure on consumer goods (especially if these have to be imported and use up precious foreign currency). These savings may be used to finance infra-structure and industrial developments. Such economies are more likely to be of interest to companies operating in industrial goods markets. There may be significant demand for construction services, railway and transportation systems, technology transfer, computing equipment and so on.

2.3) Concentration

A study of the basic demographic pattern of some export markets, particularly in developing countries (sometimes categorised as the "Lesser Developed Countries" or LDC's) will often reveal *population concentrations*. A significant proportion of the total population may be concentrated in the larger cities, and especially in the national and provincial capitals. The rest of the population will often be diffused across those areas of the country that are agriculturally productive, or which contain extractive industries like coal-mining, and fishing. A basic segmentation and stratification of the market, therefore, will be based on *urban and rural population distributions*. More detailed segmentation and stratification may then be carried out on the basis of such factors as:

* *relative income distributions:* wealth may be unevenly distributed as between rich and poor; between urban and rural areas; between ethnic groups making up the society (as in Latin America); or between the state, industrial investment and consumer expenditure.

* *access to channels of distribution:* which will reflect the factors described above. Channels of distribution will tend to be concentrated on the more densely populated areas. In countries with an uneven distribution of income, they will tend to favour those locations in which there is effective demand for the product.

* *access to decision-makers:* government ministries and industrial decision-makers tend to be concentrated in national and provincial capitals. Promotional and selling effort may therefore have to be concentrated on these locations.

2.4) Communication

The means by which the exporter chooses to organise his efforts in overseas market territories is discussed in later sections in this chapter. Suffice it to say that consideration must be given to the following items:

a) the communication media available to the overseas territory, and available within it. It may be easy enough to contact the capital, and to send documents by FAX, or whatever. Communications *within* the country may not be quite so highly developed, however, and may not always be totally reliable! This is particularly true of the poorer Third world countries.

b) how may the exporter keep in contact with his channels of physical distribution? Loss of communication may mean loss of control over goods in transit. Old Africa hands have a wealth of anecdotes about what could happen to goods in transit between the coast and an inland destination over a thousand miles away or more!

c) how may the exporter keep in contact with his channels of distribution? Again, this has control implications.

d) the choice of promotional media: the exporter will have to investigate the alternative promotional media available, and establish promotional strategies which are appropriate to the country and its culture. For instance, where there is a low degree of literacy, television may be an important media. Newspapers may be regional rather than national, or based on language or ethnic differences.

e) language: the marketing effort and the communications involved in it must be carried out in whatever language (or languages) are relevant to the target market segments. There will be no substitute *to learning those languages, and to employing and training multi-lingual nationals within the territory*.

2.5) Channels of distribution

Channels of distribution were analysed in Chapter 25. Such an analysis is as relevant to overseas territories as it is to home ones. However, export strategies for distribution channels involve a more complex set of considerations and these are dealt with in the next chapter.

2.6) Capacity to pay

The viability of an international marketing proposal is dependent upon the capacity of the target market to pay for the goods and services it has ordered. This is true whether we are considering individual consumers buying television sets or toothpaste; industrial companies purchasing computers or technology; or governments investing in massive infrastructure projects, hospitals or defence systems.

This capacity to pay will be a function of many factors, some of which might include:

* Gross National Product; resources available for investment; personal disposable income (etc);

* government restrictions on the expenditure of foreign currency reserves;

* the pattern and terms of financing packages made available by the supplier;

* guarantees of payment, whether made overseas or by home government agencies;

* loan terms; interest and capital repayment requirements. Readers should be aware of the serious nature of this problem in some developing countries. These have borrowed so much money that there is a question as to whether all of the interest can be paid, and the total capital ever paid back to the lenders.

2.7) Currency

The value of overseas sales is, in part, dependent on the currency involved. Firstly, is the local currency *acceptable* (or "convertable") in international trade, or is it worthless from that viewpoint? Where the local currency is not acceptable in trading terms, then payments will have to be made out of "hard currency" reserves (such as dollars, pounds sterling, Swiss francs, German marks etc). Payment is then dependent upon the availability of such currency reserves. This is the source of the terrible conundrum facing some Third World countries, who are not able to earn enough foreign currency to cover their needs. One alternative may be the making of payment for imported goods *in kind,* at an equivalent value. So, for instance, one country might pay for its imports of machinery with an equivalent value of tea or coffee. This then depends upon how well such *countertrade* arrangements can be made to work in the country supplying the machinery, and on tea or coffee prices there.

Secondly, the value of an export-import transaction to both supplier and buyer is dependent *on the value of the currency* involved. All currencies accepted in international trade are subject to fluctuations in their value against other currencies. So, a rise in the value of the mark or yen against other currencies makes German or Japanese goods more expensive in world markets. And a fall in the relative value of the pound sterling, or Italian lira makes British or Italian goods cheaper. Currency fluctuations, therefore, affect the transaction value involved, and determine the revenue return to be obtained. Given any particular level of costs this will determine the profitability of the transaction to the supplier, and hence influence his view of the viability of the overseas market in question.

2.8) Control and co-ordination

The viability of any export marketing or international trading activity is also partly dependent on *the degree of control* that may be exercised over that activity. The principles of control are the same for any activity, and are shown in simplified form in Figure 28.1.

Within the context of export marketing and international trade, therefore, the effectiveness of the control process will depend on:

a) *the clarity and realism of the strategies, plans, policies and objectives upon which the activity is to be based.* Are the plans *achievable* within the context of a particular country or trade? For instance, airline operators wishing to reduce air fares in order to attract more customers have consistently fallen foul of powerful international cartel arrangements, especially in Europe, that have the effect of maximising prices and minimising competion.

b) *the number of agencies and individuals involved in the chain of command.* The greater the involvement of outside agencies, companies, distributors (etc), the more difficult it will be for the marketer to co-ordinate what is going on. And, as any basic management textbook will tell you, *the poorer the co-ordination, the poorer the control.*

c) *the performance measurement criteria or standards available.* The problems of measuring value have already been considered in section 2.7 above. Secondly, what performance standards can be applied to outside agencies, such as import-export enterprises, wholesale and retail distributors (etc) in overseas countries? How can these intermediaries be motivated to achieve the exporter's performance targets? What are the consequences of under-achievement or poor performance, and what relative power does, say, the distributor have relative to the supplier in the particular country in view?

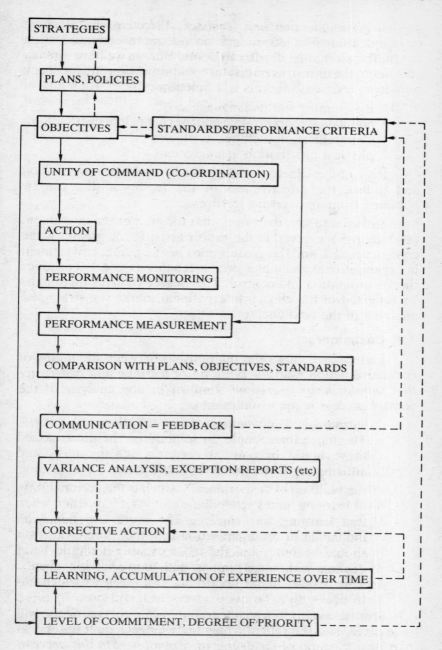

Figure 28.1. The Control Process.

d) *communication and feedback*. Effective co-ordination and control is dependent on adequate communication links, so that feedback can occur. But, as we have already seen, the unrestricted flow of communication and feedback from overseas markets is a function of:-

* the country and its language;
* population concentration and the channels of distribution;
* communication facilities available;
* physical distribution arrangements.

Each of these factors may act as *a barrier to communication* and reduce the effectiveness of the feedback that can be obtained from an overseas territory.

Suffice it to say, therefore, that the greater the investment (and the risk) involved in the export activity, the greater is the control needed, and the greater must be the parallel investment in organisational and managerial mechanisms that will produce this co-ordination and control. This degree of investment must be reflected in the chosen international marketing strategies, analysed in the next chapter.

2.9) Commitment

Figure 28.1 shows the relationship between the taking of corrective action, and *the build up of learning and experience that should occur over time*. Implicit in any analysis of the control process is the assumption of:

* learning and movements down the "learning curve". The more that people do something, the more skilled they should become at carrying out the task, and anticipating when things will go wrong;
* the build up of "experience", which is the accumulation of learning, and knowledge about what happened when that learning was applied. The more experience an individual or an organisation has, the more efficient it should become, and the more capable it should be at dealing with uncertainties and unpredictable events. This is particularly important to a business which has to deal with a variety of overseas territories.

But the extent to which learning from past experience will take place, and the rate at which knowledge is built up, will in part be a function of *the degree of commitment to this process*. The level of commitment, in turn, will depend on the perceived priority of the learning process.

It is important that the international marketing activity builds up knowledge and experience of the territories in which it is operating. International marketing, by definition, is an activity that will be sure to give rise to a high level of uncertain, unpredictable and uncontrollable events. *But the build-up of experience will depend upon the commitment of the enterprise to the international marketing activity.* This commitment, in turn, will depend upon the stated and perceived priority of international marketing. This will be a function of the kinds of strategies and objectives that the enterprise sets for itself.

Local knowledge, skill and experience will only be built up if the enterprise commits itself *to a determined and long-term presence within the territory,* and treats its activities within that territory as a priority. Hence the success of Japanese exporters throughout the world. Once the Japanese arrive, they stay. And they involve the local populace by employing them, training them and working with them. It is a recipe for success.

2.10) Choices

The exporter must study the marketing mix choices available in the target territories in which he or she is interested. This point has already been made above. The international marketer needs to find out what alternative elements of the marketing mix work most effectively within the local context. This again calls for long term involvement in the territory, the learning of local languages and customs, and the use of local resources and personnel. If people need training, then train them! Investment in people usually yields positive benefits, and is an essential part of the long term view that is so essential to the international trader.

2.11) Contractual obligations

The study of the contractual terms upon which international trade is carried out is a highly specialised one. Normally, the enterprise will employ specialist agencies to deal with this matter. Nevertheless, the exporter needs to look carefully at the contractual obligations of any proposed deal, under such headings as:-

* financial deposits (in hard currency) required as evidence of the exporter's "good faith";
* payment terms and conditions, and their agreement with the customer;

387

* guarantees of delivery;
* penalties for late delivery or failure to deliver;
* stage payments to be made by the customer, and the circumstances under which the final payment is to be made.

It is sometimes the experience of construction companies that the final payment, due upon completion of the project, is not always made. For instance, the price agreed on Project X was Pq, and the number of instalments or stage payments the customer had to make was negotiated at n, so that:-

$$Pq \div n = \text{Value of each agreed contractual stage payment}$$

The contractor can actually cover his costs and required profit margin at value Va, which is lower than Pq. He knows that the final instalment is unlikely to be paid (as, having completed the project he has little remaining leverage over the customer), but he has calculated Va so that:-

$$Va \div (n\text{-}1) \text{ covers his costs and profit margin}$$

As long as the customer makes (n-1) instalment payments, then the contractor will cover his costs and profit margin, even though the customer fails to make the final payment.

2.12 Caveats

There are a number of specific points to which the international marketer should pay particular attention. Failure to give these points sufficient consideration may lead to ineffective marketing and sales performance within the territories concerned.

a) *Company reputation:* the reputation of the exporter's company may depend upon:-
- the quality of its products (buyers are less embarrassed to criticize imported goods than home produced ones);
- delivery on time: which is particularly important in industrial goods markets;
- long term presence in the market, based on local offices and plant (etc).

b) *motivation of export salesmen:* export selling can be a frustrating, exhausting and lonely occupation. The motivation of export salespeople will need considerable thought and careful management.

c) *local risk:* the assessment of which may require specialist expertise. International marketing and selling in some parts of the Middle East, for instance, requires well briefed and well supported operations.

d) *political stability:* which is related to local risk. Exporters need a clear picture of the trends in local political conditions, since these will affect government investment decision-making, consumer spending, currency reserves and so on.

e) *how business is done:* the export marketer or his agent must establish how buyers, import agencies, industrial companies, government ministries (etc) *actually do business.* The exporter must find out who to deal with, and how to approach them. Must there be conformity to *protocols?* How important are prior diplomatic contacts, especially in negotiations for large construction, infra-structure or defence contracts? Foreign buyers may insist upon peer group negotiation, only negotiating with people of their own rank. This phenomenon was noted in an earlier chapter. And to what extent will the successful conclusion of deals be dependent upon financial and credit packaging, home government guarantees and support, promises of local manufacture, and so on?

3) THE 12 C's SUMMARISED

The 12 C's of international marketing are summarised in Table 28.2.

The 12C's	SUMMARY
2.1 Country	Policy towards imports; import regulations; marketing and commercial infrastructure; marketing and distribution structures.
2.2 Culture and consumer behaviour	Individual motivation, life-styles, reference groups, family life-cycle; culture, whether traditional, achieving or affluent.
2.3 Concentration	Population concentration, urban and rural population distribution; relative income distributions, access to channels of distribution, access to decision-makers.
2.4 Communication	Communication media available to and within overseas territories; available promotional media; language(s) used.
2.5 Channels of distribution	Chapter 25 and Chapter 29.
2.6 Capacity to pay	Resources available for expenditure; currency reserves, financing packages.
2.7 Currency	Acceptability of currency; fluctuations in currency value.
2.8 Control and co-ordination	Clarity of objectives; number of intermediaries involved; performance measurement and criteria; communication and feedback.
2.9 Commitment	Experience in the market and long term commitment are related, as are company reputation and commitment.
2.10 Choices	Marketing mix choices available.
2.11 Contractual obligations	Deposits; payment terms and conditions; penalties for late delivery; stage payments.
2.12 Caveats	Company reputation; motivation of export salesmen; local risk; political instability; how business is done.

Table 28.2. The 12C's of International Marketing.

29 International Marketing Strategies

INTRODUCTION

This chapter continues the analysis of international marketing. It begins by looking at the assessment of market and political potential. It then analyses some of the alternative international marketing strategies from which the enterprise may choose. And it reminds the reader of the importance of effective pricing policy and risk assessments. These are essential to the financial viability of international marketing activities.

The chapter concludes by analysing the specific effect for UK companies of 1992 and the establishment of the Single European Market.

CHAPTER CONTENTS

1) ASSESSING MARKET POTENTIAL

Sales and market forecasting was analysed in detail in Chapters 7, 8 and 9. The analysis contained therein is as relevant to overseas markets as it is to home ones. Nevertheless, it is reasonable enough to suggest that making assessments of overseas market potential is an additionally difficult activity, if for no other reason that:

* there may be language problems;
* the scope and variety of published information may be different, or limited;
* the forecaster may have to build up knowledge and go through a learning process in order to gain a qualitative understanding of the territory.

Suffice it to say that an assessment of the market potential for *your product* in the foreseeable future may be based upon:

i) present demand for the product;

ii) predicted future demand for the product, which may be indicated by such factors as trends in current Gross National Product, the relative distribution of income and expenditure as between industrial and consumer markets, and the relative distribution of personal income on a per capita basis.

As with all forecasting, the problem lies in producing a specific assessment of the market potential for a particular product or product range, rather than producing vague economic generalisations.

2) ASSESSING POLITICAL POTENTIAL

This matter was also dealt with in Chapter 9 and Chapter 28. The export marketer, and indeed all of those people involved in international trading activities, will need to make assessments of the likely effect of political events on the nature and level of economic and trading activity in a particular country. Some examples of these assessments could include:

a) *political policy* towards imports, foreign companies and multinational companies (whilst possessing a domestic base, a "multi-national" company operates on an international basis. Its production, marketing and selling activities are organised across national boundaries, as well as within them).

b) *the effect of East-West differences on trade:* socialist and communist countries are highly selective about the imports they will accept. Their exports, on the other hand, tend to be of foodstuffs, raw materials and industrial goods, since the manufacture of consumer goods is usually given low priority. They may, in any case, only accept certain types of foreign manufactures on a "joint-venture" or "local manufacture" basis (see Section 3 below).

c) *popular nationalism,* which has its roots in zenophobia. The traditional dislike of one country by another takes the form of consumer resistance towards the products of that country. Some French people will not buy British or German goods; trade between Greece and Turkey can be difficult, and exchange between Israel and her Arab neighbours can be highly variable!

d) *political risk:* some regimes are unstable or just plain dangerous! Trading with such regimes may become impossible, even if these regimes do refrain from damaging their own local economy. The economies of Uganda and Cambodia, for instance, were both virtually destroyed by horrific dictatorships during the 1970's. Uganda, in particular, is a potentially wealthy and agriculturally productive country, but sadly has been unable to realise her potential.

3) INTERNATIONAL MARKETING STRATEGIES

3.1) Overcoming trading restrictions

The choice of international marketing strategies is briefly analysed in Section 3.2 below. However, the choice of strategy must first be informed by a knowledge of whatever trading restrictions the company may face. The chosen strategy must be capable of overcoming the effect of these restrictions, or at least minimising their impact. Trading restrictions include:

* tariffs or taxes imposed on imported or foreign goods;
* restrictions on the remittance of revenues earned from trading, and especially on hard currency movements out of the country;
* quotas imposed on the import of foreign goods;

* ownership regulations in which trading, distribution or manufacturing operations undertaken by foreign enterprises can only be undertaken by local companies in which at least (say) 51% of the shareholding is owned by nationals of that country, or its government.

3.2) Operational strategies

The choice of operational strategies listed below *vary directly in the degree of enterprise control and local involvement*. The further down the list, the greater the local involvement and the less the exporter's control is likely to be.

a) *direct export:* in which products are shipped overseas, marketed and sold direct to the customers by the company's own salespeople. This may involve the establishment of a local office in the territory, and a management structure there to control and monitor operations. Direct export activity may be subject to the imposition of a variety of trading restrictions.

b) *direct export using local agencies:* the use of such a channel was described in Chapter 25 (Section 3.2). It is the responsibility of the agent to handle the marketing, distribution and sale of the product within the territory. This strategy is as good as the agent, and its effectiveness depends on how well motivated the agent is towards putting energy and commitment into selling your product. It is also subject to the effects of trading restrictions.

c) *local assembly:* sub-assemblies and components, "kits" of parts (etc) are shipped overseas for assembly in local plants owned by the company. This course of action increases the level of involvement required but retains enterprise control. At the same time it meets territory requirements for a degree of "local manufactured content", and may overcome quota restrictions.

d) *local manufacture:* this is the most expensive option. However, whilst meeting local demands for a higher level of locally manufactured content than in (c) above, it allows the enterprise to retain control of manufacture and distribution. It also overcomes quota restrictions.

e) *licensing and contract manufacture:* in this case, the company arranges for its products to be assembled or manufactured by local companies who have either been awarded licences or contracts to undertake the work on its behalf. Marketing and distribution may remain within the control of the company's local representatives or it may make use of local agents, distributors (etc) to do this on its behalf.

f) *franchising:* this is a variation on (e) above, and is more common in the service sector. The local representatives of the company award franchises to local companies, who then carry out the activity to the standards laid down in the franchise document. The local representatives of the company will enforce these standards, and failure to achieve them will result in the withdrawal of the franchise. International franchises are to be found, for example, in the hotel and fast-food trades.

g) *joint ventures based on joint ownership:* manufacturing and/or distribution are undertaken by a company established and jointly owned by the exporting enterprise and local shareholders or the government. This is now a popular form of business organisation as it means that the joint venture is truly a "local" company, controlled from within the territory. Exporting companies may have little or no choice but to accept this type of structure, even though it weakens their control at the same time as committing them to an agreed level of investment in plant and distribution facilities. The requirement to establish a joint venture may be the price of access to the market in an overseas territory.

4) PRICING POLICY AND FINANCIAL RETURN

Pricing and pricing policy were discussed in detail in earlier chapters. It is vitally important that, whatever the operational strategies chosen, the enterprise sets appropriate prices within its international trading activities. For a start, international trading may incur addition costs of shipping, distribution and investment in territory organisation. Do the prices set allow the enterprise to cover these extra costs? Indeed does it know the consequences for its fixed cost structure of trading on an international basis? This will be especially important where the company runs these activities through a fully established and autonomous "international division". Similarly, can the enterprise charge prices which will allow it to cover the investment cost involved in local assembly, local manufacture or the establishment of joint ventures?

Secondly, what level of financial return can be obtained from international trading activities? This level of return will be dependent upon the factors listed above, and those described in the previous chapter. In particular, the enterprise will have to weigh up:

* *the level of risk* attaching to the trading or manufacturing venture;
* the likely effect on revenues and profits of fluctuations in currency values;
* the length of time over which the return calculation is to be made. This is in part a function of a company's *commitment* to trading in a particular overseas market.

5) 1992 AND THE SINGLE EUROPEAN MARKET (SEM)

The Chartered Institute of Marketing notes that 'the stated objective for 1992 is to have goods, services, capital and people moving freely between the ... member states of the European Community. By then, the *Internal Market* will be an area without internal frontiers. To achieve this will require the elimination of physical, technical and fiscal barriers, and action to this end is already well under way.

If this goal is achieved as planned ... new business opportunities will arise, and ways of doing business in Europe will change significantly'.

5.1) What 1992 means and does not mean

What it does not mean is that there will be a huge single, uniform 'European market' of 320 million people. There will still be twelve different national markets, and most small and medium sized companies will only be able to trade in a few of them. Languages, cultures, lifestyles; industrial, retailing and commercial operations will still vary considerably from country to country, and region to region. There will also continue to be separate national banks, individual currencies, education, legal systems, and other fundamental differences.

What 1992 also does not mean is that other international markets should be ignored, whether in North America, the Middle East or the Far Eastern Pacific basin. The achievement of a Single European Market is not only intended to provide internal market opportunities, but should also give Community companies the stronger base they need in order to compete more effectively in these wider global markets.

So, although cross-border movement within the Community should be barrier-free by 1992 and will therefore make international trade much easier and cheaper, the actual gaining of business may become much more difficult. This is because what were formerly national markets with varying degrees of protection will be opened up to greatly increased, aggressive competition. This competition will come not only from other Community members, but also from countries outside who will see European markets with free movement as even more attractive than they presently are. Many leading companies from these countries are already well established in what they have considered for some years to be their *European Market*.

5.2) Some major changes brought about by the Single European Market

a) *European technical standards*

Most Member States have their own standards and laws which are important in setting quality and safety requirements for goods sold in their national home market. The standards are drawn up by national standards bodies, such as the BSI in the UK, AFNOR (France) and DIN (Federal Republic of Germany).

National technical barriers will be progressively eliminated as the Single Market is completed. By then any product which can be sold in the member state in which it is produced will be freely marketable in all other parts of the EC, unimpeded by different national standards and testing and certification practices.

This process is being assisted by the work of the European standards organisations CEN (European Standardisation Committee) and CENELEC (European Standardisation Committee for Electrical Products) who are establishing European standards for a wide range of products, and monitoring the pace of technical harmonisation.

b) *Public purchasing*

Purchasing by governments and other public bodies accounts for as much as 15 per cent of the Community's gross domestic product. In theory, all have freedom to seek public contracts. In practice, local and national companies stand a better chance of success, whilst trade and non-trade barriers discourage others through discriminatory specifications, complex tendering procedures, lack of information etc.

Completing the Single Market will mean that purchases by governments and public bodies should reflect fair competition, not national identity.

c) *Company Law*

As the Single Market is completed more companies are becoming involved in intra-Community operations, resulting in an increasing number of links with associated companies, creditors and other parties outside the Member State in which their registered office is located. The Commission has a series of proposals aimed at harmonising Member States' laws governing limited companies. Their aim is to secure equivalent protection for shareholders and others involved with companies in all Member States and, by improving the legal relationships between companies through the co-ordination of company law, to make co-operation between them easier.

d) *Professional and financial services*

Freedom to work anywhere in the Community is one of the basic rights laid down by the Treaty of Rome. However, in most cases Member States refuse to recognise professional qualifications which have been obtained in another Member State. The result is that professionals often have to requalify, in whole or in part, before they can pursue their profession in another Member State. An accountant would in theory have to spend 50 years qualifying and requalifying if he or she wished to audit in every Member State. Similar problems face lawyers, teachers, engineers, physiotherapists and many other professions.

In 1985 the Commission suggested a major new approach to tackle the remaining restrictions. It put forward a draft directive on higher education diplomas, under which the qualifications necessary to pursue a profession in one Member State will be recognised throughout the Community. The directive will apply to all professions to which access is in some ways restricted by the State and which requires at least three years' university level training or equivalent. It will therefore apply to lawyers, accountants, engineers, teachers, surveyors, physiotherapists and all will be covered by the directive.

The Council of Ministers reached agreement in principle on the directive in 1988, and it is expected that the directive will come into force at the beginning of 1991.

The directive will not require Member States to change their present professional training systems: its aim is to ensure that professional qualifications issued in one Member State are recognised in another. The distinctive features of the UK system of professional training and regulations are fully reflected in the directive.

e) *Transport*

Liberalising transport services has a central place in completing the Single Market, because of the economic importance of the transport industry itself and because of its vital role in moving goods between Member States.

Completion of the Single Market will virtually coincide with the opening of the Channel Tunnel in 1993. There will be increased choice and competition in the vital cross-Channel market, leading to better, faster and keenly priced services which will benefit travellers and consumers. Moreover, direct rail freight access into the European network will open up a major new opportunity for British manufacturers to sell their goods in the European Community (EC) on equal terms with EC competitors.

EC transport ministers agreed in 1988 that international road haulage within the Community will be liberalised by the end of 1992. All road haulage permits and quotas for trade between Member States will then be abolished.

Proposals to allow hauliers registered in one Member State to operate transport services wholly within another Member State ('cabotage' as it is known) are still under discussion. But once these proposals are accepted, EC hauliers will be able to operate freely within the Community carrying out their business wherever they wish.

Within the fields of industry, distribution and commerce the effect of all these major changes will be far-reaching. It is intended that EC dedicated customs organisations will remain solely for drug surveillance and security purposes. There is now one single form (SAD) for all EC customs clearance. And after 1992 there will be freedom to conduct business anywhere within the European Community, with whoever the enterprise chooses.

This will raise many issues. Who does the enterprise work with? Does it form joint-ventures, co-operatives or networks? Can it issue franchises? Does the business attempt mergers with, or takeovers of other European companies? Does it seek partnerships, and if so, how does it find the right partners? 1992 will confront all European businesses with these questions, and force them to find answers if they are to take advantage of the new opportunities it will bring.

5.3) Some marketing implications of 1992

The European Economic Community is already a major international market for UK companies. The percentage of UK exports going to the EC has risen from 22% in 1960, to 43% in 1980 and 50% in 1987. UK companies cannot opt out of the Single European Market after 1992. They may decide not to trade in the newly freed EC markets, but they will still face increased competition in their own markets. This threat to existing business will be particularly serious in the *undifferentiated* and *commodity* type markets described in Chapters 43 and 44. And those companies *that do decide that the survival of their business depends upon them taking an international view,* as opposed to a local one, will need to confront a whole series of marketing issues, many of which are dealt with in detail in other chapters of this book.

For instance, has the company thought through and defined its business objectives, and formulated the marketing strategies and marketing mix required to achieve them? The majority of small and medium sized enterprises will have to pursue the *selective* or *segment-specific* policies described in Chapter 44. Each company will have to identify the particular segments or niches that provide the best business opportunities. Only the biggest companies will be able to operate on a 'Europe-wide'' basis. And will the chosen markets require modified or new products and services?

Will the company have to change its existing brand policies, packaging and promotional strategies in order to meet the needs of its new markets?

i) *Marketing intelligence:* companies will have to decide whether they have adequate levels of marketing intelligence about the European markets in which they plan to operate. Do they know how to build up this intelligence, and how to go about carrying out or obtaining the necessary market research? Does the company understand how its chosen segments behave, and what factors influence them? Does it know what kind of competition it faces, and what the strengths and weaknesses of that competition are?

Whilst the individual EC countries are very different, most are well documented on the basic data necessary for making marketing decisions and preparing a marketing plan. Compiling this information will require effort and imagination, and in many areas commissioned market research will be needed. Information on EC markets and trading therein is available from the British Overseas Trade Board (BOTB) division of the DTI. Information on the 1992 legislation is available from the DTI, CBI, British Standards Institute (BSI), Chambers of Commerce and European Documentation Centres.

ii) *Marketing mix:* having defined *where* it is going to compete, the enterprise must work out *how* it is going to compete. Why should a European customer buy from your company rather than from one of its competitors? What is the source of the company's *competitive advantage*? Is the advantage meaningful to potential customers within the chosen market segments, and how may it best be communicated? Just because a particular marketing mix has proved successful in the UK is no guarantee that the same mix will be successful in a European context.

Similarly, the company will need to establish where it considers itself to be vulnerable within its existing markets and segments, and decide what action needs to be taken to counter new competitive threats. The strategy of *segment protection* is described in Chapter 44.

The company will then have to decide how well its technology and operating assets, its products and their quality, its cost structure and prices, selling and distribution capacity match up to the European Market environment and the competition as it is likely to develop. Indeed, to what extent is the *culture* of the organisation open-minded and capable of flexible response to the changing environmental, market and competitive conditions that will apply after 1992?

iii) *people:* the company will have to decide whether it has the *skills, competencies,* and *organisational capacities* necessary to competing effectively within its chosen European markets. Do they have the necessary languages and logistical skills to make the business work? Do they understand the culture and thinking of their new European customers?

Are they properly trained, equipped and motivated to promote and sell in Europe?

Have responsibilities for European development been clearly defined and allocated, and what form will the operation take? Will the company use direct operations, subsidiaries, links with local firms, agents, partnerships or acquisitions?

iv) *commitment:* is the enterprise fully committed to making a success of its European operations? Have European marketing strategies and plans been properly developed, and communicated effectively throughout the organisation? And what kind of return will be made on the company's investment in its European strategy? How and when will the commitment be successful and profitable?

5.4) Strategies

A selection of marketing strategies are outlined in Chapter 45. UK companies facing the challenge of the Single European Market after 1992 can use any or all of such strategies as:

* *defending* existing segment provision, for instance within the home market. This defence can itself be *reactive* (reacting to competitive threats as they occur), or *proactive* (anticipating competitive threats and counter-attacking competitors on their own home ground);

* *attacking* (or *offensive*) strategies in which the enterprise enters fully into competition with a European focus, treating the SEM as its true 'home market';

* *going it alone*: maintaining total independence of strategy and action;

* *seeking co-operation*: seeking to share the burden and spread the risk by considering acquisition or merger, partnership, joint ventures or alliance. The loss of independence inherent in this strategy may be counterbalanced by the more rapid build-up of experience (whose importance was described in Chapter 28), and the sharing of decision making, resources and *people skills* amongst the various partners.

5.5) How will it affect accountants?

The Certified or Chartered Accountant in *public practice* is likely to have the opportunity to practice throughout the EEC after 1992. The *management accounting* profession is not well established in many countries, and the opportunities for promoting and selling management accounting services and consultancy are likely to develop rapidly for those Chartered Management Accountants who have the appropriate language skills and commitment to working in Europe.

Certified, and Chartered Management Accountants working in industry or commerce may be affected:

* by the need to budget for currency fluctuations within the company's European operations;

* by the need to develop new or more extensive ways of dividing up revenue and cost centres for the purposes of

planning, analysis and control. This will have implications for planning for Management Information Systems (MIS);

* by the need to develop effective mechanisms for monitoring the performance of *all* competitors, whether UK or European;

* by the need to develop more effective methods of monitoring and analysing *customer and segment profitability*. This issue is briefly discussed in Chapter 40. The greater variety of customer types and trading conditions, increased competition, increased risk and the potential for currency fluctuations all combine to increase the need for proper monitoring and control of the company's sales performance.

SUMMARY

The contents of this chapter are summarised in Table 29.1.

TABLE 29.1
Summary : Chapter Twenty Nine

SECTION	MAIN POINTS
1. Assessing market potential	Forecasts of sales and market share potential in overseas markets are complicated by language problems, variations in the range and scope of published information, and the need for the forecaster to build up a qualitative understanding of the territory.
2. Assessing political potential	Assessments must be made of the likely effect of political events on the level of economic and trading activity in a particular country. These may include political policy; the effect of East-West differences on trade; the effect of popular nationalism; political risk.
3.1 Overcoming trading restrictions	The chosen strategy must be capable of overcoming the effect of restrictions on trade, which include the imposition of import tariffs, taxes or quota restrictions; restrictions on the re-mittance of revenues and currency; ownership regulations.

3.2 Operational strategies	May include direct export; direct export using local agencies; local assembly; local manufacture; licensing and contract manufacture; franchising; joint ventures based on joint ownership. These strategies vary in the degree of enterprise control and local involvement they contain.
4. Pricing policy and financial return	The prices at which international trade is carried out must be adequate (i) to cover the additional costs incurred in overseas trade, and (ii) to ensure a level of financial return which is commensurate both with the risks attaching to such a venture, and with the company's commitment to the territory.
5. 1992 and the Single European Market (SEM)	The stated objective for 1992 is to have goods, services, capital and people moving freely between the member states of the European Community. The Single European Market (SEM) will be a free market, without internal frontiers acting as barriers to trade.
5.1 What 1992 means and does not mean	1992 does not mean that there will be a huge, single and uniform European market. There will still be twelve different national markets, each containing many smaller markets and segments. What 1992 also does not mean is that other international markets should be ignored. The SEM should provide European companies with a stronger base from which to compete in global markets. 1992 does of course mean that trade within European markets will become much more competitive.

5.2 Some other major changes brought about by SEM	These include changes to (a) European technical standards, (b) public purchasing, (c) company law, (d) professional and financial services, (e) transport. Customs organisations will remain solely for drug surveillance and security purposes associated with the EC.
5.3 Some marketing implications of 1992	These include increased competition, and the need to protect existing segment provision. Companies will need to take an international view towards trading in Europe, and need to think carefully about their business objectives. This process will require them (i) to obtain and use adequate levels of market intelligence; (ii) to formulate appropriate and segment − specific marketing mixes; (iii) to develop the right people, skills, competencies and organisational capacities to compete effectively in the SEM; (iv) to show commitment to making a success of their European operations.
5.4 Strategies	Strategies appropriate to 1992 and the SEM include defence (reactive or proactive); attack; going it alone; seeking co-operation and sharing people skills.
5.5 How will it affect accountants?	1992 may bring increased opportunities to undertake public practice, and to sell management accounting services and consultancy. Accountants working in industry and commerce will have to budget for the effect of currency fluctuations; to find better ways of budgetary planning for wider varieties of revenue and cost centres; and to find better ways of monitoring/analysing customer and segment profitability.

RECOMMENDED READING

Dudley J.W.   1992 − Strategies for the Single Market
                                    CIMA/Kogan Page

Kinsey J.   Marketing in Developing Countries.   Macmillan

Majaro S.   International Marketing.   Allen and Unwin

Paliwoda S J.   International Marketing.   Heinemann

SOME USEFUL ADDRESSES

Commission of the European Communities
Information Unit,
Millbank Tower,
LONDON SW1P 4QU; and

8 Storey's Gate
LONDON SW1P 3AT

Department of Trade and Industry
1−19 Victoria Street
LONDON SW1H 0ET

British Overseas Trade Board (BOTB)
1 Victoria Street
LONDON SW1H 0ET

Export Intelligence Service
DTI
Lime Grove
Eastcote
Ruislip
Middlesex HA4 8SG

Centres for European Business Information, located at:

Birmingham Chamber of Industry and Commerce
75 Harborne Road
BIRMINGHAM B15 3DH

Newcastle Polytechnic Library
Ellison Building
Ellison Place
NEWCASTLE UPON TYNE NE1 8ST

Strathclyde Euro Infocentre
Scottish Development Agency
25 Bothwell Street
GLASGOW G2 6NR

Centre for European Business Information: Small Firms Service
Ebury Bridge House
2 – 18 Ebury Bridge Road
LONDON SW1W 8QD

Irish Export Board
Merrion Hall
PO Box 203 Strand Road
Sandymant
IRL Dublin 4
Eire

Shannon Free Airport Development Co Ltd
The Granary
Michael Street
IRL Limerick
Eire

European Community SME Task Force
Rue d'Arlon 80
1040 Brussels
Belgium

CENELEC ASBI
Rue Bréderode 2
BTE 5 – 1000
Brussels
Belgium

Other addresses

Association of British Chambers of Commerce
Sovereign House
212a Shaftesbury Avenue
LONDON WC2H 8EW

International Chamber of Commerce (British National Committee)
Centre Point
103 New Oxford Street
LONDON WC1A 1QB

London Chamber of Commerce and Industry
69 Cannon Street
LONDON EC4N 5AB

Export Credits Guarantee Department
Aldermanbury House
Aldermanbury
LONDON EC2P 2EL

Confederation of British Industry
Centre Point
103 Oxford Street
LONDON WC1A 1DU

United Nations
London Information Centre
Ship House
20 Buckingham Gate
LONDON SW1E 6LB

British Export Houses Association
16 Dartmouth Street
LONDON SW1H 9BL

QUESTIONS FOR SELF-REVIEW

1)   Why do companies undertake international marketing activities?

2)   What factors must the marketer take into account when analysing international markets?

3)   Why is international trade often a technically complex activity for a company to undertake?

4)   In what ways may other countries place restrictions on imports and inward trade activities? How and to what extent may the marketer overcome these restrictions?

5)   Why is it important for those involved in international trade to analyse and understand the culture of the countries in which they wish to market their products, or set up manufacturing operations?

6)   Why must the international marketer consider the capacity to pay, and the currency of his target markets?

7)   Why are communication, co-ordination and control factors important to companies undertaking international trading activities?

8)   Why is company commitment important to successful international trading?

9)   *Describe and comment on some of the alternative inter-national marketing strategies available to a company engaged in overseas trade.*

10)   *Analyse and comment on the implications of 1992 and the emergence of the Single European Market for European companies. What will be some of the principal changes brought about by the SEM, and what will be their effect?*

EXAMINATION QUESTIONS

Q54   *Your company is considering exporting for the first time. As newly appointed Marketing Manager prepare a brief report outlining the relative merits and potential problems of this course of action.*

(CIM)

Q55   *What are the essential requisites of successful marketing overseas?*

(SSM)

Q56   *"No company is likely to be successful in overseas markets if it ignores or offends cultural behaviour patterns." Do you agree with this statement? Give reasons.*

(IIM)

Promotion

What some reviewers said about the First Edition of this book:

* '. . . a classic DPP publication . . . the book provides excellent value for money, with a "no frills" coverage of a wide subject with the minimum of verbal wastage. There is a wealth of vital detail . . .' *Certified Accountants Students' Newsletter.*

* '. . . a real winner . . .' *Middlesbrough Evening Gazette.*

* '. . . it is a really impressive book . . .' *Polytechnic Director.*

* '. . . the text is excellent. It is well laid out and comprehensive . . .' *Professor and Dean of polytechnic business school.*

* '. . . very impressive . . .' *Professor and Director of polytechnic business school.*

* '. . . very useful . . .' *Professor and Director of university management centre.*

* '. . . brilliant book . . .' *professional institute review.*

* '. . . can be recommended unreservedly . . ." *professional institute review.*

The next eight chapters deal with the role of Promotion within the marketing mix. Promotion is an essential activity within marketing. It creates awareness and stimulates interest in the product or brand. It persuades people and finally sells the product. These activities are all part of the "promotional" mix. This section of the book commences with an analysis of the promotional mix, and continues by dividing into two parts the actual activities involved. Part One deals with advertising and techniques of sales promotion. Part Two deals with personal selling and salesforce management.

30 The Promotional Mix

INTRODUCTION

This chapter begins by analysing marketing communication within the context of communication theory. It then deals with the promotional mix, and considers the relative effectiveness of promotional techniques at different stages of the persuasion process. It concludes by looking at a number of other marketing factors which are relevant to promotional mix decisions.

CHAPTER CONTENTS

1) COMMUNICATION AND PROMOTION

Organisations promote their goods or services to the market, and to the users of these products or services. They make use of a variety of *promotional methods,* such as advertising, personal selling, publicity or exhibitions. Such promotional methods may be used by *any* type of organisation, whether commercial or non-profit making, to *communicate to and persuade* a target recipient or potential customer that they should avail themselves of the product or service on offer.

A study of marketing communication and promotion is therefore relevant to many different types of organisation. Promotional activities are undertaken by commercial companies, trade associations, government bodies, educational institutions, health advisory councils, political parties, charities and the like. It is an important area of study for the marketer because of the large financial investments (expenditure) made in promotional activity. The advertising industry, in particular, is a large and important sector in any western economy. This industry is also showing signs of rapid growth in the lesser developed economies and in some socialist countries.

All promotional activities are forms of *marketing communication,* and must therefore be first analysed in terms of *communication theory*.

1.1) Communication Theory

The process of "communication" attempts to use messages (ie transmit information) to create AWARENESS and UNDERSTANDING on the part of someone who is receiving the message. Conventional communication theory shows communication in terms of a standard communication process model. This is illustrated in Figure 30.1.

The message flows as *information* through the various stages of the model until it reaches the receiver. *There is no guarantee, however, that the receiver will get the full message or understand it.* This is because the communication process is subject to "interference". This interference takes the form of "barriers" and "impediments" to the smooth flow of information. Barriers and impediments can occur at any of the stages within the communication process model, and reduce the chance of the receiver effectively understanding the message transmitted to him. Interference can take any (or all) of the following forms:

* *barriers* such as physical distance; language and cultural differences; inappropriate, ineffective or hostile channels of communication;
* *filtering* of message content, such that some of the original message is removed;
* *distortion* of message content, such that the original meaning of the message is changed before it gets to the receiver;

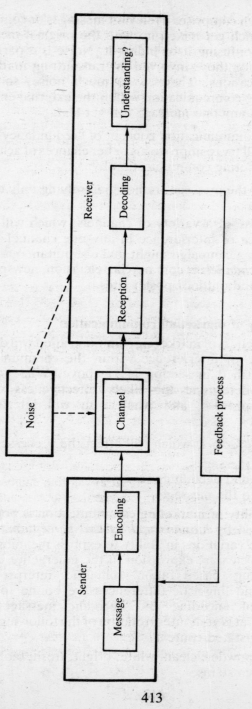

Figure 30.1. The communication process model.

    * *noise* which comprises irrelevant messages or communication which get mixed up with the original message, thereby confusing it or hiding it. Noise is a particular problem for those involved in transmitting marketing communications. There is so much noise, so much competing communication within the external environment that any one message can get lost.

Hence the communication concept of "redundancy". The communicator will try to improve his or her chances of achieving a successful marketing communication by:

    a) repeating the message, rather than relying only on one transmission.

    b) making use of a variety of channels, which will offset the incidence of interference in any one channel. Thus, an advertising campaign might make simultaneous use of such *media channels* as commercial television, newspapers, magazines and outdoor poster sites.

1.2) The viability of marketing communication

The effectiveness of marketing communication will depend on the incidence of interference within the communication process, as described in section (1.1) above. What factors, therefore, will determine the likely effectiveness of the communication process, and what form will interference actually take?

    i) *Personal factors:* which will affect the processes of:
    * encoding messages;
    * receiving and decoding messages;
    * reaction to the message.

    The quality of marketing communication is bound to be influenced by *human capacity and perception*. There will be wide variations in ability to express meaning. This will find its clearest expression in the emergence of misunderstanding based upon semantic interpretation. Semantic and linguistic differences are bound to cause problems of encoding and decoding messages. For instance, what is your interpretation of the following words within their stated context?

    * washing powder: clean, white, bright, fresh, biological, deep-down stains;

* foodstuffs: tasty, nourishing, flavoursome, healthy, original, quick, take-away, traditional, economical;
* cosmetics: exciting, tangy, subtle, gentle, natural, exotic, hint.

Human capacity will also find its expression in the level of personal command over communication methods, modes and skills. Can your advertising *copy writers* express an idea so that the target market can understand it? And what level of communication skills does that target market possess? Communication effectiveness will also depend upon the level of attention and retention, emotional state and individual perceptions of the receiver. How does he or she perceive the intentions of the sender of the message?

ii). *Group factors:* In general terms, the behavioural analysis of group influence suggests that family, reference groups, peers and so on will have the capacity to affect individual behaviour in response to communications. This issue was dealt with in the earlier chapters on consumer behaviour. One example of group influence might be the placing of "confidence limits" upon a message, or its sender. Fleet car buyers, for instance, may become highly sceptical of advertising or sales claims for cars made by manufacturers with whose products they have had poor operational experience in the past. Individual scepticism becomes much more deeply rooted when it is reinforced by group experience and opinion.

iii) *Message factors:* effective communication will depend on the *clarity* of the message, and on whether the recipient perceives the message to be *meaningful. Immediacy* will also affect reception, for in general terms the more immediate communication drives out the less.

Further, the *strength* and *duration* of the transmission will affect its viability. This will be determined by the "power" of the media channel chosen, and on the frequency with which the message is repeated. Media channel power is relative to the target market or target recipient. The larger and more widely spread the target, the more powerful must the media channel be. Commercial television, national, regional and local newspapers are regarded as powerful media, which is why they are relatively expensive to use. Trade journals, magazines and sales representatives are powerful channels when the target is more closely defined, segmented or restricted.

The number of occasions (frequency) with which the message needs repetition, and the length of time over which this repetition should take place is a complex issue. The problem was discussed in Chapter Eight, and is illustrated in Figure 30.2.

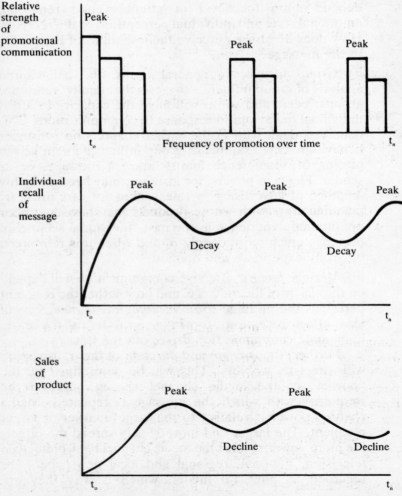

Figure 30.2. Promotional Message Effectiveness.

The shape of the sales curve in Figure 30.2 depends upon the relationship between promotion and sales: for the sake of illustration a simple direct relationship is assumed here. Individual recall of promotional messages is shown to rise and decay according to the relative strength and frequency of the promotional communication. This curve can be seen in a "flatter" form when translated into actual sales, given the promotion-sales relationship shown above. Note how the peaks show the effect of "lags" over time, moving to the right as the promotional effect works through to actual sales.

The modelling program "Dysmap" is particularly useful for modelling these kinds of dynamic relationships. Dysmap was discussed in Chapter 8.

2) THE PROMOTIONAL MIX

The *promotional mix* is the combination of marketing and promotional communication methods used to achieve the promotional objectives of the marketing mix. There are two main types of communication method within the promotional mix. These are "non-controllable" and "controllable" methods.

2.1) Non-controllable methods

Here, the communication of marketing messages takes place on the basis of:

* independent word-of-mouth information dissemination;
* independent and objective publicity;
* individual personal recommendation.

The enterprise is not normally in a position to control such communication. *Indeed its value to the enterprise lies in its independence and objectivity*. These non-controllable methods are effective and valuable precisely because they will not be perceived as containing much commercial vested interest. Their recipients will tend to accept them as more trustworthy than the controllable methods to be described in section (2.2).

These methods are of particular importance where market trends are determined by the views of influential opinion leaders or reference groups. The importance of opinion formulators, family influences (etc) on brand loyalty, customer attitudes and purchasing patterns was discussed in detail in the earlier

417

chapters on consumer behaviour. One example is the travel trade. Independent word-of-mouth information dissemination, and individual personal recommendation is known to be highly influential in determining customer choice of tour operator and holiday destination.

The benefits of non-controllable communication do not, of course, come free! The enterprise will have to *earn the respect and trust of the general public,* by years of consistent, market-sensitive performance. The company will have to *deliver* its promised satisfactions, year in, year out, building up customer trust, loyalty and approbation. In the UK, companies such as Rolls Royce, Marks and Spencer and Sainsbury have built up such a reputation. So have some Japanese suppliers of cars, televisions and hi-fi's. If the customers of such companies have a justified complaint, a swift remedy will always be forthcoming. In the meantime, customers have come to take the appropriateness and quality of the goods on offer as a matter of fact. The supplier has positioned the right products on the right market segments.

On the other hand, of course, independent word-of-mouth or editorial *condemnation* can have an equally potent but opposite effect. Soundly-based bad publicity can have a significant negative effect. Look at the effect of football hooliganism and loutish behaviour on the attendances at association football matches in Great Britain. Bad publicity has driven the paying customer away.

2.2) Controllable methods

There are four main types of promotion under this heading. They are:

a) *ADVERTISING:* which is defined as purchased non-personal communication using mass media, such as television and newspapers. Described in Chapters 31, 32 and 33.

b) *SALES PROMOTION:* which includes purchased activities like in-store displays, exhibitions, sponsorship, money-off coupons, on-pack offers and so on. Described in Chapter 34.

c) *PERSONAL SELLING:* which is based upon direct face-to-face communication and persuasion. Described in Chapter 35, 36 and 37.

d) *PUBLICITY:* which is non-personal communication using mass media. Unlike advertising it is not paid for on a direct basis. One of its key components is "Public Relations" or PR. Publicity is briefly described in Chapter 31 and in the next major section of this text.

2.3) "Above-the-line" and "Below-the-line"

Sometimes these controllable methods of promotion are categorised on the basis of the terms "above-the-line" and "below-the-line":

a) *above-the-line:* comprises mass media advertising (eg TV, newspapers) from which the advertising agency receives a *commission* (sometimes 15% of the value of media time or space purchased). Typically, agency-client relationships are based on *negotiated fees* rather than on the volume of client expenditure on mass media space or time. The negotiated fee is likely only to be indirectly related to expenditure on mass media. The client is therefore not so easily put under pressure to spend more (which might only be to the benefit of the agency who receive the commission). Indeed, commission received may be refunded to the client, and excluded from the fee negotiation which actually determines the net worth of the transaction to the agency.

b) *below-the-line:* comprising all media and promotional types from whose use neither the company nor its agency will receive a commission.

The terms "above-the-line" and "below-the-line" have their origins in past UK tax regulations. All types of promotional expenditure are nowadays allowable as costs against UK corporation tax.

2.4) Consumer and industrial markets

It is reasonable in general terms to make the assumption that companies operating in consumer goods markets, and especially those marketing *fast-moving consumer goods* ("fmcg") will commit most of their promotional resources to media advertising and sales promotion techniques. Fast moving consumer goods include such items as branded groceries and confectionery, household wares, toys, washing powders and detergents (etc). Such a strategy might allocate up to 80% of their available budget to such promotion. Such a strategy is described as being based upon *demand pull*. The effect of advertising and sales promotion gives rise to customer demand that "pulls" the product through the channels of distribution. Distributors stock the product because they know that advertising will maintain a level of customer demand. This strategy has other objectives:

* media advertising and sales promotion are used to maintain and reinforce product differentiation in the perception of the target market segment;

* the promotional activity maintains consumer awareness and loyalty towards the product or brand. It should thereby encourage and reinforce brand loyal purchase behaviour;

* channels of distribution will stock the product because promotional activity will encourage demand for the product. Indeed, some retail chains will *only* stock lines that are supported by what *they consider* to be an adequate level of promotional activity.

Companies operating within industrial goods markets, on the other hand, are likely to place much more reliance on personal selling, and secondarily on forms of publicity. They might allocate up to 80% of their promotional budget in the form of personal selling and publicity. Personal selling is more appropriate to specialist or concentrated industrial markets. Other reasons for its use follow from the analysis contained in Chapters 2, 14 and 15:

* catalogues, technical data sheets, written specifications (etc) must be distributed to potential customers before they can order;

* sales staff need to find out who has influence and authority over purchasing decisions;

* face-to-face contact is necessary in order to allow discussion over technical specifications, customer requirements, costs, prices and terms of business;

* negotiations may take place over price, delivery, contractual arrangements (etc);

* peer group negotiations may be necessary, especially prior to the completion of contracts;

* publicity may be a useful means of establishing awareness and credibility on the part of people who are influential within the industrial buying process.

Where personal selling is the mainstay of the promotional and persuasion process, a strategy of *demand push* may be identified. Sales effort pushes the product through the channels of distribution, and there is emphasis on the salesman "making the sale".

3) THE PERSUASION PROCESS

It is possible to identify generalised but distinct stages of a process within which a potential customer becomes aware of a product for which he or she may have a demand, and moves to a stage at which the customer makes a purchase decision (which can be positive or negative). This is described as the *persuasion process*. Two examples of persuasion process models are given, thus:

i) **AIDA,** whose stages are:-
Attention – Interest – Desire – Action

ii) **DAGMAR** ("Defining Advertising Goals for Measured Advertising Results"), whose stages are:-
Unawareness – Awareness – Comprehension – Conviction – Action

Each of the various types of promotional activity identified in section (2.2) above are likely to have a varying value, in terms of their capacity to communicate and persuade, at different stages in the persuasion process described above. These variations are best explained diagramatically, using Figure 30.3

For example, whilst media advertising is effective at creating awareness and comprehension, personal selling is a better means of establishing conviction in the mind of the potential customer, and moving him or her to the point at which they take action (by purchasing the product or deciding against it).

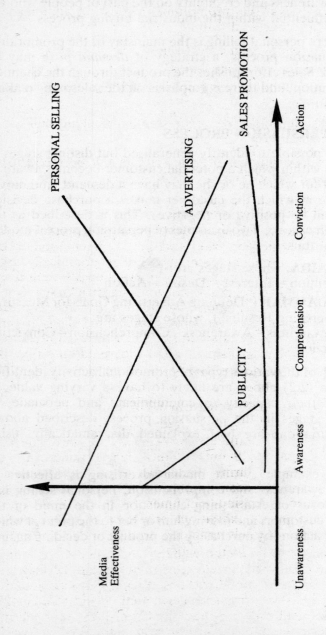

Figure 30.3. Promotional Effectiveness.

4) OTHER PROMOTIONAL MIX FACTORS

The analysis of the promotional mix can be summarised so far as being concerned with:

* its communication effectiveness;
* its persuasion effectiveness;
* its credibility in the perception of the potential customer;
* marketing objectives expressed as "demand pull" and "demand push".

However, a number of other factors will be relevant to promotional mix decisions.

4.1) Market size and segmentation

Promotional requirements will vary with geographic size, demographic dispersion and market segmentation. For instance, the promotional requirements in geographically large and demographically dispersed markets will be different from the more targeted approach possible for concentrated segments. *Indeed, the more clearly defined the segment, the more accurate may be the targeting of the promotional mix.* This in turn minimises the necessary expenditure. The less clearly identified is the market, the more disparate and widespread must be the promotion and the greater its cost.

4.2) Correlation with Product Life Cycle stage

The nature and balance of the promotional mix must correlate with stage on the Product Life Cycle. This issue was dealt with in Chapters 19 and 20. For instance, the creation of customer awareness during the early stages of a product's existence is likely to mean proportionately high promotional expenditures on advertising (consumer goods markets) or new literature, catalogues, exhibitions and new product demonstrations (industrial goods markets).

Similarly, the marketer will be concerned to maintain customer loyalty to the product or brand during the maturity stage. In consumer goods markets this may be achieved by advertising and sales promotional activities. In industrial goods markets this need will keep the salesforce busy, and call for ranges of customer or dealer incentives to maintain their loyalty and support.

423

4.3 Product complexity

Where detailed technical evaluation by prospective buyers in industrial goods markets provides an important pre-purchase assessment, the supplier's promotional mix needs to be designed to furnish the necessary information about the product or service under consideration. Such information will include Technical Data sheets and catalogues. Additional support to the evaluation process may come from demonstrations, testimonies from other satisfied customers and visits to their premises, the secondment of sales engineers, the use of "demonstration" products on a trial basis, and so on.

4.4) Personal service

Some markets, especially within the service sector, are very sensitive to standards of personal service and visible operational efficiency. The promotional mix must reflect this customer concern. So, for example:

* one contract cleaner in Northern England invites prospective customers to discuss business in its luxurious (and spotless) office premises, which it (of course) cleans to a very high standard;

* petrol filling stations run by the major oil companies are bright, modern establishments offering fuel self-service (preferred by most motorists) and retail facilities for sweets, tobacco, soft drinks, oil and car accessories (etc). They carry the corporate colours and attempt to differentiate the brand and product (which is difficult with petrol!) by the level of service and convenience offered.

4.5) Competitor promotional mix

Any one business, whether it be in a consumer or industrial goods market, needs to have a convincing reason *for not using* a promotional mix that compares favourably with that employed by its main competitors. Indeed, matching competitors' promotional activity is frequently the basis for market competition. As we have already seen, this is particularly true during the maturity phases of the Product Life Cycle when competition tends to centre around *market share*. And where a market segment has become dominated by promotional activities, the company will have little or no choice but to follow suit. This, for example, is true of branded f.m.c.g. such as washing powder or instant coffee. Competition amongst manufacturers for space on retail shelves ensures that matching promotional mixes and expenditure levels has become the norm.

SUMMARY

The contents of this chapter are summarised in Table 30.4

TABLE 30.4
Summary : Chapter Thirty

SECTION	MAIN POINTS
1. Communication and promotion	Organisations promote their goods or services to the market using a variety of promotional methods. Promotion is used to communicate to and persuade a potential customer to take advantage of the offer.
1.1 Communications theory	The process of communication attempts to use messages (i.e. transmit information) to create awareness and understanding on the part of the receiver. However, the communication process is subject to interference. This interference takes the form of barriers, filtering, distortion and noise within the channels of communication. This interference may be offset by redundancy, which is the process of duplicating messages and using different channels.
1.2 The viability of marketing communication	The effectiveness of marketing communication will depend on (i) personal factors, (ii) group factors; (iii) message factors. Message factors include the strength and duration of the transmission. This will be determined by the power of the media channel chosen, and by the frequency with which the message is repeated.

2.1 Non-controllable methods of promotion	These comprise independent, word-of-mouth information dissemination, personal recommendation, and objective publicity. Their promotional value lies in their independence and objectivity. They are of particular importance where market trends are determined by the views of influential opinion leaders or reference groups.
2.2 Controllable methods of promotion	These comprise (a) advertising, (b) sales promotion techniques, (c) personal selling, (d) publicity.
2.3 Above-the-line and below-the-line	Above-the-line promotion comprises mass media advertising, from which the agency receives a commission. Below-the-line promotion comprises all media and promotional types from whose use no commission is received.
2.4 Consumer and industrial markets	Media advertising and sales promotion techniques dominate promotion within consumer goods markets. This may be described as a "demand pull" marketing strategy. Companies in industrial goods markets will place much greater emphasis on personal selling and publicity. This may be described as a "demand push" strategy.
3. The persuasion process	Persuasion process stage models include AIDA (attention – interest – desire – action) and DAGMAR (unawareness – awareness – comprehension – conviction – action). Each type of promotion is likely to have varying effectiveness (in terms of their capacity to communicate and persuade) at different stages within the persuasion process.
4. Other promotional mix factors	Promotional mix decisions are also affected by (4.1) market size and segmentation, (4.2) correlation with

Product Life Cycle stage, (4.3) product complexity, (4.4) personal service, (4.5) competitor promotional mix.

The Promotional Mix – Part One Advertising and Techniques of Sales Promotion

31 Advertising media

INTRODUCTION

This chapter lists and describes some of the main types of mass media used by advertisers, and considers the role of publicity within the promotional process. It outlines some of the advantages and disadvantages of each mass medium in terms of its advertising value, and anticipates the analysis of advertising effectiveness which follows in the next chapter.

CHAPTER CONTENTS

1) Printed media
   1.1) Advantages of printed media
   1.2) Disadvantages of printed media
2) Broadcast media
   2.1) Advantages of broadcast media
   2.2) Disadvantages of broadcast media
3) Cinema
   3.1) Advantages of cinema as an advertising medium
   3.2) Disadvantages of cinema as an advertising medium
4) Outdoor media
   4.1) Advantages of outdoor media
   4.2) Disadvantages of outdoor media
5) Publicity
   5.1) Advantages of publicity as a promotional medium
   5.2) Disadvantages of publicity as a promotional medium
6) Direct marketing

Summary

1) PRINTED MEDIA

Printed media include:

* national daily newspapers;
* national Sunday newspapers (and colour supplements);
* regional and local daily newspapers (published in the morning or in the evening);

* regional Sunday newspapers;
* local newspapers published weekly (either purchased by the customer or distributed free);
* national magazines and periodicals;
* regional and local magazines and periodicals;
* trade press;
* professional journals;
* children's magazines and periodicals;

(etc)

The majority of such publications will be purchased by their subscribers, although in some categories the publication will be distributed free. This is particularly true in the UK of local "free sheets" distributed direct to homes on a weekly basis. Free sheets are financed solely by advertising revenue.

1.1) Advantages of printed media

a) *accurate targeting of promotional communications* on customer segments identified as making up the readership profile. This is of particular value in the case of professional publications, such as "Marketing" or "Management Accounting". It is of prime importance to the trade press, and to special interest or hobby publications connected with homes and gardens, musical and teenage publications, sports magazines (etc). This potential for the accurate targeting of promotional messages is the main advantage of printed media.

b) *Printed word:* the message is durable and may be read repeatedly, as in the case of the UK "Radio Times" and "TV Times".

c) The advertisement may take on *the prestige of the publication*. This may be true, for instance, in such UK publications as the quality daily and sunday newspapers, sunday colour supplements, county magazines, or prestige magazines given free to airline or railway passengers.

d) *colour quality* in full colour periodicals.

e) use of tear-off *reply coupons* so that the reader can follow up the advertisement and obtain brochures, free estimates or whatever.

f) printing is a *flexible technology* and facilitates rapid editorial and publication response to market changes, readership attitudes (etc).

1.2) Disadvantages of printed media

i) can the advertisement *gain and hold the reader's attention?* The reader is not forced to read advertisements. In any case, any one advertisement will suffer *noise* in the channel, since it may not be easy to effectively distinguish it from other messages competing for the reader's attention.

ii) *lack of colour* in black and white printed media. Newsprint quality paper may limit the quality of colour reproduction in newspapers.

iii) the advertisement is *static* – it cannot have any dynamic quality.

2) BROADCAST MEDIA

Broadcast media include:

* commercial television;
* commercial radio.

2.1) Advantages of broadcast media

a) *media power:* radio and especially television are perhaps the most "powerful" media channels available. Television viewing figures can exceed 20 million in the UK for certain programmes. The repetition of advertising messages builds and maintains general public and customer awareness. UK readers can try a *recall test:* with what event was "Sid" connected in 1986?

b) *presentation quality:* radio and television *commercials* can be of a very high creative quality. This quality will have a direct effect on their communication and persuasion effectiveness.

c) promotional messages using broadcast media are *dynamic.* They have voice, feeling and colour. Above all, they have *movement.* The listener or viewer can react to the advertisement over a period of time, especially if the message is repeated.

2.2) **Disadvantages of broadcast media**

i) *absolute cost:* television is the most expensive medium to use.

ii) *direct restrictions:* broadcast media often impose restrictions on the advertising they will carry. Restrictions are often placed on the promotion of tobacco products, alcoholic beverages and the like.

iii) *wastage:* the broadcasting of promotional messages implies a "shotgun" approach. It is not so easy to target the message on a specific market segment. Inevitably many recipients will be uninterested in the communication since it will not be relevant to them.

iv) *noise:* any one broadcast advertisement may get lost in the welter of competing messages. This is why creative quality is so important. Good advertisements may build up awareness, poor ones are forgotten.

v) *viewers/listeners switching off:* the recipients of broadcasting may "switch-off" when advertisements occur. They may switch-off by reducing their attention level; or they may physically obliterate the advertisements by switching-off the set, or by channel hopping using a remote control selector facility.

vi) *alternative uses of the television receiver:* people increasingly use their television receivers to watch video recordings, play computer games or act as a VDU for their personal computer. As such, they cannot receive broadcast messages. The increasing cost of television advertising and the growing trend towards the alternative use of television sets has had the effect of:

– reducing the power of commercial television companies within the market for advertising media;

– reviving the interest of advertisers in the printed media;

– increasing the interest of advertisers in direct mail and other forms of direct marketing.

vii) *quality of programming:* the incentive to watch television, or listen to the radio, is in part determined by the quality and range of programmes. The better or *more appropriate* the programme schedules are to the demands of the viewing or listening public, the more people will switch-on and stay tuned-in. Hence, for instance, the popularity of "soap operas" on television the world over. The programme controllers of commercial television walk a tightrope. Their programmes must consistently appeal to the widest possible range of viewers, so that they can bring in the advertising revenue upon which their operations depend.

viii) *increasing competition:* competition for the advertiser's custom is increasing. Dissatisfaction with radio and television as advertising media has revived the fortunes of other channel media. At the same time, competition amongst television broadcasters in Europe and the USA is likely to increase with the arrival of satellite broadcasting. The advertiser who wishes to use television may find new opportunities opening up, and his bargaining power relative to the television companies increasing for the first time since the emergence of commercial television broadcasting.

CINEMA

3.1 Advantages of cinema as an advertising medium

a) *large screen impact:* the cinema screen offers the greatest scope for the scale and intensity of visual and creative impact.

b) *accurate targeting:* as with printed media, the cinema allows the targeting of promotional communications on specific customer segments identified as making up the audience profile. It should not be too difficult for market research to establish the demographic and socio-economic backgrounds of audience groups.

c) *captive audience:* a cinema audience cannot switch-off, however much it may try to ignore advertisements being screened. The sheer size and sound volume of cinema advertisements make them difficult to ignore!

3.2) Disadvantages of cinema as an advertising medium

i) *dependence on trends in cinema attendance:* cinema audiences can fluctuate widely. They are partly dependent on the quality and popularity of the films being shown, and on the cost of the cinema ticket. They are also dependent on whatever factors influence "going-out" for entertainment. These include:

- the relative attractiveness of competing entertainments;
- weather, transport facilities;
- the fear of older people about going out at night;
- cinema location and comfort.

ii) *competitiveness with home-based entertainment:* home-based entertainment, based around the radio, television set, hi-fi (etc) has replaced the cinema as a staple form of family entertainment in the UK. This trend has been reinforced by the widespread use of video recorders, the availability of feature films on video cassettes, and the making of feature films for television and video rather than cinema audiences.

4) OUTDOOR MEDIA

Outdoor media include:

* fixed posters, hoardings and showcards;
* posters on the outside or inside of transport vehicles (buses, trains, underground trains etc);
* electric and neon signs;
* electronic screens, message units (etc).

4.1) Advantages of outdoor media

a) *size, visibility and situational impact* may be considerable if the media is correctly or appropriately sited. Advertising cards in underground trains tend to get looked at if for no other reason that there is not much else to look at, except for one's fellow passengers!

b) *colour, movement and impact of electric signs:* electrical, electronic and message transmitting media can have an immense visual effect, especially after dark. Think of Piccadilly Circus in London, or the centres of great cities like Hong Kong or Hamburg. Each is a blaze of changing lights and colours.

4.2) Disadvantages of outdoor media

i) all forms of outdoor media suffer from noise and information clutter within the immediate environment. They are surrounded by a plethora of other communications, some directly competing and others just getting in the way.

ii) *mixed image:* outdoor media have a variable image in the minds of advertiser and general public alike. Posters, for instance, whilst undeniably effective, may appear old-fashioned and out of date to advertisers who have something more sophisticated in mind. Similarly, it is an undeniable fact that the siting of advertising posters and hoardings can generate a certain amount of public dislike. This dislike centres around the environmental impact and visual disturbance caused by the more obtrusive forms of outdoor media. Such media can also distract drivers when they are sited near to main roads, motorways (etc);

iii) *risk of damage:* outdoor media such as fixed posters and showcards are subject to damage by vandalism and graffiti. Whilst this is bad enough in itself, what may be worse is a concerted attack on the advertising campaign itself. This has happened to posters promoting, for example, tobacco products and high performance saloon cars. Counter-messages have been sprayed onto the posters by individuals who hold views hostile or opposed to those communicated by the advertisement.

5) PUBLICITY

Publicity can occur through the means of the printed media, the broadcast media, the cinema, film and video, and direct communication. It can include:

* news items and announcements;
* editorial comment;
* features, feature articles and pictures;
* regular consumer affairs columns or new product spots;
* documentary, magazine and consumer affairs programmes on the broadcast media;
* documentary and newsreel films shown in the cinema;
* documentary films shown to "interested groups", clubs, societies (etc);
* talks to interested groups, clubs, societies (etc).

Such publicity can take two forms. The first is independent, objective and non-controllable. The information will be researched, compiled and formulated under the editorial control of the particular media. The second form will be based upon information and assistance provided by the company source. It will use an information department or Public Relations function to provide this information and guidance.

5.1) Advantages of publicity as a promotional medium

Publicity *may be perceived* by the general public as relatively objective and free from bias, especially when compared with direct advertising. Publicity also carries by *implication* the endorsement of the medium in which it appears. This may add to its persuasiveness in the mind of the public at large. So, a documentary film about holidays in Austria shown by a local travel agent to a meeting of a Women's Institute or Townswomen's Guild may have more effect on sales than a series of advertisements in the local newspaper. Indeed, television and radio programmes about holidays, travel and tourism are often highly influential in shaping purchase attitudes and behaviour in that market.

5.2) Disadvantages of publicity as a promotional medium

i) publicity is an *unpredictable and uncontrollable medium*. The enterprise cannot be sure that publicity will occur, nor can it be sure of the treatment the subject will receive. For the quality and character of the publicity may depend upon the interpretation and opinions of other people. These people may or may not agree with the company's philosophy and line of approach.

ii) *the effect of publicity may be unpredictable*. There is no guarantee that publicity will always be presented in "the right way", or that it will always be favourable. The launch of a new car may be heralded by a fanfare; but it may also be accompanied by a catechism on the faults of the model it replaces. Is the new car tainted with the faults of the old?

6) DIRECT MARKETING

Direct mail and other forms of direct marketing were analysed in Chapter 27.

SUMMARY

The contents of this chapter are summarised in Table 31.1.

TABLE 31.1
Summary : Chapter Thirty One

SECTION	MAIN POINTS
1. Printed media	Main advantage: accurate targeting of promotional communications on customer segments identified as making up the readership profile. Main disadvantage: gaining and holding the reader's attention.
2. Broadcast media	Main advantages: media power and dynamic presentation quality. Main disadvantages: absolute cost, wastage (ineffective targeting), and alternative uses of television receiver (especially video).
3. Cinema	Main advantages: accurate customer targeting and visual impact. Main disadvantages: dependence on trends in cinema attendance, lack of competitiveness with home-based entertainment.
4. Outdoor media	Main advantages: size, visibility and situational impact. Main disadvantages: noise and information clutter, variable image, risk of damage.
5. Publicity	Main advantage: perception of objectivity and freedom from bias. Main disadvantages: unpredictable and uncontrollable occurence, unpredictable and uncontrollable effects.
6. Direct marketing	See Chapter 27.

32 Advertising Effectiveness

INTRODUCTION

This chapter deals with the analysis and assessment of advertising effectiveness. It looks at the reasons why companies make such an assessment. It summarises the objectives of advertising within the persuasion process, and looks in detail at the constituents of advertising effectiveness. These constituents are advertising quality and media effectiveness. The chapter goes on to outline some of the UK sources of audience research data, and concludes with a comment on the practical difficulties of evaluating advertising effectiveness.

CHAPTER CONTENTS

1) Evaluating advertising effectiveness

2) Advertising objectives within the persuasion process

3) The constituents of advertising effectiveness

4) Advertising quality

5) Media effectiveness
   5.1) Impact on attitudes
   5.2) Audience research

6) UK Audience research
   6.1) Printed media
   6.2) Broadcast media
   6.3) Mixed media

7) Direct response

8) Conclusion

Summary

Chapter Appendix 32(1) Illustrative examination question and suggested answer.

Chapter Appendix 32(2) "Ads in a tight spot".

1) EVALUATING ADVERTISING EFFECTIVENESS

Advertising is a crucial part of the promotional mix. It is highly visible and, particularly in consumer goods markets (especially f.m.c.g.) may require very high levels of company expenditure. It is hardly surprising, therefore, that companies should be interested in making some kind of evaluation of the effectiveness of the advertising in which they have invested.

The assessment of advertising planning and effectiveness is, however, fraught with difficulties. In essence, how can one relate an investment in advertising to the level of sales that may follow an advertising campaign? And how can the marketer relate the current level of sales and market share to long-running and consistent advertising, without stopping the advertising to see what might happen!

A variety of factors are likely to affect consumer attitudes and sales levels. We have examined some of these in earlier chapters. Nevertheless, advertising is undoubtedly a powerful tool in shaping attitudes and brand loyal behaviour, so some attempt needs to be made to evaluate it. Even if a direct correlation with sales level and market share cannot be drawn, an evaluation of advertising effectiveness will help the company improve and refine its promotional skills, and contribute to the build up of *experience*. Building and retaining marketing experience is a key organisational and managerial task.

2) ADVERTISING OBJECTIVES WITHIN THE PERSUASION PROCESS

The persuasion process was defined and described in Chapter 30. Advertising may be used to achieve a number of different objectives across the various stages of the persuasion process. It is particularly valuable at the *awareness* and *comprehension* stages, whilst a key role at the *conviction* stage is that of encouraging brand-loyal attitudes and behaviour. Advertising objectives within the persuasion process may be summarised thus:

AWARENESS

Advertising is used to establish a basic awareness of the product or service in the mind of the potential customer, and to build up knowledge about it. This is of particular importance during early stages of the Product Life Cycle. Repetition of the message over time should build up recall on the part of the target market. Successful and consistent advertising should build up a relationship in the mind of potential customers between the advertising and the product or service. What matters, of course, is that advertising keeps the product or service in the mind (or "frame of reference") of the potential buyer, so that he or she includes it within the available purchase alternatives. The advertising of branded grocery products, for instance, reminds consumers of their existence and offsets the tendency to select own brands when shopping.

COMPREHENSION

Advertising is used to build up an understanding of the product and its benefits, in the mind of the potential customer. Effective advertising will be the catalyst for a process in which the potential customer reduces his or her doubts about the product, and begins to establish favourable attitudes about it. Obviously, other factors will come into play here. Existing attitudes; reinforcing messages of a positive or negative nature (such as personal recommendation or the views of opinion leaders); past experience with similar products, (etc), will all shape the build-up of individual attitudes towards the product.

CONVICTION

A more difficult role for advertising to play will be the conversion of emergent favourable attitudes into feelings that are *actually positive and preferential* towards the product or service. Advertising may be able to enhance the process by which the potential customer establishes feelings of "rightness" or "contentment" about the product. Similarly, customers may come to feel that they should make repeat purchases of a product with which they have already had experience, but towards which they had no prior feelings of preference or commitment. This is a crucial advertising role. Much advertising expenditure, particularly in mature markets, is aimed at encouraging and maintaining *brand-loyal behaviour,* so that repeat purchases continue to be made. In fast moving consumer goods markets, advertising is also a major manufacturer weapon against the encroachement of retailer own brands on their market share. Retailers have to stock branded goods (even though they might prefer to concentrate on their own brands, over which they have greater control), because advertising creates and maintains custom for them on a "demand-pull" basis.

ACTION

Advertising objectives at this stage include:

* helping the potential customer to overcome personal doubts and barriers to action;

* reinforcing feelings of rightness and preference about the product or service;
* helping or encouraging the individual to make the purchase decision;
* encouraging repeat purchase of the product or service;
* encouraging the customer to increase his usage and level of purchase of the product;
* reinforcing the customer's feelings that he or she *has made the right purchase decision.*

The final objective in this list is an interesting one. Advertising may be used to reinforce the customer's feelings that he or she has made the right decision. At the same time, such advertising may offset *post-purchase dissonance.*. Post-purchase dissonance comprises negative feelings and attitudes that may emerge from experience with the product. No advertising in the world can offset genuine feelings of dissatisfaction with the product. The personal criticism or condemnation that can result from it may constitute a powerful and non-controllable form of negative communication. Nevertheless, many customers worry about whether they have done the right thing, and advertising may have a role to play in providing them with the reassurance that they would genuinely like to receive.

3) THE CONSTITUENTS OF ADVERTISING EFFECTIVENESS

The evaluation of advertising effectiveness depends on analysing two related factors, namely:

– COMMUNICATION EFFECTIVENESS

– PERSUASION EFFECTIVENESS

Communication effectiveness can be tested by analysing (i) the reach and penetration of promotional communications; (ii) advertising recognition and recall; (iii) the degree of brand or company awareness; (iv) the degree of brand or company knowledge on the part of target market segments.

Persuasion effectiveness can be tested by establishing the degree of customer interest, preference and loyalty to the product or service.

The more effective the advertising, the more it will have been seen to achieve the various communication and persuasion objectives outlined in section (2) above. In practice the assessment of this effectiveness is carried out under two headings namely:

* ADVERTISING QUALITY;
* MEDIA EFFECTIVENESS.

These are analysed in Sections (4) and (5) below.

4) ADVERTISING QUALITY

Assessments of advertising quality are concerned with the communication and persuasion effectiveness of the advertisement or advertising campaign itself. Advertising quality is a function of such factors as:

* timing and frequency of repetition;
* message content;
* message construction and formulation;
* creative content, style and impact;
* appropriateness to the target audience.

Take, for example, the famous PG Tips television commercials. These form one of the longest-running television campaigns in the U.K. They are described in Box 32.1.

Box 32.1

PG TIPS

The UK market for tea is a large and mature one, worth in excess of £500 million per year. Brooke Bond Oxo's PG Tips has been brand leader in this market for something like thirty years, during which time it has run the UK's longest advertising campaign. The campaign features its renowned chimpanzee advertisements.

The PG Tips chimpanzees have become synonymous with the brand. PG Tips commercials are instantly recognised and their association with the product is universally made. The chimpanzee advertisements have, therefore, become a classic case of how good and consistent advertising can be used to maintain and reinforce product awareness and brand loyalty.

Perhaps the best known of these commercials is Mr. Shifter, the furniture removal man. This is the UK's most screened commercial, holding the record at 1900 showings.

Other famous sketches have been based on James Bond, Ada and Dolly, and Jean Pierre Burke. These commercials are based on a "slice of life" storyline. *Marketing* commented that "the British public loves them. They parody family life, and the British like making fun of themselves. The basic parallel is with situation comedy. The jokes are music hall jokes (and) they are ... funny because they're delivered by chimps."

Marketing also comments that "however obvious the link between chimpanzees and tea parties, it took a brave marketer all those years ago to link his brand to a pack of unruly apes. If someone brought the idea to us today, would we accept it?"

There are a number of methods by which an assessment of advertising quality can be made. These are described follows.

a) *tests of recall:* which indicate the percentage of a sample of respondents who could (i) remember a particular advertisement: (ii) recall parts of its format and message. Tests of recall might be undertaken after the initial placing of an advertisement, or after the completion of an entire campaign. Recall tests are used to assess the level of recognition and memory of advertising and promotional messages on the part of a target audience, in order to ascertain its level of awareness and knowledge about the product, brand or company in question.

b) *attitude tests:* may be used to establish the degree to which advertising and promotional activities have been successful in:

* strengthening preference, commitment and conviction towards the product or service;
* establishing a degree of "intention to purchase" (ie encouraging positive action).

The build up of preference, and the movement through the *purchase process* (described in an earlier chapter) are dependent upon the development of increasingly favourable buyer attitudes towards the product. These attitudes can be measured, and to some extent the impact of advertising on their development can be deduced.

The relationship between advertising, attitude formation and the establishment of preference or intention to purchase can best be illustrated in the case of new products or brands. The potential customer must be moved through the stages of the persuasion process, such that he or she moves through the purchase process towards a decision. Whilst opposing opinions, past experience, the attitudes of opinion leaders (etc) will "get in the way", there will be fewer impediments to the analysis of attitude formation and change as compared with those associated with longer-established products.

c) *linguistic tests:* are carried out to assess the process of *concept formation* on the part of the recipients of advertising. It will be important to understand the recipient's *perception and understanding* of a promotional message. The advertiser will need to know how the recipient interprets the message and goes on to form concepts on the basis of it. Attitude formation will in part depend on this process of interpretation and concept formulation. Try this yourself. What do you understand by the following descriptions used in the motor trade, and what interpretations do you put on them?

– mini	– fleet car
– hatchback	– high performance
– hot hatchback	– engineered
– notchback	– aerodynamic
– family saloon	– European styling
– sports car	– American styling

Similarly, advertising research appears to show that "whiteness" as a property of washing powder is perceived as a *favourable* concept, whilst "brightness" is viewed as an *unfavourable* concept. Hence, many soap powder advertisements stress whiteness in the wash, not the brightness.

d) *visual tests:* can be used to assess the impact on an individual subject of the visual content of advertising material. For instance, "tachistoscopes" can be used to indicate visual reaction and visual priority. Does the recipient look at the product, and for how long? Is he distracted by some other element in the picture in front of him? Visual tests may also be used to show the *effect of movement* in a commercial. Does the movement help the recipient to concentrate his attention on the product or message, or does it distract and confuse him?

5) MEDIA EFFECTIVENESS

The main types of media were listed and described in Chapter 31. They are:

* printed media;
* broadcast media;
* cinema;
* outdoor media;
* publicity;
* direct mail (etc)

It is normal for marketing specialists to carry out regular analysis of the effectiveness of printed and broadcast media, and this section will concentrate upon them. However, the principles involved are equally applicable to the other types of media, and reference will be made to these where appropriate. The assessment of media effectiveness can be divided into two areas, namely:

5.1) Impact on attitudes

5.2) Audience research

Each is described, as follows.

5.1) Impact on attitudes

The effectiveness of any particular media for promotional purposes will depend, in part, on *its ability to influence audience attitudes*. Advertising that is contained in a prestige journal, for example, may be viewed by some people with greater attention than the same advertisement published in one of the less reputable tabloid newspapers! The choice of media is bound to have some impact on the attitude of the recipient of the promotional messages contained within it. So, how may the choice of media affect attitude formation?

a) *stability and consistency of patronage:* where a particular media is known to have a stable and consistent patronage, then the advertiser may choose this media for long-term and consistent advertising. In the same way that customers have developed loyalty and favourable attitudes towards this media, so may they come to develop favourable attitudes towards promotional messages from advertisers whom they come to regard as an accepted part of the format of the media. Indeed, they may come to *expect*

445

this advertising, relying on it for information about likely future purchases. This happens with special interest periodicals, motoring magazines and so on.

b) *media appropriateness to market segment:* the marketer needs to use the promotional medium that is most appropriate to the target market segment. This point has already been made in earlier chapters. Just as products need to be designed and positioned on the needs of the target market segment, so must the promotional support. The marketer needs to understand how his or her market is segmented, and what are the most effective media to use for promotional purposes. Segment-specific media will yield the greatest access to the market, and have the greatest chance of developing favourable attitudes on the part of the recipients.

c) *media prestige:* attitude formation, whether by editorial comment, publicity or promotional message, will in part depend on the prestige of the media in the eyes of the recipient. The marketer may seek the most prestigious segment-specific media. Media which are held in esteem by their recipients will be trusted. They are likely to be effective in influencing attitude formation, and often serve as *opinion leaders.* Advertisers may therefore seek to be associated with such media prestige, in the hope that recipient esteem will be transferred to the promotional messages.

5.2) Audience research

Direct assessments of advertising effectiveness are made on the basis of *audience research.* This is based upon two criteria, namely *reach* and *frequency.*

i) *reach:* the advertiser will be concerned with the comparative cost of transmitting one message, or a series of messages, to his target audience. This comparative cost is often expressed in terms of "the cost per thousand people reached by the media". Some media will be more expensive than others when compared on this basis, but the advertiser may wish to know which is the most *cost-effective* means of reaching the target audience. For instance, in the UK:

* whilst commercial television is the most expensive advertising medium in absolute terms, it is the most cost-effective at reaching *large* regional and national audiences. This assumes, of course, that its programming choices enable it to maintain its share of the total available audience when compared, say, with the BBC (and independent satellite channels when they commence broadcasting). Effective programming choices are essential to maintaining advertising patronage and revenue;

* commercial radio is also relatively expensive, but is cost-effective for promoting to large but specific market segments known to make up the audience profile. Such segments include young people and housewives in socio-economic categories C and D, male householders in manual and transport occupations (etc);

* national press is less expensive but arguably less cost-effective at reaching and reinforcing messages aimed at large audiences. Nevertheless it is a powerful and flexible medium and, used consistently, may be particularly effective in attitude formation and development;

* regional and local press is highly cost-effective per thousand reached: indeed, on a local basis it is probably the most powerful advertising medium;

* cinema is cost-effective if the target market segment is known to be part of the audience profile. The problem for cinema advertisers is *the frequency of attendance,* which can be variable and unpredictable. Cinema attendance is dependent upon a variety of factors, as well as film quality;

* magazines and periodicals are highly cost-effective when used to reach specific audience segments, large or small. These publications are close to specific market segments and can promote to a *self-selecting* audience. For instance, advertisers of bathroom fittings, fitted bedrooms and kitchens, garden equipment, cars, (etc) make extensive use of specialist and hobby magazines and periodicals such as "Homes and Gardens", "Prima", "Woman's Own", "Autocar", (etc). The principle also applies to the *trade press.* Advertisers make heavy use of specialist trade publications, and it

447

is often true that readers will actually *expect* to see their advertisements, as part of the current trade scene;

* outdoor media are seen as a cost-effective means of *reinforcing* campaigns being run in other media. The effectiveness of such media is dependent on siting and visual quality. Good posters, for instance, may be large and create strong visual impact.

ii) *frequency:* the advertiser will also have to consider the number of times the message needs to be repeated in order to obtain the necessary recall and *impact. Impact is a function of advertising objectives and "media planning".* It will be determined by the extent to which the advertising campaign aims to develop:
– awareness and recall
– comprehension
– conviction
– action

The relationship within media planning between the **chosen media, reach, frequency and impact is a complex** subject, largely beyond the scope of this book. Suffice it to say that the advertiser *will be looking for the most cost-effective combination of media reach and message frequency that will produce the desired impact on the target audience,* thus:

Media planning = f(optimum combination of media reach and message repetition)

The relationship is summarised in Figure 32.1

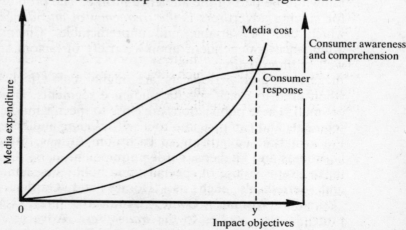

Figure 32.1. Impact Cost-Effectiveness.

Media expenditure up to the point x will yield increases in customer awareness and comprehension. Beyond this point there is no further benefit, and advertising impact objectives can only be fulfilled to the point y. The diagram assumes a proportionate relationship between media expenditure and the build-up of awareness and comprehension. If the advertiser wishes to achieve greater impact, then, given the shape of the consumer response curve, he will have to increase his expenditure on reach and frequency, so as to move the media cost curve upwards and to the right. This should also cause a proportionate change in the shape and position of the consumer response curve.

iii) *wastage*

The analysis of advertising effectiveness must not only consider reach and frequency factors that derive from the advertising objective, but also the wastage that is inherent in any advertising media. Whatever channel is chosen, the advertiser will be paying for the message to be transmitted to some recipients to whom this message is not relevant. For instance, non-car owners may see advertisements for cars, fuel, oil (etc) but will largely ignore them. Nevertheless, the advertiser has had to incur the cost of reaching them as part of the price of gaining access to potential customers.

During the "media planning" process the advertiser, therefore, *will seek media which will maximise access to interested recipients, and minimise reach to uninterested ones, which is wasted.* He or she will seek media whose audience or buyer profile is known, and concentrate on those which contain the highest proportion of whatever customer target it is at which the promotion is aimed. The more specific the media, therefore, the lower is the wastage likely to be. Several implications follow from this:

* national media, such as TV and newspapers, are powerful but inevitably incur very high wastage. Given such inherent wastage, therefore, such media are particularly suited to large areas of population concentration (such as London and the South East). In such areas both reach and wastage may be maximised, but the media also maximises the advertiser's chances of gaining access to the largest proportionate number

of interested recipients relative to the cost incurred. In geographically large areas in which there is a much lower population density, there is a statistical probability of achieving a much higher relative wastage rate as compared with the reach to interested recipients, for a similar cost.

* more *selective* media may be effective at maximising reach to interested recipients, and minimising wastage, especially where the relationship between media and customer segment is known. This point has already been made above. It accounts for the popularity of magazines, local press, local radio and so on. It also accounts for the popularity of direct marketing techniques such as direct mail. Direct mail, despite its current popularity, does however carry an inherently high risk of wastage. This point (and its consequences) were examined in an earlier chapter.

6) U.K. AUDIENCE RESEARCH

Research into media audiences in the UK is carried out by a number of specialist agencies, and their results are made available to subscribers such as advertising agencies, company marketing departments, market researchers, and so on.

6.1) Printed media

British Rate and Data (BRAD) is the national guide to UK printed media. Amongst the publications it lists, research into circulation and readership is carried out by the:

a) *Audit Bureau of Circulation (ABC)* which publishes audited sales figures, which it terms "circulation". Circulation, however, is not always an accurate guide to *readership*. Have *you* purchased this book even though you are reading it!? Advertisers are more concerned with readership figures, which will usually be larger than sales figures. Hence, for instance, the:

b) *National Readership Survey (NRS),* which is carried out by JICNARS (Joint Industry Committee for National Readership Surveys). This comprises a twice yearly sample of 30,000 individuals, who are asked to report on their reading of national newspapers and magazines. The results are published on a segmented basis, for instance detailing the percentage of total "Sun" readership made up by socio-economic groups C,D,E.

c) *Business Readership Survey (BRS)* which is an annual survey of the reported reading of a sample of business managers and executives. The BRS covers national newspapers and the more important commercial, business and trade journals, such as "Management Today", "Electronics Weekly", "Baking Today", "The Grocer" etc. The BRS is of particular interest to advertisers who wish to reach business readers (both in their business and home environment) and need to know the segment profile of business readers of the various business publications.

6.2) Broadcast media

i) *Television Ratings (TVR),* which are carried out by BARB (Broadcasters' Audience Research Board) on behalf of the BBC and IBA. Television audiences in the UK are sampled on a continuous basis by meters and individual recorders, using a permanent national panel of 3000 homes. The Television Rating is an estimate of the percentage of the total available audience viewing at any one time. The statistics can also be segmented on a demographic basis to yield the TVR for specified subgroups like children, housewives, specific socioeconomic categories or age groups.

ii) *Commercial radio ratings,* which are carried out by JICRAR (Joint Industry Committee for Radio Advertising Research) on a sample basis for all the independent commercial radio networks in the UK. Audience research for BBC Radio programmes is carried out by the BBC. Listening figures for commercial and BBC radio are not published on a uniform basis (unlike television ratings).

6.3) Mixed media

Independent audience research is carried out by agencies such as the British Market Research Bureau (BMRB), who make available to subscribers their "Target Group Index" (TGI). This is a mixed twice yearly postal survey of 24,000 individuals. The TGI covers product purchase, printed media readership and TV viewing. It is segmented on a demographic basis and also by **ACORN** categories.

There are a number of other specialist agencies, such as MEAL (Media Expenditure Analysis Ltd) who provide subscribers with specialist information on advertising media, audience composition and market segmentation. A detailed analysis of their activities is beyond the scope of this manual.

7) DIRECT RESPONSE

Where advertising is based upon the direct response principle, it is possible to make some judgement about the communication and persuasion effectiveness by analysing:

* coupons or address slips returned which seek further information;
* coupons or address slips returned which ask a salesperson to call;
* actual sales figures where the product is sold on a direct response basis.

Direct response was discussed in an earlier chapter.

8) CONCLUSION

In reality it is quite difficult to establish the relationship between advertising expenditure and its results, especially in terms of sales. This is because the effect of advertising is difficult to isolate from the other elements in the promotional mix, and indeed from other factors in the marketing mix, such as price. Nevertheless, it is clear that, especially in consumer goods markets, advertising has a very important role to play. Well-presented advertising campaigns using carefully targeted media will always be a major part of the promotional activity in such markets.

SUMMARY

The contents of this chapter are summarised in Table 32.2.

TABLE 32.2
Summary : Chapter Thirty Two

SECTION	MAIN POINTS
1. Evaluating advertising effectiveness	Whilst advertising is undoubtedly a powerful tool in shaping attitudes and brand-loyal behaviour, the large expenditures incurred (especially in consumer goods markets) call for evaluation of the effectiveness of advertising planning and policy.
2. Advertising objectives within the persuasion process	Advertising may be used to achieve a number of different objectives at the awareness, comprehension, conviction and action stages within the persuasion process.
3. The constituents of advertising effectiveness	The evaluation of advertising effectiveness depends on analysing its communication effectiveness and persuasion effectiveness.
4. Advertising quality	An assessment of advertising quality can be made on the basis of (a) tests of recall; (b) attitude tests; (c) linguistic tests; (d) visual tests.
5. Media effectiveness	The assessment of media effectiveness is divided into the analysis of (5.1) impact on attitudes; (5.2) audience research.
5.1 Impact on attitudes	The capacity of a media to influence audience attitudes may depend on (a) stability and consistency of the media's patronage; (b) media appropriateness to target market segment; (c) media prestige.
5.2 Audience research	Audience research is based on two criteria, namely reach and frequency. Measurements of reach will be expressed in terms of the "cost per thousand people reached by the media". The advertiser wants to know what is the most cost-effective means

of reaching the target audience. Frequency is concerned with the number of times the promotional message needs to be repeated in order to obtain the necessary recall and impact. Impact is a function of advertising objectives. Wastage comprises recipients to whom the message is irrelevant. During the media planning process the advertiser will seek media that will maximise access to interested recipients, and minimise reach to uninterested ones, which is wasted.

6. UK audience research	Specialist agencies produce audience research information for (6.1) printed media eg Audit Bureau of Circulation, National Readership Survey, Business Readership Survey; (6.2) broadcast media eg Television Ratings, commercial radio ratings; (6.3) mixed media eg Target Group Index.
7. Direct response	The effectiveness of direct response advertising can be indicated by sales achieved, requests for further information (etc).
8. Conclusion	In reality it is difficult to establish the relationship between advertising expenditure and its results, especially in terms of sales. This is because the effect of advertising is difficult to isolate from other elements in the promotional and marketing mix.

CHAPTER APPENDIX 32(1)

Appendix 32(1) contains an illustrative examination question, and suggested answer.

QUESTION:

A manufacturer of frozen foods decided to plan a national TV advertising campaign for a particular product and to assess the results in terms of sales achieved. A sample survey undertaken before the campaign over a period of four weeks revealed the following:

Channel	Sales (units)		
	Product A	Product B	Total
Multiple stores	160,250	71,300	231,550
Independent stores	40,500	18,160	58,660
Total:	200,750	89,460	290,210

The advertising campaign (for product B) lasted for four weeks, and immediately thereafter, a further sample survey over a period of four weeks showed the following changes:

Channel	Sales (units)		
	Product A	Product B	Total
Multiple stores	176,275	89,125	265,400
Independent stores	42,525	20,430	62,955
Total:	218,800	109,555	328,355

a) What conclusions can be drawn from these results?

b) What other information would you require before making any positive statements on the effect of the campaign? (CIMA)

Suggested answer:

a) What conclusions can be drawn from these results?

Calculation of percentage changes:

Channel	Product A	Product B	Total
Multiple stores	+ 10%	+ 25%	+ 14.6%
Independent stores	+ 5%	+ 12.5%	+ 7.3%
Total	+ 9%	+ 22.5%	+ 13.1%

The advertising campaign has produced proportionately much better results in multiple stores than independent stores for the sales of Product B. Evidently, the television campaign reached market segments for products A and B who shop at multiple rather than independent retailers. The campaign had a close relationship to the market for Product A, which has also enjoyed sales increases of a proportionate level in each channel type. The campaign could have resulted in a reduction in sales of Product A. Instead, has it increased the total market for the product type?

b) What other information would you require before making any positive statements on the effect of the campaign?

i) what is Product A and how does it compare with Product B? Why have its sales also gone up? Has this been due to the campaign for Product B, or would A and B's sales have increased in any case (perhaps to a lower extent) without the campaign?

This relates to:-

ii) how seasonal is the market? Some frozen food purchases show seasonal variations.

iii) why have the sales increases for Product B varied between the two channel types, and why have sales in multiple stores increased at a proportionately greater rate?

iv) how are stocks of Products A and B distributed across the two channel types? Have the multiple stores reacted more quickly to the advertising campaign and increased their stock levels faster than the independents? Indeed, have some of the multiple stores been undertaking their own promotional activities for the two products, at the same time?

v) *what was the objective of the campaign?* Was the campaign a "one-off" or seasonal? It would have been helpful to have information on sales trends over a longer period of time. Was the campaign launched to support a sales drive by sales staff, and to what extent do selling and advertising activities complement each other in moving products through this market? At whom was the campaign aimed? Who were the target audiences and in what market segments are they to be found?

vi) *what was the relationship of the campaign to competitor activity?* What (if any) was the relationship to product or promotional activity undertaken by competitors? The campaign may have been mounted to protect market share at a time of increasing competitor activity in an apparently rising market.

vii) *role of channel type:* the results could indicate that the distribution system (wholesalers?) supplying independent retailers is relatively inefficient, and that it has responded more slowly than the multiples, who have built up and moved stock more quickly in response to the advertising campaign.

c) Conclusion

This sample question deals with the extent to which the manufacturer could hope to show a *direct* relationship between a single advertising campaign, and the sales results that followed it. The manufacturer will have to consider what other factors (within its control or outside it) might have given rise to the varying increases in channel sales performance.

CHAPTER APPENDIX 32(2)

ADS IN A TIGHT SPOT

"There was a time when (UK) TV commercials were relatively simple to plan and evaluate. Advertisers were predominantly in the business of selling mass market products, and therefore their interest was simply in the number of people who saw their ads. At most, segmentation was merely 'all housewives', or for the really fastidious, 'older housewives'.

Naturally, TV research was designed to meet the needs of TV advertisers. In its time, starting in the late sixties, the old JICTAR (Joint Industry Committee for TV Audience Research) system was probably the most advanced in the world. It produced masses of reasonably accurate information within, by research standards, an amazingly short time – weekly and within ten days of the end of the week covered.

But the information produced in this way was rather poorly segmented, partly because such segmentation would have greatly increased the amount of effort in processing and publication, but also because there was little demand for such extra sophistication.

The basic categories were men, women and housewives, within which it was normal to show one class and two age breakdowns. It was always possible to analyse the data far more thoroughly, but the work was laborious and therefore expensive, and few advertisers or agencies felt that it was worth going to that degree of effort.

Over the past few years, the nature of TV advertising has changed. Table 1 shows the shifts in the type of advertiser between 1973 and 1984. The most obvious movement is the fall in advertising for fast moving consumer goods (FMCG), and the growth in areas such as financial and durables advertising.

Table 1. TV Revenue base (1973-84)

	Percentage	
	1973	1984
FMCG	70	50
Durables	14	20
Financial	1	5
Services	6	8
Retail	4	6
Other	5	11

Source: AA/MEAL

The table itself probably fails to bring out the degree of change, since even in FMCG, a number of new types of product targeted at specific groups of consumers have moved to TV in recent years. The newer TV advertisers tend to cater for smaller and more sharply defined markets than those which dominated in the early 70s.

In principle, it should not be sufficient for the newcomers to be given information covering broad aggregates. They need something considerably more detailed. But although JICTAR has changed to BARB, and the research techniques have greatly improved, with the great strides made in electronic technology, the basic form of data publication remains very similar to what it was 15 years ago.

In particular, the demographic breakdowns remain wide and bland. The question is how far this affects the ability of advertising agencies to recognise and buy the optimum schedules on behalf of their clients, and whether anything can be done to make their task easier.

Recent developments at AGB TV Audience Research have helped to provide answers to both parts of the question. Thanks to improved computer systems and the greater accuracy and detail provided by PeopleMeters, it is now possible to look at the viewing behaviour of smaller sectors, and see how far these differ from the larger aggregates with which they have normally been lumped in the past.

Table 2 shows the top ten programmes in the week beginning 12 January 1987, for all adults, for the over-55s, which is the age category normally shown in BARB reports, and then splits this group into its two obvious components, the 55 to 64-year-olds and those above 65. It can be seen immediately that there are great differences in the viewing patterns of the two groups.

Table 2. Top ten programmes by age (week starting 12 Jan 1987)

Position	All adults	55+
1	Coronation Street ITV	Coronation Street ITV
2	Coronation Street ITV	Coronation Street ITV
3	Eastenders BBC 1	News at 5.45 ITV
4	Eastenders BBC 1	News at 5.45 ITV
5	News at 5.45 ITV	News at 5.45 ITV
6	Bergerac BBC 1	News at 5.45 ITV
7	Inspector Morse ITV	Inspector Morse ITV
8	Three Up Two Down BBC 1	News at 5.45 ITV
9	Weather News BBC 1	Never the Twain ITV
10	Wish You Were Here ITV	This Is Your Life ITV

	55-64	65+
1	Coronation Street ITV	Coronation Street ITV
2	Coronation Street ITV	News at 5.45 ITV
3	News at 5.45 ITV	Coronation Street ITV
4	Inspector Morse ITV	News at 5.45 ITV
5	Bergerac BBC 1	News at 5.45 ITV
6	Sporting Triangles ITV	News at 5.45 ITV
7	News at 5.45 ITV	News at 5.45 ITV
8	The Equaliser ITV	This Is Your Life ITV
9	Never The Twain ITV	Never The Twain ITV
10	News at 5.45 ITV	Crossroads ITV

Source: AGB/BARB

Naturally, these reflect differences in their lifestyle - most men between 55 and 64 have full-time jobs and their viewing patterns differ greatly and systematically from those over 65, few of whom work.

AGB has written several papers on the purchasing power of older people which show that there are major differences between those above and those below 65. It is important to many advertisers to be able to distinguish between them when buying spots for their campaigns.

If there is one area of particular interest to the newer advertisers on TV, it is the upper classes. Much advertising for financial institutions and expensive durables is aimed primarily at people with high incomes. One determinant of this is social class, which, although far from perfect as a guide to disposable wealth, is the best available.

In the past, TV viewers have normally been divided simply into sheep and goats: ABC1 and C2DE, with the obvious assumption that those looking for higher class and richer consumers should aim predominantly at the first group.

This view is not false, but its accuracy leaves a great deal to be desired. There are considerably more C1s than ABs, and most of them are far from being affluent. Of course, if ABs and C1s watched the same programmes, there would be no problem for advertisers, but, as Table 3 shows, this is not the case. In fact, the list of top ten programmes for ABs bears little resemblance to the corresponding list for C1s, or to the joint ABC1 list.

Table 3. Top ten programmes by class
(Week starting 12 Jan 1987)

Posit-ion	ABC1
1	Miss Marple/Murder BBC 1
2	Bergerac BBC 1
3	Eastenders BBC 1
4	Eastenders BBC 1
5	Coronation Street ITV
6	Weather News BBC 1
7	News and Weather BBC 1
8	Coronation Street ITV
9	Inspector Morse ITV
10	Holiday 87 BBC 1

	AB	C1
1	Miss Marple/Murder BBC 1	Eastenders BBC 1
2	Bergerac BBC 1	Coronation Street ITV
3	Weather News BBC 1	Coronation Street ITV
4	News and Weather BBC 1	Miss Marple/Murder BBC 1
5	Last of the Summer Wine BBC 1	Bergerac BBC 1
6	Weather News BBC 1	Eastenders BBC 1
7	Eastenders BBC 1	Inspector Morse ITV
8	Mastermind BBC 1	Weather News BBC 1
9	News, Sport, Weather BBC 1	Three Up Two Down BBC 1
10	Weather News BBC 1	News and Weather BBC 1

Source: AGB/BARB

One problem for advertisers is that many of the most popular programmes among categories of interest to them are on BBC, and therefore not open to commercials. Of course, a top ten could be prepared covering only the commercial channels, and advertisers would probably find this of more immediate interest than a general top ten. But it is possible to go beyond this in producing material of interest to advertisers.

Table 4 looks simply at ABs and shows the top ten programmes by commercial value to the advertiser for the same week covered in Table 3. It considers the ratio of ABs to all adults watching a particular programme. If the same proportion of ABs as of all adults watched it, the ratio would be 1:1, but as can be seen from the table many programmes do far better than this. For example, if 10% of all ABs watched it but only 5% of all adults the ratio is 2:1.

Table 4. Top ten programmes by commercial value*

Position	Programme	Ratio ABs:All adults
1	News Summary BBC 1	2.01:1
2	Audience with Dame Edna Everage C4	1.23:1
3	World According to Smith and Jones ITV	1.20:1
4	News at Ten ITV	1.18:1
5	Superfrank C4	1.10:1
6	American Football C4	1.10:1
7	News BBC 1	0.99:1
8	The Big Match Live ITV	0.98:1
9	Bonnie and Clyde ITV	0.97:1
10	The Challenge ITV	0.94:1

* for week starting 12 Jan 1987

Source: AGB/BARB

The system described here has one obvious weakness - it is necessarily historical, showing what has happened, whereas advertisers are buying spots for the future. However, this weakness is not as great as it may appear. Many programmes are in series, and it is generally the case that if one is popular with a particular sub-group, the succeeding episodes will be equally popular, although changes in external factors such as opposition programmes or the weather can make a significant difference.

The figures shown here are only the tip of the very large iceberg of potential uses for this type of detailed demographics. For example, different sub-groups do not differ only in the programmes they watch, but also in their general viewing patterns: both the amount they watch, the channel they watch most frequently and in the time of day they watch. ABs, for example, are light viewers generally, but heavier late at night.

This type of information, allied to more detailed programme preferences, could do a great deal to help sophisticated spot buying."

(*Source:* "Marketing" Reproduced with permission)

33 Advertising Expenditure

INTRODUCTION

This chapter completes the analysis of advertising by looking at the methods by which companies establish their advertising budgets. A variety of methods are compared, some of which are more systematic than others. The chapter then goes on to illustrate the extent and scope of advertising by giving some examples of actual UK advertising expenditures for the year 1989. During that year, expenditure by the top ten advertising categories amounted to £3 billion. This figure gives a clue to the absolute importance of advertising within the promotional mix, especially in the markets for consumer goods and services.

CHAPTER CONTENTS

1) Determinants of advertising budgets

2) Objective and task budgeting

3) UK advertising expenditures

Summary

Recommended reading

1) DETERMINANTS OF ADVERTISING BUDGETS

There are a number of methods by which annual advertising budgets can be determined. These are described below.

a) *percentage of actual sales:* the advertising budget for the forthcoming year is based upon estimated sales revenue achieved for the current year, perhaps weighted for actual sales achieved in the year previous to that. A variation on this approach is:

b) *percentage of forecasted sales:* the advertising budget for the forthcoming year is based upon the forecasted level of sales to be achieved during the forthcoming year.

The use of either of these approaches is, in theory, based upon the assumption that the marketer knows what the relationship is between advertising and sales volume achieved. In other words, the marketer must have some assessment of the effectiveness of advertising, carried out this year and in previous years. This must be so, as sales levels are in part determined by investments in promotional activity.

Whether or not this is, in reality, a reasonable assumption to make, it contains one major disadvantage. Where marketing management sticks closely to this percentage formula, advertising expenditures may *decrease* if sales levels decline, say as a result of recessionary circumstances. What is much more likely to be needed, of course, is an increase in advertising under such circumstances.

c) *matching competitor spend:* the level of advertising budget is set at a level which is equal to (or proportionate with) the advertising expenditures of competitors. Such information is made available in the UK by specialist agencies such as *MEAL* (mentioned in the previous chapter) and on an annual basis by *The Media Register.* Matching competitor spend is a "safety-first" strategy, and assumes that all advertising within the trade is equally effective. The main disadvantage of such an advertising strategy is that it ignores qualitative differences between the promotional mix of the differing companies in the trade. The promotional activities of some companies will be more effective on a "pound-for-pound" basis than others.

d) *spending "the money available":* advertising budgets are based on the money available. In the absence of any analysis of advertising effectiveness, this can be regarded as an unsystematic strategy. The professional marketer will prefer to avoid being seen to use it as a means of determining his or her advertising objectives.

2) OBJECTIVE AND TASK BUDGETING

Objective and task budgeting, in theory, is a more systematic approach to setting advertising and promotional budgets. It contains a number of steps, as follows:

i) target market segments are identified;

ii) the most effective media are identified by which to reach the target audiences within these market segments;

iii) advertising objectives for communication and recall, persuasion and desired sales levels are established;

iv) time-scales for the achievement of advertising objectives are established.

Advertising objectives, in turn, will be related to the requirements of company sales forecast for the period ahead, and to the needs of marketing and corporate plans.

Once this *promotional strategy* has been established, the marketer and the advertising agency will work out the specific advertising activities or Tasks that will be needed to put this strategy into effect. This will include:

* media planning (the choice of media and frequency of advertising, etc);
* campaign planning (the creative content, message, consistency with previous campaigns, etc).

The costs of these various component tasks are then calculated and the final budget assembled. This will comprise the budget for the year ahead, unless there are resource limitations. Where there are not enough funds available for the whole strategy, then funds will be allocated to its component parts on a priority basis. The task requirements of the promotional plan must, therefore, be allocated *priority indicators,* so that a systematic choice can be made amongst them.

Objective and task budgeting for advertising will be greatly assisted where assessments of the effectiveness of past advertising are available. This will enable the formulation of more effective and accurate objectives for communication and recall, persuasion and sales levels to be achieved.

3) UK ADVERTISING EXPENDITURES

The importance of advertising (and the need to evaluate its effectiveness) can be indicated by the total annual UK expenditure by the top ten advertising categories, which for 1989 is analysed in Table 33.1.

Table 33.1 Top ten advertising categories in 1989

	Category	Total spent (£ million)
1	Financial	515
2	Food	451.5
3	Motors	433.9
4	Retail	421.8
5	Business to Business	343
6	Drink	241.3
7	Cosmetics and Toiletries	190.2
8	Household Stores	167.3
9	Travel	166.7
10	Publishing and Broadcasting	165.3
	TOTAL	3096

(Source: Marketing)

Most of this advertising relates to markets for consumer goods and services. The 1989 figures for the top ten advertisers using press and television are listed in Tables 33.2 and 33.3 respectively.

Table 33.2 Top ten advertisers using press in 1989

	Advertiser	Total spent (£ million)
1	Currys	13.7
2	B & H Special Kingsize	13.6
3	B & Q	13
4	Sky	12.9
5	MFI/Hygena	12.4
6	Dixons	11.7
7	Woolworths	11.6
8	Water Share Offer	10.8
9	Texas Homecare	10.5
10	Tesco	10.1
	TOTAL	120.3

(Source: Marketing)

Table 33.3 Top Ten advertisers using television in 1989

	Advertiser	Total spent (£ million)
1	McDonalds	14
2	Water and Sewage Businesses	12
3	Water Share Offer	11.6
4	British Telecom	10.9
5	Woolworths	9.4
6	Ariel Automatic Powder	8.9
7	Yellow Pages	8.9
8	Carlsberg Lager	8.4
9	Milk (NDC/MMB)	8
10	Maxwell House	7.8
	TOTAL	99.9

(Source: Marketing)

These figures are given for illustrative purposes only, to give the reader a feel for the scope and extent of advertising expenditure in the UK. Two trends can be identified:

* advertising by *financial institutions* (banks, building societies, etc) maintains its number one position. The top ten financial advertisers are shown in Table 33.4. The marketing of financial services is the subject of a later chapter.

* advertising by *foodstuffs manufacturers* remains heavy. The reasons for this have already been explained. The food market is mature and slow growing. Advertising is needed to encourage repeat purchase behaviour, maintain market share, and to ensure that retail multiples stock the product on a consistent and long term basis. The top ten food brands in 1989 are listed in Table 33.5.

Table 33.4 Top ten financial brands in 1989

	Advertiser	Total spent (£ million)
1	Water Share Offer	22.4
2	Midland Orchid	6.2
3	Halifax Property Services	6.1
4	Black Horse Agencies	5.8
5	Royal Life Estates	5.5
6	Prudential Property Services	5.1
7	General Accident Property Services	5
8	T.S.B.	4.9
9	Nat Savings Capital Bond	4.6
10	Halifax B S Mortgages	4.6
	TOTAL	70.2

(Source: Marketing)

Table 33.5 Top ten food brands in 1989

	Advertiser	Total spent (£ million)
1	Milk (NDC/MMB)	10.1
2	Nescafé Coffee	9.3
3	Maxwell House	8.2
4	Nescafé Gold Blend	8
5	Weetabix	5.8
6	Brook Bond PG Tips Bags	5.8
7	Kelloggs Cornflakes	5.7
8	Walkers Crisps	4.7
9	Kelloggs Raisin Splitz	4.6
10	Kelloggs Toppas	4.4
	TOTAL	66.6

(Source: Marketing)

Advertising by *retailers* during 1989 was affected by further concentration amongst grocery multiples, and a general downturn in consumer expenditure over the previous years. The top ten retail advertisers in 1989 are listed in Table 33.6.

Table 33.6 Top ten retail advertisers in 1989

	Advertiser	Total spent (£ million)
1	Woolworths	21.1
2	B & Q	15.2
3	McDonalds	14.3
4	MFI/Hygena	14.1
5	Currys	14
6	Tesco	13.2
7	Dixons	12.2
8	Texas Homecare	12
9	Comet	11.6
10	Asda	9.6
	TOTAL	137.3

(Source: Marketing)

Other major advertisers in 1989 included car manufacturers and importers, who are consistently heavy advertisers. The top ten car advertisers in 1989 are listed in Table 33.7.

Table 33.7 Top ten car advertisers in 1989

	Advertiser	Total spent (£ million)
1	Rover 200 Series	11.2
2	Ford Fiesta	10.5
3	Vauxhall Nova	9.8
4	Citroen AX	8.5
5	Peugeot 405	8.3
6	Renault 19	7.1
7	Citroen BX	6.9
8	Fiat Uno	6.9
9	Ford Sierra	6.4
10	Volvo 440	6.3
	TOTAL	81.9

(Source: Marketing)

Advertising expenditure by the top ten spenders in 1989 amounted to £463 million, as detailed in Table 33.8.

Table 33.8 Top ten spenders in 1989

	Company/organisation	Total spent (£ million)
1	Unilever	81.3
2	Procter and Gamble	71.4
3	Kellogg	48.3
4	Kingfisher	47.9
5	Mars/Pedigree	46
6	Water Authorities	38.7
7	News International	36.5
8	Nestlé/Rowntree	31.4
9	Rover Group	31.1
10	British Telecom	30.4
	TOTAL	463

(Source: Marketing)

SUMMARY

The contents of this chapter are summarised in Table 33.8.

Table 33.8
Summary : Chapter Thirty Three

SECTION	MAIN POINTS
1. Determinants of advertising budgets	Advertising budgets may be determined on the basis of (a) percentage of actual sales revenue; (b) percentage of forecasted sales revenue; (c) matching competitor spend; (d) spending "the money available".
2. Objective and task budgeting	Is a more systematic approach to setting advertising budgets. Advertising objectives derive from the company sales forecast and marketing plan. They are based on target market segments and the most effective media by which to gain access to these

	segments. Advertising tasks, time-scales and costs are then used to formulate the budget.
3. UK advertising expenditure	Advertising in the top ten UK categories totalled £3 billion in 1989. The heaviest advertisers were (1) the financial institutions; (2) foodstuffs manufacturers; (3) motor manufacturers and importers; (4) retail multiples. The heaviest advertising is concentrated on the markets for consumer goods and services.

RECOMMENDED READING

Jefkins F.   Advertising Today.   Intertex Books

Hart N A. and O'Connor J.   Practice of Advertising.
Heinemann

Wilmshurst J. The fundamentals of Advertising. Heinemann

Davis M P.   The Effective Use of Advertising Media.
Business Books

34 Sales Promotion Techniques

INTRODUCTION

This chapter analyses a number of techniques to which the term "sales promotion" is applied. These techniques range from consumer incentives such as coupons and cash-refunds to exhibitions and sponsorship. Consideration is also given to the evaluation of the effectiveness of these techniques.

CHAPTER CONTENTS

1) Sales promotion techniques

2) Immediate consumer incentives
   2.1) Free samples and trial packs
   2.2) Bonus packs
   2.3) Premiums and give-aways
   2.4) Price promotion on pack
   2.5) Competitions
   2.6) Industrial markets

3) Delayed consumer incentives
   3.1) Coupons
   3.2) Tokens and trading stamps
   3.3) Cash refunds on mail-in basis
   3.4) Premium giveaway offers on mail-in basis
   3.5) Charitable offers on mail-in basis
   3.6) Self-liquidating offers
   3.7) Competitions

4) Performance-related trade or industrial incentives

5) Point of sale display (POS) and merchandising
   5.1) Integrating POS

6) Exhibitions
   6.1) Advantages in consumer goods markets
   6.2) Advantages in industrial goods markets
   6.3) Disadvantages of exhibitions

7) Sponsorship

8) Evaluating sales promotion effectiveness

Summary

Recommended reading

Chapter Appendix 34(1): In-store merchandising

Questions for self-review

Examination questions

1) SALES PROMOTION TECHNIQUES

The term "sales promotion techniques" is used in this book to describe a general category of promotional activities which do not fit the other groupings within the promotional mix. In particular, they can be treated separately from advertising and direct selling. The term will be used, for the sake of convenience, to cover a variety of techniques. These techniques are to be found in both consumer and industrial goods markets. They are listed in Table 34.1, along with their application to the two types of market.

The application of sales promotion techniques is likely to be most familiar to the reader within the context of consumer goods markets. Heavy users in such markets include manufacturers, distributors and retailers of branded packaged foodstuffs and household products, alcoholic drinks and consumer durable goods. Not surprisingly these kinds of products often face intense competition within concentrated channels of distribution, and sales promotion techniques are used as part of a wider array of promotional methods.

Whether or not we are dealing with consumer or industrial goods markets, sales promotion techniques appear to have two broad objectives, namely:

* to enhance promotion and sale to *the trade;*
* to assist the trade in promoting and selling products to *the final customer.*

How these objectives are achieved forms the main content of this chapter.

The application of techniques of sales promotion is highly variable in its effect and an assessment of its effectiveness can be a complex and uncertain investigation. Sales promotion experts stress the importance of a creative approach to the

TECHNIQUE	APPLICATION TO CONSUMER GOODS MARKETS	APPLICATION TO INDUSTRIAL GOODS MARKETS
Immediate customer incentive	Frequent	Rare
Delayed customer incentive	Frequent	Rare
Performance – related trade or industrial incentives	Occasional	Frequent
Point of sale display	Frequent	Occasional
Exhibitions	Frequent	Frequent
Sponsorship	Frequent	Occasional

Table 34.1. Sales Promotion Techniques.

subject, warning that repeated "off-the-shelf" methods can quickly lose their effectiveness as sales motivators. Bad use of sales promotion does not work, and may offend, disgrace or demean either or both the product or customer.

Good use of sales promotion assists the enterprise to achieve the following marketing objectives:

i)   to develop the image of the brand or product;

ii) to complement other elements of the marketing mix, for instance by reinforcing advertising messages. Once promotional messages are directly associated with "the pack on the shelf", there is a greater chance that the customer will be motivated into purchasing it.

iii) to achieve harmony or consistency with promotional activities being undertaken by distributors or retailers. This is of particular importance in consumer goods markets where goods and services are sold through independent retail outlets and multiples.

2) IMMEDIATE CONSUMER INCENTIVES

Immediate consumer incentives include the following:

2.1) Free samples and trial packs

Free samples are given to customers, or trial packs sold at low prices (in both consumer and industrial markets) in order to encourage them to try the product, in the hope that they will eventually purchase it. Free sample promotions may be supported by the direct leafleting of homes with coupons which may be redeemed against samples in retail outlets. In industrial markets, products such as commercial vehicles, buses and railway equipment may be provided free for long term use and assessment by the potential customer, with the eventual objective of being able to make a full sales presentation to him.

2.2) Bonus packs

Bonus packs offer the customer more product for the same price. The customer is being offered greater value for money, whilst the increased incentive to purchase the product makes the technique popular with the trade.

2.3) Premiums and give-aways

Premiums may take the form of "more product for your money" – for instance buy two packs and get one free. Alternatively, the customer may receive a different item once he or she has made the requisite purchase. For instance, some readers will associate purchases of petrol with "merry sherry glasses" and other assorted glassware! Much older readers may remember the plastic daffodils given away with packs of washing powder! Others will associate "Club Class" flights with half bottles of champagne!

2.4) Price promotions on pack

The pack will carry "money-off" offers on the packaging, thereby reducing the cost to the customer. This is a form of *price competition*. Its use is somewhat controversial within the marketing fraternity, and some retailers will refuse to stock any items carrying such on-pack offers. Price promotions of this sort are used to gain relatively short-term enhancements in sales, especially in mature markets with low growth rates (such as foodstuffs, groceries and household consumables).

The critics of this technique argue that its use may damage brand reputation, image and loyalty that have been built-up by long-term and consistent pricing and advertising. They suggest that price promotions may not build sales volume *but merely trade market share*. This may only generate short term increases in sales, which then disappear with the end of the promotion. At best, argue the critics, on-pack price promotions may only be a suitable strategy for the third or fourth largest share-of-market brand whose manufacturer is seeking to enlarge his market share. They may not be suitable for the market share leader, or number two in the market, where there is effective product differentiation and where the main hope for long-term growth *lies in expanding the total market*. Many marketers argue that price is only a secondary factor here, as lower prices *cannot* be guaranteed to increase total market demand. They argue that expanding market size can only be achieved by expenditure on the development of better or value-added products, and on investments in advertising that build up customer awareness, interest and eventual loyalty to the product and the brand.

An equally compelling argument against on-pack price promotion is that where a supplier starts price competition, he or she will need to be sure that they are *the lowest cost producer*.

Otherwise they may lose a price war, with potentially damaging results. Markets rarely benefit from excessive price competition: the quality of service may decline and investment in research and new product development may be impossible to fund.

2.5) Competitions

The purchase of a product may give the buyer access to a competition which yields instant results. For instance, "scratch cards" are popular, and the consumer has a chance of winning a prize with the one card. Often such cards can be built up over time to give their collector more chances of winning prizes. Scratch cards are popular in the petrol retail market. Alternatively, many retail stores run competitions, free draws (etc) to which only those shopping in the store have access.

2.6) Industrial markets

Occasional use of immediate buyer incentives is made in industrial markets. One tractor importer in the UK offers farmers a free long weekend in Moscow if they purchase one of their tractors! Incentives in industrial markets often take the form of free trips and holidays, day conferences and visits, free lunches and the like.

3) DELAYED CONSUMER INCENTIVES

3.1) Coupons

Brand-specific coupons are made available to consumers who can redeem them against the purchase of the product (thereby gaining a price reduction). Coupons may be made available in press advertisements, by direct leafleting of households or may be printed on-pack (etc). The use of coupons is widespread in consumer goods markets. Their advantages include:

* giving the customer a discount whilst leaving the product's price structure unchanged;
* reinforcing brand loyalty by focussing the consumer's attention on the brand;
* encouraging repeat purchase behaviour.

The use of coupons is less popular with retail outlets because of the administrative effort involved in collecting and sorting coupons and obtaining refunds.

3.2) Tokens and trading stamps

Whilst the use of trading stamps has largely disappeared from the retailing scene in the UK, to be replaced by discount-orientated trading policies, trading stamps and tokens are still used, for instance in petrol retailing. A certain quantity of stamps or tokens are given to the customer each time he makes a purchase, and specified quantities of the stamps can later be redeemed for goods or services. This kind of use of tokens is aimed at reinforcing brand loyal behaviour and encouraging repeat purchase. This is a particular problem for petrol companies.

3.3) Cash refunds on mail-in basis

The consumer can obtain a specified cash refund if he or she saves up and sends in the required number of "proofs of purchase" (cut off from the labelling or packaging, or made up of printed can ring-pulls, bottle tops or whatever). Cash refund schemes are popular with the retail trade and their effectiveness as a sales motivator can be directly evaluated by the number of proofs of purchase mailed in.

3.4) Premium/giveaway offers on mail-in basis.

The consumer can obtain a specified product or service if he or she sends in the required number of proofs of purchase. This form of sales promotion can be an effective means of increasing sales if the offer made is perceived by the customer to be distinctive or attractive, or to offer particular value for money.

From the marketer's point of view, premium or giveaway offers are seen as effective where they clearly relate to the product and *enhance its image,* thereby complementing other elements of the promotional mix. Two examples can be given. The UK manufacturer of the drink "Babycham" gave away sparkling earrings to customers who mailed-in the appropriate number of proofs of purchase. These earrings complemented the product's brand image, which is that "nothing sparkles like Babycham". Similarly, a free silk bandeau was offered by a shampoo manufacturer. The objective of the bandeau was to associate (and reinforce) the concept of "silk" with hair and the particular brand of shampoo and conditioner.

478

3.5) Charitable offers on mail-in basis

A variation of (3.3) and (3.4) above involves the manufacturer making a donation to a specified charity, dependent upon the number of proofs of purchase mailed-in. This is now a very popular form of sales promotion in UK consumer goods markets. It has the major advantage of a *strongly positive* association with the product, since both the purchaser and the manufacturer are visibly seen to be acting in a socially responsible manner. Charitable offers allow the manufacturer to build both positive *and* corporate images, hence their popularity within the current social climate. For instance, one manufacturer of toilet tissue donated 5p for each batch of returned proofs of purchase. In one year it donated £100,000 to Guide Dogs for the Blind, and the next year gave £250,000 to the National Society for the Prevention of Cruelty to Children.

3.6) Self-liquidating offers

A self-liquidating offer is a promotion that partly or fully pays for itself. For instance, customers may be offered specified goods or services which can be obtained by sending in the required number of proofs of purchase, plus an additional sum of money. This income, added to the funding attributed to increased sales, covers the cost of the promotion which is continued until the supply of products or services is sold out or "self-liquidated". *Marketing* recalls a self-liquidating promotion run by Quick Brew Tea. The consumer could purchase two garden chairs for the equivalent of £2.99, or one sun lounger for £1.99. This promotion was so successful that 150,000 pairs of chairs and 250,000 sun loungers were sold.

The main advantage of self-liquidating offers lies in the additional revenue they generate. This advantage is, however, offset by the additional administration costs involved.

3.7) Competitions

Consumers may enter competitions by submitting the relevant proofs of purchase with their entry. Often competitions are spread across a number of packs or products, so that a number of purchases is needed before the entry can be made. The reaction to competitions can be very mixed, and generally they have low consumer appeal. Where consumers do enter them, on the other hand, their attention is focussed strongly on the product, and so competitions have some benefit in enhancing brand loyalty as well as increasing sales.

4) Performance-related trade or industrial incentives

Within industrial markets, sales promotion techniques may take the form of performance-related incentives. For instance:-

a) *performance-related bonuses:* bonuses or prizes may automatically be awarded to dealers, agents or distributors once they have reached or passed specified sales or market share targets. The effectiveness of such bonuses will of course depend upon their relative value: the higher the value the greater the incentive. These incentives may be financial in form, or instead they may be non-financial. Non-financial incentives will include sales conferences or holidays abroad, or gifts in the form of goods and services.

b) *performance-related competitions:* bonuses or prizes may instead be awarded on a competitive basis. For instance the agents with the greatest level of sales in excess of target may receive annual incentive awards.

c) *performance-related supply bonuses:* the dealer or distributor may receive supply bonuses comprising extra product for the same price. The quantity of the extra product made available will be dependent on the volume of sales already achieved.

5) POINT OF SALE DISPLAY (POS) AND MERCHANDISING

Within consumer goods markets it is important to present, display and promote the product *in the location where it is sold.* This is described as "point-of-sale" (POS) display. There is no doubt that effective display in retail or trade premises sells products, and that poor presentation and display undoes the good work achieved by other elements of the promotional mix.

Good POS display attracts customer attention, encourages the would-be buyer to approach, inspect and touch the product; and assists the customer in making the final product selection and purchase decision. POS display is also central to distributor/retailer "merchandising". *Merchandising is the physical process of stocking retail and distribution outlets with goods,* such that:

i)   the right merchandise is in the right place at the right time;

ii) the merchandise is appropriate to the target customer segments who make up the outlet's customer profile;

iii) the merchandise meets retailer/distributor segmentation objectives for the achievement of (a) principal benefit within the usage context; and (b) contribution/turnover objectives (described in the chapter on market segmentation);

iv) the merchandise is assembled, arranged and displayed *in situ* such that the physical arrangements of the shop or distribution outlet make easy and enjoyable for the customer the processes of:

* moving around the store;
* identifying, reaching and selecting merchandise;
* transporting, paying for and taking away the goods they have selected.

Good merchandising gives competitive advantage to both the retailer and the manufacturer. Given the nature of the relationship between the two, however, (both are independent organisations, each trying to achieve its own objectives), in-store merchandising can provide considerable difficulties for the manufacturer. This is especially true of fast moving consumer goods markets. The issue is therefore more fully discussed in the Appendix 34(1) to this Chapter.

Within the merchandising process, therefore, POS promotes the product by involving the customer physically and mentally with the product. Physical (and mental) "closeness" to the product in the retail or distribution setting will mean that the interested customer moves through the kind of purchase process described in an earlier chapter towards the final purchase decision. Many other factors will be responsible for increasing the level of customer awareness, interest and conviction that the purchase may be necessary or desirable. Appropriate merchandising (for instance allowing the potential customer to make comparisons between competing brands) and effective display may move the customer to the actual point of decision and action. This may be as true for a car displayed in a motor showroom as for a pack of washing-up liquid on the shelves of the local supermarket.

POS layout, in consequence, is an important determinant *in situ* of:

* visual and presentational impact of the product, or range of products;
* customer access to the product;
* secure retention of the product, product protection;
* the ease with which low level of stocks are indicated, and re-stocking facilitated.

POS display units must, as a result, be serviceable. They must work. They need to be able to fulfil their display objectives whilst standing up to use by the retailer or distributor, and handling by the customer. They must neither intimidate the customer nor make it difficult for him or her to reach and select the product, yet they must not collapse as a result of some heavy-handed treatment. As in all things, there is a balance to be struck. For instance, display units of cosmetics must make it easy for the customer to find and compare their choice from amongst a number of relatively small packs. Yet the packs must be held securely, since many contain glass bottles, and they must offer a clear field of view to the sales assistant. POS and merchandising are an open invitation to shop-lifters and thieves!

There is evidently a fair degree of psychology attached to Point of Sale promotion. POS psychology stresses such factors as:-

* the importance of the product's location relative to eye-level: eye-level locations are the most favoured;
* display location relative to height: the next time you are in your local supermarket look for the display of crisps. They are at *child-height!*
* access and reach for the physically handicapped, for instance shopping in wheelchairs.
* display location relative to competing products: retailers place displays of own-brands near to well-known manufacturer brands so as (a) to reveal the price difference between the two, and (b) to benefit by association from customer awareness and interest in the branded product created by promotional activities undertaken by its manufacturer.
* closeness to the cash register of items purchased on an "impulse" basis, such as sweets and special offers on lines that the retailer wishes to clear out.

5.1) Integrating Point of Sale

In order to be successful, POS must be integrated with other elements of the marketing mix. In particular, POS must be designed to co-ordinate with the shape, style and form of *packaging* used. Packaging has considerable promotional value, and this promotional value must be enhanced by effective and co-ordinated display *in situ*. Similarly, POS must be integrated with *other promotional mix* elements. Each must have complementary messages, shapes, style and design. Each must be colour co-ordinated. And changes in one element need to be considered in the light of the need to make corresponding changes elsewhere. For instance, a decision to change "house-style" may affect:

* packaging design;
* vehicle livery;
* shop livery;
* POS display design and colour;
* advertising format.

Design is dealt with in the next section of this book.

The marketer will also have to deal with the problem of reconciling brand POS displays *with a different retailer in-house style*. Where the products are sold through an independent retailer or multiple, then some kind of compromise over POS display may have to be found, such that the branded POS display is complementary to the retailer's own in-house style and display arrangements. This problem is symptomatic of the marketer's need *to manage the relationship with retail distributors*. As far as integrating POS display is concerned, the retailer view may be that the most favourable outcome is one in which they integrate POS with their own house-style, using own-brands, and that POS displays of branded goods should be designed (ie subordinated) to their specific in-house requirements. Manufacturer control over branded POS arrangements may, therefore, be a function of its relationship with its retail distributors. Unless the branded goods manufacturer is prepared to compromise over POS arrangements, he may lose control. Ultimately, he may find that his brands are no longer stocked by the retailers with whom he is unable to come to satisfactory agreement.

6) EXHIBITIONS

Exhibitions are used as a form of sales promotion in both consumer and industrial goods markets. Exhibitions can range from small, localised "Ideal Homes" exhibitions held in town halls, to massive International trade fairs and biannual jamborees, such as the UK "Motor Show". Some of the advantages and disadvantages of exhibitions as a promotional technique are listed as follows.

6.1) Advantages in consumer goods markets

a) *creation of awareness and recall:* exhibitions create awareness, and may be particularly effective at promoting recall, both of the exhibition itself and of promotional messages associated with a product. The experience of visiting an exhibition may render an individual more receptive to advertising messages, and may create a more positive attitude towards a product associated with the exhibition.

b) exhibitions offer scope and potential for *promotional scale and creativity.* Large and spectacular displays can be used, incorporating a variety of creative or innovative activities. For instance, the indoor UK Boat Show usually incorporates an actual harbour setting. The UK Garden Festivals, held at Liverpool, Stoke-on-Trent, Glasgow, Gateshead (etc), offer massive scope to plantsmen, seed merchants, manufacturers of garden equipment (etc) to promote their wares for a whole season, amid spectacular scenes, to huge numbers of visitors.

c) exhibitions may be used as the *high point* of a more general promotional activity. The promotional campaign can be reinforced or boosted by the kind of spectacular display or event that can be staged at an exhibition.

d) the exhibition may become a *well-known event* associated with the promotion of a product. People may recall the product in association with the exhibition, and look forward to attending on the next occasion. The result is a positive or favourable association between the product and the exhibition. Certainly, the great UK and European Motor Shows are eagerly awaited events attended by enormous numbers of people.

e) exhibitions offer an individual supplier the chance to *inspect and evaluate competitors' products and promotional strategy.*

6.2) Advantages in industrial goods markets

a) exhibitions are at their most effective as promotional tools in industrial goods markets *where potential buyers, and representatives of target market segments are known to use the exhibition* to inspect, compare, assess and evaluate products or services which it is their intention to purchase.

b) Similarly, the technique is effective where the exhibition has become *a major annual forum* for display, promotion, buying and selling. The annual "trade show" often develops this kind of reputation or cachet. Everyone in the trade feels that they need to be there, and that everybody else's presence makes the effort worthwhile.

c) exhibitions are often regarded as cost-effective in *overseas markets.* They can be used for "one-off" promotions; or better, to support international marketing operations or the activities of local offices, and so on. In some countries, would-be exporters are "expected" to use trade fairs as a basic form of promotion and display. This is especially true in socialist countries where the means of promotion and distribution are controlled by the state.

6.3) Disadvantages of exhibitions

a) the use of exhibitions may become *an expected pattern of promotion* within a trade. Exhibitions may be held for reasons of *inertia:* you exhibit because your firm has always exhibited. The company may have lost sight of the value of exhibiting, as compared with alternative promotional forms.

b) exhibitions *offer competitors the chance of inspecting and evaluating your products and promotional strategy.*

c) the most serious disadvantage of the exhibition as a technique of sales promotion is *wastage.* Many of the people who attend an exhibition will have no interest in particular products, nor will they have any intention of buying. Yet it will cost the exhibitor to accommodate those people. It is difficult to assess the effectiveness of exhibitions as a promotional technique, especially where no direct selling is taking place. From this point of view, exhibitions are a better medium in industrial markets, since some actual selling activity often takes place.

7) SPONSORSHIP

Sponsorship has shown rapid growth as a technique of sales promotion during the last decade. This growth in interest is international. The Olympic Games have been sponsored by Coca Cola; the World Cup by a consortium of well-known multinational brands, such as Philips. Sponsorship involves a number of inter-related elements, namely:

* direct funding of the event or activity to be sponsored;
* guarantees of a minimum level of media advertising being accepted at a time when the event or activity is occurring (for instance whilst a sporting event is being screened on commercial television);
* guaranteed association of the sponsor's name with the event or activity eg the Cornhill Test Series in UK cricket; Embassy World Professional Darts; Dulux Snooker (etc).

The objective of sponsorship is two-fold. Firstly there is direct promotion of the sponsor's brand or company name. The name is used in conjunction with publicity for the event, and will be seen or heard if the event is broadcast on television or radio. The audience at the event will of course also be made aware of the name of the sponsor. Secondly, the sponsor may gain *by association* with the activity or event. International cricket matches or top class opera performances are highly prestigious events: by being associated with them the sponsor obtains a certain amount of "reflected glory". This may help to create a more favourable attitude toward the product or brand on the part of those who see or hear the event. It may also promote recall of the sponsor's name and of the product or service with which it is associated.

The use of sponsorship is concentrated on two areas, namely sport and the arts. Sports sponsorship is popular for a number of reasons, which include:

* large audiences, both in the stadium and for radio and television audiences;

* sports audiences can be clearly segmented. Sponsorship may be an effective means of promoting to a specific target segment, which is known to make up the audience profile of the sport's following;

* sporting activities often have lengthy duration and extensive media coverage. The sponsor's name will, in consequence, receive frequent mention and remain constantly visible;

* individual involvement in the sport may increase recall of the name where it is associated with key events in the calendar of that sport.

Sponsorship of the arts tends to be more discreet. Association with the arts is seen as prestigious. It may also be a means of promoting to, and gaining access to senior decision-makers whilst they are in a *non-work role* and their "defences" (described in an earlier chapter) against sales and promotional pressures are less effective.

Sponsorship is seen as an effective form of sales promotion where the product-brand relationship can be clearly identified. For instance, Cornhill Insurance, who sponsor the UK cricket Test Series, suggest that their sponsorship has greatly increased public awareness of the company's name and its product. Because many people purchase insurance through channel intermediaries (brokers), it is important to get customers to *specify* the company's name. Otherwise the broker may sell the customer insurance from another company. Cornhill attribute to their cricket sponsorship a "very significant" growth in sales turnover.

Sponsorship of the arts has value both in terms of promoting a company's product and name, and in building "corporate image". The role of "image-building" is dealt with in a later chapter.

Marketing publishes periodic summaries of sponsorship arrangements made in the UK. The reader should consult such summaries for up-to-date information about sponsorship deals.

8) EVALUATING SALES PROMOTION EFFECTIVENESS

There are considerable problems associated with the measurement and evaluation of the effectiveness of sales promotion techniques. Some of the analysis contained in Chapter Thirty Two, relative to advertising effectiveness, is also relevant to sales promotion techniques. Nevertheless, a number of indicators are available, and these are listed in Table 34.2.

Immediate customer incentive	New product trial and re-purchase rates. Sales volume trends. Sales revenue trends.
Delayed customer incentive	Coupon redemptions (can be physically counted). Token redemptions (can be physically counted). Cash refunds ⎫ Premium offers ⎬ proofs of purchase can be physically counted. Charity offers ⎭ Self-liquidating offer results. Competition entrant numbers: proofs of purchase can also be physically counted. Sales volume trends. Sales revenue trends.
Performance–related trade or industrial incentives	Correlation of bonus awards with dealer sales performance (especially as indicated by trends over a number of years).
Point of sale	Maintenance of product presence in-store. Turnover (sales volume) trends. Brand awareness/brand recall.
Exhibitions	Raw attendance statistics. Number of visitors to Stand. Sales Enquiries received. Sales Enquiries followed up by sales staff. Sales Enquiries resulting in actual sales. Brand awareness/brand recall. Attitude measurements taken immediately after exhibition, and later in time.
Sponsorship	Raw attendance and viewing/listening statistics. Trends in brand awareness/brand recall over time. Periodic attitude measurements. Turnover (sales volume) trends.

Table 34.2. Indicators of Sales Promotion Effectiveness.

SUMMARY

The contents of this chapter are summarised in Table 34.3.

TABLE 34.3
Summary : Chapter Thirty Four

SECTION	MAIN POINTS
1. Sales promotion techniques	These are promotional activities which do not fit other groupings within the promotional mix. Found in both consumer and industrial goods markets. They have two broad objectives, namely (i) enhancing promotion to the trade; and (ii) assisting the trade in promoting and selling products to the final customer. Good use of sales promotion technique develops product/brand image, complements other elements of the supplier's marketing mix, and enhances promotional activity undertaken by distributors or retailers.
2. Immediate consumer incentives	Comprise (2.1) free samples and trial packs; (2.2) bonus packs; (2.3) premiums and giveaways; (2.4) price promotions on pack; (2.5) competitions; (2.6) use in industrial markets. The objective of their use is to achieve short-term increases in sales. Their effectiveness may be relatively easy to assess.
3. Delayed consumer incentives	Comprise (3.1) coupons; (3.2) tokens and trading stamps; (3.3) cash refunds on mail-in basis; (3.4) premium/giveaway offers on mail-in basis; (3.5) charitable offers on mail-in basis; (3.6) self-liquidating offers; (3.7) competitions. The objective of their use is also to achieve short-term increases in sales. Their effectiveness may be relatively easy to assess.
4. Performance-related trade or industrial incentives	Comprise (a) performance-related bonuses; (b) performance-related competitions; (c) performance-

489

	related supply bonuses. Their effectiveness may be assessed by correlation with dealer sales performance.
5. Point of Sale display (POS)	POS presents, displays and promotes the product in the location where it is sold. POS attracts customer attention; encourages the would-be buyer to approach, inspect and touch the product; and assists in the making of the final purchase decision. POS display is central to distributor/retailer merchandising. Merchandising is the physical process of stocking retail and distribution outlets with the appropriate goods. Within the merchandising process, POS promotes the product by involving the customer physically and mentally with it.
6. Exhibitions	Used in both consumer and industrial goods markets. Exhibitions (6.1) create awareness and recall; offer a chance to inspect competitors' products; (6.2) may be most effective in industrial markets where potential buyers and representatives of target market segments are known to use the exhibition to inspect and compare products or services on offer; offer scope for promotion in overseas markets. The main disadvantage (6.3) is wastage.
7. Sponsorship	Involves direct funding of the event or activity to be sponsored; guarantees of a minimum level of media advertising being accepted when the event or activity is occurring; and guaranteed association of the sponsor's name with the event or activity. Sponsorship is a direct means of promoting a brand or company

name. The sponsor should also gain by association with the prestige of the event or activity. Sponsorship is usually concentrated on sport and on the arts.

8. Evaluating sales promotion effectiveness

Summarised in Table 34.2.

RECOMMENDED READING

Petersen C.

Sales Promotion in Action.
Associated Business Press

CHAPTER APPENDIX 34(1)

IN-STORE MERCHANDISING

As the multiples reinforce their dominance in most retail markets, the traditional sales rep's ability to influence the order at the point of sale decreases day by day. But it is still vital for a supplier to have a regular physical in-store presence – to maintain agreed fixture layouts, for instance.

And as media and sales force costs continue to escalate, manufacturers are showing a renewed interest in the basics of selling and display in-store. Though not as glamorous as a multimillion pound TV advertising campaign, a well planned and carefully managed in-store sales merchandising operation can make a sizeable contribution to company profitability.

A well trained, well managed and highly motivated team of sales merchandisers can improve a manufacturer's presence where it counts – in-store. A recent survey by the Market Research Society found that 20% of all purchasing decisions are made by housewives in the shop, right at the point of sale. In the grocery business, that proportion accounts for £1bn worth of sales.

Once a manufacturer has decided to mount an in-store merchandising operation, it must define its objectives carefully. How many outlets are to be visited, and how often? Is it just retailers who are involved, or do cash-and-carries and wholesalers need coverage too? What are the operational objectives of display and distribution? The manufacturer must then decide whether to develop an in-house team or contract the project out to a specialist organisation. Although some manufacturers still set up their own operations, many have placed the responsibility for their merchandising function in the hands of specialist companies.

If the second route is chosen, two types of merchandising coverage are available: the shared service, where personnel work for a number of manufacturers in the same store, or the solus method, where personnel work for only one manufacturer.

Shared merchandising lowers the operational cost, whereas the solus route encourages loyalty to the manufacturer as opposed to any individual retail outlet. The style of the operation will depend on whether what is required is a tactical campaign, say to exploit seasonal bursts of activity, or a long-term, continuing presence in-store.

Whichever operation is chosen, pre-call planning must be meticulous. Reference should be made to all records made on previous visits, and supporting equipment such as visual aids, point-of-sale material and samples should be checked, as should any essential information on pricing, products and current or future promotions. Retailers that continue to raise their standards of professionalism expect no less from the sales merchandiser.

It is also vital for merchandisers to strike up a good relationship with the retailer. On the first visit to a store, merchandisers should introduce themselves to the retailer, and explain why they are there and what they intend to do. Only then can the full co-operation of the staff be achieved.

The merchandiser must then run an outlet check, focusing on levels of stock, point-of-sale and product displays. If these do not meet expectations, initial objectives may have to be revised to take account of the situation in an individual outlet.

Another basic activity is a thorough brand 'spring clean' – re-stocking empty shelf spaces, and cleaning up dusty or dirty fixtures if necessary. As one merchandiser puts it: 'Good displays sell products. An eye-catching, well stocked display shows that both retailer and manufacturer do care about the brand.'

On-pack branding should be arranged to face the front of the display, and new stock should be priced. Stock should also be rotated to allow for the product's shelf life. Weetabix, for example, generally introduces a new on-pack promotion every two months. Once the promotion has changed the pack immediately becomes obsolete. Part of a merchandiser's brief will be to ensure that the older packs are positioned at the front of the display, so that they sell out as quickly as possible. ,

Although companies such as Heinz and Weetabix will generally limit themselves to this kind of shelf filling and pricing operation, other merchandisers will extend their range of activity to include the building of feature displays.

To be effective, these must be well sited – usually at the end of a fixture, to create maximum impact. All manufacturers are aware of the selling power of off-shelf displays. A good merchandiser will try to requisition one of these 'hotspots' to highlight a particular product or promotion. If a merchandiser identifies a space, the rapport that has been built up with the retailer will enable them to make the most of the opportunity.

In recent years supermarket managers have put greater restrictions on the amount of manufacturers' point-of-sale material they will allow in-store. It is more important than ever, therefore, that the merchandiser takes care to place any point-of-sale material to its best advantage. Point of sale that identifies a special offer can create an eye-catching feature.

Alternatively, companies such as H.P. Bulmer will use the product itself at point of sale by building attractive displays to encourage off-take at key periods such as Christmas. Walls mounts an annual merchandising campaign through Counter Products Marketing Ltd to re-dress the nation's freezers in 20,000-plus retail outlets, replacing old point of sale in time for the peak summer season.

Merchandisers can also be used to influence sales directly. Those representing Dairy Crest Foods, for example, make weekly stock and order calls on cash-and-carry outlets, and telephone the orders taken direct to Dairy Crest.

An in-store 'concept' can also be sold by merchandisers. Mars, for example, uses its network of merchandisers to sell in its summer 'Cool 'Em' promotion, which recommends retailers to keep Mars confectionery in the fridge.

A good merchandiser will not only ensure that the correct amount of space has been allocated to the brand, but will actively encourage the store manager to increase the facings for the fastest selling lines. It is possible to boost sales dramatically in this way.

In addition, merchandisers can be the manufacturer's mouthpiece to the trade, fulfilling a valuable communications role. They are in an ideal position to talk to the retailer about new products, line extensions, promotions and other new developments.

Thomson Holidays employs a regional network of merchandisers to inform, educate and motivate counter staff in the travel industry. A visit to a travel agent might involve providing information on new promotions and programmes, talking staff through the Thomson brochure, and promoting trade competitions to encourage retail staff to study the literature.

Finally, the merchandising operation can provide a valuable and immediate research opportunity. Careful record keeping and well planned methods of assessment will ensure that the cost, coverage and operational objectives are measurable against budget and in-store performance targets.

Something that is often over-looked is the added value to the manufacturer of the market information provided by the merchandiser on product turnover, pricing, stock, distribution and facing levels of both its own and its competitors' products.

If the manufacturer is to get maximum value from what has become an increasingly sophisticated activity, great care must be exercised in the recruitment, training, control and motivation of a highly professional and powerful human resource.

Source : Marketing (reproduced with permission)

QUESTIONS FOR SELF-REVIEW

1) Describe the communication process and comment on its relevance to marketing and promotional communications.

2) What communication factors will determine the effectiveness of marketing communications?

3) Compare and contrast 'controllable' and 'non-controllable' communication methods within the promotional mix.

4) Compare and contrast the alternative promotional mix policies applied to consumer goods markets and industrial goods markets.

5) Describe the persuasion process and comment on its relevance to marketing communication and the promotional mix.

6) How may a company determine the objective and content of its promotional mix?

7) Describe and comment on the role of advertising within the persuasion process.

8) Describe and compare the main types of mass media used by advertisers. What are the relative advantages and disadvantages of each type?

9) Why do companies evaluate the effectiveness of their advertising?

10) How may a company evaluate the effectiveness of its advertising?

11) Describe and comment on the means by which a company can assess the effectiveness of its advertising quality.

12) Describe and comment on the means by which a company can assess the effectiveness of its chosen advertising media.

13) What factors are likely to determine the level of a company's advertising budget? How should that budget be constructed?

14) Outline and describe the main techniques of Sales Promotion. What are their objectives?

15) Compare and contrast immediate consumer incentives and delayed consumer incentives.

16) Why is Point of Sale (POS) display an important Sales Promotion technique in consumer goods markets?

17) Describe and comment on the role of Point of Sale (POS) display within the merchandising process.

18) What are the advantages and disadvantages of using exhibitions as a promotional tool?

(19) What are the advantages and disadvantages of using sponsorship as a tool of Sales Promotion?

20) How can the marketer evaluate the effectiveness of Sales Promotion techniques?

EXAMINATION QUESTIONS

Q57 Analyse the relevant factors that would help determine a company's promotional mix. (IOMS)

Q58   Describe, and justify, the difference between the communication mix that is typically used in industrial markets and that typically used in consumer markets.

(CIM)

Q59   What is the purpose of advertising?   *(CIM)*

Q60   What are advertising media? What factors govern the use of various media in advertising campaigns?   *(IOE)*

Q61   How might a company attempt to measure the effectiveness of its advertising effort?   *(IIM)*

Q62   Using examples discuss the effective use of sales promotion activities.

(CIM)

The Promotional Mix

Part Two

Personal Selling
and
Sales Force Management

35 Personal Selling

INTRODUCTION

This chapter describes personal selling and outlines its role within the total promotional mix. It examines the role of the sales force, and looks at some of the factors that determine the nature of this role. It considers the problem of prospecting for new customers, and concludes with a brief analysis of sales technique.

CHAPTER CONTENTS

1 PERSONAL SELLING AND THE PROMOTIONAL MIX

Personal selling and salesmanship are of critical importance to the marketing mix. The objective of personal selling is TO MAKE THE SALE. The sales activity is the culmination of the many other activities which have been described in earlier chapters in this book. The activities of market research, product design, distribution, pricing (etc) will determine whether there is to be an *opportunity* to sell the product or service. But in the end, the salesperson is responsible for the final act, *that of making the sale*.

In fulfilling this important role, personal selling must be seen within the context of the promotional mix as a means of:

* changing personal attitudes towards the product;
* changing personal attitudes and inclination towards purchasing the product;
* establishing conviction in the mind of the would-be purchaser;

* moving the potential customer to the point of decision to purchase;

* encouraging and facilitating the actual purchase decision and action;

* re-assuring the customer that he or she has made the right decision.

From the viewpoint of marketing management, further, this process ought to be relatively cost-effective in terms of achieving sales as *a proportion of the number of potential customers reached.* In other words, marketing management will be concerned to optimise the value of its investment in the sales activity in the same way that it will be interested in the effectiveness of advertising, techniques of sales promotion, and so on.

This concern with the effectiveness of the selling activity is a strong one. Personal selling is *relatively* and *absolutely* expensive as a promotional medium in terms of "people reached". At the time of writing it is likely to cost a company in the UK *at least* £25,000 to keep one salesperson "on the road" per year. 40 salesmen will directly cost £1 million per year. This direct cost includes salary and commission, National Insurance and other payroll costs, cost of car, fuel and maintenance, cost of subsistence and entertainment (etc). But the £25,000 figure does not include costs of sales management, sales offices and sales administration. All of these are needed to guide, direct and support the sales effort out in the marketplace. Personal selling, especially in industrial goods markets, is an expensive activity.

THE ROLE OF THE SALES FORCE

The sales force has two main roles. These are:

– personal persuasion and selling activities;
– personal contact for non-selling tasks.

a) *activities involving persuasion and selling* are to be found in both consumer and industrial markets. The reader can think of his or her own experience of personal selling from the viewpoint of being a customer in a bookshop, clothing store, travel agent, motor dealer or wherever. As a proportion of total promotional expenditure, however, selling activities are most important in industrial markets. In consumer goods markets the salesperson assists a process in which advertising is often the driving force in *pulling* the product through the market. In industrial goods markets it is the job of the sales-force to *push* the product through the market. The salesforce provides the main sales drive in such markets.

Personal persuasion and selling is also important in the *marketing of services* whether in consumer or industrial goods markets. It may be more difficult to sell services than products, because:

i)   services are *intangible*, unlike products;

ii) it may be difficult for the potential customer *to persuade himself* of the need to make the purchase;

iii) it may be easy to put off the purchase, especially if the service being considered is perceived as having a low personal priority;

iv) it may be difficult to define the benefits (especially long-term ones) relative to the cost of the service.

Services may therefore need to be sold hard. This can be the case of personal and life assurance, holidays, business services and consultancy (etc).

b) *activities involving personal contact for non-selling tasks* are also to be found in both consumer and industrial markets. These tasks include:

*   providing customer service and dealing with complaints, returned goods (etc);

*   carrying out market research, feeding back market intelligence;

*   briefing or training retail sales staff about new products, guarantee arrangements (etc);

*   providing technical advice.

In industrial markets the sales representative may be reponsible for providing the basic technical training in how to use the product. If you sell welding and flame cutting equipment, the customer may well expect you to be able to demonstrate the virtues of your product by making skillful use of it! In addition, the sales representative will be a major source of detailed *feedback* on product quality and performance. This customer feedback must be incorporated into the company's new product development process.

3 DETERMINANTS OF THE SALESFORCE ROLE

There are a number of factors which are likely to determine the kind of role to be fulfilled by the company's salesforce. Reference has already been made to the importance of personal selling in industrial markets. Other factors are listed below.

a) *size and location of markets:* large and widespread markets, such as retail outlets for fast moving consumer goods, can only be covered at great cost by massive salesforces. Some manufacturers of branded, packaged foodstuffs employ such salesforces. These sell to retail and wholesale customers who vary in size from giant national multiples down to independent corner-shops. Such salesforces are very expensive to maintain, and many have seen reductions during recent years. This issue is dealt with in the next two chapters.

Concentrated markets, on the other hand, are ideal for personal selling. Industries like ceramics, steel or commercial vehicle manufacture tend to be clustered together in a few places, making personal selling cost-effective.

The difference between these two market types highlights a major policy choice for marketing management. Can it distribute and sell its products throughout a large and widespread market? If it chooses to do so, it will be pursuing a policy of INTENSIVE DISTRIBUTION. If on the other hand it faces a concentrated market, or wishes only to supply certain key distributors (perhaps such as wholesalers or selected retailers only) in a large and widespread market, then it will be pursuing a policy of SELECTIVE DISTRIBUTION. Manufacturers and importers of high quality Hi-Fi equipment often concentrate their sales effort through carefully selected retail outlets. Their reputation for quality, plus their advertising policy, should overcome consumer resistance towards the travelling necessary to view the goods in the appointed dealers. It will then be up to (what should be well-trained) retail sales staff to make the final sale.

b) *inertia:* in many companies, the marketing activity is still dominated by sales managers and the salesforce, especially if sales managers and sales representatives are in the majority. Despite changes in the market, or changes in marketing practice which favour the development of other promotional activities such as direct marketing, use of agents (or whatever), it may be very difficult to dismember a large sales force. This is hardly surprising. Firstly there will be massive inertia within the organisation. There will be resistance to change and a desire to maintain the "status quo". And the reduction in size of a sales force will be fiercely resisted by a large, important and vociferous group who are skilled at making a case and negotiating terms. Interfering with a large sales force is often the equivalent to stirring up the proverbial hornet's nest!

c) *customer expectations:* in some markets, customers may have become used to personal selling and demand its continuance. For instance, older retail customers in parts of the UK which have become retirement areas (such as the Sussex and Hampshire coasts and the New Forest) are used to personal selling and may prefer to patronise shops with counter-service rather than self-service. For older (and sometimes lonely) people, contact with the salesman or the sales assistant is an important source of company, human contact and reassurance.

Up-market fashion and department stores also make heavy use of personal selling. Firstly, their customers expect to receive the personal attention of sales staff. Secondly, the type of merchandise stocked, and the prices charged make necessary an element of selling. High priced goods often need active and effective selling, especially to price conscious customers.

d) *channel expectations:* channel intermediaries may also expect, or even come to rely on the activities of their supplier's salespeople. Industrial buyers may expect regular visits from salesmen or saleswomen, even if they have no orders to place. A good salesperson will capitalise upon this expectation by building a friendly and long-term relationship with the buyer. The development of such relationships is often a crucial factor in achieving consistent sales to a particular customer, especially where there is not much to choose between competing products.

Similarly, wholesalers and middlemen (for instance in the grocery distribution trade) may be quite happy to organise *both their work and their stockholding levels* around frequent visits from suppliers' sales representatives. Effectively, the sales rep. is doing the wholesaler's work for him. The sales rep. can take care of stock calculations and will keep the wholesaler's stock sufficiently high to avoid stockouts. Frequent sales rep. visits and deliveries make the problem of customer supply and service a relatively easy matter for the wholesaler.

e) *competitors' use of personal selling:* where the company's main competitors rely heavily on personal selling activities as a key constituent of their total promotional mix, it is going to be very difficult for that company to do anything but follow suit. Companies can become "locked-in" to the use of large salesforces by a combination of the factors described above, and by a fear of the consequences of attempting to "break the mould" and do something different.

4) PROSPECTING FOR CUSTOMERS

A traditional role fulfilled by the sales person is that of *prospecting for customers.* Where the salesman is under pressure to maintain or increase his sales, then he must find new customers. Sometimes this will involve the salesperson in carrying out "cold calling". The salesman will attempt to interest a potential buyer in dealing with his company, never having visited that person before. This initial visit, or "cold call", may have been set up by the company's sales office. Or the salesperson may have identified the new "prospect" (as a potential customer is sometimes called), arranged a meeting with him beforehand, or even called upon him without any prior enquiry or announcement.

Cold-calling by sales representatives can be highly variable in its effect. Many companies will not see sales representatives without a formal appointment, whilst others will only deal with recognised contractors. This restriction on sales activity was analysed in detail in an earlier chapter. Within the context of this section of the book, further, the reader should by now have recognised the problem that the use of the sales representative's time to undertake cold-calling may not be cost-effective. The concept of *opportunity cost* requires that the salesperson's time be spent on selling and customer relations activities that are likely to prove the most rewarding for the company. So, how can the marketing function replace cold-calling and find new prospects or potential buyers?

4.1) Alternatives to cold-calling

These can include:

i) the use of *canvassers,* whose job it is to find potential customers. The details are then passed on to the sales representative who will meet the prospect at a later date. Canvassers may be paid on an hourly basis, with a bonus paid in proportion to the number of prospects passed on to the salesperson. Door-to-door canvassing is widely used in the UK market for home improvement products. Canvassers are also to be found in large retail stores, hypermarkets and so on.

ii) the use of *independent agents,* whose job it is to find potential customers. Agents, who are often paid on a *commission-only* basis (ie payment for results achieved), are usually involved in the selling process. (Insurance is often sold this way). The company may use agents as part of its sales strategy, restricting its use of full-time sales staff to dealing with existing large accounts, and to developing large volume new business. Agents may handle a large volume of relatively low value accounts, to which it would be too expensive to sell and provide service with full-time salespeople.

iii) the use of *appointed agents,* who handle low volume and low value accounts. These official agents are responsible for finding, developing and servicing business *below a certain value per customer.* The agents act as an integral part of the company's operation, even though they are independent. They are often under a contractual obligation to pass on to the company they represent that business which has reached or gone beyond a stated threshold value. They may receive a bonus upon the transfer of such business (which it has not cost the company anything to develop). This kind of agency structure is to be found in the UK microcomputer market. Several manufacturers, including IBM, use agents to sell basic microcomputers and work-station facilities. Agent-based systems are also widely used in international marketing. This point was dealt with in earlier chapters.

iv) the use of *direct marketing techniques,* for instance direct mail, which facilitates a customer response requesting the salesperson to call", or indicating "offers to tender" etc. These techniques must make clear what is on offer, and explain what the potential customer must do next in order to signal the sales procedure to commence.

v) the use of *telephone selling* or "telemarketing". Telephone selling is growing in popularity, and it is regarded as a cost effective means of cold calling. Successful contacts can then be passed on to the field sales staff to follow up. The advantage of telephone canvassing is that it remains under the control of the company. The disadvantage is that consumers, and buyers in industrial markets in the UK are often resistant to telephone selling or canvassing. The use of the telephone in this way may not be regarded as acceptable, in which case it can hinder or damage the efforts of field sales staff.

Certainly, whatever means are used to seek new custom, the development of new business must be closely integrated with other elements of the promotional mix, whether this be advertising, actual telephone selling, direct mailing or whatever. The promotional machine must move as one, and it must all move in the same direction!

5) SALES TECHNIQUE

This section makes brief reference to some items of sales technique. A full description of such techniques is, however, beyond the scope of this book.

a) *the selling opportunity:* in industrial markets, and in selling to wholesalers, retailers (etc) the field sales person *must obtain or create the opportunity to make his or her sales presentation*. This might take the form of a sales interview, or a full-scale sales presentation. This opportunity may come from the build-up of rapport with the potential customer over a period of time. It may derive from cold-calling techniques, or from the stimulus of other promotional techniques such as advertising or direct mail. However this is achieved, the salesman faces the problem of *getting access to the right person*. This issue has been dealt with in Chapters Fourteen and Fifteen. Can the salesperson get past the "gatekeeper" role to the "influencers" and "decision-makers" in a multi-role industrial purchasing procedure or Decision Making Unit? Does the company have to become an approved contractor before it can tender for orders? Creating the selling opportunity is the first main hurdle the salesperson must surmount. This is why thorough experience of a trade, and knowledge of the buyers in it, can make a salesperson such a valuable marketing resource.

b) *the sales pitch:* the salesperson must make his case, or presentation, on the basis of a strategy which derives from the *unique selling propositions* (USP's) possessed by the product being sold. The potential customer must be *convinced* about the product's advantages, and the benefits to be gained from its purchase. These advantages and benefits can take many forms, such as:

– superior operational performance;
– cost savings;
– technological advantage;
– good design;
– (etc).

Product advantages were outlined in more detail in Chapter Twenty.

c) *overcoming objections:* at the same time, the salesperson must endeavour to overcome the objections of the potential customer. Possible objections (such as a high price, or expensive after-sales service) must be thought about beforehand, and the answers to them thoroughly researched and rehearsed. The salesperson must try to build a positive attitude towards his product, even if this takes many discussions. The process of building up such an attitude may take a long time, especially in export markets. Selling products in Russia or China can take months or years of persistent negotiation. The salesperson will have to overcome the customer's objections at the speed at which *the customer* changes his attitude, however long this takes.

d) *negotiating techniques:* sales people must possess the necessary negotiating skills. The larger and more complex the order under discussion, the more complex will be the negotiations over price and conditions of supply, and the more the people that will have to be involved. Sales staff in industrial goods markets, or selling to retailers or wholesalers are likely to encounter buyers who are highly trained and effective negotiators. Similarly, negotiators in international markets, say in the Middle East, the Far East and the USA are likely to provide export salespeople with a demanding and professional challenge.

e) *sales aids:* some aids that will help the selling effort include:

* product demonstrations, the offer of demonstrator products or vehicles for trial use and assessment;
* product samples, the offer of samples to test and use;
* presentation media, whether printed or visual. Catalogues, printed specifications, illustrations, films or videos need to be professionally prepared and of a high quality;
* presentation techniques (see recommended reading at the end of this chapter);
* personal self-presentation. *The salesperson represents the company* and should be clean, tidy, well-dressed and self-confident. (If you are a student looking for a job, what impression do *you* create at an interview? *Can you sell yourself?*)

f) *closing the sale:* the professional sales person is trained to recognise signs of "closure". This means that the potential customer is ready to come to a decision. At this point the salesperson moves the business to its close, settling contractual arrangements and getting the customer's signature on the order. It is important to recognise closure signals so that the salesperson can finalise matters before the customer changes his mind, or finds reasons to prevaricate further.

SUMMARY

The contents of this chapter are summarised in Table 35.1.

TABLE 35.1
Summary: Chapter Thirty Five

SECTION	MAIN POINTS
1. Personal selling and the promotional mix	The objective of personal selling is to make the sale. In fulfilling this important role, personal selling must be co-ordinated and integrated with the rest of the promotional mix. Because personal selling is a relatively expensive activity, it needs to be cost-effective in terms of achieving sales as

	a proportion of the number of potential customers reached.
2. The role of the sales force	The salesforce has two main roles, which are (a) persuasion and selling activities; and (b) personal contact for non-selling tasks.
3. Determinants of the salesforce role	These include (a) size and location of markets (which lead to the consideration of intensive or selective distribution); (b) inertia; (c) customer expectations; (d) channel expectations; (e) competitors' use of personal selling.
4. Prospecting for customers	Maintaining sales and finding new business will involve the salesperson in prospecting for customers. This may mean "cold calling" to find new prospects. Cold-calling can be highly variable in its effect, and may not be cost-effective in opportunity cost terms. Hence 4.1.
4.1 Alternatives to cold-calling	These can include the use of (i) canvassers; (ii) independent agents; (iii) appointed agents; (iv) direct marketing techniques; (v) telephone selling.
5. Sales technique	This includes (a) obtaining the selling opportunity; (b) formulating the sales pitch; (c) overcoming customer objections; (d) negotiating technique; (e) the use of sales aids; (f) closing the sale.

RECOMMENDED READING

A concise but valuable guide to presentation technique will be found in the booklet "Making Your Case" published by Video Arts Ltd.

36 Salesforce Management I

INTRODUCTION

This chapter introduces the issue of sales force management. Sales force management is an important part of the marketing management process. Sales managers must set sales objectives, determine the size of the sales force needed to achieve these objectives, and control salesforce activity. This process is a complex one, and it can give rise to some major problems and difficulties.

The analysis of salesforce management is continued in the next chapter.

CHAPTER CONTENTS

1) Setting sales objectives

   1.1) Sales objectives within the marketing context

   1.2) Sales objectives

2) Determining the size of the sales force

   2.1) Sales territories

   2.2) Territory sales potential in consumer goods markets

   2.3) Territory sales potential in industrial goods markets

   2.4) Sales force workload

3) Controlling sales force activity

   3.1) The control process

   3.2) Sales objectives, performance standards and performance criteria

   3.3) Performance standards

   3.4) Performance criteria

   3.5) Some problems of salesforce control

Summary

1) SETTING SALES OBJECTIVES

1.1) Sales objectives within the marketing context

Sales objectives derive from the company's marketing plans and marketing objectives. These in turn are established by the wider process of corporate planning and strategic management. The analysis of sales objectives must therefore be placed within the wider context of marketing mix planning and objectives, since salesforce activity must be co-ordinated with other promotional and marketing mix activities, such as advertising, special price campaigns (etc). The achievement of sales objectives is in part dependent upon the effect of these other elements on the market environment.

Detailed sales objectives will be quantified and formulated on the basis of two main variables, namely:

* *the annual sales forecast* (described in detail in Chapters 7, 8 and 9);
* *specific sales targets* set for market segments, products and product groups. These specific targets will derive from the requirements of corporate and marketing plans. For instance, a manufacturer of branded food-stuffs may wish to increase his turnover by further seg-menting the market and introducing a new product to position on a redefined segment. This will produce an entirely new sales target to be achieved by advertising and selling activities.

Total sales objectives are then broken down *so that ultimately they are specific to individual salespersons and individual sales territories*. A sales "territory" is the geographical area or product group assigned to one salesperson. Sales objectives must be broken down and allocated in this way so that the salesperson is clear about what he or she is expected to achieve. This has control and *motivational* implications; these implications are dealt with in later sections in this chapter and in Chapter 37.

The process by which sales objectives are set must also be *flexible*. The company must always be prepared to revise its sales objectives as a result of changes in market or customer circumstances, changes in marketing plans and policies, and unexpected contingencies. Similarly, the company's perfor-mance appraisal procedures must be flexible when it comes to appraising and evaluating the performance of salespeople. Remember, whilst the salesperson is undertaking a persuasive and selling role, he or she is, in turn, the *representative of the company* as far as the customer is concerned. To the customer the salesperson may be a communication channel, consultant, friend, and "whipping boy" (for instance when faulty goods are returned, or a product already purchased fails to live up to expectations).

1.2) Sales objectives

Individual sales objectives (for instance as described below) will result from a *composite* of quantitative and qualitative variables including:

* annual sales forecasts;
* specific sales targets;
* targets by product group, product or brand;
* targets by geographical area, viz countries, regions, territories;
* company policy towards use of channels of distribution.

The resultant sales objectives can take any of the following forms:

a) *sales volume:* as indicated by the number of *units* sold. Annual and monthly statistics of sales volume in the UK car market are, for instance, widely publicised.

b) *distribution:* objectives for distribution relate to the level of penetration of the company's products within the available channels of distribution. Data for the level of distribution may be obtained from specialist distribution audits, which were described in an earlier chapter. These audits provide data on where the product is stocked, on the level of customer off-take, on stock levels, and on the level of competitor penetration. Such data can be used in fast moving consumer goods markets to inform annual sales forecasts, and to set specific distribution targets. For instance, a popular bookseller might wish to increase the proportion of relevant retail outlets selling its publications from 20% to 40%, and also to increase the range sold by such outlets from fifty titles to seventy five titles per outlet.

c) *market share:* volume sales targets may be based on market share objectives. Market share was analysed in Chapter 9, and will include objectives for distribution as in (b) just described above. Market share targets will have to be broken down into individual sales objectives. In view of the composite nature of a market share figure (and the number of marketing influences to which it is subject), this preparation of individual territory, product or brand sales/share targets may be a complex calculation.

d) *sales revenue:* as indicated by the *value* of the units sold. The relationship between sales volume and sales value achieved is most important where the salesperson is free to negotiate *price* with the customer. Where the salesperson has no such freedom, he or she is more likely to concentrate on the volume of business achieved rather than its value. A variation is:-

e) *contribution targets:* sales staff may be set the objective of achieving a sales mix that maximises the amount of contribution earned by the company. In such a case it is important that sales staff are told of the "contribution margin" of all of the lines they are to sell. Contribution margin is the proportion of the sales price that is represented by contribution. This approach to pricing and selling is described in Chapters 23 and 40.

f) *profit:* may be used as a sales objective where sales staff have sufficient costing information to make the necessary calculations. Because of the difficulties involved in calculating the likely profitability of deals under negotiation, the use of contribution targets (described in (e) above) is likely to be preferable. So many factors affect company profitability that it may be impossible to provide meaningful assessments of the profitability of the sales performance achieved by an individual sales representative.

g) *service objectives:* the previous chapter noted that the sales role includes personal contact for non-selling tasks. The maintanance of good customer relationships is essential to a continuing and mutually beneficial business relationship between sales representative and customer. Whilst such an objective can only be expressed in qualitative terms, poor customer service levels will eventually show up in decreasing sales value.

DETERMINING THE SIZE OF THE SALES FORCE

2.1) Sales territories

The number of sales representatives required by a company is a function of the following variables:

* objectives for reach and frequency (a promotional mix variable already introduced in earlier chapters in this section), which is dealt with in section (2.4) below;
* geographical territory to be covered;

* sales potential of the geographical territory to be covered (section (2.2) and (2.3) below).

Sales representatives are assigned to clearly defined "territories". These territories must be defined so that:

i) they are manageable: (if a company bases its UK sales territories on counties, what logic is there to giving its export salespeople territories like "West Germany", or "the Far East"!);

ii) they offer approximately equal sales potential (which means that some territories will be larger than others but, making allowance for extra travelling time, should yield similar sales levels to smaller but "denser" territories);

iii) there is no confusion of responsibilities, or overlap between sales representatives;

iv) the incidence of "difficult" areas is widely spread across the territories and not just concentrated in a few;

v) the expense of operating them is minimised relative to the benefits to be gained from the territory allocation. This is particularly important in export markets;

vi) customers within the territory know who their representative is, and are not confused by visitations from several different people from the same company, each with different responsibilities.

a) *Geographic territories:* local government and census enumeration districts are often used as a basic territory constituent or "building block". Such building blocks will be based on counties and electoral districts. The manner in which these geographic constituents are combined into actual territories may, however, be adjusted for the density and distribution of key trading areas. This adjustment depends upon the sales potential available in these trading areas (see (b) below). Some companies also adjust their territory allocation to meet regional definitions employed by commercial television contractors, so that advertising and salesforce efforts can be co-ordinated and monitored.

b) *Estimates of territory sales potential:* once sales management has decided upon its basic territory building block, it needs estimates of the sales potential contained within each. This is described in sections 2.2 and 2.3 below. Territorial blocks can then be combined to give final sales territories which meet the definition criteria listed from (i) to (vi) above. There will also have to be some kind of trade-off between:

– increasing the size of the territory to maximise its sales potential; and
– minimising the size of the territory to keep it manageable, to minimise travelling time between customers and to minimise travelling costs.

Operations research techniques may be useful in assisting sales management to finalise the definition of sales territories.

2.2 Territory sales potential in consumer goods markets

Estimates of territory sales potential may in this case be based upon such variables as:

* the total population (available from Census data);
* demographic data, income and housing type (available in detail, for instance, from the ACORN system);
* the nature and location of retail outlets;
* retail sales data (available from specialist audits such as those compiled by AGB, and from the ACORN system).

Companies such as CACI specialise in providing estimates of sales potential in consumer goods market territories.

Where territory sales representatives are selling to retail outlets, however, they are likely *to be restricted to selling to independent retailers*. Regional and national retail multiples purchase on a central basis, and normally control stock levels in their retail outlets by using computerised systems. Suppliers can only sell to them on a *national account* basis, whilst the territorial activities of the sales representative have largely been replaced by the merchandiser. Merchandising was examined in Chapter 34. National account selling is dealt with in Chapter 37.

2.3) Territory sales potential in industrial goods markets

Estimates of territory sales potential may be based upon such variables as:

* the location of the relevant industry and its level of output;

514

* the number of employees in that industry within the territory;

* the location of purchasing functions, and of purchase influencers and decision-makers within Decision Making Units;

* the impact of specific industry trends upon the output of target companies within the territory.

The dispersal of companies who make up a particular industrial market is likely to make for larger territories than in consumer goods markets. Territories are often based upon regions or groupings of counties, or provinces and departments in overseas markets.

2.4) Sales force workload

Once sales management has defined its sales territories, and estimated their sales potential, *sales force workload* can be calculated and the size of the sales force determined. The calculation of sales force workload is based upon:

the number and duration of calls needed in each territory to achieve the company's objectives for reach and frequency.

This calculation is based upon the following variables:

* sales potential, as indicated by the number of actual and potential customers, and by the size and relative importance of these customers;

* required reach, which is indicated by *the degree of coverage to be achieved* as a proportion of the total available sales potential within the territory;

* required frequency, which is indicated by the frequency of calls, or "call rate" for the different categories of customer. For instance, large accounts may need more calls *and* lengthier calls than small accounts.

Once sales management has calculated the approximate number and duration of calls needed in a particular territory to achieve the company's objectives for reach and frequency at the estimated level of sales potential, it has an indicator of the *sales effort required.*

This level of required sales effort is then matched with the *sales effort available,* which is a function of selling hours available per sales representative per unit of time. Therefore:

515

$$\text{number of sales representatives needed} = \frac{\text{sales effort required (expressed in hours)}}{\text{sales effort available (expressed in selling hours per sales representative)}}$$

This calculation is illustrated by an example, thus:

* *a mixed territory example:* all 270 actual and potential customers in Territory XYZ (in an industrial goods market) are to be reached in the year, but on a differential frequency according to the size of the account, viz:

> 20 largest accounts to be visited twice monthly ie 24 calls per annum.
>
> 50 medium-sized accounts to be visited once per month ie 12 calls per annum.
>
> 200 small accounts to be visited once per quarter ie 4 calls per annum.

This gives a workload (expressed as sales effort required) of:

$$((20x24)+(50x12)+(200x4)) = 1,880 \text{ calls per annum.}$$

Let us assume that one sales call should last one hour, but that one sales representative can only carry out four calls per 8 hour day. The remaining four hours would be taken up by travelling, completing reports and documentation, and carrying out non-selling tasks whilst at customer premises. So, each sales representative has an available effort of:

$$((5 \text{ days} \times 4 \text{ calls}) \times 48 \text{ weeks}) = 960 \text{ selling hours per year.}$$

Therefore, the number of sales representatives required in Territory XYZ is:

$$\frac{1,880}{960} = 1.9 \text{ or two sales representatives}$$

3) CONTROLLING SALES FORCE ACTIVITY

The subject of sales force control is a complex and sometimes controversial one. This section will be limited to an overview of the subject, and will summarise a few of the major problems attaching to the attempt by sales management to monitor and control sales force performance.

3.1) The control process

At a *strategic* level in the company, marketing management will be involved in setting *objectives* for the marketing function. At a *tactical* level, marketing and sales management will need to establish:

a) *performance standards* to be achieved by sales staff, upon the basis of which staff appraisal may be carried out.

b) *performance criteria* in which the performance standard is to be carried out, and by which marketing and sales objectives are to be achieved.

At an *operational* level, marketing and sales management will be responsible for:

i) measuring performance actually achieved against the relevant standards and criteria.

ii) comparing this with the targets set for performance standard and criteria.

iii) stating variances.

iv) justifying variances and/or taking "corrective action".

v) reviewing objectives, performance standards and performance criteria.

3.2) Sales objectives, performance standards and performance criteria

The major sales objectives were listed in section (1.2) above, and included objectives for:

* sales volume
* distribution
* market share
* sales revenue
* contribution
* profit

These objectives are set at a *strategic* level. In order that they may actually be achieved at an *operational* level, marketing and sales management must render these objectives practicable and meaningful at a *tactical* level. This will mean establishing:

a) performance standards or "targets" to be achieved by sales staff (section (3.3) below); and

b) performance criteria in which this performance standard is to be carried out (section (3.4) below).

3.3) Performance standards

By "performance standards" sales management actually means *the target level of performance to be achieved by the sales*

517

representative within his or her territory. This specification of a target level of performance is a tactical concept designed to guide, direct or inform operational activity. The target might be based on two inter-related variables thus:

* an estimate of the available potential within the territory, for instance as expressed as the maximum achievable sales volume or value;

* the results achievable by (say) an effectively trained and motivated salesperson of average experience and ability, after any time needed to build up sales if the territory had been previously underdeveloped.

This target level of performance must exclude all factors which are outside of the control of the salesperson (for instance price increases that result from company policy towards increases in raw material costs). It should take into account previous sales performance within the territory. And the setting of the target level of performance should involve the individual representative. This is a basic participative concept derived from the behavioural sciences, and is best expressed in the form of "management by objectives". Where an individual is to be held responsible for the achievement of a specified level of performance or objective, then he or she should be involved in the process by which that objective is formulated. There should be general agreement about the form, context and viability of the target or objective as it is expressed for the purposes of comparison and appraisal.

Like all standards, sales targets should be formulated in such a way that they are:

i) relevant.
ii) timely.
iii) free from ambiguity or misinterpretation.
iv) understood by sales manager and representative alike.
v) known to enjoy the confidence of the representative.

This section has paid particular attention to the setting of targets and performance standards, since it is important that *the relationship between target and result is clearly understood* by sales management and sales representative alike. The company's expectations of the performance level to be achieved must be crystal clear. The sales representative, in turn, must be in agreement that such expectations can actually be achieved. For the job of the sales representative is unusual in that performance and results are *clearly measurable*. Relatively few other occupations contain such a clear relationship between target and results achieved. And given the importance of these results to the company as a whole, it is not surprising that sales representatives are sensitive to the kinds of targets set for them, and to the processes by which these performance requirements are established.

The potential clarity of the target-results relationship is shown in Figure 36.1. This illustrative chart shows actual sales achieved in a territory plotted against monthly forecast targets.

3.4) Performance criteria

It is usual to describe performance criteria, for which performance standards are set, in two categories. Effective sales management is likely to make use of both. These categories are:

a) input criteria;

b) output (or productivity) criteria.

a) *Input criteria:* of which three illustrations will be given.

    i)   *work load:* as measured in terms of the number of sales calls made per day over the measurement period in question. This criteria is used as an indicator of effort. The call rate is related to the standard call rate, and to other required persuasive/selling activities such as standard hours to be spent on demonstrations, exhibitions (etc). However, whilst work load criteria may indicate the level of effort put into the job, it does not indicate anything about the desired outcome. As a result, pressure from sales management to increase the call rate (and hence increase the apparent input of effort) may actually result in *decreased* sales if, in reality, sales calls have a minimum critical required duration in order to have any individual or cumulative effect in persuading the customer to buy from the company.

    ii) *selling cost:* as indicated by comparisons of cost per call, selling cost per product/range, or selling cost per customer with the relevant cost standard. Such comparisons may yield variances, which will in turn require justification or the taking of corrective action. Whilst indicators of selling cost do not have a direct relationship to sales results, it will be of particular importance to

519

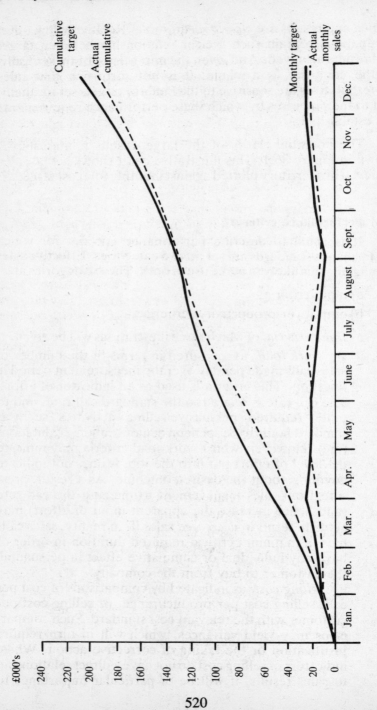

Figure 36.1. Sales Performance Chart.

monitor and control selling costs, which may be very high.

iii) *ability to self-manage time:* given the finite level of selling time available to any sales force, it is essential that sales representatives *maximise their productive selling time* as a proportion of the total hours available. At the same time they need to keep under control the time spent on non-selling tasks at customer premises, and to reduce unproductive administrative tasks to a minimum. Information Technology developments may be useful here, for instance by:

* making use of personal computers/telecommunication links for compilation and transmission of reports, summaries, memos, instructions (etc);
* making use of telecommunications facilities to minimise the need for sales office visits;
* making use of cellular car telephones, so that sales call schedules can be made more flexible and travelling time used for communication with the sales office;
* using wordprocessing facilities to prepare both standard and customised documentation contracts (etc) which can be called off from the sales office on demand.
* (etc)

The need to improve self-management of time is now widely recognised as a particular training need of sales representatives, as their cost per hour increases.

b) *Output (or productivity) criteria*

Output criteria relate effort to the results achieved. A number of examples are given.

i) *sales quality:* as indicated by such ratios as:
 − sales orders to sales call ratio;
 − sales volume to sales call ratio;
 − sales orders/volume to sales call ratio per customer;
 − sales value to sales call ratio;
 − sales value to sales call ratio per customer;
 − contribution earned to sales call ratio;
 − average order size;
 − sales proposals to sales achieved ratio;
 − (etc).

ii) *achieving quota:* which indicates that the sales representative has met his monthly or annual sales target.

iii) *orders in excess of quota:* which indicates the level of effort and achievement put in above the basic target requirement.

iv) *sales mix:* which indicates the relative emphasis given to selling different products in the product range. The results will show up in the relative levels of contribution earned per product line, and in total. The importance of this point is made in Chapters 23 and 40; the sales representative should be encouraged to maximise sales of those lines that generate the most contribution.

v) *sales expense to sales revenue ratio:* indicates the level of cost incurred by sales staff in selling to customers. A problem with this calculation is the apportionment of sales office and sales administration costs to individual sales staff or customers. These are better treated as departmental fixed costs and only directly variable costs may be included in the calculation of sales expense.

vi) *business development:* as represented by the rate of generation of new business, and by increases in the volume and value of existing business. The latter may be indicated by the value of the average customer order.

vii) *customer service:* which indicates the adequacy of the salesforce as perceived by customers. The perceived quality of customer service may be established by attitude surveys carried out by an independent agency.

3.5 Some problems of salesforce control

The control of a sales force is a complex matter. To members of the sales management team, and the sales representatives it may also be the cause of considerable controversy and conflict. These difficulties arise from a number of problems that face sales management in drawing up sales force controls. These problems include:

a) *type of business:* the kinds of standards and criteria described in sections (3.3) and (3.4) above may be more appropriate to selling activities in consumer goods markets, and to re-purchase/re-buy decisions in industrial goods markets. This kind of selling is repetitive and relatively predictable. It is often based upon targets or quotas. The standards and criteria described may, however, be less applicable to many (less predictable, or more innovative) aspects of selling in industrial goods markets, especially where the use of targets may not be feasible.

b) *time-lags:* where there are time lags between arousing customer interest and the receipt of orders, the use of such ratios as sales orders to sales calls may be meaningless. Business may take a long time to develop, especially in industrial goods and contract markets. All that sales management can do is to monitor (i) the size of customer orders; and (ii) the ratio of sales proposals to sales achieved.

c) *assessment time-period:* the time period of assessment provides a monitoring and measurement problem. Should the period of account be weeks, months, quarters or years? Long periods may be essential in industrial and international markets. Yet lengthy assessment periods may obscure problems, which may have become serious by the time sales management has become aware of them.

d) *incidence of unproductive tasks:* where control and reward systems (see Chapter 37) are based on results achieved, sales representatives will complain about what they perceive as the incidence of unproductive tasks such as completing paperwork, reports and answering requests for information from the sales office and marketing department. This problem is compounded by the inclusion in the role of the sales representative of non-selling customer activities. After all, as far as the customer is concerned, the sales representative *is* the company. This point has already been made. Some of the representative's time has to be spent on customer service activities, the quality of which may have an eventual effect on the level of sales achieved.

e) *selling is person-centred:* irrespective of the control or motivation systems in operation, sales performance will inevitably vary with individual ability, experience, motivation and application. Some individuals will react differently to control systems than others. Sales representatives would argue that if company selection procedures are effective, sales representatives should be involved in setting objectives and left alone to get on with the job. What they want from sales management, and the wider marketing function, is *support, guidance and direction,* not control. Controls may be seen by some representatives as mechanisms for stifling personal initiative and entrepreneurship, applied in circumstances where the salesperson needs freedom to produce results.

SUMMARY

The contents of this chapter are summarised in Table 36.2.

TABLE 36.2
Summary : Chapter Thirty Six

SECTION	MAIN POINTS
1. Setting sales objectives	(1.1) Sales objectives must be analysed within the wider context of marketing mix planning and objectives, since sales force activity must be co-ordinated with other marketing mix activities. Detailed sales objectives are based upon the annual sales forecast and additional specific sales targets. Total sales objectives are then broken down so that they are specific to individual sales representatives and individual sales territories. (1.2) Sales objectives include (a) sales volume, (b) distribution, (c) market share, (d) sales revenue, (e) contribution targets, (f) profit, (g) service objectives.
2. Determining the size of the salesforce	The number of sales representatives required by a company is a function of (2.1) the geographical territory to be covered, (2.2) and (2.3) the sales potential of this territory, and (2.4) the salesforce workload. The calculation of salesforce workload is based upon the number and duration of sales calls needed in each territory to achieve the company's objectives for coverage of customers (reach) and frequency of sales visit. This

calculation yields an indicator of sales effort required. This is then divided by the sales effort available to determine the number of sales representatives needed. Sales effort available is indicated by the number of hours per representative per working day available for selling activities.

3. Controlling sales force activity

(3.1 to 3.3) Performance standards will be set for various performance criteria derived from basic sales objectives. Actual performance will be monitored and compared with standard, and the control process operated. (3.4) Performance criteria for sales staff may be (a) input based (using indicators such as work load, selling cost, ability to self manage time); or (b) output (productivity) based (using indicators such as sales quality, achieving quota, orders in excess of quota, sales mix; sales expense to sales revenue ratio, business development, customer service). (3.5) Some problems of salesforce control include (a) type of business, (b) time-lags, (c) assessment time-period, (d) incidence of unproductive tasks (e) selling as a person-centred activity.

37 Salesforce Management II

INTRODUCTION

This chapter continues the analysis of sales force management. It looks in detail at sales force motivation which, in sales management terms, involves three main areas of consideration. These are field management and communication, training, and systems of remuneration and reward. The chapter then concludes with a brief look at some of the developing trends in personal selling and salesforce management.

CHAPTER CONTENTS

1) Sales force motivation

2) Field management and communication

3) Training

4) Systems of remuneration and reward
   4.1) Salary based remuneration
   4.2) Payment by Results based remuneration
   4.3) Other financial and non-financial incentives
   4.4) Payment by Results thresholds

5) Trends in personal selling and salesforce management
   5.1) Team selling
   5.2) Selling to multi-individual buying structures and Decision Making Units
   5.3) Selling to national accounts
   5.4) Telephone selling

Summary

Recommended Reading

Chapter Appendix 37(1) Telephone ways to raise promotion performance

Questions for self review

Examination questions

1) SALES FORCE MOTIVATION

The previous chapter analysed the related issues of setting sales objectives and controlling salesforce activity. The control of salesforce activity is a problem area within sales management. The job of the sales representative is an individualistic one, and it is often lonely. The sales representative is isolated from the company, his sales manager and his colleagues. Yet the work done by sales people is critical to the company's success, and it can be easily measured. So, apart from monitoring and controlling salesforce activity, it will be of equal importance for sales management to maintain and encourage *the motivation and morale* of each and every sales representative. The maintenance of a consistent level of sales force motivation is one of the most important responsibilities of sales managers.

After all, the role of the sales representative is a *co-ordinative* one, with considerable potential for *role stress*. Role stress may derive from:

a) *task dependency:* the work of the sales representative is at "the end" of the marketing activity. All sorts of different activities come to fruition in a situation in which the customer also has his or her expectations. The sales representative is dependent on a whole series of inter-dependent policies and events for his or her success. Yet at the same time the representative *is the company* to the customer and will receive the full force of customer comment, criticism or complaint.

b) *workflow uncertainty:* the workflow of the sales representative is characterised by a high degree of *variability and unpredictability*. Sudden changes may occur, new pressures may come from company management, and the representatives may have to channel unpalatable adverse comment back to senior management on behalf of irate customers.

Hence, it will be important for sales representatives to maintain a high degree of:

* self-reliance;
* resilience
* self-confidence
* self-motivation

There are a number of ways in which these necessary qualities can be maintained. These include:

- effective field management and communication;
- effective training;
- effective systems of remuneration and reward.

Each is described in turn.

2) FIELD MANAGEMENT AND COMMUNICATION

Sales managers need to maintain effective contact with sales representatives working "in the field" (that is, out in the market). This contact is needed for a variety of reasons, which include:

* providing support, guidance and direction to sales staff;
* monitoring the activities, achievements and problems of field sales staff;
* providing training and advice *in situ* to inexperienced salespersons;
* acting as a "sounding board" and assistant in solving problems faced by experienced salespersons;

Planned and systematic contact and communication is needed to achieve these sales management objectives. At the same time, communications, field visits, meetings of sales staff (etc) should serve to foster a feeling of *team spirit and identity* on the part of field sales staff. Given the independent nature of the role of the sales representative, it is essential to pay particular attention to the maintenance of a feeling of identity with the company and fellow sales-representatives. By this means feelings of isolation are overcome and some feeling of "esprit de corps" (team spirit and enthusiasm) are maintained.

The communication process (whether in written or verbal form, at meetings, briefings, conferences or whatever) must fulfil basic requirements for information dissemination, such as for new campaigns, forthcoming product launches (etc). It will also be part of the control process (communication and control are two sides of the same coin). But it is important that sales managers operate the communication process such that representatives do not perceive it as a bureaucratic source of unnecessary and unproductive administrative tasks that should instead be undertaken by the sales office. The communication process must be perceived in a positive light, as a source of help and an opportunity for the individual sales representative to *feedback* whatever information he or she thinks sales and marketing management ought to know.

3) TRAINING

The field sales representative works independently. He or she faces the company's customers whilst carrying out persuasive and selling activities. He or she is the first line in the achievement of customer service objectives. And he or she represents the company to the customer. In consequence, sales management, in conjunction with the company's personnel function, needs to make effective selection decisions. The company must recruit the right staff, *and then it must train them*. Remember, the prosperity of both company and country depend on adequate and effective education and training. The more complex the technology, and the more competitive the market, the more essential become well educated and trained people. This is critically true for sales representatives, especially in industrial goods markets. The *content* of sales representative training can include some or all of the following:

* market knowledge (or "market intelligence") and trends in market requirements;
* knowledge of the company's products and their applications, plus new product developments (etc);
* knowledge of competitors' products and their applications, plus their strengths and weaknesses;
* sales and presentation technique;
* pricing (and pricing consequences) where the sales representative is involved in price negotiations;
* customer purchasing techniques; how to deal with multi-individual buying (DMU) situations in industrial goods markets;
* how to sell to *national accounts* (especially in retail multiples);
* how and where to obtain specialist support and assistance within the company.

Training in these areas is essential if the sales representative is to be able to do his or her job properly. Other relevant training needs include:

i) *training to improve skills:* for instance in negotiating sales to highly-motivated professional buyers, perhaps qualified in the UK to the standards of the Institute of Purchasing and Supply.

ii) *training to increase motivation:* some UK readers will be aware of a whole array of motivational training which is available, ranging from high cost "management and motivation" courses for senior sales management (based on the applied behavioural sciences), to the famous half-day or evening "roadshows" marketed in the UK by sales trainers like John Fenton or Sales Boosters International. This kind of training is an industry in itself: *you pays your money and you takes your choice!*

iii) *training in sales management skills:* essential to producing top quality sales managers whose previous experience has been "on the road".

iv) *training for change:* for instance training sales managers to cope with a shift in emphasis to selling to national retail accounts in fast moving consumer goods markets, or showing them how to get their salesforce to increase productivity by making use of appropriate Information Technology developments.

Training methods can be lecture based, for instance for basic information dissemination purposes. Or instead, participative classroom methods can be used. These will include sales and negotiation case studies, role plays, presentations and CCTV work. Such methods must complement training and development activities carried out in the field. And they must be related to performance feedback, staff appraisal and the process by which training needs are identified.

4) SYSTEMS OF REMUNERATION AND REWARD

A variety of remuneration and reward systems have long been associated with the motivation of sales representatives. In particular, people often think of remuneration systems based on *Payment By Results* (PBR) in which there is a direct relationship between effort and results on the one hand, and reward on the other. In fact, salesforce remuneration and reward is not a straight-forward issue, and some forms of Payment By Results are now relatively unpopular. The use by sales management of a variety of systems of remuneration and reward for the purposes of salesforce motivation can, in general terms, be explained by the following reasons:

* people react differently to the incentives on offer. Some people will derive greater motivation from one particular system than others of their colleagues. Money may motivate one group, whilst another is more interested in enhanced prestige.

* sales representatives are faced with a variety of tasks. These tasks will vary in their timescale, their results and their urgency. Different tasks will need different motivations, and therefore call for a variety of incentives.

4.1) Salary based remuneration

Many sales representatives are now paid a straight salary, receive an expense allowance and have a company car (or a preferential car purchase loan scheme plus mileage rate). There is no commission and no bonus payments are made. The main justification for salary based remuneration is the view that sales orders achieved are not an effective indicator of the performance needed to carry out the job. Straight salary is seen as preferable where business development activities, the gathering of marketing intelligence, and technical or customer service activities are an important part of the sales representative's role. These activities will not yield immediate sales, yet they are important within the context of the marketing mix. Salary is also held to be preferable where sales staff operate as a team, and the efforts of the individual cannot easily be discerned and measured.

Salary based remuneration is the most appropriate system where a high level of technical or professional service is to be provided. This is particularly the case in industrial goods markets with a high technological content, such as electronic engineering, avionic systems (etc). Indeed, salary based remuneration may be essential to attract sales staff or technical representatives of the required calibre. The employment market for sales and technical representatives in such markets as electronics, computer system specification, or pharmaceuticals is very competitive. The quality of staff that can be recruited will be a reflection of salary prospects on offer.

Where a company operates a large sales force, a salary based system may render the remuneration system more manageable. The gains in operational and administrative simplicity may be offset against the motivational advantages of PBR based systems that have to be foregone. In any case, salary systems may have to be used where PBR *cannot* be applied to all products. Products subject to supply shortages and excess demand, or products with variable margins may not be suitable for Payments by Results based reward systems.

Salary based remuneration systems have a major advantage in that they avoid completely the problems that can be associated with *complex PBR based reward systems.* These systems can contain:

– a variety of basic salary rates;
– commission rates that vary according to product group;
– individual and/or group bonus payments;
– regional incentives (for instance for selling in "difficult" areas such as inner cities, or in areas in which the company wishes to develop its business);
– variable adjustments against the value of returned goods.

Such payment systems are complex to calculate and administer, and they are a fruitful source of conflict between sales representatives and sales management. Such systems are also open to abuse and manipulation, especially where the constituent data comes from records and documentation originated by the sales force.

Salary based systems also avoid a problem associated with PBR in times of economic downturn and recession. Remuneration based upon a significant proportion of commission will decline, as the commission received from sales declines. As remuneration declines, so will morale and motivation. Yet what is needed is quite the opposite! Recession calls for *increased effort and increased incentive,* not a reduction.

Where remuneration is based on salary, performance appraisal procedures become an important element of sales-force monitoring, motivation and control.

4.2) Payment By Results (PBR) based remuneration

Where sales representatives are paid on the basis of PBR, this usually means that added to a basic salary will be any of the following:

    * *Commissions and bonuses* based on total sales achieved, or based on sales performance relative to target or

quota. Commission and bonus may be earned individually or on a group basis. Typically, such additions comprise up to 20% of total remuneration earned;

* *Bonus to reward exceptional effort or achievement,* for instance in recording the highest sales figure in the salesforce;

* *Bonus related to urgency or importance of an activity,* for example to achieve a rapid short-term increase in sales of a product for which demand has suddenly increased beyond forecast, perhaps as a result of hot weather or additional shelf-space becoming available in retail multiples.

PBR based systems exploit the *incentive value of money.* However, to be effective as a motivator, such systems must be based upon a close relationship between effort and sales achieved. This means that PBR can be problematic where sales staff operate in teams and individual effort cannot be separated out. This point has been made above. Group PBR systems will be unpopular where "workers" (high performers) suspect they are carrying "shirkers" (low performers) who are receiving the same commission or bonus.

Suffice it to say that *commission-only* remuneration is now unusual in the UK and Northern Europe. In the UK it is only found in self employed or agency selling, for instance of insurance, home improvement products and the like.

4.3) Other financial and non-financial incentives

Many companies make use of financial and non-financial incentives which are awarded separately from sales representative remuneration. These include:

* *achievement awards,* usually accompanied by publicity within the company. Such awards can take the form of cash, vouchers redeemable against goods, prizes in kind, holidays and travel facilities, annual conferences held at exotic resorts (etc).

* *status symbols* such as bigger cars, increased expense accounts and prestigious charge card facilities;

* *promotion,* for instance to a senior sales post and then into sales management;

* *published "league tables"* comparing the performance of the sales team or salesforce, (such tables also having

a potentially de-motivating effect on the lower positions, especially if the bottom place tends to be relegated back to the sales office, or even to the local Job Centre!);

* *contests and competitions,* which are used to foster a competitive spirit amongst individual representatives and sales teams. The winners receive achievement awards. Contests and competitions are often used as incentives in specific sales and promotional campaigns. They increase interest in the particular campaign and concentrate salesforce effort on it.

These kinds of financial and non-financial incentives are most appropriate to specific tasks or sales campaigns. They are used to stimulate sales of a particular line for a relatively short time (say in the autumn stocking of shops prior to the Christmas rush), to reward outstanding presentation or demonstration performance, or to congratulate a representative on receiving a specific level of praise from customers for the level of customer service achieved.

4.4) Payment By Results thresholds

Where sales representative remuneration contains some element of PBR, the motivation value of the PBR element (commission, bonus etc) will in part depend upon the *threshold* at which the PBR element comes into operation. There are a number of considerations here, including:

a) *the basis* of the commission or bonus: PBR might come into effect at a different sales level if the basis is *sales volume* rather than sales value. The representative may be tempted to sell a large volume of low-margin or low contribution items in order to reach a volume-based PBR threshold. The company, on the other hand, will be more interested in PBR becoming operational after a certain *value of sales* has been achieved. Secondly, should the threshold figure exclude returns, or instead be calculated *net of returns?* After all, the quality of the firm's products (which will determine the level of returns) is beyond the control of the individual sales representative.

b) *the level of quota:* Commission or bonus will become payable after the salesperson has reached a certain volume or value of sales quota. It is therefore important to establish effective quota or target setting procedures so that:

* reaching the quota is itself a challenge, but not such a demanding task that the quota-commission structure can have a demotivating effect;
* the value of the commission or bonus element is sufficient to make it worthwhile striving for;
* the quota set is not too low, allowing the representative a chance to exploit the commission system. In this case, the remuneration system would have lost its capacity to motivate the sales representative into making the maximum effort. It would have instead achieved a "sub-optimal" result.

c) *incentive system behaviour:* the motivation value of the PBR element will in part depend on its design pattern. Is there a *straight line* relationship between enhanced effort and reward? Such a relationship is shown in Figure 37.1.

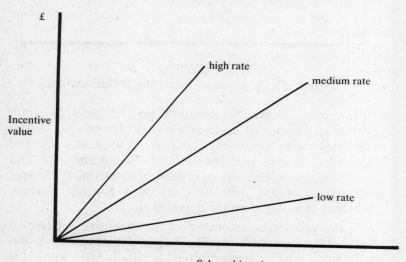

Figure 37.1. Straight-Line Incentive Relationship.

Whilst such a relationship may maximise the incentive value of the PBR element, it can mean that an outstanding salesperson can achieve a dramatic increase in earnings. In theory this should be an acceptable outcome to the company (especially where the incentive is based on sales value). However, some companies are not prepared to accept what they see as such a potentially "open-ended" commitment, and design incentive relationships with a *decreasing rate of increase.* This is illustrated in Figure 37.2.

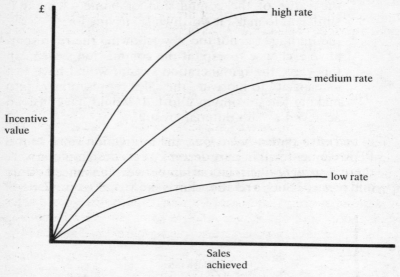

Figure 37.2. Decreasing Incentive Relationship.

d) *timing of payment:* incentives may be paid (i) upon receipt of order; (ii) upon delivery of the product to the customer; (iii) upon the receipt of payment by the customer. The longer the delay between the sale and receipt of order, delivery or receipt of payment, the longer the representative will have to wait for his reward. Whether this is important depends upon:

* the proportionate value of the incentive relative to total remuneration. The larger the proportion, the more the representative is likely to want his commission quickly;

* the degree to which *immediacy* of reward is perceived as an important element of the motivation value of incentives based upon PBR.

5) TRENDS IN PERSONAL SELLING AND SALESFORCE MANAGEMENT

Marketing and selling are dynamic activities, subject to review and change. Because personal selling is an important but expensive part of the marketing mix, it is not surprising that its role within the promotional mix will periodically be questioned, and adapted to meet changing circumstances. Some of the changes to which personal selling and salesforce management have been subject are described below. But this is not an exclusive list, doubtless other changes will occur during the years to come.

5.1) Team selling

The size or complexity of some customer accounts may call for a *teamwork effort* in selling, and in providing customer service. Within industrial markets, such as electronics, the selling and customer service roles will be fulfilled by technical sales representatives or sales engineers, supported by designers, engineers, production accountants and so on. Within consumer goods markets, selling and customer service may be carried out by national account sales staff (section (5.3) below), local sales order-takers and van-driver salespersons, and merchandising teams. The role of merchandisers was explained in Chapter 34.

Where team selling is used, sales management *will have to ensure that team efforts are co-ordinated and that the total team activity is properly integrated.* Team and individual roles and objectives will have to be clearly stated and inter-related, and effective management mechanisms established to achieve and maintain the required levels of co-ordination and integration.

5.2) Selling to multi-individual buying structures and Decision Making Units

One of the themes that has run throughout this book has been the complexity of markets, and of purchase and buying behaviour. In particular, several chapters examined the problems of selling to retail buyers and industrial markets where:

- buying is done under contract from approved suppliers;
- the buying process contains a variety of roles and individuals;
- the buyer role is differentiated from influence and decision-making roles.

The point was made in Chapter 15 that the promotion and selling effort in such markets would have to proceed consecutively along a number of paths. These would require the involve-

ment of senior company personnel, as well as sales representatives and sales management. In order to be effective, the
promotion and selling process would have to be targeted upon
a variety of different levels within the organisational hierarchy
of customer companies, and might have to be carried out on a
long-term and continuous basis.

5.3) Selling to national accounts

Another important theme that has run throughout this
book has been the incidence of *concentration in buying
power*. The concentration of buying power, both in consumer
and industrial goods markets has been a key feature of post-1945
economies in Europe and the USA. The process of concentration
has meant that supplying companies are often faced with the
problem of selling to a relatively small number of relatively
large customers. Each customer is therefore highly significant
in sales and profit terms to the supplier. *This level of significance
must be reflected in the way in which suppliers deal with such
customers.*

Some UK examples of selling to national accounts include
the following:

* selling to centralised buying departments in national
  retail multiples such as Tesco, Rumbelows and Boots
  the Chemist;
* selling to centralised buying departments in major
  national manufacturers such as Ford Motor Company,
  Plessey or ICI;
* selling to centralised buying departments in government
  agencies, National Health Service, and nationalised
  industries such as British Rail;
* selling to centralised buying departments in major
  companies in the service sector, such as Trust House
  Forte Hotels or British Airways.

The development of *national account management* within
the sales management process involves a number of elements,
including:

a) the allocation of an adequate degree of selling and
customer service resources on a continuing or permanent
basis *to each account.*

b) the involvement of senior company management in the
sales and customer service activity, in addition to sales

staff and sales management. This requirement was also mentioned in paragraph (5.2) above.

c) the permanent availability to the customer of access to the relevant staff in the supplying company. This access is made available for the communication of queries, problems or complaints, new or changed customer requirements, requirements for technical advice (etc). The staff and management of the national accounts function provides the *continuing link* between the customer and the company.

d) obtaining market intelligence and feedback about: customer satisfaction with the products supplied and the level of service offered, customer attitude towards the supplier, and new requirements which may lead to a new product development response. Close contact with the customer will, in addition, assist in the formulation of sales forecasting (for instance on the basis of *buyer intentions* as described in Chapter 7). More generally, well managed contact and communication will consolidate the position of the supplier *as a company who deliver, and who care about the customer*. This is what the marketing concept is all about.

e) the likelihood of wide-ranging negotiations on products and specifications, price, promotion, delivery, credit terms and financing arrangements, product guarantees and contractual obligations. The latter include supplier liability for claims under guarantee or warranty, and the rights of the supplier to pass on to the customer increases in raw material costs.

The development of national account management has highlighted the need for sales staff and sales management *to have an adequate background in basic management accounting,* or to have access to *sales-orientated* accountants (perhaps qualified members of the Chartered Institute of Cost and Management Accountants or the Chartered Association of Certified Accountants). Such accounting knowledge will be essential in cost and price calculations, product mix contribution calculations, break-even and profitability calculations. Supplying companies cannot afford to make mistakes when dealing with large-scale customers, nor to appear unprofessional in their preparation and negotiations over prices and terms of supply.

5.4) Telephone selling

The use of the telephone to sell products and services, make appointments and conduct market research is not new. However, during recent years, there has been a large growth in the use of the telephone for promotion and selling purposes. The reasons for this growth in the UK include:

* the increasing cost of personal selling, compared with which telephone selling may be cost-effective;
* increasing marketing by British Telecom of telephone promotion and selling;
* the increasing use of toll-free 0800 and Freefone numbers for in-bound calls to suppliers and advertisers.

Parallel developments in telephone selling are to be found in Western Europe, the USA and the industrialised Far East.

Companies use the telephone for the *direct selling* of products and services, especially to dealers, retailers and agents who are buying regularly on a re-buy or re-order basis to replenish stocks. This may be more economical than the use of personal sales representatives, especially where sales telephonists can be trained to make "add-on" sales. Add-on sales may expand the ranges or stocks held by dealers, agents or retailers, and so increase the total volume and value of orders received. An example is given in Box 37.3.

Box 37.3

M6 Cash and Carry

'Marketing' notes that "half of Crewe-based M6 Cash and Carry's business is delivery to shopkeepers. The company's use of out-bound telesales at its operations centre has turned its telephonists from order takers to sales people. At set times the telesales people call the shop-keepers, who order from customised lists – of which M6 and the customer have identical copies. Orders are entered into the computer, made up and delivered. M6 found that a phone order can be processed immediately and at one third of the cost of a sales staff visit. According to the M6 sales manager, after a training course for the telephonists to prepare them for their new role, sales increased by approximately 7%"

Companies also use the telephone *to make appointments and carry out cold-calling.* This is particularly advantageous because it is not cost-effective to use the time of sales staff on the road to carry out such activities if it can be at all avoided.

Promotional activities can also be carried out by telephone. Retailers, dealers or agents can be kept up to date on forthcoming promotional campaigns, special offers, new products and dealer incentives. Trade customers are thereby "kept in the picture" on a more frequent basis than would be possible using field sales staff. Advocates of the telephone approach would also point to the motivational benefits of relatively frequent calls from the supplier. Frequent but short communication may "involve" the customer more than infrequent personal visits, and will enhance and support the undoubted (but more costly) value of direct field visiting and promotion by sales representatives.

The Appendix to this chapter continues the analysis of telephone selling, by suggesting ten areas in which use of the telephone can help to improve sales performance.

SUMMARY

The contents of this chapter are summarised in Table 37.4.

TABLE 37.4
Summary : Chapter Thirty Seven

SECTION	MAIN POINTS
1. Sales force motivation	As well as monitoring and controlling sales force activity, it will be of critical importance for sales management to maintain and encourage the motivation and morale of sales staff. The role of the sales representative contains considerable potential for role stress, due to the inherent task interdependence and workflow uncertainty. Hence the need to maintain self-reliance, personal resilience, self-confidence and self-motivation.
2. Field management and communication	Sales managers must maintain effective field management and communication in order to provide support, guidance

and direction to sales staff, to monitor salesforce activity, to provide training and to foster team spirit and identity with the company. Communication methods must appear supportive, not bureaucratic.

3. Training

Effective sales performance requires effective sales force training. Training should cover markets, products, competitors' products, sales and presentation technique, pricing, customer purchasing techniques, how to sell to national accounts (etc). It should also cover skill improvement, self-motivation, sales management skills (etc).

4. Systems of remuneration and reward

(4.1) Salary based remuneration is used where sales management considers that sales orders achieved are not an effective indicator of individual performance, especially where business development activities, the gathering of market intelligence, and customer service activities are an important part of the sales representative's role. This system is common in industrial selling, technical sales representation (etc). (4.2) Payment by Results based remuneration exploits the incentive value of money. PBR additions to basic salary include performance-related bonuses and commission payments. (4.3) Other financial and non-financial incentives include achievement awards, status symbols, published league-tables, contests and competitions, and promotion. (4.4) Payment By Results thresholds (the point at which the PBR element comes into operation) affect the motivation value of the PBR element. Considerations here include the basis of the commission or bonus, the level of

	quota or target, incentive system pattern, and timing of payment.
5. Trends in personal selling and salesforce management	Current developments include trends towards (5.1) team selling, (5.2) selling to multi-individual buying structures, (5.3) selling to national accounts, (5.4) increased use of telephone selling.

RECOMMENDED READING

Gilliam A.   Principles and Practice of Selling.   Heinemann
McDonald M.   How to Sell a Service.   Heinemann

CHAPTER APPENDIX 37(I)

TELEPHONE WAYS TO RAISE PROMOTION PERFORMANCE

1. Direct selling to launch new products

Outlets can be contacted and informed of new products, discounts and special offers. Orders can be taken at the same time. The speed of the operation enables a supplier to adopt a blitz approach if needed. And telephone ordering cuts down paperwork, which the retailer always appreciates.

2. Opening new accounts.

The telephone is ideal for opening and expanding marginal accounts, allowing the sales force to concentrate on the major ones. Apart from selling a product, the call can qualify the retailer, by getting details of the outlet – including vital matters such as bankers' references – at low cost and with little fuss.

3. Setting up qualified appointments

The sales force can be freed from the job of setting up appointments, allowing them to spend time on what they have been trained to do best: selling face to face. Because the telephone is interactive, there is the possibility of overcoming resistance, and if a 'next week' appointment is not on, there is the chance of leaving it open for the medium or long term.

4. Market research

The telephone can be used to track marketing and sales campaigns daily. People do talk on the telephone and, while long conversations push up the price, it is still much more cost effective than direct interviewing.

5. Maximising mail shot response

The telephone is integrated with direct mail to check a mailing list, prompt non-respondents to action, and ascertain resistance. In this way, a marketing campaign can be modified on the run. Well planned, integrated mail and telephone campaigns can increase response four or fivefold over direct mail used alone.

6. Invitations to seminars, exhibitions and launches

Apart from increasing the response of a direct mail or advertising campaign, the instant feedback of telephone activity means that flexible date and time arrangements can be implemented to meet demand, if necessary. Establishing direct contact also enables other opportunities to be explored. For example, non-attenders might be interested in other dates or events.

7. Incoming orders

Orders from dealers can be handled quickly and efficiently on the telephone, and can often be inputted directly into a computerised system. The growth in credit card distribution has led to a huge growth in direct telephone ordering by the public, often across national borders.

8. Screening enquiries or exhibition leads

Telephone screening of leads is a quick and cost effective way of minimising lead wastage. Positive leads can be verified and names and addresses checked for future action.

9. Locating distributors/dealers

Potential distributors can be contacted initially through a telephone campaign, making this a cost effective way of qualifying a list. Used internationally, the savings could be huge.

10. Renewing subscriptions

The telephone can be used not only for renewing subscriptions, but also for cross-selling new products at the same time, such as diaries. Because it is interactive, reasons for non-renewal can also be elicited, and fed back to the marketing division.

(Source Marketing; reproduced with permission)

QUESTIONS FOR SELF REVIEW

1.   Describe and comment on the role of personal selling within the promotional mix.

2.   Outline and comment on some of the factors that are likely to determine the nature and role of the company's sales force.

3.   What is cold-calling? Outline and comment on other ways of prospecting for new customers, alternative to cold calling by the sales representative.

4.   Research, describe and comment on some of the major elements of sales technique.

5.   Outline and comment on the various types of sales objective that may be used by sales management.

6.   How may a company determine the size of the sales force it needs to achieve its sales objectives?

7.   What factors are relevant to the control of sales force activity?

8.   Compare and contrast Input performance criteria and Output performance criteria as indicators of sales force performance.

9.   Outline and comment on some of the problems associated with the monitoring and control of sales force activity.

10.   What factors are relevant to the analysis of sales force motivation?

11.   Why must sales managers maintain communication with, and effective field management of the company sales force?

12.   Why is effective sales force and sales management training an essential pre-requisite to company success and profitability?

13.   Analyse, compare and comment on the alternative systems of sales force remuneration and reward available to sales management.

14.   Outline and comment on recent and current trends in personal selling and sales force management.

EXAMINATION QUESTIONS

Q63 What advantages does personal selling have over other elements of the communications mix? (CIM)

Q64 What factors, both within and outside of a company, determine the role and size of a sales force? (CIMA)

Q65 Discuss the tasks which the sales representative undertakes in the course of his/her contact with customers. (CIM)

Q66 For a business of your own choice describe the ways by which you would motivate the field sales force. (CIM)

Q67 In view of increasing labour costs and a reduction generally in the number of buying points, assess the changing role of personal selling as an element in the marketing mix. (CIMA)

Marketing within the Organisation

The effective implementation of the marketing concept depends upon organisational factors, and these are examined in this section. It also deals with the evaluation and control of the marketing effort, which is a basic managerial task. The section analyses some Information Technology applications; and the relationship of the Public Relations (or PR) function with marketing is considered. The section ends with an analysis of the relationship with Design, which is of increasing concern to the marketer as the importance of good design becomes more widely accepted.

38 Organising for Marketing Management

INTRODUCTION

This chapter looks at a variety of ways in which the enterprise may organise the marketing and marketing management activity. It shows how the development of marketing organisation has consolidated the position of the marketing function. And it comments on how the culture and values of the organisation will determine the degree to which the marketing concept (or 'customer-orientation') will pervade both the marketing organisation, and the wider enterprise structure of which it is a part.

CHAPTER CONTENTS

1) MARKETING ORGANISATION

It is possible to identify a variety of different types of marketing organisation. Each type represents a different approach to the management of the marketing activity. The choice of marketing organisation may depend, amongst other things, upon:

* the priority of the marketing function in the affairs of the enterprise (which is dependent upon the degree to which the *culture and values of the organisation* have espoused the marketing concept);

* the stage to which the organisation has evolved and developed;

* the relative importance of the salesforce within the promotional and marketing mix;

* the size and structure of the organisation.

The following sections describe and analyse some of the different types of marketing organisation. The character of each will be influenced by some or all of the four factors just outlined.

2) PRE-MARKETING FUNCTIONAL STRUCTURES

A pre-marketing functional structure is illustrated in Figure 38.1.

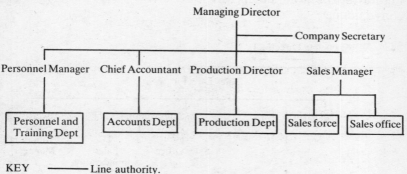

KEY ————— Line authority.

Figure 38.1. Pre-Marketing Functional Structure.

In such a structure, there is *no* marketing function. The sales manager is responsible for the sales force and for the sales office, which receives and processes orders and deals with customer enquiries or complaints.

Research and development, product planning, distribution and customer service might be controlled by the production director. Sales forecasting and budgeting, sales analysis and control would be the responsibility of the accounts department. The recruitment and training of sales staff would be undertaken by the personnel department. Advertising and marketing planning (if this is carried out at all) might be the responsibility of the Managing Director. Market research might well be difficult to carry out, and where the need for it is recognised, the work would be sub-contracted to an outside agency.

Such a structure may be effective in a small company in which there are close personal relationships between management, and where an *entrepreneurial style* pervades the organisation. Such a style is usually strongly marketing orientated. But where such an entrepreneurial style is missing, or where the organisational culture is production or accounting orientated, such structures are likely to become ineffective if market and trading conditions become subject to change, or become increasingly competitive.

3) SALES ORIENTED STRUCTURES

A sales-oriented structure is illustrated in Figure 38.2. The Personnel, Accounting and Production functions shown in Figure 38.1 have been left out merely for the sake of convenience.

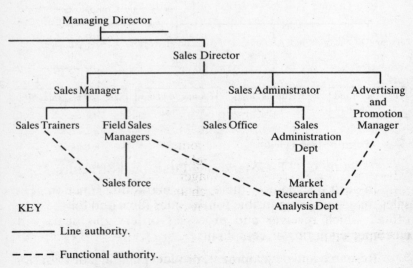

Figure 38.2. Sales-Oriented Structure.

Sales oriented structures may develop out of pre-marketing functional structures. The reason for this development would be (i) a perceived need to be more sensitive to the

550

needs of the market, and (ii) a greater requirement for promotional, persuasive and selling activities. These requirements would stem from changing market circumstances, and increasingly competitive trading conditions. Typically, a sales director will be responsible for:

* sales management, the sales force and sales training;
* sales administration and the sales office;
* customer service activities; and marketing activities previously carried out by other departments, such as market planning, advertising and sales analysis;
* newly identified "marketing" activities such as market research, market analysis and the gathering and systematic build-up of a marketing intelligence database.

At this stage, the non-selling areas of the sales function will be seen as providers of marketing intelligence, market information and customer support. The role of this information and support *will be perceived directly as an input to the selling effort.* The marketing activity is subordinate to the sales activity.

The reader will have noted that Figure 38.2 includes both "line" and "functional" authority. G. A. Cole ("Management Theory and Practice" DP Publications) defines *line authority* as the authority that each manager exercises directly over his own subordinates and department. *Functional authority* is the authority to command the staff of *other managers* as *to what to do and how to do it,* within an agreed specialist responsibility context of that functional manager. Thus, whilst the sales force are the direct responsibility of the Field Sales Managers, the Sales Trainers may direct and control their training on a functional basis. Similarly, the Field Sales Managers and the Advertising and Promotion Manager can exercise functional authority over the Market Research and Analysis Dept. where this is necessary to the carrying-out of their own work.

4) THE EMERGENCE OF THE MARKETING FUNCTION

Pre-marketing functional structures, or sales oriented structures may work effectively under stable trading conditions in which production-orientation, or sales-orientation are appropriate. They may, however, become ineffective under trading circumstances characterised by some (or all) of the following conditions:-

i) increasing competition, pressure on operating margins, etc.

ii) an increasing need for accurate market research.

iii) a need for better informed sales and market planning.

iv) a need for detailed market segmentation to inform product development and sales/market planning.

v) the maturing of markets and the shortening of Product Life Cycles, making New Product Development (NPD) a more critical activity needing market rather than production orientation.

vi) increasing NPD and promotional costs, which in turn call for (a) a greater awareness of the relationship between market segmentation and product positioning, and (b) strategies to maximise the likely success of NPD and new marketing initiatives. Only in this way can the cash flow needed to finance NPD and promotion be assured.

vii) the emergence of centralised buying as a result of concentration in both consumer and industrial goods markets. This has focused attention on product specification, position and pricing in industrial goods markets. In retail markets it has had the effect of changing or reducing the role of the sales force, and has increased the need for advertising and sales promotion techniques.

Adaptation to such conditions brought with it the almost inevitable enhancement of the role of the marketing activity. For instance, marketing as opposed to sales activities might have been grouped under a Marketing Manager responsible to the Sales Director. This organisation structure is shown in Figure 38.3.

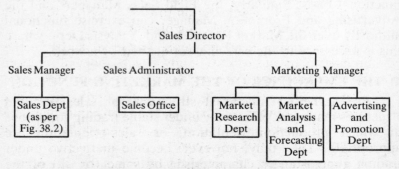

Figure 38.3. Emergent Marketing Function.

Alternatively, corporate decision-makers may have been persuaded to separate the Marketing department from the sales functions, to prevent the latter attempting to strangle the former at birth! This route would have been chosen to allow the marketing function to develop in its own way, free from the direct pressure of the day-to-day sales activity. This structure is shown in Figure 38.4.

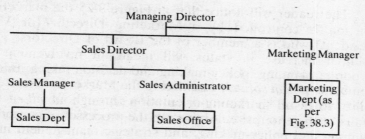

Figure 38.4. Separate Marketing Function

5) MARKETING STRUCTURES

A fully developed functional marketing structure is illustrated in Figure 38.5. Its establishment may follow from a combination of the following circumstances:-

a) a further perceived diminution of the relative organisational role of the day-to-day selling activity, with its short-term focus. This is now particularly a characteristic of companies who supply fast moving consumer goods markets in the UK.

b) an enhanced need for a medium and long term focus on product, market and business development.

c) an enhanced need for sophisticated and accurate market intelligence and segmentation to support NPD, Research and Development, marketing planning (etc).

d) an increasing need for more extensive and effective management and control of advertising, sales promotion, direct marketing (etc).

e) the need to eliminate the rivalry and lack of co-ordination between separate sales and marketing functions that can characterise the emergent marketing function described in section (4) above.

f) a corporate need to establish and consolidate the organisational position of the marketing activity such that the implementation of market orientation can be carried out *with authority throughout the company*. Secondly, to consolidate the position of the marketing function vis a vis other functions and departments (such as production and accounts) with whom co-ordinated and integrated activity is needed to put the marketing concept into operation within the enterprise as a whole.

The reader will notice that in Figure 38.5 the marketing function is controlled by a Marketing Director (or Vice President) who is a member of the Board of Directors. This essential increase in status will mean an involvement in corporate planning, policy-making and decision taking. Board membership is *absolutely essential* to the Marketing Director's ability to instill marketing-orientation throughout *all* of the affairs of the enterprise. Above all, the processes of corporate planning and policy-making, and strategic management must be market-led, if the company is to survive and prosper in the competitive markets of the world.

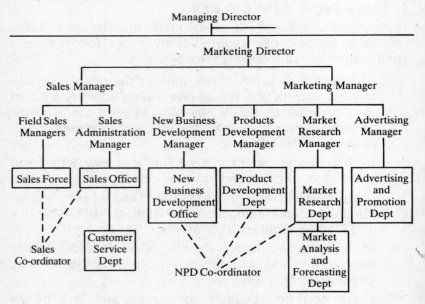

Figure 38.5. Functional Marketing Structure

Figure 38.5 shows a marketing structure organised on a functional basis. The various specialisms are organised on a departmental basis, and each has its own supervisor or manager.

The main advantage of this type of structure is its simplicity. Identifiable divisions of labour can be departmentalised without too much overlap or competition between the various sections. The co-ordination and integration of internal activities takes place, as usual in such functional structures, by means of:

* management roles;
* committees, meetings and other forms of co-ordinative communication;
* co-ordinating roles. For instance, Figure 38.5 shows two such "in-between" roles, namely the Sales Co-ordinator who liaises between Sales Management and Sales Administration; and the NPD Co-ordinator, who liaises between the Market Research Department, the Products Development Manager, and the New Business Development Manager. The organisational basis of such roles is usually based upon the application of functional authority to such co-ordinating roles.

As a result of the development of the kind of structure described in Figure 38.5, and Board membership for the Marketing Director, the marketing function ought to be in a position to instil market orientation throughout the organisation by means of:

i) involvement in marketing and corporate planning, and its implementation through the process of strategic management.

ii) leading and guiding Research and Development policy; directing New Product Development, product specification and design.

iii) determining the content of the marketing mix and co-ordinating those areas which overlap with other functional areas (such as pricing; credit control; manufacturing, production and stock-level planning; customer service policy; (etc))

Ultimately, the corporate role of the marketing function will be to provide marketing intelligence and plans that should act as the cornerstone of the company's total planning and strategic management effort. This issue is dealt with in the final section of this book.

6) PRODUCT-BRAND BASED STRUCTURES

The effectiveness of functionally based marketing structures will depend upon two factors, namely:

* the effectiveness of mechanisms of co-ordination;
* the ability of the structure to cope with a variety of products and markets.

Where the company faces a variety of product-markets, it may decide that the difficulties that arise from co-ordination, decision-making and the prioritisation of resource allocation give rise to the need for a more complex (and more expensive) form of marketing structure. This is the *product-brand based structure*. An example of such a structure is illustrated in Figure 38.6.

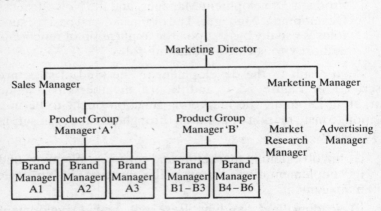

Figure 38.6. Product-Brand based Marketing Structure

The essential features of such structures are that:

* the various products and brands are grouped together in Product and Brand Groups, each of which will have its own manager. There should be some logic or "common thread" which underlies each grouping. This criterion is then used to allocate products and brands, and to balance the relationship between each group;
* activities such as New Product Development, brand policy and new business development (which were shown as separate functional specialisms in Figure 38.5) become the responsibility of Product Group or Brand Managers.

The key to understanding Product-Brand based structures lies in an analysis of the responsibilities of the Product-Brand Manager.

6.1) The Product/Brand Manager

The Product or Brand Manager *acts as the champion of his or her products/brands.* He or she looks after a group or range of products or brands (or just one individual brand), seeking to promote their cause within the total marketing activity, and injecting a degree of *entrepreneurship* at product/brand level. This type of organisation is used where there is a wide range of products/brands, any one of which may receive inadequate attention if it was not the responsibility of an individual person to champion its cause. This allocation of individual and specific product/brand responsibility should minimise the potential for brand neglect.

The Product/Brand Manager plans the strategy for his/her brands, supervises and encourages their development, and recommends the mix to be used for their promotion and sale. This will involve him/her in co-ordinating and integrating the efforts of whatever marketing functions (and other functions in the business) that are needed to develop, promote and sell the brand. In terms of Figure 38.6 this will include market research and market segmentation analysis, advertising and sales effort through the chosen channels of distribution. Each of these activities are the responsibility of other functional managers.

In other words, the Product/Brand Manager acts as a *general manager* for his brands, although his authority is limited to functional responsibility for the product or brand. In other words, the Product/Brand Manager's responsibilities *cross organisational lines,* and depend upon co-ordinative and inter-departmental relationships. This has the inevitable result that Product/Brand Managers *compete for resources and the available time* of functional specialists in market research, advertising, sales (etc). They have no direct line authority over these functional specialists, any more than they do over engineers, technologists (etc) involved in New Product Development activities relevant to their brand or product group. Nevertheless, the success of the Product or Brand management process depends upon these functional specialists, and on how the Brand Managers can maintain and operate the organisational and personal relationships with them.

As a result, Product-Brand based marketing structures can generate friction or even conflict between product groups or brands. Each may be vying with the others for resources and the available time of functional specialists in market analysis, product development, or sales (etc). These functional specialists will be supposed to respond equally and without favour to all product/brand needs, *within the time and resources available.* Yet each functional specialist will have his or her own priorities and objectives to work to, and each may come to establish individual, unofficial or unpredictable preferences (or personal relationships) which tend to favour one brand as compared with another, or one Brand Manager rather than another.

Product-Brand structures therefore raise the thorny organisational problem of *the definition of responsibility and authority.* To what extent can Brand Managers be held responsible for brand success when they possess limited authority over those functional specialists who implement brand plans and mixes?

Certainly, successful Product Group or Brand management would seem to depend upon:

* a clear definition of the organisational and managerial role and responsibilities involved in the job; relative to other functional managers and specialists within the marketing department (and outside it);

* agreement of other marketing and management functionaries to this definition;

* the build up of *expertise* within the Product/Brand management area. Expertise builds up the likelihood of successful product or brand management. This in turn reinforces the organisational position of the brand management role and increases the level of authority and prestige attaching to it.

* the build up of *interpersonal skills,* without which an individual working in a co-ordinative and inter-departmental role will find it difficult to achieve the objectives set.

7) MATRIX STRUCTURES

A matrix marketing structure is illustrated in Figure 38.7, based upon a hypothetical manufacturer of lubricants.

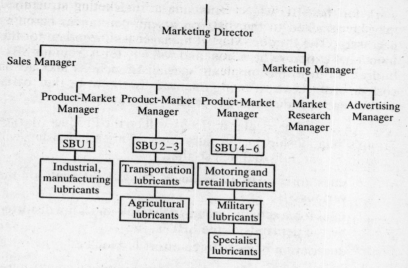

Figure 38.7. Matrix Structure.

This structure retains certain features of the previous types, including separate sales, market research and advertising functions. What is new is the designation of Product-Market Managers *for specific business areas* (not simply for products or brands as in section (6) above). These business areas are based upon STRATEGIC BUSINESS UNITS (SBU's), which are based upon specific market segments and products positioned thereupon. In Figure 38.7, these hypothetical SBU's are:

SBU 1 – Industrial and manufacturing lubricants.
SBU 2 – Transportation lubricants.
SBU 3 – Agricultural lubricants.
SBU 4 – Motoring and retail lubricants.
SBU 5 – Military lubricants.
SBU 6 – Specialist lubricants.

Each Product-Market Manager will be responsible for:

* SBU marketing strategy;
* Marketing mix policy;
* Business development and innovation;
* New Product Development.

The Product-Market manager *will have full line authority* over these activities. He or she will have access to functional expertise and sales effort, as needed. Functional specialists may work for the SBU whilst remaining in their function, or they may be attached to the SBU on a semi-permanent basis, as necessary. The Product-Market manager will negotiate for the functional expertise he needs, and will pay for it from his SBU budget. In turn, the supplying specialist functions may act as cost or profit centres, being financed by the work they carry out for each product-market group.

An area of particular difficulty will be the Product-Market group's relationship to the sales force. This relationship will have to be carefully defined so that:

* sales force activity achieves the sales targets of the various SBU's;
* sales force activity remains coherent, and is not distorted by the demands of the SBU's;
* duplication of sales force effort is avoided.

Matrix structures represent an organisational compromise as an adaptive form. They give more authority to the Product-Market Manager than to the Product/Brand Manager. But they stop short of *full divisionalisation* based on separate Strategic Business Unit product-markets, which is a comprehensive but more expensive solution to the organisation and management of a variety of inter-related product and marketing activities.

The concept of the Strategic Business Unit is also examined in the final section of this manual.

8) ADDITIONAL ORGANISATIONAL VARIATIONS

The need for additional organisational variations may stem from:

a) *a requirement for regional sub-divisions,* especially within geographically dispersed markets like the USA or Canada, and in international marketing.

b) *a requirement for sub-divisions based upon individual customers,* such as large industrial or government buyers, Ministry of Defence (etc).

In either case, these requirements may be organised and managed on the basis, as appropriate, of:

* sales force sub-divisions;
* establishment of specialist functions;

* the establishment of product or brand groups;
* the establishment of product-market groups or SBU's;
* fully autonomous divisions.

9) CULTURE AND VALUES

The priority and effectiveness of the marketing function within the affairs of the enterprise are dependent upon two things, namely:

* the structure of marketing organisation, described in Sections (2) to (8) above; and

* the *culture and values* of the organisation, which are briefly discussed in this Section.

The structure of the marketing organisation will provide an appropriate *framework* within which the marketing function can achieve its objectives, whilst the culture and values of the organisation will determine the degree to which the marketing concept, or *customer-orientation* pervades the whole of its activities.

Where the enterprise has been successful in espousing the marketing concept, it will visibly become customer-oriented in its outlook and behaviour. The importance of being *close to the customer* has been emphasised by Tom Peters and others in a series of recent books, a brief comment on which can be used to discuss the importance of organisation culture and values to organising for marketing management.

9.1) 'In Search of Excellence' (Tom Peters and Robert Waterman 1982)

Peters and Waterman suggest that companies who consciously pursue *excellence* place a high value on being "close to their customers", and are "unfailingly externally focussed." Implementing the marketing concept means paying close attention to the market, and *listening to customers*. From such closeness to the customer, for instance, may come major product or service innovations. Peters and Waterman's sample of "excellent companies" go to great pains to understand customer needs, to innovate in response to these needs, and where possible to involve potential users in the New Product Development process. In particular, the "best listeners" pay special attention to those customers who are the leaders in their own field. The leading edge user (not the average customer) may be years ahead, whether in terms of technology or operating systems. Learning from such customers may give competitive advantage as the experience gained diffuses down into the more mundane markets served by the company.

Listening to customers also means that the excellent companies described by Peters and Waterman *are good at segmenting their market*. Their capacity to differentiate and categorise customers then results in an ability to *fine tune*:

* problem solving activities carried out for customers;
* the provision of technical, operational or business advice and solutions in response to customer requirements;
* product and service differentiation and positioning;
* pricing skills, thereby enhancing company profitability.

This skill in market segmentation and product/service differentiation and positioning is then reinforced by a commitment to provide high levels of *customer service and quality*. The sample of excellent companies define themselves as SERVICE BUSINESSES. Senior management is actively involved in promoting and encouraging a high quality of customer service. This process is termed "service statesmanship" and derives from a company culture and philosophy that views the achievement of excellence of service and quality as the prime objective of the business (and from which "profitability naturally follows").

At the same time, there will be effective operational mechanisms of measurement and feedback, whose role is to monitor, control, reinforce and give incentive to the people within the organisation whose job it is to put quality and customer service into practice, in the marketplace. Peters and Waterman suggest that *a strong sense (or value) of involvement, personal responsibility and accountability amongst ordinary employees is critical to the achievement of company objectives for quality and customer service*. Objectives for profit, whilst important, are internally focussed and do not inspire most ordinary employees. Objectives for quality and service, on the other hand, can be made meaningful to most people. *Indeed, Peters and Waterman conclude that those companies that emphasise innovation, quality and customer service have chosen the most effective source from which to generate excitement and interest on the part of the average employee. And excitement, interest and a commitment to quality and customer service that run throughout the organisation are hallmarks of a company that takes seriously the implementation of the marketing concept.*

9.2) 'A Passion for Excellence' (Tom Peters and Nancy Austin 1985)

Peters and Austin develop some of the themes first published in Peters and Waterman's "In Search of Excellence". They suggest that whether in big business or small there are two main ways of creating and sustaining superior market and operational performance. These are:

* take exceptional care of customers via superior service and superior quality of product or service offered; and
* constantly innovate.

The achievement of effective customer care and innovation will in turn depend upon a corporate philosophy *that listens to, trusts and respects the dignity and creative potential of every person within the organisation.* People are the means by which customer care may be made successful (or ineffective), and people are the source of ideas and innovation.

Peters and Austin then propose a basic model by which the marketing concept may be implemented. It comprises care of customers, constant innovation, and "switched on" employees, distributors, agents (etc). And the element that links each of these is *leadership.* Leadership within the organisation should show a breadth of vision, encourage and motivate staff, develop others, and exhibit trust and respect. That is, leaders should act as a force for change and progress.

Corporate leadership should at the same time be externally focussed, and remain adaptive and sensitive to market and environment alike. This means that people at all levels in the organisation should spend time listening to, empathizing and staying in touch with customers, distributors and innovators alike.

Peters and Austin's excellence model is illustrated in Figure 38.8.

Figure 38.8
Peters and Austin's excellence model

9.3) 'Thriving on Chaos' (Tom Peters 1987)

Within the continuing theme of implementing the marketing concept and achieving customer orientation, Tom Peters suggests that contemporary national and international competition will force companies *to create a total responsiveness to customer and market needs*. The organisation and management of the enterprise may in the future need to be based upon a framework of objectives, strategies and asset utilisation illustrated in Figure 38.9.

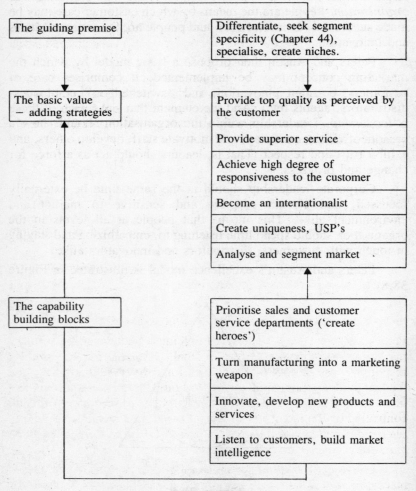

Figure 38.9
Creating total customer responsiveness

564

Whilst a number of issues involved in creating total customer responsiveness are dealt with throughout this book, particular emphasis can be placed upon two features:

a) *become an internationalist:*

Peters encapsulates the growing acceptance of the fact that trade has become global. Marketers and managers *need to think globally* about their business and its customers. At the same time, marketers must recognise the contrasting *need to act locally*, and to meet localised needs. There will always be a limit to what such 'global brands' as Pepsi-Cola, Philips or Sony can achieve, and there will always be a market for localised, segment-specific products such as real ale, speciality cars and agricultural vehicles, books, music and industrial equipment.

Becoming an internationalist will require the enterprise to show long term commitment and persistence in building up contacts and credibility within international markets. International marketers must become part of the local scene, and remain that way. Tom Peters suggests the following:

* build local relationships;
* learn the culture;
* specify and position products or services to meet local needs or segment attributes;
* meet other people's quality requirements: don't prejudge them:
* decentralise the organisation and encourage local autonomy.

Many of these issues have already been analysed in Chapters 28 and 29.

b) *turn manufacturing into a marketing weapon:*

Peters suggests that "manufacturing must become a ... primary marketing tool in the firm's arsenal. Quality, maintainability, responsiveness (length of lead times for delivery), flexibility, and the length of the innovation cycle (for both incremental improvement of current products and major new product development) are all controlled by the factory." *Customer orientated manufacturing and operations management are at the heart of the process by which the marketing concept is implemented.*

The use of manufacturing and operations management as a marketing tool is discussed in more detail in Chapter 44 Section (4).

SUMMARY

The contents of this Chapter are summarised in Table 38.8.

TABLE 38.8
Summary : Chapter Thirty Eight

SECTION	MAIN POINTS
1. Marketing organisation	The choice of marketing organisation may depend on: the priority of the marketing function in the affairs of the enterprise; the stage to which the organisation has developed; the importance of the salesforce within the marketing mix; and the size and structure of the organisation.
2. Pre-marketing functional structures	Contain no marketing function, only sales. All other marketing related activities are carried out by other functions.
3. Sales-oriented structures	Are dominated by sales management and the sales force. Some marketing activities will be carried out by non-selling functions. The marketing role will be to provide information input and customer support as a direct input to the selling effort. Marketing is subordinate to sales.
4. The emergence of the marketing function	Adaption to increasingly competitive trading conditions leads to an enhanced organisational role for the marketing function. The marketing function may now equal the position of sales, or be separated from it so that it can develop free of pressure from the sales function.
5. Marketing structures	Contain the full range of marketing activities, with the sales function as a subordinate element. The function should be controlled by a marketing director, and the position of marketing consolidated such that the implementation of market orientation can be

carried out with authority throughout the enterprise. The internal organisation of marketing may be based upon the various functional activities.

6. Product-brand based structures	Are differentiated from simple functional structures in that the various products and brands are grouped together in Product and/or Brand Groups, each of which has its own Product or Brand Manager. This individual is responsible for NPD, brand policy and new business development in his product or brand area.
6.1 The Product/Brand Manager	Acts as the champion of his or her product or brand; plans its strategy; supervises and encourages its development; and co-ordinates the promotional mix. The job is co-ordinative but lacks authority over functional areas (such as advertising or market research), whose resources and time have to be sought in competition with other brand managers. Friction is possible between the various product/brand managers, and so it is important to clarify the responsibility and authority of the role. The product or brand manager, in turn, needs to build up interpersonal skills and expertise to enhance personal authority and brand success.
7. Matrix structures	Contain Product-Market Managers for specific business areas or Strategic Business Units, which are based on market segments and products positioned thereon. The Product-Market Manager has full line authority over marketing strategy and marketing mix, business development and innovation, and NPD. He or she will have access to functional expertise and sales effort, as needed.

8. Additional organisational variations	May stem from (a) a requirement for regional sub-divisions; and (b) a requirement for sub-divisions based on individual customers.
9. Culture and Values	The priority and effectiveness of the marketing function within the affairs of the enterprise are dependent upon (i) the structure of marketing organisation, and (ii) the culture and values of the organisation. The structure of the marketing organisation will provide an appropriate framework within which the marketing function can achieve its objectives, whilst the culture and values of the organisation will determine the degree to which the marketing concept, or 'customer-orientation' pervades the whole of its activities. Where the enterprise has been successful in espousing the marketing concept, it will visibly become customer-oriented in its outlook and behaviour. The importance of customer-orientation has been emphasised by Tom Peters and others in a series of recent books, a brief comment on which is used to discuss the importance of organisational culture and values to organising for marketing management. These studies are (9.1) 'In Seach of Excellence'; (9.2) 'A Passion for Excellence'; (9.3) 'Thriving on Chaos'.

RECOMMENDED READING

Peters T.J. and Waterman R.H. In Search of Excellence Harper and Row

Peters T.J. and Austin N.K. A Passion for Excellence Fontana

Peters T.J. Thriving on Chaos Pan

Goldsmith W. and Clutterbuck D. The Winning Streak Penguin

568

39 Marketing and Information Technology

INTRODUCTION

The purpose of this chapter is to recap, revise and collect together the various Information Technology and information system applications in Marketing, whether these be at a planning or a control level in the organisation. The chapter categorises the main types of IT application, and lists the various detailed applications described throughout this book.

CHAPTER CONTENTS

1) Information Technology applications

2) IT at control level

3) IT at planning level

4) Information Technology applications in marketing

Summary

Chapter Appendix 39 (1) Smart Money Goes Plastic

1) INFORMATION TECHNOLOGY APPLICATIONS

Information Technology (IT) applications are of particular importance to the marketer, whether these applications are based on software run on mainframe computers, minicomputers or personal computers. These applications take a variety of forms, and each is listed and described below.

a) *Data and Transaction Processing:* which is a general term for the processing of information which derives from the various transactions with which the organisation is involved.

b) *Database:* which is the compilation and storage of information. In the past there was usually a close link between *application programs* and *data files*. Each application accessed its own set of data files, and each file was relatively unique. However, some items of similar data resided in a number of different data files, and these items varied in value across these files if each application had a different processing cycle. This meant that there was duplication of stored data, which is not cost-effective; and an inconsistency between stored values, which made the co-ordination and synthesis of a variety of information inputs more difficult.

A preferable method of data storage is the single database, in which only one version of each data item is stored. Each item is related to other data items as required, and applications programs can then "access" the database. Applications programs and data storage are thus separated, and changes or additions can be made to one without affecting the other.

c) *Wordprocessing:* which separates information input from written output, and permits a variety of textual manipulations prior to printing out the final text. The computer based wordprocessor has yielded massive productivity improvements in clerical and secretarial activities, and has made direct mail shots and desk top publishing an economic proposition in a whole range of different marketing situations.

d) *Spreadsheets:* which permit the operator to carry out complex and interrelated calculations speedily and cheaply, for instance for the purposes of sales forecasting or assessing media effectiveness.

e) *Graphics:* which convert information into more easily visually understood graphical form, essential in the *presentation process*.

f) *Telecommunications:* which have made possible the speedy and inexpensive transmission of data over national and international telecommunications networks. IT applications under this heading include:

* Telex and Teletex, which directly transmit and receive typed or wordprocessed information;

* Facsimile transmission (or FAX), which transmits and receives documents which have been photocopied and converted into digital outputs suitable for electronic transmission;

* access to external databases, which permit the user to access large volumes of up-to-date information in external databases such as TELETEXT (Ceefax (BBC) and Oracle (ITV)) and the much larger and specialist VIEWDATA system. A wide variety of specialist external databases are also now available in the business and technological field, many of which are relevant to the marketing activity.

g) *Electronic Funds Transfer at Point of Sale*(EFT – POS): which is a system whereby goods and services may be purchased and paid for by transmitting details of the transaction to the bank accounts of the customer and the retailer without the need for supporting documentation. EFT-POS is a form of electronic clearing system which can accept both credit cards and charge cards. Terminals are installed at retail outlets and magnetically striped plastic cards containing the cardholder's personal identification number (PIN) are used to make purchases. The purchase transaction credits the retailer's account and debits the cardholder's account, using an automated message transmission facility which links the computers of the banks and the various account holders.

2) IT AT CONTROL LEVEL

Information Technology applications are relevant at the *operational and control level* in marketing, for instance:

* speeding up transactions involving the customer and customer response, thereby improving the level of customer service and increasing company cash flow;

* making possible frequent mail shots and customer communications, using mailing lists and wordprocessor/ desk top publishing facilities;

* speeding up and making more comprehensive such standard, recurring administrative activities and decision-making as the preparation and dissemination of sales progress summaries, sales mix variance reports, and limitations on supply to customers with excessive outstanding debts;

* facilitating the more effective use of Budgetary Control, the identification of variances from target, and the use of Management by Exception. Appropriate, adequate and relevant information flows are essential to the monitoring and control of the marketing activity, and of the resources invested in it.

3) IT AT PLANNING LEVEL

Information Technology applications are relevant at the *planning level* in marketing, for instance in supporting decision-making where alternatives can be evaluated and compared, or *sensitivity analysis* ("What if ?" questions) carried out. For example, electronic spreadsheets can be used to carry out sensitivity analysis of the implications of price negotiations and credit terms for the profitability of an order, and its cashflow implications. More sophisticated financial modelling of the relationship between sales forecasts, credit policy and debtor payment rates could be carried out on a mainframe package like DYSMAP to assess the cashflow and working capital implications of strategic marketing plans.

More generally, IT applications in *Decision Support* can use analysis tools and access to database to carry out such inter-related tasks as:

* Search – seeking relevant data or information;
* Assimilation – seeking relationships amongst data, re-ordering facts and making patterns;
* Calculation – processing and re-calculation of information;
* Analysis – examining and analysing constituent elements of information, problem or decision;
* Synthesis – putting together constituent elements so as to make up a whole construct in answer to a problem or decision requirement.

4) INFORMATION TECHNOLOGY APPLICATIONS IN MARKETING

This section lists and recaps the various IT applications described under specific headings throughout this manual. The order in which this list appears approximates to the order of the sections and chapters.

i) *Market research:* the compilation and analysis of market research may be undertaken using specialist software, or general packages like SPSS (Statistical Package for the Social Sciences) and Minitab. Increasing use is being made by multiple retailers and specialist audit agencies of *bar code analysis* derived from electronic checkout and scanning systems located at point of sale (EPOS or Electronic Point of Sale). Some market research agencies are also making increased use of Computer Aided Telephone Interviews (CATI). Telephone respondents are asked questions by the researcher on the basis of a standardised questionnaire specified for whichever CATI package is being used. Answers are keyed in, processed and the results are immediately available once all of the telephone interviews are complete. CATI packages can generate random samples of telephone subscribers, or can instead provide quotas based upon constraints (such as segment characteristic, geodemographic variable, age group (etc)) as specified by the client.

ii) *Sales and market forecasting:* to which may be added sensitivity analysis using probabilities, Discounted Cash Flow (DCF); competitor performance analysis; market trend analysis using spreadsheets, the Systems Dynamics DYSMAP programme, (etc).

iii) *Market segmentation analysis:* for instance using SPSS, or purchased from specialist agencies who use ACORN type computer programs.

iv) *Consumer targeting and market analysis:* using ACORN type programs. Chapter 17 noted that the computer-based linking of large, geographically based databases (of which published census statistics are a key component) with other sets of marketing information has made possible a whole variety of new insights into market patterns and marketing opportunities.

v) *NPD and product planning:* product planning, development and launch can be formulated, monitored and controlled by specialist software, or by standard network analysis programs, based on Critical Path Analysis (CPA).

vi) *Price:* price and financial planning can be carried out on a wide variety of spreadsheet, accounting and modelling programs. Such programs are available for the largest mainframe and the smallest personal computer. Such IT applications make possible sensitivity analysis of price during contractual negotiations; the calculation of cost-volume, profit/contribution relationships; or the analysis of the impact of changing competitor discount policies, (etc).

vii) *Distribution planning:* computer based Operations Research (OR) techniques are widely applied to problems of physical distribution management, customer service level planning, stock control and vehicle routing.

viii) *Direct marketing:* chapters 17 and 27 noted that the massive revival of direct marketing can largely be explained by developments in wordprocessing and printing, database marketing and mailing list availability, accurate consumer targeting (etc). These developments have made possible the revival of direct marketing as a major marketing strategy to counter increasing retailer power, and to offset increases in the cost of advertising media.

ix) *Currency exchange rates:* companies operating in overseas markets will need to calculate and plan for variations in currency exchange rates. The potential impact of such variations will be calculated on a "what if" basis when final prices are being formulated, and price negotiations undertaken. Again, spreadsheets may be useful for this purpose.

x) *Advertising, publicity and promotion:* graphics applications are widely used in creative design and artwork, proposal and story-line presentation, copy-writing (etc). Advertising and Public Relations agencies make use of FAX to send advertising copy, press releases (etc) to both clients and final recipients. Such agencies also use FAX for communication with clients and printers during proof preparation and correction. This speeds up the process by which documents are prepared and finalised, especially when this process takes place on an international basis.

Advertising and Public Relations agencies are also making increasing use of *desk-top publishing* to prepare reports and written presentations. Desk-top publishing combines a variety of wordprocessing and graphics facilities with high quality printed output to produce small to medium sized runs of documentation needed for presentation purposes, which it would otherwise be uneconomic to have printed. Desk-top publishing facilities can also be used to produce professional quality output on a small scale more quickly and flexibly than is possible with full printing technology.

xi) *Analysing the effectiveness of advertising and sales promotion techniques:* most UK advertising media now make use of demographic based **ACORN** type programs to evaluate their effectiveness and to target their own promotional activity more precisely on readership/viewer segments. Press advertising schedules can be analysed by **ACORN** in terms of reach and frequency, whilst a variety of specialist agencies make available market segment data about readership, viewing, listening and purchase patterns in consumer goods markets.

Similarly, specialist agencies like CACI are increasingly making available computer based analysis of sales promotion effectiveness. For instance, how representative of the heaviest users of the brand are respondents to promotional offers? To what extent has a particular promotional campaign been successful in encouraging trial use amongst people who have hitherto not purchased the brand? To what extent do sales promotion campaigns actually enhance brand image, and what is the effect of on-pack price reductions on this image?

xii) *Sales force planning:* specialist programs are available for carrying out sales territory construction, and for planning sales force workload allocation. Alternatively, OR based programs may be used for this purpose. Spreadsheets may also be effective for this purpose if the requisite variables and equations (and their inter-relationship) are known and understood. OR techniques may also be used to evaluate and optimise sales journeys where representatives must achieve pre-set weekly sales call targets.

xiii) *Field sales communication:* direct personal contact with field sales personnel has been made much easier by the introduction of cellular car telephone systems, such as "Cellnet" and "Vodaphone" in the UK. The use of electronic mail is also becoming increasingly important. This will use a network of remote terminals (which are personal computers) in the homes of sales representatives. These remote terminals are linked by telephone line to a central processor, which can be used to transmit to the appropriate representative such information as:

* customer records (from the customer database);
* new prospect details;
* sales analysis and variances;
* visit and appointment schedules, personal diary, bring-forward schedules;
* memos and reports (etc).

In turn, the sales representative can input, store and transmit orders, reports, memos. The advantage of such electronic mail systems is that the timing of despatch and receipt of communication can be arranged to suit both the sales office and the sales representative in the field – freeing the representative from unnecessary contact and communication with an office that may be situated a long way away. Such electronic mail systems also offer a considerable potential for improvements in sales office efficiency and productivity.

xiv)*Evaluating the sales-marketing effort:* IT applications have long been established in the area of performance monitoring and control. They include Budgetary Control and Variance Analysis. Available programs and packages range from simple systems based on spreadsheets to fully-integrated management accounting suites of programs operated on large mainframe computers. Whatever the system, the marketer should look at the form, level of summary and presentation of the information output, so that he or she can be sure that it will be relevant and appropriate to the particular situational and managerial requirement of the enterprise.

xv) *Supplier-retailer interface:* financial service retailers are probably in the best position to use customer data to facilitate sophisticated retail analysis, but computerised customer and transaction data has also opened up new opportunities for many other types of retailer. Transaction data, based upon customer records, credit and charge cards, EFT-POS all link customer details to retail branch. This permits the retailer to see where his customers are coming from, what they buy and how much revenue is being generated from each sector of the store catchment area. Retailers are using census data with increasing sophistication to evaluate site potential, and to target new retail propositions prior to committing themselves to increasingly expensive construction developments. Demographic programmes can be used to give accurate quantification of localised market sizes, and databases detailing the size and distribution of retail competitors can then be used to build an even more complete picture of the retail market place.

The implication for the marketer in the supplying company, especially in f.m.c.g., is that of enhanced retailer control over stock and merchandise policy, and advertising and promotional activities. The retailer may come to insist on advertising and promotion that fits *its* analysis of the market, rather than being based upon the supplier's perceptions.

xvi) *Marketing planning and strategic marketing management:* a wide variety of IT applications, ranging from suites of marketing and strategic planning programs, to spreadsheets and graphics packages for personal computers, can be used in marketing planning and strategic management.

SUMMARY

The contents of this chapter are summarised in Table 39.1.

TABLE 39.1
Summary : Chapter Thirty Nine

SECTION	MAIN POINTS
1. Information Technology applications	IT applications of relevance to the marketer may be based on software run on mainframe or mini computers, or personal computers. The main categories are (a) data and transaction processing, (b) database, (c) word-processing, (d) spreadsheets, (e) graphics, (f) telecommunications, (g) EFT-POS.
2. IT at control level	IT applications are relevant at the operational and control level in marketing eg preparation of frequent and accurate sales control data; making possible frequent mail shots and customer communications.
3. IT at planning level	IT applications are relevant at the planning level in marketing. For instance in Decision Support (where decision alternatives can be evaluated and compared), and Sensitivity Analysis (asking "What if?" questions using spreadsheets (etc)).

4. IT applications in marketing	Include (i) market research, (ii) sales and market forecasting, (iii) market segmentation analysis, (iv) consumer targeting and market analysis, (v) NPD and product planning, (vi) pricing, (vii) distribution planning, (viii) direct marketing, (ix) currency exchange rate conversions, (x) advertising, publicity and promotion, (xi) analysing the effectiveness of advertising and sales promotion techniques, (xii) sales force planning, (xiii) field sales communications, (xiv) evaluating the sales-marketing effort, (xv) supplier-retailer interface; (xvi) marketing planning and strategic marketing management.

Chapter Appendix 39(1)
Smart Money Goes Plastic

In the big borrowing, instant credit (1990's) it is a shock to realise that plastic cards were first introduced over (20) years ago . . . In the past two decades, credit cards have graduated from being a mistrusted novelty to an indispensable payments system for 25 million people. But the next 20 years will see such technologically advanced developments as the inventors of the plastic card never dreamed.

Soon, we will be getting to grips with the *smart card*, meaning a plastic card that is clever.

Its intelligence comes from an integral microchip on the back of the card where existing credit cards have a magnetic stripe. This mini computer can store full details of the customer's bank account, credit limit, past transactions and a security code. Details on the chip will dictate how much you can borrow, or overdraw, or even how many times a week you are permitted to use the card.

In another 20 years' time, the "smart" card, which will combine credit card, debit card and cash card, will be all you need. But remembering your PIN (Personal Identification Number), your only access to your account, will be more crucial than ever.

Whether you believe that society will ever operate totally without small change depends on your attitude to shopping. Those involved in this new technology do not believe that cash could ever become as outdated as bartering. To cater for all tastes, the card being developed to encourage cashless shopping will also be used for withdrawing cash from the popular through-the-wall dispensers.

The technical name for cashless shopping is Electronic Funds Transfer at Point of Sale (EFTPoS). When a customer buys goods with EFTPoS, he hands his debit card to the cashier. Eventually there will be EFTPoS machines at every till, like credit card imprinters now. Either he will tap his PIN into the machine (making sure no-one can see the number) or he will sign a counterfoil.

The cashier then runs the card through a slot at the back of a telephone-type piece of equipment. The machine reads the information on the magnetic stripe, which travels via a central switch in the UK, and authorises acceptance (or not) almost immediately.

The customer has a printed receipt and the whole transaction will take between 10 and 15 seconds. By that time, the goods will have been wrapped and the customer's account debited with the cost, which has been transferred to the shop's account.

There is still debate about customer acceptance of instant debiting when we are used to a three-day cheque clearing delay. While the system is designed to remove funds instantly, banks could impose an artificial 24-hour, or two-day, delay before the money leaves your account.

EFTPoS machines will be used anywhere that handles a lot of cash and cheque sales. The most popular sites will be garages but high street chain stores, supermarkets, department stores, theatres and railway stations will eventually take EFTPoS.

Garages have been at the forefront of plastic card trials and Barclaycard have a national network of Pinpoint petrol pumps in Shell petrol stations from Scotland to Cornwall. The petrol pump is activated by the EFTPoS card, so petrol stations can stay open 24 hours a day, not needing any staff at night.

Buying rail tickets from a machine to avoid the queue is a time-saver which Barclaycard users can already enjoy. Pinpoint machines can be found at railway stations in London at Euston, Paddington, King's Cross, Victoria and Waterloo; and at Birmingham, Cardiff, Manchester Piccadilly, Newcastle, Edinburgh, Leeds and Gatwick.

There are a few pilot EFTPoS schemes already taking place with Midland Bank, National Westminster Bank and the Anglia Building Society. But the immense cost of installing new equipment means that EFTPoS is unlikely to become commonplace for another decade?

The difference in cost between a credit card and EFTPoS card is enormous: a credit card today costs no more than 40p to produce; a 'smart' card could cost between £3 and £6, depending on the size of the order. Showing the advantage of its bulk purchasing, Barclaycard pays about 11p for a Barclaycard, but reckons it will cost £2 for a 'smart' card.

Altogether, the banks would have to replace between 40 million and 50 million existing cards.

As a half-way step to EFTPoS Barclays has launched terminals called PDQ (Process Data Quickly). The system collects the data and authorises the transaction but it does not transfer the funds as an EFTPoS system would. Barclays would like this eventually to form the basis of a national EFTPoS scheme. Already it has taken over the Anglia Building Society's 200 terminals in Northampton.

There are another 300 in places like Brent Cross shopping centre, London's Oxford Street, and the Duty Free Shop at Heathrow's Terminal 4. Barclays will soon have several thousand.

Before too long, customers will have just three different types of cards; the debit card attached to a cheque account for immediate purchases and cash withdrawal; a credit card and, for the wealthier, a gold card. That is a long step from the very first Barclaycard.

(Reproduced with permission from InterCity Magazine)

40 Evaluating the Marketing Effort

INTRODUCTION

This chapter describes and analyses some of the main criteria by which the marketing activity may be appraised and evaluated. The first criteria is that of Unit Measurement. The second and third criteria, namely Contribution analysis and Budgetary Control, derive from Management Accounting. The fourth criterion, accounting ratios, derive from financial accounting. The final evaluation technique is based upon Customer Profitability Analysis.

CHAPTER CONTENTS

1) The evaluation process

2) Units

3) Contribution

4) Budgetary Control
   4.1) Revenue budgets
   4.2) Marketing expense budgets
   4.3) Variance analysis

5) Financial ratios

6) Customer Profitability Analysis

Summary

Recommended Reading

1) THE EVALUATION PROCESS

The evaluation process is one in which actual performance is compared with *desired results*. These desired results are represented by predetermined functional goals, standards and objectives. These goals and objectives derive in turn from corporate strategies and plans, and from the process of *strategic management*. Strategic management is the process by which the enterprise implements the achievement of its corporate strategies within defined time and cost limits.

This process of corporate and functional *comparison and review* is dependent upon the effectiveness of the company's

Management Information System (MIS) in providing information flows that are appropriate, relevant, accurate and timely, so that evaluation can take place and the control activity implemented. The Information Technology implications for MIS were dealt with in the previous chapter. The organisational *control loop* (described in an earlier chapter) requires information feedback for comparison of actual performance with plan and standard, so that variances can be identified and corrected for. Similarly, information feedback within the predetermined exception tolerances is needed so that the limits of Management by Exception (dealing only with significant variances, and merely monitoring the rest) can be operated.

2) UNITS

The actual performance of the sales and marketing function can be evaluated by a comparison with *unit or volume targets*. For instance, did Company X achieve its market share percentage target in volume terms, as expressed in the number of units sold? The nature of these unit/volume targets has received extensive treatment in earlier chapters, and derives from:

* market research;
* market segmentation analysis;
* sales and market forecasting;
* consumer targeting;
* sales force targets;
* (etc).

Unit or volume targets provide the basic quantification for the evaluation process, and are used as the basis of the calculations needed to carry out financial appraisal of the marketing activity.

Financial appraisal of the marketing activity derives from two disciplines, namely:

– management accounting
– financial accounting

Whilst a detailed analysis of marketing evaluation under these two headings is beyond the scope of this book, they provide the structure for the summaries given in the next few sections of this chapter.

3) CONTRIBUTION

Contribution was defined in an earlier chapter as the difference between net sales revenue and the variable costs incurred by that volume of sales, ie:-

CONTRIBUTION = NET SALES REVENUE – VARIABLE COST AT THAT VOLUME

Contribution Margin is the ratio between Contribution and Sales. It expresses the relationship between contribution value and sales value, and may be calculated as a decimal, a fraction or a percentage, ie:-

CONTRIBUTION MARGIN = CONTRIBUTION ÷ SALES

Where a company sells a variety of products within its product mix, or is developing and pricing new products or services, it may appraise the marketing function on the basis of any or all of the following contribution criteria:

a) *achieving break-even:* for instance in selling new products or when establishing and developing new business. Break-even point can be calculated thus:

SALES VALUE AT BREAK EVEN = FIXED COSTS x (NET SALES REVENUE ÷ CONTRIBUTION).
SALES VOLUME AT BREAK EVEN = FIXED COSTS ÷ CONTRIBUTION PER UNIT.

For example, Crump, who is an inventor, has produced a revolutionary new domestic labour-saving device, which he has called a Gigo. With the help of small business consultants at the local Polytechnic he has tested the market and is sure that there will be a satisfactory demand for Gigos. Crump has estimated the costs of producing a single Gigo as:

Direct Material £4
Direct Labour £1

and has in mind a selling price of £10 per unit. The Fixed Costs of running the business are expected to be £10,000 per annum.

Break-even can be calculated in volume terms at:

$$£10,000 ÷ (£10 - (4 + 1)) = 2000 \text{ units}$$

Crump must therefore sell two thousand Gigos in order for his new business to break-even.

b) *maximising contribution:* the marketing function may

be appraised on the basis of a strategy of maximising the absolute level of contribution earned by the company. This criteria may be of particular importance in divisionalised companies, where divisional performance appraisal can be based on the concept of "Residual Income". The objective of the division is to maximise its total annual absolute contribution as a form of Residual Income, having paid to the corporate centre a charge which is proportionate to the cost of capital of the assets invested in the division during that year. All income above this charge is residual, and it is this income (expressed as contribution) which divisional management endeavours to maximise.

c) *maximising contribution relative to target:* where contribution targets have been established, the marketing function will be appraised on the degree to which it has attained, or exceeded the target set. Contribution targets may result from the sales forecasting process, and from the analysis of territory sales potential.

d) *optimising the generation of contribution:*where a company markets a wide range of products, some of which are *value-added* versions of more basic lines, the marketing function may be appraised on its success in optimising the rate at which it generates contribution. For instance, the Krumbell company can supply three varieties of widgets, namely brands A, B and C. The widget cost structure is as follows:

Brand	A	B	C
Price per unit	30	40	50
Variable Cost per unit			
Material	17	20	21
Labour	5	6	11
Selling	3	6	8
Total Variable Cost	25	32	40
Contribution per unit	5	8	10

Whilst all of the three brands generate some contribution, it will be most profitable to maximise sales of brand C, followed by brand B. The relative attractiveness of sales of brands C and B, as compared with brand A, is reflected in the higher sales cost needed to sell the more expensive but more profitable brands.

In other words, the greatest marketing effort should be concentrated on the lines with the highest Contribution Margin, if appraisal is to be based on this particular criterion.

e) *maximising contribution under limiting conditions:* The marketing function may be required to maximise contribution under conditions which contain *operational limitations.* The factor which will determine the rate of generation of contribution will be a limitation on activity imposed by some capacity or operating constraint, such as:

* market limitations;
* processing capacity;
* operating time;
* product characteristics restricting supply;
* (etc).

The objective for the marketing function will therefore be that of obtaining *the highest contribution per unit given the operation of the limiting factor.* For instance, Neasden Ltd sell two products, P and Q, for which prices and costs are given below:

Product	P	Q
Price per unit	10	15
Variable costs	7	9
Contribution	3	6
Contribution Margin	30%	40%

At first glance, Q looks more profitable than P. However, if you knew that the production department had 1,000 hours of capacity available, and that three units of P could be turned out per hour as compared with only one unit of Q per hour, your choice would be to maximise sales of P. This is because it contributes most *per hour,* which is the limiting factor in this case, thus:

	P	Q
Units per hour	3 units	1 unit
Contribution per hour	9	6
Total contribution : 1000 hours	9,000	6,000

Another example is given by the Haddock Company, below.

i) *The Haddock Company*

The Haddock Company can produce three products, namely Uno, Duo and Trio. Given the information below, which mix of products will be the most profitable?

Product	Uno £	Duo £	Trio £
Price per unit	10	30	6
Variable costs	9	15	2
Contribution	1	15	4
Production hours required	1	10	2
Market limitation	None	4000 units	40,000 units

Fixed costs are £180,000 p.a. Production hours available are 200,000.

First step: calculate contribution per production hour:-

	Uno	Duo	Trio
	1÷1	15÷10	4÷2
	= £1	= £1.5	= £2

Second step: decide product mix:-

	HOURS	UNITS
Trio (2 hours x 40,000 units) =	80,000	40,000
Duo (10 hours x 4,000 units) =	40,000	4,000
Uno (1 hour x 80,000 units) =	80,000	80,000
	200,000	

The first choice is Trio (£2 contribution per production hour) and this is made in the market limitation quantity. The second choice is Duo (£1.5 contribution per production hour) and this is also made up to the market limitation quantity. The balance of production hours (200,000 − (80,000 + 40,000)) is used up on making Uno, which has the lowest contribution per production hour.

Third step: calculate net profit of this mix:-

Product	Units	Contribution (£)	Total (£)
Trio	40,000	4	160,000
Duo	4,000	15	60,000
Uno	80,000	1	80,000

Total Contribution	300,000
Less Fixed Costs	180,000
NET PROFIT	120,000

4) BUDGETARY CONTROL

Short and medium term evaluation and appraisal of the sales and marketing activity will be based upon *Budgetary Control*. A Budget was defined in Chapter 7 as "a quantitative and financial plan of the activity to be pursued during the financial year to achieve that year's objectives".

Budgetary Control was defined as "the establishment of budgets which relate the responsibilities of departments and employees to the requirements of plans and policies; and the continuous comparison of actual results with the budgeted targets, so that the latter may be achieved, or amendments made to the objectives upon which they were based". Budgetary Control is shown diagramatically in Figure 40.1.

Budgetary Control employs the managerial concept of *Responsibility Accounting*. Areas of employee responsibility, such as sales or advertising, are used as *control centres* within the organisation. There are two main types of responsibility or control centre, namely:

* cost centres – responsible only for costs;
* profit centres – responsible for costs and revenues.

Given the responsibility of the marketing function for the company's sales revenue, it would be usual to establish marketing as a *profit centre*, whilst individual departments within the function, such as advertising or market research, would be constituted as *cost centres*, responsible only for their expenditure.

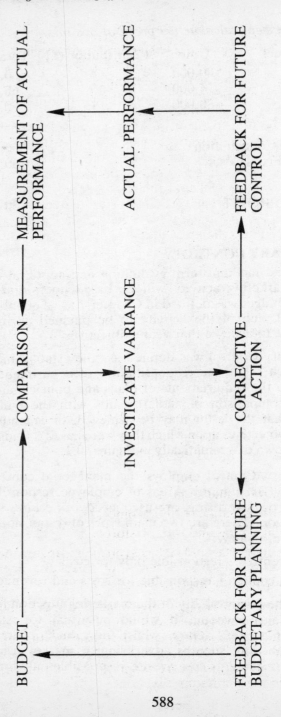

Figure 40.1. Budgetary Control.

4.1) Revenue Budgets

The pivotal role of the sales forecast and the sales budget was described in Chapter 7. In most business enterprises the sales forecast is the factor that determines the scale of activity in the coming period, and other functional and departmental budgets (such as manufacturing, working capital requirements (etc)) will be geared to the sales budget. Some of the factors which determine the budget for sales revenue were described in Chapters 7, 8, 9 (sales and market forecasting); 22,23,24 (pricing); 35, 36, 37 (personal selling and salesforce management). These factors will find their clearest expression when the budget for sales revenue is actually formulated on the basis of *sales force output standards*. Where sales force output standards are used, their calculation will have to take into account the various determinants of demand and sales revenue to be expected in the target market.

4.2) Marketing Expense Budgets

The marketing function may contain a variety of cost centres for which budgets are prepared. In terms of the order in which this book has been written, these could include expense budgets for:

* market research and analysis;
* sales and market forecasting;
* Information Technology and data processing;
* product planning and development;
* product and brand management;
* direct marketing;
* international marketing;
* advertising, publicity and promotion;
* personal selling and the salesforce.

Expense budgets would be based on management and staff costs, expenditure on the services of specialist agencies, materials, travelling, data processing (etc).

Preparation of the budgets for product and brand planning, development and management will often be complex, because of the integrated nature of these activities. Expenditure budgets in Research and Development, Design, Production Engineering (etc) will all be relevant to the setting of NPD budgets within the marketing function.

The budget for the sales force may be calculated upon the basis of *input standards and territory workload*. This was described in an earlier chapter. Whilst commission payments may vary, the costs of personal selling and salesforce management are usually fixed in any one year, since the role of the salesforce within the promotional mix is a major policy decision, not usually changed on the short term. Expenditure for which budgets must be prepared include salaries and payroll costs, vehicles and fuel, training, field communications, materials and subsistence. Separate budgets are likely for sales administration, the sales office, and international selling.

The budget for promotion should be based upon *objective and task*. This was described in an earlier chapter. Given the very large expenditure on advertising and sales promotion in consumer goods markets, the process by which budgets are formulated and expenditure is controlled will provide a major task for marketing management.

4.3) Variance Analysis

Management control within Budgetary Control is based upon the determination and analysis of *variances*. The variation of actual costs from the budget (or *standard cost* where this is applied) is measured and analysed, so that the cause of the variance can be understood. Management action can then be applied to correct these variances, or to change the budget or standard (for instance by using the technique of *flexible budgets,* which *relate cost to activity level achieved* rather than to a predetermined and fixed activity level.)

The application of variance analysis to the marketing function may usefully be illustrated by the example of *sales mix analysis*. The analysis of sales mix achieved can be based upon:

* volume variances;
* mix variances;
* price variances.

In this example, Rainbow Ltd sells two brands of de luxe pens, the Gold and the Silver. Each is sold to retailers in unit size boxes of one dozen pens. The details of budgeted and actual sales performance are shown overleaf:

	Brand	Quantity (units)	Sales Mix (%)	Sales Price (£)	Sales Revenue (£)	Total Revenue (£)
1) *Budget*	Silver	180}	60	72	12,960	
		}300				
	Gold	120}	40	120	14,400	27,360
2) *Actual*	Silver	182}	70	60	10,920	
		}260				
	Gold	78}	30	129	10,062	20,982

Total variance (which in this case is Adverse (A))   6,378(A)

This total variance comprises:

a) *Volume variance*
Actual sales are 40 units below budget (ie 300-260)
Budgeted sales   27,360
Actual volume at budget mix at budget price:
260 x .6 x 72 = 11,232
260 x .4 x 120 = 12,480   23,712
Volume variance   3,648(A)

b) *Mix variance*
Actual volume at actual mix at budget price:
260 x .7 x 72 = 13,104
260 x .3 x 120 = 9,360   22,464
Mix variance is therefore 23,712 ((a) above) – 22,464 = 1,248(A)

c) *Price variance*
Actual mix at actual quantity at actual price   20,982
Actual mix at actual quantity at budget price   22,464
Price variance   1,482(A)

The variances can therefore be summarised as follows:

Volume variance   3,648(A)
Mix variance   1,248(A)
Price variance   1,482(A)
Total variance   6,378(A)

Rainbow Ltd must therefore concentrate on improving its sales volume and sales mix, since volume is below target and the mix is badly down on sales of Gold brand pens. The company also needs to review its pricing policy for the Silver brand, which may be too expensive at £72 per dozen. On the other hand, the positioning and promotion of the Gold brand need re-consideration. Whilst volume is below target the sales price achieved is above budget. Perhaps this pen should be re-positioned on its target market, priced up to, say, £144 per dozen, and more effectively promoted?

5) FINANCIAL RATIOS

The performance of the marketing function within a company can be evaluated by an outside observer by making use of *accounting ratios*. Accounting ratios may be calculated from published company reports and accounts. The interpretation of accounting ratios, and the relative value to be obtained from the exercise depend upon the availability of:

* past trends in these ratios;
* inter-firm comparisons;
* accepted norms or yardsticks by which to judge the results.

The ratios of relevance to marketing fall mainly under the financial accounting headings of:

- *profitability:* which indicates the return being generated by the assets employed;
- *solvency:* which indicates the degree to which the enterprise is liquid, and is able to repay its debts. Solvency ratios also indicate the level of working capital being used to finance the operation of the business;
- *cover:* which indicates the adequacy of profit margins when compared with the desired rate of dividend payment, and with the interest and capital repayments attached to the use of loan finance.

These ratios include:-

a) *sales : capital employed:* which indicates the degree of effectiveness with which management uses its capital employed to generate sales. The greater is the ratio, the more efficient is the enterprise at generating sales turnover. Sometimes called the "turnover ratio". This ratio can be divided up as in (b) and (c) below.

b) *sales : fixed assets:* may be used on a comparative basis to see if too many fixed assets are being used to generate a given level of turnover. Alternatively, a low ratio of sales to fixed assets may indicate that the business is under-capitalised, and over-reliant on current assets (such as short term bank overdrafts and loans).

c) *sales : current assets:* which indicates the level of working capital used to generate sales, and the speed at which the working capital cycle moves.

All of these three ratios will give some indication of how efficient the sales and marketing functions are in achieving sales, for these ratios work in both directions. Good marketing performance may offset the effects of poor asset utilisation; whilst poor marketing can ruin the operations of the most efficient manufacturer, rendering the activity unprofitable.

d) *gross profit : sales:* which, by indicating the gross profit margins obtained from company trading, give a clue to the company's competitiveness and the marketing function's ability to deal effectively with its customers. Gross profit margin trends also give the outside observer an idea about the developing competitiveness of the market generally.

e) *costs : sales:* which gives an indication of the company's operating efficiency and productivity. This ratio will also show up the degree to which the company has either been able to absorb, or to pass on to the customer, increases in raw material costs, wages and salaries, rates and so on. Where the accounts enable the observer to analyse sales and marketing costs as a clearly identifiable item, he or she can plot the developing trend of the relationship between sales and the marketing costs incurred in obtaining them. Again, this will be useful if the information can be compared across a number of companies in the trade.

f) *Return on Capital Employed:* which is calculated as:-

(Profit ÷ Sales x 100)% x (Sales ÷ Capital Employed)

This ratio reveals the return earned on the total capital employed in the business, and includes some of the ratios described in (a) to (e) above. The ROCE formula is a basic indicator of the financial success of the business, and as such will show how effective are the activities of the marketing function in achieving profitable trading results.

g) *sales : stock:* which is the *stock turnover ratio*. This ratio gives some indication of the company's stockholding and customer service policy. It also shows how much working capital is tied up in stock and how successful is the sales and marketing activity in moving the product through from manufacture to the customer. A decline in this ratio (ie a build-up in stock) may indicate:

- a build-up of unsaleable or uncompetitive products;
- declining efficiency of the sales and marketing function;
- high or uncompetitive prices;
- excessive rates of manufacturing output;
- ineffective sales and market forecasting.

h) *debtors : sales:* which indicates the amount of *credit* being given to customers, and the time taken to pay the supplier. Ratios in this area are monitored regularly as they are a crucial factor in maintaining company solvency (as is ratio (g) above). These ratios may take the form of :

debtors : average daily sales
debtors : total credit sales

These ratios will indicate whether indebtedness is increasing or decreasing, and how long on average debtors take to pay their bills. They give a clue to the importance of credit in the marketplace, and to the liberality (or otherwise) of a supplier's credit policy. The determination of a company's credit policy is often a point of conflict between marketers and accountants, since accountants are likely to take a more prudent view of credit sales, and of the company's working capital tied up by such sales.

6) CUSTOMER PROFITABILITY ANALYSIS

The increasing level of competition that characterises many contemporary trading environments is a function, amongst other things, of:

— increasing retailer buying and bargaining power relative to suppliers in consumer goods markets;

— maturing markets, whether consumer or industrial. Mature markets make *the protection of existing segment provision a necessity for business survival.* Whatever market share or segment penetration a company already has it must at least try to hold, protecting this segment provision from (a) existing competitors and (b) new entrants seeking a share of such markets. Mature markets are, by their nature, only likely to show slow growth.

Many suppliers have reacted to this increasing competition by:

(i) giving increased trade discounts on the gross price negotiated with retailers or distributors; and/or

(ii)   increasing the level of customer service offered to buyers or distributors.

By so doing, suppliers hope to maintain or expand the volume and value of business done with that sector or segment.

However, the additional level of discounts offered, the increased volume of business attained, or the enhanced customer service offered may all have the effect of increasing costs, or decreasing margins on sales, or both. *But there is no guarantee that companies will be in a position to calculate this effect.* Some will instead simply resign themselves to a belief that decreasing margins and profitability are the inevitable consequence of trading in such competitive environments. Such a generalised response is based upon the not unreasonable perception that trading 'is becoming more difficult'. One solution to the problems to which this negative perception then gives rise is the use of *Customer Profitability Analysis*.

Customer Profitability Analysis is a technique *by which all revenues and costs attributable to any one customer or distributor are individually and separately analysed.* The technique can be used to manage trading performance at the level of the individual customer. It can be used to confront trading questions such as:

* which customer accounts generate the greatest contribution or profit? Why is this the case?

* which customer accounts generate the least contribution or profit? Why is this the case?

* do the company's largest customer accounts provide adequate margins? Is the volume business they provide justifiable in terms of profit, or contribution to fixed costs?

* what are the maximum discounts/improvements in customer service that the company can afford to offer during the next round of negotiations with these larger customers?

* upon what type of customer should the company's new business development efforts be concentrated?

* does product X yield a contribution sufficient to justify retaining it in the product line, given its current market performance?

* should the company continue to trade in market Y? What would be the strategic consequences for the business of a decision to withdraw from that market?

Customer Profitability Analysis accounts for, and analyses all revenues and costs attributable to the trading relationship with any one customer outlet or market segment. The costs incurred may vary with customer type, level of volume and timescale, and could include:

- handling enquiries and orders; transaction costs
- quality control costs; costs of 'non-conformance' in systems of Total Quality Management (TQM)
- costs of merchandising and sales promotion
- advertising and sales force costs
- costs of inventory management and physical distribution
- financing costs, credit cost
- special purchasing requirements
- cost incurred by special production or operations management requirements

It is not reasonable to assume that these kinds of costs all behave in the same way, irrespective of customer type or size. Each cost needs instead to be analysed in order to identify what aspect of the relationship with the customer it supports, how it varies with the level of activity or volume of business, and how it responds to changes in the nature of customer demand. The potential for cost variations can be illustrated by the following examples:

a) variations in the degree of salesforce and sales office support devoted to individual customer service;

b) more advertising, merchandising and promotional support required by some outlets than others (for instance as in the case of retail grocery multiples in the UK, whose hold over suppliers was described in Chapter 25);

c) variations in packaging requirement and quality;

d) variations in transportation and delivery requirement. Can bulk orders be accumulated and shipped, or are individual consignments called for? Does the customer specify physical distribution facilities and delivery schedules, for example in delivering bulk supplies of fresh produce to retail branch locations?

Customer Profitability Analysis therefore accumulates revenues and costs on the basis of transactions with individual customers or clients. *Each customer is a profit centre.* Each customer has a time-related statement of revenue, cost and profit/loss.

6.1) How is Customer Profitability Analysis achieved?

Customer Profitability Analysis will require:

i) agreed categories of standard costs attributable to servicing customers. These might include the transaction, quality control and other costs described above; or

ii) agreement on the differential allocation per customer of such costs where the actual expenditure cannot be calculated. What would be required in this case will be some agreed scale of apportionment, or a set of rules which approximate the reality of cost behaviour (perhaps based upon past experience or computer modelling);

iii) recording systems capable of allocating actual or agreed expenditures (for instance on advertising or sales promotion) to individual customer accounts;

iv) a Management Information System (MIS) capable of handling this level of information processing, summary and presentation over the time-scale chosen.

6.2) Customer Account Management

Customer account management is a process by which the relationship between the supplier and any one customer or distributor *is individually and separately managed.* The need for customer-specific account management is obvious in the case of large or dominant customers, and is also dealt with elsewhere in this book, for instance in Chapters 22, 23, 24, 29 and 44. But the technique of Customer Profitability Analysis calls for the process to be extended to all customers, whether account-managed individually or in groups with common characteristics.

The customer-specific monitoring of revenues, costs and profitability may then, for instance, permit the enterprise to make customer-specific decisions about:

* the variation and 'accuracy' of pricing of product lines needed to enhance product profitability, especially where distributors are known to use *Direct Product Profitability* assessments and comparisons of the individual lines they hold;

* the degree of fine-tuning of the product mix offered to the customer;

* the potential for manufacturing retailer/distributor own brands where the maintenance of company brands in a particular segment is calculated to be of marginal financial and marketing value;

* the objective and task budgeting *per customer* of promotional

activities, and the evaluation of past promotional activities associated with the account;

* seeking to use customer distribution systems rather than the company's, for instance in delivering in bulk to the customer's national or regional distribution centres, and not delivering individual orders to branches;

* the use of wholesalers or intermediaries to service all customer accounts under a pre-set level of turnover. IBM sell personal computers and office technology this way;

* franchising low value regions on a fixed term, performance-assessed basis to owned venture companies or independent operators who can operate with a lower fixed or overhead cost structure. Such a policy may be preferable to abandoning low contribution activites altogether (which would represent a loss of market share and market presence). The franchisee may indeed be in a position to build up the business where it would be uneconomic for the company to do this.

Customer account management may be used to prioritise customer service decisions using customer account profitability. Similarly, *re-aggregated* information that can be generated may be used to make informed decisions on the strategic priority to the company of different customer segments, and ultimately on whether to get out of certain lines of business altogether.

SUMMARY

The contents of this chapter are summarised in Table 40.2

TABLE : 40.2
Summary : Chapter Forty

SECTION	MAIN POINTS
1. The evaluation process	Is one in which actual performance is compared with desired results. These desired results are represented by pre-determined functional objectives and standards.
2. Units	The actual performance of the marketing function can be evaluated by a comparison with unit or volume targets.
3. Contribution	The actual performance of the marketing function can be appraised

on contribution based criteria such as (a) achieving break-even; (b) maximising contribution; (c) maximising contribution relative to target; (d) optimising the generation of contribution; (e) maximising contribution under limiting conditions.

4. Budgetary control

Short and medium-term appraisal and control of the marketing function will be based on budgetary control. This uses the managerial concept of Responsibility Accounting and identifies responsibility centres on a "cost centre" or a "profit centre" basis. Budgetary control in the marketing function comprises (4.1) revenue budgets; (4.2) marketing expense budgets; (4.3) variance analysis, especially of the sales mix achieved.

5. Financial ratios

The performance of the marketing function within a company can be evaluated by an outside observer by making use of accounting ratios, calculated from published reports and accounts. The most relevant ratios will indicate profitability, solvency and cover. Some ratios include (a) sales to capital employed; (b) sales to fixed assets; (c) sales to current assets; (d) gross profit to sales; (e) costs to sales; (f) return on Capital Employed; (g) sales to stock; (h) debtors to sales.

6. Customer Profitability Analysis

Customer Profitability Analysis is a technique by which all revenues, costs and profits attributable to any one customer or distributor are individually and separately analysed. The technique can be used to manage trading performance at the level of the individual customer, or market segment. It can also be used to prioritise customer service decisions, and to inform strategic decisions on the relative importance of different customer segments.

RECOMMENDED READING

Lucey T.   Management Accounting.   D.P. Publications
Sizer J.   An Insight into Management Accounting.
Penguin Books

41 Marketing and Public Relations

INTRODUCTION

This chapter describes the Public Relations activity, and briefly analyses some of its main functions. Public Relations, or PR, is responsible for creating and maintaining a positive and beneficial "corporate image" within the company's external environment. Given the importance of effective marketing performance and customer satisfaction to a company's external reputation, it is important to provide the reader with at least a brief overview of the relationship between the marketing and Public Relations functions within the organisation.

CHAPTER CONTENTS

1) Public Relations and the external environment

2) Public Relations activities

3) Public Relations, perceptions and corporate image

4) Marketing and Public Relations

Summary

Recommended Reading

1) PUBLIC RELATIONS AND THE EXTERNAL ENVIRONMENT

All business and public organisations have to take account of those elements or forces in their *external environment* that are capable of affecting their operations. These elements or forces may be institutional, economic, political, ethical, sociocultural or technological. They may be represented by organisations, or by influential individuals and groups. Each may be capable of exercising a considerable influence over the policies, practices and procedures of the organisation.

The organisation will have to try to identify and evaluate these elements, and decide how best to react to them. This is usually the role of a company's *Public Relations* function. *The purpose of a Public Relations function is to help the organisation develop and maintain an external climate or environment in which it can prosper best.* Such an external climate will derive from favourable organisation performance and behaviour as seen from *the viewpoint of specific interest groups and the general*

601

public, rather than just the customer. It will be the role and responsibility of the PR function to ensure that this performance and behaviour is publicly acknowledged and appreciated.

2) PUBLIC RELATIONS ACTIVITIES

Specific PR activities include:-

a) *identifying specific interest groups.* These groups are likely to be able to influence the activities of the organisation or the attitude of the wider public towards it. This may involve the PR function in:-

- identifying the objectives of these interest groups (such as investors, consumer or environmental pressure groups, etc), and assessing the resources available to them;
- identifying their attitude towards the organisation, the manner in which they operate, and their capacity to exercise influence over the firm's external environment;
- formulating and implementing PR strategies which may influence these interest groups, thereby creating more favourable public attitudes, offsetting the effect of criticism, or building up a desired *corporate image* in the perception of individual members of these interest groups.

b) *counselling,* which is the provision of advice to the management of an organisation about what is happening in a society or environment. Such advice may also be based upon forecasts or "scenarios" about *what might happen,* and could suggest what the organisation should do if the events predicted by that scenario do actually occur.

c) *product publicity,* which means publicising products and services offered. Such publicity should be integrated with marketing promotional activity, for instance associated with new product development and launch. This kind of publicity means informing both the general and *specific* publics (such as investors, banks, professional institutions, trade associations, chambers of commerce (etc)) about developments and events connected with these products and services.

d) *media relations,* the aim of which is to secure media coverage of newsworthy information, so as to attract public attention to a particular product, service, activity or enterprise. Media relations may also be used to inform, educate and persuade the public, and to correct the effects of *misinformation* that may have arisen in the recent past.

e) *corporate communications,* which are internal and external communications intended to create awareness, understanding and positive attitudes towards the organisation itself. Corporate advertising, for instance, is now widely used in the UK. For example, oil companies such as Shell, Esso and BP have been particularly effective in using it over a long period of years.

f) *lobbying,* which means attempting to dissuade legislators, influential government officials or professional bodies from implementing "undesirable" legislation or regulation and persuading them to promote "favourable" legislation or regulation.

3) PUBLIC RELATIONS, PERCEPTIONS AND CORPORATE IMAGE

Perception is a concept which denotes how a person senses or interprets a situation or experience. The PR function will be responsible for developing a favourable corporate image within the external environment. This image will, in part, be fostered by the process of "perceptual re-organisation", by which inputs to the public's perceptual process are re-ordered or presented in a fashion most favourable to the organisation. Ideally, "good" public perception is that in which a situation or experience is sensed from a favourable or positive viewpoint presented by the company's Public Relations function.

It should also be argued that a business or public organisation normally exists only by public consent, and its continued existence is justified in terms of its contribution as viewed (i) by society as a whole, and (ii) by those people or groups of particular relevance or influence within specific external environments (such as customers and markets, consumer representatives, investors and employees). Both of these categories make demands upon the organisation based upon their expectations of it. Both categories constitute the source of opportunities and constraints. These opportunities and constraints may be economic, legal, social, ethical or political.

The most basic expectation of both general and specific external publics is, however, that the organisation should behave in a *socially responsible* manner. Society's expectations of socially responsible behaviour have changed substantially during this century and there is a greater demand for social responsiveness. This is in part due (i) to better public education, (ii) to a demand for increased information disclosure, and (iii) to changing attitudes to what constitutes acceptable and non-acceptable organisation behaviour.

Public perceptions and expectations therefore provide business and public organisations with a *response problem*. Should they pursue a PR strategy that is limited to *reacting* to environmental or social pressures, once these pressures have become widely accepted? Or should they instead take a more positive or *proactive* stance towards environmental response? If organisations implement a proactive strategy, they may attempt to forecast and pre-empt problems, modify environmental or market expectations, create public standards and generally influence public opinion. In other words, the organisation may choose not to wait until problems occur (or legislation forces the issue) before planning how to deal with at least some of them.

This response problem may in part be solved by the pursuit of a strategy of building up Corporate Image in the mind and perception of the relevant publics. Corporate image may be used to achieve both reactive and proactive PR objectives by:

* building public goodwill in the wider community;
* enhancing public perceptions of consistent social responsibility, and organisational flexibility in response to changing environmental circumstances;
* providing direct benefits within specific external marketing, commercial, financial and technological environments.

4) MARKETING AND PUBLIC RELATIONS

There are a number of ways in which the marketing function can contribute to the development of a more favourable external corporate image, and assist in *reinforcing* the Public Relations activity. The first, and probably the most important, is the creation of market awareness and sensitivity throughout the company, that is, *implementing the marketing concept*. An effective and well managed company which is market-sensitive should create customer satisfaction within its markets. The commercial consequences of this will benefit employees and investors alike, and encourage the development of goodwill within the company's immediate locality. On the other hand, no amount of PR can make up for inept and inadequate performance. Outstanding trading performance and customer loyalty are the keystones for the development of a positive external image. In the UK, companies with such positive images include Marks and Spencer, Sainsburys, BP, Rolls Royce and British Aerospace. Readers may care to think of their own examples of companies with a good public image. Other ways in which marketing can reinforce PR include:

a) *counselling,* which may be informed by wider interpretations of information derived from market research, market forecasting and market analysis. For instance, environmental forecasts may be produced by qualitative forecasting methods described in Chapter (9). Such forecasts may be used in marketing and corporate planning, and in the development of PR strategies.

b) *product publicity,* which ought to be integrated with the normal processes of promotion within the marketing mix. Marketing and PR management should *both* be aware of the PR benefits of NPD, the launch of new products and brands, technological and market "firsts" and so on. For instance, product demonstrations on such television programmes as BBC TV's "Tomorrow's World", "Blue Peter" or "Top Gear" have enormous viewing figures, and can reap large promotional and PR benefits.

c) *media relations,* which again ought to be co-ordinated with media usage within the promotional mix. The enterprise needs to formulate a cohesive media relations strategy with its advertising and PR agencies, and co-ordinate advertising campaigns, news and press releases and media briefing. The media are always seeking good stories; there is much more to be gained by giving them access to news than denying such access. Denial of access to company information, on the other hand, encourages the printing of negative stories and the dissemination of misinformation.

d) *corporate communications* include external communications intended to create awareness, understanding and positive attitudes towards the organisation. The formulation of company policy towards corporate communication should be co-ordinated with marketing promotional policy. By this means any one promotional message can reinforce its corporate counterpart, and vice versa. There is no reason why promotional campaigns cannot build corporate image as well as influence customer attitudes towards products – if *this is what the company wants*. If the company's reputation adds attractiveness to the product or service, then make use of it. If the company's reputation is less certain, keep the company's name well away from the promotional mix, and concentrate on brand reputation instead!

e) *corporate image development,* which may be assisted by the marketing function in such ways as:-

* using market research within the market and commercial environment to gain an understanding of environmental expectations about the company, and to achieve an awareness of the relevant concepts of socially responsible behaviour that are applied by general or specific groups of the public;

* understanding image formation and attitude development by making use of the analysis (given in earlier chapters of this book) of consumer and buyer behaviour, market segmentation, consumer targeting, advertising and personal selling. Each of these subjects may be used to assist the PR function to influence or re-order perceptions within the external environment;

* optimising market and marketing opportunities, which allows the company to communicate its *successes* to its employees and investors, and so build up external confidence. Genuine honesty about mistakes or failure also builds confidence, and offsets the effect of the inevitable bad publicity that is associated with faulty products, disasters, failures and the like;

* using promotional skills (and understanding how best to apply these promotional skills) to make presentations, to disclose information, to publicise successes or communicate failures. It is important that both the marketing function, and its chosen agencies, develop presentational and promotional skills, and pass these on to other functions of the company when they are needed.

f) *competitive advantage,* whilst technology can be purchased or transferred by competitors, and imitative or "me-too" products manufactured, *brand values and corporate identities cannot so easily be imitated or built-up.* Brand identity and corporate image can be used to reinforce each other, building up external perceptions of:-

- the best product in the market from the best supplier or manufacturer;
- quality products or services supplied by a caring company;
- environment − friendly products from a company whose concern for the environment is clearly visible and publicly acknowledged.

Similarly, an *internal image* of quality and service may be built up by communication to, and motivation of managers and employees within the organisation. That may serve to develop a positive internal identity, and build an appropriate customer service orientated culture. This is important, since internal identity and corporate culture affect external perceptions about the quality, reliability, service, value-for-money (QRSV) and level of *customer care* offered by the organisation. These external perceptions have a direct impact on the company's marketing mix (and on its likely effectiveness). In particular they will shape the company's reputation for product quality, the level of service offered, and customer care. To be effective, customer care programmes need to be based on internal perceptions of quality and customer service as important values within the organisation. Otherwise, customer care programmes can become a charade. Bad customer care programmes can backfire, having aroused and then dashed customer expectations that improvements in service are really on the way.

SUMMARY

The contents of this chapter are summarised in Table 41.1.

TABLE 41.1
Summary : Chapter Forty One

SECTION	MAIN POINTS
1. Public Relations	All business and public organisations have to take account of those elements or forces in the external environment that are capable of affecting their operations. The purpose of a Public Relations function is to help the organisation develop and maintain a climate within this environment in which it can best prosper.
2. Public Relations activities	Include (a) identifying specific interest groups likely to be able to influence the activities of the organisation; (b) counselling; (c) product publicity; (d) media relations; (e) corporate communications; (f) lobbying.
3. Public Relations perception and corporate image	Perception is a concept which denotes how a person senses a situation or experience. The PR function may attempt to foster a favourable corporate image by the process of perceptual reorganisation, by which inputs to the perceptual process are re-ordered or presented in a fashion more favourable to the organisation.
4. Marketing and Public Relations	The marketing function can contribute to the creation of a more favourable external environment, and assist in reinforcing the PR activity. The most important method is creating a customer-centred and effective business, which will benefit customers, employees, investors and the local community alike. Additionally, the marketing function can (a) provide information inputs to the counselling

process; (b) integrate product publicity with the promotional mix; (c) co-ordinate media relations with the promotional mix and provide the media with access to positive and honest news/information; (d) reinforce corporate communications; (e) assist in the development of corporate image; (f) yield competitive advantage, for instance from external perceptions about customer service and customer care.

RECOMMENDED READING

Jefkins F.   Public Relations.   Heinemann
Jefkins F.   Public Relations for Marketing Management.
                                                       Macmillan

42 Marketing and Design

"Design is first and foremost an attitude." Roger Tallon

INTRODUCTION

This chapter comments on the importance of design to the marketing activity. Good design has marketing value. Products and services must meet customer needs, they must be functional and serviceable, and their shape and form must appeal to the market. Effective design meets all of these requirements. Even from its earliest days, the process of design has been as much concerned with selling as with specification and manufacture.

CHAPTER CONTENTS

1) Design definitions

2) Design and marketing

3) Design and the marketing mix

4) Design and client-agency relations

Summary

Recommended Reading

Questions for self-review

Examination Questions

1) DESIGN DEFINITIONS

Design gives form, shape and style to an idea or a concept. Each one of us can think of a product that we have seen or purchased, which, as well as being functional, is pleasing to see, own and use. We often prefer one product to another on the grounds of aesthetic quality; in our perceptions it has better design than other similar products.

The subject of design covers a wide range of activities, from materials technology and Computer Aided Design (CAD) at one end, to creative styling and marketing at the other. Design is relevant to products and services in terms of:

* specification;
* structure;

* form;
* shape;
* style;
* pattern;
* colour;
* presentation;
* space and environment.

Design is an integral part of modern industry and the modern economy. Indeed, as a fundamental part of the process which provides us with goods and services, design is a significant component of our contemporary visual, aesthetic and material culture.

Sir Terence Conran has said of design that "everything that man makes is designed, but not everything is well designed. Good design only comes about when things are made with attention both to their functional and their aesthetic qualities. Designers are necessarily concerned with the ordinary, everyday things that we use, but design is by no means a purely utilitarian discipline. Quite the opposite: good design starts from the premise that living is more than just a matter of existing, and that everyday things which are both effective and attractive can raise the quality of life … things designed with commonsense and with style are better than those made without them … and the more things that are designed this way, the better for everyone. Design is more than a particular style, it is an attitude to a product's intrinsic qualities. This is why we react against things which are coarse, bogus or puny, and are drawn to things which have guts, wit and ingenuity."

2) DESIGN AND MARKETING

Sir Terence Conran also notes that "the term design is a modern invention, a product of the machine age: before then the same person who created an object in his mind went on to build it. The great achievements in design of the nineteenth century were civic monuments, the bridges, structures and steamers of Telford, Paxton and Brunel; those of the twentieth century are … more personal … in scale: think of … Ferdinand Porsche's Volkswagen, or the Sony 'Walkman'. In today's mass market every consumer can be a design critic. That gives the consumer the power to affect his or her environment. The more discriminating people become, the more manufacturers will have to realise that merchandise must meet the demands made of it; as a result good design will have to become a fundamental part of any successful business."

Good design, therefore, is an essential component of the marketing mix. Products and services must meet customer needs, they must be functional and serviceable, and their design must appeal to the market. *Good design has marketing value.* It adds value and enhances the total appeal of the product. The better the design, the more the characteristics of the product or service are "augmented". The concept of the augmented product was analysed in the first section of this book. Such product enhancement increases the value for money obtained from the purchase, and makes product differentiation more effective.

Indeed, design competence and creativity is a *distinctive competence,* or distinctive strength possessed by a company within its market environment. Design competence and creativity give competitive advantage within the market place. This is hardly surprising. Customers are bound to favour products which, if competitively or reasonably priced, offer better functional and aesthetic value than their competitors. This is true in both consumer and industrial goods markets. Good design will sell industrial products just as much as it will sell fast moving consumer goods, consumer durables and the like.

3) DESIGN AND THE MARKETING MIX

Design competence and creativity is relevant to every part of the marketing mix, thus:

a) *Product and packaging:* effective design and creativity must be an integral part of the New Product Development process, brand development, and the development of existing products. Product or brand specifications, functional/usage factors and Unique Selling Propositions will take their shape or form in the design process. Design will therefore be a major contributor to the degree to which the product or brand can effectively be differentiated from its competitors. Design features will also give the product or service its visual and psychological impact. Consider the revolutionary shape and styling of the Volkswagen, a car that lasted for three decades and became perhaps the best known of all motor vehicles. Other products known for their shape and style include the Anglepoise desk lamp, the Parker pen, the Boeing 747, the Concorde, Habitat furniture and Laura Ashley clothes.

Design and creativity are also crucial inputs to product stretching. The process of product stretching was described in an earlier chapter as one in which the product's life is prolonged during the later stages of the Product Life Cycle. Functional enhancements and design improvements are the twin ingredients of the process. The results are visible in the case of cars and other consumer durables which have an obvious shape or form. Other products, such as washing machines or Hi Fi's may have visual embellishments put on them to signal that changes have been made, even though the basic form and technology remains the same.

Service activities are ideally suited to periodic re-design. Shops, railway or airport buildings, financial and insurance services (etc) are all ideal candidates for the talents of the designer to refresh and revive customer interest and enthusiasm.

Good design is essential in the development of *packaging*. Packaging must be both functional and visually appealing. Packaging gives full scope to the skill of the designer. The shape of the Coca Cola bottle is universally known; indeed glass is an ideal material for the designer because it is cheap and yet holds a great potential for shape. The Persil packet and the Guinness label are equally well known within the consumer's experience and recognition of packaging.

b) *Promotion:*
Creative design is an essential ingredient in the formulation of advertising campaigns, sales promotion, and the presentation of sales literature and sales aids. Good design reinforces the promotional or sales message, and aids customer recall. The reader should think, for example, of an advertisement which he found particularly memorable. Invariably the impact of such messages is due to creative design and copy.

c) *Place*
The relevance of design to Place has already been mentioned in section (a) above. Spatial and environmental design is important in retailing, and in service activities

such as transportation, banking and insurance, building societies, hotels, institutions of further and higher education and so on. Good spatial and environmental design makes a visit to such service institutions attractive and stimulating. For instance, shopping in the modern galeria or regional shopping centre is a contemporary equivalent to visiting some great cathedral or palace. Shopping in such environments becomes an experience in itself, offering excitement and interest to what would otherwise be a necessary but tedious and unattractive routine.

Similarly, the large architectural scale of motorway service areas, railway stations and airports, banks or hotels (and even stock exchanges and insurance centres like Lloyds in London) give great scope for innovation and creativity in design. Such environments must be functional, but there is no reason why they should not also be exciting and stimulating. Such excitement promotes the business, increases customer interest, and sells goods or services.

Good design is also important on a less grand scale. Point of Sale (POS) promotion was described in an earlier chapter. The three dimensional design characteristics of POS facilities offer the designer the opportunity to involve the customer physically and mentally with the product on offer. The potential customer is attracted to view, touch, pick-up and inspect the product. This often has the effect of moving the customer to the point of the purchase decision. Good POS focusses customer attention upon the product, and away from competing products situated in close proximity. Effective POS facilities:

* must be functional and serviceable;
* must allow access to the product;
* must co-ordinate with the design and shape of product and packaging;
* must co-ordinate with the creative design of brand image and advertising;
* must "fit" the design characteristics and colour schemes of retailer/distributor's premises. The designer of POS facilities needs to ensure that the visual image and impact of these facilities (whether shelf units, free standing units, product demonstrations or whatever) do not clash with the design and colour scheme used by the

retailer or distributor. Ideally, POS facilities should blend with, or complement, the environmental and spatial design features, colour schemes, graphics and logos used by the retailer.

d) *Price:* good design is not cheap design. Allowance must be made for the necessary design requirements within product costing and pricing. As with advertising, design budgets should be based upon "objective and task". What are the design objectives? What design tasks are needed to achieve these objectives, and what will they cost?

4) DESIGN AND CLIENT – AGENCY RELATIONS

Design is a creative and *person-centred* activity. Design competence benefits from the build-up of experience by individuals and teams. *Indeed, design often requires a teamwork effort.* Ideally, therefore, marketing and company management need to organise their relationship with chosen design agencies and consultancies so as to develop and enhance the long-term client-agency teamwork relationship. Design agencies and consultancies are widely used because, in general, individual companies cannot afford to develop and maintain the level of design expertise and capacity available from design specialists. Total reliance on in-house design facilities is something that only the larger companies can contemplate, and even then such facilities are frequently supplemented by the specialist services of outside agencies.

The development of a consistent and long-term relationship between client and agency enhances the agency's understanding of the client's design needs, and allows design expertise and creativity to develop in both client and agency on a teamwork basis. Effective design will result from such a development of mutual experience, understanding and familiarity.

It may be much less desirable to "buy-in" design on an *ad hoc* or job-by-job basis. This reduces the agency's level of understanding of the client's business and his needs, and therefore reduces the agency's scope for creativity, innovation or risk-taking. Yet a clear understanding of the client's business, and a mutual preparedness to take risks may result in a crucial design "break-through", the result of which may be a significant gain in competitive advantage. Examples of such design break-through include the plastic PET bottle for carbonated drinks;

the digital watch in all its forms; the "Walkman" type personal Hi-Fi, and so on.

Ad hoc design briefs are likely to be met with greater caution and less commitment by design agencies. There will be no opportunity to build up a longer-term client-agency teamwork relationship. Yet this would allow a positive and beneficial build-up of experience in refining the objective and specification of design briefs and projects, develop the client's own skill at using design, and increase his understanding of the marketing opportunities it offers.

The problems of using and managing design are amongst the most important marketing justifications for the role of the UK Design Council. The role of this Council is to support, encourage and promote good design. UK readers may have seen or purchased specific products whose good design has been rewarded by a Design Centre Award.

SUMMARY

The contents of this chapter are summarised in Table 42.1.

TABLE 42.1
Summary : Chapter Forty Two

SECTION	MAIN POINTS
1. Design definitions	Design gives form, shape and style to an idea or concept. Design is relevant to products and services in terms of specification, structure, form, shape, style, pattern, colour, presentation, space and environment.
2. Design and marketing	Good design has marketing value. Products and services must meet customer needs, they must be functional and serviceable, and their design must appeal to the market. Good design adds value and enhances the total appeal of the product. Additionally, design competence and creativity is a distinctive competence, or distinctive strength possessed by a company within its market environ-

ment. Design competence and creativity give competitive advantage, whether in consumer or industrial goods markets.

3. Design and the marketing mix

Design competence and creativity is relevant to: (a) product and packaging: NPD, brand development and the development of existing products. Product or brand specifications, functional/usage factors and USPs will take shape and form in the design process, as will the form and visual impact of packaging; (b) promotion: creative design is essential to advertising campaigns, sales promotion, and the presentation of sales literature and sales aids. Good design reinforces the promotional message and aids customer recall; (c) Place: spatial and environmental design is important in retailing, and in service activities such as transportation, financial services, hotels (etc). Design is also important to POS facilities within the retail environment; (d) Price: appropriate allowance must be made for the necessary design requirements within product costing and pricing, preferably on the budgetary basis of "objective and task."

4. Design and client-agency relations

Design competence benefits from the build-up of experience by individuals and teams, both within in-house design departments, and outside agencies where these are used. Companies often draw on the specialist skills of design agencies, and ideally, a consistent and long-term relationship between client and agency should be built up, to the benefit of mutual

| understanding, awareness and teamwork in solving the client's design problems. |

RECOMMENDED READING
Bayley S. (Ed.)   The Conran Directory of Design.
Guild Publishing

QUESTIONS FOR SELF REVIEW
1.   What factors have lead to the development of a fully effective marketing organisation?

2.   Describe and compare the various different types of marketing organisation. What are the advantages and disadvantages of each in terms of marketing management?

3.   Describe and comment on the role of the Product or Brand Manager.

4.   Describe and comment on some of the ways in which Information Technology can be applied to marketing operations and management.

5.   By what criteria may the marketing activity be appraised and evaluated?

6.   How may an analysis of Contribution earned facilitate the appraisal of marketing effectiveness?

7.   What is the relevance of Budgetary Control to marketing operations and management?

8.   What is "corporate image" and why does a company attempt to develop such an image about itself?

9.   What are the objectives of Public Relations (PR) and how are these objectives achieved?

10.   Compare and contrast the objectives of the Public Relations and marketing functions in a business enterprise.

11.   In what ways can the marketing function contribute to the development of a more favourable external corporate image?

12.   What is Design? Why is good design important to the marketing activity?

13.   In what ways is design relevant to marketing strategy and the marketing mix?

EXAMINATION QUESTIONS

Q68   *It is sometimes suggested that the modern marketing department evolved through several stages. Using simple organisation charts trace the nature of, and reasons for, this evolution. (CIM)*

Q69   *State the main objectives for the evaluation of marketing activities. Give examples of two practical evaluation techniques and discuss the strengths and weaknesses of each of them. (CIM)*

Q70   *How do contribution analysis and break-even analysis relate to each other? What use is made of them in Marketing? (CIM)*

Q71   *More and more organisations are beginning to realise the advantages of projecting an appropriate corporate image. What is the objective of establishing a corporate image? (CBSI)*

Q72   *Use examples to show how public relations might be used as an effective marketing tool. (CIM)*

Q73   *It is sometimes suggested that marketing adds to the quality of life. Present a case either supporting or refuting this proposition. (IIM)*

Strategic Marketing Management

"Planning is an activity which involves decisions about ends as well as means ... Planning is a process which has to start at the top ... the first priority has to be given to the strategic goals of the organisation. An organisation that does not know where it is going and how, broadly, it will get there is, to put it mildly, at a considerable disadvantage compared with its competitors!"

(from G A Cole *Management* D.P. Publications)

The penultimate section of this book contains an analysis of selected principles and practices associated with marketing strategy. Chapter 43 looks at the specific problem of volume markets to which the "experience effect" may be relevant. Chapter 44 examines the role of market segmentation in marketing and business planning. Chapter 45 analyses marketing strategy and planning. Chapter 46 takes a brief look at strategies for the marketing of financial services. Chapter 47 analyses 'green marketing', and examines the implications for enterprise product-market strategy of an increasing environmental awareness on the part of the public.

43 Volume Markets and the Experience Effect

INTRODUCTION

This chapter introduces the reader to the subject of *marketing strategy* by looking first at volume markets for commodity-type products, and products which are capable of only a limited degree of product differentiation. Such markets are becoming increasingly characterised by the "Experience Effect", in which volume, cost, price and market share may become inter-related. Application of the Experience Effect shows up problems of market share dominance, and points to the importance in marketing strategy of product differentiation and market segmentation. These are analysed in Chapter 44.

CHAPTER CONTENTS

1) What is the experience effect?

2) Sources of the experience effect

3) The relationship between volume, cost, price and market share

4) Experience curve pricing

5) The experience effect and marketing strategy

Summary

Recommended Reading

1) WHAT IS THE EXPERIENCE EFFECT ?

Experience effect theory begins with the assumption that *increases in the scale* on which an activity is carried out may yield both:

    i) proportionate decreases in the unit cost of production or provision; and

    ii) a build up of EXPERIENCE, whose accumulation will also affect unit cost.

The theory postulates a relationship between the total unit cost, and the volume of units produced, such that (production + marketing + distribution + capital) cost will decrease at a certain rate each time the volume of total output is doubled.

The *rate* at which this unit cost will decrease will decline as volume increases, and may eventually reach a zero value. At this point, cost decreases may be offset by the emergence of diseconomies of scale (especially of an organisational and managerial nature). The theory can be illustrated by a simple example of an *experience curve,* shown in Figure 43.1

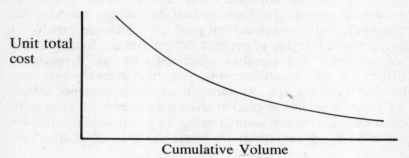

Figure 43.1 An Experience Curve

2) SOURCES OF THE EXPERIENCE EFFECT

There are two sources of the experience effect.

a) *economies of scale:* which will yield proportionate decreases in the unit cost of production or provision as the scale of activity is increased. There are many examples, including:

* increases in the physical size, scale and volume of operation;
* decreases in unit cost obtained from bulk buying – a feature of the retail trade;
* the absorption of Fixed Costs over a greater volume of output, thereby reducing the contribution required from each unit sold to pay for these Fixed Costs.

b) *gains in Value-Added:* which are more than proportionate to the cost incurred in obtaining these gains. They include:

* increases in labour productivity, which result from downward movements on the *learning curve.* The more that an individual carries out the task, the more efficient he or she is likely to become at accomplishing it, and the greater is the productivity that may be achieved;
* resource specialisation, for instance in manufacturing equipment, physical distribution systems (etc);

* new operational processes and improved methods. For instance, the introduction of the "Chorleywood" process permitted the large-scale baking of bread on a continuous flow basis, speeding up the manufacturing process and ending the need to leave large quantities of dough (working capital) waiting to prove and rise.
* product and process standardisation, the effects of which are widely visible in car manufacture, where many parts are standardised and interchangeable between models and ranges, and even between different manufacturers.
* substitution in the product, whereby cheaper but equally effective materials or processes are used to replace more expensive ones. Why use a bolt to secure a nut when a spring clip or a self-tapping screw will perform equally as well?
* product redesign, yielding cost decreases or value-added gains. Compare the modern electronic typewriter or wordprocessor with the complex and heavy electro-mechanical electric typewriters of a decade ago. The electro-mechanical typewriter had reached its ultimate point of development, and was expensive to purchase and maintain. Technological changes have increased the capacity and applications of script preparation, and decreased its cost.

3) THE RELATIONSHIP BETWEEN VOLUME, COST, PRICE AND MARKET SHARE

Experience effect theory is relevant to conditions in which the products being marketed are broadly similar, and cannot be fully differentiated from each other. The most extreme conditions to which it may apply are those in which the products are of a *commodity* nature, and which cannot easily be differentiated. Commodity type products include non-processed foodstuffs; standard foodstuff lines such as bread, tinned vegetables and soup; bulk industrial purchases of paint; steel (etc).

The theory suggests that whichever manufacturer or supplier is able to produce more units than its competitors can, given (i) the similarity between available products, and (ii) any particular level of market demand, become *the market share leader. This is because the supplier with the greatest volume of output is furthest down on the industry's experience curve,* has the lowest cost per unit, and can therefore enjoy a price advantage.

The reasoning can then become cyclical. The greater the supplier's volume of output, the lower the unit cost. The lower the unit cost, the lower can be the price per unit at which the product or service is offered for sale. The lower the price (given the nature of the kind of products with which we are dealing), the larger will be the sales and the greater will be the market share. The greater the market share, the greater the volume of manufacture or supply. And so on.

In theory, at least, the market share leader should be able steadily to increase its market share at the expense of those competitors whose unit costs *of producing a similar product* are higher. This kind of pattern can be illustrated by the following examples;

* the UK bakery industry, which is dominated by two major companies;
* the personal and home computer industry, which is showing the classic pattern of a decreasing number of increasingly dominant manufacturers such as IBM, ICL and Apple; and Sinclair in the home computer market;
* the manufacture and distribution of petrol, diesel fuel, oil (etc), which is carried out by a very small number of very large multi-national companies;
* the supply of fertilisers, agricultural chemicals and feedstuffs, which is again dominated by a very small number of large firms;
* the manufacture and distribution of synthetic fibres, the best known of which are sold under the brand names owned by ICI, Du Pont and Courtauld.

In all of these cases, the products illustrated are of a commodity nature or can only ineffectively be differentiated.

The motor industry provides a variation on this theme. This industry is, again, dominated by a small number of national and multi-national manufacturers based in Europe, the USA and Japan. At the lower end of the market most model ranges are broadly similar and, in those countries like the UK and the USA which permit a high level of import penetration, market competition is severe, and price is an important product attribute. The market becomes less price sensitive the further up-market the prospective purchaser moves, and this is why Japanese importers, subject to quota restrictions, concentrate on selling up-market, differentiated models. Their production volumes are so large, and their unit costs so low, that sales of such up-market models *are highly profitable*. The profits generated are ploughed back into NPD, and new models appear with great regularity. Car buyers like new models, and so the market position of the Japanese manufacturers is reinforced. Giants like Nissan now rival even General Motors in car output, whilst domestic European manufacturers like Renault and Fiat have a difficult commercial path to tread, often relying on government subsidy and protection to maintain market share.

4) EXPERIENCE CURVE PRICING

Under market conditions where the product cannot effectively be differentiated, and competition centres around price, a manufacturer or supplier may follow a strategy of experience curve pricing. In order to maintain or increase market share, the supplier will base his price (and hence profit margin) *on the experience curve costs of the estimated sales volume to be obtained at that chosen market share*.

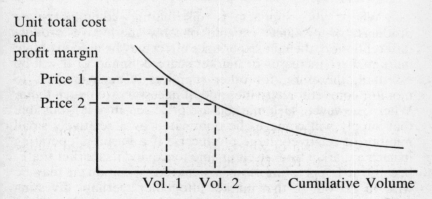

Figure 43.2. Experience Curve Pricing.

For, if it can calculate the experience curve, a company may be in a position to estimate its probable costs at any particular level of sales volume. By reducing his price the supplier will be forced to accept lower profit margins in the short term (because of the lowered prices), but *may* gain a long term increase in market share and profitability. This is shown in figure 43.2. A reduction in price from Price 1 to Price 2 yields an increase in volume (and hence market share) from Vol 1 to Vol 2.

The three classic examples of experience curve pricing usually quoted were to be found in the markets for:

* integrated electronic circuits or "silicon chips";
* electronic calculators;
* electronic digital watches.

In each case, the products are difficult to differentiate, and increases in production volume yielded both economies of scale and gains in value-added. Once into their growth stages these markets grew rapidly in volume, and were characterised by substantial price reductions and the emergence of dominant manufacturers, who came to hold significant market share.

5) THE EXPERIENCE EFFECT AND MARKETING STRATEGY

Where the supplier is distributing commodity-type products, or products capable of only ineffective product differentiation, then the experience effect may be used to obtain market share increases or market share dominance. It will be essential, therefore, for other suppliers in such markets to monitor competitor activities and, if necessary, to match them. Where, however, such markets are price sensitive it is possible that supply will come to be dominated by a relatively small number of relatively large producers. If a business operating in such a market finds itself unable to expand its market share, because it is operating from a weak cost position, it may be wise to get out of that market altogether, perhaps divesting (selling off) its interests to one of the dominant suppliers.

The experience effect is less important in terms of marketing strategy where markets are not strongly price sensitive, and where segmentation and product differentiation are more effective. The roles of segmentation and product differentiation within marketing strategy and business planning are analysed in the next chapter.

SUMMARY

The contents of this chapter are summarised in Table 43.3.

TABLE 43.3
Summary : Chapter Forty Three

SECTION	MAIN POINTS
1. What is the Experience Effect?	Experience effect theory postulates a relationship between total unit cost and the volume of units produced, such that (production + marketing + distribution + capital) cost will decrease at a certain rate each time the volume of total output is doubled.
2. Sources of the Experience Effect	The two sources of the experience effect are (a) economies of scale, and (b) gains in Value-Added.
3. The relationship between volume, cost and market share	Where markets are characterised by commodity – type products capable of only ineffective product differentiation, experience curve theory suggests that whichever manufacturer or supplier is able to produce more units than its competitors may become market share leader. This is because the supplier with the greatest volume of output is furthest down on the industry's experience curve, has the lowest cost per unit, and can enjoy a price advantage.
4. Experience curve pricing	In order to maintain or increase market share, the supplier may base his price on the experience curve costs of the estimated sales volume to be obtained at that chosen market share.
5. The Experience Effect and marketing strategy	Where markets are characterised by commodity-type products, or ineffectively differentiated products, the experience effect may be used to obtain market share increases or market share dominance. Such price-sensitive

markets may come to be dominated by a small number of relatively large suppliers. Suppliers with a weak cost position may be better off by divesting themselves of this particular activity.

RECOMMENDED READING

"Note on the use of experience curves in competitive decision making." Harvard Business School (available from the Case Clearing House of Great Britain and Ireland).

44 Market Segmentation and Business Planning

INTRODUCTION

Market segmentation and customer targeting were analysed in detail in Chapters 16 and 17, but the importance of these concepts has constituted a theme that has run throughout the text. This chapter turns to a consideration of the application of market segmentation to the formulation of business objectives and marketing strategy.

CHAPTER CONTENTS

1) MARKET SEGMENTATION AND BUSINESS PLANNING

The role of market segmentation as a marketing tool was analysed in Chapters 16 and 17. These chapters looked at market segmentation, product positioning and customer targeting. Market segmentation is also, however, an important input to the formulation of marketing strategy. And marketing strategy is a vital component of the total corporate or company-wide process of business planning and policy-making. So it is to the role of market segmentation as a cornerstone of business strategy and planning that this chapter now turns.

2) UNDIFFERENTIATED, DIFFERENTIATED AND SEGMENT-SPECIFIC MARKETING STRATEGIES

The degree to which a company's marketing strategy is determined by market segmentation and customer targeting will be evident from the extent to which that strategy is *"differentiated"*.

2.1) Undifferentiated marketing strategies

Companies that are not market-orientated and especially those that are characterised by production orientation, may not make any great attempt to differentiate their products. They may rely instead for their business success on product or customer familiarity and the length of time for which they have been trading in the market; on customer inertia; on a monopoly position; or on lack of effective competition. Such companies will make what they think they can sell. They may have considerable experience of the market, but the low priority of the marketing function means that a lack of market research and analysis will result in an ineffective (or non-existent) market segmentation input to the business planning activity. And since there will be a lack of market segmentation analysis, products cannot be differentiated and positioned according to specific segment requirements. As a result there are several disadvantages attaching to such an undifferentiated marketing strategy. These include:

* maximising business risk: the success rate is unpredictable since the enterprise has limited its use of market analysis and intelligence in the business planning process. Such strategies may, in part, depend on *luck* for their success;

* maximising NPD risk: ineffective market analysis and product positioning is a major cause of the high rate of new product failure;

* inappropriateness under contemporary market conditions: these conditions are characterised by market fragmentation, increased customer awareness and consumer self-confidence, the availability of greater choice, and increased market competition. Undifferent-

iated and unsegmented marketing strategies may be inappropriate and ineffective under such market conditions;

* volume-commodity business: companies marketing undifferentiated products may be forced into the kind of Experience Effect business conditions described in the previous chapter;

* manufacture for own-brands: companies who have been unable to position effectively differentiated products on clearly identified target segments may be forced to undertake manufacture of retailer own-brands. This contains a high risk of loss of company identity and control.

2.2) Differentiated marketing strategies

The use of differentiated marketing strategies as a means of implementing the marketing concept has been described at various stages throughout this book, and it has been one of the most important themes. Products containing appropriate characteristics or attributes are positioned or targeted upon specific market segments, and are promoted by the means of a segment-specific promotional mix. Differentiation can be achieved both by the characteristics possessed by the product, and by the analysis of the market segment(s) upon which it is to be positioned.

The extent to which this strategy may be carried out is a matter of degree. It will be a matter of judgement for marketing management as to the extent to which the product or service mix must be modified, adjusted or differentiated to meet the demands of the various segments into which the enterprise wishes to trade. The more competitive the conditions, however, the more accurate must be the segmentation and the positioning, and the more carefully selected must be the promotional mix. Ultimately, products or services may have to be marketed on a *segment-specific* basis.

2.3) Segment-specific, "concentrated" or "niche" marketing strategies

Where a company's marketing strategy is segment-specific, it will market one or a limited number of products or services into one or a limited number of segments. This specialised strategy is sometimes described as a *"concentrated"* or *"niche"* marketing strategy. Such a strategy requires the enterprise to be highly sensitive in the degree to which it anticipates and adapts to the requirements of the market segment it serves. And given the reliance or *dependence* of the enterprise on one or a small number of target segments, a company pursuing a segment-specific strategy must always try to be "number one", to minimise the risk attaching to operations of this kind. The greatest strategic risk attaches to a "one product company" selling into one target market segment; hence the need to remain the market leader and most favoured supplier. The issue of segment risk is dealt with in more detail later in this chapter.

3) MARKET SEGMENTS AND COMPANY ASSETS

In establishing company objectives and strategies for products and markets, *the enterprise must also be able to relate the requirements of target customer segments to its operational capacity to fulfil these market needs.* This strategic relationship has two components, namely *asset based marketing* and *capacity planning.* Each is examined in turn.

4) ASSET BASED MARKETING

Business planning must eventually lead to the use of enterprise resources to produce *customer value.* The generation of customer value comes from *the planned and flexible integration of (i) market segment opportunities and (ii) the profile and development of company assets.* For a company must seek to develop its asset structure in such a way as to find the most effective use for these assets within its market context. At the same time, it should aim to put its assets to uses in which the weaknesses of competitors are exploited.

The categories used in describing and evaluating the asset profile or structure include the Balance Sheet items of Fixed Assets and Working Capital, to which should be added:

* research, development and technological capacity;
* marketing, financial and operations management expertise;
* quality, skill training and teamwork of employees and management.

An asset based marketing approach then requires that the enterprise should attempt to plan in four major stages, thus:

i) define and evaluate company assets, analysing their marketing strengths and weaknesses.

ii) identify the marketing strengths and weaknesses of competitor asset profiles.

iii) use existing assets to maximum effect in the target market segments identified by the company's marketing strategy.

iv) adapt the asset profile over time to supply new markets, and to develop new operational strengths.

The maintenance and development of this asset profile may be a strategic requirement that the enterprise feels confident enough to deal with on its own. Or instead it may prefer to operate on a joint basis, so that its asset profile may gain the combined benefit of "joint effect", "critical mass", or "synergy". Joint profiles may for instance, be obtained:

* by acquisition, as in the case of Beecham's purchase and development of formerly under-utilised UK brands such as Ribena or Horlicks;

* by co-operative ventures, however these are formalised. For instance, both the Automobile Association (AA) and Royal Automobile Club (RAC) are highly effective in the direct marketing of a variety of insurance services. They possess large member database assets, and can negotiate preferential terms with insurance companies who, in turn, can minimise the marketing and administration costs of the business they obtain from these motoring organisations.

Whichever method is used to achieve the required asset profile, the business will have clearly to define *what business it is in*. For example, it may choose to shape its asset profile (i) in order to serve those market segments it knows best (its *"core businesses"*); and (ii) to find market opportunities in which it possesses *distinctive advantage*. It may attempt to harness its distinctive advantage and whatever *distinctive competence* it possesses to the process of more clearly defining its objectives for those segments in which it wishes to operate. Such logical and self-imposed constraints contain obvious common sense. The cost and risk of diversifying into activities in which the enterprise currently possesses no distinctive competence or advantage (or must build it), may not be commensurate with the kinds of financial returns that may eventually be obtained.

4.1) Turn manufacturing into a marketing weapon

Reference was made in Chapter 38 (Section 9.3) to Tom Peters' suggestion in '*Thriving on Chaos*' (1987) that 'manufacturing must become a . . . primary marketing tool in the firm's arsenal'. The achievement of customer-orientated manufacturing and operations management was described in Chapter 38 as being at the heart of the process by which the marketing concept is implemented. Tom Peters suggests that decision-makers within the organisation need to recognise that the use of assets and people skills in manufacturing or operations management is the prime source of:

* superior output quality, reliability, or value for money;
* superior customer service and customer care;
* day-to-day product, service, design or process innovation;
* the capacity to respond quickly or flexibly to changing customer or segment needs. This is a key source of competitive advantage in contemporary markets and business development;
* the capacity to reduce manufacturing and delivery lead-times, ultimately making possible flexible operations based upon the principles of *Just In Time* (JIT) manufacturing.

Peters also suggests that it is important to 'get customers into the factory (and) get factory people out to the customers', arguing that 'every production worker should make at least three customer visits per year.'

Such an attitude and approach to manufacturing and operations management aims to increase customer orientation and responsiveness, thereby increasing the degree to which the marketing concept is applied to all aspects of the business. This approach aims to focus (i) the activity and skills of people (designers, engineers, factory floor operatives, production planners and managers), (ii) the application of technology, and (iii) the use of plant and equipment on meeting customer needs, *thereby generating customer value.*

This focused customer orientation may in turn lead to better planning, operation and control of productive assets and operations management. It will emphasise the need to make investments in assets (and to analyse the financial return therefrom) that are exactly appropriate to the needs of the core business. And it should concentrate management attention on reinforcing the competitive advantage that comes from gains in distinctive competence and value-added that the use of these assets, combined with cumulative experience in the business, should confer.

5) CAPACITY PLANNING AND USE

Capacity planning is concerned with *the level of productivity of the assets to be used in serving the chosen market segment opportunities*. The enterprise will have to manage the relationship between the desired standard of segment customer service, and the level of operational productivity that must be maintained. This issue has already been raised in Chapter 26. For instance:

* should a company guarantee the same delivery rate to all customers, irrespective of order size?
* how may the level of customer service be defined as "urgent" and what is to be its permitted effect on the process of production planning?
* what is to determine the speed by which a supplier is to meet a level of segment demand that is significantly above or below the usual call-off rate?
* what happens when the timing of customer service comes into conflict with the direct demands of operational productivity?

The establishment of the marketing and productivity dimension of the asset structure is further complicated by *"system problem characteristics"*. These will influence *the rate, manner and order in which assets may be used*, and their consequences for the level of customer service. System problem characteristics will include the need to maintain a certain speed of the working capital cycle, for instance where large volumes of working capital are required (perhaps to pay large wage or frequent supplier bills, or to cover lengthy production periods). This might inhibit the customer credit content of the marketing mix. Other examples might include the ability to maintain stocks to meet fluctuations in demand (impossible in the case of highly specialised machinery or heavy capital goods), or the time required to reset machinery, make new jigs or design new control electronics.

Ultimately a *trade-off* may have to be established on the basis of a comparison between:

* the additional revenue obtainable from the market segment; and
* the additional variable and fixed costs incurred by the required alteration to a given pattern of operating productivity, for instance see Figure 44.1.

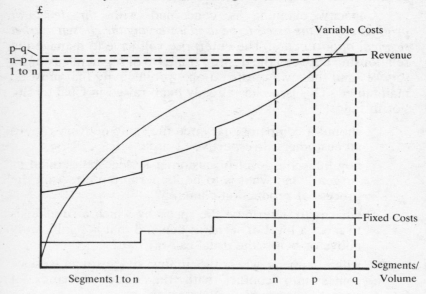

Figure 44.1. Segment Profitability.
(Source: Quarterly Review of Marketing.
Vol. 10 No. 2 Jan 1985).

Augmenting existing customer service (segments 1 to n) with the additional segment n-p would be profitable, even though it resulted in an increase in fixed costs. Adding segment p-q would however not be profitable if the shape of the Variable Cost curve indicated a proportionate decrease in asset productivity brought about by extending marketing activity into segment p-q.

The risk of productivity losses arising from an over-extended segment provision may similarly be shown in Figure 44.2, in the "worsened IRR" (Internal Rate of Return) curve. This would indicate a suboptimal outcome to an expansion of segment provision whose intended objective is shown by the "desired IRR" curve. The net result would be a reduction, rather than an increase, in the number of segments which would yield a Return on the asset profile employed equal to, or greater than the company cost of capital K%.

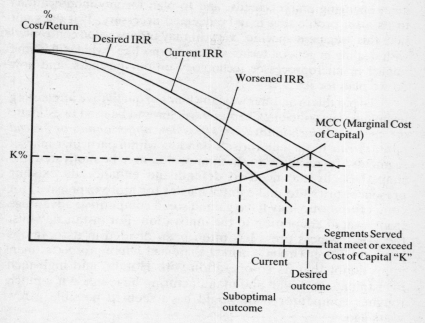

Figure 44.2. Segment Return.
(Source: Quarterly Review of Marketing.
Vol. 10 No. 2. Jan 1985.)

6) SEGMENTATION AND INNOVATION

Segmentation may be used to render more manageable the *commercial pressures that result from technological and market innovation*. When seen from a general viewpoint, the effects of innovation may be confusing, being perceived to lead off in all sorts of different directions. Marketing management must reduce this general perception problem to more specific proportions, so that it does not lose sight of the *probable direct impact of the particular change* in view. Specifically, the effects of innovation should be looked at:

* from the detailed viewpoint of likely changes within existing patterns of segment demand;

* in terms of the emergence of specific new segment opportunities that will result from the innovation.

In both cases, the enterprise will need to examine the likely impact of the innovation on the capacity of its existing assets to meet changing market needs, and to plan for any modifications to its asset profile that may be deemed necessary. If it does not take this "segment-specific" view, it may otherwise be confronted with dealing in general terms with questions like "what will be the impact of microprocessor technology on our business, and how do we plan for it?"

To put this in another way, the kinds of qualitative forecasting techniques described in Chapter 9 will have to be used to estimate *the degree to which innovation offers new opportunities or instead poses threats* to the enterprise's standing within particular market segments. Its response to that innovation may be motivated and shaped (i) by the need to defend and enhance its existing presence; or (ii) to make entry harder (or more expensive) for competitors who may have gained some competitive advantage from a rapid adaptation to the innovation. For instance, whilst the UK business press has often been divided in its opinions about the Rover Group's market share and future prospects, there is no doubt that its co-operation with Honda, and high tech investments in design and manufacturing have made it a much tougher competitor than would have seemed possible a few years ago.

Innovatory pressures also make sensible a periodic review of the enterprise's current segment provision, so as to ensure that there is not too much potential "virgin territory" close to the business which a competitor could use as the base for an eventual attack on the wider segment range. The obvious example is the change in the computer market brought about by microcomputer manufacturers and software houses. These changes were initially ignored by the great mainframe manufacturers, who eventually woke up to the fact that the likes of Apple, Visicalc and Lotus had introduced products for which there was a ready and unsatisfied market demand.

6.1) Innovation and Volume Markets

Volume markets which are characterised by:

* a relatively small number of large market segments; and
* ineffective product or brand differentiation (such as is the case with home computers, toys, household cleaning products, paint and do-it-yourself products); or
* commodity products (such as bread or groceries)

present serious marketing problems. Competition and long term survival in such markets is likely to require *volume operation,* so as to offset the inevitable downward pressure on manufacturer or distributor margins. This point was made in the previous chapter. Such levels of operational volume, further, become indispensable where there are conditions of innovation. *The absolute cost of innovation may only be sustainable if there is a sufficiently large rate of cashflow and profitable sales revenue to pay for it.* The motor industry is often quoted as an example, but the same logic may be seen, for instance, in pharmaceuticals or electronics.

The situation may be made more difficult if these large market segments show *at the same time* (i) expansion, (ii) a requirement for continuous (or increasing) Research and Development expenditures, and (iii) evidence of shortening product life cycles. Quite apart from the likely effect on the enterprise's percentage return on the assets employed to service its chosen market segments, the business is likely to be confronted with a difficult problem of working capital management.

6.2) Innovation and Fragmenting Markets

Fragmentation was described in Chapter 16 as one of the major qualitative changes to have affected markets. Market fragmentation may force companies into using segmentation as a means of innovative response. This response may take the form of the accurate positioning and support of new or updated products or services *against specific segments or niches within this fragmented market.* These products must be exactly appropriate to customer buying and usage requirements within these specific segments. One example is the targeting of relatively low cost and "segment-specific" textbooks and manuals in the student and professional textbook market. Changes in the popularity of academic subjects, the emergence of interdisciplinary approaches, increasing consumer resistance to high textbook prices and the general inappropriateness of many publishers' lists have combined to make an accurate and flexible segment-specific approach a key to the future of textbook publishing.

These segment-specific product ranges need, of course, to "fit" the distinctive competence and strengths of the asset profile (current or planned) of the existing business. And they should be designed to maximise their *position potential* within the target segments. In the case of Rank Hovis McDougall, for example, RHM Foods pursue a strategy in which it attempts to obtain market share leadership in very specific segments where it has developed technological and marketing expertise. These segments include:

* the food processing trade, which, for example, requires crumb coatings for fish fingers, fishcakes, rissoles, chicken portions (etc). RHM coatings are positioned *to supply a series of principal benefits sought within specific manufacturing contexts.*

* housewives seeking combinations of specific principal benefits (such as convenience, economy, traditional flavours, fibre content etc) *within family usage contexts* for foodstuffs such as crispbread, stuffing, gravy powders and tinned mushrooms.

7) SEGMENT PROFITABILITY AND RISK

Business planning for segment provision and investment in operational assets must take into account the *risks* involved relative to the *potential return*. Available market segment opportunities may be ranked according to their relative risk, and plotted against their Return on Investment (ROI) potential, as in Figure 44.3.

Whilst six segment opportunities are shown in Figure 44.3 as being available, only numbers 1 to 5 are acceptable in terms of risk, and number 1 offers an inadequate ROI since it is below the company's minimum acceptable return (or cost of capital) at K%. Justification for continuing to service segment 1 would then have to be found on non-financial grounds, for instance that it was essential to the maintenance of demand in other segments. On financial grounds the strategic choice might be the shaded area a – b – c – d within segments 2 to 5 inclusive, assuming limited resources for investment in operational assets and marketing activities. There are two main reasons for thus limiting the target segments:

a) ideally, segments should be sought that *maximise the scope* (or position potential) on either side of the *centre line*. Such positions allow a maximum sales potential within the segment, and offer the greatest room for manoeuvre when adapting to changes in demand patterns, or technological innovation.

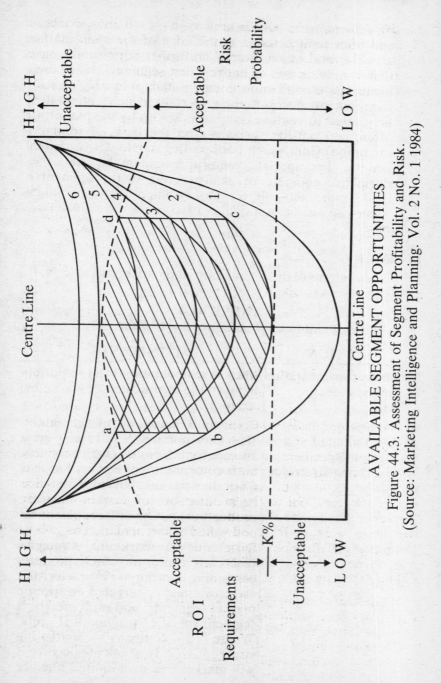

AVAILABLE SEGMENT OPPORTUNITIES

Figure 44.3. Assessment of Segment Profitability and Risk.
(Source: Marketing Intelligence and Planning. Vol. 2 No. 1 1984)

b) segment areas outside area a – b – c – d are specialised and offer limited scope at the edge of the main market area, beyond which there is no further opportunity, save that of moving into an entirely new segment. Hence their higher risk classification, compensated for by a higher ROI requirement. Access to these specialised niches might then be offered to venture companies set up by the parent, or offered to outside specialists on the basis of joint co-operation, from which both parties should derive mutual benefit. The specialist enterprise can make use of its distinctive competence, whilst access to the segment is made more difficult for large competitors who might otherwise use it as a springboard to attack the main market base.

SUMMARY

The contents of this chapter are summarised in Table 44.4.

TABLE 44.4
Summary : Chapter Forty Four

SECTION	MAIN POINTS
1. Market segmentation and business planning	Market segmentation is an important input to the formulation of marketing strategy.
2. Undifferentiated, differentiated and segment-specific marketing strategies	Companies that are not market orientated may not make (2.1) any great attempt to differentiate their products. Such companies will make what they think they can sell, but since there has been little or no market analysis, products cannot be differentiated and positioned on target market segments. Differentiated marketing strategies (2.2) are those in which products containing appropriate characteristics are positioned or targeted on specific market segments, and supported by a segment-specific promotional mix. Where a company's marketing strategy is (2.3) segment-specific, it will market one or a limited number

of products or services into one or a limited number of segments. This is sometimes called a "concentrated" or "niche" marketing strategy.

3. Market segments and company assets

In establishing marketing strategies, the enterprise must be able to relate the requirements of target customer segments to its operational capacity to fulfil these market needs.

4. Asset based marketing

Company strategy must aim to integrate market segment opportunities with the profile and development of company assets. It must develop its asset structure so as to find the most effective use for these assets within its market context. Ideally, the business should aim to turn its manufacturing and operations management into a marketing weapon. The achievement of customer-orientated manufacturing and operations management lie at the heart of the process by which the marketing concept may be implemented throughout the enterprise.

5. Capacity planning and use

Capacity planning is concerned with the level of productivity of the assets to be used in serving the chosen market segments. The enterprise will have to manage the relationship between the desired standard of customer service, and the level of operational productivity that must be maintained.

6. Segmentation and innovation

Market segmentation may be used to render more manageable the commercial pressures that result from technological and market innovation, whether, for example, this is in (6.1) volume markets, or (6.2) fragmenting markets.

7. Segment profitability and risk

Business planning for segment provision and investment in operational assets must take into account the risks involved in that segment, relative to the potential financial return.

45 Marketing Strategy and Planning

INTRODUCTION

This chapter reflects the importance of marketing strategy and planning to company and marketing management. Marketing strategy involves the identification of marketing objectives, the analysis of the marketing environment, the choice between alternative strategies, and the implementation of these strategies. Detailed functional and marketing mix strategies were described in earlier chapters. This chapter puts these strategies into the wider context of marketing and corporate strategy, using the approach of "Strategic Management" as a convenient means of categorising and structuring the analysis.

CHAPTER CONTENTS

Recommended Reading

Chapter Appendix 45(1): Case Study — Babb Foods Plc

1) STRATEGIC MANAGEMENT

The process of *Strategic Management* can be divided into three main components. These are:

i)   strategic analysis (Fig 45.3)

ii)   strategic choice (Fig 45.6)

iii) strategic implementation (Fig 45.7)

The process is one in which the enterprise analyses its market environment, chooses amongst whatever feasible courses of action are open to it, and puts its chosen strategies into operation. The process is completed by the organisational and managerial activities of feedback, control and review. Each of these three components will be examined in turn, within the specific context of *strategic marketing planning and management*.

2) STRATEGIC MARKETING ANALYSIS

Strategic marketing analysis has a number of components or steps, which can be described in the logical order used below. It includes SWOT analysis (strengths, weaknesses, opportunities and threats). The process of strategic analysis is illustrated and summarised in Figure 45.3.

2.1) The marketing audit or strengths/weaknesses analysis

It will be important at an early stage to undertake a major and comprehensive marketing audit, in which the various *marketing strengths and weaknesses* are analysed, and their strategic implications considered. For instance:

* is the company aware of, and utilising the kind of segment and *asset strengths* described in the previous chapter, and what is it doing about its identified weaknesses in segment provision or asset capability?

* does it have specific strengths or weaknesses in the areas of product or brand management, NPD or distribution, (etc); and what are their likely consequences?

From this analysis of strengths or weaknesses it may be possible to construct a *gap analysis* (illustrated in Figure 45.1), which identifies gaps between actual and desired (or target) levels of performance or achievement.

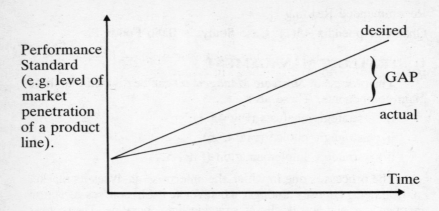

Figure 45.1. Gap analysis

2.2) Competitor analysis

Another important step in strategic marketing analysis (and one that requires continuous activity), is the construction and up-dating of *an evaluation of the strengths and weaknesses of the enterprise's competitors*. This issue was anticipated in the two previous chapters. To what extent, in volume markets, do competitors possess a cost advantage deriving from the Experience Effect? Or instead, to what extent does their possession of some particular competitive advantage or distinctive competence account for their level of penetration and customer service in market segments in which the company itself competes? Does their asset structure and operational capability put them at an advantage, or is this a weakness that can be exploited?

Competitor analysis will lead to the identification of marketing *opportunities and threats* faced by the enterprise. The identification of such opportunities should be followed at the *Strategic Marketing Choice and Decision-Making* stage (Section 3 below) by the establishment of strategies and actions by which these opportunities can be exploited, and defensive or offensive enterprise responses taken towards major threats.

A widely used technique of competitor analysis is the competition model of M E Porter. Porter suggests that market competition is a function of five major variables, namely:

* extent of industry rivalry
* bargaining power of buyers
* bargaining power of suppliers

* threat of new entrants

* threat of substitutes

These five variables are inter-related and can be illustrated by Porter's competition matrix shown in Figure 45.2.

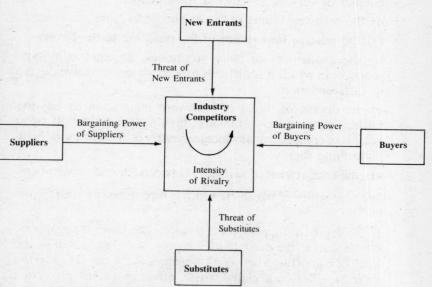

Figure 45.2. M.E. Porter's competition model.

a) *extent of industry rivalry:* which is determined by such factors as:

i) the number of competitors, and the degree of balance (or equality) between their relative market strengths;

ii) the degree or effectiveness of product differentiation. The worst competitive case, that of commodity products, was described in Chapter 43 of this book;

iii) the degree to which operational capacity is "lumpy", that is increased in large increments. The addition of large increments in operational capacity leads to the risk of over-capacity in the market, and excessive price competition;

iv) high exit barriers, causing companies to remain in a market (however unattractive) because of the costs and risk attached to leaving it. Hence the importance of the segment protection policies described in the previous chapter, and the *consolidation* product-market strategy described in Section 3 of this chapter.

b) *bargaining power of buyers:* which is determined by such factors as:

   i) the degree of buyer concentration. Frequent reference has been made in this book to the exercise of "buyer power" in the UK grocery market, which is dominated by a very small number of very large national retail chains;

   ii) the relative volume of buyer purchases, *and*

   iii) the relative importance of the purchase to the buyer;

   iv) the availability of close substitutes, or commodity-type products in which it is difficult to achieve any effective degree of differentiation;

   v) the degree of threat of backward integration by buyers, wishing more closely to control their sources of supply or to achieve a competitive advantage over *their own competitors* by controlling supply;

   vi) the relative *cost of switching* between alternative suppliers.

c) *bargaining power of suppliers:* which is determined by such factors as:

   i) the degree of supplier concentration. The fewer the suppliers, or the scarcer the product they supply, the greater will be the level of competition between companies in the market *to secure their supplies,* especially where effective patent protection renders any attempt at copying an illegal act. Access to secure supplies of necessary inputs may, on occasions, confer significant competitive advantage. This is related *to*

   ii) the relative importance to the buyer/user of the input product being purchased from the supplier. This is also related *to*

   iii) the availability (or otherwise) of close substitutes as inputs;

   iv) the degree of threat of forward integration by suppliers, wishing more closely to control *their own market outlets.* Hence, for instance, the control of UK retail outlets for petrol and diesel fuel by the oil companies that refine them. Forward integration has become a feature of competition in the automotive fuels market, but has affected the traditional owner-operated "garage trade" in the UK as a result.

d) *threat of new entrants*: the degree of competitive threat from new entrants to the market will be determined by *the ease of entry to that market*. This will, in turn, be a function of the relative strength of "barriers to entry", including:

i) the effectiveness of product differentiation and the degree of customer loyalty to brand (as described in the Products and Product Management Section, and Chapter 44) of existing suppliers already in the market;

ii) capacity of would-be entrants to gain access to channels of distribution (described in the Place section of this book);

iii) the capacity of existing competitors to deter new entrants by using entry-deterring prices and price strategies (described in the Pricing section of this book);

iv) the possession by existing competitors of economies of scale, or a pre-eminent position on the industry's Experience Curve, such that they possess an *absolute cost advantage* (as described in Chapters 43 and 44 of this book). This absolute cost advantage may be reinforced *by*

v) the absolute size of capital cost incurred in establishing representation in the market. Given the likely returns on the investment this represents, it may simply not be worthwhile entering the market through such a route. The likely preferred option would be to take-over or merge with an existing supplier in the market;

vi) government policy discouraging further entry to the market, for instance to protect home suppliers from the entry of foreign competitors.

e) *threat of substitutes*: the competitive threat imposed by substitute products or services will be determined by such factors as:

i) the relative profitability (and hence market attractiveness) of existing products/services in the market;

ii) buyer propensity to substitute between products/services on offer; which is related *to*

iii) the relative price (and price-performance perception by customers) of existing and substitute products;

iv) the relative cost and risk involved in switching between the existing and substitute products;

v) the ease with which customers (and existing suppliers) can *identify* substitute products and the nature of the competitive threat they pose. Home entertainment in the form of the video recorder/TV set and pre-recorded video tape libraries, for example, competes with a wide variety of other entertainment services, whether availed of at home or externally.

Porter suggests that the intensity of competition within a market,⁻ and hence the opportunities and threats to which it gives rise, *will depend upon the relative strength and interaction of these five groups of variables*. The effect of this competition may take various forms, *for example*:

* price competition, reducing industry margins and profits;

* non-price competition in mature markets, based upon innovation, New Product Development and product differentiation (discouraging newcomers and decreasing the threat of substitutes); advertising and sales promotion (building brand loyalty and securing representation on retailer shelf space); and "locking-in" the necessary channels of distribution (again discouraging potential entrants) by a web of discounts, credit and preferential financial arrangements;

* mergers and take-overs of existing suppliers to consolidate and strengthen competitive position in the market.

2.3) Market analysis and intelligence

Detailed strategic, tactical and operational market analysis and intelligence will be derived from:

— market research (chapters 4 to 6);

— market segmentation analysis (chapters 16 and 17)

The role of market segmentation in business planning was analysed in Chapter 44.

2.4) Sales and market forecasting

Both *medium to long term*, and *annual* sales and market forecasts provide essential inputs to the process of strategic marketing analysis. Sales and market forecasting were described in Chapters 7 and 8. Specifically, Figure 7.1 illustrates the role of the sales forecast in the annual budgetary planning cycle.

2.5) Environmental analysis

It is important to supplement detailed competitor and market analysis with a wider view of the environment in which the enterprise is operating. For instance, what technological, political, social or cultural developments are likely to have a direct effect on the company's products, markets and customers? Market analysis cannot be separated from the environment in which that market operates, and there are many ways in which marketing strategies can be influenced by broad environmental factors and trends.

This book has described the application of quantitative forecasting techniques (Chapter 8) and qualitative forecasting techniques (Chapter 9) to environmental analysis and forecasting.

Marketing management may find it useful to *categorise* environmental circumstances in terms of criteria that describe *the degree of stability* of that environment. For instance, the business environment may be categorised as being:

* stable;
* moderately dynamic;
* turbulent;
* turbulent with increasing rates of change

The further down this list is the appropriate description that can be applied to the prevailing environment, the greater may be the opportunities and threats facing the enterprise, and the more comprehensive must be the strategic marketing response, for instance in terms of:

- The management of change and innovation
- Research and Development
- Product Life Cycle analysis and New Product Development (NPD)
- Marketing communications, the promotional mix and Public Relations (PR)
- Cashflow and financial management
- Pricing
- Information systems bringing feedback from the market place
- Market orientation of functional strategies for design, production, physical distribution, personnel and training
- Marketing Management Development
- Customer service
- Customer care policies and staff training in customer care

2.6) Corporate strategic analysis

The process of strategic marketing analysis cannot be carried out in isolation from the wider processes of *corporate strategic analysis*. Whilst both types of analysis are inter-dependent, strategic marketing analysis forms the most essential input to corporate strategic analysis. This is why effective strategic marketing analysis is so important in a wider, corporate context.

The process of strategic marketing analysis is illustrated and summarised in Figure 45.3.

2.7) Practical applications

Where readers have to do *case study work* as part of their coursework assessment, or are assessed upon the basis of case study examination, they will find that strategic analysis is an important component of such case study work. They should be prepared to carry out:

* an analysis of internal company strengths and weaknesses, and external opportunities and threats (the "SWOT" analysis);
* market analysis;
* competitor analysis;
* environmental analysis;
* gap analysis;
* an analysis of the inter-relationship of existing or proposed marketing strategies with other corporate or functional strategies.

A short strategic marketing case study is contained in Chapter Appendix 45(1).

3) STRATEGIC MARKETING CHOICE AND DECISION-MAKING

The process by which company and marketing management make choices amongst the various alternative strategies, tactics and activities which may be open to them is a complex one. This section will summarise some of the choices, and describe some of the methods used by which these choices may be identified, categorised and analysed. A more detailed analysis of strategic choice is beyond the scope of this book. The process of strategic marketing choice and decision-making is illustrated and summarised in Figure 45.6.

3.1) Marketing Mission and Objectives

The enterprise must make fundamental decisions about what its *marketing mission* should be. This basic question can only clearly be settled when the company *has decided what business it is in, and how it may best carry on that business*. For instance, a shipping line may define its commercial purpose as that of 'operating cargo ships', or instead as 'offering a door to door international cargo transportation

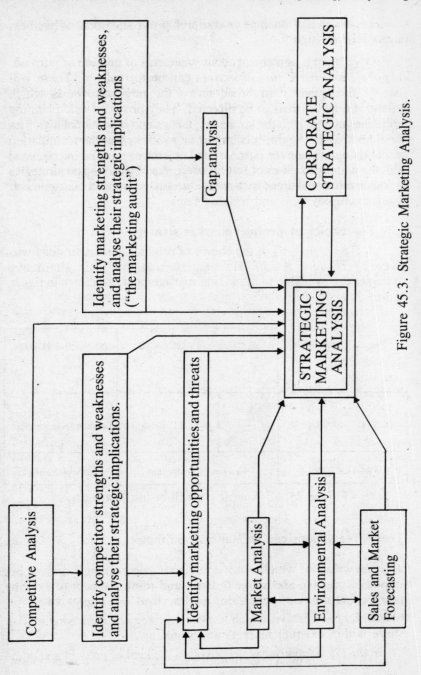

Figure 45.3. Strategic Marketing Analysis.

service', which is a much more comprehensive statement of business purpose or mission.

Once there is agreement about statements of mission or purpose, *corporate and marketing objectives* can be formulated. These will specify and quantify in broad terms the targets towards which organisational effort is to be directed. They provide basic planning guidelines upon which the strategies, tactics and operational activities should be based. Again, it is important to stress that the formulation of marketing mission (or purpose) and objectives must be inter-related with the wider processes of setting corporate objectives and strategies for other functional areas such as production, operations management, finance, employment and training (etc).

3.2) The choice of product-market strategy

A classic analysis of the choice of product-market strategy was given by *H. Igor Ansoff*. He suggests that *five* main alternative strategies are available to marketing management, as shown in figure 45.4.

PRODUCT MARKET	EXISTING PRODUCTS	NEW PRODUCTS
EXISTING MARKETS	*consolidation* Market Penetration	Product Development
NEW MARKETS	Market Development	Diversification

Figure 45.4. Ansoff's product-market matrix

These five options can be summarised thus:-

a) *consolidation*: which is not a negative "do nothing" option, but implies a positive and active defence and reinforcement of existing market and segment provision, as described in Chapter 44.

b) *market penetration*: which implies a strategy of increasing market share within existing markets and segments.

c) *product development*: which involves the kind of product and brand

654

management, and new product development (NPD) described in the Product and Product Management section of this book.

d) *market development*: which could be based upon new market research findings, or on the results of more detailed market segmentation and customer targeting. Or instead, advertising and promotion may be used to develop market demand from existing or latent needs which, up to now, have remained unsatisfied. New markets may also open up for new products derived from technological change and innovation. Market development may take place within either or both national and international contexts.

e) *diversification*: which itself has four alternatives, thus:-

* *horizontal integration*, in which the enterprise expands its activities in a direction similar to its existing strategy. For instance, a clothing retailer may take over or merge with another, similar retailer.

* *concentric diversification*, in which the enterprise diversifies into related activities. A stationery retailer may diversify into newspaper wholesaling. Clearly, these two business activities are closely related.

* *vertical integration*, in which the enterprise diversifies 'backwards' into supply or manufacturing activities necessary for its existing activities, and/or diversifies 'forwards' into further manufacture or distribution of that product.

* *conglomerate diversification*, in which the enterprise diversifies into unrelated activities to which it can apply particular skills, competencies and resources (eg strong marketing or financial management, investment finance etc), thereby gaining distinctive or competitive advantage.

3.3.) Strategic product-market development and management

Once marketing management has made its selection of product-market strategy, for instance by using Ansoff's approach as described above, this product-market strategy must be managed and developed over the planning period in view. This may, for instance, be accomplished by means of the Boston Consulting Group's *market growth-share matrix*, as illustrated in Figure 45.5.

The management and development of strategic product-market activities may be based upon two main variables, namely *market growth rate* and *market share*. This is because the Boston Consulting Group (BCG) correlates success under these two headings with long term company profitability.

655

Once a product-market strategy has been implemented, it becomes a real strategic activity or "Strategic Business Unit" (SBU) (as introduced in Chapter 38 section 7), requiring monitoring, control, management and development. Whatever the actual nature of the particular strategic product-market activity or SBU in view, the Boston Consulting Group suggest that it could find itself *at one of four possible development stages*, depending upon its market share, and the rate of growth of the market. These development stages are:

i) *stars:* which are high growth rate, high market share activities or SBUs. They may be highly profitable (for instance being at an early stage in the Product Life Cycle) but will require large cash inputs to finance their growth. Eventually their growth will slow down, they will become mature and, if they have a high share of what has become a low growth market, they will become 'cash cows'.

ii) *cash cows:* which are low growth, high market share activities whose role is to generate cash to support innovative, technological, market and new product development (NPD) activities taking place within "stars" (described above), or "question marks".

iii) *question marks:* which are low market share activities in high growth rate markets. Question marks will consume finance (supplied by cash cows). Marketing management will have to make judgements based on experience, probability and risk assessment as to whether these question-marks will develop into stars, or instead fail to fulfil their promise. In the latter case they would become "dogs".

iv) *dogs:* these are low share activities in markets characterised by low growth rates. They may generate enough cash to support themselves, but worst of all, they may require financial support from other activities. Dogs may be products situated at an uncertain distance from the end of their life cycle.

The Boston Consulting Group specify *four management strategies* which can be used to achieve, maintain or change the development stages described above. These management strategies are:

a) *build:* which is the strategy whose aim is to develop and improve market position. This implies a willingness to provide the necessary financial resources from wherever these may be available (and in particular from cash cows). This strategy is particularly appropriate for stars (in order to ensure their eventual transition to cash cow status), and question marks (to achieve eventual star status).

b) *hold:* which strategy is designed to preserve the market position of an activity or SBU. This strategy is particularly appropriate for the management of cash cows, so that their capacity to yield large positive cash outflow is prolonged for as long as possible.

c) *harvest:* this strategy aims to achieve the maximum short-term cash flow, regardless of the longer term effect. This strategy is appropriate for a weak cash cow near the end of its life cycle, and may be applied to question marks and dogs where it is thought that these have uncertain future prospects in the market.

d) *divest:* this strategy is based upon selling off business activities and applying the resulting finance elsewhere, for instance in financing the growth of stars or question marks. The strategy will be appropriate to dogs and question marks whose maintenance or growth the company decides to discontinue funding, and for which buyers can be found to whom the activity in question is more appropriate or desirable. Such activities might instead be sold off to their managers and employees, and established as independent specialist or "venture" companies.

Ideally, therefore, the development and management of the company's product-market strategies should concentrate on developing stars and cash cows, so that there is a movement over time concentrated on the upper and lower quadrants of the left hand side of the matrix shown in Figure 45.5.

3.4) Strategic market position

Strategic product-market choice (section 3.2 above) and strategic product-market development and management (section 3.3 above) will require marketing management to make specific decisions about strategic market position. Some examples of these decisions include those concerning:

* market position — is the company to strive for market leadership or dominance: to be a challenger; a follower; or a specialist operating on a concentrated basis in a niche market?
* market share objective — which decision is related to objectives for market position listed above;
* market position in volume or commodity-type markets to which the Experience Effect and the concept of "critical mass" are applicable;

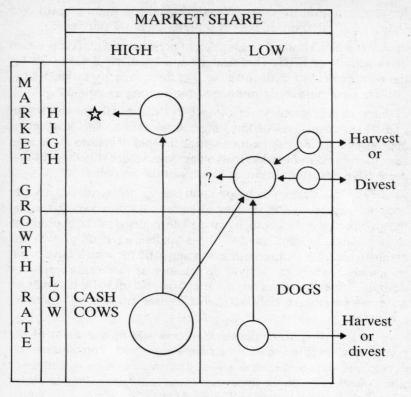

Figure 45.5. The B C G Market Growth-Share Matrix.

* price; quality; level of customer service; search for excellence (etc), as described in previous Chapters.

Once the appropriate decisions have been taken, the company's marketing strategy can then be applied to the formulation of strategies and tactics for the Marketing Mix.

3.5) Marketing Mix strategies

Strategies and operational tactics for the Marketing Mix were described in detail in previous chapters, under Sections entitled Product, Price, Place and Promotion.

3.6) The Test of Consistency

The Test of Consistency is a strategic test which compares:

+ strategic choice, and
+ strategic viability

In other words, are the strategic choices that have been made by marketing management *feasible and achievable*? Can the enterprise *actually put into practice* what it would like to do? What constraints does it face and how will these affect the achievement of its stated objectives? Submitting strategic marketing decisions to the Test of Consistency may, for example, highlight the following issues for resolution:

* the extent to which the company's assets and capacity are *appropriate* to the achievement of marketing objectives (an issue discussed in Chapter 44);
* the extent to which proposed strategies exploit corporate strengths or offset company weaknesses;
* the extent to which marketing strategies need to defend existing provision, and deal with known threats, whether these be competitive or environmental;
* the financial implications of strategic choice and strategic product-market management;
* the organisational implications of strategic choice and strategic product-market management.

The process of strategic choice is illustrated and summarised in Figure 45.6

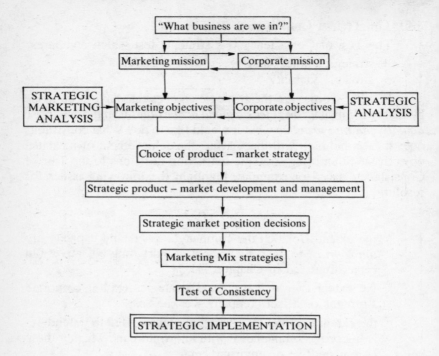

Figure 45.6. Strategic Marketing Choice and Decision-Making.

4) STRATEGIC MARKETING IMPLEMENTATION AND MARKETING PLANNING

The process of strategic marketing implementation and marketing planning is summarised in Figure 45.7. *Each of the components of this process has received detailed consideration in earlier Sections and Chapters.*

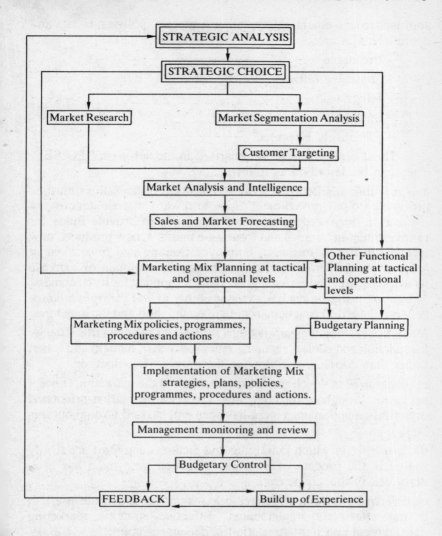

Figure 45.7. Strategic Marketing Planning and Implementation.

4.1) ''Offensive Marketing'': an approach to strategic implementation

Hugh Davidson (see Recommended Reading) suggests that *Offensive Marketing* provides an effective approach to practical strategic marketing implementation. Offensive Marketing takes an approach to implementing marketing strategies, policies, tactics and operations that are:

- Profitable
- Offensive (attacking or pro-active)
- Integrated
- Strategic
- Effectively Executed

These criteria can be summarised in the acronym "POISE". They can be described as follows:

a) *Profitable:* marketing activities in business organisations must be profitable (to pay government taxes, to reward shareholders or pay interest on borrowed funds, and, above all, to provide funds for re-investment in "stars" and "question marks", new products, new technologies, new business, employee training and *investment in people*). At the same time the business must maintain or increase its market share, and provide good value for money for its customers. Marketing management has a responsibility *to find the right balance* between these differing demands, both on the short and the long term.

b) *Offensive:* which means taking a *positive attitude* towards strategy formulation and choice, retaining independence of thought and action rather than copying or following the moves of competitors.

c) *Integrated:* in which market-orientation and the marketing concept permeate throughout the company. The need for market-orientated organisation and management has been emphasised throughout this book.

d) *Strategic:* in which marketing and business activities are firmly rooted in the process of Strategic Management, which has been described in this chapter.

e) *Effectively Executed:* Strategic Management is of little use if it is not effectively implemented. Effective strategic marketing management and implementation is dependent upon:

* coherent marketing strategies and plans;
* an integrated relationship between marketing and other business functions;
* well trained, adaptable and motivated staff;
* teamwork effort in pursuit of agreed objectives;
* organisational capacity to encourage creativity, innovation and change;
* effective financial and resource management.

4.2) Strategic implementation and the work of Tom Peters (et al)

Chapter 38 section 9 described the relevance of *Culture* and *Values* in determining the degree to which the marketing concept and customer orientation will pervade the planning and implementation of strategies and policies by the enterprise as a whole. That section examined the work of Tom Peters (et al) and notes as relevant to this Chapter the importance to marketing planning of:

— being close to the customer;
— effective market analysis and segmentation;
— listening to the customer;
— seeking to innovate;
— defining the mission of the business in terms of *service*, and placing the achievement of high levels of customer service as an operational priority;
— pursuing excellence;
— attempting to involve all levels of staff in Quality, Service, Reliability and Value for Money (Q, S, R, V) programmes, but placing particular emphasis upon *quality* and *customer service*;
— taking an international view;
— effective leadership by marketing management.

Ultimately, Tom Peters suggests that contemporary national and international competition will confront companies with the need to create a total responsiveness to customer and market requirements. *This need lies at the heart of the process of strategic marketing planning and implementation.*

SUMMARY

The contents of this chapter are summarised in Table 45.8.

Table 45.8
Summary: Chapter Forty Five

SUMMARY	MAIN POINTS
1. Strategic Management	Comprises strategic analysis, strategic choice, and strategic implementation.
2. Strategic Marketing Analysis	Summarised in Figure 45.3.
3. Strategic Marketing Choice and Decision Making	Summarised in Figure 45.6. The enterprise must decide what business it is in, and how it may best carry on that business, in order to define its marketing mission and set marketing objectives. Strategies are derived from objectives. Analysis of the alternative product-market strategies available to marketing management may be based on (3.2) Ansoff's Matrix. Strategic product-market development and management may be based on (3.3) the Boston Consulting Group's market growth-share matrix. Chosen marketing strategies must pass (3.6) the Test of Consistency, to indicate their feasibility and viability.
4. Strategic Marketing Implementation and Marketing Planning	Summarised in Figure 45.7. The implementation of marketing strategies and plans may be accomplished on the basis of (4.1) "Offensive Marketing", and (4.2) Culture and Values (the work of Tom Peters et al).

RECOMMENDED READING

Ansoff H. Igor	Corporate Strategy	Penguin Books
Chisnall P.M.	Strategic Industrial Marketing	Prentice Hall International
Davidson Hugh	Offensive Marketing	Penguin Books

| Foxall G.R. | Strategic Management | Croom Helm |

Foxall G.R. Strategic Management Croom Helm
Johnson G. and Scholes K. Exploring Corporate Strategy
Prentice Hall International
McDonald M.H. Marketing Plans Heinemann
Porter M.E. Competitive Strategy Collier Macmillan
Porter M.E. Competitive Advantage Collier Macmillan
Thomas M.J. and Waite N.E. (Editors) The Marketing Digest
Heinemann

CHAPTER APPENDIX 45(1)
CASE STUDY
BABB FOODS plc

Babb Foods plc is a medium sized food processor/manufacturer. It has several factories throughout the UK, each of which is responsible for marketing and distributing its own products. These factories are autonomous units, responsible for their own profit targets and performance, and each maintains its own sales force.

The company manufactures and markets a range of processed and packaged foodstuffs. These include:

* dried vegetable concentrates sold to other food processors;
* dried and preserved fruits;
* cake mixes;
* packet spices and flavourings;
* packet desserts requiring the addition of milk;
* fruit sauces used on meat, fish and cheese dishes. The company's 'Relish' brand of brown sauce is its best known brand (the company uses a variety of brand names for its different products), and is thought by the company to hold at least 10% of the brown sauce market in the UK. 'Relish' also obtains significant overseas sales, particularly in the Commonwealth and the USA.

The company's *branded products* are sold under a wide variety of company brand names. Some carry the name 'Babb Foods' whilst others carry the name of the manufacturing division from which the product derives. The company also manufactures *own brands* for wholesalers and retailers. The company's products are sold and distributed through the following channels:

* wholesalers;
* major retail multiples;
* independent retailers;
* Co-operative Wholesale Society;
* import agencies in overseas territories

There are a number of other companies in the market, and market share percentage estimates are given in Table I. The balance of company sales as between its branded goods, and sales of manufactured own brands sold to wholesale and retail distributors is shown in Table II and Table III.

REQUIREMENT:

You have recently been appointed as the new Managing Director of Babb Foods plc. The previous incumbent retired at 65, having admitted to you that he "had got a bit out of touch with the sharp end of the business over the last few years". You have rapidly become extremely concerned at the recent performance of the business and particularly with its apparent loss of market share.

You have decided to establish a strategic plan for the company, starting with a strategic marketing plan. What form do you think this strategic marketing plan should take, and upon what principles and objectives should it be based? What other information will you need to obtain in order to draw up the plan in detail?

Present your findings in report format.

Table 1
Market Share Percentage Estimates:

COMPANY	19x7 %	19x5 %	19x1 %
General Food Processors	16	15	10
Associated British	15	12	11
Rank Hovis McDouglas	11	9	4
Whiteworth	8	8	9
HB Smedley Foods/BRN	8	7	8
Beresford Cheshire	7	8	9
Babb Foods	5	6	11
Other companies	30	35	38
TOTAL	100	100	100

Table II
Babb Foods Sales Distribution Percentage

DISTRIBUTION CHANNEL	19x7 CB	19x7 OB	19x5 CB	19x5 OB	19x1 CB	19x1 OB
Wholesalers/cash & carries	35	40	38	30	51	25
Major retail multiples	41	60	37	55	19	40
Independent retailers	6	0	8	0	12	0
Co-operative Wholesale Society	8	0	10	15	14	35
Exports	10	0	7	0	4	0
TOTAL	100%	100%	100%	100%	100%	100%

CB — Company brands OB — Own brands

Table III
Own brand manufacture as a percentage of total Babb Foods sales

	19x7 %	19x5 %	19x1 %
Babb Foods brands	77	81	89
Own brands manufactured	23	19	11
TOTAL	100	100	100

46 Marketing Financial Services

INTRODUCTION

This chapter contains a brief analysis of the marketing of financial services. It looks at some of the alternative marketing strategies available to companies, and at the marketing mix used to put these strategies into operation. It makes reference to the Building Societies Act 1986 and the Financial Services Act 1986, both of which have had a significant effect on the marketing of financial services to the customer. The Social Security Act 1986 is also relevant to this chapter, because of its effect on the market for personal pension products. The specific implications of the Financial Services Act for the marketing of life assurance, pension and investment services is examined in the last section of the chapter.

CHAPTER CONTENTS

1) The marketing of financial services

2) Asset base

3) Marketing strategies for financial services
   3.1) Segment consolidation strategies
   3.2) Market penetration strategies
   3.3) New markets
   3.4) New products
   3.5) Diversification

4) The marketing mix
   4.1) Media advertising and P.R.

5) The marketing of life assurance, pension and investment services

6) Volume markets and specialist segments

Summary

Questions for self review

Examination Questions

1) THE MARKETING OF FINANCIAL SERVICES

There are four main types of financial institution involved

in the marketing of financial services to the consumer in the UK. These are:

* the major clearing banks;
* the building societies;
* the insurance companies;
* licensed intermediaries such as insurance brokers.

The past decade has seen a re-definition by the banks and building societies of the basic business *mission* which shapes and guides their strategies and actions. These two groups of institutions have moved away from being providers of a limited range of consumer and specialist services (such as current and deposit accounts in banks), to a broader provision of *financial services*. As a result, there has been a "blurring at the edges" between these two types of institution, and a *convergence* of the type and range of financial services which they promote and sell.

This convergence has been formalised by two major pieces of legislation, namely:

* The Financial Services Act 1986;
* The Building Societies Act 1986

and affected by the Social Security Act 1986, which has deregulated the market for personal pension schemes.

Insurance companies are also affected by the Financial Services Act. Insurance companies market insurance policies against risks associated with fire, accident, motoring, industrial, marine and aviation activities (etc). Often these policies are underwritten at Lloyds. Insurance and Life Assurance companies also market life assurance and personal investment policies, the risk attaching to which they carry themselves. These kinds of policies are not underwritten at Lloyds. The marketing of insurance services to the consumer is examined in the final section of this chapter.

As a result of these strategic and legislative changes, the market for financial services has become more competitive. Financial institutions selling to the consumer have, as a result, had to become more market and marketing orientated. They have had to develop skills and make use of the various principles and practices described throughout this text. *These principles and practices are as relevant to the marketing of financial services as they are to other goods and services sold in consumer goods markets.* Indeed, several examples taken from the insurance industry have been used as illustrations during earlier chapters.

2) ASSET BASE

The relationship between a company's asset base and its marketing strategies was analysed in chapter 44. In the case of all four types of financial institution in the UK the nature and size of the asset base is of critical importance. These asset bases include:

investment funds from customers, mortgages and secured property;

customer database, which can be segmented (for instance by **ACORN**) and accessed by means of direct marketing, or through retail outlets;

banks, building societies and insurance brokers have their own retail outlets, many of which are in prime High Street locations and shopping centres. This maximises customer access (although bank opening hours and patchy Saturday opening patterns are a controversial issue to some bank customers who require access to more than external card-operated cash withdrawal machines outside "normal" trading hours);

operational and managerial experience in the market. This is, for instance, important in the sale of insurance services to which high, increasing or unpredictable risks are attached; or in the unsecured lending/consumer credit market;

flexibility of operation, which gives advantage based upon people, experience, skill and effective information systems;

specialist channels of insurance promotion and selling (through controlled salesforces or independent brokers).

3) MARKETING STRATEGIES FOR FINANCIAL SERVICES

A variety of marketing strategies are visible. These are listed below, using the categories described in Ansoff's Matrix (Chapter 45).

3.1) Segment consolidation strategies

a) *capitalising on existing strengths:* for instance, insurance brokers and licensed intermediaries will always be able to claim that they are in the strongest position to give *"best advice"* to the customer. They can make a variety of comparable policies from different insurance companies available, and select that policy *according to their experience* which best fits the customer's needs. This form of segment-protection strategy was described in theoretical terms in Chapter 44.

b) *increasing utilisation of existing assets:* this strategy was also described in Chapter 44. Within the context of financial services marketing, this strategy can be illustrated by the development of customer database direct marketing by the banks and building societies.

c) *widening service provision:* for instance illustrated by the flotation of the Trustee Savings Bank and its full emergence as one of the major clearing banks, and more recently, the flotation in 1989 of the Abbey National Building Society as a *public limited company* (PLC). By this public flotation, the Abbey National voluntarily terminated the *mutual company status* under which the activities of UK building societies are normally regulated in law.

d) *adding complementary products:* which are also described below.

e) *increasing the strength and depth of segment provision:* achieved in this case by merger and acquisition, for instance between building societies. This was also one of the stated aims of the flotation of the Abbey National Building Society as a public limited company. Some of the aims and objectives of that flotation are summarised in Box 46.1.

3.2) Market penetration strategies

i) *increased competition within existing markets and segments.* In some cases this has turned into a classic battle for market share, with the participants supporting their products in particular with heavy media advertising.

ii) *expanding the available market.* The UK market for financial services is very far from saturated. For instance, there is a significant degree of under-insurance, and plenty of scope for the further development of home ownership, requiring additional

BOX 46.1
THE ABBEY NATIONAL FLOTATION

In recommending PLC status to its customers, prior to flotation, the Abbey National Building Society stated in one of its publicity documents that ' . . . we recognise that we have to keep on striving to provide our customers with better facilities and services if we are to remain competitive in the years ahead. All around us, the financial world is changing. The banks and others compete with us for mortgages. They offer savings accounts. You can even go to a department store for a personal loan. None of the business we do today is safe from competition.

Our ability to compete on equal terms with other large financial institutions is still restricted. We are faced with increasing competition from Japanese and American financial institutions and, from 1992, we expect an influx of European competition following the removal of trade barriers within the European Community. PLC status would enable us more cheaply to fund expansion and improvements to our branch network, to improve our traditional business of savings and lending for house purchase, and to provide better services in healthy competition with other financial institutions . . . we must, in competing, be able to provide the full range of personal financial services our customers want. Too often we have been handicapped legally or otherwise in adapting or extending our services in ways our customers deserve and expect.'

In response to the question *'if Abbey National became a public limited company would it be just the same as any High Street bank?'* the Society responded that ' . . . Abbey National would be free to offer the same services but will retain its own special character. Abbey National will be concentrating on providing personal financial services, rather than banking services for companies and the financing of overseas business loans. It is in personal financial dealings and services that our reputation is most enviable. It is in this field that we believe we can offer the customer better service than our competitors.'

mortgage services. Given the importance of the City of London as a world financial centre, there remains plenty of opportunity for the marketing of international financial services, and overseas sale of insurance and investment services.

3.3) New markets

It may be possible to identify new markets and niches by the use of accurate market segmentation and customer targeting. For instance, companies may be able to identify the need for, and position specialist segment-specific services on newly identified customer segments. This point was made in Chapter 27. Insurance companies, for instance, may be able to offset increasing competition from the banks and building societies (who also sell insurance services) by applying their cumulative experience to identifying new markets, and then differentiating and targeting segment-specific services. Banks and building societies may face higher levels of under-writing risk in competing at this level, whilst the resulting business may be less viable as far as they are concerned. The advantage possessed by insurance companies and licensed insurance intermediaries may be enhanced where legislation has the effect of limiting the *source range* of insurance services that other institutions can sell.

3.4) New products

a) *complementary products:* sold within the context of "financial services" marketing. The bank or building society is nowadays in a position to service a whole variety of customer needs. The customer need no longer have to deal with a number of different institutions.

b) *new products:* include the following:
* current account-based cash dispenser systems using magnetic stripe cards carrying PIN (Personal Identification Numbers), and cash dispensing machines eg Halifax Building Society's "Cash Card".
* credit and charge cards based upon the Visa and MasterCard systems. Recent developments include the introduction of preferential interest rates coupled with annual account service charges; and the issuing of 'affinity' cards which involve donations to nominated charities. Payments are made by the

affinity card operator to the chosen charity (i) when the account is opened, and (ii) as a proportion of total usage per year (eg 25p per £100 spent);

* current account debit cards, which are used as substitutes for cheque payments but may include credit or overdraft facilities. Such cards make use of the Visa payment system in the UK;
* retail store account (charge and credit) cards marketed by finance houses owned by major retailers;
* "cashflow" type personal loan accounts;
* insurance-based income protection plans, tailor-made pension plans for the self employed, and investment plans in many different formats from both lump-sum and regular payments;
* private health insurance schemes, competing with the long established BUPA policies.;
* EFT-POS based payment/credit systems (described in Chapter 39);
* portable personal pensions.

3.5) Diversification

i) *horizontal integration* between the major clearing banks and, more recently, between the building societies. For instance, in proposing a merger between the two, the Anglia and Nationwide Building Societies suggested that a combined society would:-

"–have greater financial strength to provide for the future security of the Society, in a highly competitive environment, to the advantage of investors and borrowers alike.

– command larger resources to be able to provide a very wide range of services now made possible by the Building Societies Act 1986, at competitive prices.

– have a much wider network of branches and agencies throughout the country, for the benefit of members.

– achieve greater influence in the savings and mortgage markets and housing policy generally.

– have the ability to make greater use of modern technology.

– have opportunities to keep costs down, once the operations of the two societies are integrated and economies of scale begin to emerge.

– offer staff wider career prospects in a larger and increasingly diverse financial organisation."

ii) *concentric diversification* to provide complementary services. For instance, the clearing banks offer mortgage services, whilst many building societies offer personal loans and personal banking services. Some building societies are now members of the bank funds clearing systems. A number of banks, building societies and insurance companies have diversified into estate agency services, whilst some building societies have become directly involved in building and construction, for instance of rented or housing society accommodation in inner city areas. A number of building societies have entered the unsecured lending and consumer credit market. Some have acquired their own personal finance subsidiary companies whilst others are developing their own operations themselves. This development contains considerable risk because, whilst unsecured lending on a personal or credit finance basis can be highly profitable, it is a different kind of operation to the traditional secured lending of which building societies have long experience. The societies must pay for, or build up the relevant specialist skills and managerial assets to manage and control a large scale unsecured lending and personal credit operation.

iii) *vertical integration* which may best be illustrated by the operation by some insurance companies of "tied" brokerage arrangements and sales forces to sell their products, in accordance with the regulations laid down by the Financial Services Act 1986.

4) THE MARKETING MIX

a) *Product:* the convergence of segment provision by banks, building societies and insurance companies has already been described above. These companies have tended to become service-orientated rather than product-orientated.

b) *Price:* the marketing of financial services varies considerably in the degree of price competition amongst its suppliers. General insurances and motoring cover are subject to a certain amount of price competition. Premiums for household property insurance, specified valuables (etc) have, on the other hand, risen in line with rising crime figures, especially in the major cities. Prices charged to borrowers are related to Bank Base Lending Rates, and in the case of credit cards, retailer account cards and unsecured personal/credit finance, rates of interest charged are relatively high. Even here, however, a degree of price competition has emerged in the form of differential interest rates on credit cards, combined with annual service charges on preferential interest accounts, and zero service charges on high interest rate accounts. Credit cards are also subject to an increasing degree of non-price competition, for instance centering on free travel insurance, special offers to card holders, and discounts on holidays purchased with the card.

c) *Place:* banks and building societies own their retail outlets, and are also represented in shopping centres, stations, airports, ports (etc). They also make use of direct marketing techniques. Insurance companies make use of retail intermediaries (licensed brokers and insurance consultants), direct marketing and, in some cases, employ their own personal sales forces.

d) *Promotion:* financial services are promoted and sold in a variety of ways, and as the market becomes more competitive, so the level of investment in promotional expenditure has risen.

* retail selling *in situ* is used by all four main types of institution;
* field sales forces are used in the sale of Life Assurance, Personal Pensions and Investments;
* direct marketing based upon customer databases and purchased mailing lists is used by all types of institution;
* media advertising – see section (4.1) below;
* corporate advertising and Public Relations – see section (4.1) below;
* sponsorship of sport and the arts, which is used by all types of institution. Sponsorship has proved particularly effective in the promotion of services, which are inherently less "visible" or "tangible" than products. This point was made in an earlier chapter.

4.1) Media advertising and P.R.

Banks, building societies and insurance companies now compete heavily on the basis of media advertising. This advertising has two main directions, thus:

\# promotional support for specific services and brand names, such as high interest/easy access personal savings accounts, life assurance plans (etc);

\# corporate promotional campaigns, for instance run by Prudential Assurance, Access, TSB, Midland Bank and Norwich Union Assurance. Investments in corporate advertising are used for P.R. purposes, and *build corporate image.* This promotes and reinforces perceptions of company "friendliness", expertise (important in the Life Assurance sector), and *reliability.* Supplier reliability is particularly important in the marketing of financial services. Public Relations was described in Chapter 41.

5) THE MARKETING OF LIFE ASSURANCE, PENSION AND INVESTMENT SERVICES

Insurance, life assurance, pension and investment services are made available by a variety of companies and trusts. These services are promoted and sold either:

* on the basis of direct marketing and selling to the customer; or

* through insurance brokers or licensed intermediaries.

General insurance, such as fire, theft, accident, motoring, commercial and industrial (etc) can at the present time be sold by anyone, whether this be the supplying company, a licensed broker or an unlicensed insurance "consultant". Such services are promoted and sold direct, or through intermediaries.

Life assurance, pensions and personal forms of investment (unit trusts, etc) can, however, now only be sold direct by their supplier, or through a *licensed intermediary.* This is a requirement of the Financial Services Act 1986. The Act then goes on to stipulate *how* these services may be sold, and its requirements are very specific. Life assurance, pensions and personal investments can only be sold in one of two ways, namely:-

i)   through a *tied agency,* in which the supplier may sell his own products direct, for instance using a field sales force, or through intermediaries who can *only* sell the products of that company. Whether the sales representatives are employed directly by the supplier, or by the agent is largely immaterial for the purposes of this chapter. The important point is that the agent can only sell *one* brand or service line. A tied agent *cannot* also act as an "independent agent".

ii) through a licensed intermediary who has chosen to act as an *independent agent.* This agent must sell a variety of brands and products, and is required by the Financial Services Act to *offer best advice* in the light of the particular needs of the customer. The independent agent cannot restrict his service lines to those of a selected few suppliers, as previously was often the practice. If he wishes to continue doing this, he must become a tied agent for one company.

The concept of "best advice" is one which is designed to provide consumer protection. The independent agent must always be able to show that, in his judgement at least, he or she has given the customer a choice from amongst the products which are most likely to satisfy the customer's requirements. The broker can no longer restrict the products on offer to those lines marketed by a selected group of suppliers, from which the broker may have hitherto chosen on grounds other than "best advice" (for instance because one company was offering additional incentives to brokers who promoted and sold its products).

Independent agents would claim that the requirements of the Financial Services Act protect the interests of the customer in that their experience of the market, plus the requirement to make available a wide choice of competing brands and products, will put them in a position to give good effect to the "best advice" stipulations of the Act. Suppliers such as assurance companies or banks who choose to sell their own life assurance, unit trusts (etc) direct to the market or through sales forces operated by tied agents will now have to rely (and depend) upon the market positioning, performance, reputation and competitiveness of their products. And the effectiveness of their promotional and selling activities will become of critical importance to them, since they can probably no longer rely on additional sales through independent brokers.

This accounts for the great increase in the development and application of sales and marketing skills within this sector. Companies selling direct or through tied agents must now rely on their own marketing efforts. Companies relying on independent brokers, on the other hand, have to promote their products through advertising (etc) so that people will ask for them or at least be aware of them when they go to their broker. And, increasingly, there will be supplier company promotional support for the independent brokers, upon whose efforts they are now reliant, to compete against the efforts of companies choosing the direct supply and tied agency route to the market.

6) VOLUME MARKETS AND SPECIALIST SEGMENTS

The contents of Chapters 43 and 44 are also relevant to the marketing of financial services. For instance, the logic of Chapter 43 suggests that a relatively small number of large organisations will eventually come to dominate the supply of financial services in the UK (and indeed, internationally).

There is a growing belief that, what with the continuing processes of merger, concentration and public flotation, the workings of the *experience effect* are becoming visible. It is possible that, say a dozen only major national financial insitutions, based upon existing banks, building societies and insurance brokers, will by the end of this century supply up to 80% of the financial services sold in the UK. The parallel with the five or so leading UK grocery supermarket chains can be cited as a useful illustration of this potential development in the field of financial services. For whilst these grocery supermarkets provide a quality service and convenience for all basic food purchases, there remains a substantial market for specialist and segment-specific or niche products. The demand for these products is met by a variety of other suppliers, large and small.

This may also be the key to the survival and success of the independent financial adviser or agent, offering ''best advice'' under the regulation of FIMBRA. FIMBRA is one of the *Self-Regulatory Organisations* (SROs) of the UK *Securities and Investment Board* (SIB) shown in Figure 46.2.

Basic financial products, such as mortgages, life assurance, pension plans, home and personal insurances, private health insurance, unit trust investments (etc) may in the main be sold through the small number of large ''retailers'' of financial services described above. Such products are essentially commodity products. They are all basically very similar (and likely to be increasingly price-competitive) in spite of the efforts made by their suppliers to differentiate them.

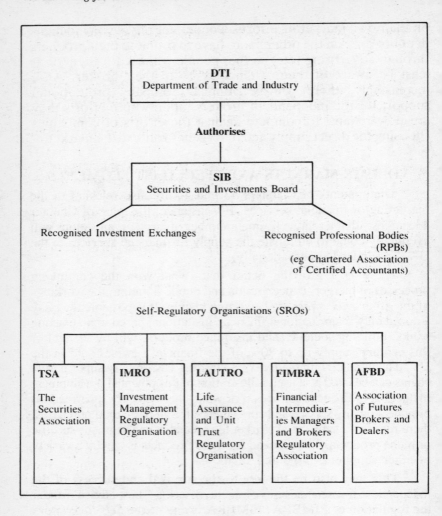

Figure 46.2
UK Financial Services: the Regulatory Matrix

As a result, there may be reduced custom for the services of the independent financial adviser. The independent agent or broker will therefore have to turn increasingly to segment-specific or niche demand (Chapter 44) for those value-added services that the large financial institutions will not be equipped to supply. Such services might include:

* specialist financial services, for instance within the insurance sector;
* tailor-made or personalised packages of financial services, whose value to the customer stems from the integration of the package. Examples might include combined mortgage, endowment, investment and pension programmes characterised by variations over customer life span, income and personal circumstances;
* computer-based search and selection amongst a range of UK and European financial products, giving the customer the best choice and combination of specialist services.

Marketing suggests that under such circumstances 'independent advisers will flourish. But only if they ... cut loose from their traditional relatively easy markets, and become experts in the sophisticated products of the next decade.

SUMMARY

The contents of this chapter are summarised in Table 46.1.

TABLE 46.1
Summary: Chapter Forty Six

SECTION	MAIN POINTS
1. The marketing of financial services	Competition between the banks, building societies and insurance companies has itensified as convergence has occured between the type and range of financial services they promote and sell. This process has been formalised by the Financial Services Act and the Building Societies Act (both 1986). As a result, financial institutions selling to the customer have had to become more marketing orientated.
2. Asset base	Include investment funds, customer database, owned retail premises, operational and managerial experience in the market, flexibility of operation , specialist channels of insurance promotion and selling.

3. Marketing strategies for financial services	Include: (3.1) Segment consolidation (capitalising on existing strengths, increasing utilisation of existing assets, widening service provision, adding complementary products, increasing the strength and depth of segment provision). (3.2) Market penetration (increased competition within existing markets and segments, expanding the available market). (3.3) New markets. (3.4) Complementary and new products. (3.5) Diversification (horizontal, concentric, vertical).
4. The marketing mix	Described under the 4 P's. (4.1) Media advertising and P.R. are particularly important, both in promoting specific services and brand names, and in promoting corporate image.
5. The marketing of life assurance, pension and investment services	These can only be sold direct by the supplier, or through a licensed intermediary such as an insurance broker. This is stipulated by the Financial Services Act 1986, which also lays down that supplying companies must either (i) sell direct or through "tied agents", who may only sell that company's products; or (ii) through intermediaries who act as independent agents. These must sell a variety of services (not restricted to those of a few companies), and offer "best advice" to the customer in the light of his stated needs. The concept of best advice, as applied to brokers, is designed to provide consumer protection.
6. Volume markets and specialist segments	There is a growing belief that, what with the continuing processes of mergers, concentration and public flotation, the workings of the experience effect (Chapter 43) are becoming visible. It is

possible that a relatively small number of large organisations will eventually come to dominate the supply of financial services in the UK and internationally, since many of the financial services they supply are in effect 'commodities' which are difficult to differentiate. The key to the survival and success of the independent financial adviser may, on the other hand, be to turn increasingly to segment-specific or niche demand (Chapter 44) for those value-added services and advice that large financial institutions are ill-equipped to supply.

QUESTIONS FOR SELF REVIEW

1)   What is the Experience Effect?

2)   What are the sources of the Experience Effect?

3)   How may volume, cost, price and market share be related?

4)   Describe and comment on experience curve pricing.

5)   Describe and comment on the implications of the Experience Effect for company marketing strategy.

6)   Describe an undifferentiated marketing strategy, using an actual example known to you.

7)   Describe and comment on differentiated and segment-specific marketing strategies, using actual examples known to you.

8)   In what ways must a company manage the relationship between its marketing strategies and the assets it uses to carry out its business?

9)   How may company strategies for market segmentation assist the process of adapting to conditions of market change and technological innovation? Illustrate your answer with actual examples known to you.

10)   Describe and comment on the steps involved in carrying out a strategic marketing analysis within a business enterprise.

11)   How may marketing management make choices amongst the various alternative strategies, tactics and activities open or available to the company?

12)   What is "offensive marketing"? Illustrate your answer with actual examples known to you.

13)   What are the implications of the Financial Services Act 1986 and the Building Societies Act 1986 for the marketing of financial services?

14)   Why have financial institutions selling services to the consumer become more marketing orientated?

15)   Describe and comment on some of the marketing strategies available to the suppliers of financial services.

EXAMINATION QUESTIONS

Q74   *'A marketing strategy is a consistent, appropriate and feasible set of principles through which a particular company hopes to achieve its long-run customer and profit objectives in a particular competitive environment.' (P. Kotler)*
       Outline the principal marketing strategies which a company may adopt in pursuit of these objectives and give at least one example of each type of strategy. (SCOB)

Q75   *How can the Boston Consultancy Group approach help the company to manage its business better? (IIM)*

Q76   *Explain the difference between an undifferentiated, a differentiated and a concentrated marketing strategy. Illustrate your answer with examples. (CIMA)*

Q77   *How might the marketing concept be applied to the services of banking and insurance? (CIMA)*

Q78   *Is there any difference, in principle, between the marketing of detergents and the marketing of financial services? Discuss. (SCOB)*

Q79   *Financial services can easily assume the role of a commodity in the consumer's perception where no product differentiation is apparent and selection is made almost entirely on price and convenience. Petrol is an example of such a product.*

Examining mortgage and investment products separately, comment upon:

i) The role and importance of price in the marketing of financial services;

ii) Creating product differentiation by enhancing a basic service with added value features. (CBSI)

47 Green Marketing

INTRODUCTION

This chapter concludes the Strategic Marketing Management section of this book. It is a new chapter, written for the Second Edition.

Its inclusion as proper material for a textbook of this kind reflects the growing public concern over a wide variety of *environmental issues*. These issues have specific implications for consumer attitudes, values and behaviour within product-market contexts. There is an increasing need for marketers to understand these specific implications, and to judge how best to adapt to the "greening" of their markets.

Its inclusion in this Section of the book is appropriate for a related set of reasons. Green principles are becoming increasingly diffused through western markets. The adoption of these principles, and their effect on consumer behaviour has *direct implications* for the product-market policies and strategies adopted by supplying organisations. These product-market strategies (and the *technologies* associated with them) are increasingly likely to have to be changed and adapted in order to meet the wider public concerns over environmental issues described above.

CHAPTER CONTENTS

1) Some green issues and product-market response
2) Some key principles for the 1990's green consumer
3) Some potential future trends
4) The implications for marketers of green marketing
   4.1) sustainability
   4.2) technology and innovation
5) Green marketing — a developing issue
Summary
Recommended Reading
Questions for Self Review

1) SOME GREEN ISSUES AND PRODUCT-MARKET RESPONSE

John Elkington and Julia Hailes (see Recommended Reading) identify a series of *environmental* or *green* issues. These are likely, within the foreseeable future, to bring about changes in the way that individuals behave as consumers. These changes will feed back into the channels of distribution, and into those consumer/industrial markets associated with them. Some of these green issues are summarised below, along with examples of product-market responses that have occurred or which can be foreseen.

1) The ozone layer

It has become clear that the thinning and puncturing of the earth's protective ozone layer has been brought about by the use of the chemical compounds of the chlorofluorocarbons or CFC's. These chemical compounds have been used in aerosols and packaging, and are extensively employed in refrigeration and air-conditioning plants.

a) *product-market response:* whilst CFC's have largely been removed from aerosols, they will remain an environmental hazard associated with packaging, refrigeration and air-conditioning until displaced by other chemical compounds or technologies.

2) The greenhouse effect

The potential for unpredictable (and uncontrollable) global warming is caused by emissions of carbon dioxide, nitrogen oxides, methane and CFCs into the atmosphere. The long-term consequences for climatic conditions can only be guessed.

a) *product-market response:* can only be based upon the wholesale reduction of such emissions, and the elimination of the use of CFCs. In part, solutions will be associated with:

− less use of hydrocarbon based energy, more efficient use of energy, more energy conservation;

− recycling materials to "save" their energy content;

− ending the destruction by burning/logging of tropical forests.

The greenhouse effect could become the major environmental issue of the twenty first century, with *enormous marketing implications*.

3) Tropical deforestation

Forests act as "sinks" for carbon dioxide and return oxygen to the atmosphere. They also darken the surface of the earth and so absorb heat. Deforestation by burning returns carbon dioxide into the atmosphere in huge quantities, which contributes to the greenhouse effect. The remaining land suffers soil erosion and deteriorates, rivers silt up and cause flooding, and the flora and fauna of the area is lost. The opportunity of finding new crops, new biochemical substances, and new drugs is lost, with unknown consequences for mankind.

a) *product-market response:* many western customers will no longer purchase furniture or fittings made from endangered tropical hardwoods. Foodstuffs and pharmaceutical producers (etc) are increasing their search for rainforest products whose successful commercial exploitation will require that the forests remain untouched.

Fortunately Brazil nuts will only grow in the tropical rainforest. Tourism, too, may lead to the conservation of tropical forest. Word of mouth condemnation or negative publicity may eventually discourage fast food chains (say, in the USA or Japan) from sourcing their beef from ranches cleared from the Brazilian rainforest. Re-afforestation, and increasing use of timber in construction, paper packaging (etc) may become a major issue in the decades to come. One recent sales promotion response is shown in Box 47.1.

4) Acid rain

Moisture in the atmosphere combines with such emissions as sulphur compounds and oxides of nitrogen to form acid rain, which causes extensive damage to trees, soils, rivers and lakes. These emissions come from power stations (in particular coal-burning), factories and car exhausts. The UK is a major polluter, by acid rain, of northern and western Europe.

a) *product-market response:* reductions in the level of emissions which cause acid rain can only be associated with energy conservation, recycling, the use of renewable energy sources (wind, tidal power, etc), and *alternative technologies* for energy generation, vehicle propulsion etc. The price of energy is almost bound to rise as power station emissions are cleaned up and energy consumption is discouraged. Clean, electric rail traction may become a dominant long-distance passenger transport mode during the next century, with rechargeable electric cars used for urban journeys in which convenience, not speed, is the principal customer benefit compared with public transport. That the motorist and the heavy goods vehicle are now on a collision course with the environment seems in little doubt. The only question (with all the marketing implications that go with it) is *when* that collision will really be felt?

Box 47.1

You can plant a tree in our one million tree

ETHIOPIAN 'TREES FOR LIFE' PROJECT

with World Vision, in the Shone Valley, Ethiopia

For every three tokens you send us, we will plant a tree for you and your family in our 'Yorkshire Trees for Life Forest', part of World Vision Charity's Shone Afforestation Project, in Southern Ethiopia.

Jeffrey Thindwa, World Vision's Overseas Director explains:

"As the mass destruction of forests in the Third World continues, our planet has begun to shout out its warnings loud and clear. A depleted ozone layer and the 'greenhouse effect' are vast scale alarms, calling the Western World to action. There must be something we can all do. Right now in Africa — where I come from — there are glimmers of hope even in famine-stricken Ethiopia. There, just a few years ago, 40% of the land was forest; now only 4% remains. Because millions of trees have been cut down, the top-soil has eroded and neither vegetation nor tens of thousands of people have been able to survive. Who 20 years ago would have considered trees so important? In 1986 we started our first Ethiopian afforestation project at Ansokia. The results are now there for all to see. Crops are growing; streams have miraculously reappeared; wildlife is back; it even rains! Now nature and human beings can flourish — all because of trees! We need to create our Ansokia success all over Ethiopia. Our next project is in the south, in the Shone Valley. We aim to plant nine million trees over a seven year period. By sending in tokens, Yorkshire Tea Drinkers can help plant the first million trees, which will form a plantation to be called 'The Yorkshire Trees for Life Forest. PLEASE HELP.''

HOW TO HELP: For every three tokens you send us, we will plant a tree for you in the Shone Valley, Ethiopia. To reduce postage costs and save paper why not collect tokens with your friends and family. Send your tokens to:
Taylors Tea & Coffee Ltd . . . .

Yorkshire Tea Bag paper is made without any chlorine bleaching . . . (the) carton is made using recycled board.

With acknowledgements to Taylors Tea and Coffee Ltd., Harrogate, UK.

5) Water pollution

The pollution of streams, rivers, lakes and the seas results in part from:

* intensive farming methods associated with cheap food policies ('encouraged' by supermarket buying power and competition which keeps agricultural margins low and forces farmers to use such methods);

* the use of artificial fertilisers, pesticides (etc) associated with intensive agriculture and fish rearing, which build up in the water resources and escape into rivers;

* the use of phosphates and bleaches in household chemicals which are inadequately treated and subsequently escape as effluent. *Marketing* notes of phosphate-free detergents that 'in West Germany ... they are the norm, and in ... Switzerland, use of phosphates is banned.'

* the dumping of wastes into rivers and sea.

a) *product-market response* may be categorised in terms of product and price, thus:

i) *product:* the need to reduce, restrict or change the use of environmentally harmful chemical constituents will affect *product specification*, as in the case of phosphate-free detergents, unbleached paper, organic foodstuffs (etc).

ii) *price:* price increases are likely to be associated with less intensive or organic food production; and the proper treatment and disposal of wastes, whether these be industrial effluents or slurry/silage liquor from intensive livestock operations.

Changes in consumer behaviour are already visible, for instance favouring products whose growing process or manufacture avoid water pollution, or indeed *consuming less in quantity, and seeking quality* whose attributes are not associated with water pollution. This is a theme to which this Chapter will return.

6) Waste

The generation and disposal of large quantities of waste, whether in the form of *used packaging or the residues of agriculture, production or consumption*, is now a key environmental issue.

The disposal of waste can involve the process of incineration (which gives rise to the contentious issue of the safe burning of toxic waste), or by *landfill*. Landfill, a process that uses up land, can give rise to what Elkington and Hailes describe as a mixture comprising "a potentially deadly cocktail of domestic, commercial and industrial waste" (p.23). Landfill may also generate methane gas, which is potentially explosive. Methane gas also contributes to global warming. Worst of all, there are varying degrees of *dumping* of waste, ranging from the legitimate disposal of household refuse at sea (a practice being halted throughout Europe), to the illicit (and dangerous) international trade in toxic waste.

The disposal of waste also uses up finite resources and 'loses' the energy associated with original manufacture or processing. Indeed, the generation and disposal of waste must, ultimately, have finite limits.

a) *product market response — the implications for packaging*

Packaging is an essential feature of the Marketing Mix. The objectives of packaging were described in Chapter 21 Section 3. The issue for this chapter is *which packaging materials should be used, and how*. Packaging is highly visible. It is an obvious and easy target for environmental questioning and criticism. Marketers are therefore now having to give increasing attention to:

* avoiding overpackaging;

* simplifying packaging;

* avoiding the use of non-renewable resources (such as oil) in the manufacture of packaging;

* decreasing the total quantity of resources used up in packaging;

* maintaining existing returnable systems (eg returnable glass bottles packaging milk, soft drinks and beer) and stimulating their use by the public;

* creating effective recycling systems, for instance for glass, metals, cardboard and paper. Recycling conserves the resource itself, plus the energy used in its original production. The manufacture of such packaging materials as glass, paper and plastic is highly energy intensive;

* highlighting, reducing reliance on, or eliminating the use of environmentally unfriendly packaging eg foam plastics, non-biodegradeable plastic bags and films.

Eventually, substantial competitive advantage is likely to be gained by those countries and companies who innovate and develop appropriate technologies/systems for *environment friendly* specification, manufacture, recycling and disposal of packaging. The heat generated from waste incineration is already widely used to provide communal hot water or domestic heating in a number of European countries. Environment friendly steam trains once burned cane waste (dried stems) in bringing sugar cane from the cane fields to the sugar factories in some South East Asian countries. These trains have been displaced by diesel lorries which pollute the air with fumes from using a fuel whose hard-currency import costs must be paid for by the export of raw sugar — a nonsense for countries whose hard currency earnings are a limited and vital national resource!

7) The disappearing countryside

The spread of urban development, afforestation through the planting of pinewoods, and pressures to produce a wide range of cheap food have brought about a drastic change in the UK's countryside, for instance in:

* the loss of traditional woodland
* the loss of lowland grassland and heath
* the loss of hedgerows

At the same time, the loss of moorland valleys in the construction of reservoirs may accelerate as demand for water increases, or if potential climatic changes caused by the greenhouse effect bring about drier weather in the UK.

Supermarket chains and other retailers have also been criticised for the scramble during the 1970's and 1980's to develop *out of town sites*. These sites permitted large new stores to be built, surrounded by car parking space. Access by public transport was not always considered to be necessary. This development is now under criticism because of the use of *green field sites*. The current trend towards the conservation of land has encouraged recent retail developments (such as Newcastle's Metro Centre) to *redevelop existing industrial sites,* especially where suitable sites are available with road and public transport links that could be upgraded.

a) *product-market response:* apart from a positive attitude towards land conservation by retailers and developers, the marketing process may help the countryside for example by:

* developing and promoting countryside or green leisure pursuits associated with wildlife and flora, for instance

through the National Trust, Woodland Trust, Royal Society for the Protection of Birds (etc);

* promoting organic food production;
* promoting the replanting and management of indigenous woodland, whether for leisure or as a source of natural hardwoods for use in furniture manufacture, windows and the construction industry.

8) Endangered species and animal welfare

Housing and urban development, roadbuilding, intensive farming (etc) have all had a severe effect upon wildlife and flora in the UK. Wildlife and flora have become *marginalised*, through loss of habitat and/or food source, or directly threatened.

Excessive fishing can drastically reduce fish stocks (*overfishing*), and *at the same time threaten other animals in the food chain* that feed on the species. This affects seals, dolphins, whales and birds. Worse, some fishing methods endanger animal lives: many dolphins can be drowned when tuna fish are netted.

The destruction of tropical rainforests (and the impoverishment of *other* tropical habitats through tree clearance, soil erosion, ineffective farming methods, overpopulation and desertification) is associated with an acceleration of the pace at which plant and animal species (many unknown to us) become extinct. Even putting aside the *moral argument* against this loss on the grounds of man's stewardship of planet Earth for future generations, there are *practical criticisms*. Plants and animals are being lost whose use as potential sources of food, plant strains, pharmaceutical and bio-chemical substances will never be available to us when otherwise they should have been maintained for posterity.

Animal welfare

There is a long and sad tradition of animal abuse and cruelty, whether it be in the form of:

— the testing of products and substances;
— the over-intensive rearing of livestock such as poultry and pigs;
— the rearing or killing of animals for fur, skin, ivory or feathers.

a) *product-market responses* are already many and varied. They include:

i) eliminating products from sale which are *associated with cruelty or the destruction of wildlife,* whether it be veal, pate de foie gras, fur coats, animal skin products, ivory.

ii) stimulating the sale of free range eggs and poultry.

iii) marketing *cruelty-free cosmetics* which contain no animal ingredients and are not tested on laboratory animals. The success of Anita Roddick's "Body Shop" chain is a famous example of this product-market strategy.

iv) eliminating products from sale which come from countries with a poor record of promoting animal welfare.

v) sponsoring threatened species as a promotional theme, as in the case of barn owls, hedgehogs, pandas and whales.

vi) promoting domestic gardening as *a source of alternative wildlife habitats.*

vii) promoting spatial design, locality planning and building construction as *a source of alternative wildlife habitats.* This may give space for flora and fauna. Or instead it may help wildlife cope with man. Tunnels may be built under roads for frogs, hedgehogs and other animals to cross, so avoiding the potential carnage above. New buildings may have special locations for bats or owls, whilst the provision of nesting boxes for birds and bats is an ideal tool of sales promotion (Chapter 34).

viii) encouraging tourism to conservation zones and national wildlife parks, thereby saving tropical rainforests and other tropical habitats in South America, Africa and Asia.

ix) promoting natural or indigenous forestation to combat the greenhouse effect, to provide hardwood by proper timber management and replanting, and to provide substantial wildlife and flora habitats.

2) SOME KEY PRINCIPLES FOR THE 1990's GREEN CONSUMER

Given the rapidly increasing awareness on the part of the general public of the importance and urgency of the green issues summarised above, Elkington and Hailes identify some key principles for the 1990's green consumer. These are that (p.4−5) "in general, the

Green Consumer should avoid products (*or services*) which are likely to:

* endanger the health either of the consumer or of others;
* cause significant damage to the environment during manufacture, use or disposal;
* consume a disproportionate amount of energy during manufacture, use or disposal;
* cause unnecessary waste, whether because of over-packaging, an unduly short useful life or because they are not suitable to re-use or recycle;
* use materials derived from threatened species or from threatened environments;
* involve the unnecessary use of, or cruelty to animals, whether this be for toxicity testing or other purposes;
* adversely affect other countries, particularly in the Third World.

The more widely these basic principles are promoted and understood by the *general public as consumers*, the greater will be the effect on *consumer behaviour*, and the greater the resulting impact on the product-market strategies pursued by suppliers to consumer and industrial markets.

Consumer behaviour was analysed in detail in Chapters 10 to 13. Behavioural determinants of demand that are likely to be of particular significance within the context of this chapter include:

- individual motivation
- culture
- life-style
- social class
- the family
- reference groups
- opinion leaders (and innovators)

Environment consciousness, and green consumer behaviour are likely to diffuse through consumer, then industrial markets in the west at an increasing rate, showing an increasingly potent "cascade effect". This increasing public awareness and propensity to act in an environmentally conscious manner will simply reflect the wider socio-cultural and political climate as it develops in response to a (potentially) deteriorating environmental context, over-population (etc).

695

3) SOME POTENTIAL FUTURE TRENDS

In addition to the general impact of environment consciousness on the marketing process and the development of green consumer behaviour, some specific trends appear to be emerging. These could have a direct impact on the provision of goods and services during the next decade. These trends include:

a) *organic food production:* the value of organic food sales will rise significantly as shoppers become more willing to pay the price premium involved. Marketing notes that "in the short term it remains a niche market because demand outstrips supply. Stock needs to be imported as land has to be left unfarmed for a minimum of five years before its yield can rightly be called 'organic' .... but that will change ... instead of the European Community funding farmers to churn out ordinary food, it will channel those funds into organic produce."

b) *woodland and forestry:* which will be re-established as a vital component of the landscape, ecology and habitat for flora and fauna. The marketing implications are based upon the eventual increase in (i) the use of indigenous hardwoods, produced through proper timber management, in construction and furniture manufacture, and (ii) the increasing use of softwoods in paper, packaging and construction.

c) *ethical investment policies:* for instance based upon the principles described in Section 2 (above). The financial services sector may find considerable growth potential and competitive advantage in the marketing of such policies to "deep green" and "light green" customers alike.

d) *consumer education:* a clearly visible trend within western societies is one in which:

* there is greater consumer awareness and demand for product information;

* there is a trend towards a more open and accountable society (as witnessed by recent developments in Eastern Europe);

* specific consumer education is now well established in schools and colleges;

* Information Technology developments make information more easy to generate and disseminate;

* significant competitive advantage may be obtained from the marketing use of Management Information Systems (MIS), and the provision of information to trade and customer alike.

e) *the decline of the "throwaway society":* it may be the case that some consumers are beginning to see the following product attributes as *negative selling propositions:* −

i)   excessive packaging

ii) short product usage life, coupled with disposability (eg throwaway cameras, pens or torches)

iii) no repair or servicing potential (eg throwaway watches, clothes and shoes).

Positive selling propositions may increasingly become associated with product quality, reliability, durability, longevity in use, and *thrift.*

f) *the politicisation of consumption not production:* the politics of the next century may, in part, be dominated in the West by the consequences of consumption and consumer behaviour on economy and ecology. The green movement, and its principles, are likely to be absorbed into mainstream political philosophies. This will have a direct effect on marketers and the process of marketing.

At the same time, the concept of *state interference in* (as opposed to *regulation of*) the productive process is being seen as an increasingly outmoded one. The uncontrolled and unchecked pollution of East Europe and Russia by state-run industries is now becoming evident to all, as country after country abandons centralised control and seeks to replace it with open regulatory frameworks, democratic sanction and consumer persuasion.

4) THE IMPLICATIONS FOR MARKETERS OF GREEN MARKETING

The issues involved in green marketing may eventually imply a change (i) in the prevailing *quality of living standard* in western countries; and (ii) in *the basics of consumer behaviour.* For instance, consumption or purchase *convenience* may become qualified. Socks, hosiery and clothing will for example be of higher quality, last longer and not need darning or mending too often! But the customer will pay more for convenience, reflecting the value of the time that this convenience affords him or her. *He or she may consume more quality but less quantity.*

Forecasters suggest that consumers may return to demanding product attributes favouring *quality, reliability, durability and safety.* This change in behaviour reflects the beginning of a rejection of the "throwaway society". The concept of the throwaway society is increasingly seen as untenable and unsustainable.

Forecasters also suggest that consumers may return to placing value on *personal and communal thrift*. Thrift has been an unfashionable concept for thirty years in the UK. The re-emergence of positive attitudes towards thrift reflects the increasing importance attached to the need to conserve and protect the environment.

4.1) Sustainability

Sustainability is seen as a key issue within green marketing. A fundamental question is whether the marketing process is *environmentally sustainable*, or does it exploit that environment on an irrecoverable basis? For instance:

a) tropical deforestation, short term ranching, soil erosion, flooding and desertification; OR

b) the planting of tropical or temperate hardwoods; the use of properly managed hardwood forests for furniture and construction materials (etc); proper replanting to maintain ecology and habitat.

i) excessive use of chemical fertilisers and pesticides damaging soil structure (for instance through continuous wheat growing), eliminating habitats (birds and bats are nature's pesticides) and placing at risk insects, bats and birds that carry out plant pollination necessary to proper plant development, OR

ii) the sympathetic use of agro-chemical and organic farming that respects soil structure, respects the landscape, makes space for flora and fauna, and involves fauna (in pollination, pest control) to a proper degree.

The issue of sustainability can be placed within the *context of consumption*. The context of consumption, and usage context were analysed in Chapter 16 Section 5 Product Segmentation, which looked at usage requirement and principal benefit. *Sustainability may become a key benefit required within the attribute set considered appropriate for any particular usage requirement.*

4.2) Technology and innovation

It will be reasonable to assume that those organisations who can innovate and implement technologies, products and processes *favourable* to the environment and its conservation/improvement will gain significant, and increasing competitive advantage within the markets they serve. For instance, see Box 47.2.

Box 47.2

GREEN SCIENCE

Modern industry, it cannot be denied, has created a lot of pollution, and still does so. But it is science, technology and industry ... who will find the answers to these problems ... ICI ... is committed to phasing out production of CFC's and is working flat out to produce substitutes ... At Billingham, ICI is using specially cultivated reed beds to treat and purify effluents ... At the same time ... comes ICI Coastguard, a revolutionary product which will reduce the bacteria and viruses released into the sea with sewage, and thus help purify our ... water ... It is science and industry that will win the battle for the environment and if it is ICI that does it that is very good news, because saving the environment is going to be good business and good for jobs in the decades ahead.

Middlesbrough Evening Gazette
13.4.1990
Reproduced with permission

5) GREEN MARKETING – A DEVELOPING ISSUE

The issue of green marketing is a *dynamic* one. It is a changing and developing subject, growing rapidly in importance. The interested reader will need to update the analysis given here, using contemporary published media, advertising campaigns, information on new product launches (etc) as appropriate.

SUMMARY

The contents of this chapter are summarised in Table 47.3.

TABLE 47.3
Summary: Chapter Forty Seven

SECTION	MAIN POINTS
1. Some green issues and product-market response.	John Elkington and Julia Hailes identify a series of environmental or green issues. These issues are likely to bring about changes in consumer behaviour, thereby affecting markets and the channels of distribution associated with them. These issues, and the product-market response analysed with them, include (1) the ozone layer; (2) the greenhouse effect; (3) tropical deforestation; (4) acid rain; (5) water pollution; (6) waste and packaging; (7) the disappearing countryside; (8) endangered species and animal welfare.
2. Some key principles for the 1990's green consumer	Elkington and Hailes identify a series of key principles for the 1990's green consumer. The more widely these principles are understood by the general public as consumers, the greater will be the effect on consumer behaviour, and the greater the resulting impact upon the product-market strategies pursued by suppliers to consumer and industrial markets.
3. Some potential future trends	Some specific marketing trends are associated with (a) organic food production; (b) woodland and forestry; (c) ethical investment policies; (d) consumer education; (e) the decline of the throwaway society; (f) the politicisation of consumption not production.

4. The implications for marketers of green marketing	The issues involved in green marketing may eventually imply changes (i) in prevailing living standard; (ii) in attitudes to customer convenience; (iii) in preference to quality rather than quantity, favouring attributes such as reliability, durability, safety; (iv) favouring personal and communal thrift. A further issue (4.1) concerns the degree to which the marketing process is seen by the general public as environmentally sustainable within the context of consumption. Competitive advantage is likely to be gained (4.2) from technology developments and innovation which are perceived by consumers/buyers as favourable to the environment and its conservation.
5. Green marketing – a developing issue	The issue of green marketing is a changing and dynamic one.

RECOMMENDED READING

Elkington J. and Hailes J.   *The Green Consumer Guide*
Gollancz

Elkington J. and Hailes J.   *The Green Consumer's Supermarket Shopping Guide*   Gollancz

QUESTIONS FOR SELF REVIEW

1)   What are "green issues" and why are they of concern to the marketer?

2)   Analyse the implications for product-market strategy of any (or all) of the following environmental issues:

– *thinning of the ozone layer*
– *the greenhouse effect*
– *tropical deforestation*
– *acid rain*
– *water pollution*

- waste generation and "excessive packaging"
- the disappearing countryside
- endangered species
- animal welfare

3)   Explain and comment upon the implications for marketers of Elkington and Hailes' "key principles for the 1990's green consumer".

4)   In what ways may a concern for environmental and green issues affect consumer behaviour?

5)   What behavioural determinants of demand are likely to be of particular significance to the adoption of green marketing, and why?

6)   Describe and comment in detail on a specific environmental/green trend, and on its likely impact on the provision of goods and services within the market(s) to which it is relevant.

7)   What are the medium and long-term implications of an increasing public environmental consciousness for marketers and managers in (i) consumer goods OR (ii) industrial goods markets?

8)   What are the medium and long-term implications of an increasing public environmental consciousness for marketers and managers in (i) a specific consumer goods, OR (ii) a specific industrial goods market in which you/your group has an interest?

9)   What is "sustainability" and why is it a key issue within green marketing?

10)   Why do technology development and innovation play a crucial role in adapting enterprise product-market strategies to respond to green/environmental pressures within the marketplace?

The Marketing of Services

". . . become a fanatic, emphasising service in the customer's terms. Consider every customer to be a potential lifelong customer, generating word-of-mouth referrals; therefore, emphasise the relationship with the customer over time. Attend especially to the intangible attributes of the . . . service. Service pays!"

from Tom Peters *Thriving on Chaos* Pan Books 1989 (p 88)

The final section of this book comprises an analysis and illustration of selected principles and practices associated with the marketing of services. Chapter 48 examines some of the principles of services marketing. Chapter 49 contains four detailed case examples by which to illustrate and reinforce some of the issues raised in Chapter 48.

48 The Marketing of Services

INTRODUCTION

This chapter analyses the marketing of services. This is clearly an important subject (i) given the size and scope of the "service sector" in the UK and the West. An increasing proportion of the total expenditure in consumer and industrial (also business-to-business) markets is being made on services of one kind or the other.

It is also important (ii) *given the increasingly market-orientated trend appearing within the UK public sector*, in which defined 'internal' markets are becoming of increasing relevance to the organisation and management of the affairs of that service sector.

It is also an important subject for consideration (iii) given the increasing emphasis being placed by suppliers of both products and services on the achievement of improved levels of customer service. Many private and public sector activities are now being redefined as *service businesses*.

The chapter begins by looking at the nature of services. It illustrates some of the services that require marketing in the UK. It then analyses some of the marketing characteristics of services. It goes on to consider some of the special characteristics of the service marketing mix.

The chapter incorporates a variety of illustrative service examples and marketing techniques. Chapter 49 contains some additional detailed case examples by which to further illustrate the contents of this chapter.

CHAPTER CONTENTS

3)   The Service Marketing Mix

4)   Personal Selling

    4.1) Some guidelines to selling services

5)   Operations Management

    5.1) Some operations management problem characteristics associated with the provision of services.

6)   People and Customer Service

    6.1) Managing service personnel.

7)   Physical Evidence

    7.1) Physical evidence associated with the service itself

    7.2) Design and specification of the service environment.

Summary

1) WHAT ARE SERVICES?

Services are defined by Donald Cowell (see Recommended Reading) as 'those separately identifiable but intangible activities that provide want-satisfaction, and that are not of necessity tied to (or inextricable from) the sale of a product or another service. To produce a service may or may not require the use of tangible goods or assets. However, where such use is required, there is no transfer of title (permanent ownership) to these tangible goods.' Similarly, P. Kotler has defined service as 'any activity or benefit that one party can offer to another that is essentially intangible and does not result in the ownership of anything. Its production may or may not be tied to a physical product.' Services are characterised by five general properties, being:

    – intangibility

    – inseparability

    – heterogeneity

    – perishability

    – ownership

The marketing implications of these five properties are analysed in Section 2, below.

1.1) What services may need marketing?

Box 48.1 illustrates a variety of service categories that may be marketed in the UK. Some of these services are to be found within the commercial or private sector, and some within the non-profit or public sector.

BOX 48.1
WHICH SERVICES MAY NEED MARKETING IN THE UK?

ILLUSTRATIVE SERVICE CATEGORY	Commercial/ private sector	Non-profit/ public sector
Personal recreation, leisure and holidays	✓	✓
Personal services (eg hairdressing, dry cleaning, personal security)	✓	
Industrial services (eg plant/asset maintenance, vehicle servicing)	✓ ✓	✓ ✓
Public and industrial transportation, physical distribution	✓	✓
Communications (postal, telecommunications) whether domestic or corporate	✓	✓
Distribution, whether wholesale or retail	✓	
Financial services, whether personal or corporate	✓	✓
Business, professional and scientific (marketing services, market research, advertising, legal services, accountancy and financial management, consultancy, research and development, etc)	✓	✓
Education and training	✓	✓
Utilities (gas, electricity, fuel oil, water supply, public environmental services, environmental protection)	✓	✓
Charities	✓	✓
Marketing people and personalities (eg politicians, media)	✓	✓
Community campaigns, the marketing of ideas (eg health education)	✓	✓
Public sector services (whether marketed to 'internal markets' or to 'external markets') eg museums, direct labour/direct works depts, environmental protection agencies, property maintenance (etc)	✓	✓
Private health care services	✓	
Public hospital/treatment services (whether marketed to 'internal markets' or to 'external markets')		✓
Public community health care services (whether marketed to 'internal markets' or to 'external markets') eg dentistry, ophthalmics, residential care for the elderly	✓	✓
Innovation (research and development, new product/ service development, patenting, innovation training etc)	✓	✓
Enterprise training	✓	✓

2) THE MARKETING CHARACTERISTICS OF SERVICES

2.1) Intangibility

It may not be possible to taste, feel, see, hear or smell a service before its purchase is undertaken. Ultimately, the customer may have no prior experience of a service in which he or she is interested, nor any conception of how it would satisfy the requirements of the purchase context for which it is intended. Opinions and attitudes may be sought beforehand, previous experience may inform a similar type of purchase, or the customer may be given something tangible to represent the purchase. But in the end, the purchase of the service remains essentially intangible.

Tangibility is a matter of degree. Tangibility has been defined as varying from:

* intangibles making a tangible product available eg financial services, retail and distribution; or

* intangibles adding value to a tangible product eg house decorating, hairdressing, vehicle or plant servicing; to

* complete intangibility eg entertainment or leisure services.

The degree of intangibility is likely to give rise to *substantial problems of operations management* within the organisation. This will affect the asset profile (and its capacity) required to serve the market segments made up by customers for these services. Operational capacity may be affected by such intangible characteristics of service provision as:

* precise standardisation of the service offering may be difficult to achieve;

* perceptions of what is good (or bad) *customer service* are important. Yet these perceptions may be difficult to influence or control, since they are developed and held by customers facing an entity which is intangible to them.

The importance of enterprise asset profile and operational capacity within a marketing context was analysed in Chapter 44.

a) *Marketing implications*

The marketer may attempt to reduce the level of difficulty to which the characteristic of intangibility gives rise, for instance by:-

i) *increasing the level of tangibility*, for instance by providing physical or conceptual representations/illustrations.

ii) *focussing the attention of the customer upon the principal benefits of consumption*, for instance as described in Chapter 16 Section 5 Product Segmentation, in which it was suggested that people seek the benefits that products provide within the defined usage contexts. Can the marketer so communicate the benefits of purchasing the service in question that the potential customer visualises its appropriateness to the usage requirement within which the principal benefit is being sought? Such an approach may reduce the customer's perception of risk attaching to the purchase of the service. A clear connection will have to be established in the customer's mind between the usage context and the benefit sought, on the one hand, and what the service has to offer, on the other.

iii) *differentiating the service and building up its reputation*, for instance by enhancing perceptions of customer service and customer value by offering *excellence* of Quality, Service, Reliability and Value for Money. Such customer perceptions of quality and excellence must then be attached as *values* to *brands*, and the brands managed to secure and enhance their market position. Singapore Airlines, for example, offer air transportation services in a highly competitive international market, but are consistently rated by business travellers as providing outstanding quality of service. Such a positive reputation develops the brand name and value, and enables Singapore Airlines to enhance its market position.

2.2 Inseparability

The creation of a service may be coterminous with its consumption. Products may be manufactured, stored, sold and consumed separately, but services may have *at the same time* to be made available, sold, produced and consumed. Personal services or medical treatment, for instance, are characterised by this coterminous pattern.

Similarly, the provision of a service may not be separable from the person or personality of the seller. Hence the importance described in an earlier chapter of establishing strongly held values about Quality, Reliability and Customer Service in the operational culture within which staff in service industries work. Organisations providing services need to instil a clear *customer service ethic* amongst management and operational staff alike. Otherwise, negative customer experience of the service received will be translated directly into negative perceptions about the provider and its market position.

(a) Marketing implications

The importance of establishing values which place emphasis on *excellence* and *customer-orientation* was analysed in Chapter 38. Effective customer service training will emphasise the need for Quality, Service and Reliability. At the same time, a service organisation will need to maximise the standard of the people it recruits and employs. Where the service is inseparable from the person providing it, there will be a clear need for the enterprise to *invest in people* in order to achieve success. This investment will include employing the right people, training and motivating them properly, managing them effectively and rewarding them for quality performance.

2.3) Heterogeneity

It may prove difficult to maintain a high degree of *consistency of output standard* when providing services. Variations between units of service are almost inevitable, whether the context of supply is a restaurant, a polytechnic lecture, or medical treatment! It may in consequence be difficult to maintain a heterogeneity (or consistency) of perception amongst customers *across a series* of purchases/consumption. As a result, there is likely to be a need to monitor customer reaction to the service provision on a continuous basis, and to feed back current perceptions of service quality into the operational process. Such a process of feedback is potentially a much more immediate and "painful" process than in the manufacture of products, since individual staff are intimately and immediately involved in providing the service to which customers are reacting.

a) Marketing implications

There will again be a need to establish and maintain attitudes and culture that emphasise

- consistency of quality control;
- consistency of customer service; and
- effective staff selection, training and motivation.

The process of quality control will require clear and understandable standards of output quality (such as restaurant food always served at the correct temperature and presented in a specific manner, or customers addressed by retail, railway or airline staff in a helpful and courteous manner — British Rail's "second-class passengers" are now "customers" who travel "standard class"!).

It may also be possible for the operations management process to standardise or 'pre-package' as much of the total offer as possible prior to its delivery. This is the principle upon which air Inclusive Tour holidays are offered. The operations management process attempts to standardise or 'control' those parts of the service that can be organised before delivery. It then concentrates staff training, management and motivation, operational monitoring and control on the potentially variable parts of the service offer. This is simply the application of Pareto's principle, under which the service operator may assume that 80% of the problems will come from 20% of the events associated with the provision of the service. The application of the Pareto principle minimises the total control and management inputs required, concentrates the resources that these inputs represent on the most important issues, and yields a build-up in experience.

2.4) Perishability

Generally speaking, services are perishable and cannot be stored in advance of demand. Worse, that demand may fluctuate, especially if it is person-centred (for instance, travel and tourism, leisure services, painting and decorating). Yet operational capacity may have to be made available to meet a level of customer demand that may or may not materialise. This may make the economics of providing such services as transportation, holidays, restaurant and hotel accommodation both uncertain and unpredictable. As a result:

i) an inadequate level of customer demand still results in the incurring of a substantial Variable and Fixed Cost burden, simply to make the capacity available in case there is demand for the service.

ii) excess demand, on the other hand, may simply have to be turned away.

Decisions on the minimum and maximum service capacity that can be made available will in turn determine:-

* the level of operational capacity lying idle at off-peak times;
* the degree to which the level of service quality may be reduced (if at all) to cope with excess demand that would otherwise be turned away. UK customers for high season air inclusive tours will be well aware of what this means for flight and hotel availability in some Mediterranean resorts!

a) *Marketing implications*

The operations management process may attempt to optimise (or 'smooth') the relationship between supply and demand, for instance by:

* using pricing variations to encourage off-peak demand, and discourage demand at peak times;

* using promotions to stimulate off-peak demand.

Both of these tactics were analysed in Chapters 24 and 26.

2.5) Ownership

The purchase of a service may only confer upon the customer the access to, or use of a facility (such as a hotel room or train seat). The customer does not obtain ownership of that facility, unlike the case of purchasing a product in which there is transfer of title (full ownership) and control over the use of the item. For example:

– a hired car vs own car

– hotel room vs own tent/caravan/holiday home.

Lack of ownership may in some way lessen the perceived customer value of the service, and render that perception (and the lack of control that goes with it) less desirable than a more tangible alternative. Compare, for instance:

– private vs public transport

– owned vs rented housing

a) *Marketing implications*

There are at least three alternatives available to the marketer. These alternatives are:

i)   promoting the advantages of non-ownership, such as the ''built-in'' maintenance or periodic upgrading of leased cars, rented televisions or leased industrial plant and equipment.

ii)   making available to the customer a tangible symbol or representation of ownership, such as a certificate of membership of a professional institution.

iii)   increasing the chances or opportunity of ownership, as in the time-shared ownership of holiday accommodation, or making available to regular customers shares in the providing organisation.

3) THE SERVICE MARKETING MIX

The extensive analysis of the Marketing Mix given in this book has not differentiated between tangible products and intangible services. In general terms, the approach to the Marketing Mix contained in Chapters 18 to 37 applies equally to products and services. However, Cowell suggests that the marketing of services will require extra emphasis to be placed upon the analysis of:

— Personal Selling (Section 4 below)
— Operations Management (Section 5 below)
— People and Customer Service (Section 6 below)
— Physical Evidence (Section 7 below)

Each of these items will be considered in the following four Sections of this Chapter.

4) PERSONAL SELLING

The nature of service marketing means that *personal selling and personal contact* are likely to constitute a significant component of the total Marketing Mix. There are a number of reasons for this level of importance.

In principle, *it may be more difficult to sell services than it is to sell products*. This will give rise to a greater need for personal selling inputs to the marketing process. The difficulty may derive from the effect of the uncertainties or subjectivities associated with service intangibility on customer purchase decision-making. As compared with the purchase of a tangible product:

* there may be greater perceived risk attaching to the purchase decision;
* there may be greater uncertainty on the part of the potential customer about quality and reliability aspects of the service offer, and lack of clarity about 'what you get for your money';
* the reputation of the supplying organisation may be of greater significance to the customer;
* the customer may perceive that there is likely to be greater reliance or dependence upon the honesty and integrity of the salesperson.

At the same time, it may be the case that the purchaser will derive lower levels of customer satisfaction from service purchases, as compared with tangible products, given the problems of perishability, ownership (etc) described in Section 2 above.

Indeed, the problem of generating an adequate level of customer satisfaction may itself be directly exacerbated *precisely because of the relatively high levels of salesperson-customer contact required in the marketing of services* such as life assurance or industrial cleaning. The situation is one in which the salesperson may have to put much greater effort into reducing customer uncertainty about the purchase (for instance because of its intangibility or inseparability) as compared with a tangible product. Tangibility may render the purpose and market positioning of a product relatively self-evident, minimise the effort required to sell it, and reduce the incidence of the 'sales-resistance' that may develop from high levels and frequency of salesperson-customer contact.

4.1) Some guidelines to selling services

a) *develop effective personal relationships with customers*, building up *trust* on the basis of individual efficiency, honesty and integrity. Such trust may for instance be an essential prerequisite to selling complex financial products like personal pensions and life assurance. The use of proper courtesy, attentiveness and personal empathy also assists in the development of personal relationships, and enhances the seller's personal image and status. The development of effective personal relationships reduces perceptions of purchase risk and serves to reassure the customer. At the same time, the communication of the 'official status' of the salesperson as representative of the supplier may have the desired effect of enhancing the supplier's corporate prestige, and reduce the general level of sales resistance to the marketing efforts of that organisation.

b) *adopt a professional approach*, communicating personal (and corporate) competence and a thorough technical knowledge of the service being sold.

c) *enhance personal and supplier (corporate) reputation* within the wider context of customer reference and peer groups, and especially amongst opinion leaders influential within those groups. The supplier will attempt to communicate and publicise evidence of existing satisfied customers, special problems solved for clients, and its reputation within relevant professional organisations or government bodies. The objective will be to encourage the kind of word-of-mouth publicity and personal recommendation described in Chapter 30.

d) *make the purchase easy* by reducing the level of risk and uncertainty associated with the purchase decision, and by placing minimal demands upon the customer during the purchase process. This will be important where, as in the case of life assurance or house purchase, the service may be conceptually difficult for some customers to understand. It will also be true where customers are under stress, as in the case of obtaining medical treatment or funeral services, or making claims upon insurance policies after accidents, fire (etc) — 'we won't make a drama out of a crisis.'

5) OPERATIONS MANAGEMENT

Chapter 26 referred to *place of availability* and *frequency of availability* as key customer service variables. Chapter 44 analysed *capacity planning* as being concerned with the level of productivity of the assets to be used in serving the chosen market segment opportunities.

The level and quality of customer service within the service sector *is particularly sensitive to the effectiveness (or otherwise) of the process by which services are made available to the market.* This process may be less sensitive where products are made because, being tangible, they can be stored ready for sale as stock or inventory. The perishable nature of services makes such a physical buffer between production and consumption impossible.

Indeed, the efficiency of service delivery process (or system) may be a significant source of competitive advantage, especially where it is otherwise difficult to achieve effective differentiation between the competing services on offer. Hence the importance of punctuality and in-flight service to the operation of airlines, the need for prompt and courteous attention to customers in a restaurant, or the availability of car servicing within (say) 24 or 48 hours of the customer request being made.

5.1) Some operations management problem characteristics associated with the provision of services

i)   *capacity utilisation*: a basic decision in managing service operations is the level of capacity that is to be made available. This issue has already been discussed in the section on service perishability above. Too much capacity may render the operation uneconomic. Too little capacity will cause bottlenecks in service delivery, give rise to customer resentment, and risk a longer term loss of business.

ii) *the degree of contact with customers*: the greater the degree of customer contact, the more difficult may be the organisation, management and control of the operational system, for instance because:

- customers make some kind of input to the process or can disrupt it (eg crowded motorway service station at peak holiday season);
- customers determine the timing of demand and it may be difficult to balance the capacity and 'fine-tuning' of the system to meet the varied demands upon it (eg hospital facilities and medical treatment);
- employees have a great influence upon the quality of service provided and help shape customer's reaction to that service.

iii) *establishing objectives in the non-profit sector:* Cowell notes (p. 246) that 'in non-profit services and the social services sector in particular, establishing system objectives may be difficult and complex at both the general level and at the operational unit level. Typically, objectives for public services will have to incorporate measures of the level and quality of service which is provided ... and these pose particular difficulties' in such areas as health care, community care, General Practitioner (GP) budgetary planning, and education at all levels.

6) PEOPLE AND CUSTOMER SERVICE

Chapter 38 refers to the importance of *people* in (i) implementing the marketing concept, and (ii) in establishing an appropriate degree of customer orientation throughout the organisation. Peters and Waterman, and Peters and Austin stress the crucial role of people and the *values they hold* in offering a proper level of customer service.

People as providers of service are important because, in the absence of the clues/reinforcement/reassurance available from tangible products, customers will tend to form impressions of the organisation and its offering on the basis of the attitudes and behaviour of its staff.

Indeed, the greater the degree of customer contact in obtaining the service, the more critical becomes the role of the staff providing that service in generating customer service and customer value. Ultimately, in the case of (say) hairdressing, dentistry or business consultancy, the selling of the service, the rendering of the service, and the visibility of the person providing that service cannot be separated. The technical competence and level of interpersonal skill of that provider are of paramount importance, since these qualities will determine the generation of customer value and shape perceptions of the standard of customer service received by the purchaser. Does the person providing the service inspire confidence within the customer about the service being received, and about the organisation supplying it?

As a result, service companies will need to include *assessments* of the degree of staff customer—orientation, and of the perceived level of customer service amongst its operational measures of performance effectiveness and efficiency. Making such assessments, which are bound in part to be subjective, may be a traumatic and controversial step to take. Yet the making of such assessments may be essential in such competitive markets as air travel, tourism, hotels, restaurants (who will be seen to be 'serving meals to eaters' rather than 'catering'!) etc.

Service organisations will also need to ensure *that all levels of staff are involved in customer service*. This means senior managers as well as counter-staff, stewardesses (etc). The involvement of senior management in 'service statesmanship' contact with customers will be a prime source of *corporate values and culture*. It will provide a powerful role model and example for those staff who spend much of their working lives dealing with customers.

6.1) Managing service personnel

The importance of the effectiveness of service staff management was noted in Section 2 above. The effective management of service personnel may include such features as:

* careful staff selection. Tolerance, empathy, discretion, self-discipline (etc) may be seen as desirable personal qualities in potential recruits;

* thorough training and development;

* the use of standardised operational practices to maximise the incidence of consistent task performance and behaviour;

* the use of standardised operational rules to ensure consistent appearance and presentation of the service offer;

* motivating service personnel such that an appropriate degree of customer orientation becomes 'second nature';

* the careful selecting, training, motivating and rewarding of the managers of service personnel, such that they set an appropriate example, establish values and provide role-models;

716

* the careful monitoring and control of the service offer and the perceived level of customer satisfaction indicated by purchasers;

* clearly thought-out policies of *reward and remuneration* to help maintain and encourage a high degree of customer orientation and customer service over long time periods. This process may also involve the periodic withdrawal of staff exposed to high levels of customer contact for 'spiritual and physical refreshment and recovery'. Maintaining high levels of attentiveness to, and empathy with customers will impose stress and strain on staff over long periods of time, even for the toughest salesperson or customer service representative. It may call for systems of job rotation to maintain personal enthusiasm and customer centredness.

7) PHYSICAL EVIDENCE

The effective marketing of intangible services may be assisted by the use of *physical evidence*. This physical evidence may be associated with the service itself, or instead be incorporated in the design and specification of the service environment.

7.1) Physical evidence associated with the service itself.

Physical evidence may be used to provide tangible clues to the nature of the service. For example:

a) *develop a tangible representation of the service:* for instance reports specifying work carried out for existing clients for consultancy services; or bank credit cards which represent the service to the customer and serve to differentiate it from its competitors.

b) *associate the service with tangible objects* thereby rendering the service more meaningful than it would otherwise be, or differentiating it from the competition. For instance, British Rail's celebrated 'Relax' promotional campaign associated Intercity rail travel with relaxing events like kicking-off shoes, comfortable carpet slippers, quiet chess games and physical and mental 'unwinding'.

c) *focus on the buyer-seller relationship*, in which the customer is encouraged to identify with a person or group of people in the providing organisation. Examples include admissions tutors in a polytechnic or university; 'personal' bankers; 'customer service representatives' at counters or holiday destinations (etc).

This encourages the customer to focus on (and develop a relationship with) people performing the service, rather than the (more amorphous) service itself.

7.2) Design and specification of the service environment

The service environment refers to the *context* (location, building, atmosphere) in which the service is made available, and where the provider and the customer interact. It includes any facilities which influence the communication and performance of the service. Such a service environment:

* can imply purpose and signify action (eg purpose built conference centres and exhibition halls);

* can be used to transmit meanings and communicate motivational messages (eg travel agencies; study environments);

* can imply aesthetic, social and cultural qualities which make up the prevailing *image*. This issue was analysed in Chapter 42;

* can reinforce and reassure. This is of crucial importance in the provision of such services as medical treatment, accountancy, banking, investment and financial services. In such cases it may be important that the customer or client feels confident and secure within the service environment;

* can create *atmosphere*. The quality and sensation of the environment will give tangible clues to the customer. For instance:-

  – the smell in restaurants, bakeries and coffee shops

  – a warm and welcoming hotel

  – solid and prestigious office accommodation for a company involved in accountancy, investment or security

  – hi-tech office accommodation for an advertising or marketing service agency, etc.

The influences on atmosphere can include:

  * visual stimuli, visual clues, colour and form
  * corporate house style and colour combinations
  * scent and smell
  * sound

* touch, texture and feel (eg furnishings, choice of construction materials favouring (say) brick, natural wood, stone, steel and glass, tile and slate)
* people's behaviour and personal body-language, dress and presentation
* general *design quality* (see Chapter 42)

SUMMARY

The contents of this chapter are summarised in Table 48.2.

TABLE 48.2
Summary: Chapter Forty Eight

SECTION	MAIN POINTS
1. What are services?	Services may be defined as those separately identifiable but intangible activities that provide want—satisfaction, and that are not of necessity tied to (or inextricable from) the sale of a product or another service. A wide variety (1.1) of services are marketed in the UK, both in the commercial or private sector, and within the non-profit/public sector.
2. The marketing characteristics of services	Services are characterised by five general properties. The marketing characteristics of each are analysed. (2.1) Intangibility means that it may not be possible to experience or evaluate a service before its purchase is undertaken. (2.2) Inseparability means that the provision of a service may not be separable from the person or personality of the seller, nor from the incidence of sale and consumption. (2.3) Heterogeneity implies that special efforts may have to be made in order to maintain an acceptable degree of consistency of output standard between

similar units of service. (2.4) Perishability means that services cannot be stored in advance of demand, so that there is no guarantee that demand and supply can be evenly matched. (2.5) Ownership means that the purchase of a service may only confer on the customer the access to, or use of a facility, not ownership of it.

3. The service marketing mix

In general terms, the treatment of the Marketing Mix contained in Chapters 18 to 37 applies equally to products and services. However, the marketing of services will require extra emphasis to be placed upon (4) Personal Selling and personal contact, (5) Effective Operations Management, (6) People and Customer Service, (7) Physical Evidence associated with the service itself, or incorporated in the design and specification of the service environment.

49 Some Case Studies of the Marketing of Services

INTRODUCTION

This chapter continues the analysis of the marketing of services with four illustrative case studies. Two case studies are taken from the commercial sector and, by way of balance, two are taken from the non-profit public sector. It was noted at an early stage in this book, in Chapter 2, that the marketing concept can apply just as much to non-profit making organisations as to those making goods or services available in consumer or industrial markets.

CHAPTER CONTENTS

CASE STUDY ONE : FINANCIAL SERVICES

Intangibility is a major feature of financial services marketing. However, the degree of intangibility varies from product to product. For instance, at one extreme there is the fixed term life assurance which will cost an annual premium, but which the purchaser fervently hopes will never yield any return (since only his heirs would reap the rewards as a result of his death!). At the other extreme are endowment policies yielding a lump sum or pension at a due date in the future.

The intangibility of financial services is also manifest in *conceptual difficulties* (such as complex financial and actuarial calculations), associated with lengthy time spans and uncontrollable variables like interest rates. The process of marketing financial services may therefore need:

　　— to focus customer attention on the principal benefits of
　　　　purchase;

- to establish some degree of differentiation between the products on offer, and those marketed by competitors. There is otherwise the danger of a market perception that 'all brands or specifications of financial service are really the same';
- to build up supplier reliability, quality and reputation;
- to reduce customer perceptions of *lack of urgency/necessity* ('why worry about your pension when you are 23?'); *purchase inappropriateness* ('what have endowment policies got to do with house purchase or paying taxes?'), or *purchase risk* ('the value of unit trust investments can go down as well as up').

The marketing of financial services is also associated with *inseparability*. The provision of financial services is often associated with the person or personality of the seller, whether this be an agent or broker, or the manager of a bank or building society. Hence the critical importance of personal professionalism and technical competence, empathy towards the customer, and a capacity effectively to represent and enhance the reputation of the organisation supplying the service.

The Marketing Mix

Personal selling and customer contact, and *the quality of the people* involved in that process, are important features of the marketing mix for financial services. This follows from the intangibility and inseparability characteristics discussed above (and in Chapter 48). Personal selling may therefore have a major role to play throughout the promotional and persuasion process described in Chapter 30. For instance, personal selling and people contact may:

* *create awareness* of technically specific products or generate proper understanding of customer problems associated with personal or corporate finance;

* *create comprehension* of how financial products on offer can meet personal financial needs, solve problems or create solutions; or instead give rise to desirable principal benefits within purchase contexts that were not hitherto properly acknowledged or understood by the customer;

* *create conviction*, whether by giving reassurance or reinforcement, reducing perceptions of inappropriateness or purchase risk, or creating conditions under which the purchase will lead to enhanced customer satisfaction;

* *create action*, for instance by persuading the customer that it is the right or appropriate occasion to make the purchase decision, or to help the customer with the actual purchase process (for instance by minimising the technical or emotional demands placed upon the client, or removing issues that would otherwise give rise to dissatisfactions).

Physical evidence

The marketing of financial services may create *tangible representations* of the service (Ch 48.7.1.a) by issuing substantial and prestigious documentation, such as certificates printed on high quality paper. The process may instead *associate the product* (Ch 48.7.1.b) with such tangibles as peoples' lives or those of their children, schooling or medical treatment, housing, personal possessions (etc). It may *focus on the relationship* (Ch 48.7.1.c) between the customer and the broker or agent, the salesperson or the personal banker. And it may make use of a *service environment* (Ch 48.7.2) which implies and communicates permanence, professionalism and confidence, and which has an *atmosphere* of purpose and reassurance.

The marketing of financial services was also analysed in Chapter 46.

CASE STUDY TWO : ACCOUNTANCY AND CONSULTANCY SERVICES

The characteristics of *intangibility, inseparability, heterogeneity* and *ownership* are relevant to the marketing of accountancy and consultancy services. The implications of each are analysed in turn.

i) *intangibility. Auditing* is an intangible service required to meet legislative and stewardship requirements. Given that the level of service must achieve certain statutory standards, the quality of provision may be marketed on the basis of the *price − service* relationship and the offer of value for money to the client.

Services associated with *financial* and *management accounting,* and *financial consultancy* may be regarded as an intangible whose objective is to add value elsewhere. The physical evidence of the success (or otherwise) of this value-adding process may eventually become demonstrable. It may then be used to focus the attention of other clients (or potential clients) upon the benefits of purchase.

Where it will prove difficult to differentiate the service, the supplying organisation may choose to build up a reputation for providing quality, reliability, value-added or value for money.

Where there is potential to do so, the supplying organisation may gain competitive advantage by differentiating the service, for instance by making use of Information Technology to add customer value. Alternatively, the nature of the service offer may be changed, perhaps by making an *augmented product* (Chapter 14) available to the client. Such a service may be based upon problem definition and solving in areas of technical difficulty associated with accounting and finance, business planning and control, international transactions (etc).

ii) *inseparability*. The provision of accountancy and consultancy services may be characterised by inseparability. It will therefore be important for the enterprise *as a whole* to create unified and consistent perceptions of excellence and customer orientation within the existing client base. This image must then be communicated and established within external publics containing the customers of competitors and potential new customers. Whilst any one individual consultant may have a personal reputation for competence and skill, the implication of inseparability is that the enterprise must ensure a uniform standard of output and customer care amongst all its consultants, and not just outstanding performance from a few achieved on an unpredictable basis.

iii) *heterogeneity*. The intangibility and inseparability of some accountancy and consultancy services may make it important to provide (and communicate) *a consistent level of technical and customer service*. Variations between units of service across a series of purchases may simply be unacceptable to clients in the markets for these kind of business to business services. Effective quality control mechanisms will need to establish clear and consistent standards of output quality to which the operational or creative process can adhere, and which can be used to guide, co-ordinate and motivate the efforts of the people who actually produce the service output.

iv) *ownership*. Many large organisations operate their own internal accounting, financial and consultancy services. Thereby they effectively compete with accountancy companies in public practice, and with consultancy firms. Can the providers of such services therefore *promote the advantage of non-ownership* such that clients *contract out* such business services as:

- financial accounting, as well as auditing ('take all the worry away from the client')
- management accounting
- Data Processing and MIS management
- payroll systems
- management consultancy, problem solving, 'trouble shooting' (etc)
- recruitment, selection
- staff training, management development.

The advantages of non-ownership may be based upon *access* to the services of experienced specialists, software and hardware facilities. Any one client could not himself afford (on opportunity cost grounds) to employ such staff or facilities for intermittent use only. The variety of problems contributed by different clients, further, *will build up the experience and knowledge base of the supplier* in a manner impossible for any one client alone to achieve. This is simply a development of the concept of 'core business' analysed in earlier chapters.

Alternatively, where ownership is seen as a level of *client commitment* (or 'brand loyalty') to an existing supplier of accountancy or consultancy services, that supplier may enhance client commitment by providing segment or customer-specific services. Tailor-made, client-specific services may be sold in such a way as to build up customer loyalty (and hence increase *client ownership of the service being made available*). This may encourage or facilitate further *related* purchases and new service trial by the client. This is a variation of the segment-specific or niche marketing decribed in Chapter 44.

The Marketing Mix

Personal selling and customer contact, and *the quality of the people* involved in that process are also important features of the marketing mix for accountancy and consultancy services.

The process of establishing client perceptions and conviction about the urgency or immediacy of the need for problem-solving services associated with financial or management consultancy depends, in part, upon the accountant or consultant (i) being able to identify and state problems that clients had not hitherto acknowledged or understood, and (ii) persuading clients, of the relevance of these problems and the need to accept ownership of them. The selling process will then concentrate upon communicating and convincing the client of the cost or risk of *not acting* to resolve these issues, and of the rightness/benefit of the consultant's proposal for dealing with them.

Effective client contact skills will also be needed to establish or maintain the level of customer satisfaction with services being purchased. Quality, reliability or value for money (*customer value*) will have, in particular, clearly to be demonstrated and reinforced in circumstances in which the purchase decision is characterised by *organisational features* described in Chapters 14 and 15. In such circumstances a number of different roles or individuals will have to be taken into account in assessing customer motivation and satisfaction with the purchase decision and its outcome.

The objective of *the development of effective personal relationships with clients* (Ch 48.4.1.a) will be to build up long term trust and loyalty. This may achieve continuing patronage and a downgrading of the desire to try the services of competitors.

It will be essential for the suppliers of accountancy and consultancy services *to develop a professional reputation* (Ch 48.4.1.b/c) for technical competence, integrity and reliability. These qualities are essential to maintaining client confidence in the supplier.

Physical evidence

Existing satisfied clients can be used as *tangible evidence* (Ch 48.7.1.a) of the capacity of the organisation to deliver to specification, or to exhibit quality, excellence or added value (for instance, being number one in receivership or computer fraud investigations, etc). Similarly, the service offered may be *associated with such tangible objects* (Ch 48.7.1.b) as the operational processes of business management and control, or the value enhancements obtained by existing clients from the use of the service.

The *design and specification of the service environment* (Ch 48.7.2) should be one that provides easy access and a prestigious context. A professional and problem-solving oriented atmosphere within this context will in turn create trust and reassurance amongst clients.

Promotion

The suppliers of accountancy services currently operate within the constraint of institutional restrictions on advertising and sales promotion. In consequence, professional reputation, client perceptions of supplier competence, reliability and value for money, and *word of mouth recommendation* are crucial to promotion and business development. Similarly, the development of *corporate image* (Chapter 41) is playing an increasingly important role in helping to retain or develop business, especially with corporate customers.

CASE STUDY THREE : THE UK NON-PROFIT PUBLIC SECTOR (I)

ESSENTIAL SERVICES

The public sector is largely funded through taxation, and provides what are classed as *essential services*. These include environmental, educational, health and social services. Since financial allocations made by local and central government to these services are limited by available funds, increasing emphasis is being placed upon the quality of service and value for money obtained. That is, the best possible service should be given by the providing agency within its available resources. The providers of these essential services are *accountable* through local and central government to the general public as taxpayers for the quality and value of the services provided.

Unlike the private sector who would not provide goods or services which were not profitable, the public sector cannot cease to provide essential services for which it is responsible. However, the provision of these services is influenced by two opposing pressures, being:

i) upward or inflationary pressures on operating costs; and

ii) increasing public expectations of the level of quality of customer service that may be obtained from such essential services.

The implications of higher costs will affect the general public through:

— higher taxation; or

— reduced service provision

Reductions in the level of service provision are however incompatible with increasing expectations of quality and customer service.

The public sector has therefore been faced in the UK with paying increased attention to:

* controlling costs and obtaining increased value for money from the operation of essential services; *and*
* maintaining or improving the standard of provision, *and*
* improving the level of customer service for recipients (who are 'customers', 'clients', 'people', 'taxpayers' and 'voters' all at the same time).

a) *Internal Markets.* The solution to achieving improved quality and value for money in the provision of essential services has been seen in terms of establishing the *element of competition* by means of the introduction of *internal markets.* For instance, the Local Government Act 1988 introduced *Compulsory Competitive Tendering. Purchasing departments* (buyers) put out tenders, say for building and construction work, or refuse collection services. *Supplying departments* (sellers) are then required to bid for the contracts represented by these tenders, often in competition with outside contractors. Compulsory Competitive Tendering has, therefore, a major impact on so-called 'Direct Works', 'Direct Labour' or 'Direct Services' departments within local authorities. These departments must now compete within the local authority's internal market for services with such outside contractors who can mount effective bids for the available work.

The reasoning behind these changes is that competition in such internal markets will lead to the provision of better services and better value for money, at the same time increasing the choice available to departmental buyers and hence to the actual customers for these services. Put in this light, these essential services may, at least in part, be marketed in exactly the same way as other services described in Chapters 48 and 49.

b) *Customer Care.* In the UK, public sector proponents of customer-care and customer orientation include John Stewart and Michael Clarke. Their work with the Local Government Training Board and the Institute of Local Government Studies has considered customer care in the public sector. In their book 'The Enabling Council' (see Recommended Reading) their main thesis is that, because of the introduction of Compulsory Competitive Tendering, the role of local authorities will change from direct provision of services to that of *enabling* services to be provided. Their criticisms of the public sector are that (i) too often services have been *administered* to the public rather than *developed for* the customer and (ii) services are only of value if they are *customer valued* by the people who receive them.

This second point then raises the issue of marketing. In the private sector companies spend significant proportions of their turnover on marketing. In the public sector expenditure on marketing is minimal: services have been seen largely as undifferentiated products which could not be made any different from the way in which they have always been provided. The introduction of Compulsory Competitive Tendering has brought about a change in this attitude. Local Authorities are being forced to examine how they provide services currently, and, more importantly, how they and their customers want the service provided in the future *in order to draw up specifications for contracts*. In some boroughs, buying departments or final customers have been able directly to compare service provision by the Local Authority with that of a private contractor when tenders have been awarded outside (say) that Authority's Direct Labour Organisation.

As Stewart and Clarke point out, customer orientation tends to become a key feature in the face of competition. If an organisation is good at meeting customer needs, it tends to get more customers and they tend to have greater loyalty. In order to judge customer service a standard is required *which should be set by the customer*. Local authorities may therefore have to become committed (i) to a programme of research to identify, monitor and review the attitudes of customers to its service offering; and (ii) to become much more responsive to customer demand and expectations, that is, to become more market orientated than hitherto. Notwithstanding the fact that such a re-orientation will, at least initially, place some supplying departments at a disadvantage when bidding for competitive contracts to provide services.

c) *Social Services departments and the Griffiths Report 1989 "Caring for People"*. The basic philosophy and principles described in sections (a) and (b) above also find their expressions in the 1989 White Paper "Caring for People". One of the objectives of the Report is 'to promote the development of a flourishing independent sector alongside good quality public services'. It will become the responsibility of local authority social services departments to make the maximum use of private and voluntary providers of care, in order to widen consumer choice and increase the range of care options available. *At the same time* local authorities as providers will have to market some care services in competition with private providers, for instance in the area of Residential Care for the Elderly. Such competition will be based upon two criteria, namely *quality of care* and *cost of care*.

This principle illustrates the nature of the internal market described above. On the one hand, social services departments as *providers* will compete with outside agencies for some types of care service contracts. On the other hand, as *buyers,* social services department staff:

 — retain responsibility for the welfare of those people that they are charged with looking after (especially the elderly);
 — act as *enablers*, ensuring that the best choice of care is available within the local authority area, at the highest quality and the most competitive price, whether this be provided by the department itself, or by outside agencies.

The complexity of this dual departmental role, its impact on the capacity of social services departments to safeguard the interests of those people with whose care they are charged, and the pressures to achieve value for money within the enabling role are all controversial issues whose discussion is beyond the scope of the services marketing context within which this issue is being analysed.

CASE STUDY FOUR : THE UK NON – PROFIT PUBLIC SECTOR (II)
MARKETING HEALTH CARE PACKAGES

The government White Paper "Working for Patients" 1989 will bring about radical changes to the National Health Service (NHS). The principles underlying the new *NHS internal market* are:

 — that District Health Authorities as agents of the government will *purchase* health care on behalf of their clients (patients, those undergoing treatment);
 — that General Practitioners (GP's or doctors in public practice) and others with budgets will also *purchase* health care on behalf of their clients;

— that the *providers* will be semi-autonomous district 'Units'.

The mechanism for implementing this market is *the contract for service*. The marketing process will then take place on all three 'levels', namely General Practitioner or budget holder, Providing Unit, Health District.

It is therefore the responsibility of the District Health Authority as the *purchasing agency* to identify the needs of the local population and offer contracts to competing providing organisations to satisfy that need. The contract will specify volume, quality and cost.

The providers will be required to market their health care packages in order to inform the purchaser of the pattern of facilities which the organisation proposes to provide, identifying criteria such as quality, access, (etc).

The providers may also seek to influence customers over the heads of the purchasing authorities, e.g., campaigns aimed at General Practitioners or other budget holding agencies such as Social Service Departments within the local authority sector.

THE MISSION OF THE PROVIDING AGENCY

It is the role of a District Health Authority to promote good health, and where illness occurs, to provide health care packages designed to restore health. The providing unit/agency must therefore provide the appropriate service of the right quality, at the right time and in the right place. At the same time the provision of health care packages must meet the required standards of reliability, consistency and value for money.

---

a) *Who are the customers (purchasers)?*

Health care packages will be purchased on behalf of individuals or the general public by any of the following:

i)   Health Authorities (in their purchasing role)
ii)   General Practitioners (budget holding)
iii) Family Practitioner Committees
iv)   Social Services Departments within Local Authorities
v)   Voluntary Organisations
vi)   Private Care Agencies
vii) Any other organisation holding a budget for health care.

731

b) *What is to be marketed?*

An important step in the process is to analyse all the health care packages being currently provided to the various market segments (or segment as appropriate) for which the particular assets and operational capacity are appropriate. Using:

i) Epidemiological studies

ii) Statistics of existing levels of service

iii) Projections of service levels

iv) Department of Health White Papers and Guidelines

v) Customer and purchaser perceptions and information from surveys

the manager can construct and *position* appropriate health care packages to target on the requirements of these market segments. In constructing health care packages, providing agencies will need to review the:

* *Competition* − identify all sources of competition (be it private care organisations, other Health Authorities, etc) and assess their strengths and weaknesses.

* *Opportunities* − market research and analysis should enable the provider to identify gaps in the market for which appropriate packages can be designed or modified.

* *Risks* − consider any risks in the market, e.g., manpower constraints, perhaps due to difficulty of recruitment in certain professions; and political risks.

Health care packages being made available are likely to reflect national policy and Unit objectives, but may be based upon a segment-specific view of what is most appropriate or most excellent in available health care, for instance within a health district.

c) *Quality of care*

An essential element of a contract for a health care package will be the identified quality standards it has to meet. The purchasing authority, by specifying the standards, *aim to define exactly what has to be provided to what level* (and thus cut out unfair competition in quality and quantity terms). The essential standards identified are likely to be limited to six, thus covering only what is considered central to the main purpose of the contract. Quality standards must be set for each package.

One of the main functions of the purchasing authority will be to monitor standards of care provided by the supplying organisations, measuring outcomes to ensure contract effectiveness. The six dimensions of the Robert Maxwell's (King's Fund) Formula should be followed, thus:

1. Access
2. Relevance
3. Effectiveness
4. Social acceptability
5. Efficiency and economy
6. Equity

For example:

Essential Element of Package	**Standards of Performance**
1) Access to Service. Maximum access of population to provision of package.	95% of new customers should be offered an appointment for assessment within 4 weeks, and receive first treatment within 4 weeks of assessment.

2) Customer satisfaction (a criterion of social acceptability)

Maximum personal satisfaction with services provided:

a) Clinical	X% satisfied with a 'bench mark' aspect of the service
b) Clerical/Admin	Y% satisfied with a 'bench mark' aspect of the service
c) Facilities	Z% satisfied with a 'bench mark' aspect of the service

d) *Pricing*

Purchasing authorities can offer three types of contract, namely:

1) Cost and volume
2) Block
3) Cost per case

Health Authorities as suppliers (providing Units) cannot run loss leaders to gain a foothold in a market, but packages must be seen to provide *value for money* and thus will be appropriately priced.

The largest component in the cost of any Community Healthcare package is likely to be manpower. Managers, therefore, will need to consider the appropriate skill mix and the appropriate level of expertise required for any particular procedure, as the use of an inappropriate grade could disproportionately increase the manpower costs associated with the contract.

Overhead costs will be absorbed into contract prices. Overheads are calculated proportionate to the work being carried out, and will include WACC — the weighted average cost of capital of the providing Unit. This implies that providers will have to exercise skill and care in pricing healthcare package proposals, and that an adequate volume of work must be obtained across which to spread the overhead cost burden. The relationship between costs and prices was analysed in Chapter 23.

There will be an interaction between price and quality, e.g. a twenty-four hour nursing service would be priced higher than a traditional twelve hour service. Thus the purchaser may be offered an appropriate choice.

e) *Public Relations and corporate image*

In the forseeable future it is unlikely that Health Authorities will be taking extensive advertising space in newspapers, radio and television, but it is possible to use these media to purvey a positive image. Any one provider of healthcare services will need to establish a successful reputation within its region (and nationally in some specialities), both as a market leader in quality care, and as a good employer, able to attract and retain all types of staff, even those in shortage categories. For instance see Box 49.1.

Box 49.1

'BY PEOPLE FOR PEOPLE IS THE KEYNOTE OF OUR ACTIVITIES

Early last year the government published a White Paper "Working for Patients". This White Paper will set the framework for the National Health Service to the end of the century and beyond. One of its stated objectives is to give people better health care and a greater choice of services.

This represents an exciting challenge, not only in providing a high quality service, but also one which is flexible, personal and local. People have a right to expect that they will be treated with respect and dignity in good facilities by highly committed and high quality staff.

Any organisation is only as good as the people who work in it and no matter how much is spent on buildings and equipment, we rely mainly on people to get things done. Northallerton Health Authority spends in excess of 70% of its revenue on staffing and is therefore very much an organisation run by people for people.

We strive to provide and maintain to the highest standards possible, a range of health services which are balanced to reflect the specific health care needs of the local community and to develop these services in accordance with national guidance and good practice. Put simply we are here to provide:-

The best of health ...Giving the highest quality of care as effectively and efficiently as we can.

... From us ... 1,500 staff all playing our part in keeping you well and caring for you when you are ill.

... To you ... The people in the towns and villages we serve.'

Northallerton Health News, in Darlington and Stockton Times 24.3.90

(reproduced with permission)

Managers should therefore be pro-active as regards P.R., ensuring that there is a favourable perception amongst the public of what the providing organisation does best. For instance:

i) identify the stakeholders and special interest groups, and manage the relationship with them proactively, e.g. with G.P.'s, Community Health Councils, Voluntary Agencies (etc).

ii) media relations — seek the right kind of coverage, make it positive, and ensure that harmful information is immediately acted upon such that any damage is limited.

iii) internal counselling — encourage all staff to be positive about their employer. Use the available communication systems (team briefings, etc.) to involve them in initiatives and health promotions. Encourage, motivate, reward and praise those who are good at promoting the services of the organisation. Ensure there is *ownership* of the organisation, that staff are proud to be a part of it, and that they are proactive in promoting its services to their customers at all times (*inseparability* characteristic is relevant here).

Ultimately, the success of the providing organisation will depend upon whether it takes care of its customers (who are purchasing agencies), and whether *their clients* (patients and those in need of care) receive an improving quality and standard of care within an increasingly competitive internal market.

RECOMMENDED READING

Cowell D.   *The Marketing of Services*   Heinemann

McDonald M.H.B.   *How to Sell a Service*   Heinemann

Kotler P. and Andreason A.R.   *Strategic Marketing for Non—Profit Organisations*   Prentice Hall International

Kotler P. and Roberto E.L.   *Social Marketing*   Macmillan

Lovelock C.H. and Weinberg C.R.   *Marketing for Public and Non-Profit Managers*   Wiley

Stewart J. and Clarke M.   *The Enabling Council*   Local Government Training Board MS 0105

QUESTIONS FOR SELF REVIEW

1) What are services, and how may their marketing differ from that applied to products?

2) What is service intangibility and how does this characteristic affect the marketing of services?

3) What is service inseparability and how does this characteristic affect the marketing of services?

4) What is service heterogeneity and how does this characteristic affect the marketing of services?

5) What is service perishability and how does this characteristic affect the marketing of services?

6) How does the characteristic of non-ownership affect the marketing of services?

7) Why are personal selling and personal contact with customers key features of the marketing mix for services?

8) Why is operations management a key determinant of the effectiveness of the marketing mix for services?

9) Why are people and customer service key features of the marketing mix for services?

10) How may service personnel be so managed that their efforts maximise the effectiveness of the marketing mix?

11) Why is physical evidence an important constituent of the marketing mix for services?

12) What kinds of physical evidence may be associated with the marketing of a service to reduce the problems caused by service intangibility, heterogeneity (etc)?

13) In what ways are the design and specification of the service environment important constituents of the marketing mix for services?

14) 'The marketing concept is applicable to all commercial organisations, irrespective of the nature of the goods or services they market.' Discuss this statement from the viewpoint of a company or partnership which offers (i) financial services, OR (ii) accountancy services; OR (iii) consultancy services.

15) In what ways is the analysis of services marketing relevant to the provision of (i) local authority 'essential services'; OR (ii) public sector healthcare, within the UK non-profit sector?

Appendix 1

Q2

Objective: to define the marketing concept and to comment on its relationship to other business orientations.

Suggested answer

The marketing concept can be defined as a management orientation that holds that the key task of the organisation is to determine the needs and wants of target markets, and to adapt the organisation to delivering the desired satisfactions more effectively and efficiently than its competitors.

The marketing concept implies that a business communicates with potential markets prior to taking new product or marketing mix decisions, and incorporates feedback from existing markets into its decision-making processes. It accepts that there should be some degree of consumer sovereignty and that policy and decision-making should be market sensitive.

The marketing concept can be contrasted with three other business orientations, which are:

i) The production concept in which the business concentrates on the volume, level of productivity and cost of the productive process. The customer, it is assumed, is only interested in product availability and price, and it is up to the manufacturer to decide what products or services he thinks the customer will buy. This approach pays little or no attention to what people want to buy, whilst the production department is seen as central to the operation of the enterprise.

ii) The product concept which assumes that the market place demands a quality product at a 'reasonable' price. Quality is seen as the over-riding component of market demand, and hence the business must invest heavily in research and development, design and quality control. This approach ignores the shape and length of the product life cycle curve and the likelihood of periodic changes in consumer tastes and preferences, nor does it recognise

738

that customers often look at their purchases from the viewpoint of usage contexts in which product quality may, or may not, be of major importance to them.

iii) The selling concept which assumes that people are not naturally inclined to buy, and will resist making purchase decisions. Purchasing is seen as a negative reaction and consumers have to be pushed into buying by a positive sales effort. The solution is to make, package and price the product or service, and then to sell it. The sales department is seen as central to the business effort, and expenditure on sales and promotion activity, advertising (etc) figure large in investment decisions. Similarly, the volume of business done is seen in terms of how hard the salesmen work, and so there will be a whole array of incentives, commissions and other forms of motivational techniques to goad them on to higher results.

Each of these three orientations to business contain necessary activities. But the marketing concept suggests that any one of these other concepts in isolation is not adequate. The marketing concept is an attempt to recognise that all of these three orientations to business have an essential part to play, but that the starting point must be the overall orientation of the business activity towards understanding, anticipating and fulfilling the needs and wants of the customer and the market place.

Q6

Objective: to describe market research and how it is carried out; and to comment on why it is an important input to setting business objectives and judging enterprise performance.

Suggested answer:

Market Research is the term given to the process of finding out what the customer wants or needs, and what he/she will buy. This means establishing which consumers comprise which market segments, and what are the characteristics and buying behaviour of these consumers. Further, market research may be used to estimate demand volume, potential company sales, intention to buy and price elasticity.

Market Research is based on two main sources of information, namely desk research and field research. Desk research makes use of:

* Internal company records, eg objective sales records, subjective judgements, etc;
* Published data, eg trade information and press, company reports and accounts, company ratio analyses, government and international statistics and reports.

Field research aims, by 'sampling', to confirm or elaborate on the view of the market or segment obtained from desk research, or provide information to clarify and quantify the implications of a new product or service proposal. There are several research methods, including (i) personal interview (ii) telephone interview (iii) consumer/user panels and test panels (iv) panels of expert opinion (v) mail survey.

Field research findings are as good as the method used. For a start, a reasoned judgement must be made to define the relevant population. In the case of medium to large sized saloon cars, is the relevant population made up of individuals, or the fewer institutional buyers who buy large numbers of cars per order for business or fleet use?

There are two main methods by which a sample of this relevant population may be obtained. The choice of sampling method will determine how "representative" of the total population this sample will be.

* "random" samples are objectively determined, and the degree of 'sampling error' can be calculated as an indication of the level of representativeness of the chosen population.
* "quota" samples are not based on random choice, and no quantification of the accuracy or representativeness can be made. On the other hand, quota samples may be constructed on the basis of objective criteria so as to make them as sufficiently accurate as may be needed for the research objective. Quota samples may be a more cost-effective sampling device.

Role in setting objectives and judging enterprise performance

Market research provides an important input to business planning by:

* informing the company about market trends and changes which affect objectives for product/service range and cost-volume-profit relationships;

* identifying life cycle changes, new product/service requirements, and 'gaps' emerging in the market;
* identifying changing consumer attitudes to the company and its products/services, or image;

Market Research provides an important input to operational planning in supplying quantifications for annual sales forecasts (which are basic to setting operational objectives and budgetary control), in terms of market segments, volumes, prices and revenues. In business and operational planning, actual enterprise performance will give rise to:

a) indications of the organisation's market research effectiveness;

b) indications of the organisation's capacity to respond to market research (and, therefore, market needs), and thus operate in a market sensitive manner;

c) indications of the organisation's capacity to interpret and translate generalised statements of environmental analysis and forecasting into concrete statements of how market opportunities and threats relate to company strengths and weaknesses.

Q4

Objective: to describe, justify and comment on factors selected in the answer which have caused companies to become marketing orientated.

Key points:

- end of colonialism, which was associated with protected markets;
- international dislike of trade protectionism; emergence of free trade zones and "common markets" eg EEC, EFTA;
- increased sources of supply, leading to:-
- increased domestic and international competition; competitor marketing orientation;
- more universal quality and delivery consciousness, making it harder to differentiate products by quality or delivery advantages;
- fragmenting markets requiring effective market research, market segmentation and market analysis;

- greater customer education and awareness, resulting in more discerning purchase evaluation and behaviour;
- increasingly effective organisational buying, and professional purchasing and supply management;
- shortening product life cycles, increased NPD (new product development) risk, increased business risk. This increases the pressure for a more effective management response to this risk, to ensure the generation of adequate financial returns;
- increasingly sophisticated marketing strategic input to competitor company corporate planning.

Q5

Objective: to differentiate consumer and industrial marketing, illustrating answer with appropriate examples.

Key points:

- consumer markets consist of all the individuals and households who purchase goods and services for their own personal use or consumption. Consumers buy "non-durable" goods (eg foodstuffs, cosmetics); "durable" goods (eg clothing, furniture); "services" (eg painters and decorators, hairdressing);
- industrial goods markets consist of individuals and organisations who buy products and services used in manufacture or business, or which are eventually resold to other customers. Buyers purchase "consumable" products (eg lubricating oil, welding rods); "capital" goods (eg machinery, buildings); "services" (eg machinery repair, advertising services);
- demand in industrial goods markets is "derived". Goods/services are purchased as inputs to a manufacturing or operational process whose objective is the supply of a product or service to another customer;
- as a result, industrial market prospects depend upon the demand for the product sold to the next customer in the chain of supply. In consequence, industrial markets tend to suffer from a much greater sensitivity to variations in demand than do consumer markets. These variations in demand manifest themselves as "business cycles" (eg as found in shipbuilding, construction, or the manufacture of machine tools);
- other differences between the two include:-
  * number of potential customers.
  * relative size and frequency of purchase.

* technical content of purchase decision.
* purchase procedures.
* prices, terms and conditions of supply.
– the basic principles of marketing apply to both, but each requires different emphasis and approach to:-
    * market research, market forecasting.
    * market segmentation, market analysis, customer targeting.
    * product management, product development.
    * pricing strategies.
    * use of direct supply, channels of distribution.
    * advertising, which is more important in consumer goods markets.
    * personal selling and technical sales representation, which is more important in industrial markets.

Q9

Objective: to describe and comment on factors that affect questionnaire design and construction, so as to facilitate an efficient and accurate analysis and application of market research findings.

Key points:
– a well constructed questionnaire will elicit more information than a badly constructed one. Clarity, simplicity and logic will make answering it, and collating the results more straight-forward;
– specific factors include:-
    * objective and scale of the research.
    * language used (should be simple and free from ambiguity).
    * relationship between questions (should be logical to respondents).
    * attitude of respondent as generated by presentation.
    * length of questionnaire.
    * facility for coding and computer processing. Can answers be structured so that they can be coded? (this is essential in large scale sampling).
– structured use of closed direct questions enables responses to be standardised and hence coded. This makes the responses easy to collate and analyse;
– use of specified criteria to restrict/limit/categorise answers to questionnaires containing open and indirect questions. These need structure in order to gain some element of standardisation;

– unstructured questionnaires containing open and indirect questions also need a framework for extracting useable information. Questionnaire design and interviewer approach must guide answers if categorisation and comparison is to be possible, otherwise analysis and comparison will be very time-consuming. Such questionnaires can only be used for in-depth or attitudinal research, for instance within industrial market research;

– the recording of attitudes and opinions requires the use of numerical scales applied to all respondents, so that results can be collated and compared. Likert and Semantic Differential scales are used for this purpose. Semantic Differential scales are good for comparing and rating attributes.

Q10

Objective: to analyse the relative advantages of quota sampling used in preference to the theoretically more accurate random sampling.

Key points:

– give definition of random and quota sampling;

– the objective of sampling within this context is the achievement of a selection of individuals from the total relevant population that is representative of it for market research purposes;

– random sampling is statistically accurate, and sampling error can be calculated. But achieving representativeness will call for an appropriate sample, which may be large, widely dispersed and expensive;

– quota sampling is not statistically accurate in that sampling error cannot be calculated;

– quota sampling is popular because it can be carried out on a predetermined scale and may be much less expensive. It is viable for market research purposes because the sample can be matched to objective criteria or statistical proportions that are appropriate to the particular research objective;

– quota sampling may be adequately or appropriately representative (relative to the market research objective) if stratified sampling is carried out on the basis of known demographic proportions eg from Census of Population Data, housing type, company customer database;

– Such demographic proportions are relatively stable. They have been computerised eg in the **ACORN** system. Stratified quota samples can be designed which contain objective statistical proportions at whatever scale of sampling is possible. This may be perfectly adequate for market research purposes, and more cost-effective than random sampling.

Q13

Objective: to describe the main short term methods of sales forecasting used to generate the annual sales forecast input to company budgetary planning.

Key points:

– quantitative forecasting methods take three forms, namely subjective, statistical and explanatory;

– subjective forecasting techniques comprise:-
  * salesforce composite method (estimates of future sales made by sales staff/sales management).
  * juries of executive opinion (combined internal and external executive opinion about market trends).
  * surveys of buyer intention (based on expected purchases in industrial goods markets).

– statistical forecasting techniques include moving averages, exponential smoothing, time-series analysis, trend extrapolation, curve fitting;

– forecast of market share, which is based on the likely available market for the period and the company's forecast of its likely share of that market. This may be calculated using the quantitative methods already listed;

– explanatory forecasting techniques (based upon Operations Research, and macroeconomic/econometric modelling) may be used to augment the more specific methods already described. They can provide a broad context by which to shape and guide the more specific assumptions and calculations that make up the annual sales forecast, or forecast of market share.

Q16

Objective: to describe and justify the application of two contrasting types of forecasting technique (namely exponential smoothing, time series analysis; and econometric modelling, scenario writing).

Key points:

i) exponential smoothing and time series analysis:-

– statistical methods applied to the construction of specific sales, market and market share forecasts at the level of sales territory, market segment, product or brand, within the firm. Based upon historical data directly derived from the sales pattern/market under consideration;

– short term application, say up to 6 – 12 months ahead;

– use values, patterns, trends derived from past data, and directly projects these forward;

– identify trends indicated by data time-series, which will have direct implications for sales;

– identify specific seasonal variations, cyclical variations, and variations which can be attributed to specified events/ occurences. The impact of these variations can be directly projected into company sales forecasts.

ii) econometric modelling and scenario writing:-

– these are explanatory/quantitative, and qualitative forecasting methods respectively;

– they are used to forecast broad and longer term economic, marketing, technological, political and social conditions within which short-run statistical methods are to be used, whether this be at a macro or industrial level;

– used to inform, assist and augment short-run statistical forecasting, and to give depth, understanding and context to it;

– both techniques are often described in terms of "environmental forecasting". Their application is a recognition that sales and market forecasting is not carried out in isolation from the environment within which the firm operates;

– these techniques are used at the level of the firm, the industry and the economy. Nevertheless, the context to which they are applied should be sufficiently specific to be of use in the company's forecasting process.

Q18

Objective: to analyse and comment upon behavioural factors relevant to the existing state and development of consumer attitudes towards the purchase of a product or service.

Key points:

i) motivation – a direct reflection of need or want into attitude formation and behaviour pattern. The marketer needs to understand the nature and causes of needs/wants, and their impact upon motivation and attitude formation. The marketer also needs to understand consumer perceptions of these needs/wants (are they positive or negative?), and how (if at all) they can or should be satisfied.

ii) personality – which is the sum total of traits defining individuality. Traits are ingrained and stable dispositions to respond in particular ways to external stimuli. Can the marketer understand the sources of personality development and align marketing messages to "fit" this development? Can marketing messages be targeted upon personality "stereotypes", thereby relating attitude and purchase behaviour?

iii) culture – which is defined as distinctive patterns of attitude and behaviour which result from basic beliefs, traditions and experience. People's attitudes towards purchase and consumption will, in part, be determined by the process by which people are "socialised" into the prevailing culture.

iv) life-style – which is based upon distinctive attitudes towards a desired way of living. If life-style attitudes can be accurately described, then marketers can design and target products and promotion upon a particular life-style group. These products and promotion should enjoy a favourable attitudinal response.

v) social class – which is a major determinant of buying behaviour. Marketers will have to accept as given many social class derived attitudes, since the rate at which these change (if at all) is likely to be very slow. Products or services will have to be perceived as "appropriate" within a social class context.

vi) family – which is also a major determinant of buying behaviour. Marketers will have to position products and promotion so that these are seen as appropriate or desirable within the context of family purchase decision-making. Marketing messages may be used to influence and develop family attitudes towards new product acceptance (etc).

vii) reference groups and opinion leaders – product development and promotional messages will be targeted upon opinion leaders and those of influence within a reference group. A change of attitude towards the product may, as a result, "trickle down" into the reference group as a whole. This factor offers considerable scope to the marketer for changing consumer attitudes.

Q20

Objective: to analyse and comment on the relevance and relative influence of family roles and family decision-making processes in household purchases of products and services.

Key points:

– influence of mother relative to husband and children. The mother often plays a "pivotal" role in household purchase decision making, exercising influence over the alternatives being considered, and the final decision that is taken. Husbands often defer to their wives during such decision-taking, irrespective of the degree to which their financial contribution to the household budget is the most significant one;

– influence of mother on daughter (or daughter-in-law) as a young housewife. Maternal influence is often very strong here, just at a point at which major expenditure is incurred in setting up the new household. This increases the significance for marketers of the maternal role;

– influence of older family members, though more subtle, is still considerable. Older family members may act as "sounding board" or "devil's advocate" during the discussion about major household expenditure decisions;

– influence of children and teenagers, which is nowadays considerable within purchase decisions for foodstuffs, clothing, and personal expenditure. Parents will have to make decisions about pocket money, the level of saving to be encouraged, and the level of personal discretion to be given to younger family members in making personal expenditure decisions;

– decision process roles will also be important. It is usual to identify initiator, influencer, decider, purchaser and user roles. Key roles will be the influencer (often taken by the mother) and the decider (mother and father);

– the relative influence of family and decision making roles will vary with stage in the family life cycle.

Q25

Objective: to analyse and comment on the importance of identifying the Decision Making Unit (DMU) in the marketing of industrial products.

Key points:
- in industrial goods markets the importance of the role of the buying department may vary widely. In general terms, the more complex and expensive the decision, the more people will be involved, the more will senior management be involved, and the less important will be the role of the buying department;
- it will be important for the marketing function in supplier companies (i) to understand how buying decisions are made, and (ii) to find out who are the most influential figures in that process;
- the problem is specifically that of how to promote and sell the product to the potential customer. Promotional and sales effort needs to be correctly targeted. These targets may be categorised and analysed on the basis of the buying process roles (gatekeeper, user, influencer, decision-maker, buyer) as these can be identified within the potential customer's organisational arrangements;
- supplier companies must establish a mix of inter-related promotional and selling activities aimed at:-
  * building awareness in gatekeeper roles and encouraging them to permit access to influencer and decision-maker roles.
  * persuading influencers and making the sales presentation to decision makers. This is the most difficult part of the process, especially where access is limited by gatekeeper roles, or a number of people are involved.
- supplier companies may make use of the following as promotional tools:-
  # catalogues.
  # trade and technical press.
  # direct marketing techniques aimed at influencers/decision-makers.
  # Public Relations.
  # peer group promotion.
- use of illustrative examples.

Q27

Objective: to suggest marketing policies by which the potential new supplier may persuade an industrial buyer to change supplier, or at least to try the products of the new supplier on a limited basis.

Key points:
- buying behaviour in industrial goods markets tends to be "conservative" and buyers often develop strong loyalty to their suppliers. Changing from a known to a lesser-known supplier involves the loss of a past performance record, loss of the familiarity and ease of dealing with an established supplier, and incurs administrative disturbance. The new supplier must be able to offer incentive to try his product that will visibly outweigh the disadvantage (to the buyer) of changing supplier;
- the new supplier could:-
  * offer the product for trial at a cost-price basis, for a limited period.
  * offer an "augmented" product as a means of securing competitive advantage. This means offering a greater collection of benefits (relative to usage context) than the existing supplier. These additional benefits could include:
    - product reliability and stringent quality control;
    - improved after-sales service;
    - faster and more reliable delivery than existing suppliers;
    - preferential credit terms or financial assistance to the buyer;
    - Research and Development activities for the product, funded by the new supplier;
  * ensure that ordering and supply is administratively easy and free from problems for the buyer.
  * encourage the buyer to move to a "dual source" of supply position, emphasising to him the advantages of increased security of supply, and competition between the two suppliers benefitting the customer.

Q29

Objective: to describe and comment on the main criteria by which a marketing manager may segment the market.

Key points:
- there are two main categories of segmentation criteria, applicable to both consumer and industrial goods markets;

i) consumer/user characteristics:-

consumer markets	*industrial markets*
geographic distribution.	geographic distribution.
demographic factors.	customer size.
consumption rate.	usage rate.
life-style.	industry classification.
personality.	

ii) product segmentation, which focusses on how consumers or buyers perceive, group together and differentiate between available brands, products or services:-

consumer markets	*industrial markets*
principal benefit sought within perceived usage context.	principal benefit sought within perceived usage context. Vendor segmentation. Contribution per unit of limiting factor (especially in retail outlets).

– use of illustrative examples.

Q32

Objective: to analyse and comment on the relationship between market segmentation, market targeting and product positioning.

Key points:

– *market segmentation* is the analysis of a particular total demand into its constituent parts, so that sets of buyers can be identified and differentiated. Detailed market segmentation may differentiate and group customers on the basis of "sets of attributes" which they possess;

– *market targeting* enhances and develops the basic market analysis provided by market segmentation. It allows the marketer to build up detailed and accurate market intelligence about target customer groups, for instance in terms of demographic profiles, area analysis, retail catchment areas and shopping centre planning;

– market targeting exploits Census Data (demographics), and Information Technology developments (for instance, as combined in the **ACORN** system);

751

- market targeting facilitates the planning and focussing of the most cost-effective promotional activity on specific target customer segments eg TV and press advertising whose audience/readership profile is accurately known on the basis of **ACORN** categories (housing, socio-economic group);
- market targeting may maximise company sales penetration through retail and distribution channels, by which target customers actually gain access to products, and whose (geographic and demographic) position is a crucial determinant of marketing success;
- *product positioning* requires the enterprise to develop and position products/product ranges whose specification or attributes are appropriate to the requirements of specific customer segments upon which they are to be targeted. People seek the benefits that products provide, so that products or brands should therefore contain those combinations of characteristics, benefits and costs sought by a particular set of potential customers;
- the logic of market segmentation, market targeting and product positioning is that of "differentiating" products and promotional activity according to the characteristics and requirements of target customer groups. Market segmentation, customer targeting and product differentiation are essential features of the marketing concept.

Q35

Objective: to analyse and comment on the complexity of marketing mix management and decision-making.

Key points:
- the marketing mix can be defined as the combination of detailed strategies, tactics, operational policies, programmes, techniques and activities, to which resources may be allocated such that the marketing objectives of the enterprise can be achieved. This gives a clue to the complexity of marketing mix management and decision-making;
- the role of the marketing mix is to move marketing objectives and plans into the reality of implementation and achievement. It must therefore comprise a complex of:-
  * strategic elements.
  * planning elements.
  * tactical elements.

* operational and implementation elements.
* resource commitment elements.

There must be a logical, consistent and integrated relationship between these elements, so that strategies and plans are financially viable, and implemented in a cost-effective manner;

– this complex of elements,decisions and activities should be managed such that it ensures that the right *product* is available at the right *price* in the right *place* at the appropriate time. This process must be supported by timely and appropriate *promotion*. These are the 4 P's;

– the component activities of each marketing mix category are inter-related and inter-dependent;

– the four marketing mix categories are inter-related and inter-dependent;

– marketing management must take account of this complex of inter-relationships and inter-dependencies. This may make management decision-making difficult, and its results unpredictable. Alterations to one element of the marketing mix can have repercussions (positive or negative) within a category, or elsewhere in another category. Similarly, a problem in one element of the marketing mix may be solved by an adjustment in another;

– the skill of the marketing manager therefore lies in understanding how the four categories of the marketing mix interact, and in being able to combine them in a cost-effective manner to achieve marketing objectives.

Q37

Objective: to describe the main features of the Product Life Cycle, and to explain how and why the marketing mix for an illustrative product/service example would be managed over its life cycle.

Key points:
– the Product Life Cycle has four stages, namely:
  * introduction.
  * growth.
  * maturity.
  * decline.

These should be illustrated diagrammatically, using sales and profit curves;

– use of illustrative example to describe the management of the marketing mix over the Product Life Cycle:-

i) Product: developed, differentiated and the range expanded up to the maturity stage; rationalised in the decline stage;

ii) Promotion: heavy at introduction stage to secure and expand distribution, to develop consumer awareness and confidence in the new product, and to encourage personal conviction to make the initial purchase. Maintained at growth stage to achieve increases in sales, and still relatively heavy in maturity to maintain trade distribution, maintain customer loyalty and repeat sales, and compete on non-price basis with competitors;

iii) Place: selective distribution at introduction stage, need to consolidate and expand distribution at growth stage, most intensive at maturity, selective or rationalised in decline stage;

iv) Price: "penetration" price at introduction (to maximise market penetration) or "skimming" (to maximise profit). Price in growth stage needs to be as high as possible to maximise profit (and perhaps pay off R and D costs) before competition enters the market. Price competition emerges thereafter and there is likely to be downward pressure on prices and profit margins. Price may be lowered or increased during the decline stage.

Q42

Objective: to suggest and comment on reasons for the increased importance of packaging as an element of the marketing mix.

Key points:

– packaging fulfills its traditional, functional role of protecting the product from damage, deterioration, climate (etc), and facilitating physical distribution;

– but its importance within the marketing mix has increased dramatically, for some of the reasons listed below:-

i) consumer convenience, to which the relationship between design, shape and form of the product and its packaging should be added, as this enhances the functional properties of the product.

ii) trade appeal, in which promotional and presentational factors will encourage distributors and retailers to stock the product (in an environment where competition for shelf-space is intense).

iii) sales promotion – changes in patterns of retailing, the increase in the number and variety of products available, and the growth of retailer power have meant that packaging must give any one product impact in situ. Packaging communicates and promotes the product, it enhances its appearance and differentiates it from its competitors. Packaging should be co-ordinated with, and assist the wider efforts of in-store sales promotion and external media advertising. The perceptions about the product in the consumer's mind that result from advertising and sales promotion should be focussed and reinforced by packaging and its presentation. After all, in self-service environments it may well be that the product's packaging is ultimately responsible for making the sale!

Q45

Objective: to distinguish between market "skimming" (or premium) pricing, and market "penetration" pricing, and to discuss the factors favouring management choice between these two strategies.

Key points:

– market-skimming (or premium) pricing means the setting of high prices which will limit demand but render each sale made relatively profitable. The concept derives from the notion of "skimming the cream" at the top of the market demand profile;

– penetration pricing means setting low prices which are used to obtain as large a market share as possible in the shortest possible time, and maintain that market share thereafter. Penetration pricing can only be used when the market is price-sensitive, and production/supply costs will decrease in proportion to increases in volume sold;

– skimming prices will be applicable where:-
   * there is restricted market demand, restricted supply and competition, or low price elasticity of demand, for instance in market segments to which price is a relatively unimportant product attribute. High prices may be based upon effective product differentiation, with products accurately targeted upon such price-insensitive segments. Quality, reliability and availability may be regarded as more important attributes than price, and buyers will adjust their price perceptions accordingly.

* a price-unique selling proposition (USP) relationship has become clearly established within customer perceptions, and before competitive products carrying similar USP's enter the market.
* to maintain a price-brand relationship.
* to cover heavy R & D costs involved in NPD activities, especially where competition is eventually inevitable.

– penetration prices will be used:-
   # where there is a high degree of price elasticity of demand, and where price is a relatively important product attribute.
   # to establish a strong market share during the introduction and growth stages of the product life cycle, so as to maximise sales during the growth and maturity stages. This is regarded as being critically important in f.m.c.g. type markets.
   # where low price equates with consumer perceptions of "value for money".
   # where channels of distribution are themselves price sensitive, and will not accept premium pricing tactics from their suppliers.

Q47

Objective: to comment on percentage mark-up and target rate of return pricing, and to analyse other factors that apply to the pricing of a new product.

Key points:

– pricing on the basis of a percentage addition to cost is a simple policy, easy to understand and calculate;

– the method involves the addition of a percentage "mark-up" to the total cost of producing/distributing the product. A more sophisticated variation is the addition of a percentage which is calculated to achieve a target rate of return;

– the percentage addition must, in addition, take into account:-
   * what the supplier can reasonably charge (which depends upon what the market will bear).
   * expectation of "traditional" or "normal" mark-ups to be found in the trade.

– other factors relevant to the pricing of a new product include:-
   # financial and marketing objectives for the new product, and the degree to which these objectives are comple-mentary.

market segment and target customer type upon which new product is positioned.
consumer attitude and sensitivity to price of similar types/categories of product.
attitude of trade/channels of distribution to price set.
requirement to cover R and D costs involved in product development, and to cover promotional costs at introduction and launch.
early feedback about the level of market demand.
consequences of price set in encouraging/discouraging early competition in the market.
the expression of the decision made in terms of setting a "penetration" or a "skimming" (or "premium") price.

Q51

Objective: to outline and analyse the circumstances in which selective and intensive distribution policies may be used by a manufacturer, within the context of the customer service objectives set by the company.

Key points:

– the choice depends, initially, on the marketer's channel objectives. These may be expressed in terms of objectives for market penetration, competitive position and market share, and will indicate the desired level of representation in the market. They will determine the level of reseller effort required, and will decide the revenue returns to be obtained;

– however, channel objectives are a function of the company's objectives for customer service, (this is why the question is much more complex than would first appear). Customer service objectives are a function of:-
  * place of availability.
  * frequency of availability (which is a time-related concept).
The greater the number of places, and the more frequent the product availability, the more intensive is the distribution. Intensive distribution is often associated with high volume, low value items such as f.m.c.g. categories like foodstuffs, soap and detergents, housewares (etc);

– but the achievement of customer service objectives (and hence the choice between selective and intensive distribution) will depend upon:-
  # available distribution channels and their density relative to the market.

757

    # timing and reliability factors in physical distribution, relative to stockholding policies and the importance of supply economics.

    # relative costs of selective and intensive distribution.

- intensive distribution policies render the product accessible in many locations throughout the land;

- selective distribution policies restrict access to the product to target locations containing specific customer types and channels of distribution;

- given the company's channel and customer service objectives, the choice of distribution policy will then depend upon relative cost-effectiveness in terms of access and transaction value. The supplier will use the distribution method that yields a positive benefit relative to the costs incurred. The more intensive the distribution, the greater the access but the greater its cost and the lower the transaction value may be (for instance because more channel intermediaries are involved as resellers). The opposite may apply for a selective policy of distribution, which will succeed or fail on account of the level of access to the product that is effective in gaining custom;

- the choice between selective and intensive distribution also depends on the type of product or service.

    * high volume low value items (eg f.m.c.g.) need intensive distribution, backed by heavy promotion.

    * consumer durables may require controlled or preferential selling, and after-sales service. This will encourage selective distribution;

    * luxury goods will be made available through restricted outlets positioned on target segments.

    * services must be made available when and where they are wanted. The less differentiated the service (eg hairdressing), and the more competitive the market, the more intensive is supply likely to be.

Q53

Objective: to analyse and comment on the growth of non-shop selling within the (UK) channels of distribution.

Key points:

- non-shop selling is based in the UK on direct selling, and direct marketing techniques comprising mail-order, direct response advertising, and direct mail. Mail order marketing is based on a lengthy tradition and experience of non-shop selling in this country;

- there has been a considerable increase in the direct selling of household improvement products and financial services (personal investment, life assurance, etc)
- reasons for the growth of non-shop selling include:-
  * potential for widening the market.
  * cost-effective method of targeting promotional activities.
  * counteracts the development of retailer/intermediary power and increases the value of transactions to the supplier.
  * makes use of Information Technology and **ACORN** type developments. Database and customer list marketing make possible the accurate targeting of products and promotion on customer segments and specialist niches.
- retailers themselves are increasing their use of non-shop selling. Reasons for this development include:-
  # use of account customer/customer database to target direct marketing via catalogues on customer segments, thereby increasing sales of existing lines without the need for increased investment in shop premises.
  # restricted availability, and competition for prime retail sites; combined with increasing cost of city-centre sites.

Q55

Objective: to analyse and comment on the essential requisites for successful overseas marketing.

Key points:

- the company will need to have a thorough knowledge of the target country, its policy towards inward trade, and its ability to pay. It will also need to understand (i) the country's marketing, commercial and industrial infrastructure, (ii) its culture and patterns of consumer behaviour (for instance whether based on traditional, achieving or affluent cultures). This knowledge or intelligence should be backed up by an objective view of the country's political potential;
- the company must position appropriate products on target market segments. These should contain characteristics suitable to the particular market demand. Product modification is usually an essential feature of overseas marketing;

- other requisites include knowledge of:-
  * communication patterns to and within the territory.
  * available channels of distribution (and their relative effectiveness).
  * how the activity is to be managed, co-ordinated and controlled.
  * the relevant contractual obligations to be incurred.
- the company must be prepared for unexpected events, but more important, it must be committed to the overseas marketing activity;
- its marketing strategies must:-
  * overcome (as far as is possible) trading restrictions imposed upon it.
  * implement effective operations (use of agents, local manufacture, etc).
  * utilise effective pricing policies.
  * ensure effective financial management and control of overseas operations.

Q57

Objective: to analyse the factors that determine a company's promotional mix.

Key points:

- the promotional mix can be defined as the combination of communication methods used to achieve the promotional objectives of the marketing mix;
- marketing communications are used to create awareness, understanding and conviction within the recipient, and to persuade him/her to take positive action to purchase the product. Communication theory is relevant to this process, and to the requirement to overcome the barriers to effective communication. The principle of communication "redundancy" may be used in this context;
- the variety and complexity of the promotional mix may be determined by market segmentation;
- the required strength and duration of promotional communications will determine the power or "reach" of the media to be used, and the "frequency" with which messages are repeated;

– communication objectives within the persuasion process are often analysed on the basis of DAGMAR (unawareness – awareness – comprehension – conviction – action). The promotional mix must reflect persuasion process stage;

– the promotional mix for a brand or product must be correlated with its stage on the product life cycle;

– promotional mix decisions will also be affected by the marketing choice between "demand pull" and "demand push" strategies;

– other determining factors include:-
  * the degree of reliance (if any) on "non-controllable" promotional methods.
  * the budget available for, and past experience with "controllable" methods.
  * the promotional mix strategies employed by competitors.

Q61

Objective: to analyse methods by which a company may measure the effectiveness of its advertising effort.

Key points:

– The company will wish to assess the effectiveness of its advertising effort within the context of the persuasion process, for instance:-
  * awareness – name/brand/product recall: inclusion by customers as a purchase alternative.
  * comprehension and conviction – positive/favourable attitudes created towards the brand/product; evidence of brand loyalty.
  * action – sales figures; repeat purchase behaviour; retailer stocking of brand/product on continuous basis; ineffective own-brand competition; confirming customer perceptions of "rightness" about purchasing the product.

– advertising effort may be evaluated in terms of communication and persuasion effectiveness. This may be achieved by:-

(i) advertising quality – evaluated by tests of recall, attitude tests, linguistic tests, visual tests.

(ii) media effectiveness – evaluated by the effectiveness of the media in influencing audience attitudes; and by promotional effectiveness as indicated by factors such as:-

the size of target audience reached.

the cost per thousand reached.

the frequency of message repetition needed for persuasion process objectives to be achieved.

the level of wastage (non-receptive audience) incurred by use of the media.

– assessments of media effectiveness are available from Audience Research Data, such as readership levels, television programme ratings (etc).

– despite the availability of these measures, the evaluation of advertising effectiveness in terms of a direct relationship to sales achieved, provides marketing management with a major problem.

Q64

Objective: to analyse the factors which determine the role and size of a company's sales force.

Key points:

– the emphasis and approach taken to this answer may, in part, depend on whether the company is operating in a consumer or industrial goods market;

(i) salesforce role determinants:-

* the salesforce has two main roles, namely personal persuasion and selling activities, and personal contact for non-selling tasks.

* personal selling is the dominant promotional and sales technique in industrial markets.

* size, location and dispersion of markets. Decisions on salesforce coverage must be integrated with strategic decisions as between demand push (salesforce orientated) and demand pull (advertising oriented), and whether distribution is to be selective or intensive.

* other factors include salesforce and organisational inertia; customer and trade expectations; competitors' use of personal selling; the requirement to prospect for new customers and the availability of resources which can relieve sales staff of the need to carry out cold-calling.

ii) determinants of salesforce size:-

sales territories to be covered; the company's objectives for reach and frequency of coverage by sales staff; and the sales potential of these territories.

salesforce workload, which is a function of: sales potential (number of customers); required reach (coverage of available/potential customers); required frequency (call rate); length of call for different categories of customer (the larger the account, the more frequent the calls and the longer should these calls last).

field management implications: sales management must shape and structure the salesforce organisation so that it can effectively be motivated and controlled.

Q66

Objective: using an illustrative example, to describe some of the ways in which a company can motivate its field sales force.

Key points:

i)   field management and communication: is needed to provide support and guidance to sales staff; to monitor and control field sales activities; to provide advice *in situ* and to assist in problem solving. Field visits, sales meetings (etc) also serve to foster a feeling of team spirit and identity.

ii) training: the performance and motivation of field sales staff is dependent upon effective training. In addition to knowledge of products and markets, salesforce motivation will be enhanced by skills training, training in sales management skills (to improve promotion prospects and retain talented staff), and specialist "motivation training" which is widely developed in the sales area.

iii) systems of remuneration and reward: experience has shown that sales staff can effectively be motivated by both the main forms of financial reward, depending upon the kind of work they have to do, and on the varying reactions to incentive systems. The two main reward systems are:-

*   salary based remuneration: used where sales orders achieved are not seen to be an effective indicator of job performance, and where commission payments would be inappropriate. This remuneration system is widely applied in selling to industrial goods markets, particularly where there is a high technological content to the work.

*   payment by results (PBR) based remuneration: which relate effort to reward, and exploit the incentive value of money as a motivating force. Motivation is achieved by the use of commission payments, bonus payments,

achievement awards, contests and competitions. The effectiveness of the PBR based systems as a motivator is dependent upon the level or threshold at which the system comes into operation, and the behaviour of the effort-incentive relationship.

– use of illustrative example(s) within answer eg selling industrial products, national account selling to retail multiples (etc).

Q69

Objective: to state the main objectives for the evaluation of marketing activities, and to analyse two practical techniques used to carry out this evaluation process.

Key points:

i) objectives for the evaluation of marketing activities include:-
  * feedback, comparison and review. The evaluation process is one in which actual performance is compared with desired results. These desired results are represented by predetermined functional objectives and standards.
  * control. This requires feedback and comparison, so that variances can be identified and corrected for, and the process of Management by Exception operated.

ii) Contribution Analysis:-
  # advantages include the ease of relating units to financial results for evaluation purposes; simplicity of calculation (compared with absorption costing); variety and flexibility of application to performance evaluation; comparison using Contribution Margin.
  # disadvantages include the need to understand how the principle works and is applied; the need for detailed cost information on items to be evaluated; the need to define and categorise Variable Cost and Fixed Cost; the problem of defining some Fixed Cost items (eg loan interest).

iii) Budgetary control:-
  * budgetary control is the basic management control mechanism based upon the concept of responsibility accounting. It permits control through variance analysis and correction, and feeds forward (as a technique of "feedforward" control) into future budgetary planning.

* disadvantages include the critical nature of the revenue budget (which is dependent upon the accuracy of sales forecasting); the level of detailed definition needed for the expense budgets; the definition of the limits of Management by Exception; the need for a management accounting system and appropriate information flows, Information Technology facilities (etc); the cost, complexity and integrated nature of budgetary control systems.

Q71

Objective: to outline and comment on a company's objective of establishing a positive corporate image within its external environment.

Key points:

– all business and public organisations have to take account of those elements or forces in their external environment that are capable of affecting their operations. These elements may be represented by individuals, groups or organisations;

– the company's reaction to the external environment should be managed and controlled by the Public Relations (PR) function. PR may attempt to create a favourable "corporate image" of the company within its external environment by presenting or re-ordering inputs to the perceptual process in a manner favourable to the organisation;

– this external environment may be widely defined to include specific interest groups and organisations within political, commercial, financial and technological contexts. The company's image may be fostered by the use of corporate advertising and communication. Alternatively, lobbying may be undertaken on a proactive or reactive basis where favourable external perceptions may affect forthcoming legislation, regulation or investment potential;

– the cultivation of a favourable external image should be integrated with marketing activities, thereby enhancing the latter. This may be achieved through effective media relations and product publicity;

– the process of establishing corporate image should also enhance public perceptions of socially responsible behaviour on the part of the organisation.

Q74

Objective: to outline and illustrate marketing strategies required to achieve customer and profit objectives, relative to the prevailing competitive environment in which the company is trading.

Key points:

- consolidation strategy involves defending and reinforcing existing market and segment provision; also seeking a sufficiently strong position on the industry experience curve in volume markets characterised by the experience effect;

- market penetration strategy involves increasing market share within existing markets and segments, which has implications for (i) advertising, promotion and selling; (ii) for volume markets characterised by the experience effect;

- product development strategies require brand and product management, innovation and NPD relative to product life cycle. Differentiated products may be positioned on a variety of segments, or product strategies may be concentrated, niche or segment-specific. Product development and differentiation may become essential in volume markets whose products are coming to be perceived as commodity products, or dominated by retail own brands, and to which the experience effect can be applied;

- market development strategies may be based on increasingly detailed and accurate market research, market segmentation and customer targeting. Advertising and promotion may instead lead to the development of latent demand, and NPD may also open up new markets (eg as in the personal and microcomputer markets);

- diversification strategies comprise:-
  * horizontal diversification: doing more of the same eg retailing foodstuffs.
  * concentric diversification: doing closely related activities eg wholesale and retail distribution.
  * vertical integration: diversifying backwards and forwards in the chain of manufacture and supply eg oil companies extract, process, distribute and retail oil-based and related products.
  * conglomerate diversification: applying skills and distinctive competences to unrelated activities so as to gain

competitive advantage eg entrepreneurial skills, expertise at marketing f.m.c.g.

- the development and application of marketing strategies must be appropriately related to the profile of company assets (and their operation) so as to minimise risk and achieve reasonable objectives for company profitability.

Q78

Objective: to analyse the differences, in principle, between the marketing of detergents and the marketing of financial services.

Key points:

- the basic marketing principles apply to both cases, although the actual marketing strategies chosen depend on the degree to which financial services marketing can be equated with f.m.c.g.; Financial services marketing is however, more tightly regulated by law;

- consumer behaviour determinants are more complex in financial services marketing, and the analysis of consumer motivation and attitude is of particular importance in market research. The purchase decision process may be longer, and more subject to evaluation and comparison. Impulse buying behaviour is less likely in the purchase of financial services;

- market segmentation analysis and product positioning are much more critical to financial services marketing than to detergents. However, much more information is available for the purpose of customer targeting and direct marketing;

- there is a problem in differentiating both types of product, and both suffer the risk of being perceived as a "commodity" type product. Effective branding may be difficult (or expensive) to create and maintain, and may depend on heavy and sustained promotion;

- financial services marketing is less likely to be sensitive to price than detergents;

- channels of distribution and distribution arrangements differ as between the two product types. The purchase situation is more complex and confusing for the consumer of financial services. Within the insurance market, the Financial Services Act is likely to restrict certain types of competition, but encourage it elsewhere within the channels of distribution;

– the markets for financial services face a much more complex marketing communication problem compared with detergents, and call for a correspondingly complex promotional mix. Services are intangible and may be harder to sell. The promotional mix may attempt to instil some urgency (or fear) into the purchase process. Potential buyers may need more motivation, and personal selling is often used. Detergents, on the other hand, are sold by resellers and would only be subject to personal selling in small independent shops.

Appendix II

SAMPLE MARKETING ASSIGNMENTS AND PROJECTS FOR INDIVIDUALS AND GROUPS (ALSO BTEC CMA'S, PIA'S, ETC).

1) Draw up a specification, and carry out (i) a consumer market research OR (ii) industrial market research exercise for a local SME (small or medium sized enterprise). This will involve deciding

* objective
* research methodology
* sampling methodology
* research and questionnaire format
* appropriate use of Information Technology packages to process and present results

Present your findings to the client in the form of (a) formal oral presentation using OHP slides derived from the use of appropriate graphics package, and (b) a written report using word processing and graphics facilities.

2) Draw up a specification, and carry out a market segmentation exercise for a local SME in (i) consumer market OR (ii) industrial market. This will involve deciding

* objective
* segmentation method to be used
* research methodology
* appropriate use of Information Technology packages to process and present results

Present your findings to the client in the form of (a) formal oral presentation using OHP slides derived from the use of appropriate graphics package, and (b) a written report using word processing and graphics facilities.

3) Draw up a specification, and carry out a market forecasting exercise for a local SME in (i) consumer market OR (ii) industrial market. This will involve deciding

* objective
* forecasting method to be used
* forecasting methodology to be used
* appropriate use of Information Technology package to process and present results

769

Present your findings to the client in the form of (a) a formal oral presentation, and (b) a formal written report.

4) Carry out a qualitative forecasting exercise for a product-market, or service-market of your choice, or of interest to a local SME or company. Make use of market, technological, social, and political forecasts to construct three five-year scenarios for this product or service-market. These scenarios should be

(1) Optimistic

(2) Likely

(3) Pessimistic

Present your findings.

5) Specify and carry out a project for a local shop to investigate the pattern and relationship between (i) the number of shoppers per time period passing by in the street directly outside the shop, and (ii) the number of people entering the shop. Present your findings and comment on the adequacy (or otherwise) of the location of the shop within the surrounding shopping context.

6) Using a specific example with which you are familiar comment on the importance to the marketer of the buying department in an organisation to which he/she would like to sell goods or services.

7) Using a specific example with which you are familiar, explain why it may be difficult for a supplier to sell its products to an organisation that makes use of multi-individual buying processes to make purchase decisions. How may it attempt to overcome this difficulty?

8) Specify and carry out a consultancy exercise to identify, explain and analyse the behavioural determinants of demand for a specific product/service, or range of products/services marketed by the client. Present your findings.

9) Specify and carry out a consultancy exercise to identify, explain and analyse the likely behavioural influences on demand for a new product/service to be introduced by the client. Present your findings.

10) Specify and carry out a project for a local SME/company to identify, explain and analyse the buying pattern and process in an industrial goods market into which the company wishes to introduce a new product or service. Present your findings.

11) Carry out a competitive product/brand analysis for a local manufacturer. Analyse, test and compare competitive products with those of the client company, reporting on the relative strengths and weaknesses of each brand.

12) Assist a local SME in the specification and design of a promotional campaign to launch a new product or service.

13) Assist a local non-profit/public sector organisation in the specification and design of a new promotional campaign.

14) Carry out a competitive price analysis for a local manufacturer. Analyse and compare the prices of competitive products with those of the client company, commenting on the apparent relationship between price charged and the market position of each product.

15) Draw up a pricing manual for use in a newly established SME. Include pricing guidelines and relevant calculated examples as illustration.

16) Draw up a set of guidelines by which a client organisation can analyse its customer service capability, and make improvements to its customer service offering.

17) Analyse one specific product or service offered by a client organisation, using product management criteria. What Unique Selling Propositions does it have? How might the product or service be developed in the future?

18) Draw up a promotional guide for use in a local SME. Rate the available promotional media in order of objective and task effectiveness for its purposes.

19) Draw up a manual for use in a local SME by which the objective and task budgeting of promotional activities may be planned.

20) Draw up a manual for use in a client organisation by which the effectiveness of expenditures on promotion may be analysed and evaluated.

21) Advise a local non-profit/public sector organisation on how best to make use of sponsorship as a tool of marketing and promotion.

22) Carry out a project for a local company to advise its Sales Office about the latest Information Technology developments affecting sales office administration, and how the company might implement and use these technologies.

23) Carry out a project for a local company to advise its Sales Managers about the latest Information Technology developments affecting sales force management, and how the company might implement and use these technologies.

24) Draw up a report for a local company that wishes to compete in European (EC) markets, advising it of the various official sources of information, assistance and advice available to it. List, compare

and comment on these sources, in their relative merit order of value and relevance to the company's needs.

25) Draw up a report for a client company that wishes to compete in a specific international market, advising it of the various official sources of information, assistance and advice available to it. List, compare and comment on these sources, in their relative merit order of value and relevance to the company's needs.

26) Assist a newly established SME to draw up its strategic marketing plan.

27) Assist a local company to draw up guidelines for the formulation and presentation of company strategic marketing and business plans. Include all necessary documentation, pro-formas etc.

28) Assist a local non profit/public sector organisation to draw up guidelines for the formulation and presentation of strategic marketing and business plans. Include all necessary documentation, pro-formas etc.

29) Compile and present a manual containing guidelines for the formulation and presentation of company strategic marketing and business plans. Include all necessary documentation, pro formas etc.

30) Compile and present a manual containing guidelines for the use of spreadsheet and graphics packages in the formulation and presentation of company strategic marketing and business plans.

Appendix III

SAMPLE MARKETING ASSIGNMENTS AND PROJECTS FOR THE NON-PROFIT/PUBLIC SECTOR

1) Can the marketing concept be applied to non-profit making organisations?

2) Draw up a draft Instruction Manual on "Getting to know your market" for discussion and use within your organisation. Include sample questionnaire formats and illustrative questionnaires.

3) (a)   What behavioural factors will be determinants of the demand for

* museum services, or

* preventative health care services; or

* Citizen's Advice Bureau

or (b)   What behavioural factors will shape public attitudes towards

* residential home care for the elderly; or

non-residential care for the elderly "within the community"

or (c)   What behavioural factors are relevant to promoting public subscription to

(i)   an existing charitable organisation; OR

(ii)   a new charity

A   Write a report based upon one of the above questions; OR

B   Write a report based upon the format of one of the above questions, but using your own chosen example.

4) Is the Product Life Cycle concept applicable to the marketing of products or services in the non-profit sector?

5) Analyse one specific product or service offered by your organisation, using product management criteria. What USP's does it have? How might it be developed in the future?

6) Draw up a set of guidelines by which your organisation can analyse its customer service capability, and make improvements to its customer service offering.

7) Draw up a pricing manual for use in your organisation. Include pricing guidelines and relevant calculated examples as illustrations.

8) Draw up an outline specification of a promotional campaign for a service of your choice. Include details of:

* the target audience/segment
* the objective to be achieved
* the theme of the campaign
* the media to be used
* the frequency of media use.

9) Draw up a promotional guide for use in your organisation. Rank the available promotional media in order of objective and task effectiveness for its purposes.

10) Draw up a manual for use in your organisation by which the objective and task budgeting of promotional activities may be planned.

11) Draw up a manual for use in your organisation by which the effectiveness of expenditures on promotion may be analysed and evaluated.

12) How may your organisation make use of sponsorship as a tool of marketing and promotion?

13) Your agency wishes to promote industrial or business relocation to . . . Draw up an outline promotional plan, to include:

* objective(s);
* main tasks required to achieve the objective;
* evaluation criteria.

14) "A high degree of customer-orientation is not necessary to the achievement of the objectives of the organisation for which I work, nor is it relevant to the effective management of its affairs". Comment on this statement.

15) "A customer care objective should underlie all operational and control activities, even within the non-profit sector". Comment on this statement.

16) What are the objectives of Public Relations (PR) within the non-profit sector?

17) Why should an organisation in the non-profit sector need to develop a corporate image towards its clients and external public?

ALSO: see Chapter 49 Questions for Self Review (1)-(15)

Useful Addresses

Association of Business Executives
William House, 14 Worple Road, London SW19 4DD, England

Chartered Association of Certified Accountants
29 Lincoln's Inn Fields, London WC2A 3EE, England

Chartered Building Societies Institute
19 Baldock Street, Ware, Hertfordshire SG12 9DH, England

Chartered Institute of Management Accountants
63 Portland Place, London W1N 4AB, England

Chartered Institute of Marketing
Moor Hall, Cookham, Maidenhead, Berkshire SL6 9QH, England

Institute of Bankers in Scotland
20 Rutland Square, Edinburgh EH1 2DE, Scotland

Institute of Export
64 Clifton Street, London EC2A 4HB, England

Institute of Purchasing and Supply
Easton House, Easton on the Hill, Stamford, Lincolnshire PE9 3NZ, England

Institute of Sales and Marketing Management
31 Upper George Street, Luton, Bedfordshire LU1 2RD, England

Marketing Institute of Ireland
12 Fitzwilliam Place, Dublin 2, Ireland

Market Research Society
175 Oxford Street, London W1R 1TA, England

Society of Sales Management Administrators
40 Archdale Road, London SE22 9HJ, England

Index

Accounting and Finance for Business Students

M BENDREY, R HUSSEY & C WEST

400pp 1989

This book provides a comprehensive introduction to accounting and finance. It includes numerous examples, with solutions in the text, to assist the student in understanding each topic. Also, for directed private study, there are student activities (assignments, objective tests, etc.).

Courses on which this book is known to be used

BTEC National and HNC/D Business and Finance; BA Business Studies; CMS/DMS; IPM; BSc Engineering; BSc Computing; BEd in Business Studies; BA in Modern Languages and other management development courses.

CONTENTS

LECTURERS' COMMENTS

'..concise and easy to follow by students..' '..good, comprehensive coverage..' ' superior in number of examples and explanations compared with alternative texts..' '..book is very good for nonspecialists..' '..assignments are excellent for classroom activities..' '..very clearly written..' '..I have recommended your book for all students on HND...' '..gives a good introduction at an excellent price.'

Free Lecturers' Supplement

Management Theory and Practice
3rd Edition
G A COLE

608pp 1990
(Also available as ELBS edition in member countries at
local currency equivalent price of £2.50)

This book aims to provide, in one concise volume, the principal ideas
and developments in the theory and practice of management as
required by business and accountancy students.

This edition revises and updates in such areas as employment law and
employee relations and has a number of new chapters, including
Japanese Approaches to Management.

Courses on which this book is known to be used
CIMA; ACCA; AAT; BTEC HNC/D; IIM; BA Business Studies; BA
Accounting; MSc Information Technology; BSc Software Engineering;
Hotel and Catering Management courses; CIB; CIM; IAM; DMS.

CONTENTS

LECTURERS' COMMENTS
'Excellent textbook for any management student.' 'One of the clearest
presentations available.' 'Very clear - excellent chapter design.' 'The right
mix of diagrams, charts and reading text.' 'Our students find your approach
to topics and logical progression beneficial and easy to understand.'

Free Lecturers' Supplement

Personnel Management
2nd Edition
G A Cole

508pp 1988

This book is intended to meet the needs of students and lecturers for an introductory textbook that can offer a variety of learning opportunities in the form of discussion questions, case studies, examination questions and suggested answers.

Courses on which this book is known to be used

IPM; ICSA; Association of Business Executives; BTEC HNC/D Business and Finance; CNAA Diploma in Personnel Management; CNAA Degrees in Business Studies (Personnel Management Options); CIB; Institute of Training and Development.

On reading lists of CIMA and ICSA

CONTENTS

Free Lecturers' Supplement

A First Course In Statistics
D BOOTH

304pp 1988

This book provides a core text for introductory level courses in statistics. It assumes the student has no prior knowledge of statistics whatsoever and no more than an ability to handle simple arithmetic.

Courses on which this book is known to be used
BTEC Business and Secretarial Studies; RSA; LCCI; AAT Certificate.

CONTENTS

LECTURERS' COMMENTS

'The book is a breath of fresh air to those who think statistics is an essentially practical subject, as it has not only a section on the derivation of individual statistics but also three sections dealing with the practical details and problems associated with 'Asking the question', 'Collecting the data' and 'Communicating the results' which are so often given such little emphasis in introductory statistical texts ... Each chapter of each section ends with a short series of exercises, answers being provided only to alternate questions, a nice tough to cut out the 'right answer/wrong calculation' effect yet still giving students some answers...'
The Mathematical Gazette

Free Lecturers' Supplement

A First Course In Marketing

FRANK JEFKINS

192pp 1989

This book has been specially prepared for those with no prior knowledge of marketing and who need to get to grips with the subject in a simple and straight forward manner. It has quickly gained wide use as support material on BTEC First and National courses.

Courses on which this book is known to be used
BTEC First and National; RSA; LCCI; CAM Certificate in Communication Studies.

CONTENTS

THE NATURE OF MARKETING
WHAT IS MARKETING ?
WHAT IS THE MARKETING MIX?
HOW DOES COMPETITION AFFECT
   MARKETING STRATEGY?
WHAT IS THE PRODUCT LIFE CYCLE?
SALES FORECASTING, PRICE AND
   MARKETING RESEARCH
HOW ARE SALES FORECASTS AND RISKS
   ASSESSED?
WHAT DETERMINES PRICE?
WHAT IS MARKETING RESEARCH?
DISTRIBUTION
HOW ARE GOODS AND SERVICES
   DISTRIBUTED?
HOW HAS DISTRIBUTION CHANGED IN
RECENT YEARS?
HOW IS DIRECT RESPONSE
   MARKETING CONDUCTED?

PROMOTION AND PUBLIC RELATIONS
WHAT IS THE ROLE OF ADVERTISING?
HOW CAN PUBLIC RELATIONS HELP
   MARKETING?
WHAT IS THE ROLE OF SALES
   PROMOTION?
HOW CAN SPONSORSHIP HELP
   MARKETING?
HOW ARE INDUSTRIAL GOODS AND
   SERVICES MARKETED?
CONSUMERISM, LEGAL AND
   VOLUNTARY CONTROL
HOW DOES CONSUMERISM AFFECT
   MARKETING?
LEGAL CONTROLS AFFECTING
   MARKETING
SELF-REGULARTORY CONTROLS
   AFFECTING MARKETING

LECTURERS' COMMENTS

'Another superb DPP book - ideal for the BTEC National Diploma Introduction to Marketing module!' '...useful on any basic marketing course...' 'Well planned - is British with British examples...' '..accessible to students ...'

Free Lecturers' Supplement

A First Course in Cost and Management Accounting

T Lucey

256pp 1990

This book provides a broad introduction to cost and management accounting for those who have not studied the subject before. It is written in a clear, straight forward fashion without technical jargon or unnecessary detail. The text includes many practical examples, diagrams, exercises and examination questions. Features include several objective tests for self-assessment and assignments for activity-based learning.

Courses on which this book is expected to be used

BTEC National Business and Finance; RSA; LCCI; AAT; Management and Supervisory Studies; Business Studies and Marketing courses; Access courses; Purchasing and Supply and any course requiring a broad, non-specialist treatment of cost and management accounting.

CONTENTS

Free Lecturers' Supplement

Financial Management
5th edition
R BROCKINGTON

600pp 1990

This book gives a full coverage of the subject of financial managment
to the level required by students taking the subject to a professionally
qualifying level. It deals with both the basic and more advanced
elements of the subject in logical way, helping the student to develop
understanding through manageable steps. It contains a large number
of worked examples together with exercises and examination
questions to enable the student to test understanding.

Courses on which this book is known to be used
ACCA; CIMA; CIPFA; CIB; IMI; DMS; BTEC HNC/D Business Studies;
Degree courses; short courses for managers and executives.

CONTENTS

FUNDS FLOW STATEMENTS
SOURCES OF FINANCE
FINANCIAL INSTITUTIONS
COST OF CAPITAL
CAPITAL STRUCTURE
RELEVANT COSTS
FORECASTING AND PLANNING
CAPITAL BUDGETING
RISK
CAPITAL ASSET PRICING MODEL
CAPITAL RATIONING
INFLATION AND FINANCIAL REPORTING
INFLATION AND INVESTMENT
  APPRAISAL

TAXATION IN FINANCIAL DECISIONS
DISTRIBUTION POLICY
FINANCIAL RATIOS
STOCK MARKET INVESTMENT
MERGERS AND TAKEOVERS
MANAGEMENT OF WORKING
  CAPITAL: STOCK; DEBTORS; CASH
FOREIGN CURRENCY TRANSACTIONS
EXERCISES WITH ANSWERS
EXERCISES WITHOUT ANSWERS
GLOSSARY
DISCOUNT TABLES

REVIEW EXTRACTS

'...written in a note format, the style is very clear and the development
logical.'
AUTA
'Ideal for giving non-accounting students an overall coverage of the subject
area.' 'Good, useful, practical book, reasonably priced.'
Lecturer
'Makes very easy reading and understanding of such an involved subject.'
Student

Free Lecturers' Supplement

Management Accounting
2nd Edition
T LUCEY

560pp 1988

This book provides comprehensive coverage of the Management
Accounting syllabuses of the major professional bodies. It includes
many graded exercises, examination questions (with and without
answers) and case studies.

Courses on which this book is known to be used

ACCA; CIMA; CIPFA; ICSA; BTEC HNC/D; BA Accounting; BA
Business Studies..
On reading lists of CIMA and ICSA

CONTENTS

WHAT IS MANAGEMENT ACCOUNTING?
COST ACCOUNTING AND COST
  ASCERTAINMENT - A REVISION
COST BEHAVIOUR
INFORMATION AND MANAGEMENT
  ACCOUNTING
PLANNING - SYSTEM CONCEPTS
LONG TERM PLANNING
BUDGETING
NETWORK ANALYSIS
CONTROL - CONCEPTS AND SYSTEM
  PRINCIPLES
BUDGETARY CONTROL
STANDARD COSTING
STOCK CONTROL
DECISION MAKING - AN
  INTRODUCTION

MARGINAL COSTING AND CVP
  ANALYSIS
PRICING DECISIONS
LINEAR PROGRAMMING
INVESTMENT APPRAISAL
DIVISIONAL PERFORMANCE
  APPRAISAL
TRANSFER PRICING
RATIO ANALYSIS
MANAGEMENT ACCOUNTING AND
  COMPUTERS
MANAGEMENT ACCOUNTING CASE
  STUDIES
EXAMINATION TECHNIQUE
SOLUTIONS TO QUESTIONS SET AT
  END OF CHAPTERS

REVIEW EXTRACTS

'This text is astonishingly comprehensive, well written and nicely laid out.
As a manual for professional examinations it has no obvious competitor.'
British Accounting Review Service

Free Lecturers' Supplement

Business Law 5th edition
K R ABBOTT AND N PENDLEBURY

608pp January 1991

This book provides comprehensive coverage of the Business Law requirements of ACCA, CIMA and ICSA syllabuses.

The **Fifth Edition** incorporates changes introduced by the Employment Act 1988, the Copyright, Designs and Patents Act 1988 and the Companies Act 1989. A new Appendix of BTEC assignments has also been included.

Courses on which this book is known to be used
ACCA; CIMA; ICSA; AAT; BTEC National and HNC/D Business and Finance; Foundation Accountancy course; BA Accounting.
On reading lists of ACCA, AAT and SCCA

CONTENTS

LECTURERS' COMMENTS

'The text is clear and concisely written. The material is well presented and it is very easy to follow because it is broken down into short sections. Each section is clearly headed with the name of the topic under discussion. The principles of law expounded are well illustrated and supported by relevant cases and statutes. The names of all the cases and statutes are displayed in bold type. The adoption of this style of presentation should enable students to read it quickly and to obtain a good grasp of the basic principles involved in a relatively short period of time.'
Accounting Technician

Free Lecturers' Supplement

Company Law
4th Edition
K R Abbott

512pp 1990

This book is intended for anyone studying company law who needs to get a good grasp of the subject in a relatively short period of time. It covers all areas of company law, presenting complex legislation in a clear and readable style and format. The new edition incorporates all the relevant provisions of the Companies Act 1989. It also includes, for the first time, 21 short progress tests with answers, and a number of new past questions from recent ACCA and CIMA examination papers. In addition it contains a new short section on European Community Company Law Harmonisation.

Courses on which this book is known to be used
ACCA; CIMA; ICSA; CIB; AAT; BTEC HNC/D Business and Finance; BA Business Studies; SSVA Taxation and Law; LLB
On *reading lists of ACCA, CIMA and SCCA*

CONTENTS

LECTURERS' COMMENTS
'It's very readable. A good balance to the more substantial reference works and a very valuable alternative to the study manual approach.' 'A clear, concise text with good explanations - it is a core text on the second year of our HND.'

Free Lecturers' Supplement